AUTOMOTIVE
ELECTRONICS
AND ELECTRICAL EQUIPMENT

NINTH EDITION

AUTOMOTIVE
ELECTRONICS
AND ELECTRICAL EQUIPMENT

WILLIAM H. CROUSE

GREGG DIVISION/McGRAW-HILL BOOK COMPANY

New York ○ Atlanta ○ Dallas ○ St. Louis ○ San Francisco ○ Auckland ○ Bogotá ○ Düsseldorf
Johannesburg ○ London ○ Madrid ○ Mexico ○ Montreal ○ New Delhi ○ Panama ○ Paris
São Paulo ○ Singapore ○ Sydney ○ Tokyo ○ Toronto

ABOUT THE AUTHOR

William H. Crouse

Behind William H. Crouse's clear technical writing is a background of sound mechanical engineering training as well as a variety of practical industrial experience. After finishing high school, he spent a year working in a tinplate mill. Summers, while still in school, he worked in General Motors plants, and for three years he worked in the Delco-Remy Division shops. Later he became director of field education in the Delco-Remy Division of General Motors Corporation, which gave him an opportunity to develop and use his writing talent in the preparation of service bulletins and educational literature.

During the war years, he wrote a number of technical manuals for the Armed Forces. After the war, he became editor of technical education books for the McGraw-Hill Book Company. He has contributed numerous articles to automotive and engineering magazines and has written many outstanding books. He was the first editor in chief of the 15-volume McGraw-Hill *Encyclopedia of Science and Technology*.

William H. Crouse's outstanding work in the automotive field has earned for him membership in the Society of Automotive Engineers and in the American Society of Engineering Education.

Library of Congress Cataloging in Publication Data

Crouse, William Harry [Date]
  Automotive electronics and electrical equipment.

  First-8th ed. published under title: Automotive electrical equipment.
  Includes index.
  1. Automobiles—Electric equipment.   2. Auto-mobiles—Electronic equipment.   3. Automobiles—Electric equipment—Maintenance and repair.
  4. Automobiles—Electronic equipment—Maintenance and repair.   I. Title.
TL272.C73   1981   629.2'54   79-24438
ISBN 0-07-014831-7

AUTOMOTIVE ELECTRONICS AND ELECTRICAL EQUIPMENT
Ninth Edition

        9   SMSM   8 9 8 7 6 5 4 3 2

Sponsoring Editor: D. Eugene Gilmore
Editing Supervisor: Paul Berk
Design Supervisor: Caryl Valerie Spinka
                  Tracy Glasner
Production Supervisor: Kathleen Morrissey
Art Supervisor: George T. Resch
Text Designer: Linda Conway
Cover Designer: David Thurston
Cover Illustration: Calibre Studio

CONTENTS

PREFACE

This is the ninth edition of *Automotive Electrical Equipment,* a textbook whose purpose is to provide students with easily understood information on the operation, construction, diagnosis, and servicing of automotive electric systems. The addition of the word *electronics* to the title reflects recent advances in automotive technology and the changes made in the text to account for them. Material taken from previous editions has been revised, rewritten, and updated. Several completely new chapters describing the many new and redesigned components in use or soon to be introduced in the automobile have been added.

Although the book's title is now *Automotive Electronics and Electrical Equipment,* its purposes and methods remain the same as those of the previous editions. Care has been taken to ensure that the text is written in simple, everyday language and that it can be used at any level automotive technology is taught: high school, trade school, technical institute, or community college.

Just how extensive are the advances in automotive technology? Nearly all automobiles now have electronic alternator regulators and ignition systems. Fuel systems, distributor spark advances, exhaust gas recirculation, and air-injection pollution control devices are also electronically controlled in many automobiles, and some have electronic load-leveling devices and braking systems. In other words, electronic components are now used in every automotive system, and even more of these devices will be used in automobiles in the immediate future. In addition, the automotive industry has made notable improvements in the construction of standard electric equipment—starting motors, alternators, regulators, and ignition systems.

Automotive Electronics and Electrical Equipment accounts for all these changes. It contains the following new chapters:

Chapter 2, "Electronics and the Automobile," introduces the student to electronic fundamentals and devices.

Chapter 16, "Electronic Ignition Systems," includes the latest in electronic spark-advance controls, such as the Chrysler Lean Burn system, the Ford Electronic Engine Control, and the General Motors Electronic Spark Timing system. The chapter also covers electronic control of the exhaust gas recirculation and air-injection systems, the antidetonation electronic spark control for turbocharged engines, and retrofitting electronic ignition to contact-point systems.

Chapter 18, "Servicing Electronic Spark-Advance Systems," details diagnosis and repair procedures for three electronic ignition systems.

Chapter 19, "Electronic Carbureted Fuel Systems," explains how electronic components are used with carburetors to precisely control the air-fuel mixture.

Chapter 20, "Electronic Fuel Injection," covers general operating principles and servicing procedures for one particular fuel-injection system.

Also, samples of the various new diagnosis charts recently developed by the major automotive manufacturers are included and explained. This prepares the student for the type of material that actually is used in the automotive shop.

Hundreds of new illustrations have been added. Dual dimensioning, which was very well received in the previous edition, has been retained. United States Customary measurements are followed by their metric equivalents. As an example, the dimensions of this book would be shown as 8½ × 11 inches [216 × 279 mm (millimeters)].

The text is accompanied by a new workbook, the *Workbook for Automotive Electronics and Electrical Equipment,* which serves as an excellent self-teaching guide. The workbook contains the basic servicing jobs recommended by the Motor Vehicle Manufacturers Association–American Vocational Association Industry Planning Council.

The text covers the subject matter tested by the National Institute for Automotive Service Excellence (NIASE). Used together, *Automotive Electronics and Electrical Equipment* and its workbook supply the student with the background information and "hands on" experience needed to become a qualified and certified automotive technician.

To assist the automotive instructor, an updated *Instructor's Planning Guide for Automotive Electronics and Electrical Equipment* is available. This guide will help the automotive instructor do the best possible job by most effectively using the available materials. It also contains information on the automotive service industry: the growing need for properly trained mechanics, their testing and certification, and new laws affecting them.

Used singly or together, these instructional materials ensure congruency between the school curriculum and the future needs of students entering the automotive service field. There are minimum standards of competence demanded of entry-level employees, and these materials will help the instructor to tailor the learning experience of the student around tested and proven competency-based objectives. The student will then be able to develop locally demanded career skills while mastering the necessary job competencies and performance indicators covered in *Automotive Electronics and Electrical Equipment*, Ninth Edition.

William H. Crouse

ACKNOWLEDGMENTS

During the preparation of this new edition of *Automotive Electronics and Electrical Equipment,* the author was given invaluable aid and inspiration by many people in the automotive industry and in the field of education. The author gratefully acknowledges his indebtedness and offers his sincere thanks to these many people. All cooperated with the aim of providing accurate and complete information that would be useful in the training of automotive mechanics.

Special thanks are owed to the following organizations for information and illustrations they supplied: AC Spark Plug Division of General Motors Corporation; Allen Testproducts Division of The Allen Group, Inc.; American Motors Corporation; Autoscan, Inc.; Bendix Corporation; Buick Motor Division of General Motors Corporation; Cadillac Motor Car Division of General Motors Corporation; Chevrolet Motor Division of General Motors Corporation; Chrysler Corporation; Delco-Remy Division of General Motors Corporation; Digital Equipment Corporation; Fisher Body Division of General Motors Corporation; Ford Motor Company; General Motors Corporation; Lumenition, Limited; Oldsmobile Division of General Motors Corporation; Monroe Auto Equipment Company; Pontiac Motor Division of General Motors Corporation; Robert Bosch GmbH; Sun Electric Corporation; Toyota Motor Sales, Limited; TRW Corporation; and United Delco Division of General Motors Corporation.

Special thanks should also go to Michael Firczuk and the late Jim Johnson for the suggestions they made for improvement of the manuscript.

William H. Crouse

THE LANGUAGE OF ELECTRICITY

After studying this chapter, you should be able to:

1. List and explain the purpose of the major electric devices and systems in the automotive electric system.
2. Explain alternating and direct electric currents in terms of electrons.
3. Define voltage, amperage, and resistance.
4. Describe parallel and series circuits.
5. Describe the characteristics of magnetism and electromagnetism.

1-1 The fundamentals This chapter introduces you to the fundamentals of electricity. All the devices in the automotive electric system operate on a few fundamental electrical principles. An understanding of these principles leads to an easier understanding of the electric devices themselves. Also, this chapter lays the foundation for Chapter 2, Electronics and the Automobile. Electronic systems operate on the same electrical principles we discuss in this chapter. But the electronic systems use such electronic devices as transistors and diodes to switch current on and off, store information in memory banks, accept instructions, receive and interpret information from various sources, and put it all together to produce a controlling action. We cover all these electronic fundamentals in Chapter 2. Later in the book, we apply these fundamentals as we describe the construction and operation of the components in the automotive electric system. First, however, we introduce you to these components (Fig. 1-1).

1-2 Need for the electric system Beneath the hood of every modern automobile is a remarkable electric system. This system produces electric energy, stores it (in chemical form), and delivers it either at low voltage or in high-voltage surges of up to 40,000 volts or more. The electric system cranks the engine, automatically controls the voltage in the electric system, and supplies electric energy for lights, radio, heater, and other accessories. The system produces as many as 12,000 high-voltage surges each car-mile. It distributes these surges to the proper spark plugs at the correct time, with an error not greater than one ten-thousandth of a second. Without the electric system, the modern automobile would not be possible. The engine would be cranked by hand, lights would be produced by gas, radios and heaters would probably still be a dream. Motoring would be a hobby for the rich, as it was at the turn of the century.

But in spite of the importance and variety of jobs it does in today's automobile, the automotive electric system is remarkably simple. Its varied actions are based on a few fundamental rules of electrical behavior. Anyone who understands these rules can intelligently service the electric system.

1-3 Components in the electric system Before we get into electricity's rules of behavior, let us see what makes up the automotive electric system and what part each component plays in the operation of the automobile (Fig. 1-1).

1. The storage battery The *storage battery* (Fig. 1-2) supplies current for cranking the engine. It also supplies current for other electric devices when the engine is not driving the alternator fast enough to handle the current demands. The battery also helps stabilize the voltage in the electric system.

The storage battery stores energy in a chemical form. When any electricity-consuming device, such as the starting motor, lights, or radio, is connected to the battery, a chemical action takes place within the battery. This chemical action produces a flow of current. The amount of current that can be delivered by the battery is limited. If current from some external source, such as the car alternator, were not forced back into the battery (to recharge it), the battery would soon run down or go "dead." That is, it would not be able to deliver any further current.

2. The starting motor The *starting motor,* or *starter* (Fig. 1-3), is a special direct-current (dc) electric motor. It operates on the same principles as the electric

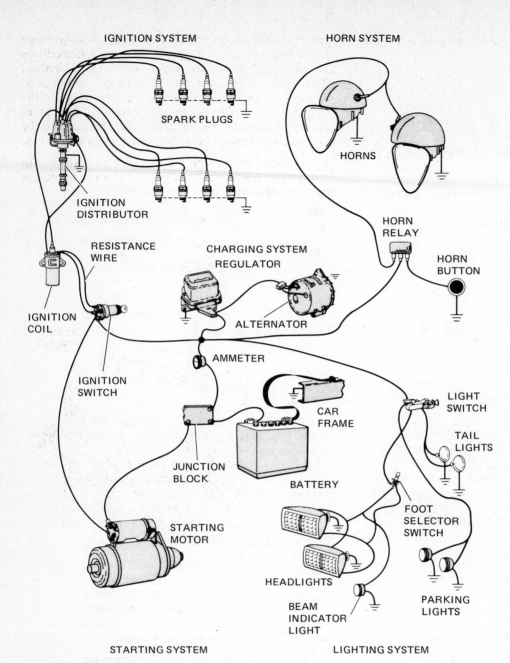

IGNITION SYSTEM

SPARK PLUGS

IGNITION DISTRIBUTOR

RESISTANCE WIRE

IGNITION COIL

IGNITION SWITCH

CHARGING SYSTEM REGULATOR

ALTERNATOR

AMMETER

CAR FRAME

JUNCTION BLOCK

BATTERY

STARTING MOTOR

HEADLIGHTS

BEAM INDICATOR LIGHT

STARTING SYSTEM

HORN SYSTEM

HORNS

HORN RELAY

HORN BUTTON

LIGHT SWITCH

TAIL LIGHTS

FOOT SELECTOR SWITCH

PARKING LIGHTS

LIGHTING SYSTEM

Fig. 1-1 Typical automobile electric system, showing the major electric components and the connections between them. The symbol ⏚ or ⏚ means ground, or the car frame or engine. Using the car frame or engine as the return circuit requires only half as much wiring. *(Delco-Remy Division of General Motors Corporation)*

motor in a vacuum cleaner or an electric fan. When the starter switch is closed, the starting motor is electrically connected to the battery. Current flows from the battery through the starting motor, and the starting motor rotates the engine crankshaft to crank the engine. The starting motor differs from most electric motors in that it is designed only for intermittent service under great overload.

3. The alternator The *alternator* converts mechanical energy supplied by the engine into electric energy. Until about 1961, all automobiles made in the United States used dc generators. Since that time, all have switched to alternating-current (ac) generators, commonly called *alternators*.[1] Both alternators (Fig. 1-4) and generators provide a dc output to recharge the battery (drained by cranking). They also supply current to operate other electric devices on the vehicle, as long as they are running fast enough. The alternator is usu-

ally mounted to the side of the engine block and is driven by the engine fan belt.

4. The regulator Since an unregulated alternator could produce too much voltage and damage the battery and other electric devices, alternators have *regulators*. The regulator limits the voltage the alternator produces. Therefore, the alternator produces only the amount of current the electric system demands. When the battery is in a discharged condition or when many electric devices are turned on, the current output from the alternator is high. But when the battery comes up to charge and electric devices are turned off, the current output of the alternator drops off. Many alternators today have the regulator inside the alternator. In other

[1]In this book we will use *generator* to mean a dc generator and *alternator* to mean an ac generator. However, some manufacturers' shop manuals still call the alternator a *generator*.

systems, the regulator is a separate component outside the alternator.

5. **The ignition system** The ignition system (Fig. 1-5) produces high-voltage surges of 40,000 volts or more. It delivers these surges to the cylinders in the engine. The engine operates and produces power because of a continuing series of explosions (triggered by the high-voltage surges) in the cylinders. Here is how it works.

In each cylinder vaporized gasoline and air are drawn in and compressed. At the right instant during compression, the ignition system delivers a high-voltage surge to the spark plug in the cylinder. This action produces an exceedingly hot spark, which sets fire to, or ignites, the mixture of gasoline and air. An explosion occurs, and tremendous pressure is created. The piston in the cylinder is forced down by the pressure. This movement is transmitted by the crankshaft and gears to the automobile wheels. The wheels turn and the car moves.

NOTE: Diesel engines do not use ignition systems. Instead, they use the heat of compression to ignite the fuel (see ⚙12-4).

CONVENTIONAL BATTERY

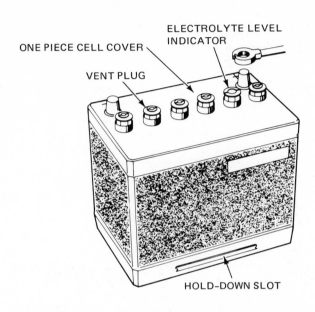

SIDE-TERMINAL BATTERY

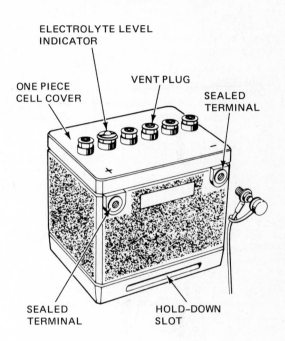

SECTIONAL VIEW OF CONVENTIONAL BATTERY

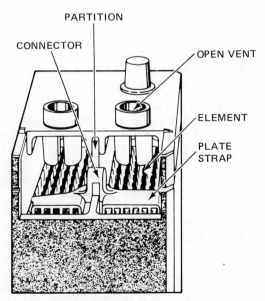

SEALED BATTERY

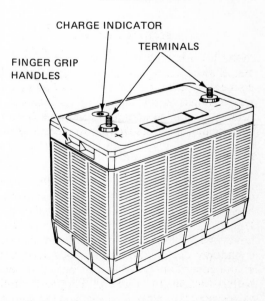

Fig. 1-2 Typical storage batteries. *(Delco-Remy Division of General Motors Corporation)*

Fig. 1-3 Typical starting motor. *(Delco-Remy Division of General Motors Corporation)*

6. Switches   Switches of several types are incorporated in the electric system. Their function is to make connections between the various electric devices and the source of electric power (alternator or battery). This completes the electric path or circuit so current will flow and the electric devices will operate.

7. Indicating devices   On many cars there are four gauges on the instrument panel that indicate engine condition: the fuel gauge, the oil-pressure gauge, the temperature gauge, and the ammeter. The fuel gauge indicates the amount of fuel in the fuel tank. The oil-pressure gauge indicates the pressure at which the oil pump is delivering oil to the engine. The temperature gauge indicates the temperature of the engine coolant. The ammeter indicates whether the battery is being charged or discharged.

Many cars use indicator lights instead of oil-pressure or temperature gauges and an ammeter. If the oil pressure is low, or the alternator is not charging, or engine temperature is too high, an indicator light comes on as a warning.

8. Lights, heater, radio   Electricity for operating these devices is supplied by the battery or alternator.

9. Electronic devices   Several electronic devices are used on most of today's cars. Automotive electronic devices will become increasingly common in the years to come. At present these devices are found in electronic systems to control:

Ignition operation and timing

The ratio, or richness, of the air–fuel mixture being fed to the engine

Automatic car rear-end levelers

Braking systems

Gasoline engine fuel-injection systems

Shifting of gears in automatic transmissions

We describe these, and other systems, later in the book.

Rules of behavior

Electricity does many jobs in the automobile. Yet the rules of electrical behavior governing these jobs are simple. Once understood, these rules will make automobile electrical service easier. The automotive electrician who understands why electric components operate can intelligently diagnose and correct troubles in the electric system.

☸ 1-4 Electricity and atoms   We start our study of electricity with atoms. Atoms contain particles that are made up, at least in part, of tiny positive and negative electric charges. There are more than 100 varieties of atoms. Each variety has a special structure and a special name, such as iron, copper, hydrogen, tin, oxygen, etc. Copper, for instance, is made up of one kind of atom. Oxygen is made up of another kind of atom. Any substance made up of one certain kind of atom is called an *element*.

Atoms compose everything in the world. However, they are far too small to be seen, even with the most powerful microscope. There are billions upon billions of atoms in a single drop of water. To give you an idea of how small the hydrogen atom is, imagine a cubic inch of hydrogen. At 32 degrees Fahrenheit (°F) [0°C (degrees Celsius, or centigrade)] and atmospheric pressure, the cube would contain about 880 billion billion atoms. Now, suppose we could expand this 1-inch [25.4 mm (millimeter)] cube until it was large enough to contain the earth. The expanded cube would measure 8000 miles [12,872 km (kilometers)] on each edge, and a single atom in the cube would measure about 10 inches [254 mm] in diameter.

Fig. 1-4 Alternator (ac generator). *(Chrysler Corporation)*

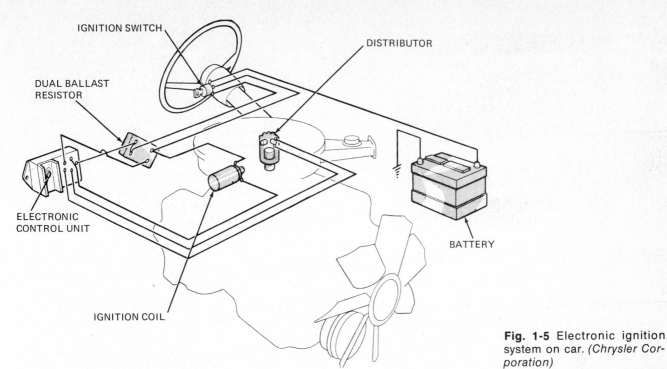

IGNITION SWITCH

DISTRIBUTOR

DUAL BALLAST
RESISTOR

ELECTRONIC
CONTROL UNIT

BATTERY

IGNITION COIL

Fig. 1-5 Electronic ignition system on car. *(Chrysler Corporation)*

Even though atoms cannot be seen, scientists have studied their actions and have been able to work out some clear ideas of how they are constructed. For instance, an atom of the gas hydrogen consists of two particles. These are a tiny particle in the center, or nucleus, of the atom and a still smaller particle whirling about the first at terrific speed (Fig. 1-6). The center, or nucleus, particle is called a *proton,* and it has a charge of positive electricity. The outer particle is called an *electron,* and it has a charge of negative electricity.

☼ 1-5 Electricity and electrons The electron in the hydrogen atom is kept whirling in its circular path (or orbit) around the proton by a combination of forces. One force is the attraction that the two oppositely charged particles have for each other. Opposing electric charges always attract. Thus, the negatively charged electron is pulled toward the positively charged proton. This attraction is opposed by the tendency of the electron to fly away from the proton. This tendency results from its movement in a circular path around the proton. The attractive force balances the tendency of the electron to fly away, and the electron is held in its orbit.

You can see the same balancing of forces when you swing a ball attached to a rubber band in a circle (Fig. 1-7). As you swing the ball, the rubber band stretches because of the tendency of the ball to fly away from your hand. But the rubber band (the attractive force) keeps the ball moving in a circle around your hand.

It is not uncommon for atoms to lose electrons. When such free electrons gather in the same place, we call the effect a *charge of electricity.* When the free electrons begin to move together—for instance, along a wire—we call the effect a *current of electricity.* Thus, electricity is made up of electrons.

Electrons are very tiny. It would take something like a hundred thousand billion of them, side by side, to measure an inch. You might think of them as tiny spheres. Remember that each electron has a negative charge of electricity.

☼ 1-6 Electricity in motion Free electrons exert a powerful repulsive force against each other. They therefore tend to move away from each other. If we arrange a path along which free electrons can move, they will always move away from areas in which there are many electrons into areas where there are few electrons.

+ MEANS PLUS OR POSITIVE
– MEANS MINUS OR NEGATIVE

Fig. 1-6 The hydrogen atom consists of two particles: a proton with a positive charge, at the center, and an electron with a negative charge circling the proton.

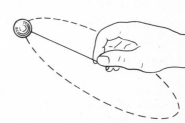

Fig. 1-7 The electron in a hydrogen atom circles the proton like a ball on a rubber band swung in a circle around your hand.

Basically, an alternator or a battery is a device that concentrates large numbers of electrons at one place, or terminal. It removes electrons from another place, or terminal. When these two terminals are connected by an electron path, or electric circuit, the electrons can move from one terminal to the other (Fig. 1-8). This movement of electrons through a circuit is called an *electron flow,* or more familiarly, a *current* of electricity.

The terminal that has large numbers of electrons massed in it is called the *negative* terminal (electrons being negative). The terminal from which electrons have been removed is called the *positive* terminal. Removing electrons leaves atoms that are positively charged (from the protons).

NOTE: The negative terminal is also called the *minus* terminal and is indicated by a minus (−) sign. The positive terminal is also called the *plus* terminal and is indicated by a plus (+) sign.

☸ 1-7 Conductors, semiconductors, and insulators

Electrons require a path or a circuit in which they can move. Electrons can move through some substances more easily than through others. Some substances—such as copper, iron, aluminum, and other metals—form good paths through which electrons can move. Since such substances conduct the electrons through easily, they are called *conductors.* Other substances, such as rubber and glass, strongly oppose movement of electrons through them. These substances are called *nonconductors,* or insulators. In a third category are substances, such as germanium, which are neither good conductors nor good insulators; these are called *semiconductors.* Whether a substance is a conductor, a nonconductor, or a semiconductor depends on its atomic structure. Semiconductors play a major part in electronics, as we explain in Chapter 2.

One of the best conductors is copper. The wires between the electric components of the automobile are usually made of copper. To find out why copper is such a good conductor, look at a single copper atom (Fig. 1-9). The copper atom has 29 electrons circling the nu-

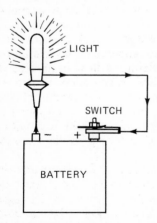

Fig. 1-8 When the switch is closed, electrons (or electric current) move from one battery terminal to the other through the circuit.

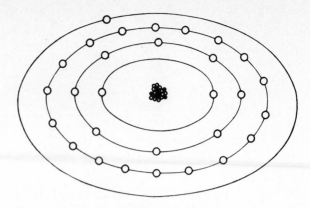

Fig. 1-9 One atom of copper.

cleus in 4 separate orbits. The inner orbit has 2 electrons, the next larger orbit 8, the third 18, and the outer orbit 1. This outer electron is not very closely tied to the atom. Therefore a copper atom can lose its outer electron.

Copper atoms are too small to be seen under a microscope. But if it were possible to make the copper atoms visible, we could observe this electron-losing activity. We would see copper atoms losing their outer electrons and then capturing new electrons in place of the old (Fig. 1-10). We would see this happening to each atom many times a second. In a copper wire, then, there are always many free electrons moving about in all directions between the copper atoms.

If we attached this copper wire between the terminals of a battery or an operating alternator, we would see something strange. Instead of moving about in all directions, all the electrons would tend to move in the same direction. The electrons would still move from one atom to another as before. But in general their movement would be in one direction along the wire.

☸ 1-8 A further explanation of conductor action

Imagine countless numbers of electrons massed at one terminal of the alternator. They are repelling, or pushing against, each other, but they have no place to go if there is no electric path or circuit. However, if we connect a copper wire from this terminal to the other alternator terminal (which has an electron shortage), we establish an electric circuit. The electrons at the negative terminal push against the free electrons in the wire. These free electrons are, therefore, pushed away from the terminal. These electrons push against the electrons farther along the wire, and this push makes itself felt almost instantly from one end of the wire to the other. As a result, free electrons immediately begin to move out of the far end of the wire into the positive alternator terminal, which has a shortage of electrons.

A particular electron does not necessarily move from one end to the other end of an electric circuit. It may move only a small fraction of an inch a minute. But the electron "push" is felt almost instantly from one end of the circuit to the other. To illustrate, let us follow the action of a single electron from the instant the circuit is closed between the alternator terminals. Let us assume that this electron is on the negative terminal,

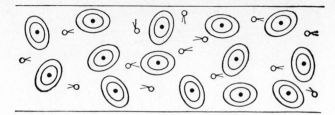

Fig. 1-10 In a copper wire, there are many free electrons moving from atom to atom.

where great numbers of electrons are massed. The electron is pushing against adjacent electrons and is, in turn, being pushed by them. When the circuit is closed, this electron is pushed off the terminal and into the copper wire forming the circuit. It is momentarily captured by a copper atom which has just lost its outer electron. Almost instantly, however, it breaks free from the atom and is pushed along the wire to another atom. Meantime, it is repelling electrons ahead of it. These electrons, in turn, repel other electrons farther along. This push is felt all along the wire, so that almost instantly electrons are pushed out of the other end of the wire and onto the positive alternator terminal.

☼ **1-9 Atomic structure and conductivity** We have noted that for a substance to be an electric conductor, it must have free electrons. Also, it must furnish these electrons from the outermost orbits of its atoms. Inner-orbit electrons are bound much more closely to the atom and do not normally take part in the electron flow that we know as electric current.

If the outermost orbit of an atom is nearly empty (with only one, two, or three electrons, for example), the outer-orbit electrons can get away from the atom fairly easily. Therefore the substance is a good conductor. If, on the other hand, the outermost orbit is filled with all the electrons the orbit can hold, then these electrons are tightly bound to the atom. This type of atom is a good insulator.

☼ **1-10 Insulators** Insulators are composed of atoms or combinations of atoms that do not lose or take on electrons easily. Insulating material is placed around the negative terminal of an alternator, for example. It keeps electrons from escaping from the terminal. Insulation is placed around the positive terminal to keep electrons from flowing into the terminal. That is, even though the terminal lacks electrons (and is thus positive in charge), it cannot pull electrons from the insulating material.

Insulators are, of course, essential to the operation of any electric device. The wires and other parts through which electrons flow are usually covered with insulation. This prevents electrons from flowing away from the circuit and thus prevents electrical loss. Current-carrying (electron-carrying) parts are covered or supported by mica, rubber, plastic, Bakelite, or fiber insulating material. Also, wires are often covered with insulating varnish, a liquid that dries to form a smooth, hard insulating coating.

NOTE: Air is a good insulating substance, particularly when it is dry. The atoms of the different gases in air are normally neutral electrically and do not take on or give up electrons.

Insulation will fail for a number of reasons. If the insulation becomes water-soaked, for example, the water will fill all the tiny pores or openings in the insulation and form an electron- or current-carrying path. Also, heat may char or burn the insulation, so that its chemical properties are changed and it becomes a conductor instead of an insulator. In addition, if the electrons continue to mass more and more heavily at the alternator terminal, that is, as voltage goes up, they will push harder and harder against each other. If this push increases too much, it may go up enough to push electrons entirely through the insulation. Such a condition is called a *short,* or *short circuit,* because the electrons take a short circuit instead of taking the longer circuit through the outside wires.

Automobiles use the *ground-return* system of wiring. This system utilizes the car frame, body, and engine to form half the electric circuit. Since it is necessary to run only one wire to many of the electric components (the ground return forming the other part of the circuit), considerable wire is saved and the system is simplified. Short circuits between the insulated and grounded parts of a circuit are often called *grounds.*

NOTE: In automobiles such shorts, or grounds, most often develop because of (1) mechanical damage; (2) accumulations of dirt, oil, or moisture; or (3) ultimate deterioration of the insulation due to all these.

☼ **1-11 Voltage** Electric current is a flow of electrons. The more electrons there are in motion, the stronger the current. Also, the greater the concentration of electrons, the higher the repulsive force, or pressure, between electrons. And the higher the pressure goes, the more electrons will flow.

In the last sentence, substitute "voltage" for "pressure" and "current" for "electrons." The sentence then reads, "And the higher the voltage goes, the more current will flow." A high voltage means a high electric pressure, or a massing of many electrons. Voltage is measured in units of electric pressure called *volts.*

☼ **1-12 Amperage** Electric current, or electron flow, is measured in amperes of electric current. When relatively few electrons flow in an electric circuit, the amperage is low. When many electrons flow, the amperage is high. The actual number of electrons flowing is enormous. For example, a 1-ampere alternator (a small unit capable of lighting a small light bulb) will supply more than 6 billion billion electrons a second.

☼ **1-13 Direct and alternating current** A battery furnishes direct current. That is, this current (or electrons) always flows out from the negative terminal through the circuit connected to the battery and back into the positive terminal. The current always flows in the same direction when the battery is furnishing current. With alternating current, the current flows first

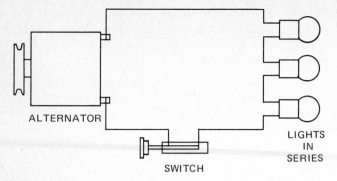

Fig. 1-11 When light bulbs are connected in series, the same current flows through all.

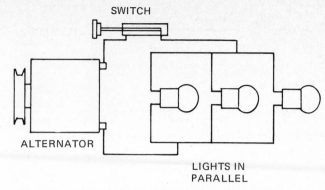

Fig. 1-12 When light bulbs are connected in parallel to the current source, the current divides, part of it flowing through each light bulb.

in one direction and then in the other. Alternating current is induced in the generator or alternator windings. The direct current generators have commutators which change this alternating current to direct current. Alternators use diodes to rectify, or change, the alternating current to direct current. (Diodes are explained in Chapter 2.) Since the battery and most other automotive electric units are direct-current devices, they can operate only on direct current. Direct current is usually referred to as *dc* and alternating current as *ac*.

The electricity used in your home is probably alternating current: 60-cycle ac to be exact. This means that the current goes through a complete cycle of changing directions 60 times a second. That is, it flows in one direction for a fraction of a second, reverses direction, and then switches back again. When this occurs 60 times a second, it is 60-cycle alternating current (called 60 hertz [Hz] in the metric system).

✿ 1-14 Resistance An insulator is highly resistant to the passage of electrons through it. Conductors offer a relatively small resistance. Even so, the best of conductors, such as copper wire, resists somewhat the movement of electrons in it. This is because a continuing "push" or pressure is necessary to keep the electrons moving in the same direction along the wire. Without this continuing pressure (or voltage), the electrons would resume their random movements in all directions in the wire.

Resistance of any wire is measured in *ohms*. A 1000-foot [304.8 m] length of No. 10 wire (which is about 0.1 inch [3.0 mm] in diameter) has a resistance of 1 ohm. A 2000-foot [609.6 m] length has a resistance of 2 ohms. If the wire size is increased to No. 4 (which is about 0.2 inch [6.1 mm] in diameter, or four times the cross-sectional area), 1000 feet [304.8 m] has only ¼-ohm resistance. It requires 4000 feet [1219.2 m] of this wire to produce a resistance of 1 ohm.

EXPLANATION: In the No. 4 wire, there are four times as many copper atoms as in the No. 10 wire. It is thus four times easier for electrons to move in the larger wire. There are four times as many atoms for the electrons to jump between, as well as four times as many free electrons in motion. With the same voltage, or push, four times as much current will flow.

To sum up, resistance varies with four factors:

1. Material (Some materials have more resistance than others.)
2. Cross section (The larger the cross section, the lower the resistance.)
3. Length (The longer the wire, the more resistance it has.)
4. Temperature (With many materials, the higher the temperature, the greater the resistance.)

✿ 1-15 Ohm's law The relationship between resistance, electron flow (or current), and pressure (or voltage) can be summed up by a statement known as Ohm's law, which is

Voltage is equal to amperage times ohms resistance

This law can be stated as the mathematical formula

$$V = I \times R$$

Other forms of the formula are

$$R = \frac{V}{I} \quad \text{and} \quad I = \frac{V}{R}$$

In each of these formulas, V is the voltage in volts, I is the current in amperes, and R is the resistance in ohms. The basic point to remember about Ohm's law is that as the resistance of a circuit goes up, the amount of the current that flows in the circuit will go down, voltage remaining the same. In automotive electric circuits, resistance sometimes goes up. This is due to loose or corroded connections and broken strands in electric cables. When resistance goes up, current flow goes down. The result can be dim lights, poor ignition-system action, a run-down battery, and other troubles. We look into these troubles later in the book.

✿ 1-16 Series circuits In series circuits, each electric device is connected to other electric devices in such a way that the same current flows through all (Fig. 1-11). That is, there is only one path for the current to follow. If any one device is turned off, the circuit is broken and no current flows in any device in the circuit.

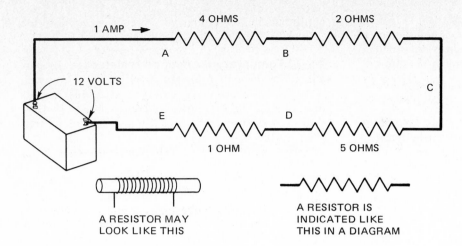

A RESISTOR MAY
LOOK LIKE THIS

A RESISTOR IS
INDICATED LIKE
THIS IN A DIAGRAM

Fig. 1-13 A series circuit made of four resistors of varying resistances.

☼ 1-17 Parallel circuits

In parallel circuits, the various devices are connected by parallel wires (Fig. 1-12). The current divides, part of it flowing into one device, part into another, and so on. Practically the same voltage is applied to each device, and each device can be turned on or off independently of the others.

NOTE: Many automotive circuits are series–parallel circuits. For instance, the headlights are connected to the battery in parallel. Both are connected in series to the battery through a lighting switch (Fig. 1-14).

☼ 1-18 Resistance in parallel and series circuits

It is simple to figure the resistance of a series circuit. The resistance will be the sum of the resistances of the various components of the circuit. In Fig. 1-13, the total resistance, ignoring the wires between the resistors, is 4 plus 2 plus 5 plus 1, or 12 ohms. Using Ohm's law, we can calculate that 1.0 ampere will flow from the 12-volt battery through the 12-ohm circuit.

The resistances of parallel circuits are more difficult to calculate. Paralleling devices reduce the resistance, so that more current flows. For example, the headlights of an automobile are in parallel (Fig. 1-14). To calculate the resistance of a number of circuits in parallel, use the formula

$$R = \frac{1}{\dfrac{1}{r_1} + \dfrac{1}{r_2} + \dfrac{1}{r_3} + \dfrac{1}{r_4} \cdots} \text{ ohm}$$

in which R is the total resistance of the group in ohms, and r_1, r_2, r_3, r_4, and so on, are the resistances of the individual circuits.

EXAMPLE: Suppose that the resistance of each of the headlights shown in Fig. 1-14 is 1 ohm. The total resistance would then be

$$R = \frac{1}{{}^1/_1 + {}^1/_1} = \frac{1}{1 + 1} = \frac{1}{2} \text{ ohm}$$

EXAMPLE: As a more complicated example, suppose we had a parallel circuit with three resistors of 1, 2, and 4 ohms. The resistance would be

$$R = \frac{1}{{}^1/_1 + {}^1/_2 + {}^1/_4}$$

$$= \frac{1}{{}^4/_4 + {}^2/_4 + {}^1/_4}$$

$$= \frac{1}{{}^7/_4} = \frac{4}{7} = 0.57 \text{ ohm}$$

☼ 1-19 Voltage drop

Voltage drops, or is used up, in overcoming resistance. The greater the resistance, the greater the voltage drop. If the voltage across each of the resistors in the circuit shown in Fig. 1-13 were checked with a voltmeter, the voltages would add up to 12 volts. For instance, the voltage between A and B, or across the 4-ohm resistor, would be 4 volts. From B to C, it would be 2 volts. From C to D, it would be 5 volts. From D to E, it would be 1 volt. If we did not know the resistance of any of the resistors, we could find it by measuring the voltage and amperage. Then we would use Ohm's law ($R = V/I$). For instance, resistance of resistor AB would be 4 volts divided by 1 ampere, or 4 ohms.

The voltage is gradually "used up" or "drops" from one end of the circuit to the other. The voltage drops 4 volts across the 4-ohm resistor so that a voltage measurement between points B and E would be 8 volts.

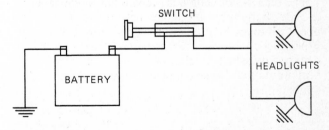

Fig. 1-14 The headlight circuit in an automobile is a series–parallel circuit. The two headlights are in parallel with each other but are connected in series with the light switch to the battery.

From C to E it would be 6 volts, and from D to E it would be 1 volt. Any resistance in a circuit causes a voltage loss, or *voltage drop*. Voltage drop is also called the *IR drop*. This comes from the formula $V = IR$.

NOTE: In a series circuit, for example, the sum of the voltage drops equals the applied or source voltage.

EXPLANATION: The electric push, or voltage, is used up along the circuit. Each unit of resistance, whether it is the wire itself or a connected electric device, "uses up" some of the electric push as the voltage forces electrons through these resistances.

☼ 1-20 Importance of voltage drop The automotive electrician must understand voltage drop. Excessive voltage drop in the headlight circuit, for example, means low voltage at the headlights and, therefore, dim headlights. Excessive voltage drop in the charging circuit between the alternator and the battery might produce an excessively low charging voltage at the battery. In this case, the battery would very likely become discharged. Another example is that a voltage drop of 1 volt in the ignition primary circuit can mean a loss of 2000 volts in the secondary circuit. This could reduce the secondary voltage so much that spark plugs might not fire and the engine would miss and run poorly.

Excessive voltage drop can be caused by wires that are too small, broken strands in a cable, bad connections, defective contact points (for instance, in the ignition distributor), and so on. These conditions set up added resistance within the circuit, and this resistance "uses up" part of the voltage. Then there is not enough voltage left to properly operate the headlights, battery, ignition coil, or other electric devices.

There is another way of looking at excessive resistance caused by a bad connection. Such a bad connection cuts down the size of the electron path, so that fewer electrons can get through. Too few electrons then reach the headlight, for instance, and it becomes dim.

☼ 1-21 Resistance heating As electric current flows through a conductor, a heating effect results. Normally, the heating effect is very slight and does no harm. But if the wire is too small, there will be considerable heating. Likewise, a bad connection will become hot.

NOTE: Any connection that becomes abnormally hot when current flows through it is not in good condition.

The reason for the heating effect is as follows. Voltage, or electric pressure, causes electrons to hop from one atom to another. There is also a certain amount of "bumping about," so that the atoms proceed to move faster. And when atoms move faster, the substance becomes hotter. That is, fast atom motion means a high temperature. Thus, the more bumping about the atoms get (from a heavier electron flow), the hotter the conductor becomes.

NOTE: An electric light bulb is simply a tungsten conductor, called the *filament*, in an airtight glass envelope. When the light bulb is connected to an electric circuit, electrons bombard the tungsten atoms so hard that the filament becomes very hot. It gets so hot that it glows brilliantly and gives off light.

☼ 1-22 Temperature effect on resistance As current passes through it, the resistance of a wire—as well as its temperature—may also increase. Most metals show this effect. A simple explanation might be this: With increased temperature, the atoms of metal that make up the wire are moving faster. The electrons, therefore, have a harder time jumping between the faster-moving atoms.

Not all substances show this increase of resistance with increase of temperature. The oxides of some metals, such as manganese, nickel, cobalt, copper, iron, and so on, show the reverse effect. That is, as their temperature goes up, their resistance goes down. They are called *negative-coefficient resistors*. This effect is made use of in electric devices called *thermistors*. Thermistors have many uses, from temperature measurement to control of many types of mechanisms. The engine-temperature gauge in many automobiles uses a thermistor.

Magnetism and electromagnetism

☼ 1-23 Magnetism Magnetism is a connecting link between mechanical energy and electricity. Magnetism in the alternator produces a flow of electrons (current) that lights the headlights, operates the ignition, and charges the battery. Likewise, a flow of electrons from the battery is transformed by magnetism into mechanical energy in the starting motor to crank the engine. Thus, magnetism can produce current (a flow of electrons), and current can produce magnetism.

☼ 1-24 Magnets Most of us have seen bar and horseshoe magnets (Fig. 1-15). Their various actions and characteristics can be shown by experiment. Following pages explain these actions and characteristics of magnets and their use in alternators, regulators, starting motors, and ignition coils.

Two basic rules of magnetism are:

Like poles repel. North repels north. South repels south.

Unlike poles attract. North attracts south. South attracts north.

☼ 1-25 Magnetic field and flux The space around a magnet is called a *magnetic field*. The magnetic field

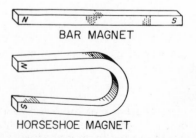

Fig. 1-15 Bar magnet and horseshoe magnet.

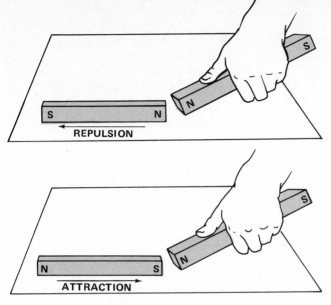

Fig. 1-16 Like magnetic poles repel each other. Unlike magnetic poles attract each other.

is assumed to be filled more or less completely with magnetic lines of force. When the magnet is weak, there are relatively few lines of force. When the magnet is strong, there are many lines of force. The lines of force as a group are called magnetic *flux*. When the magnet is strong so that there are many lines of force, the magnetic field is said to have a high *flux density*. When the magnet is weak, the flux density is low.

☼ 1-26 Characteristics of magnetic lines of force

To us, lines of force are invisible, unfelt, and, in fact, imaginary. However, they are assumed to exist because they help to explain many of the effects of magnetism. Lines of force are assumed to stretch, or "move," between the north and south poles of a magnet. On the outside of the magnet, they move from the north to the south pole. On the inside of the magnet, they move from the south to the north pole, thus completing the magnetic circuit.

Lines of force tend to parallel each other. They do not cross but tend to push adjacent lines of force away. This tendency makes the lines of force want to separate

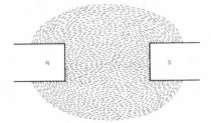

Fig. 1-17 Magnetic lines of force between two unlike magnetic poles. Magnetic lines of force stretching between poles tend to shorten, thus producing the attractive force between the unlike poles.

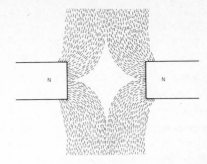

Fig. 1-18 Magnetic lines of force between two like poles. Magnetic lines of force tend to parallel each other, thus forcing the two line poles away from each other.

or spread out. Opposing this tendency is the "rubber-band" characteristic of lines of force. This characteristic tries to shorten the lines of force. They become more closely packed together as they stretch from magnetic pole to magnetic pole.

The attraction between unlike poles and repulsion between like poles, illustrated in Fig. 1-16, can be explained in terms of the rubber-band characteristic. When unlike poles approach each other, the lines of force, which are stretching between the north and south poles, tend to shorten like rubber bands (Fig. 1-17). This pulls the unlike poles together. However, when like poles are brought near each other, many lines of force are brought into parallel. The repulsions between the parallel lines of force tend to push the poles apart (Fig. 1-18). These repulsions and attractions between like and unlike magnetic poles are used in electric motors. In motors, magnetic fields are set up which attract or oppose each other, and the resulting forces make the motor armature spin.

☼ 1-27 Electromagnetism

A current of electricity (that is, a flow of electrons) always produces magnetism or magnetic lines of force. Magnetism produced by electric current is called *electromagnetism*. As we shall see in following chapters, alternators, regulators, electric motors, and ignition coils contain windings, or coils, made of many turns of wire. These windings, or coils, produce magnetism when current passes through them. They are often called *electromagnets* (Fig. 1-19).

☼ 1-28 An explanation of electromagnetism

Electromagnetism is produced by the motion of electrons. Each electron is like a tiny magnet. When electrons move about in all directions in a conductor (no current flowing), the magnetic effects of the electrons

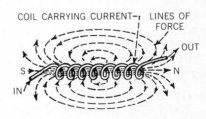

Fig. 1-19 An electromagnet is a coil of wire that is carrying electric current.

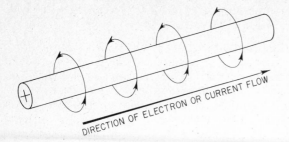

Fig. 1-20 Direction that magnetic lines of force circle a current-carrying conductor.

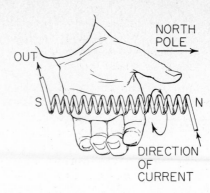

Fig. 1-22 The left-hand rule determines the north pole of an electromagnet.

cancel out. But when a voltage is applied to the conductor, electrons begin to move through the wire in the same direction. The magnetic effect then becomes apparent. The magnetism of the electrons, moving in the same direction, adds up to produce lines of force around the conductor.

NOTE: Magnets which retain their magnetism (permanent magnets) do not depend upon a flow of electricity. But their magnetism can be explained in terms of electron motion. In an unmagnetized piece of iron, the iron atoms are not lined up in any particular order. The electrons circling the nuclei of the iron atoms produce magnetic effects, but these effects cancel each other out. However, when the piece of iron is magnetized so that it becomes a magnet, the iron atoms are forced into a more definite alignment. Now, with many electrons circling many iron-atom nuclei in the same direction, the magnetic effects of the electrons in motion add up to produce the magnetic field. Heat or heavy blows may cause a magnet to lose its magnetism. These forces disturb the atomic alignment that permits the electrons of the iron atoms to add their magnetic effect.

☼ 1-29 The left-hand rule The left-hand rule lets you determine the direction of the magnetic lines of force around a conductor through which current (or a flow of electrons) moves. The rule can also be used to determine the north and south poles of an electromagnet, as explained in a following section. When electricity flows in a wire in the direction shown in Fig. 1-20, the lines of force circle the wire in the direction shown by the circular arrows. Note that the current is shown flowing away from you. This is indicated by the small

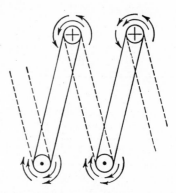

Fig. 1-23 Magnetic lines of force around two adjacent turns in a coil carrying current. The front halves of the turns are shown as broken lines.

cross in the end of the conductor. If the current were flowing toward you, this would be indicated by a dot. You can remember this by thinking of an arrow. If the arrow were coming toward you, you would see the point as a dot. If it were moving away from you, you would see the tail feathers as a cross.

In Fig. 1-20, the lines of force are shown as circling the conductor in a *counterclockwise* direction or in a direction opposite to, or counter to, the direction in which the hands of a clock move.

To use the left-hand rule, simply circle the conductor with the fingers of the left hand, with the thumb pointing in the direction of current (or electron) flow. We assume that the current of electrons, or the electron flow, is from negative to positive. The curled-up fingers will be

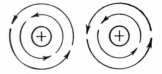

Fig. 1-24 Close-up of wire ends, showing circling lines of force.

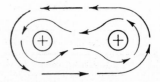

Fig. 1-25 The way lines of force merge.

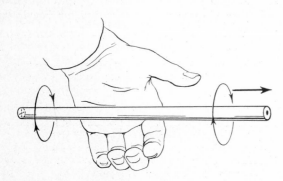

Fig. 1-21 The left-hand rule determines the direction that lines of force circle a conductor carrying current.

pointing in the direction that the lines of force circle the conductor (Fig. 1-21). The left-hand rule can also be used with electromagnets to determine magnetic polarity. This is explained in a later section.

NOTE: Before the electron theory of electricity was understood, it was assumed that current flowed from positive to negative. Therefore a *right-hand rule* was used to show the relationship between magnetic lines of force and current flow. Later, when current flow was found to be a movement of electrons from negative to positive, it was easy to change the right-hand rule to the left-hand rule. The right-hand rule is mentioned here because it is still in use to some extent and the

above explanation will enable the student to understand why there are two rules.

⚙ **1-30 Electromagnets** When many turns of wire are wrapped into a coil and current is passed through the coil, the lines of force around adjacent turns of wire add up to make a magnetic field (Fig. 1-19). If we use the left-hand rule on the coil, we can determine north and south poles. Place the hand around the coil with the fingers pointing in the direction of current flow (assuming it flows from negative to positive). The thumb will then point toward the north pole of the coil (Fig. 1-22). The coil is producing magnetism electrically and is called an *electromagnet*.

	ELECTRICAL SYMBOLS			
SYMBOL	**REPRESENTS**	**SYMBOL**	**REPRESENTS**	
(ALT)	ALTERNATOR	HORN	HORN	
(A)	AMMETER		LAMP OR BULB	(Preferred)
─┤├─	BATTERY-ONE CELL		LAMP OR BULB	(Acceptable)
─┤│├─	BATTERY-MULTICELL	(MOT)	MOTOR-ELECTRIC	
12 V ─┤│├─	(Where required, battery voltage or polarity or both may be indicated as shown in example. The long line is always positive polarity.)	─	NEGATIVE	
BAT	BATTERY-VOLTAGE BOX	+	POSITIVE	
─⊓⊓⊓─	BI-METAL STRIP		RELAY	
─┼─	CABLE-CONNECTED	─◟◞◟◞─	RESISTOR	
─┼─	CABLE-NOT CONNECTED		RESISTOR-VARIABLE	
─┤├─	CAPACITOR	IDLE STOP	SOLENOID-IDLE STOP	
	CIRCUIT BREAKER			
─<	CONNECTOR-FEMALE CONTACT		STARTING MOTOR	
─→	CONNECTOR-MALE CONTACT			
─≫─	CONNECTORS-SEPARABLE-ENGAGED			
─▶├─	DIODE			
	DISTRIBUTOR	─◦◜◦─	SWITCH-SINGLE THROW	
		─◦ ◦─	SWITCH-DOUBLE THROW	
─◠◡◠─	FUSE	(TACH)	TACHOMETER	
(FUEL)	GAUGE-FUEL	─●─	TERMINATION	
(TEMP)	GAUGE-TEMPERATURE	(V)	VOLTMETER	
─╪	GROUND-CHASSIS FRAME (Preferred)	─◠◠◠─ OR ─◡◡◡─	WINDING-INDUCTOR	
─╫	GROUND-CHASSIS FRAME (Acceptable)			

Fig. 1-26 Electrical symbols used in wiring diagrams. *(General Motors Corporation)*

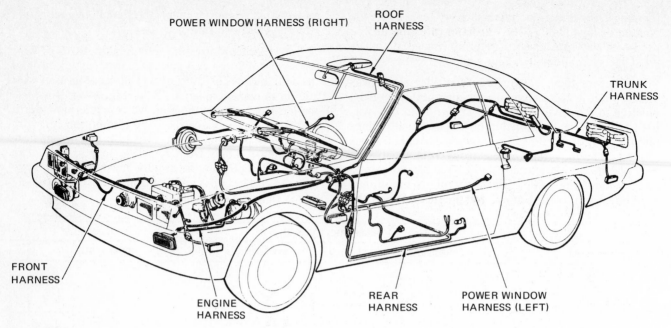

Fig. 1-27 Wiring harnesses for a late-model car. *(Chrysler Corporation)*

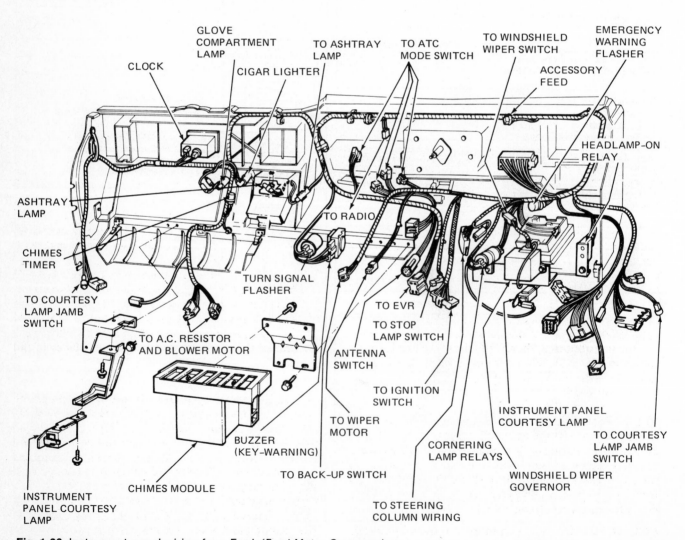

Fig. 1-28 Instrument-panel wiring for a Ford. *(Ford Motor Company)*

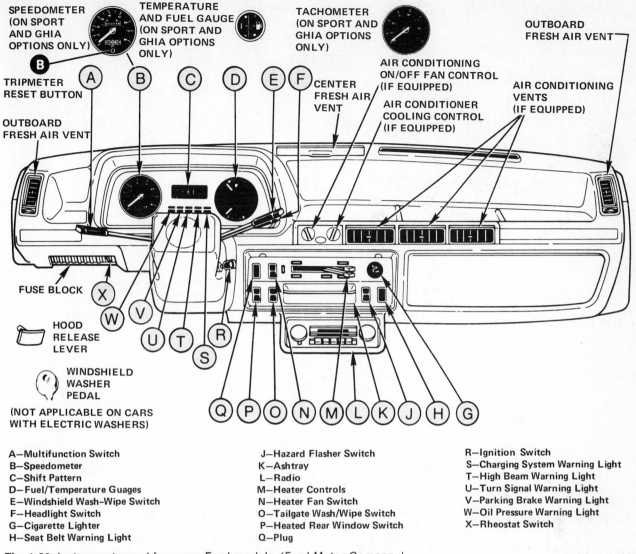

Fig. 1-29 Instrument panel for some Ford models. *(Ford Motor Company)*

A—Multifunction Switch
B—Speedometer
C—Shift Pattern
D—Fuel/Temperature Guages
E—Windshield Wash–Wipe Switch
F—Headlight Switch
G—Cigarette Lighter
H—Seat Belt Warning Light

J—Hazard Flasher Switch
K—Ashtray
L—Radio
M—Heater Controls
N—Heater Fan Switch
O—Tailgate Wash/Wipe Switch
P—Heated Rear Window Switch
Q—Plug

R—Ignition Switch
S—Charging System Warning Light
T—High Beam Warning Light
U—Turn Signal Warning Light
V—Parking Brake Warning Light
W—Oil Pressure Warning Light
X—Rheostat Switch

Let us examine only two turns of the coil so we can see how the lines of force around the conductors add up to produce the combined magnetic effect. When current flows in both turns in the same direction, the lines of force circle both in the same direction (Fig. 1-23). This means that the lines of force between the two are in opposite directions (Fig. 1-24). Since they are in opposite directions and of equal force, they cancel out, and the lines of force, therefore, circle the two turns as shown in Fig. 1-25. With additional turns, the lines of force circle them also, so that the pattern shown in Fig. 1-19 is produced.

☸ 1-31 Permeability The electromagnet discussed in the previous section has an air core. That is, the core or space inside the coil is composed of air. If we were to insert a piece of iron inside the coil or were to wrap the coil around a piece of iron, the coil would have an iron core. An iron core gives the coil a much more powerful magnetic effect.

EXPLANATION: Iron is much more *permeable* than air. Iron permits the magnetic lines of force to *permeate*, or pass through, the iron much more easily than does air. Iron is thus said to have much greater *permeability* than air.

Because iron offers an easy path for the lines of force, it is considered to be a conductor of magnetism, somewhat as copper is a conductor of electricity. Iron in one form or another is used in motors, alternators, ignition coils, regulators, and other electric machinery to conduct the magnetism to the proper places in the device.

☸ 1-32 Electrical symbols In the wiring diagrams that you will find in this book, there are many symbols that stand for specific electric items. Figure 1-26 shows most of the symbols that you will run across as you study this book. As you examine the wiring diagrams in the book, you will become familiar with the symbols and what they mean. This will be of great help to you when you go out into the shop and are required to read wiring diagrams in manufacturers' shop manuals. The manufacturers use symbols like those shown in Fig. 1-26.

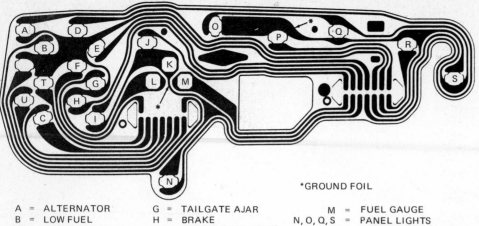

*GROUND FOIL

A	=	ALTERNATOR	G	=	TAILGATE AJAR
B	=	LOW FUEL	H	=	BRAKE
C	=	LIGHTS ON	I	=	FASTEN SEAT BELTS
D	=	ENGINE	J	=	RIGHT TURN SIGNAL
E	=	HOT	K	=	GROUND
■ F	=	FASTEN SEAT BELTS	L	=	12V (IGN)

M	=	FUEL GAUGE
N, O, Q, S	=	PANEL LIGHTS
P	=	HI BEAM INDICATOR
R	=	LEFT TURN INDICATOR
T	=	WAIT
U	=	START

Fig. 1-30 Printed circuit for instrument-cluster assembly. *(Oldsmobile Division of General Motors Corporation)*

■ USED WITH REMINDER PACKAGE ONLY

⚙ 1-33 Wiring circuits With the increasing number of electrically operated devices in the modern automobile, the wiring circuits have become rather complex. Figure 1-27 shows the wiring harnesses for one model of automobile. The wires between components are bound together into harnesses. Each wire is marked by special colors in the insulation, for example, light green, dark green, blue, red, black with a white tracer, and so on. These markings permit identification of the various wires in the harnesses.

The circuits through the bulkhead, which is between the engine-compartment components and the instrument panel, are completed by connector plugs and receptacles. Figure 1-28 shows how the wiring harnesses are positioned and how the various connections are made. In this illustration, the instrument-panel cluster is shown removed so the back of it can be seen. As many as a dozen separate wires are gathered together and connected to a receptacle. Then the matching wires are connected to the matching plug. It becomes a simple matter, then, to push the plug into the receptacle to

complete many connections at one time. Matching tangs and holes complete the connections between the wires. The plugs and receptacles have locking devices that prevent their coming loose in operation.

⚙ 1-34 Printed circuits The instrument panel carries a number of indicating devices, switches, and controls (Fig. 1-29). These must be interconnected electrically, either with separate wires or with a printed-circuit board. Because there must be a dozen or more connections in a small space and this would make separate wires hard to connect, car manufacturers use printed circuits to make the connections. Figure 1-30 shows the location of a printed circuit in the back of an instrument-cluster assembly. The printed circuit is a flat board of either rigid or flexible insulating ma-

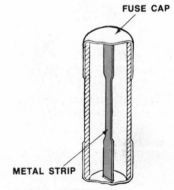

Fig. 1-32 Sectional view of a cartridge fuse.

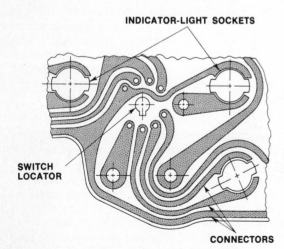

Fig. 1-31 Part of a printed circuit. The connectors are metallic strips printed on the insulating base.

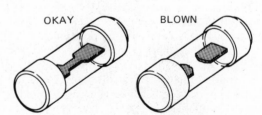

Fig. 1-33 A good and a "blown" fuse. *(Ford Motor Company)*

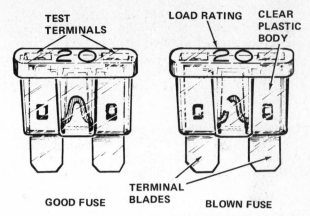

GOOD FUSE   TERMINAL BLADES   BLOWN FUSE

Fig. 1-35 A good and a blown miniaturized fuse. Note the terminals to test the fuse. *(Buick Motor Division of General Motors Corporation)*

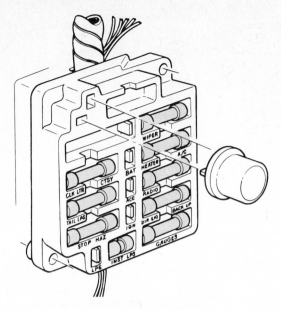

Fig. 1-34 Fuse block, with cartridge fuses in place. *(Chevrolet Motor Division of General Motors Corporation)*

terial such as plastic on which a series of metallic, conducting strips are printed or otherwise applied. Figure 1-31 shows part of a printed circuit. When it is installed as shown in Fig. 1-30, the conducting strips complete the circuits. The contacts on the indicator lights rest on the conducting strips at the light sockets when the lights are installed, thus completing the circuits to the lights.

✿ 1-35 Fuses, fusible links, and circuit breakers

Most electric circuits have fuses, fusible links, or circuit breakers. They protect the electric components from damage if a short circuit or ground develops and dangerously high currents start to flow. If this should

happen, the fuse or fuse link "blows," or the circuit breaker opens, opening the circuit.

A typical "old-style" cartridge fuse is shown partly cut away in Fig. 1-32. It contains a soft metal strip, connected at the ends to the fuse caps. It is connected in series in the circuit. All current in the circuit flows through the fuse. If excessive current flows, the metal strip overheats and melts or "blows" (Fig. 1-33). This opens the circuit and protects the rest of the circuit and connected electric devices from damage. When a fuse blows, the circuit should be checked to see what caused it to blow. Then, after the trouble is fixed, a new fuse should be installed. Figure 1-34 shows the type of fuse block that takes the cartridge fuse.

Instead of the cartridge fuse, shown in Fig. 1-32, many cars today use a U-shaped fuse (Fig. 1-35). This fuse was engineered for compactness and ease of service. The type of fuse block in which these fuses are installed is shown in Fig. 1-36.

Fig. 1-36 Fuse panel using miniaturized fuses. *(Chevrolet Motor Division of General Motors Corporation)*

A fuse link, or fusible link as it is also called, is a short length of wire in series with a circuit. It is of a smaller size (or gauge) than the circuit it protects. It burns out if excessive currents start to flow. Fuse links are covered in detail in ☀8-18.

Figure 1-37 shows a fuse block which includes circuit breakers and the horn relay. Circuit breakers do the same job as fuses except that they do not "blow" when an overload occurs. Instead, they open contact points to interrupt the circuit. When the overload condition is eliminated, the contact points close to complete the circuit again. Figure 1-38 shows how a circuit breaker works. When too much current flows, the metal blade becomes hot. The heat causes the two metal strips to expand at different rates, bending the blade upward so that the contacts separate, thus interrupting the circuit.

Summary of electricity's and magnetism's rules of behavior

1. Current is a flow of electrons and is measured in amperes.
2. Voltage is an absence of, or an excess of, electrons in sections of an electric circuit. It is measured in volts.
3. Resistance is just what its name implies—the resistance any substance has to the passage of electrons. It is measured in ohms.
4. The relationship between voltage, amperage, and resistance is expressed by the formula $V = I \times R$, $I = V/R$, $R = V/I$.
5. Magnetism is produced by a flow of electrons in a circuit.
6. A magnetic field may be thought of as lines of force.
7. To use the left-hand rule to find the direction of the lines of force around a single conductor, curl the left hand around the conductor with the thumb pointing in the direction of the current flow. The fingers will point in the direction the lines of force circle the conductor.

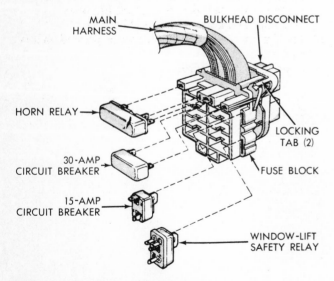

Fig. 1-37 Fuse block and related parts on one model of car. *(Chrysler Corporation)*

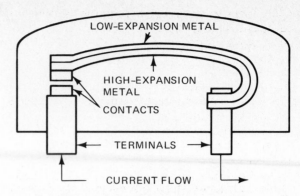

Fig. 1-38 Circuit breaker. When too much current flows and it gets hot, the bimetal strip bends and separates the contacts, as shown.

8. To use the left-hand rule to find the north and south poles of a coil, put the left hand around the coil with the fingers pointing in the direction of the current flow through the turns of wire. The thumb points toward the north pole of the coil.
9. When two magnetic fields are brought close to each other, a force will be exerted between them. This force will be one of either attraction or repulsion, according to the way the magnetic poles line up (principle of electric motor).
10. Unlike magnetic poles attract each other.
11. Like magnetic poles repel each other.

Chapter 1 review questions

Select the *one* correct, best, or most probable answer to each question. Then check your answers against the correct answers given at the end of the book.

1. A substance made up entirely of only one type of atom is called:
   a. a particle,
   b. an electron,
   c. an element,
   d. a proton.
2. The hydrogen atom is made up of two particles, which are:
   a. proton and neutron,
   b. proton and electron,
   c. proton and nucleus,
   d. element and electron.
3. The particle that has a negative electric charge is called:
   a. an electron,
   b. a proton,
   c. a neutron,
   d. an element.
4. The negative terminal of an active battery cell has more:
   a. electrons than protons,
   b. protons than electrons,
   c. neutrons than electrons,
   d. atoms than neutrons.

5. Substances that strongly oppose the movement of electrons through them are called:
   a. conductors,
   b. metals,
   c. insulators,
   d. semiconductors.
6. Electrons that form electric current in a conductor come from the atom's:
   a. outer orbit,
   b. inner orbit,
   c. nucleus,
   d. center.
7. A basic characteristic of a semiconductor is that it:
   a. usually has high resistance,
   b. is a pure element,
   c. has negative-type material,
   d. can be either a conductor or an insulator.
8. The more electrons there are crowded at one alternator terminal (and the fewer electrons there are at the other terminal), the:
   a. lower the voltage,
   b. greater the resistance,
   c. higher the voltage,
   d. faster the alternator turns.
9. When electric devices are connected so that the same current flows through all of them, then we have a:
   a. parallel circuit,
   b. series circuit,
   c. series–parallel circuit,
   d. parallel–series circuit.
10. When electric devices are connected so that the same voltage is applied to each, then we have a:
    a. parallel circuit,
    b. series circuit,
    c. series–parallel circuit,
    d. parallel-series circuit.
11. Three resistors of 2, 3, and 4 ohms are connected in series. The resistance of this combination is:
    a. 1 ohm,
    b. 2 ohms,
    c. 9 ohms,
    d. 24 ohms.
12. Three resistors of 2, 2, and 4 ohms are connected in parallel. The resistance of this combination is:
    a. 0.4 ohm,
    b. 0.8 ohm,
    c. 8 ohms,
    d. 16 ohms.

13. Voltage drop is also called:
    a. VR drop,
    b. VI drop,
    c. IR drop,
    d. CD drop.
14. Opposing the tendency of the magnetic lines of force to separate and spread out is their:
    a. repulsion characteristic,
    b. crossing characteristic,
    c. rubber band characteristic,
    d. spring effect.
15. Magnetic lines of force:
    a. are real,
    b. are imaginary,
    c. can be felt,
    d. can be seen.
16. When using the left-hand rule, place the hand around the coil with the fingers pointing in the direction of current flow; the thumb will point to the:
    a. north pole,
    b. south pole,
    c. current flow,
    d. voltage flow.
17. Magnetic lines of force between adjacent conductors, when of equal force and in opposite directions, will:
    a. attract each other,
    b. cancel out,
    c. cancel the current flow,
    d. reduce the voltage.
18. A substance which permits magnetic lines of force to pass through it with great ease is said to have a high degree of:
    a. permeability,
    b. permanence,
    c. conductance,
    d. resistance.
19. The three devices that protect the electric circuit of the automobile are:
    a. fuses, wiring, and alternator,
    b. fuses, fusible links, and wiring,
    c. fuses, fusible links, and circuit breakers,
    d. circuit breakers, relays, and battery.
20. The flat board with conductor strips printed on it is called:
    a. an insulating board,
    b. a printed board,
    c. a printed circuit,
    d. a panel.

ELECTRONICS AND THE AUTOMOBILE

After studying this chapter, you should be able to:

1. Explain what the word *electronics* means.
2. List six applications of electronics to automobiles.
3. Explain what a semiconductor is and how it can become either a conductor or an insulator.
4. Explain how a diode and a transistor work.

2-1 What is electronics?   Electronics is a specialized area of the more general study and application of electricity. Electronics depends on *solid-state* devices for its actions. A solid-state device is exactly what its name implies. It is solid, and it has no moving mechanical parts. The only thing that moves in it is a flow of electricity, or electrons. These solid-state or electronic devices can do many things:

Produce current amplification

Store information (memory systems)

Receive and analyze data

Control other electronic and mechanical devices

Solve problems and supply answers in the form of some action, a typed manuscript, or a visual display

And the electronic devices can perform these actions at incredible speeds. Modern electronic computers can do millions of calculations in a second. The electronic controls used in many cars are high-speed devices. For example, many cars have an ignition system which electronically controls the timing of the spark. A series of sensing devices continuously reports engine operating conditions to the electronic control. The electronic control compares these data with data stored in its memory system. It then sends out signals to the ignition system "telling" it what the proper timing is for the operating condition. All this is done at very high speed so that timing is continuously readjusted as engine operating conditions change.

This chapter discusses solid-state devices, computer memory, and computers. The chapter thus lays the groundwork for the later chapters in the book which describe the many electronic devices now being used on automobiles.

2-2 Electronics in automobiles   Electronics is playing an increasingly important role in the automobile, especially in the control of operating components. First we had electronic devices taking over control of the alternator. This eliminated the old-style regulator with its vibrating contact points. Next came electronic ignition systems, which eliminated the distributor contact points. Following that came electronic spark control which eliminated the centrifugal and vacuum-spark-advance devices in the ignition system. Right on the heels of that development came the electronic control of the fuel system. This control continuously adjusts the richness of the air–fuel mixture going into the engine. This improves gasoline mileage and at the same time reduces atmospheric pollution from the exhaust gases.

You do not often think of them that way, but radios are also electronic devices. Also, some cars have electronic rear-end levelers. As loads are added to or removed from the rear of the car, the electronic leveler readjusts the car suspension to maintain its level position. Some automatic transmissions now have electronic devices that decide when shifts should be made, and then they cause these shifts to occur. Many modern cars are equipped with electronic antilock brake systems. These prevent wheel lockup during hard braking to guard against skids and improve braking effectiveness. Electronic cruise controls are now appearing on cars. These maintain the speed that the driver selects even though the driver's foot is off the accelerator pedal. Some cars have visual displays that report to the driver such operating data as expressway vehicle location, miles per gallon, elapsed time since starting out, average miles or kilometers per hour, continuously updated arrival time at destination, average cost per mile or kilometer, and so on. Coming in the future are other electronic devices such as anticollision radar which

, showing only the four

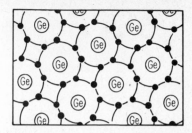

Fig. 2-2 When germanium atoms combine, they share the electrons in their outer orbits. In effect, all outer orbits are filled with eight electrons each. The germanium, therefore, becomes an insulator.

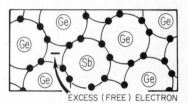

EXCESS (FREE) ELECTRON

Fig. 2-3 When a little antimony (Sb) is added to pure germanium, four of the five electrons in the outer orbit of the antimony atom are shared with germanium atoms. The extra electron is free, and it can move around.

rator and brakes to slow
pears likely. Some day
s buried in the highway
l an electronic control
s would steer the car,
and brake it when nec-
m the electronic device
informing it where the
could sit back and read
n. Electronic devices
roper lanes, move it at
ving at the destination,
the engine off.
f course, but more and
pear on cars in the near
come in. As you study
ed shop work, you will
any sort of electric or
n automobiles.

2-3 What electronics is Electronics is the branch of science and technology relating to the movement of electrons through gases, vacuum, or semiconductors. Electronics really started with Thomas Edison's discovery, in 1883, that electrons would flow through a vacuum from a hot electric light filament to a cold metal plate. Years later (in 1897), J. A. Fleming developed the first practical vacuum tube using this principle. Lee De Forest, in 1906, invented the triode vacuum tube that made possible early radio and long-distance telephoning. This tube was an amplifier. A small voltage applied could control a much larger voltage.

Electronics took a great step forward, however, when workers at the Bell Telephone Laboratories (John Bardeen, Walter H. Brattain, and William Shockley) invented the transistor. This device is also an amplifier, but it does the same job as the vacuum tube while producing less heat, using less energy, and occupying less space.

Today, electronics is all over the place, not only in automobiles, but also in space satellites and space vehicles, in control of manufacturing and chemical processes, in communications (radio, television, telephone), in computers that can make millions of calculations a second, and much more. Our concern in this book is what electronics is doing in the modern automobile. This chapter explains the fundamentals of electronics. Later chapters describe in detail the many uses of electronics in today's and tomorrow's automobiles.

2-4 Semiconductors We start our study of electronics by looking at semiconductors. In Chapter 1 we describe conductors and insulators. Recall that conductors have many free electrons "floating" around between the atoms of the conducting metal. Suppose we have many electrons massed at one terminal of an alternator and many electrons taken away from the other terminal. Electrons (current) will flow through any conductor that is connected between the two terminals.

Insulators have few or no free electrons floating between atoms. Therefore if you put insulation between two terminals, one of which has an excess of electrons and the other of which has a shortage of electrons, you get no action. That is, no electrons can flow through the insulation.

Semiconductors can be either conductors or insulators, depending on how the material is put together and how it is used. Germanium, a chemical element, is a semiconductor. Figure 2-1 represents an atom of germanium. It has four electrons in its outermost orbit. Germanium atoms can unite with themselves, or with atoms of other elements, to form either insulators or conductors.

As an example, if germanium atoms unite with each other (Fig. 2-2), they share outer-orbit electrons. This means that the outer orbits of all the atoms are filled with eight electrons. There are no electrons left over to move about freely. That is, when the germanium atoms share electrons as shown in Fig. 2-2, they become an insulator.

2-5 Turning a semiconductor into a conductor If we add a little antimony (Sb), another element, to the germanium, we have a conductor. Figure 2-3 shows

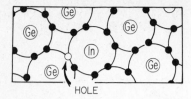

Fig. 2-4 When a little indium (In) is added to pure germanium, the three electrons in the outer orbit of the indium atoms are shared with germanium atoms. This leaves, in effect, a shortage of one electron, or a "hole."

why. The antimony atom has five electrons in its outer orbit. Four of these are shared with germanium atoms, as shown. But this leaves one electron free to move about. Free electrons moving about turn the material into a conductor. Combinations of this type, which leave electrons free, are known as *n*, or negative-type, materials because of the free electrons which are negative in electric charge.

A somewhat different sort of material results if a substance such as indium (In), another element, is added to germanium (Fig. 2-4). The indium atom has only three electrons in its outer orbit. When the indium is mixed with germanium, the three electrons in the outer orbit of the indium atom are shared with the germanium atoms. However, this leaves a shortage of one electron in the outer orbit. In effect, this shortage leaves a "hole." Since an electron has a charge of negative electricity, the absence of an electron, or the hole, results in a positive charge. The combination is known as *p*, or positive-type, material.

NOTE: Adding the impurities to the base material (germanium in this example) is called *doping* the material. The antimony added to the germanium to make *n* material is the "dope."

Free electrons can move through *n*, or negative-type, material. In the same way, the holes can move through *p*, or positive-type, materials. It may be a little hard to picture this, but think of it this way. Electrons can move from the orbit of one atom to the orbit of another atom. This fills the "hole" in the orbit of the atom getting the electron. But it leaves a hole in the orbit of the atom that lost the electron. In the end, it is all the same action—electrons moving about in the material.

⚙ 2-6 Diodes The diode is a one-way valve for electrons, or electric current. It is an up-to-date application of the effect Edison discovered in 1883—that electrons will flow in a vacuum from a hot filament to a cold metal plate. The difference here is that there is no heat, just two slices of semiconductor materials that are put together. The combination allows current to flow through in one direction but not in the other. Diodes are used in radios, television sets, battery chargers, automotive alternators, and other devices in which alternating current has to be changed to direct current. The various electronic devices in automobiles use diodes, as we learn in later chapters when we study these devices.

Changing alternating current to direct current is only one of the jobs diodes do. This process is called *recti-*

fication. The rectifier-type battery charger you see in many garages and service stations changes ordinary house alternating current to direct current to charge batteries. Diodes are used in automotive alternators, electronic ignition systems, electronic controls of fuel systems, antilock brake systems, and elsewhere.

A diode is made from a section of *n* material joined to a section of *p* material (Fig. 2-5). Since unlike charges attract, the free electrons in the *n* material move toward the holes lacking electrons in the *p* material. You might expect the two to merge at the junction, and, in fact, some crossing over does take place. But most electrons and holes are restrained by the electric charges they leave behind. Thus, a stabilized situation results, with no electrical action taking place.

If an electric charge is applied to the two sections, action may start. For example, suppose we connect a battery as shown in Fig. 2-6. The battery can now supply plenty of electrons to the *n* material. Therefore electrons can cross the junction and move from the *n* material to the *p* material. That is, electric current, or electrons, flows freely through the diode. Both the electrons and the holes move.

But the situation is different if the battery connections are reversed (Fig. 2-7). With these connections, the holes in the *p* material are attracted toward the negative terminal of the battery. The electrons in the *n* material are attracted toward the positive terminal of the battery. As a result, there are no current carriers at the junction. Therefore, no electrons—current—can flow. Current flow is blocked.

Figure 2-8 shows the use of a diode and an alternator to charge a battery. The current from the alternator flows first in one direction and then in the other. But when the diode is inserted in the circuit, as shown in Fig. 2-8, the current can flow to the battery only in the charging direction. When the current attempts to flow in the opposite direction, the diode prevents it. This protects the battery from current that would flow in the discharging direction. In an actual automotive alternator, there are three overlapping windings producing alternating current and three sets of diodes to convert the alternating current into direct current. We cover this action, and alternators, in a later chapter.

⚙ 2-7 Zener diode The Zener diode is a special type of diode which will allow current to flow in the reverse

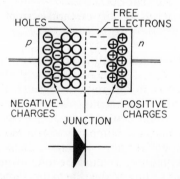

Fig. 2-5 A diode consists of thin slices of *n* and *p* materials joined together.

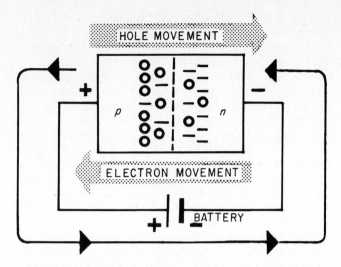

Fig. 2-6 Connecting a battery across the diode as shown permits the battery to replace the electrons leaving the *n* material and replaces the holes leaving the *p* material. Therefore, electric current can move through the diode.

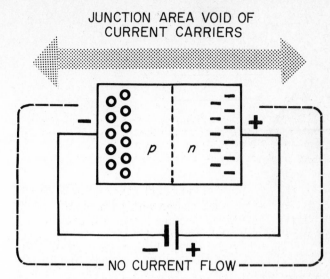

Fig. 2-7 Connecting the battery across the diode as shown prevents a flow of current through the diode. The holes and electrons are attracted away from the junction so that no current can flow through it.

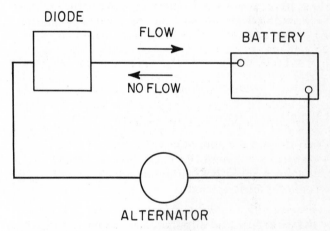

Fig. 2-8 Alternating current from an alternator can be rectified, or changed to direct current, by a diode, for charging a battery.

direction if enough voltage is applied. That is, it refuses to allow current to flow in the reverse direction as long as the reversing voltage remains low. But if the voltage reaches the breakdown level, the Zener diode will allow current to flow in the reverse direction. In other words, the resistance of the diode breaks down to near zero, and the reverse current can flow. The Zener diode is used in electronic voltage regulators to control alternator voltage and output. If the voltage reaches its regulated maximum, the diode breaks down and allows reverse current to flow. This reverse current then actuates transistors that shut off the current to the alternator field. This reduces alternator voltage. When the voltage drops below the breakdown value, the diode regains its original state and stops the flow of reverse current through it. This deactivates transistors so current can again flow to the alternator field. Alternator voltage goes up and the cycle is repeated. Actually, the complete cycle takes place several thousand times a second. This holds the voltage to a safe value. We describe regulator action in a later chapter on alternators and their regulators.

☼ 2-8 Transistors The transistor is, in effect, a diode with additional semiconductor material. This gives it the ability to amplify electric current. Figure 2-9 is a simple drawing of a transistor. The transistor shown consists of three layers of semiconductor material. The two outside layers are of the same polarity—that is, either *n* or *p*. The center layer is of the opposite polarity. If the two outside layers are of *n* material, the center layer is of *p* material. If the two outside layers are of *p* material, the center layer is of *n* material.

Figure 2-10 shows, in simplified form, the actions of a *pnp* transistor. When the switch is closed, current from the battery can flow into the center, or *n*, material which is called the *base* of the transistor. In the example shown, 0.35 ampere is flowing to the base. This floods the base with electrons. These added electrons attract

the current carriers, or holes, of the *p*-type material, and a relatively heavy current can, therefore, flow across the junctions. The important fact to note here is that a relatively small current can cause a much larger current to flow. In effect, the transistor becomes an amplifier. This amplifying effect makes the transistor useful for literally thousands of different applications—radios, television sets, electric stoves and washers, automotive alternator regulators and ignition systems, and so on.

Figure 2-11 shows what happens when the switch is open and current stops flowing to the base. Without extra current carriers being attracted to the junctions, no current can flow through the transistor.

Figure 2-12 illustrates how the two simplest types of transistors are shown in wiring diagrams. One is *npn* and the other is *pnp*. Both work the same way. In the case of the *npn* transistor, the base would be connected to the positive or plus terminal of the battery. This

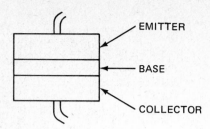

Fig. 2-9 Transistor.

would tend to drain the base of extra electrons so that plenty of holes would result. These holes become the electron or current carriers that allow a relatively high current to flow from the collector to the emitter.

There are many other more complex transistors made of more than three slices of semiconductor material. However, as a general rule, the transistors used in automotive applications are of the three-element type described above.

NOTE: You can understand, now, why diodes and transistors are called *solid-state devices*. They are solid and have no mechanical moving parts. They do their jobs with electrons and holes, as we have explained.

⚙ 2-9 Thyristor The thyristor is a semiconductor device which will not permit current flow until a small voltage is applied to it. It then permits current flow. So far, this sounds like an ordinary transistor. However, there is a difference. The activating voltage can be removed but the current still flows. It will continue to flow through the transistor until a small reverse voltage is applied. When this happens, the current flow is cut off. It will not resume until the forward, or activating, voltage is again applied.

⚙ 2-10 Integrated circuits Scientists and engineers have found ways to make diodes and transistors very small. Thus, it is possible to group thousands of these semiconductor devices in a very small package. Such packages are called *integrated circuits* (or ICs, as shown in Fig. 2-14). That is, many components are put together, or integrated, into a small package. Today, the solid-state art has progressed so far that a hundred thousand components can be crowded into a case no

larger than a half-dollar. This is called a *chip*. Chips come in many sizes and designs.

Integrated circuits on chips are used in computers and complex controlling devices. Examples in the automobile include the electronic controls used in electronic ignition systems, electronic fuel injection, electronic carbureted fuel systems, antilock braking, and others. These are described later in the book.

A chip that can receive information, perform mathematical calculations based on these data, and send out signals is called a *microprocessor*. That is, it can *process* information and is small (*micro*scopic). Many of the chips used in automotive electronic controls are microprocessors.

⚙ 2-11 Computer memory Computers must have memories. That is, they must be able to receive and store facts, or what are called *data*. There are two general types, random-access memory (RAM) and read-only memory (ROM). The difference is that the RAM starts with no memory and as it is used, data are sent in for it to retain. Then these data are used for calculations and other computer activities. The ROM has a memory already imprinted, or programmed, in it. This is the type of memory that most automotive applications use. The memory is imprinted or programmed at the automobile factory or at the computer factory where the chips are manufactured. The ROM is somewhat like a very long hall with many doors, some of which are open. These open doors lead to bits of information. The original programming opens some doors and closes others. When the chip is active, electric impulses travel down the "hall" looking for open doors. The electric impulses, in effect, enter the open doors to find bits of information. These bits of information "tell" the electric impulses what they are supposed to do. The electric impulses then carry out these instructions. For example, look at the electronically controlled fuel system using a carburetor. (We study this in ⚙ 19-17.) A sensing device in the exhaust system of the engine continuously reports on the richness of the air–fuel mixture being burned in the engine. For best engine operation with minimum atmospheric pollution, the richness must be held within narrow limits. That is, there must not be too much gasoline vapor in the mixture, nor too little. The chip has a built-in or programmed memory which remembers just what the

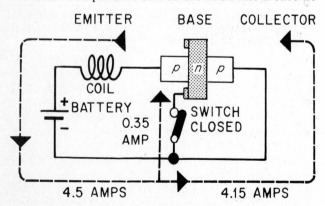

Fig. 2-10 When the switch is closed, current flows.

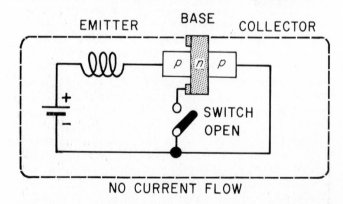

Fig. 2-11 When the switch is open, no current flows.

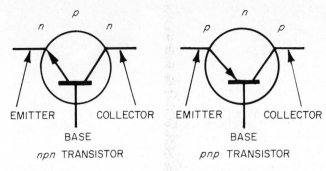

EMITTER   COLLECTOR   EMITTER   COLLECTOR

BASE   BASE

npn TRANSISTOR   *pnp* TRANSISTOR

Fig. 2-12 How two types of transistors are shown in wiring diagrams.

limits are. The sensing device continuously "tells" the chip what the mixture richness actually is. And the chip continuously compares these incoming data with the information stored in its memory bank. As long as the richness is within the limits, the chip does nothing. But when the richness falls outside the limits, the chip memory triggers some action. Through a series of diodes and transistors, signals are sent to the carburetor. These signals, or electric impulses, adjust the carburetor to return the mixture to within the proper mixture richness.

☼ 2-12 A calculator Figure 2-13 shows a hand-held calculator. It is only a little larger than a package of cigarettes. Yet it can add, subtract, multiply, and divide as fast as you can touch the buttons. It can carry out much more complicated calculations than that, also with fantastic speed. The calculator can solve problems that might take weeks for you to solve by the old pencil-and-paper method. The answers are displayed in the window at the top of the calculator. A brief study of this calculator will help you to understand just how integrated circuits work. The display in the calculator works in the same way as the trip computer, now being installed on many cars such as Cadillac, Lincoln, and Chrysler. The trip computer is described in Chapter 24 and illustrated in Fig. 24-20.

☼ 2-13 How the calculator works Now, let us look inside one specific Texas Instrument calculator to see how it works. The part that does all the calculating—the chip or IC—is shown, greatly enlarged, in Fig. 2-14. The actual size is about a quarter of an inch square [6 mm] and not much thicker than a page in this book. This chip is encased, for protection, in a package about an inch and a half long, half an inch wide, and an eighth of an inch thick [approximately 38 by 13 by 3 mm]. The package has a series of metal strips, or pins, sticking out the bottom. These are wired to the chip and provide connections to the other parts of the calculator. The package is shown at the bottom of Fig. 2-14 to a different scale than the chip.

Figure 2-15 is a schematic diagram of the connections inside the calculator. The chip, or IC, is shown as a rectangular box at the bottom. It has a series of connections to the other components of the calculator. At the top, there are nine square boxes with the numeral 8 in each. Notice that each 8 is made up of seven long,

Fig. 2-13 A hand-held computer, capable of making thousands of calculations a second. *(Texas Instruments, Incorporated)*

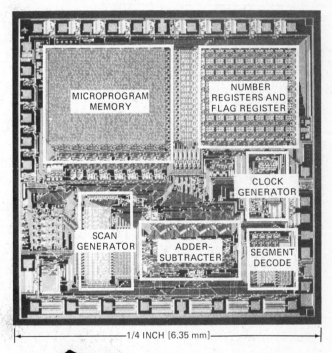

1/4 INCH [6.35 mm]

CHIP (ENLARGED ABOVE) SEALED IN IC PACKAGE

Fig. 2-14 At top, a computer chip, greatly enlarged, with its various major systems labeled. The actual chip is only about ¼ inch [6 mm] square. At bottom, shown about actual size, is the package in which the chip is sealed, for protection. The pins coming out of the package are the connectors to the chip. *(Texas Instruments, Incorporated)*

thin strips. Each of these strips is a special diode. This diode is called a *light-emitting diode* (LED). When a small voltage is applied to it, it glows, or emits light. Notice that you can form any number from 0 to 9 with

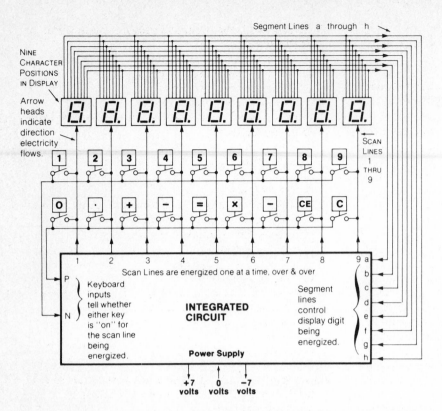

Fig. 2-15 Schematic diagram of the connectors among the integrated-circuit chip, the keyboard, and the display. *(Texas Instruments, Incorporated)*

the seven diodes. See Fig. 2-16. Each diode, or *segment* of the numbers, is connected by a separate line—called a *segment line*—to the IC. There are seven segment lines connected to each character-display box.

NOTE: The number is visible in Fig. 2-15 simply to show how the display works. In the actual computer, the 8s would be invisible until the correct segments had been lighted.

Now, all we need do to make a number appear is to connect the proper segment lines to a source of power—the battery. One additional thing is needed to complete the circuit from the segment lines through the diodes to the battery. This is a series of nine scan lines, which enter the action as explained in ☼ 2-14.

☼ 2-14 Putting a number into the display We turn on the calculator. The IC instantly applies voltage to the scan lines, one after the other, from 1 through 9, thousands of times each second. As long as no key is touched, nothing else happens. The IC applies voltage to scan line 1, then to scan line 2, and so on, at very high speed. The voltage is applied to each for only a very small fraction of a second.

Now, we press one of the number keys. The switch under the key now completes a circuit through the N (for number) input terminal to the IC. This now tells the IC to light up the proper diodes so as to display the number. Suppose it is the number 7. The segment lines connected to diodes that form the number 7 are connected to the battery. They glow to show the number 7. The number 7 is displayed in the box to the right.

When you press a second key to put a two-digit number into the calculator, two things happen. The IC gets the signal and instantly tells the first digit to move

one space to the left. At the same time, the new digit is displayed in the first space to the right. Suppose you want to put the figure 732 into the computer. The 7 appears at the right as the first key is pressed. Then when you press the 3, the 7 moves to the left and the 3 appears in the first space. When you press the 2, the 7 and 3 both move one space to the left, and the digit 2 appears in the right space. The display then reads 732.

☼ 2-15 Adding numbers Now let us see what happens when we want to add another number to our 732. First, we press the + (add) key. This alerts the computer that a new number is coming up which is to be added to the number already in the computer. As a result, the 732 disappears from the display. It is not lost, however; it is temporarily stored in the memory system that is part of the IC. Now, we press keys to put the second number into the computer. The LEDs light up to show this second number. When the number has been put in, we press the = (or equal) key. The computer instantly checks its memory, pulls out the number stored there, and adds it to the second number. The result appears at once on the display.

☼ 2-16 Multiplying The calculator handles multiplication by addition. For example, if you ask it to multiply 27 by 15 (by pressing the appropriate keys), the calculator will add 27 fifteen times. You might think this is an awkward way to do it, but remember, the calculator can perform additions at a speed of thousands of times a second.

☼ 2-17 Other calculations The simple computer we have been describing has only a limited ability to add

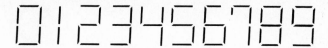

Fig. 2-16 How seven segments, or light-emitting diodes (LEDs), can form all the digits from 0 through 9.

and multiply. Actual calculators are more complex and can do many other tasks. Our purpose in discussing this simple calculator, however, was to acquaint you with the basic principle of calculators and integrated circuits. As we discuss the various electronic devices used in automobiles, you will better understand how they work.

⚙ **2-18 Servicing electronic components**   This brief introduction to the world of calculators is designed to give you some insight into the way calculators, and the electronic devices on automobiles, work. Electronic circuits are ''go–no-go'' circuits. Either they work or they do not work. If they do not work, you replace the electronic component. There are no adjustments. Simple testers are needed—simple, that is, to use. They are usually electronic. You plug a tester in, and by a series of lights or meter readings you quickly determine whether any component needs replacement.

Another advantage is that the components of electronic devices—transistors, diodes, and so on—should never wear out. They have no moving parts. Connections may go bad ultimately, but the devices themselves should far outlast the automobile if they are not overheated or given shock blows. As one example, many alternators have an electronic regulator mounted inside them. It is sealed as protection against dust and moisture. If it should ever fail, it is serviced by complete replacement. Contrast that with the long procedure that is required on the older mechanical regulators designed with vibrating contact points. We come back to this later in the book, when we deal with alternators and regulators, and other electronically controlled automotive components.

Chapter 2 review questions

Select the *one* correct, best, or most probable answer to each question. Then check your answers against the correct answers given at the end of the book.

1. All that moves in a transistor are:
   a. electrical impulses,
   b. holes,
   c. protons,
   d. electrons and holes.

2. Electronics is the branch of science and technology dealing with:
   a. the movement of electrons,
   b. the magnetic effects of electricity,
   c. electrochemical effects,
   d. electrical effects of magnets.

3. Substances that can be either conductors or insulators are called:
   a. elements,
   b. semiconductors,
   c. conductors,
   d. compounds.

4. Adding impurities to a semiconductor to turn it into either a conductor or an insulator is called:
   a. doping the material,
   b. diluting the material,
   c. reducing the material,
   d. debasing the material.

5. The device that is a one-way valve for electrons, or electric current, is called a:
   a. transistor,
   b. diode,
   c. triode,
   d. tetrode.

6. The type of diode that will allow reverse current to flow if enough voltage is applied is called a:
   a. voltage diode,
   b. thyristor,
   c. Zener diode,
   d. transistor diode.

7. Transistor action begins when current starts to flow to the transistor:
   a. base,
   b. emitter,
   c. receiver,
   d. circuit.

8. When thousands of transistors and diodes are put in a chip, the result is called a:
   a. circuit,
   b. integrated circuit,
   c. calculator,
   d. television.

9. The first electronic device to be used in the automobile aside from the radio, was the:
   a. electronic ignition system,
   b. electronic load leveler,
   c. electronic brakes,
   d. electronic alternator regulator.

10. Rectification is:
    a. correcting tests,
    b. changing alternating current to direct current,
    c. changing direct current to alternating current,
    d. tuning the engine.

THE STORAGE BATTERY

After studying this chapter, you should be able to:

1. Discuss the construction and operation of a lead-acid storage battery.
2. Describe the chemical actions in a battery during charge and during discharge.
3. Define and discuss battery ratings.
4. Explain why battery terminal voltage changes with temperature, charging rate, and state of charge of the battery.

3-1 Purpose of the battery The battery (Figs. 3-1 to 3-3) supplies current to operate the starting motor and the ignition system when the engine is being started. It also supplies current for lights, radio, and other electric accessories when the alternator is not handling the electric load. The amount of current the battery can supply is limited by its capacity. Capacity, in turn, depends on the amount of chemicals the battery contains. The battery's third job is to stabilize the voltage in the electric system. That is, it helps to prevent excessive voltage changes in the system.

NOTE: One manufacturer (Delco) uses the name ''Energizer'' for its batteries. In this book, however, we will refer to all lead-acid devices as storage batteries or batteries.

When the battery is supplying electric current, chemical actions in the battery push electrons out through one terminal and take them back in through the other terminal. After these chemical actions have gone on for a while, the battery becomes *discharged* or *run down*. Now, current (or electrons) from an alternator or battery charger must be pushed back through the

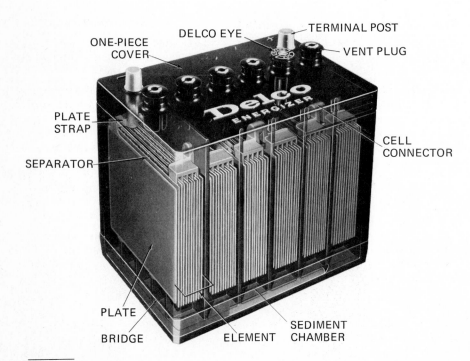

ONE-PIECE COVER

DELCO EYE

TERMINAL POST

VENT PLUG

PLATE STRAP

SEPARATOR

CELL CONNECTOR

PLATE

BRIDGE

ELEMENT

SEDIMENT CHAMBER

Fig. 3-1 Phantom view of a 12-volt storage battery. The case is shown as though it were transparent so that the construction of the cells can be seen. *(Delco-Remy Division of General Motors Corporation)*

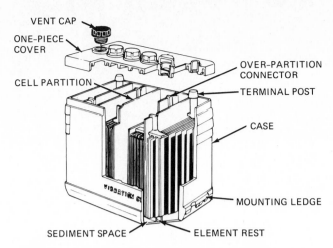

Fig. 3-2 Partly cut away and disassembled battery. *(Ford Motor Company).*

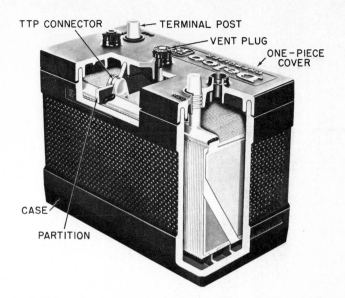

Fig. 3-3 Cutaway view of a 6-volt storage battery with through-the-partitions (TTP) connectors. *(Delco-Remy Division of General Motors Corporation)*

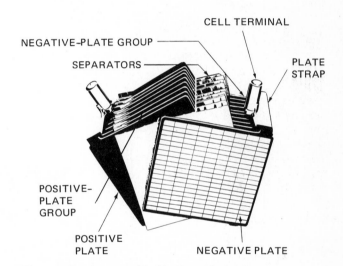

Fig. 3-4 Partly assembled battery element.

battery in the reverse direction. This reverses the chemical actions so that the battery becomes *recharged.*

⚙ **3-2 Battery cells** Before we describe battery operation, let us see how the battery is made (Figs. 3-1 to 3-3). A 6-volt battery is made up of three cells of about 2 volts each. A 12-volt battery is made up of six 2-volt cells. The internal construction and operation of all cells are identical. (Later we will discuss the way in which the cells are connected so that the voltages add up to the 6- or 12-volt total.) The cells are enclosed in compartments in the battery case. The covers are sealed on top to prevent the escape of the battery liquid (called *electrolyte*). The case is made of hard rubber or a plastic which is acid resistant and mechanically strong.

⚙ **3-3 The element** Each cell consists of an element (Fig. 3-4) submerged in a mixture of sulfuric acid and water (electrolyte). It is enclosed in an acid-proof container. An acid-proof cover is sealed in place with an acid-proof compound.

The element is made up of two *groups* of plates, positive and negative, nested together. There is normally one more negative plate than there are positive plates. (A 17-plate cell would have 8 positive and 9 negative plates.) Every positive plate thus has a negative plate on each side of it. This arrangement is desirable. More chemical activity takes place at the positive plates than at the negative, and less positive-plate area is required. Each plate is insulated from adjacent plates by separators (⚙ 3-6).

Many batteries which are sold by dealers as replacement units are "dry." They are made exactly as already described but have no electrolyte in them. Since they have no electrolyte and are sealed, they are chemically inert. They can be stored for long periods without deterioration and then be put into service as described in ⚙ 4-34.

⚙ **3-4 The group** Each group (Fig. 3-5) is made by welding (called *lead burning*) the plates to a lead-alloy

plate strap. The plate strap has a round post which protrudes through a hole in the cell cover or the side of the case and becomes a cell terminal.

⚙ **3-5 The plate** The plate (either positive or negative) is made by applying lead-oxide pastes to a rectangular latticelike grid (Fig. 3-5) molded from lead alloy. The horizontal and vertical bars of the grid hold the pastes in place and, in addition, serve to distribute the current evenly over the plate.

⚙ **3-6 The separator** The separators separate the positive and negative plates (Fig. 3-4). They prevent the negative and positive plates from actually touching. The separators are very porous, so that the electrolyte can circulate between the plates. This circulation of the electrolyte is necessary. The electrolyte must be able to get to all plate surfaces for effective battery action.

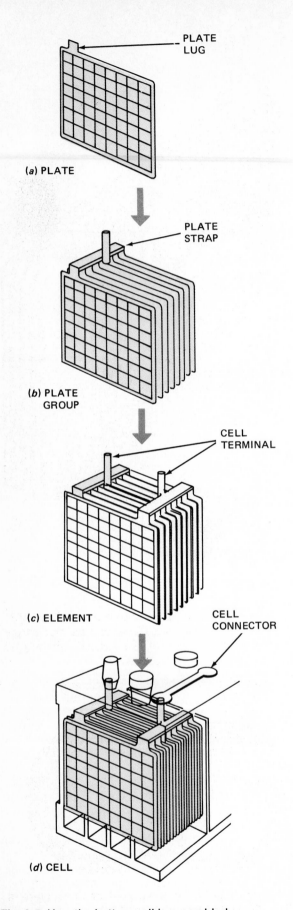

(a) PLATE

PLATE LUG

PLATE STRAP

(b) PLATE GROUP

CELL TERMINAL

(c) ELEMENT

CELL CONNECTOR

(d) CELL

Fig. 3-5 How the battery cell is assembled.

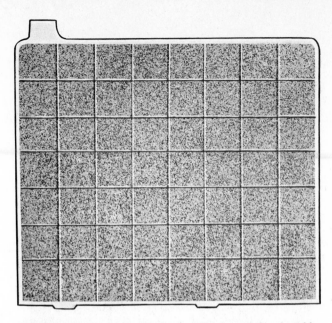

Fig. 3-6 Separator. *(Delco-Remy Division of General Motors Corporation)*

Separators (Fig. 3-6) are sheets of microporous rubber, fiberglass, or plastic (Fig. 3-7). Separators are usually ribbed (Fig. 3-6). In the assembled battery, the ribs face the positive plates (Fig. 3-4). This position gives the electrolyte extra room to circulate around the positive plates. Separators in maintenance-free batteries (✪ 3-10) are usually enclosed in envelopes of porous plastic film to prolong their life.

✪ 3-7 Cell connectors The individual cells in a battery are connected in series so that their voltages add (see ✪ 3-15). The cell connectors are heavy lead-alloy bars attached to the cell terminals. In older-style batteries, the cell connectors were located above or in the cell covers. When they were in the cell covers, they were protected with a heavy coat of sealing compound. This prevented current leakage across the tops of the cell covers. Where the cell terminals are exposed, moisture and dirt can form an electric path between the terminals so that a slow leakage of current takes place. Over a period of time, this could cause the battery to run down.

A better method of protecting the cell terminals and connectors is shown in Figs. 3-3 and 3-7. Here, the battery has a one-piece cover that covers all cells. The plate straps of adjacent cells are joined by the connector which passes through the partitions between the cells, as shown. This construction also minimizes internal resistance and thus improves battery performance.

✪ 3-8 Battery terminals In many batteries, the two main terminals are on top (Figs. 3-1 and 3-2). The positive terminal is larger in diameter than the negative terminal (Fig. 3-8). The positive terminal is larger so it is less likely that the battery would be put into a car backward, that is, so the two terminals would be connected backward. Connecting the terminals backward could cause severe damage to the electric system.

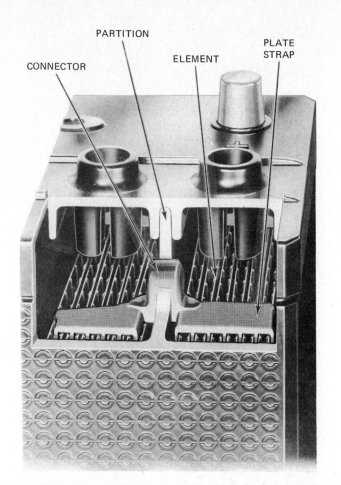

CONNECTOR PARTITION ELEMENT PLATE STRAP

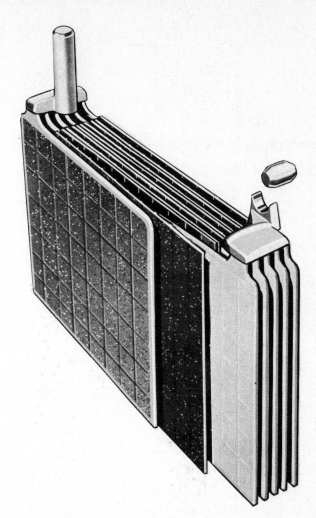

Fig. 3-7 Left, cutaway view of two cells in a battery which has a one-piece cover and cell connectors that pass through the partitions between the cells (TTP construction). Right, battery element partly assembled, showing the lead slug that forms the TTP connector in the finished battery. *(Delco-Remy Division of General Motors Corporation)*

However, since one terminal is larger, it is easy to see which cable clamp fits which terminal.

Many batteries have the two main terminals on the side of the battery case (Fig. 3-9). This type of battery is called a *side-terminal battery*. Figure 3-10 shows how the cables are connected to the battery. It also shows the battery mounting arrangement. With this battery, it is difficult to connect the terminals backward. When the battery is put into the car, it must be installed so that the side terminals are exposed. The two cable connectors will then be in position to be attached to the proper terminals.

☼ **3-9 Vent plug** Vent-and-filler plugs either push into plain holes or screw into threaded holes in the cell covers. The plugs can be removed so that water can be added to the cells when necessary. Water is lost during battery charging. Some evaporates and some is converted into gases (hydrogen and oxygen). The plug has a vent hole to permit these gases to escape. Perforated baffle plates are usually included in the plug. When the battery is being charged, it may emit gas freely. This

gas will often contain droplets of electrolyte. The baffle plates tend to trap these droplets so that the electrolyte is returned to the cell instead of escaping with the gas.

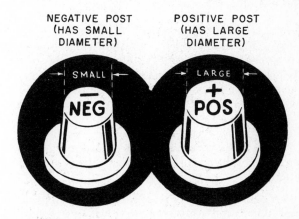

NEGATIVE POST (HAS SMALL DIAMETER)   POSITIVE POST (HAS LARGE DIAMETER)

SMALL   NEG   LARGE   + POS

Fig. 3-8 The negative terminal post of the battery is smaller than the positive terminal post.

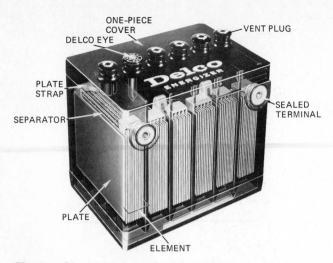

Fig. 3-9 Phantom view of a 12-volt battery with the terminals in the side of the battery case. *(Delco-Remy Division of General Motors Corporation)*

✲ 3-10 Sealed, "maintenance-free" batteries

Some batteries are sealed (Fig. 3-11) and never need extra water. This is the reason they are sometimes called *no-service batteries*. The battery contains a lifetime supply of water which is put in during manufacture. There is a small well-baffled vent in the battery that permits charging gases to escape but retains the droplets of electrolyte.

One reason the battery does not usually require water is that the grids are made of a special metal alloy. Other batteries use grids made of lead–antimony alloy. The maintenance-free battery uses grids made of lead–calcium alloy. There is less gassing with this alloy. The gases come from the split-up of water into hydrogen and oxygen (✲ 3-19). Since there is less of this, there is less water loss.

Some maintenance-free batteries are made with vent caps. These batteries can have water added in case the electrolyte level falls excessively.

Many maintenance-free batteries have a charge indicator built into the cover. The indicator tells the condition of the battery—whether it is fully charged, needs charging, or is defective (✲ 4-10).

✲ 3-11 Nonoverfill devices

If too much water is added to the battery cells, electrolyte will be forced out the plug vents when the battery is charged (due to gassing). Electrolyte is corrosive and will damage engine and body parts. Also, this electrolyte loss reduces the effectiveness of the battery. To prevent loss of electrolyte due to overfilling, various nonoverfill devices are now in use. These devices are in the cell covers and let you visually observe the electrolyte level. It is still possible, of course, to overfill most batteries.

1. Visual fill level   Figure 3-12 shows the visual fill level. When seen from above, the lower end of the vent well shows as a ring with sections cut out. When water is added so that the electrolyte level rises to contact the slotted lower end of the vent well, the electrolyte surface will distort where it touches the vent well. This distortion is easily seen and indicates that sufficient water has been added.

2. Delco eye   The Delco Eye is a special vent cap or plug used in one of the six cells in some batteries. It has a transparent rod extending down into the cell (Fig. 3-13). When the lower tip is immersed, the exposed top of the rod will show black. When the level of the electrolyte falls below the tip, indicating the need for adding water, the top of the rod will glow. This device eliminates the need to remove the vent caps to check electrolyte level in the cells.

✲ 3-12 Battery heat shield

Temperatures are higher under the hoods of late-model cars. Engines run hotter, and there is more equipment packed under the engine compartment. For this reason, the batteries on many of today's cars are protected by a heat shield (Figs. 3-14 and 3-15). The heat shield fits over the top of the battery. Outside cooling air enters the shield through an opening and flows around the battery, keeping it cool. Some heat shields have a built-in windshield-washer reservoir. There is no reason for the combination except that space is saved and car assembly simplified by uniting two separate parts into one.

✲ 3-13 "Forming" the plates

After the battery is assembled at the battery factory, it is given an initial charge. This "forms" the plates. The forming process does not change the shape of the plates. It merely

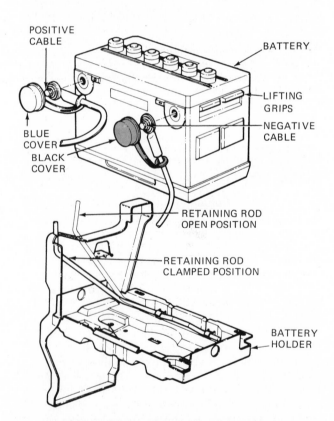

Fig. 3-10 Cable connections and battery mounting arrangement of a side-terminal battery. *(Cadillac Motor Car Division of General Motors Corporation)*

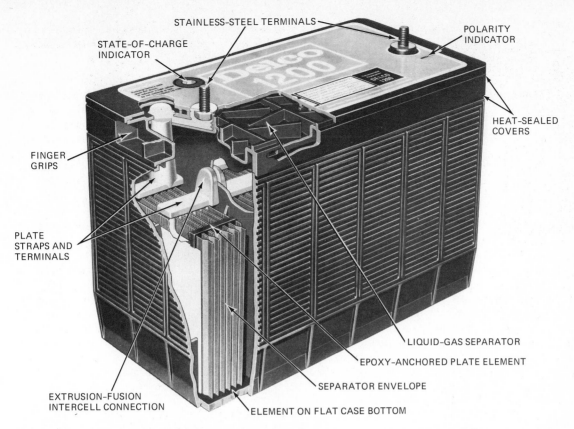

STATE-OF-CHARGE INDICATOR

STAINLESS-STEEL TERMINALS

POLARITY INDICATOR

HEAT-SEALED COVERS

FINGER GRIPS

PLATE STRAPS AND TERMINALS

LIQUID-GAS SEPARATOR

EPOXY-ANCHORED PLATE ELEMENT

SEPARATOR ENVELOPE

EXTRUSION-FUSION INTERCELL CONNECTION

ELEMENT ON FLAT CASE BOTTOM

Fig. 3-11 Sealed battery of the type that never requires water (a "maintenance-free" battery). *(Delco-Remy Division of General Motors Corporation)*

changes the lead-oxide pastes in the positive plate to lead peroxide (PbO_2) and those in the negative plate to spongy lead (Pb). The lead peroxide is chocolate brown in color, and the spongy lead is gray. The terms "PbO_2" and "Pb" are the chemical symbols for these materials. These substances are known as the *active materials* of the plates.

☼ 3-14 Cell voltage

When plates of lead peroxide and lead (PbO_2 and Pb) are placed in a mixture of sulfuric acid (H_2SO_4) and water (H_2O), an electric pressure or voltage of approximately 2.1 volts occurs between them. Even if no more than one positive plate and one negative plate were used, there would still be 2.1 volts.

NOTE: A battery cell at 80°F [26.7°C] will test on open circuit about 2.1 volts when fully charged. However, common practice is to call it 2 volts.

Table 3-1 shows how the cell voltage varies with the state of charge of the battery. A discharged cell (specific gravity 1.100) has a voltage slightly below 2 volts. A fully charged cell (1.280 to 1.300 specific gravity) has a voltage slightly above 2 volts. These figures are for a battery cell at 80°F [26.7°C]. Specific gravity is explained later. It is a measure of battery charge.

Adding plates will not increase the voltage because, you will remember, all the positive plates are burned to one plate strap and all the negative plates are burned to another plate strap. This puts the plates in parallel

which means that the electric pressure, or voltage, has not been increased.

☼ 3-15 Effect of added area

As plate area is increased—by adding plates—the voltage does not increase, but the amount of current available does increase. This seems obvious because the current is produced by chemical actions between the sulfuric acid and the active materials in the plates. The greater the plate surface that is exposed to the acid, the more chemical activity there is and hence the more current that can be produced.

TABLE 3-1 Voltage to Specific Gravity Comparison Chart

Open circuit voltage reading	Corresponding specific gravity	Open circuit voltage reading	Corresponding specific gravity
1.95	1.100	2.05	1.200
1.96	1.110	2.06	1.210
1.97	1.120	2.07	1.220
1.98	1.130	2.08	1.230
1.99	1.140	2.09	1.240
2.00	1.150	2.10	1.250
2.01	1.160	2.11	1.260
2.02	1.170	2.12	1.270
2.03	1.180	2.13	1.280
2.04	1.190	2.14	1.290
		2.15	1.300

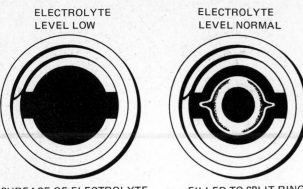

ELECTROLYTE LEVEL LOW — ELECTROLYTE LEVEL NORMAL

SURFACE OF ELECTROLYTE BELOW SPLIT RING — FILLED TO SPLIT RING

Fig. 3-12 Appearance of the electrolyte and split ring when the electrolyte level is too low and when it is correct. *(Delco-Remy Division of General Motors Corporation)*

☀ 3-16 Connecting cells in series

When we connect three battery cells in series (Fig. 3-16), we add their voltages and get 6 volts. Connecting six cells in series makes a 12-volt battery. The total current available is not increased by these connections. By raising the total voltage in this manner, however, we can push three or six times as much current through a circuit of a given resistance provided the cells are capable of delivering that much current. (See Ohm's law, ☀ 1-14.)

NOTE: As mentioned in the Note, ☀ 3-14, actual open-circuit voltage of fully charged battery cells is about 2.1 volts. This means that the six-cell battery will test, on open circuit when fully charged, about 12.6 volts. However, in common practice it is called a 12-volt battery.

☀ 3-17 Chemical actions in the battery cell

As we said, chemical actions between the materials in the plates and the sulfuric acid in the electrolyte produce the current. These actions are illustrated in simplified form in Fig. 3-17. The active material in the positive plate is PbO_2 and in the negative plate Pb. Pb is the chemical symbol for the metal lead. PbO_2 is the symbol, or formula, for the chemical lead peroxide. Lead peroxide is formed when lead and oxygen unite chemically in the proportions of one atom of lead to two atoms of oxygen. When one atom of lead unites with two atoms of oxygen, a *molecule* of lead peroxide is formed. A molecule is made up of two or more atoms.

Sulfuric acid has the chemical formula H_2SO_4, which means that every molecule of sulfuric acid has two atoms of hydrogen, one atom of sulfur, and four atoms of oxygen. In a fully charged battery, the electrolyte is about 60 percent water and about 40 percent sulfuric acid. Electrolyte in a discharged battery will be mostly water (85 to 90 percent) and only about 10 to 15 percent acid.

When the battery is discharging, that is, supplying current, the chemical actions are as shown in Fig. 3-17. To start the action, the sulfuric acid molecules split up into H_2 and SO_4. One SO_4 unites with the Pb in the negative plate, while the other unites with the Pb in the positive plate, forming $PbSO_4$ or *lead sulfate* in each plate. This action frees two atoms of oxygen (O_2) from

ELECTROLYTE LEVEL CORRECT

ELECTROLYTE LEVEL LOW

Fig. 3-13 Cutaway views showing the appearance of the Delco Eye when the electrolyte is at the proper level (top) and when it is low (bottom). *(Delco-Remy Division of General Motors Corporation)*

the positive plate. These atoms of oxygen, therefore, leave the positive plate and unite with the hydrogen left behind when the SO_4 went into the plates. The oxygen and hydrogen unite into molecules (H_2O). This is simply water. Therefore, we can see that during discharge lead sulfate ($PbSO_4$) is formed at both plates while the sulfuric acid in the electrolyte is replaced by water (H_2O).

Figure 3-17 shows only a few molecules. Actually, there are billions of them in the plates and electrolyte, and not until most of them have been broken up and reunited is the battery run down or discharged.

☀ 3-18 Direction of current flow

The flow of current, or movement of electrons, is produced by the

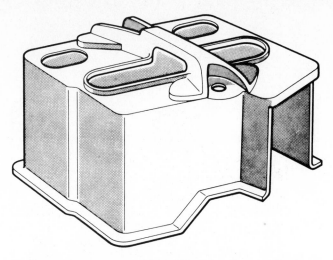

Fig. 3-14 Battery heat shield. *(Chrysler Corporation)*

shifting of the SO_4 and O_2 to and from the plates. These parts of molecules (called *ions*) carry electrons away from the positive plate and place them on the negative plate. As a result, electrons mass on the negative terminal while the positive terminal develops an electron shortage. Then, when the external circuit between the terminals is completed, electrons move from the negative terminal through the external circuit and into the positive terminal. This action can continue as long as there are enough additional PbO_2 and H_2SO_4 molecules left to be split up and reunited into $PbSO_4$ and H_2O molecules. When most of these molecules have been split and reunited, the battery is said to be discharged. It must be recharged, as explained in the following section.

☼ 3-19 Recharging the battery To recharge the battery, electrons must be forced into the negative plate and removed from the positive plate. In other words, electric current (for instance, from an alternator) must be forced through the battery. This current must flow through the battery in a direction opposite to that in which the current flowed during battery discharge. During recharging (Fig. 3-18), the water (H_2O) is broken down into hydrogen (H_2) and oxygen (O). The SO_4 moves from the plates back into the electrolyte; it unites with the hydrogen to form sulfuric acid (H_2SO_4) once again. Meantime, the oxygen atoms are driven back into the positive plate, so that lead peroxide once again appears in this plate. Thus, sulfuric acid reappears in the electrolyte, replacing water. In addition, lead sulfate disappears from both plates, leaving lead in the negative plate and lead peroxide in the positive plate. When most of the lead sulfate has disappeared from the plates, the battery is said to be recharged. During the recharging process, some of the hydrogen and oxygen (both are gases) escapes from the battery cell through the filler-plug vent. This is how water (H_2O) disappears from the battery when it is being charged. The change is known as battery *gassing*. The manner of checking the state of battery charge is explained in a following section.

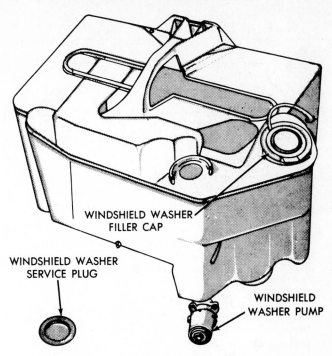

Fig. 3-15 Battery heat shield with built-in windshield-washer reservoir. *(Chrysler Corporation)*

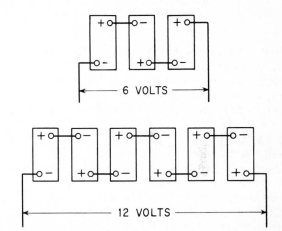

Fig. 3-16 When three 2-volt cells are connected in series, the battery of three cells produces 6 volts. When six cells are connected in series, the battery is a 12-volt battery.

Battery ratings

☼ 3-20 Battery ratings The amount of current that a battery can deliver depends on the total area and volume of active plate material. It also depends on the amount and strength of electrolyte, that is, the percentage of sulfuric acid in the electrolyte. Factors that influence battery capacity include the number of plates per cell, the size and thickness of plates, cell size, and quantity of electrolyte. The ratings most commonly used in referring to battery capacity are discussed below.

1. Reserve capacity   Reserve capacity is the length of time in minutes that a fully charged battery at 80°F [26.7°C] can deliver 25 amperes. A typical rating would

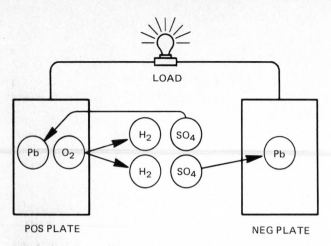

LOAD

POS PLATE NEG PLATE

Fig. 3-17 Chemical actions between positive and negative plates and sulfuric acid when a battery is being discharged.

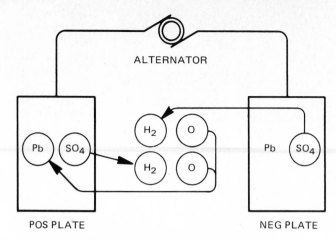

ALTERNATOR

POS PLATE NEG PLATE

Fig. 3-18 Chemical actions between positive and negative plates and electrolyte in a battery being charged.

be 125 minutes. This figure indicates the ability of a battery to carry the electric operating load when the alternator is not operating. Some engineers figure this in terms of ampere-hours. That is, they multiply the number of amperes by the number of hours. For example, the 125-minute rating means the battery is a 52.1-ampere-hour unit.

$$25 \times \frac{125}{60} = 52.1$$

2. **Cold cranking rate** One of the two cold cranking rates is the number of amperes that a battery can deliver for 30 seconds when it is at 0°F [−17.8°C] without the cell voltages falling below 1.2 volts. A typical rating for a battery with a reserve capacity of 125 minutes would be 430 amperes. This figure indicates the ability of the battery to crank the engine at low temperatures. The second cold cranking rate is measured at −20°F [−28.9°C]. In this case the final voltage is allowed to drop to 1.0 volt per cell. A typical rating for a battery with a reserve capacity of 125 minutes would be 320 amperes.

3. **Overcharge life units** Overcharge units are a measure of how well the battery will stand up when it is overcharged.

4. **Charge acceptance** Charge acceptance is a measure of how well the battery will accept a charge under normal operating conditions with a voltage-regulated automotive charging system.

5. **Watts** Delco uses an additional rating—watts. This is roughly equivalent to the battery's cold cranking rate. The watt rating of a battery is a measure of its ability to supply cranking power to the starting motor at a temperature of 0°F [−17.9°C].

☼ **3-21 Battery efficiency** The ability of the battery to deliver current varies within wide limits, depending on temperature and rate of discharge. This characteristic of the battery is known as *battery efficiency*. At low temperature, chemical activities are greatly reduced; the sulfuric acid cannot work so actively on the plates. Thus the battery is less efficient and cannot

supply as much current for as long a time. High rates of discharge do not produce as many ampere-hours as low rates of discharge. At high-discharge rates, the chemical activities take place only on the surfaces of the plates. They do not have time to penetrate the plates and to use the materials below the plate surfaces.

Here are some figures that relate battery efficiency to battery temperatures. Note that these are only approximations.

Efficiency, percent	Battery temperature, °F [°C]
100	80 [26.7]
65	32 [0]
50	0 [−17.9]
10	−45 [−42.8]

☼ **3-22 Variations in terminal voltage** Because the battery produces voltage by chemical means, the voltage varies according to a number of conditions. These conditions and their effects on battery voltage may be summed up as follows:

1. Terminal voltage, battery being *charged,* increases with:
   a. Increasing charging rate. To increase charging rate (amperes input), the terminal voltage must go up.
   b. Increasing state of charge. As state of charge goes up, voltage must go up to maintain charging rate. For example, a voltage of approximately 2.6 volts per cell is required to force a current through a fully charged battery. This is the reason that voltage regulators are set to operate at about 15 volts—slightly below the voltage required to continue to charge a fully charged battery. This setting protects the battery from overcharge.
   c. Decreasing temperature. Lower battery temperatures require a higher voltage to maintain a charging rate.
2. Terminal voltage, battery being *discharged,* decreases with:
   a. Increasing discharge rate. As larger amounts of

current are taken from the battery, the chemical activities cannot penetrate the plates so effectively. Battery efficiency and voltage are reduced.

b. Decreasing the state of charge. With less active materials and sulfuric acid available, less chemical activity can take place, and the voltage drops.

c. Decreasing temperature. With lower temperature, the chemical activities cannot go on so effectively, and the voltage consequently drops.

Since the battery terminal voltage plays a very important part in alternator output regulation and determines the efficiency of operation of all the electric devices in the car, we shall refer to these battery-voltage-variation characteristics when we study the ignition, starting motor, alternator, and regulator.

☼ 3-23 Batteries for diesel engines

Diesel engines require more cranking power to get them started. The reason is that diesel engines have much higher compression ratios. There is a discussion of compression ratios in Chapter 12. The higher the compression ratio, the harder it is to crank the engine. A larger starting motor and battery are required. On some vehicles, this means installing two 12-volt batteries in parallel to provide greater cranking power. Where still more cranking power is required, two 12-volt batteries are connected in series during cranking to produce 24 volts. A 24-volt starting motor is used. See ☼ 5-16 for details.

Chapter 3 review questions

Select the *one* correct, best, or most probable answer to each question. Then check your answers against the correct answers given at the end of the book.

1. A negative-plate group and a positive-plate group, nested together, with separators between, are called:
   a. a battery,
   b. a cell,
   c. a group,
   d. an element.
2. The liquid in the battery, a mixture of water and sulfuric acid, is called:
   a. electricity,
   b. electro-chemical,
   c. electrolyte,
   d. electroliquid.
3. In the assembled battery, the ribs on the separators face the:
   a. positive plates,
   b. battery covers,
   c. negative plates,
   d. cover.
4. Several plates welded to a plate strap are called a:
   a. plate element,
   b. plate group,
   c. plate cell,
   d. battery.
5. When the battery plates are formed, they are:
   a. flattened out,

b. changed chemically,
c. made thicker,
d. die cast.

6. During battery discharge, the sulfuric acid in the electrolyte is replaced by:
   a. lead sulfate,
   b. lead peroxide,
   c. water,
   d. oxygen.
7. According to the reserve capacity rating, a battery that can deliver 25 amperes for 2 hours would be rated at:
   a. 5 ampere-hours,
   b. 8 ampere-hours,
   c. 120 minutes,
   d. 50 amperes.
8. The cold rate of a battery is given in:
   a. degrees of temperature,
   b. amperes,
   c. minutes,
   d. hours.
9. In order to maintain a constant-current input to a battery during charge, as the battery temperature is reduced the voltage must be:
   a. reduced,
   b. held constant,
   c. decreased,
   d. increased.
10. As the discharge rate of a battery is increased, the voltage of the battery will be:
    a. reduced,
    b. held constant,
    c. increased,
    d. improved.
11. The battery most commonly used for automobiles is the:
    a. lead–acid type,
    b. nickel–iron type,
    c. nickel–cadmium type,
    d. lead–calcium type.
12. As the battery is discharged, the active materials in both negative and positive plates are changed to:
    a. sulfuric acid,
    b. lead oxides,
    c. lead sulfate,
    d. spongy lead.
13. If you counted the negative plates and the positive plates in a battery cell, you would find:
    a. the same number of each,
    b. one more negative plate,
    c. one more positive plate,
    d. two more positive plates.
14. Adding plate area to a battery cell increases:
    a. voltage,
    b. current availability,
    c. cell resistance,
    d. battery temperature.
15. Connecting battery cells in series increases:
    a. voltage,
    b. current availability,
    c. cell resistance,
    d. the charging rate.

BATTERY SERVICE

After studying this chapter, you should be able to:

1. Describe the various battery services, including testing, charging, and replacing batteries.
2. Explain how to clean battery terminals.
3. Explain how to safely start a car with a booster battery.
4. Perform the various battery services described in the chapter under the supervision of the instructor.

 4-1 Battery life Batteries wear out and require replacement. How long a battery lasts depends on three factors:

1. Original design and construction
2. How the battery is used
3. How it is maintained

Each battery has a certain useful service life built into it. Whether the battery will live that long, or longer, depends on how it is used and how it is maintained. A battery that is discharged and recharged frequently will have a shorter life. The battery in a car that is hard to start, and is used only for short trips, would be subjected to this discharge–recharge kind of operation.

A battery that is neglected will also have a shorter life. Failure to check the electrolyte level periodically could mean that it will drop below the plate level due to water loss. The plates exposed to air will then be damaged. The area below will be exposed to stronger electrolyte (stronger because of the water loss). All this means that the plates will wear out faster and so battery life is shortened.

Corroded battery terminals could mean extra resistance in the charging circuit. The battery will not get a full charge. It will operate in a partly charged condition, and this shortens battery life.

These troubles are largely eliminated by the new maintenance-free batteries which never require water. Also, many batteries have the terminals in the side of the battery where they will not corrode as readily and cause resistance.

4-2 Neglect shortens battery life What we are saying is that failure to check the battery periodically can lead to early battery failure. These periodic checks can also detect certain electric system troubles that can

cause damage to other electric devices in addition to the battery. For example, if the battery requires water frequently, chances are the charging voltage is high. The battery is being overcharged. Also, other electric devices such as the lights are being subjected to this higher voltage, shortening their life.

The whole point of periodic battery checking is to find and correct conditions that could cause serious trouble if neglected. Proper battery service means full battery life.

Battery services and checks

4-3 Battery service Battery service can be divided into two parts: servicing batteries in vehicles and servicing batteries after they have been removed from vehicles. Servicing batteries in vehicles includes:

Inspecting and testing the battery

Adding water if necessary

Cleaning the battery top

Cleaning and tightening cable clamps

Replacing damaged cables

Checking battery hold-down clamps for tightness

Servicing batteries removed from vehicles includes:

Adding water if necessary and testing the battery

Recharging the battery if necessary

Cleaning the battery and terminals

Cleaning the battery carrier

Sometimes a technician will open a battery that has failed prematurely to determine what caused the failure. This means examining the plates, internal connections, and separators. We discuss all these services in following sections.

☀ 4-4 Battery maintenance

Most people tend to forget about their car battery. That is, they forget it until one cold morning, when they try to start their car, the battery will not do its job and the engine will not start. Battery failure is one of the most common car troubles.

If people would have their batteries checked periodically, much of this battery trouble could be avoided. ☀ 4-3 lists the checks to be made.

CAUTION: Sulfuric acid, the active ingredient in battery electrolyte, is very corrosive. It can destroy most things it touches. It will cause painful and serious burns if it gets on the skin. It can cause blindness if it gets into eyes. If you get battery acid (electrolyte) on your skin, flush it off at once with water. CONTINUE TO FLUSH FOR AT LEAST 5 MINUTES. Put baking soda (if available) on the skin. This will neutralize the acid. If you get acid in your eyes, flush your eyes out with water OVER AND OVER AGAIN (Fig. 4-1). GET TO A DOCTOR AT ONCE! Do not wait!

CAUTION: The gases that form in the tops of the battery cells during charging are very explosive. Never light a match or a cigarette near a recently charged battery. Never blow off a battery with an air hose. The compressed air could lift the cell cover and splash electrolyte all over you.

☀ 4-5 Visual inspection of battery

Look the battery over for signs of leakage, cracked case or top, corrosion, missing vent plugs, and loose or missing hold-down clamps. Leakage signs, which could indicate a cracked battery case, include white corrosion on the battery carrier, fender inner panel, or the car frame. If the top of the battery is covered with corrosion and the owner complains that the battery needs water frequently, chances are the battery is being overcharged. Check the charging system.

The most common cause of a cracked top is improper installation. If the wrong tool or procedure is used to remove or tighten the cable clamps, the battery top probably will be broken. See ☀ 4-23 on how to remove and replace cable clamps.

The most common cause of a cracked case is excessive tightening of the hold-down clamps. Also, a front-end crash, even if so minor that little damage is done to the sheet metal, may cause the battery case to crack.

☀ 4-6 Checking electrolyte level and adding water

This is standard procedure at some service stations. The attendant starts the gas pump and then opens the hood of the car to check engine oil level, the battery, and other things. The attendant removes the vent caps and looks down into the cells. If water is needed, it is added. Distilled water is recommended. However, any water that is fit to drink may be used, provided it does not have excessive iron or other metallic chemicals in it. These chemicals can damage the

Fig. 4-1 If you get battery acid in your eyes, flush it out at once! Continue to flush for several minutes and see a doctor as quickly as possible.

battery, causing it to self-discharge rapidly and shortening battery life. Self-discharge is discussed in ☀ 4-13.

NOTE: You cannot visually check battery cells on sealed batteries, of course. But you can make sure connections are tight at the terminals.

Many batteries have rings in the cell covers which show whether the battery needs water (Fig. 3-12). Some batteries have a Delco Eye, which tells you at a glance, without removing the vent cap, if the battery needs water (Fig. 3-13).

Careful: Do not add too much water! Too much water will make the electrolyte leak out. This will corrode or eat away the battery carrier and any other metal around.

☀ 4-7 Cleaning corrosion off the battery

Battery terminals and cables, especially those on top of the battery, tend to corrode. This corrosion builds up around the battery and the cable clamps and also, unseen, between the terminal posts and clamps. To get rid of it, and to clean the battery top, mix some common baking soda in a pan of water. Brush on the solution, wait until the foaming stops, and then flush off the battery top with water (Fig. 4-2). If the buildup of corrosion around the terminals is heavy, detach the cables from the terminals (as explained in ☀ 4-24) and use the battery-terminal brushes, shown in Fig. 4-3, to clean the terminal posts and cable clamps. Then coat the terminals with an anticorrosion compound to retard corrosion.

☀ 4-8 Testing battery condition

The purpose of testing a battery is to determine whether it:

1. Is in good condition
2. Needs recharging
3. Is defective and must be discarded

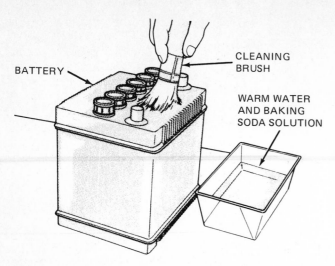

Fig. 4-2 Brushing on baking soda solution to neutralize the acid and clean the battery top.

There are two ways to check battery condition. One way uses a battery hydrometer. The other uses a voltmeter. The hydrometer checks the specific gravity of the battery electrolyte. This is a measure of the battery state of charge. The hydrometer cannot be used on sealed, or maintenance-free, batteries. These may have their own built-in hydrometer or charge indicator (☼ 4-10). The voltmeter measures the battery voltage under various operating conditions, and this tells us the condition of the battery. The voltmeter can be used on any type of battery. Testing methods are described in detail in following sections.

☼ 4-9 Hydrometer test   The hydrometer measures the thickness, or specific gravity, of the electrolyte. Recall from ☼ 3-17 that sulfuric acid disappears from the electrolyte, replaced by water, as the battery is being discharged. Therefore, measuring the percent of sulfuric acid still in the electrolyte tells us the battery state of charge, that is, how much more current we can take out before the battery goes dead. Sulfuric acid is much more dense than water. That is, it has a much

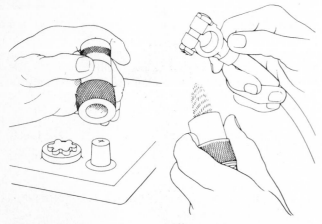

Fig. 4-3 Using special wire brushes to clean battery terminal posts and cable clamps. *(Buick Motor Division of General Motors Corporation)*

higher specific gravity. Measuring the specific gravity of the electrolyte, therefore, indicates how much sulfuric acid still remains in the electrolyte. This tells us how much charge is still left in the battery. The hydrometer measures specific gravity.

There are two types of hydrometer. One contains a series of plastic balls, the other a glass float with a stem on top of it (Fig. 4-4). Both are used in the same way. The plastic ball type is smaller and easier to use. Insert the end of the rubber tube into the battery cell so it is in the electrolyte. Then squeeze and release the bulb. This draws electrolyte up into the glass tube (Fig. 4-5). The number of balls that float tells you the state of charge of the battery cell. If all float, the cell is fully charged. If none float, the battery cell is run down, or dead. Test all cells.

To use the float type of hydrometer (right in Fig. 4-4), you draw electrolyte up into the glass tube in the same way, by squeezing and releasing the bulb. The float will float in this electrolyte. The amount the stem sticks out above the electrolyte tells you the battery gravity, or state of charge. Take the reading at eye level, as shown in Fig. 4-6.

NOTE: The vent holes in the covers of small batteries, such as those used in motorcycles, usually are too small to take the rubber pickup tube of the float-type hydrometer. Also, these small batteries may not have enough electrolyte in the cell to float the float. Therefore, you might have to use the ball type to test these batteries (Fig. 4-5).

CAUTION: Do not drip electrolyte on the car or on yourself! It will ruin the paint on the car, eat holes in your clothes, and burn you! See Caution, ☼ 4-4.

If the float sticks out so the reading on the stem is between 1.260 and 1.290, the battery is fully charged. If the reading at the electrolyte level is between 1.200 and 1.230, the battery is only half charged. If the reading is around 1.140, the battery is run down and needs a recharge. The following list of specific-gravity readings gives you a general idea of battery condition.

1.265–1.299 Fully charged battery

1.235–1.265 Three-fourths charged

1.205–1.235 One-half charged

1.170–1.205 One-fourth charged

1.140–1.170 Barely operative

1.110–1.140 Completely discharged

If some cells test quite a bit lower than others, it means there is something wrong with those cells. It could be that a cracked case has allowed electrolyte leakage, or perhaps there is internal damage to the plates or separators. If the variation is only a few specific-gravity points, then there is probably no cause for alarm. But if cells measure 25 to 50 points lower, then those cells are defective and the battery should be replaced.

The decimal point is not normally referred to in a discussion of specific gravity. For example, "twelve

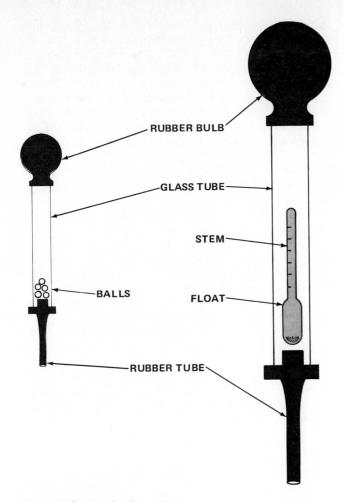

Fig. 4-4 Battery hydrometers.

twenty-five'' means 1.225, and ''eleven fifty'' means 1.150. Also, the word *specific* is dropped, so that the term becomes just *gravity*.

NOTE: The above figures give you only a general idea of what the gravity readings mean. Batteries designed for service in extreme temperatures have different readings. For example, a battery for very cold climates such as the Arctic may have a gravity of 1.290 when

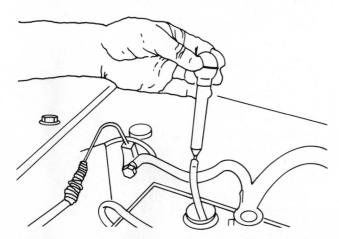

Fig. 4-5 Using a ball-type hydrometer to check a motorcycle battery. *(K-D Manufacturing Company)*

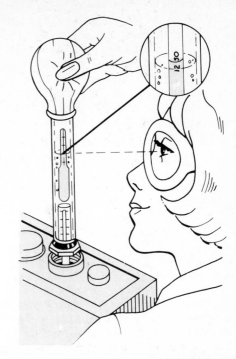

Fig. 4-6 Using a float-type hydrometer to check the specific gravity of a battery cell. Take the reading at eye level.

fully charged. A battery designed for the tropics may have a specific gravity of only 1.225 when fully charged. Batteries are built to work satisfactorily in the climate in which they are sold and normally used. This means that the gravities are adjusted to suit the climate they will encounter in service.

⚙ 4-10 Built-in charge indicator or hydrometer Many sealed, or maintenance-free, batteries (⚙ 3-10) have a built-in charge indicator in the cover. It is a small version of the ball-type hydrometer illustrated in Figs. 4-4 and 4-5. Figure 4-7 shows how the indicator is assembled into the battery cover and extends down into the cell. Figure 4-7 also shows the green ball which is held in an open cage. The green ball is immersed in the electrolyte. If the gravity is around

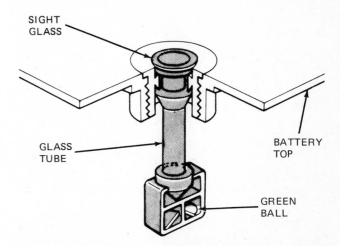

Fig. 4-7 Cutaway battery top, showing the built-in charge indicator. *(Chrysler Corporation)*

1.215 to 1.225 or more, the green ball can be seen as in Fig. 4-8a because the ball floats in gravities this high. If the indicator is all dark, as at Fig. 4-8b, it means that the green ball is not floating and the gravity is low. The battery needs charging. If the indicator shows up light yellow or clear, as in Fig. 4-8c, it means that the electrolyte is low. Of course, water cannot be added to a sealed battery—the battery must be discarded.

CAUTION: If the indicator sight glass shows light yellow or clear, do not attempt to charge the battery. Also, do not attempt to test or jump-start the car with another battery. Any of these procedures can cause the battery to explode!

☸ 4-11 Variation of gravity with temperature

Varying states of charge affect the gravity. Temperature also changes the gravity. As a liquid cools, it becomes more dense and gains gravity. As a liquid warms, it becomes thinner and loses gravity. Thus, temperatures must be considered when a gravity reading is taken. A correction must be made if the temperature varies from standard. This correction involves the addition or subtraction of gravity points, according to whether the electrolyte temperature is above or below the 80°F [26.7°C] standard. The gravity of electrolyte changes about four points, or four thousandths (0.004), for every 10°F [6.5°C] change in temperature. To make temperature correction, four points must be subtracted for every 10°F below 80°F [26.7°C]. Four points must be added for every 10°F above 80°F [26.7°C].

EXAMPLE: 1.250 at 120°F [48.9°C]: Add 0.016 (4 × 0.004). Corrected reading is 1.266. 1.230 at 20°F [−6.7°C]: Subtract 0.024 (6 × 0.004). Corrected reading is 1.206.

NOTE: The battery hydrometer in Fig. 4-9 is compensated for temperature. No temperature corrections have to be made when this hydrometer is used. Also,

the plastic-ball-type hydrometer (left in Fig. 4-4) does not require temperature compensation.

☸ 4-12 Loss of gravity from age

As the battery ages, the electrolyte gradually loses gravity. This is because active material is lost from the plates (as it sheds and drops into the bottom of the cells). Also, gassing causes the loss of acid. Over a period of 2 years, for example, battery electrolyte may drop to a top gravity, when fully charged, of not more than 1.250 from the original top gravity of 1.290. Little can be done to restore gravity, since the losses are an indication of an aging battery.

☸ 4-13 Loss of gravity from self-discharge

There is always some chemical activity in a battery even though the battery is not connected to a circuit and delivering current. Such chemical action, which does not produce current, is termed *self-discharge*. Self-discharge varies with temperature and strength of electrolyte. The higher the temperature, the faster the self-discharge. The chemical actions are stimulated by the higher temperatures (Fig. 4-10). Note that a battery kept at 100°F [37.8°C] loses half its charge in 30 days. A battery kept at 0°F [−17.8°C] suffers almost no loss of charge.

A strong electrolyte, with its higher percentage of sulfuric acid, also causes more rapid self-discharge. This was shown by the more rapid dropping off of the

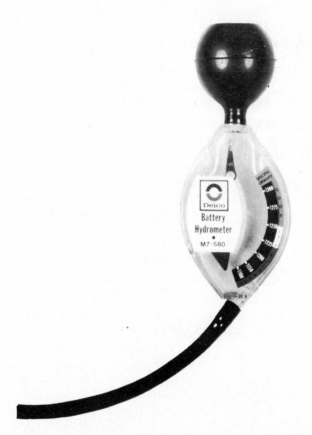

Fig. 4-9 Temperature-compensated hydrometer. (*Delco-Remy Division of General Motors Corporation*)

BATTERY TOP   BATTERY TOP   BATTERY TOP

DARKENED INDICATOR (WITH GREEN DOT)   DARKENED INDICATOR (NO GREEN DOT)   LIGHT YELLOW OR BRIGHT INDICATOR

MAY BE JUMP STARTED   MAY BE JUMP STARTED   DO NOT JUMP START

(a)   (b)   (c)

Fig. 4-8 Appearance of the charge indicator in the top of some sealed, or maintenance-free, batteries. *(a)* If the green dot shows, the battery is in a charged condition; *(b)* if the indicator shows black, the battery is low and should be charged before any test; *(c)* if the indicator shows light yellow or is clear, the battery is dead and should be discarded. Do not try to recharge a battery or jump-start a car when the indicator is yellow or clear.

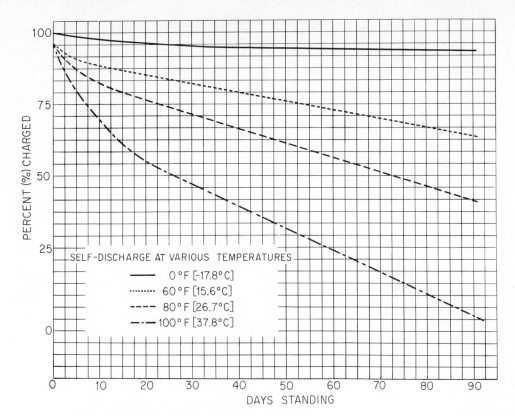

Fig. 4-10 Self-discharge of batteries at various temperatures. The four curves indicate self-discharge of four batteries kept for 90 days at 0, 60, 80, and 100°F [−17.8, 15.6, 26.7, and 37.8°C]. *(Delco-Remy Division of General Motors Corporation)*

curves during the first few days of the test (Fig. 4-10). The electrolyte was the strongest then.

The lead sulfate produced by self-discharge is harder to break down during recharging of the battery. Batteries should be recharged periodically to compensate for self-discharge. Otherwise, they may be severely damaged or even completely ruined.

Older batteries and batteries that have impurities in them (often introduced in the water) tend to self-discharge more rapidly. The maintenance-free batteries have a different plate composition that combats self-discharge. They self-discharge slower than the older-type battery.

☸ 4-14 Freezing point The higher the gravity, the lower the temperature required to freeze the electrolyte. Freezing must be avoided, since it will usually ruin the battery.

Note Fig. 4-11. The lesson we gather from this table is that a run-down battery must never be left out in the cold. Sometimes in winter, a person may try to start a car and do nothing more than run the battery down. If the car remains out in the cold, the battery may freeze. Then a new battery will have to be installed *and* the original trouble corrected.

Careful: Some of the newer 12-volt passenger-car-type batteries have sufficient capacity, even with a low gravity reading, to crank the engine. Thus, even though these batteries are still able to crank the engine, the specific gravity of the electrolyte can be so low that the electrolyte will freeze at comparatively mild temperatures. Therefore, with these batteries the ability to crank cannot be related to resistance to freezing.

☸ 4-15 Refractometer test The refractometer test uses the principle of light refraction (bending of light rays) as light passes through a drop of battery electrolyte. To use the refractometer, open the plastic cover at the slanted end of the tester, as shown in Fig. 4-12. Wipe the measuring window and the bottom of the plastic cover as shown with a tissue or clean cloth.

Close the plastic cover. Release the black dipstick. Remove a vent plug from a battery cell. Dip the black dipstick into the cell to pick up a couple of drops of electrolyte. Then put the end of the black dipstick into the cover-plate opening. This deposits the drops of electrolyte in the measuring window.

Now point the tester toward the light and look into the eyepiece (Fig. 4-13). Note where the dividing line between light and dark (the edge of the shadow) crosses the scale. This indicates the electrolyte strength and determines the battery state of charge. Test all cells in this manner. After each test, wipe the black dipstick,

SPECIFIC GRAVITY	FREEZING TEMPERATURE, °F [°C]
1.100	18 [−8]
1.160	1 [−17]
1.200	−17 [−27]
1.220	−31 [−35]
1.260	−75 [−59]
1.300	−95 [−71]

Fig. 4-11 Freezing temperatures of battery electrolyte at various specific gravities.

43

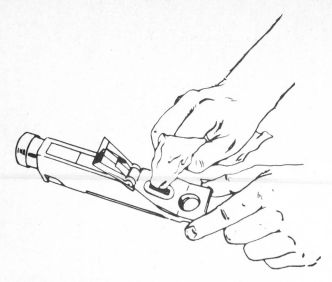

Fig. 4-12 Cleaning refractometer measuring window.

the measuring window, and the plastic cover of the refractometer.

CAUTION: Be careful not to drip electrolyte on yourself or on the car. Remember that electrolyte contains sulfuric acid, and this acid is very corrosive. It will ruin the paint on the car, and if you get it on yourself, it will burn your skin. (See Caution, ☼ 4-4.)

☼ 4-16 Voltmeter tests As mentioned in ☼ 4-8, there are two ways to check battery condition. One is with a hydrometer, the other is with a voltmeter. We have covered the hydrometer test. The voltmeter tests measure battery voltages under various conditions. There are two types of voltage checks. One is performed while the battery is being discharged at a high rate. The other is made with the battery on open circuit, that is, disconnected. The battery can be given a high discharge either by using it to crank the engine or with a battery-starter tester (BST) that applies a heavy variable resistance across the battery.

There is also a tester that applies timed discharge and charge loads to the battery after which the open-circuit voltage is checked. Chrysler also offers a "three-minute-charge" test. We cover all these tests and testers in following sections.

☼ 4-17 Starting-motor check of battery This is a relatively simple check. You use the voltmeter to check battery voltage while the starting motor is cranking the engine. Many variations enter into this test. If the engine is cold, it will be harder to crank, and the starting motor will pull more current from the battery. This means that the battery voltage is going to drop lower. Also, the voltage of a cold battery will drop more when it is subjected to high discharges. For these reasons, only approximate specifications can be given for the test. If the battery is in a charged condition, as determined by the hydrometer, and the engine and battery are warm (not hot), the battery voltage should not drop below about 9.0 volts.

☼ 4-18 Capacity or high-discharge test of battery This test procedure is much more accurate because you use a high-capacity variable resistance with the voltmeter. The variable resistance is connected across the battery (Fig. 4-14). It can be adjusted to discharge the battery at a specific number of amperes. A simple rule for determining the exact number of amperes is to multiply the ampere-hour rating of the battery by 3. That is, if the battery is rated at 50 ampere-hours, you would discharge it at 150 amperes (3 × 50). The discharge should continue for 15 seconds, after which the voltage of the battery should be noted. See Fig. 4-15 which outlines the procedure recommended by Ford. Note that the voltmeter leads are not connected to the resistance clamps (Fig. 4-14), but to the battery terminal clamps. You will need adaptors for side-terminal batteries (Fig. 4-16).

Careful: When using the ammeter, be sure to set it on the high-reading scale (0–400 or 0–600). If the ammeter is set on a low scale and is connected across the battery, it would be a direct short of the battery. A high current would flow and the ammeter would be damaged.

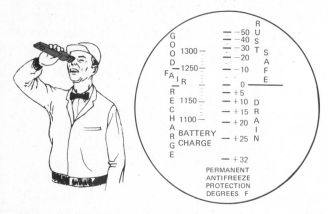

Fig. 4-13 Reading the refractometer.

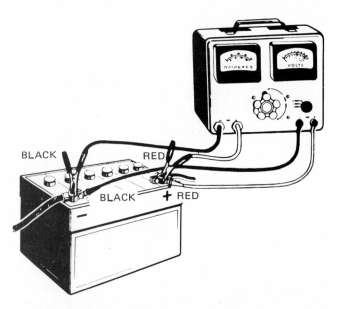

Fig. 4-14 Testing battery voltage under high discharge. *(Chrysler Corporation)*

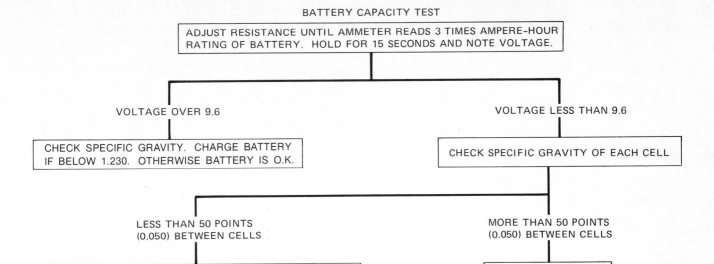

BATTERY CAPACITY TEST

ADJUST RESISTANCE UNTIL AMMETER READS 3 TIMES AMPERE–HOUR RATING OF BATTERY. HOLD FOR 15 SECONDS AND NOTE VOLTAGE.

VOLTAGE OVER 9.6

CHECK SPECIFIC GRAVITY. CHARGE BATTERY IF BELOW 1.230. OTHERWISE BATTERY IS O.K.

VOLTAGE LESS THAN 9.6

CHECK SPECIFIC GRAVITY OF EACH CELL

LESS THAN 50 POINTS (0.050) BETWEEN CELLS

MORE THAN 50 POINTS (0.050) BETWEEN CELLS

ADD WATER IF NECESSARY AND CHARGE BATTERY PER CHARGING SCHEDULE AND REPEAT CAPACITY TEST

REPLACE BATTERY

TOTAL VOLTAGE LESS THAN 9.6

TOTAL VOLTAGE MORE THAN 9.6

REPLACE BATTERY

BATTERY IS SERVICEABLE

Fig. 4-15 Battery capacity test recommended by Ford for batteries with vent caps which can be removed to check specific gravity and temperature of the electrolyte. *(Ford Motor Company)*

NOTE: Ford supplies specification charts that allow you to more accurately diagnose battery condition. Figure 4-17 shows the correct discharge rates for Ford batteries of various ampere-hour ratings. Figure 4-18 shows the minimum acceptable voltages under the specified discharge rates for various temperatures. As noted previously, battery voltage under discharge will drop as battery temperature goes down.

Chevrolet also supplies discharge rates for their various batteries (Fig. 4-19) and minimum acceptable voltages for various temperatures (Fig. 4-20). Chevrolet also specifies that first you apply a 300-ampere load to the battery for 15 seconds to remove any surface charge on the plates. Then, after letting the battery rest for 15 seconds, give it the capacity test as previously explained.

If battery voltage drops below the minimum acceptable voltage during the capacity test, the battery is defective or needs charging. Recharge and retest the battery. If it fails the capacity test again, the battery is defective.

☼ **4-19 Open-circuit voltage check** This check depends on the variations in voltages of batteries in various states of charge. Recall, from ☼3-14, that voltage varies slightly according to the state of charge of the

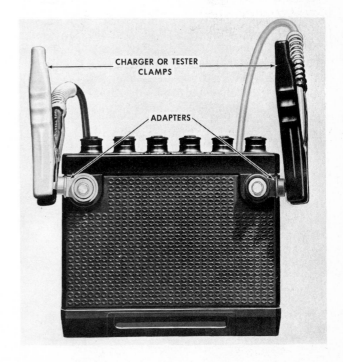

Fig. 4-16 Adaptors to permit attachment of charger or tester clamps. *(Chevrolet Motor Division of General Motors Corporation)*

AMPERE—HOURS	DISCHARGE RATES, AMPERES
36	155
41	145
45	190
53	175
53*	200
54	225
63	205
63*	215
68	220
68*	235
71	235
77	225

*Maintenance-free battery

Fig. 4-17 Recommended discharge rates for high-discharge test of various batteries. (*Ford Motor Company*)

battery. It also varies according to the internal condition of the battery. As a battery gets older, its voltage, fully charged, is lower. A good battery with a low gravity (nearly discharged) will have an open-circuit voltage of less than 12 volts. A fully charged battery in good condition will have a voltage above 12.40 volts.

Note that the voltage reading is taken with the battery completely disconnected from any circuit (Fig. 4-21). The voltmeter must be accurate within hundredths (0.01) of a volt.

For their maintenance-free batteries, Ford recommends the test that follows. First give the battery a

TEMPERATURE, °F [°C]	MINIMUM VOLTAGE ACCEPTABLE
70 (or more) [21.1]	9.6
60 [15.6]	9.5
50 [10.0]	9.4
40 [4.4]	9.3
30 [−1.1]	9.1
20 [−6.7]	8.9
10 [−12.2]	8.7
0 [−17.8]	8.5

Fig. 4-18 Minimum acceptable voltages for load tests conducted at various temperatures. (*Ford Motor Company*)

BATTERY	TEST LOAD, AMPERES
Y85-4	130
R85-5	170
R87-5	210
R89-5	230

Fig. 4-19 Recommended discharge rates for high-discharge test of various batteries. (*Chevrolet Motor Division of General Motors Corporation*)

capacity test as explained in ☼4-18. If the battery passes the test, read the open-circuit voltage with an accurate voltmeter. If the voltage is below 12.40 volts, recharge it at the rate specified in the battery high-rate charge time schedule (Fig. 4-22). For example, suppose you have a 63-ampere-hour battery which has passed the capacity test and has an open-circuit voltage below 11.85 volts. You should charge it for 13 hours at 5 amperes, or 6.5 hours at 10 amperes, or 3.25 hours at 20 amperes, or 2 hours at 30 amperes. The battery should then be in a fully charged condition. ☼4-29 to 4-32 discuss charging procedures.

If the battery fails the capacity test, charge the battery at 35 amperes for 20 minutes and repeat the capacity test. If the battery then passes the capacity test, read the open-circuit voltage as above and give it any further charge that the voltage indicates it should have (Fig. 4-22). However, if the battery fails the capacity test the second time, it should be discarded.

☼ 4-20 Chrysler three-minute charge test This is a test that Chrysler recommends for a battery that has failed the capacity test and for which you want further information. The battery should be at 60°F [15.6°C] or above. The procedure follows.

Connect a voltmeter and a battery charger to the battery as shown in Fig. 4-23. Make sure you connect the charger correctly—positive lead to positive battery terminal, negative to negative. Turn the battery charger on and set the timer switch to 3 minutes. Adjust the charging rate to 40 amperes. When the timer switch cuts off, turn the timer switch to *fast charge*. Now use the voltmeter to check the battery voltage while it is being fast charged. If the fast-charge voltage reads above 15.5 volts, the battery is probably sulfated. It should be cycled (discharged and then recharged at a

MINIMUM VOLTAGE	TEMPERATURE °F [°C]
9.6	70 [21]
9.5	60 [16]
9.4	50 [10]
9.3	40 [4]
9.1	30 [− 1]
8.9	20 [− 7]
8.7	10 [−12]
8.5	0 [−18]

Fig. 4-20 Minimum acceptable voltages for various electrolyte temperatures. (*Chevrolet Motor Division of General Motors Corporation*)

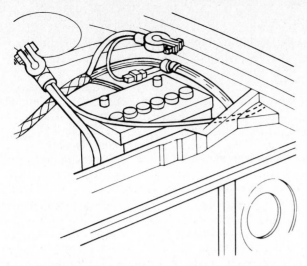

Fig. 4-21 Disconnect battery cables to check open-circuit voltage if battery is in car.

slow rate). Charge it until its gravity reaches 1.265. If the gravity does not increase to this value, discard the battery. If the gravity does stabilize at 1.265, give it another capacity test. If it fails the test again, discard the battery. It is probably about at the point of failure.

✿ 4-21 The 421 test The 421 test is somewhat similar to the Chrysler 3-minute charge test, but it uses a

tester that does the discharge-charge cycle automatically. That is, it applies a discharge load and then a charge, each for a specified number of seconds. The open-circuit voltage is read immediately after the discharge cycle and again after the charge cycle. The difference in the two voltages indicates the condition of the battery. Most 421 testers have automatic timers to control the discharge and charge cycles. The procedure for a typical test follows.

NOTE: Do not charge the battery just before the test. Battery defects can be disguised by a charge so the 421 test will not show them up.

1. Inspect the battery for damage, corrosion, and other faulty conditions, as noted in ✿4-5. Battery, cables, and connections must appear to be in good condition before proceeding with the test.
2. Connect tester leads to the battery. If the battery is still in the car, make absolutely sure that all car electric loads are turned off.

Careful: Connect the leads correctly with respect to polarity. Connecting the leads backward could ruin the alternator.

3. Start the tester. It will discharge the battery for 15 seconds at a 50-ampere rate. When it turns off, wait 5 seconds and note the open-circuit voltage as registered on the tester dial. Some testers have an in-

OPEN CIRCUIT TERMINAL VOLTAGE	AMPERE-HOURS	CHARGE RATE, AMPERES*			
		5 AMPERES	**10 AMPERES**	**20 AMPERES**	**30 AMPERES**
Below 1.185	53	11 hours	5.5 hours	2.75 hours	1.75 hours
	63–68	13 hours	6.5 hours	3.25 hours	2 hours
1.185–1.200	53	8 hours	4 hours	2 hours	1.5 hours
	63–68	10 hours	5 hours	2.5 hours	1.5 hours
1.200–1.210	53	6 hours	3 hours	1.5 hours	1 hour
	63–68	8 hours	4 hours	2 hours	1.25 hours
1.210–1.225	53	5 hours	2.5 hours	1.25 hours	45 minutes
	63–68	6 hours	3 hours	1.5 hours	1 hour
1.225–1.235	53	3 hours	1.5 hours	45 minutes	0.5 hour
	63–68	4 hours	2 hours	1 hour	0.5 hour
Above 1.235	53	2 hours			
	63–68	2.5 hours			

*CAUTION: Do not exceed 30-ampere charge rate.
If gassing or spewing of the electrolyte occurs during charging, the charge rate must be reduced.
Battery must be at a temperature of at least 40°F [4.4°C] before charging.

Fig. 4-22 High-rate charging schedule for maintenance-free batteries. (*Ford Motor Company*)

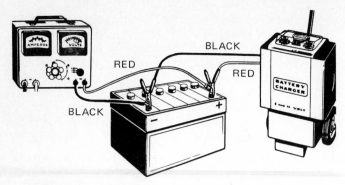

Fig. 4-23 Setup for 3-minute charge test. *(Chrysler Corporation)*

dicator light that comes on to signal the end of the 5-second period. Note the voltage immediately.

4. Charge the battery for 45 seconds, or until the indicator light comes on. Note the voltage.

Careful: Note the voltage readings immediately after the indicator light comes on even though the meter needle may still be moving.

5. A comparison of the two voltages will indicate the battery condition. Batteries indicated as "bad" by the tester should be discarded. Batteries indicated as "good" should remain in service. However, if trouble is suspected because of a customer complaint or battery age, make a further test with a hydrometer. On the type with a built-in hydrometer (maintenance-free battery), check the indicator sight glass (Fig. 4-8).

⚙ 4-22 Cadmium-tip test The cadmium-tip test was once recommended by Chrysler, but the Chrysler service manuals no longer carry this test. It requires a special tester with cadmium tips that are inserted into the electrolyte of adjacent cells (Fig. 4-24). Obviously, the test cannot be made on sealed batteries. The difference in the meter readings indicates the battery condition. If all are close, the battery is in good condition. If they vary too much, the battery either needs recharging or is defective.

⚙ 4-23 Removing and installing a battery When a battery is being removed from or installed in a vehicle, certain precautions should be taken to avoid future

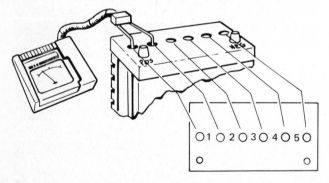

Fig. 4-24 Testing battery cells with a cadmium-tip cell analyzer. *(Chrysler Corporation)*

trouble or damage to the battery. If a new battery is being installed, it should be of a capacity at least as large as the original. A battery of a higher capacity should be installed if the vehicle has extra electric equipment that may be operating when the engine is not running. The new battery should be in a charged condition. If it is only partly charged, it might not provide satisfactory initial performance. The driver might then consider the battery defective and blame the seller. Of course, it is sometimes possible to "get by" with installing a partly charged new battery. The alternator in the car would probably bring it up to charge after the car has been operated for a few days. But it is best to give the new battery a charge before installing it. Dry-charged batteries should also be given a charge before installation. A dry-charged battery is at about 65 percent of capacity or full charge just after the electrolyte has been added. Manufacturers recommend giving the battery a charge, especially if the car is used in local service. See ⚙ 4-35 on activating dry-charged batteries.

After the new battery is in, make sure the alternator is charging the battery. Start the car and watch the indicator light or car ammeter. If the alternator is not charging the battery normally, the new battery will soon run down, and the dealer might be accused of installing a defective battery. Procedures for removing and installing batteries are described below.

NOTE: The discussion that follows refers mainly to the type of battery having the terminals in the battery top and not on the side as shown in Figs. 3-9 and 3-10. On batteries with the terminals on the side, the terminals are more protected and less likely to corrode.

1. **Removing battery** To remove the battery, first disconnect the grounded terminal cable from the battery terminal post. Then it is less likely that the insulated terminal will be grounded when it is being disconnected. If the grounded terminal is not disconnected first, there might be sparks from a short. That is, the wrench may be accidentally touched to ground while the clamp nut on the insulated terminal is loosened. In this case, there would be a direct short of the battery through the wrench, producing a shower of sparks.

Note carefully the locations of the positive and negative terminals so the new battery can be put in with the terminals in the correct locations. The negative terminal post is smaller (Fig. 3-8).

When removing the cable clamps, do not use pliers or an open-end wrench to loosen the clamp nuts. This is liable to cause breakage of the cell cover. Instead, use battery-cable pliers or a box wrench (Fig. 4-25). Never pry the clamp loose from the terminal if it is stuck. Prying will put a great strain on the battery terminal and might cause it to break loose from the battery plates. Use a special clamp puller (Fig. 4-26). This puller exerts a pulling action between the clamp and the terminal and does not put stress on the terminal itself.

Use pliers to remove the spring-type cable clamp (Fig. 4-27). Squeeze the ends so the clamp expands. It can then be lifted from the terminal port.

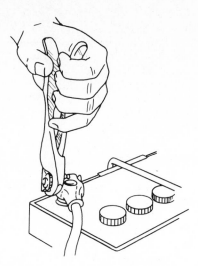

Fig. 4-25 Using battery cable pliers to loosen a nut-and-bolt battery cable.

With the terminal cable clamps disconnected, remove the hold-down bracket or clamps. Use a case-type battery carrier (Fig. 4-28) to lift the battery from its holder. Never use the type of carrier strap that fastens on the battery posts. This could break the seals around the posts. Inspect the holder for corrosion. If it is badly corroded, it may require replacement. Otherwise, it may be cleaned and repainted.

Inspect and clean the battery cables and terminals as necessary (☼4-24).

2. **Installing battery** Install the battery and connect the insulated terminal first, followed by the grounded terminal. Be sure the positive and negative terminals are connected in the proper relationship. On most cars, the negative terminal is grounded.

CAUTION: Be extremely careful not to install the battery backward. The reversed polarity would burn out

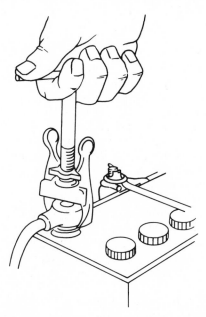

Fig. 4-26 Using a clamp puller to pull a cable from a battery terminal.

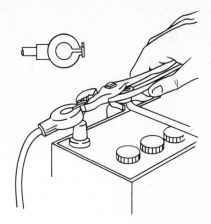

Fig. 4-27 Using pliers to loosen a spring-ring-type cable clamp.

the diodes in the alternator, and it would also damage any other electronic equipment.

☼ 4-24 Cleaning terminals and cable clamps
Corrosion tends to accumulate around the cable clamps and terminals; this is a normal condition. When electrolyte escapes from the battery cells, through overfilling or overcharging and a resulting spray of electrolyte, the corrosion speeds up. In any case, periodic cleaning of the battery top and of the terminals and cable clamps will prevent the corrosion from progressing so far as to cause a bad connection. A bad connection would, of course, cause poor starting or a run-down battery. To remove the corrosion and reestablish good connections, first detach the clamps from the battery terminal posts as explained in ☼4-23. Detach the battery ground cable first so that you will not accidentally ground the insulated terminal with a tool. If

Fig. 4-28 Using a case-type battery carrier.

this should happen with the ground cable still connected, a heavy current that might cause considerable damage would flow.

With the cable clamps off, use battery terminal brushes or steel wool to clean the clamps and the terminal posts to bright metal (Fig. 4-3). Then replace the cable clamps and tighten the nuts (on the nut-and-bolt type) with special battery-cable pliers or a box wrench. If necessary, use a clamp spreader to spread the cable clamp to ensure full seating of the clamp on the terminal post (Fig. 4-29). Figure 4-30 shows the wrong and the right way to seat the clamp on the post. Never hammer or force the clamp down on the post. This may break the cell cover or cause internal damage that could ruin the battery. Do not overtighten the nut since this could damage the clamp.

Careful: Make sure the cable clamps are making good connections with the terminal posts (see Fig. 4-31). If the jaws of the clamp come together as shown to the left, chances are the clamp is not tight on the post. This could mean starting trouble. Correct the condition by disconnecting the clamp from the post. Shave the clamp jaws so you get a gap, as shown to the right, when the clamp is installed.

A coating of petroleum jelly or special battery anti-corrosion paste spread on the clamps and posts will retard corrosion. Also, keeping the vent plugs tight will help prevent the escape of electrolyte and consequent corrosion on the clamps, posts, and other metal parts around the battery.

If battery cables are badly corroded, if insulation is damaged, or if strands are broken or loose, replace the cables. When replacing cables, always use a size at least as large as the original. Using a cable that is too small may introduce excessive resistance in the circuit, which could cause serious starting trouble.

If the battery holder is corroded, the battery should be removed while the cables are disconnected so that the holder can be cleaned and painted if necessary.

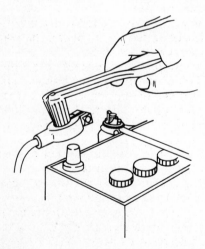

Fig. 4-29 Using a cable-clamp spreader to spread the clamp and assure good seating of the clamp on the battery terminal post.

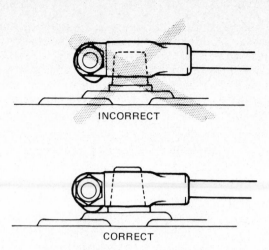

Fig. 4-30 Incorrect and correct ways to put a cable clamp on the battery terminal post.

☼ **4-25 Tightening battery hold-down clamps** The hold-down clamps should be kept tight so that the battery will not bounce around or move in its carrier. However, avoid tightening the clamps too much since this could break the clamps or cause the battery case to warp, bulge, or break. Make it "snug."

☼ **4-26 Battery trouble diagnosis** When battery trouble is found, the cause should be determined and eliminated. That way, the same problem will not occur again. Following are various battery troubles and their possible causes.

1. **Overcharging** If the battery requires a considerable amount of water, it is probably being *overcharged*. That is, too much current is being supplied to the battery. This is a damaging condition that overworks the active materials in the battery and shortens battery life. In addition, overcharging speeds up the loss of water from the battery electrolyte. Unless this water is replaced frequently, electrolyte level is likely to fall below the tops of the plates. This exposes the plates and separators to air and could ruin them. Also, battery overcharge will make battery plates buckle and crumble. Thus, a battery subjected to severe overcharging will soon be ruined. Where overcharging is experienced or suspected, check the charging system.

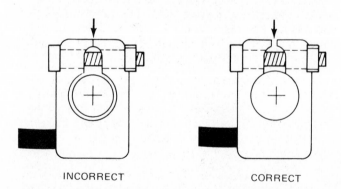

Fig. 4-31 If there is no gap between the jaws of the clamp (left), the clamp is probably loose on the terminal post.

NOTE: Battery overcharge can occur if one of the non-maintenance-free batteries (which has the older-style grids) is installed in a car having the Delcotron 10SI alternator. This alternator has a higher voltage setting and is designed to be used with the Delco-Remy maintenance-free "Freedom" battery which has a grid made of different materials.

2. Undercharging   If the battery is discharged, recharge it as outlined in ☀ 4-29 to 4-32. In addition, try to find out why the battery is discharged. This condition can be caused by:

1. Charging-system malfunction
2. Defective connections in the charging circuit between the alternator and the battery
3. Excessive load demands on the battery
4. A defective battery
5. Permitting the battery to stand idle for long periods so that it self-discharges excessively

In addition, an old battery may have a low specific-gravity reading because it is approaching failure.

CAUTION: If you connect a booster battery to start the engine, observe the procedure in ☀ 4-27.

3. Sulfation   The active materials in the plates are converted into lead sulfate during discharge, as has already been noted. This lead sulfate is reconverted into active materials during recharge. However, if the battery stands for long periods in a discharged condition, the lead sulfate changes into a hard, crystalline substance. This is difficult to reconvert into active materials by normal charging processes. Such a battery should be charged at half the normal rate for 60 to 100 hours. Even though this long charging period may reconvert the sulfate to active materials, the battery may still remain damaged. As it forms, the crystalline sulfate tends to break the plate grids.

4. Cracked cases   Cracked cases may result from excessively loose or tight hold-down clamps, battery freezing, or flying stones.

5. Bulged cases   Bulged cases result from tight hold-down clamps or high temperatures and overcharging.

6. Corroded terminals and cable clamps   Corrosion occurs naturally on batteries. You should be prepared to remove excessive corrosion from terminals and clamps periodically. Cable clamps should be disconnected from the terminal and the terminal posts and cables cleaned, as explained in ☀ 4-24.

7. Corroded battery holder   As the battery is being charged, some of the electrolyte commonly sprays from it. This lost electrolyte may cause the battery holder to become corroded. With the battery removed, such corrosion may be cleaned off with a wire brush and a baking-soda solution.

8. Dirty battery top   Dirt and grime mixed with electrolyte sprayed from the battery may accumulate on the battery top. This should be cleaned off periodically, as explained in ☀ 4-24.

9. Discharge to metallic hold-down   If the hold-down clamps are of the uncovered metallic type, a slow discharge may occur from the insulated terminal to the hold-down clamp. Discharge is more likely to happen with a dirty battery top, because current can leak across the top. The remedy is to keep the battery top clean and dry.

☀ **4-27 Starting a car with a booster battery**   If the battery in the car is too low to start the engine, another battery can be connected. This other battery, called a *booster battery*, will furnish the current the starting motor needs to start the engine. You should observe certain precautions when using a booster battery. Otherwise, you can be badly injured and could also damage the electric equipment in the car. Here are those precautions:

1. Wear eye protection to guard against getting electrolyte in your eyes if a battery should erupt or explode. See the cautions at the beginning of the chapter and also Fig. 4-1.
2. If the dead battery is the no-service type, and the charge indicator shows yellow, do not try to jump-start the car. The battery could be defective, and connecting another battery to it could cause it to explode.
3. During cold weather, the electrolyte in the low battery may freeze. If electrolyte is not visible in the battery, or if it looks frozen, DO NOT TRY TO JUMP-START! The battery could explode.
4. The battery could explode if the jump battery is connected backward (positive to negative, negative to positive). This is the same as directly shorting both batteries, and a very high current will flow. Even if a battery does not explode, both batteries would probably be ruined.

Here is the jump-start procedure. You need two jumper cables (see Fig. 4-32).

1. Remove the vent caps from both batteries. Cover the holes with cloths to prevent splashing of the electrolyte in case of explosion (Fig. 4-33).
2. Shield your eyes.
3. Do not allow the two cars to touch each other. This could damage electric equipment if the two electric systems are not compatible.
4. Make sure all electric equipment except the ignition is turned off on the car you are trying to start.
5. Connect the end of one jumper cable to the positive (+) terminal of the booster battery. Connect the other end of this cable to the positive (+) terminal of the dead battery.
6. Connect one end of the second cable to the negative (−) terminal of the booster battery.
7. Connect the other end of the second cable to the engine block of the car you are trying to start. *Do not connect it to the negative (−) terminal of the car battery!* This could damage electric equipment or cause a battery to explode. Do not lean over the battery while making this connection!
8. Now start the car containing the booster battery. Then start the car containing the low battery. After

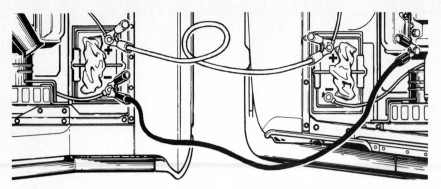

Fig. 4-32 Connections between a booster battery and the dead battery for jump-starting a car with a dead battery.

the disabled car is started, disconnect the booster cables by first disconnecting the cable from the engine block. Then disconnect the other end of this (the negative) cable. Finally, disconnect the positive cable.

9. Throw away the cloths used to cover the vent holes. They have been exposed to acid fumes.

NOTE: Never operate the starting motor for more than 30 seconds at a time. Pause for a few minutes to allow it to cool off. Then try again. It takes a very high current to crank the engine. You can overheat and ruin a starting motor if you use it for too long.

☼ 4-28 Using portable starting unit There are several types of portable starting units. They all work the same way. They furnish a high current that assists the car battery to crank the engine. Be sure to follow the instructions of the manufacturer if you use one of these units. Observe the cautions about proper connections, removing the battery vent caps, and covering the vent holes with cloth.

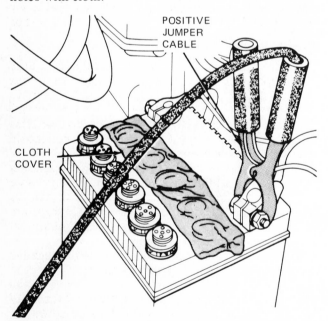

POSITIVE JUMPER CABLE

CLOTH COVER

Fig. 4-33 Connecting jumper cable and covering the cover openings with cloth. Note that the vent plugs are removed. Some manufacturers recommend leaving them in after making sure the vents are open. *(Chrysler Corporation)*

Also, and very important, this caution: Do not allow the charging voltage to exceed 16 volts. Otherwise, the car battery, starting motor, alternator, and other electric equipment could be seriously damaged.

☼ 4-29 Battery charging The purpose of charging the battery is to reverse the chemical changes that took place during its discharge. Recall, from ☼ 3-17, that the sulfuric acid, in effect, goes into the plates during discharge. When a direct current is sent through the battery in the reverse direction, the sulfuric acid, in effect, goes out of the plates and back into the electrolyte.

The charging rate, or number of amperes sent through the battery, can vary from a few amperes up to 40 or 50 amperes. The rate depends on the type of battery charger. One type, called a *trickle charger,* provides a slow charge of only a couple of amperes. This is the type of charger that some car owners have. The charger can bring a battery fairly well up to charge overnight. Another type—the type found in most service facilities that handle battery service—is able to supply a heavy charging current of up to 50 or so amperes. This gives the battery a quick charge.

The actual amount of charge that a battery gets is the charging rate in amperes multiplied by the period of time that the battery is charged. For example, a battery charged at the rate of 30 amperes for 2 hours would get 60 ampere-hours of charge. A battery charged at 3 amperes for 20 hours would receive the same amount of charge—60 ampere-hours.

Actually, a battery can be safely charged at almost any rate so long as the battery temperature does not go above 125°F [51.7°C] and the battery does not gas so heavily as to cause the electrolyte to spew out.

Before charging a battery, check the electrolyte level. If the level is low, the battery can be damaged. If the level is too high, the electrolyte can overflow because of gassing and heat. Here are cautions to observe:

1. The gases released by batteries under charge are very explosive. Be sure the area is well ventilated. Do not smoke or have open flames around charging batteries. This could cause an explosion.

2. Be sure to disconnect the battery ground strap if the battery being charged is in a car. Otherwise, you can damage the electric equipment in the car.

3. Most manufacturers recommend leaving the cell

caps in place. But make sure the vent holes are open. Cover the caps with a cloth during the charging procedure. Some manufacturers recommend removing the caps and covering the openings with a cloth.

4. Do not charge a battery that is frozen. It could explode.

5. Protect your eyes with glasses or a shield. See the cautions in ☼ 4-4 and Fig. 4-1.

6. If the charge indicator of a maintenance-free battery shows yellow or clear, do not charge it. The electrolyte level is low, and charging it could cause an explosion. The battery should be discarded.

7. Do not turn the charger on until the charger cables are connected to the battery. Turn the charger off before disconnecting the cables.

8. Check the gravity and temperature of the electrolyte periodically during charge. If the temperature goes above 125°F [51.7°C], stop the charge.

9. The battery is fully charged when the specific gravity shows no increase for 3 hours. Also, the cells should be gassing freely.

10. After charging, wash and dry the battery top. This removes any electrolyte that might have spewed out during charge.

☼ 4-30 Quick chargers There are some special points to watch when using a quick charger. These chargers (Fig. 4-34) can supply a fast charge of up to 100 amperes (for some types). Normally, you would set the charging rate for around 40 to 50 amperes and charge the battery for around 30 or 45 minutes. This boosts the battery with up to 38 ampere-hours of charge. A battery in normal condition can stand high charging rates without damage if the electrolyte temperature does not go above 125°F [51.7°C], as we have said.

Quick charging cannot, as a rule, bring the battery up to full charge in a short time. To bring it up to charge, the battery should be given a slow charge after the quick-charge cycle. Some chargers can do this. That is, they charge fast, then slow, to fully charge the battery.

Careful: A battery with discolored electrolyte (from cycling) or with gravity readings more than 25 points apart should not be quick-charged. Likewise, a badly sulfated battery should not be quick-charged. Such batteries may be near failure, but they may give additional service if slow-charged. However, quick-charging them might damage them further. During quick charging, check the color of the electrolyte. Stop charging if it becomes discolored as a result of the stirring up of washed-out active material. Likewise, cell voltages should be checked every few minutes. Charging should be stopped if cell voltages vary more than 0.2 volt.

Careful: When quick-charging a battery in a car, disconnect the battery ground strap to protect the electric system from damage due to high voltage.

Careful: If the charge indicator (in no-service batteries) shows yellow, do not try to quick-charge it. (See ☼ 4-10.)

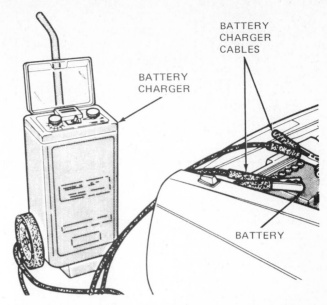

Fig. 4-34 Battery charger connected to a battery in a car in readiness to charge the battery. The grounded battery cable should be disconnected before the charger cables are connected. *(Chrysler Corporation)*

NOTE: A very low battery may not accept a quick charge. The electrolyte in a very low battery does not have much sulfuric acid in it. Therefore, the conductivity of the electrolyte is too low to allow a high current to flow through the battery. You might assume that if a battery refuses to take a quick charge, it is worn out. This may not be true. You may be able to restore such a battery to a charged condition in the following way: First, slow-charge it for a few minutes to see if it starts coming up to charge. If it does, it can then be put on quick charge. Some quick chargers have a special circuit which will slow-charge a dead battery for a short time and then switch to quick charging.

☼ 4-31 Special manufacturers' instructions Some manufacturers supply specific charging instructions, along with recommended charging rates, for their batteries. Figure 4-22 is a chart showing Ford recommendations for charging their maintenance-free batteries. Figure 4-35 is a chart of Ford recommendations for charging their non-maintenance-free batteries. This type of battery has vent caps. They can be removed to check battery gravity and temperature during charge. Note that Ford's larger batteries (63- and 68-ampere-hours rating) can be charged at 35 amperes for nearly 2 hours (115 minutes), provided the electrolyte temperature does not rise excessively.

Always follow the recommendations of the manufacturer when charging and testing batteries.

☼ 4-32 Charging sulfated batteries When a battery has been allowed to stand for some time without attention, its plates may have become sulfated to such an extent that it will not take a charge in a normal manner. In fact, the battery may be completely ruined. However, an attempt to save such a battery may be worthwhile, especially if it is not too old. Put the battery

SPECIFIC GRAVITY READING†	CHARGE RATE, AMPERES	BATTERY CAPACITY, AMPERE-HOURS			
		36	41—45	53—54	63—68
1.125–1.150	35	50 minutes	65 minutes	80 minutes	115 minutes
1.150–1.175	35	40 minutes	50 minutes	65 minutes	95 minutes
1.175–1.200	35	30 minutes	40 minutes	50 minutes	70 minutes
1.200–1.225	35	25 minutes	30 minutes	35 minutes	50 minutes
Above 1.225	5	§	§	§	§

NOTE: Battery must be at a temperature of at least 40°F [4.4°C] before charging. At no time during the charging operation should the electrolyte temperature exceed 130°F [54.4°C].
†If the specific gravity is below 1.125, use the time indicated for the 1.125 specific gravity, then charge at 5 amperes until the specific gravity reaches 1.250 at 80°F [26.7°C].
§Charge at 5-ampere rate only until the specific gravity reaches 1.250 at 80°F [26.7°C].

Fig. 4-35 High-rate charging schedule for non-maintenance-free batteries, which have vent plugs that can be removed to check the electrolyte temperature and specific gravity.

on charge at half the normal charging rate for 60 to 100 hours to see whether the sulfation can be broken down so that the battery will take a charge.

Usually, in a badly sulfated battery, the plate grids and separators are injured because the sulfate takes more room than the active materials in the plates, and the consequent swelling cracks or breaks the grid structure. A badly sulfated battery may be returned to usable condition, but it can never come back all the way; part of its life has been lost.

✿ 4-33 Additives for the battery Sometimes electrolyte may be added to a battery if some acid has been lost through spraying or spilling. But other chemicals or additives should never be put in a battery. Some of these chemicals may give a battery a temporary boost, but this condition will not last long. Shortly afterward, the battery will probably fail completely, having been ruined by the added chemicals. Furthermore, the use of such chemicals voids the battery manufacturer's guarantee. All battery manufacturers condemn the use of such substances.

✿ 4-34 Care of batteries in stock Batteries are supplied in two ways: wet or dry. The wet batteries have the electrolyte already in them. The dry batteries are in a charged condition but contain no electrolyte. They are ready for use once the electrolyte has been added. (The procedure of activation is explained in ✿ 4-35.) Dry-charged batteries require little attention in stock. They should be stored in a clean, dry place and put in suitable racks. They should not be stacked one on top of another. Wet batteries require somewhat more attention in stock because they are active and subject to self-discharge.

1. Inspection on arrival When wet batteries are delivered to the dealer, they should be inspected for damage. The specific gravity should be checked. If the

gravity is low, recharge batteries immediately before putting them in stock.

2. Storing wet batteries To store wet batteries, build a temporary rack with ¾-inch [19.05 mm] wood plank as shown in Fig. 4-36. No nails are required to build this rack. Batteries should never be stacked on top of one another since the weight on the bottom batteries might collapse the plate assemblies and ruin them. Wet batteries should be recharged every 30 days. If a battery is allowed to stand for long periods without attention, it will run down from self-discharge. In addition, the sulfate formed may become so dense that it can never be reconverted. The battery can never be fully recharged. Before charging, the electrolyte level should be checked and brought up to the proper height if necessary.

At low temperatures, self-discharge proceeds slowly. Wet batteries, therefore, should be stored at a temper-

Fig. 4-36 Storing wet batteries with temporary wood racks.

ature that is as low as possible without the risk of freezing the batteries. On the other hand, high temperatures accelerate self-discharge. If batteries are stored in a warm place, they may have to be recharged more often than once a month.

Be sure always to sell the oldest battery in stock. Otherwise, you might find yourself with some very old batteries on hand.

⚙ **4-35 Activating dry-charged batteries** Dry-charged batteries have no electrolyte in them and are sealed. Therefore, they are chemically inert and can be stored for long periods without attention or deterioration. However, since the plates may oxidize slowly if moisture is present, dry-charged batteries should be kept in a dry, clean place and protected from moisture.

Dry-charged batteries are usually packed in shipping cartons. These cartons should be inspected whenever a shipment arrives. If the cartons are damaged or damp, they should be opened so that the batteries themselves can be checked.

The electrolyte for dry-charged batteries is shipped separately in single-application cartons or in 5-gallon [18.93l (liter)] containers.

CAUTION: Handle electrolyte containers with great care, since electrolyte is highly corrosive (see Caution, ⚙ 4-4). Handle electrolyte in an area where plenty of water is available for flushing it away if it should come in contact with the skin or clothes. Wear goggles or eye shields. Refer to the side of the container for the antidotes to use if you should get any electrolyte on your body.

To prepare a dry-charged battery for use, or to activate it, proceed as follows:

1. Remove the battery from the carton.
2. Remove the vent plugs. Some batteries which are vacuum-sealed have hard-rubber seals in the vent-plug openings (Fig. 4-37). These seals must be broken by pushing the rod of the Delco Eye (⚙ 3-11) down into the vent well. The seal will drop down into the cell, where it will remain without harm.
3. Using the filler tube from the electrolyte container as shown in Fig. 4-38, fill each cell to the proper level. Wait a few minutes to allow the plates and separators to absorb the electrolyte. Then, if necessary, add more electrolyte to bring it up to the correct level.
4. Code-date the battery to indicate the day it was activated.
5. Although the battery can be put into immediate operation, good battery operation can be ensured by checking open-circuit voltage and by charging the battery if it is found to be low. For example, one battery manufacturer states that if a 12-volt battery tests 12 volts (6 volts for a 6-volt battery) or more on open circuit, the battery is good and can be put into immediate operation. From 10 to 12 volts (5 to 6 volts for a 6-volt battery) on open circuit indicates some battery-plate oxidation; such a battery should be recharged. Less than 10 volts (5 volts for a 6-volt

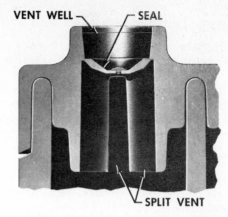

Fig. 4-37 Construction of a cell seal in a vacuum-sealed battery. *(Delco-Remy Division of General Motors Corporation)*

battery) indicates a defective or reversed cell; this requires battery replacement.

Another check is specific gravity. If, after electrolyte is added, gravity readings drop below 1.235 (new electrolyte is 1.265) or if cells gas violently, the battery should be charged. Gravity readings should be corrected for temperature.

In cold weather a battery will do well if given a short booster charge with a quick charger after it has been activated.

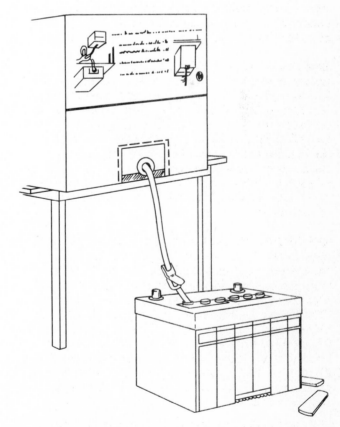

Fig. 4-38 Filling a dry-charged battery with electrolyte from a large container.

Analysis of battery failures

⚙ 4-36 Causes of battery failure Usually, when a battery fails, it is junked and that is the end of it. However, technicians may sometimes open a battery that has failed in order to determine what caused the failure. You, as a student of automotive electric equipment, should know what goes on inside batteries when they fail. We therefore include the following material on causes of failure and what the inside of a battery that has failed looks like. Most battery failures can be grouped under four headings: overcharge, cycling, sulfation, and internal short circuits. The following sections discuss each.

⚙ 4-37 Overcharge failure A badly overcharged battery will fail. There are signs both inside and outside the battery that clearly show the cause of failure to have been overcharging. The positive sides of the cell covers will have been pushed up. This results from the swelling of the positive plates. The positive plates swell because the free oxygen continues to enter the positive plates even after all the lead sulfate has been converted into lead peroxide. The free oxygen, therefore, attacks the grid structures of the plates and gradually converts them into lead peroxide. Since lead peroxide requires more room than the lead itself, the plates must swell and push upward. This raises the cell covers.

In addition, the swelling of the grids causes them to crumble and the plates to buckle (Fig. 4-39). The crumbling of the grid and the pushing upward of the plate are illustrated in Fig. 4-40. Note that the swelling of the grid has pushed the positive plate up so far that it has shorted against the negative-plate strap (at the upper right in Fig. 4-40).

The separators in a battery that has been overcharged, if they are made of wood, will be found to be crumbly and brittle. The high temperature and strong acid acting together on the wood cause this condition. The negative plates also suffer from overcharging, but the effect on them is less obvious to the eye. The negative plates become very hard and dense during overcharging. This is because the organic material which is incorporated in the negative plate to produce and maintain plate porosity is destroyed by the high temperature and strong acid brought on by overcharging. Thus the plate porosity is lost and the capacity of the negative plate is greatly reduced.

⚙ 4-38 Cycling failures A cycling failure is, in a sense, a normal failure, since a battery in normal life is being repeatedly charged and discharged. An outside negative plate from a battery that has failed because of cycling is shown in Fig. 4-41. The swelling and contraction of the active material during the discharge-recharge cycle cause the active material to loosen and gradually wash out of the plate. Inside negative plates are protected by the separators and do not lose as much active material. Sometimes, inside negative plates are flecked with white specks. These specks are material that has become detached from the plate. Since they are detached, these specks remain lead sulfate and are not reconverted into active material.

In a cycling failure, the positive-plate material becomes soft, muddy, and brown in color. It is so soft

Fig. 4-39 Appearance of a battery element that has been removed from a badly overcharged battery.

Fig. 4-40 Appearance of the inner positive plate from a badly overcharged battery. Note how the swelling of the grid has raised and shorted the plate against the negative-plate strap.

Fig. 4-41 Outside negative plate from a battery that has failed because of cycling. Note the blistered and "washed out" appearance.

that any gassing or jarring action causes the material to shed off badly and fall into the bottom of the cells. Figure 4-42 illustrates the results of this action. Figure 4-43 shows what happens when so much of the material accumulates in the bottom of the cells that it bridges over, or "trees," and produces a short circuit between the bottoms of the negative and positive plates.

Fig. 4-43 Lower end of a battery element removed from a battery that has failed because of cycling. Note that the bottom of the element is covered with "trees" that have bridged over and shorted between negative and positive plates.

It may also happen that bridging over, or "treeing," will occur at the top of the cell. This is most likely to occur when the loose material is kept floating in the electrolyte by jarring or by heavy charging currents. Under such circumstances, the loose material builds up on top of the negative plates until it finally bridges to the positive-plate strap (Fig. 4-44).

Fig. 4-42 Appearance of an inner positive plate from a battery that has failed because of cycling. Note that much of the active material has been washed out of the plate.

Fig. 4-44 Inside negative plate of an element from a battery that has failed after prolonged cycling. Note the trees that have formed on top of the negative plate and have shorted it to the positive-plate strap.

❀ 4-39 Sulfation Active materials in the negative and the positive plates are converted into lead sulfate during battery discharge. If the battery is recharged within a reasonable time, the lead sulfate will reconvert into active materials without trouble. However, if the battery stands for any time in a discharged condition, the lead sulfate will crystallize into a hard *permanent sulfate* that resists reconversion. During this process, the negative plates turn grayish white. The positive plates tend to turn milky white but appear less affected than the negative plates. In addition to this change in appearance, the plates tend to swell and break the grids. Over a period of time, a sulfated battery may become so badly damaged that it will be ruined. (The slow-charge method of recharging badly sulfated batteries was discussed in ❀ 4-32.)

❀ 4-40 Internal short circuits Internal short circuits result from two things: the treeing of material that has shed from the plates and mechanical damage. When treeing occurs, the loose material gradually builds up along the edges of the plates. Ultimately it shorts between the positive and negative plates or between the negative plates and the positive-plate strap. Short circuits also result from mechanical causes, such as the failure of a separator. Definite evidence of internal short circuits between plates or between the plates and plate straps can often be found, because such short circuits usually produce orange-colored spots either on the plates or on the separators. The heat produced by a short circuit causes the formation of an orange-colored lead compound. The orange-colored spots are usually quite small but are easily seen because of their brilliant color. Figure 4-45 shows a separator through which a short circuit has occurred. The failure has

occurred in the upper left-hand corner and was produced by buckling of the plates due to overcharging.

Chapter 4 review questions

Select the *one* correct, best, or most probable answer to each question. Then check your answers against the correct answers given at the end of the book.

1. One of the most important cautions to observe while working around batteries has to do with the battery gases. These gases are:
   a. poisonous,
   b. highly explosive,
   c. dangerous to breathe,
   d. very smelly.
2. Two of the most important battery services are:
   a. adding water and testing,
   b. adding acid and battery cleaning,
   c. installing plates and checking voltage,
   d. replacing case and recharging.
3. If you have to add water to a battery every few days, you should suspect that the battery is:
   a. excessively overloaded,
   b. overcharged,
   c. sulfated,
   d. old.
4. A bad connection at the battery could cause:
   a. battery overcharge,
   b. excessive battery voltage,
   c. overheating,
   d. a run-down battery.
5. One of the damaging effects of overcharging is:
   a. sulfation of plates,
   b. oxidation of negative-plate grids,
   c. loss of electrolyte,
   d. oxidation of positive-plate grids.
6. The two ways to test a battery under high discharge are with the:
   a. starting motor and hydrometer,
   b. ammeter and variable resistance,
   c. ammeter and hydrometer,
   d. starting motor and variable resistance.
7. Wet batteries in stock should be recharged or boosted every:
   a. week,
   b. 2 weeks,
   c. 30 days,
   d. 90 days.
8. The distinguishing feature of dry batteries is that the:
   a. battery has no electrolyte,
   b. plates have been removed,
   c. separators are dried out,
   d. battery requires infrequent charging.
9. One of the most important points to remember when installing a new battery is to make sure it is:
   a. larger than the original,
   b. fully charged,
   c. filled to vent plugs with water,
   d. of the same polarity.

Fig. 4-45 Battery element in which a short between negative and positive plates has occurred. The short has taken place in the upper left corner. See the arrow.

10. When removing a battery, disconnect:
    a. grounded terminal cable first,
    b. insulated terminal cable first,
    c. both terminal cables together,
    d. charging system.
11. When comparing the sizes of the two battery terminal posts, you will note that the negative terminal post is:
    a. smaller than the positive terminal post,
    b. larger than the positive terminal post,
    c. same size as the positive terminal post,
    d. is on the same side of the battery.
12. Installing a battery backward can:
    a. burn out the diodes in the alternator,
    b. damage electronic equipment,
    c. neither (a) nor (b),
    d. both (a) and (b).
13. You can quick-charge the battery at as much as 50 amperes provided:
    a. the electrolyte does not get too hot,
    b. you do not charge for more than 5 minutes,
    c. you make sure the battery gets fully charged,
    d. it remains connected to the electric system.
14. When jump-starting a car:
    a. leave ignition turned off so car will not start unexpectedly,
    b. do not allow the two cars to touch each other,
    c. you need only one jumper cable,
    d. crank both engines at the same time.
15. The two basic battery tests require either a:
    a. voltmeter or hydrometer,
    b. voltmeter or variable resistance,
    c. ammeter or voltmeter,
    d. quick charger or ammeter.

STARTING-SYSTEM FUNDAMENTALS

After studying this chapter, you should be able to:

1. Explain the purpose, construction, and operation of the starting system.
2. Explain why a starting-motor drive mechanism is needed.
3. Describe the various types of starting-motor controls.
4. Locate starting motors on cars.
5. Identify and name component parts of disassembled starting motors.

5-1 Purpose of the starting system The engine crankshaft must be rotated at speeds of 100 revolutions per minute (rpm)—more or less—to start the engine. This procedure is called *cranking the engine*. During cranking, the fuel system delivers air–fuel mixture to the engine cylinders. Also, the ignition system delivers sparks to the spark plugs in the engine cylinders. Ignition and fuel systems are covered later in the book. The combination of a rotating crankshaft, and air–fuel mixture and sparks being delivered to the cylinders, causes the mixture to be ignited. The engine starts and runs.

The starting system, which includes the starting motor, switch, battery, and cables, does the cranking. Figure 5-1 is a simplified drawing of the starting system. When the key switch is closed, it connects the main switch to the battery. The main switch then magnetically closes the main contacts between the battery and starting motor. The starting motor shaft begins to turn. A small pinion gear on this shaft is meshed with a large gear on the engine flywheel. When the small pinion gear turns, it rotates the flywheel. The crankshaft is attached to the flywheel so the crankshaft rotates and the engine starts.

5-2 Definition of starting motor The starting motor, or starter, is a direct-current electric motor that can deliver, for short periods of time, a high horsepower for its size. The starting motor rotates the engine crankshaft so the engine can start and run under its own power. Considerable power is needed to do this, and in order to get enough power from a motor no larger than the starting motor, the unit must have a very low electric resistance. The conductors in both the field and the armature are, therefore, very heavy. This permits a high current to flow through the motor

so that enough power to crank the engine will be developed. The starting motor operates on the same principles as any other electric motor.

5-3 Demonstrating motor principles The electric motor converts electric energy into mechanical energy. In other words, it uses current (or electron flow) to produce mechanical movement. A simple arrangement to demonstrate motor principles is shown in Fig. 5-2. When the wire is touched to the loop support, current flows from the battery through the loop. As a result, the loop will swing out of the magnetic field. The direction in which the loop moves depends upon the position of the magnetic poles and the direction in which current moves through the loop.

A closer look at the central part of the loop and the magnetic flux around it will help us to understand why the loop swings out of the way. Suppose the arrangement is as shown in Fig. 5-3, with the current flowing away from you and the north pole of the magnet at the top. With this arrangement, the conductor will be pushed to the right, as shown. A closer look, in end view, is shown in Fig. 5-4. By using the left-hand rule,

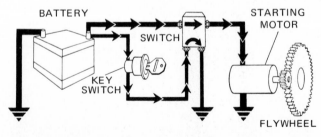

Fig. 5-1 Simplified drawing of a starting system. (*Chevrolet Motor Division of General Motors Corporation*)

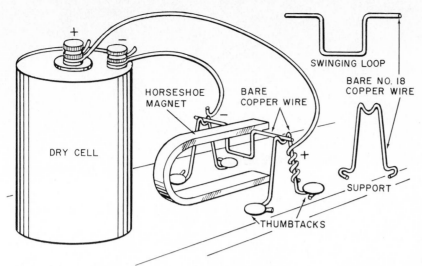

Fig. 5-2 Simple arrangement to demonstrate motor principles. When the circuit is closed, the wire loop swings out from between the magnetic poles.

we can see that the magnetic lines of force circle the conductor in a counterclockwise direction, as shown. This weakens the magnetic field to the right of the conductor for the following reason: The circular lines of force around the conductor oppose the lines of force from the magnet, and the opposing lines of force tend to cancel each other out. However, to the left of the conductor, the conductor lines of force and the magnetic lines of force are in the same direction, and they add to produce a stronger magnetic field.

Adjacent lines of force push apart and also act like rubber bands by trying to shorten. Note, in Fig. 5-4, that the lines of force are bunched on the left of the conductor and are bent around the conductor. As the lines of force try to push apart and also shorten, they exert a push that moves the conductor to the right.

If the direction of current were reversed, the push on the conductor would be in the opposite direction. The distortion and bending of the lines of force would be to the right of the conductor.

✱ 5-4 A simple motor Instead of a single conductor, as shown in Fig. 5-2, suppose we have a loop as shown in Fig. 5-5. This puts two conductors into the magnetic field. We would then have the essentials of a simple motor. For if we were able to start a flow of current into the right-hand side of the loop and take it out from the left-hand side of the loop, the loop would revolve in the direction of the circular arrow. A glance at Fig. 5-6 will show why this is so. Note that with the current entering the right-hand conductor (moving away from you), the push is down on it. Also, with the current leaving the left-hand conductor (moving toward you), the push is up on it. Therefore, the downward push on the right-hand conductor and the upward push on the left-hand conductor cause the loop to revolve in a clockwise direction, as shown.

✱ 5-5 Electric-meter principles We have seen how a push is exerted on a current-carrying conductor held in a magnetic field. In motors, many conductors are "pushed" or forced to move so that rotary motion is produced. Before we describe how this is done, however, let us look at a somewhat simpler application of the motor principle as used in electric meters.

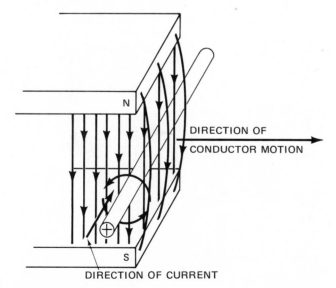

Fig. 5-3 Conductor held in the magnetic field of a magnet. The direction of current flow and encircling magnetic field are shown by arrows.

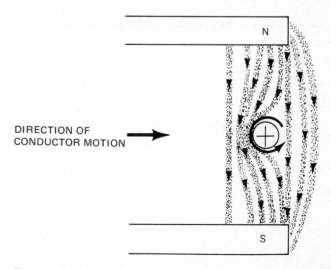

Fig. 5-4 End view of the conductor shown in Fig. 5-3.

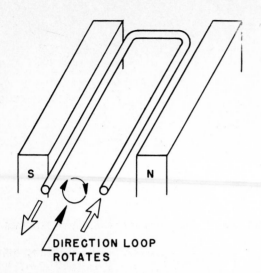

Fig. 5-5 Direction of loop rotation when it is carrying current in a magnetic field.

Electric meters are used to measure the strength of current flow in a circuit or the voltage across a circuit. Meters to measure current strength, or amperes of current, are called *ammeters*. Meters used to measure voltage are called *voltmeters*. Figure 5-7 illustrates, in simplified form, one type of ammeter. It consists essentially of a movable coil of wire held in the magnetic field of a permanent magnet by two spiral springs. An indicating needle is attached to the coil. When no current is passing through the coil, the spiral springs position the coil so that the needle points to zero on the scale. When current passes through the coil, the coil swings around much like the loop shown in Fig. 5-2. However, the coil does not swing freely, since it must move against the spiral-spring tension. Therefore, the spring tension must be overcome before the coil can move. With a weak current, the push on the coil is weak and the coil cannot move far. But the stronger the current, the farther the coil swings, or rotates, against the spiral-spring tension. Thus, the indicating needle swings around and indicates on the scale the amount of current flowing.

Figure 5-8 is the wiring diagram of an ammeter. To determine the amount of current flowing in a circuit, the meter is connected into the circuit, in series, by

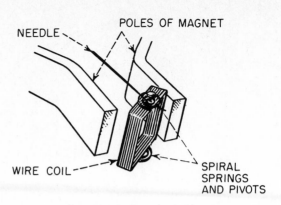

Fig. 5-7 Simplified sketch of an ammeter.

means of the two terminal posts. Note that there is a *shunt* connected in parallel with the ammeter coil. This shunt carries most of the current since it has a very low resistance. Without the shunt, the ammeter would introduce a high resistance into the circuit. This would change the circuit conditions so that proper analysis of the original conditions would not be possible. The shunt, however, is very heavy, and so the ammeter has a very low resistance. The small percentage of the total current that passes through the coil is sufficient to move the coil, and the total current is indicated.

The voltmeter is very similar to the ammeter, but its coil is connected in series with a high resistance so that only a small amount of current can flow through the meter (Fig. 5-9). This small amount of current, however, is able to produce coil movement, and total voltage is measured.

Figure 5-10 shows the manner in which an ammeter and a voltmeter might be used to measure the voltage at, and the amperage consumed by, a light.

⚙ **5-6 The motor commutator** In order for the loop pictured in Fig. 5-5 to receive current and thus rotate, there must be some means of establishing a circuit between it and a battery. The way this is done is shown in Fig. 5-11. The coil ends are connected to the two halves of a split ring. The split ring is called a *commutator,* and two brushes (which are blocks of carbon or metallic compound) rest on it. Current flows from the battery, as shown by the arrows. This causes the left-hand part of the loop to be pushed upward and the

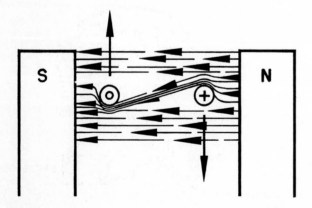

Fig. 5-6 Direction of magnetic field and conductor movement.

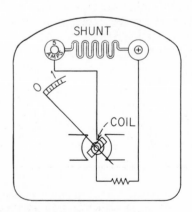

Fig. 5-8 Wiring diagram of an ammeter.

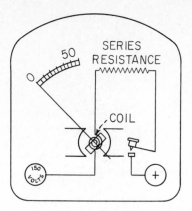

Fig. 5-9 Wiring diagram of a direct-current voltmeter.

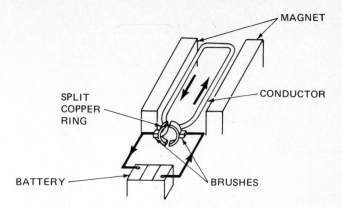

Fig. 5-11 Simplified drawing of a direct-current motor.

right-hand half to be pushed downward (Fig. 5-6). These forces cause the loop to rotate in a clockwise direction.

The commutator rotates with the loop (neither the loop nor the commutator supports are shown). When the loop has rotated half a turn, each segment of the commutator has disconnected from one brush and has connected to the other brush. Therefore, the part of the loop nearest the south pole is always pushed upward while the part nearest the north pole is always pushed downward; rotation of the loop continues.

☼ **5-7 A simple series motor** Figure 5-12 is a simplified sketch of a series motor. It is called a *series motor* because the rotating loop and the stationary windings around the magnetic poles are connected in series. The current flowing through the loop also flows through the windings. In an actual motor, the windings are called *field windings* or *field coils*. They help produce the magnetic field. They do this because the current flowing through the field windings makes them the two poles of an electromagnet. In the illustration, you might picture the electromagnet as being a special sort of horseshoe magnet with curved poles. The rest of the magnet, which is not shown, is made up of the motor field frame in which the poles are mounted (Fig. 5-13). This is discussed in later sections describing motor construction.

The purpose of the field windings or coils is to produce a strong magnetic field so that the loop will receive a more powerful push. Note that the poles are curved. They are curved so that the conductors of the loop will be very close to the poles as they move past. Since the magnetic flux is strongest near the poles, the conductors are given a stronger push.

In an actual starting motor, there are many rotating loops, all assembled into an *armature* (Fig. 5-13). The armature consists of a shaft on which are mounted a laminated iron core and a commutator. The loops, or windings, of the armature are mounted in the core and are insulated from one another and from the core, being connected only at the commutator segments. The commutator segments have riser bars, to which the ends of the armature windings are soldered or welded. The core itself is made up of thin sheets of iron (lamination) with slots around the outer edge into which the windings can be assembled.

NOTE: The core is made of soft iron because this substance has a high magnetic permeability. It is laminated to prevent excessive internal currents. If it were solid, it would act just like any other conductor being moved in a magnetic field. That is, it would have electric current induced in it. In fact, if the core were solid, it would have a very low resistance, and very high currents might be induced (remember Ohm's law). This high current not only would produce considerable heat but also would waste electric energy.

☼ **5-8 Starting-motor construction** There are two general types of starting motors in common use in automobiles: drive pinion direct drive and gear reduction. The direct drive has either a solenoid or a movable pole shoe which causes the starting-motor drive pinion (gear) to mesh with the flywheel gear teeth. We explain

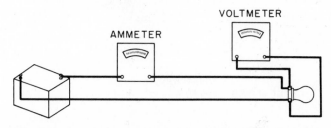

Fig. 5-10 Connecting a voltmeter and ammeter to measure voltage and current consumed by an electric light.

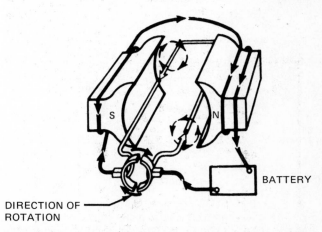

Fig. 5-12 Schematic diagram of a series motor.

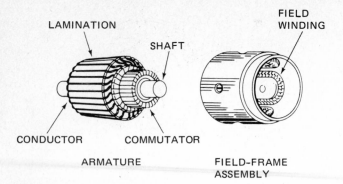

Fig. 5-13 The two major parts of a starting motor, the armature and the field-frame assembly. *(Delco-Remy Division of General Motors Corporation)*

all these terms as our story of starting-motor construction goes along.

Figure 5-14 is a sectional view of a starting motor which uses a solenoid to move and mesh the drive pinion. Figure 5-15 is a similar starting motor, disassembled. The major moving part in the starting motor is the armature. The drive pinion slides back and forth on the armature shaft. This gear is part of an overrunning clutch. The clutch allows the drive pinion to crank the engine. But it allows the pinion to run free after the engine is started. This protects the armature from damaging high speed as we explain later.

The armature is supported by two bearings, one in the commutator end and the other in the drive housing. The starting motor shown in Figs. 5-14 and 5-15 is the direct-drive type using a solenoid.

The armature loops, or windings, are all connected together so that current is flowing in all windings at the same time. This allows each winding to add its turning effort to the others so all work together to spin the motor armature.

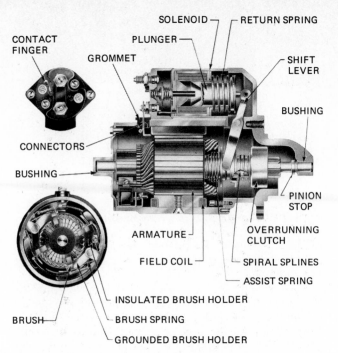

Fig. 5-14 End and side sectional views of a starting motor with an overrunning clutch and solenoid. *(Delco-Remy Division of General Motors Corporation)*

Field windings (also called *field coils*) are used to increase the strength of the magnetic field and, therefore, increase the power of the motor. The current taken through these windings greatly increases the magnetic-field strength over what it would be with permanent magnets alone.

The simplest wiring arrangement is to connect the field coils in series with the brushes and armature windings (Fig. 5-16). With these connections, the current that flows through the field coils also flows through the

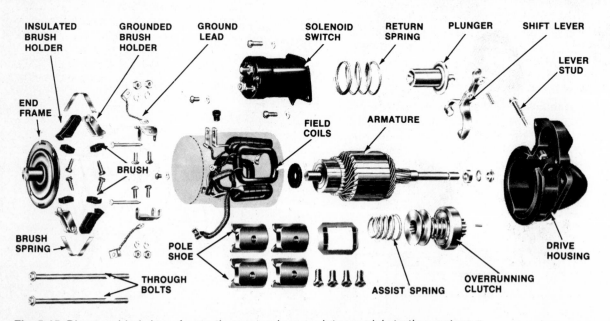

Fig. 5-15 Disassembled view of a starting motor. In many later-model starting motors, the pole shoes cannot be removed from the field frame. *(Delco-Remy Division of General Motors Corporation)*

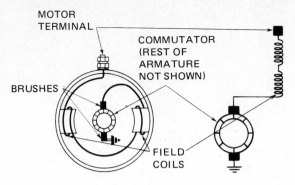

Fig. 5-16 Simplified wiring circuit of a starting motor. Right, schematic; left, simplified end view (armature windings not shown).

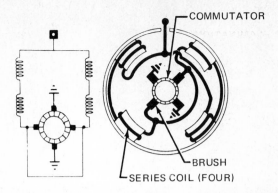

Fig. 5-18 Wiring circuit of a starting motor with four field coils. The field circuit has been split in two for lower resistance, more current flow, and higher cranking torque.

armature windings. A heavy conductor of the ribbon type is used in both the fields and the armature so that the resistance of the motor will be very low. This permits an extremely large current to flow, and as a result the motor develops high torque, or turning effort.

Some starting motors are four-pole units but have only two field coils, such as shown in Fig. 5-16. This gives a four-pole action with only two field coils, and thus resistance is low so high current can flow. Other starting motors have four or six field coils. There are several ways to connect the field coils. Figure 5-17 shows the wiring circuit for a starting motor with four field coils, connected in series. For higher torque, the field coils may be split into two circuits as shown in Fig. 5-18. This arrangement provides two parallel circuits for the current, so more current can flow. This produces a more powerful magnetic field and higher torque. Starting motors using this arrangement are designed to crank larger V-8 engines and also automotive diesel engines.

Some starting motors have a shunt coil connected as shown in Fig. 5-19. This type of unit is called a *compound motor*. The purpose of the shunt coil is to prevent excessive armature speed when the armature is running free. The armature runs free for a moment after the engine starts but before the starting motor is disconnected from the battery.

Figure 5-20 shows a variety of wiring circuits for different starting motors. Note that the three to the

right have insulated brushes. That is, instead of brushes being connected to ground (the end frame of the starting motor), they are connected to an insulated terminal on the commutator end frame. This type of circuit is required on some applications which have a completely insulated starting system. Note that the circuit to the extreme right in Fig. 5-20 is for a motor using six brushes and six field coils. This motor is a heavy-duty unit for cranking large truck diesel engines.

⚙ **5-9 Starting-motor operation** As previously mentioned, the opposing magnetic fields set up by the armature windings and the field coils cause the armature to rotate. When the starting motor is first connected to the battery and before the armature begins to rotate, a very high current of several hundred amperes flows through the starting motor. This produces, at the starting-motor drive pinion, the very high torque necessary to start the engine turning over. Once the engine is being cranked, however, the amount of current drops off. The reason for this is that, with the armature rotating, a countervoltage is produced in the armature conductors. When a conductor is moved through a magnetic field, a voltage will be produced in the conductor. This voltage in the rotating starting-motor armature is in opposition to the battery voltage. The faster the armature turns, the higher this countervolt-

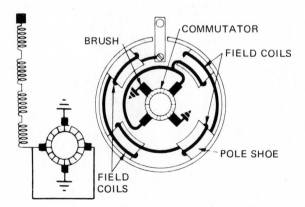

Fig. 5-17 Wiring circuit of a starting motor with four field coils.

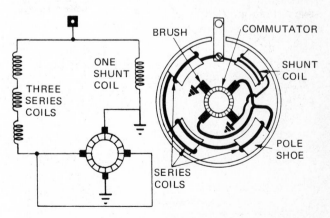

Fig. 5-19 Wiring circuit of a four-pole, series-shunt, or compound, starting motor. *(Delco-Remy Division of General Motors Corporation)*

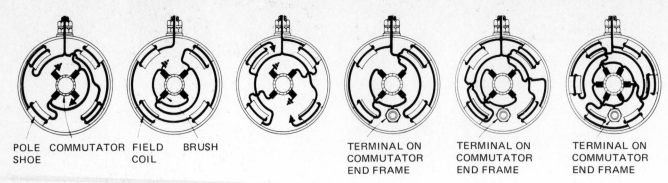

POLE SHOE   COMMUTATOR   FIELD COIL   BRUSH   TERMINAL ON COMMUTATOR END FRAME   TERMINAL ON COMMUTATOR END FRAME   TERMINAL ON COMMUTATOR END FRAME

Fig. 5-20 Wiring circuits of different types of starting motors. *(Delco-Remy Division of General Motors Corporation)*

age. The difference between the battery voltage and the countervoltage causes the current flow through the starting motor. If the armature is turning relatively slowly, as it would be when cranking during cold weather, then there would be a small countervoltage, a high differential voltage, and a high current flow. However, if the armature were turning freely, as it would be after the engine has started, then the countervoltage would be high, the differential voltage would be low, and a relatively small current would flow.

NOTE: The countervoltage is often called the *counter emf* (for *e*lectro*m*otive *f*orce).

☼ **5-10 Need for drive mechanisms** A starting motor depends on gear reduction to transmit its cranking power to the engine. It could not crank the engine if the armature were coupled directly to the engine crankshaft. The starting motor would not have enough turning power. Gear reduction uses a pinion, or gear, on the starting-motor armature shaft. In operation, this pinion meshes with teeth on the engine flywheel. There are about 15 teeth on the flywheel for every tooth on the starting-motor pinion. This means that the starting-motor armature will revolve 15 times while the flywheel and the crankshaft of the engine revolve once. Consequently, the starting motor needs only one-fifteenth the power that a directly coupled motor would require to rotate the engine flywheel, since the armature can rotate 15 times in turning the flywheel once. In operation, the starting-motor armature may revolve as fast as 3000 rpm. Thus the engine crankshaft may be spun at speeds of up to 200 rpm.

After the engine begins to operate under its own power, it may be speeded up to 3000 or 4000 rpm. If the starting-motor pinion did not demesh from the flywheel teeth, the starting-motor armature would be spun at 45,000 to 60,000 rpm. This would most certainly wreck the starting motor. The centrifugal force would throw the windings from the slots in the armature core and the segments from the commutator.

To prevent this, there must be a way of meshing the starting-motor pinion with the flywheel teeth for cranking and demeshing it when the engine starts.

☼ **5-11 Types of drives** Several different types of drive arrangements have been used that provide meshing for cranking and demeshing when the engine starts. One type, used widely years ago, is the Bendix drive. It depends on inertia for its action. Figure 5-21 shows how it works. When the armature begins to rotate, the drive pinion does not rotate at first. This is because it has a weight on one side. The spiral splines (coarse threads) on the drive sleeve cause the drive pinion to move endwise and into mesh with the flywheel teeth. The heavy spiral spring takes up the shock of meshing. When the engine starts, the flywheel spins the pinion faster than the armature is turning. The pinion, therefore, moves on the spiral splines so it backs out of mesh.

There have been a considerable variety of drives based on this inertia principle. However, inertia drives are no longer used on automobiles. You will find them only on some small engines and some farm tractors.

The drive that is used almost everywhere in starting

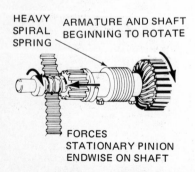

HEAVY SPIRAL SPRING   ARMATURE AND SHAFT BEGINNING TO ROTATE

FORCES STATIONARY PINION ENDWISE ON SHAFT

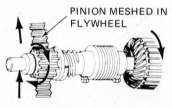

PINION MESHED IN FLYWHEEL

ALL PARTS NOW ROTATING TOGETHER, CRANKING ENGINE

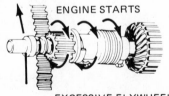

ENGINE STARTS

EXCESSIVE FLYWHEEL SPEED DRIVES PINION OUT OF MESH

Fig. 5-21 Operation of a Bendix drive. *(Delco-Remy Division of General Motors Corporation)*

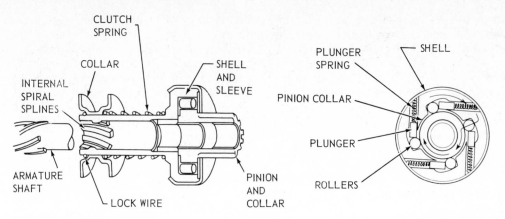

Fig. 5-22 Cutaway and end sectional views of an overrunning clutch. *(Delco-Remy Division of General Motors Corporation)*

motors is the overrunning clutch, described in the following section.

✹ 5-12 Overrunning-clutch starting motor with solenoid

The overrunning-clutch starting motor is used on almost all automobiles made today. It provides positive meshing and demeshing of the pinion and flywheel teeth. This positive action is produced by a shift lever that slides the pinion along the armature shaft. On most vehicles, the shift lever is operated by a solenoid. The overrunning clutch permits the drive pinion to run faster than the armature during the brief period that the pinion remains in mesh after the engine starts. This protects the armature from damage due to overspeeding. Figure 5-14 shows sectional views of an overrunning-clutch starting motor.

The overrunning-clutch drive (Fig. 5-22) consists of a shell-and-sleeve assembly, which is splined internally to match splines on the armature shaft. A pinion-and-collar assembly fits loosely into the shell. The collar makes contact with four hardened-steel rollers, which are assembled into notches cut from the shell. These notches taper slightly inward. There is less room in the end away from the rollers than in the end where the rollers are shown. Spring-loaded plungers rest against the rollers.

The shift lever causes the clutch assembly to move endwise along the armature shaft. It is operated either by manual linkage or by a solenoid (Fig. 5-14). When the shift lever is operated, it moves the clutch assembly endwise along the armature shaft. The pinion is pushed into mesh with the flywheel teeth. If the teeth should butt instead of mesh, the clutch spring compresses and spring-loads the pinion against the flywheel teeth. Then, as soon as the armature begins to rotate, the pinion will mesh.

Full shift-lever travel closes the starting-motor switch contacts and the armature begins to revolve. This rotates the shell-and-sleeve assembly in a clockwise direction (in the end view of Fig. 5-22). The rollers rotate between the shell and the pinion collar. They move away from their plungers and toward the sections of the notches in the shell, which are smaller. This jams the rollers tightly between the pinion collar and the shell. Now, the pinion is forced to rotate with the armature and crank the engine. Figure 5-23 illustrates the engaging action in a solenoid-operated starting motor.

When the engine begins to operate, it attempts to drive the pinion and armature much faster. This causes the pinion to spin faster than the shell. As a result, the rollers are turned back toward their plungers, where the notches are larger. This allows the pinion to spin freely without driving the armature. This protects the armature from overspeeding during the short time that the driver leaves the ignition switch in the START position after the engine has started. Then, when the driver releases the switch, it moves back to ON, opening the circuit to the solenoid. The solenoid releases the

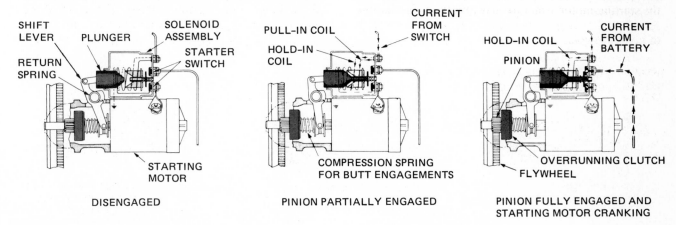

DISENGAGED   PINION PARTIALLY ENGAGED   PINION FULLY ENGAGED AND STARTING MOTOR CRANKING

Fig. 5-23 Actions of the solenoid and overrunning clutch as the pinion engages. *(Chevrolet Motor Division of General Motors Corporation)*

shift lever, and the spring action moves the shift lever and pinion out of mesh. At the same time, the starting-motor switch is opened. Solenoid action is discussed later.

⚙ 5-13 Sprag clutch Another type of clutch for medium- and heavy-duty operation uses sprags instead of rollers. A disassembled view of the sprag-clutch drive is shown in Fig. 5-24. Figure 5-25 shows how a sprag in the clutch works. The outer race is driven by the starting motor. During cranking, the sprags lock between the outer and the inner races. After the engine starts and begins to drive the pinion, the pinion spins the inner race faster than the outer race. This unlocks the sprags so that the pinion can overrun the starting-motor armature and thereby prevent damage to the starting motor. Only one sprag is shown in Fig. 5-25. Actually, there is a series of sprags.

⚙ 5-14 Overrunning-clutch starting motor with sliding pole shoe This starting motor does not have a solenoid to pull the drive pinion into mesh. Instead, it uses one of the field coils and a sliding pole shoe. Figure 5-26 is a disassembled view of a starting motor which has a sliding pole shoe. Figure 5-27 shows the pole-shoe action. When the starting motor is connected to the battery, the magnetism provided by the field coil under the sliding pole shoe causes it to pivot downward. This movement operates the shift lever so the drive pinion is moved into mesh with the flywheel teeth. Note that the field coil has a hold-in winding (Fig. 5-27). The actions in the electric circuits and control are covered in ⚙ 5-20.

⚙ 5-15 Gear-reduction starting motor This starting motor (Fig. 5-28) uses an overrunning clutch that is shifted by a solenoid, similar to the unit discussed in ⚙ 5-12. The major difference between the two motors is that the gear-reduction starting motor has a pair of internal gears. It has a small gear on the armature shaft meshed with a larger gear on the overrunning-clutch drive shaft. This provides a gear reduction of about two to one. That is, the armature rotates two times to turn the drive pinion once. This increases the torque at the drive pinion so greater starting torque is applied to the engine flywheel.

⚙ 5-16 Starting motor for automotive diesels Diesel engines require greater cranking torque than gasoline engines. The reason is that diesel engines have much higher compression ratios. There is a discussion of compression ratios in Chapter 12. The higher the compression ratio, the harder it is to turn the engine crankshaft. A larger starting motor and battery are required. In some vehicles, this means installing two batteries connected in parallel. Two batteries can furnish twice as much cranking current. One installation of this sort is shown in Fig. 5-29. The two 12-volt batteries are mounted at the front, on the two sides of the engine. The starting motor used in this vehicle is compared with a starting motor used for gasoline engines in Fig. 5-30. The larger starting motor operates the same way as the smaller one. The major difference is that it has heavier conductors so that more current can flow through. Also, all internal parts are of heavier construction so they can take the greatly increased cranking torque the motor develops.

Where still greater cranking torque is required, two 12-volt batteries are connected in series to produce 24 volts. A 24-volt starting motor is used. See ⚙ 5-25.

⚙ 5-17 Starting-motor controls Starting-motor controls have varied from a foot-operated switch to automatic devices that close the circuit when the accelerator pedal is depressed. The system used today in passenger cars and other vehicles has starting contacts in the ignition switch (see ⚙ 13-27). When the ignition key is turned against spring pressure past the ON position to START, the starting contacts close. This connects the starting-motor relay or solenoid to the battery. The solenoid or relay then operates to connect the battery directly to the starting motor. As soon as the engine starts, the driver releases the pressure on the ignition switch. A spring then returns it from the START to the ON position. This disconnects the relay or solenoid and starting motor from the battery so the starting motor stops. The ignition, however, remains connected to the battery so that it and the engine continue to function.

⚙ 5-18 Magnetic switch The starter relay is a magnetic switch. Its action depends on the fact that a flow of current in a winding creates a magnetic field. The winding is wrapped around a hollow core, and a cylindrical iron plunger is placed part way into this core. When the winding is energized, the resulting magnetic field pulls the plunger farther into the core (Fig. 5-31). A contact disk is attached to the plunger, and two contacts are placed so that the plunger movement forces the disk against the contacts. This closes the circuit between the battery and the starting motor.

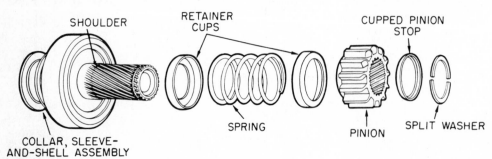

SHOULDER
RETAINER CUPS
CUPPED PINION STOP
COLLAR, SLEEVE-AND-SHELL ASSEMBLY
SPRING
PINION
SPLIT WASHER

Fig. 5-24 Disassembled view of a heavy-duty sprag-clutch drive. *(Delco-Remy Division of General Motors Corporation)*

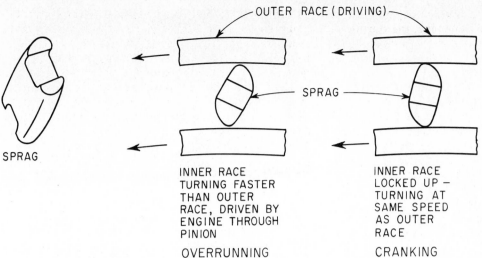

OUTER RACE (DRIVING)

SPRAG

SPRAG

INNER RACE
TURNING FASTER
THAN OUTER
RACE, DRIVEN BY
ENGINE THROUGH
PINION

OVERRUNNING

INNER RACE
LOCKED UP –
TURNING AT
SAME SPEED
AS OUTER
RACE

CRANKING

Fig. 5-25 Sprag action in an overrunning clutch.

☼ 5-19 Solenoid switch On many vehicles, overrunning-clutch starting motors use a solenoid to move the overrunning clutch and close the starting-motor switch. The solenoid is somewhat larger than the magnetic switch. It is mounted on the starting motor (Fig. 5-14). When it operates, it first shifts the drive pinion into mesh with the flywheel teeth (Fig. 5-23). Then it closes the circuit between the battery and the starting motor.

The solenoid has two windings, a pull-in winding and a hold-in winding. The pull-in winding is connected across the starter-switch contacts in the solenoid. Both windings work together to pull the solenoid plunger in and move the overrunning-clutch pinion into mesh. But once mesh is completed, it takes much less magnetism to hold the plunger in. Therefore, the pull-in winding is shorted out as the main contacts are connected by the solenoid disk.

☼ 5-20 Sliding pole-shoe motor control circuit On the Ford starting motor illustrated in Fig. 5-26, there is no separate solenoid. Instead, the starting-motor field windings do two jobs. One is to move the overrunning-clutch pinion into mesh. The other is to provide the magnetic field which causes the armature to turn. Many starting motors that use the sliding pole-shoe (Fig. 5-26) have a magnetic switch or starter relay in the circuit as shown in Fig. 5-32. This is called a *starter relay*. When the ignition switch and safety switch are in the START position, current can flow to the magnetic-switch winding. This current flow causes the magnetic switch to pull in the contact disk. The disk then connects the battery to the starting motor. One of the field coils in the starting motor has two windings, a pull-in winding and a hold-in winding (just as in the solenoid described in ☼ 5-19). The magnetic field produced by these two windings forces the sliding pole shoe to move. This

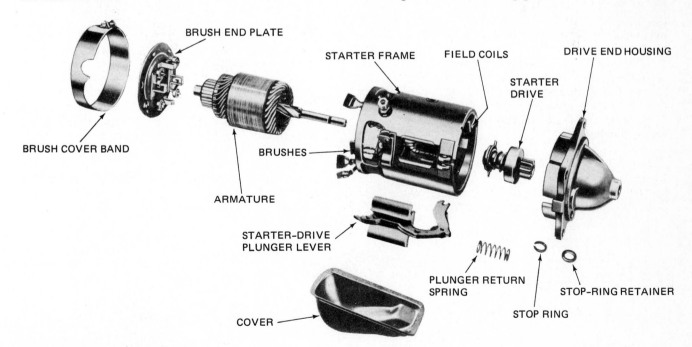

BRUSH COVER BAND

BRUSH END PLATE

STARTER FRAME

FIELD COILS

DRIVE END HOUSING

STARTER DRIVE

BRUSHES

ARMATURE

STARTER-DRIVE
PLUNGER LEVER

PLUNGER RETURN
SPRING

STOP-RING RETAINER

STOP RING

COVER

Fig. 5-26 Disassembled starting motor with a sliding pole shoe which moves the shift lever. *(Ford Motor Company)*

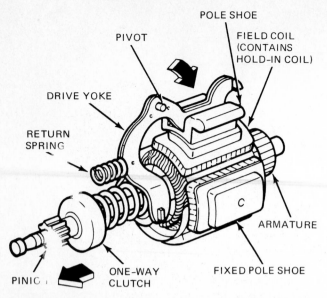

Fig. 5-27 Internal operating mechanism of the starting motor using a sliding pole shoe. *(American Motors Corporation)*

Fig. 5-29 Locations of the two 12-volt batteries for the starting motor in a diesel-engine car. *(Oldsmobile Division of General Motors Corporation)*

shifts the drive pinion into mesh with the flywheel teeth. At the same time, the armature begins to rotate, so that the engine is cranked. Also, the movement of the pole shoe opens a set of contacts—the pull-in contacts in Fig. 5-32. This opens the pull-in winding circuit. The hold-in winding has enough magnetism to hold the pole shoe and drive pinion in the cranking position.

☼ 5-21 Safety switch Many cars have a safety switch connected into the circuit between the ignition switch and the starting-motor solenoid or magnetic switch. For example, many cars with an automatic transmission and a console- or floor-mounted shift lever have a neutral safety switch. This switch is open whenever the transmission selector lever is in any gear. The switch is closed when the transmission selector lever is in N (neutral) or P (park). This prevents engine starts when the transmission is in gear.

Vehicles with automatic transmissions and column-mounted shift levers may not use the neutral safety switch. On these, the ignition switch in the steering column can be turned to START only when the selector lever is in park or neutral.

Some cars with manual transmissions and clutches use clutch-operated safety switches. The switch is closed only when the clutch pedal is depressed and the

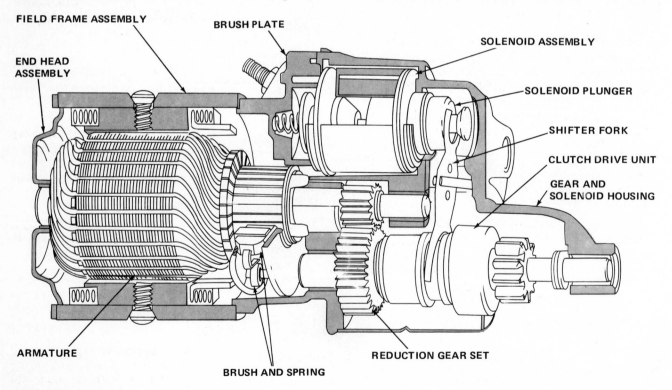

Fig. 5-28 Sectional view of a gear-reduction overrunning-clutch starting motor. *(Chrysler Corporation)*

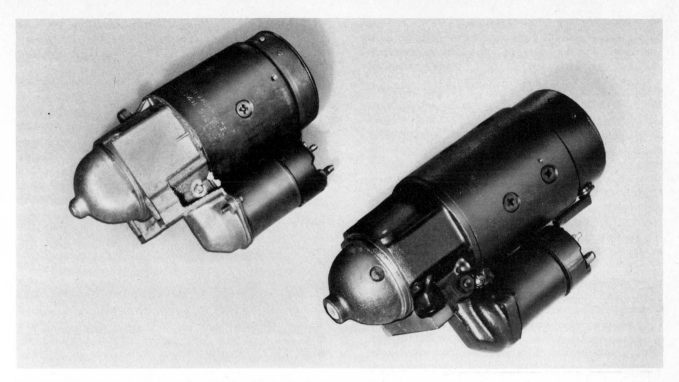

Fig. 5-30 Standard starting motor (left) compared with the starting motor used in a diesel-engine car. *(Oldsmobile Division of General Motors Corporation)*

clutch is disengaged. This prevents starting with the clutch engaged and possibly the transmission in gear.

On earlier cars without the steering-column-mounted ignition switch, the automatic transmission selector lever actuated a neutral safety switch which permitted starting only in park or neutral.

⚙ **5-22 Ignition resistance** Most ignition systems using contact points include a resistance wire. The resistance is in series in the ignition-coil primary circuit when the engine is running. This protects the ignition contact points from excessive current. However, during cranking, the ignition switch shorts out this resistance (when the key is turned to START). Now, full battery voltage is applied to the ignition coil for good performance during cranking. The resistance is also called a *ballast resistance*. On some cars, the resistance is a separately mounted part, but on most cars, the resistance is in the wiring harness.

NOTE: Electronic ignition systems, which do not use contact points, do not usually have or need resistance

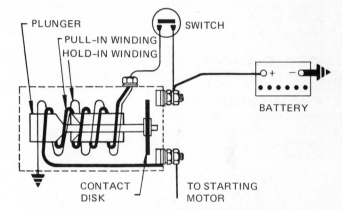

Fig. 5-31 Wiring circuit of a magnetic switch with two windings, a pull-in winding and a hold-in winding.

wire. The exception is the Chrysler electronic system (Fig. 1-5).

⚙ **5-23 Fusible link** A fusible link is a short length of insulated wire connected in series with a circuit. It

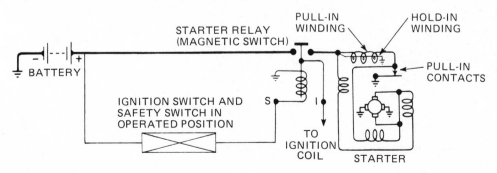

Fig. 5-32 Wiring circuit for a sliding pole-shoe starting motor with a magnetic switch (starter relay). *(Ford Motor Company)*

is smaller than the circuit it protects. If excessive current flows, it will burn out, thus protecting the circuit and connected electric equipment from damage. Wiring harnesses in cars have several fusible links. Some are connected into a feed line attached at the battery insulated terminal. This feed line takes care of supplying electric current to all electric equipment except the starting motor. It is, in effect, the master fuse for the system. If a short develops in any part of the electric system, it burns out. In other cars, the fusible link is connected to the starter relay or solenoid. Figure 5-33 shows how the feed line, which has a fusible link, is connected to the same solenoid terminal as the battery cable. Figure 5-34 shows schematically how more than one circuit feeds from the same terminal that the battery cable is attached to. Each of these circuits has a fusible link. Other circuits also have fusible links. See ☼ 8-18.

☼ **5-24 Seat-belt starter interlock system**   The seat-belt starter interlock system, introduced on 1974 cars, compels front-seat passengers to buckle their seat belts before the engine can be started. The switches shown in the box labeled SEAT AND SEAT-BELT SWITCHES (Fig. 5-35) must be closed before the circuit to the starting-motor magnetic switch is completed. Both seat-belt retractors have switches that are open when the belts are not in use. There is a switch under the right front seat that will open if someone sits in the seat. However, if the passenger then puts on the right-hand seat belt, the circuit will close.

NOTE: This system lasted only about 6 months. There were so many complaints that the United States Congress rescinded the law that had originally required the system. It is now legal for the automotive mechanic to disconnect the seat-belt starter interlock system. The approved procedure allows the interlock to be bypassed and the buzzer to be disconnected. But the seat-belt warning light must remain operative. Procedures

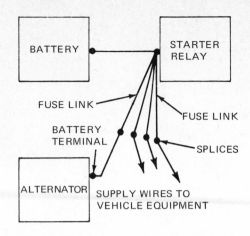

Fig. 5-34 Simplified diagram showing how more than one feed circuit, with fusible links, can be attached to the battery terminal on the starter relay. *(Ford Motor Company)*

for making the disconnect are available from the vehicle manufacturers.

☼ **5-25 Series–parallel system**   The series–parallel system is used on some heavy-duty applications, particularly big diesel engines, where the cranking requirements are especially high. This provides 12 volts for lights, alternator, regulator, and other electric accessories while still allowing a 24-volt starting motor to be used. Two 12-volt batteries are connected in parallel during normal operation of the engine. The parallel connections are made through a series–parallel switch. When the series–parallel switch is operated for starting, the parallel connections between the batteries are broken by the switch. The batteries are connected in series to supply 24 volts to the starting motor.

An electronic 12/24-volt system is shown in Fig. 5-36. It uses a transformer-rectifier combination with a 12-volt alternator and two 12-volt batteries connected in series. The two batteries, in series, supply 24 volts to the starting motor when the 12-volt magnetic switch is closed. The alternator is of the integral type, with an internal rectifier, a voltage regulator, and a transformer-rectifier unit. (Chapter 8 covers alternators and charging systems.) The S, or service, battery is charged from the plus (+) terminal of the alternator. The C battery is charged, in series with the S battery, at 24 volts through the transformer-rectifier system. The transformer steps up the 12 volts of the alternator to the 24 volts needed to charge the two batteries in series. The rectifier changes this to 24 volts direct current. The vehicle load as well as the 12-volt magnetic switch is fed from the S battery and the 12 volts from the alternator.

Note that the transformer-rectifier assembly is built into the alternator. The operation of the 12/24-volt system is completely automatic. Both batteries are charged normally at 12 volts. But the two batteries operate in series to supply 24 volts to the starting motor and are charged in series at 24 volts from the transformer-rectifier.

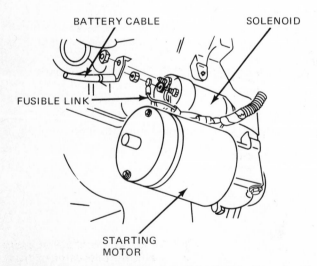

Fig. 5-33 Typical location of fusible link in the circuit feeding from the solenoid terminal to which the battery cable is attached.

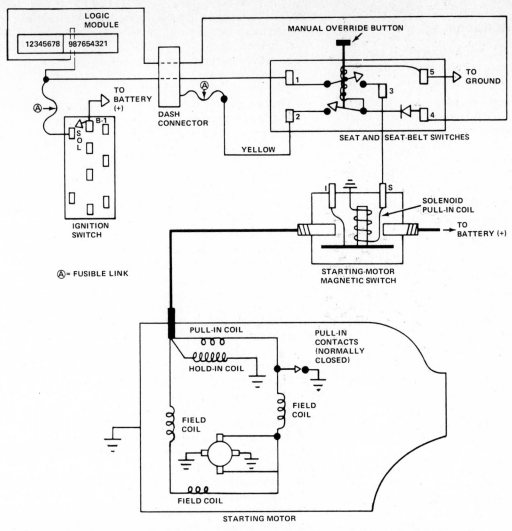

Fig. 5-35 Starting system for a sliding pole-shoe starting motor, magnetic switch, and seat-belt interlock system. *(American Motors Corporation)*

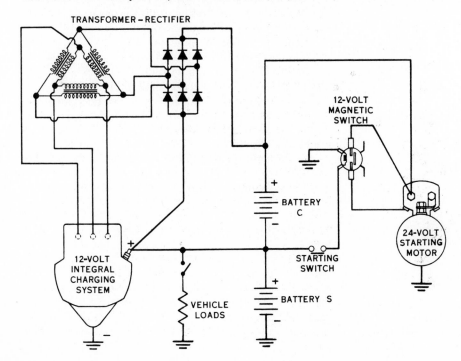

Fig. 5-36 Electronic 12/24-volt charging-starting system using a transformer-rectifier built into the alternator. *(Delco-Remy Division of General Motors Corporation)*

Chapter 5 review questions

Select the *one* correct, best, or most probable answer to each question. Then check your answers against the correct answers given at the end of the book.

1. In order to obtain enough cranking power from the starting motor, the circuit that runs through it must have:
   a. low resistance,
   b. high resistance,
   c. welded connections,
   d. three current paths.

2. A conductor that is carrying current in a magnetic field will:
   a. resist attempts to move it,
   b. tend to move,
   c. move to north pole,
   d. move to south pole.

3. In the ammeter, the shunt and the ammeter coil are connected:
   a. in series,
   b. in parallel,
   c. to separate terminals,
   d. to the battery.

4. In the voltmeter, the shunt and the voltmeter coil are connected:
   a. in series,
   b. in parallel,
   c. to separate terminals,
   d. in series–parallel.

5. The ring formed of segments and mounted near one end of the armature shaft, and through which current passes to and from the armature windings, is called the:
   a. shaft bearing,
   b. terminal,
   c. ring,
   d. commutator.

6. In the starting motor, the armature windings and the field windings are connected:
   a. in series,
   b. in parallel,
   c. to separate terminals,
   d. to the commutator.

7. The most commonly used starting-motor drive is the:
   a. inertia drive,
   b. overrunning clutch,
   c. Bendix drive,
   d. solid coupling.

8. The drive pinion in the overrunning clutch is moved into mesh for cranking action by:
   a. pinion inertia,
   b. sleeve turning in pinion,
   c. an idler gear,
   d. a shift lever.

9. The two electric devices that move the overrunning clutch into mesh with the flywheel are the:
   a. Bendix drive and solenoid,
   b. solenoid and sliding pole shoe,
   c. Bendix drive and sliding pole shoe,
   d. spur gear and splines.

10. Since starting motors draw several hundred amperes from the battery during cranking, starting-motor switches must:
    a. be mounted on the car floorboard,
    b. have heavy contacts,
    c. be operated by foot,
    d. be close to the battery.

11. As the magnetic switch operates, the contacts in the switch become connected to each other by a:
    a. heavy wire,
    b. plunger,
    c. iron core,
    d. contact disk.

12. The neutral safety switch is used on some cars with:
    a. overrunning clutches,
    b. automatic transmissions,
    c. automatic clutches,
    d. automatic starters.

13. In the starting motor with the sliding pole shoe, the pole shoe is moved by:
    a. one of the field windings,
    b. the solenoid,
    c. the magnetic switch,
    d. the clutch drive.

14. The solenoid mounted on overrunning-clutch starting motors not only closes the circuit between the battery and the starting motor but also:
    a. demeshes the pinion from the flywheel,
    b. actuates the vacuum switch,
    c. closes the throttle for starting,
    d. meshes the pinion with the flywheel.

15. The reason that vehicles with automatic transmissions and column shift levers do not need a neutral safety switch is that:
    a. the solenoid has two windings,
    b. the clutch has a safety switch,
    c. the ignition switch can be turned to START only in P or N,
    d. the engine will not start in P or N.

STARTING-SYSTEM DIAGNOSIS

After studying this chapter, you should be able to:

1. List the 10 basic starting-system problems and explain the various causes of each.
2. Describe the procedures to use for each problem to help pinpoint the cause. For example, what do you do if there is no cranking and the lights dim heavily when you try to start?
3. Perform these procedures under the supervision of the instructor.

6-1 Need for logical procedure Figure 6-1 shows a typical starting system on a V-8 engine, with various items to consider when you check starting trouble. You should follow a logical procedure when trying to find the cause of trouble. Once you find out what is wrong, it is usually fairly easy to fix the trouble. Suppose the starting motor does not operate at all. If the car has an automatic transmission, you would first check the shift lever position to make sure it is in N or P so that the circuit to the solenoid or starter relay is closed when you turn the ignition switch to START. Then you would check the battery to see if it is charged (with hydrometer or voltmeter). If the battery is okay, then you would check the circuits and connections.

A quick and simple check you can perform is to turn on the car dome light and try to start the car. Any one of five conditions will result: (1) lights stay bright, (2) lights dim considerably, (3) lights dim only slightly, (4) lights go out, (5) lights burn dimly or not at all when first turned on, before any attempt to start is made. The causes of trouble with these and other abnormal situations are outlined in the chart that follows, along with checks or corrections to be made. Following the chart are detailed explanations of the checking procedures to be used for each situation. The next chapter describes tests of the starting motor as well as starting-motor repair and overhauling procedures.

6-2 Starting-system trouble diagnosis chart Most starting-motor complaints are really battery complaints. That is, the battery is run down to the point where it cannot supply enough current to crank the engine. The result is slow cranking or no cranking at all. A low battery can also cause the solenoid to kick in and out with a clicking or chattering sound. That is,

the battery is strong enough to pull the drive pinion into mesh. But when the pull-in winding is shorted out by the closing of the main contacts, the hold-in coil is not strong enough to hold the pinion in. The spring pulls it back, and the whole process repeats. There have also been complaints of unusual noises such as a high-pitched whine or "whoop." The chart that follows lists possible causes of various troubles and the checks or corrections to be made.

NOTE: The trouble and possible causes are not listed in the chart in the order of frequency of occurrence. That is, item 1 under "Condition" does not necessarily occur more frequently than item 2, nor does item a under "Possible Cause" necessarily occur more often than item b.

6-3 Lights stay bright If the lights stay bright as the starting-motor circuit is closed and if no cranking action takes place, it means that there is no current flowing from the battery to the starting motor. The tests to locate the open circuit that produces this condition differ according to the type of system. Look for a blown fusible link on cars so equipped. If you find a blown link, determine the cause (ground, short) and correct it. Then replace the link.

There are several types of safety switch which prevent engine cranking when the transmission is in gear (5-21). One type, used on cars with manual transmission and clutch, prevents cranking unless the clutch is depressed. Some cars with an automatic transmission have a neutral safety switch that prevents cranking unless the selector lever is in PARK or NEUTRAL. Cars with a steering-column-mounted ignition switch do not need a safety switch. On these, you cannot turn the ignition switch to START unless the selector lever is in PARK or NEUTRAL.

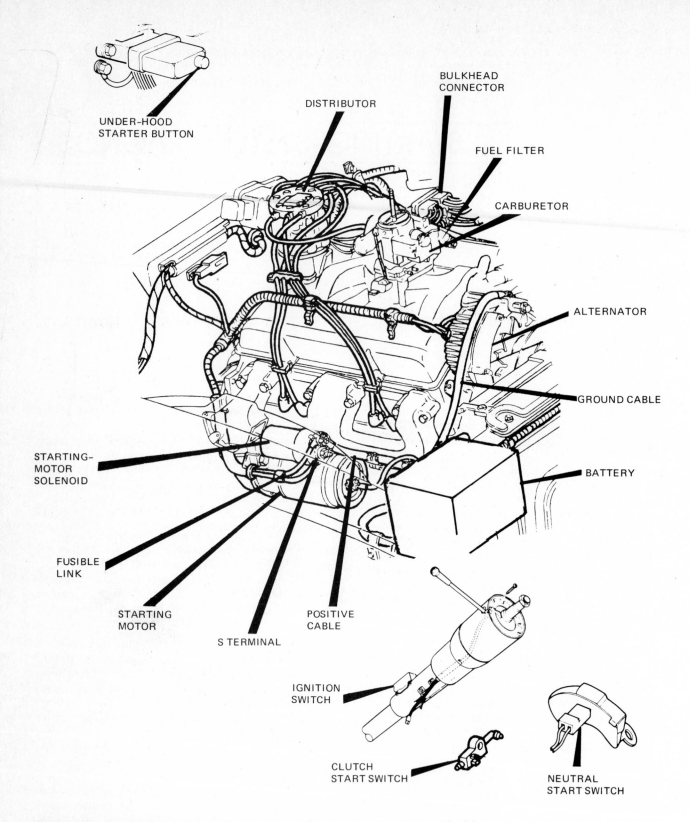

UNDER-HOOD
STARTER BUTTON

DISTRIBUTOR

BULKHEAD
CONNECTOR

FUEL FILTER

CARBURETOR

ALTERNATOR

GROUND CABLE

BATTERY

STARTING-
MOTOR
SOLENOID

FUSIBLE
LINK

STARTING
MOTOR

S TERMINAL

POSITIVE
CABLE

IGNITION
SWITCH

CLUTCH
START SWITCH

NEUTRAL
START SWITCH

Fig. 6-1 Starting-motor system on an engine, showing also the charging and ignition-system components. The air filter has been removed from the carburetor so parts can be seen. *(General Motors Corporation)*

Starting-System Trouble Diagnosis Chart

(See ☀ 6-3 to 6-9 for detailed explanations of trouble causes and corrections listed below.)

CONDITION	POSSIBLE CAUSE	CHECK OR CORRECTION
1. No cranking, lights stay bright (☀ 6-3)	a. Open circuit in switch	Check switch contacts and connections
	b. Open circuit in starting motor	Check commutator, brushes, and connections
	c. Open in control circuit	Check solenoid, relay (if used), switch, and connections
	d. Open fusible link	Correct condition causing link to blow, replace link
2. No cranking, lights dim heavily (☀ 6-4)	a. Trouble in engine	Check engine to find trouble
	b. Battery low	Check, recharge, or replace battery
	c. Very low temperature	Battery must be fully charged, with engine, wiring circuit, and starting motor in good condition
	d. Frozen shaft bearings, direct short in starting motor	Repair starting motor
3. No cranking, lights dim slightly (☀ 6-4)	a. Faulty or slipping drive	Replace parts
	b. Excessive resistance or open circuit in starting motor	Clean commutator; replace brushes; repair poor connections
4. No cranking, lights go out (☀ 6-5)	Poor connection, probably at battery	Clean cable clamp and terminal; tighten clamp
5. No cranking, no lights (☀ 6-5)	a. Battery dead	Recharge or replace battery
	b. Open circuit	Clean and tighten connections; replace wiring
6. Engine cranks slowly but does not start (☀ 6-6)	a. Battery run down	Check, recharge, or replace battery
	b. Very low temperature	Battery must be fully charged; engine wiring and starting motor in good condition
	c. Starting motor defective	Test starting motor
	d. Undersized battery cables or battery	Install cables or battery of adequate size
	e. Mechanical trouble in engine	Check engine
	f. Also, driver may have run battery down trying to start (see item 7)	
7. Engine cranks at normal speed but does not start	a. Ignition system defective	Try spark test; check timing and ignition system (Chap. 17)
	b. Fuel system defective	Check fuel pump, line, choke, and carburetor
	c. Air leaks in intake manifold or carburetor	Tighten mounting; replace gasket as needed
	d. Engine defective	Check compression, valve timing, etc.
8. Solenoid plunger chatters (☀ 6-7)	a. Hold-in winding of solenoid open	Replace solenoid
	b. Low battery	Charge battery
9. Pinion disengages slowly after starting (☀ 6-8)	a. Sticky solenoid plunger	Clean and free plunger
	b. Overrunning clutch sticks on armature shaft	Clean armature shaft and clutch sleeve
	c. Overrunning clutch defective	Replace clutch
	d. Shift-lever return spring weak	Install new spring
10. Unusual noises (☀ 6-9)	a. High-pitched whine during cranking (before engine fires)	Too much clearance between pinion and flywheel
	b. High-pitched whine after engine fires as key is released	Too little clearance between pinion and flywheel
	c. Loud "whoop," buzzing, or siren sound after engine fires but while starter is still engaged—sounds like a siren if engine is revved	Defective clutch
	d. Rumble, growl, or knock (in severe cases) as starter is coasting down to a stop after a start	Bent or unbalanced armature

ars equipped with a seat-belt
n, the car will not start unless
uence is followed (Chapter 23).
stem will also prevent starting.

automatic-control starting-motor
oid or a magnetic switch (Fig. 5-
he control system is doing its job.
edure that should produce starting-
of two things will happen: (1) The
magne... solenoid will not operate or (2) the
magnetic switch or solenoid will operate but the starting
motor will not. Check further, as follows.

**1. Magnetic switch or solenoid does not oper-
ate** This means that current is not getting to or
through the magnetic switch or solenoid. One of the
various control devices is not doing its job. Before
proceeding any further, make sure that the starting
motor will operate. Momentarily connect a heavy
jumper lead across the two main terminals of the solenoid or magnetic switch (on the nuts, not on the
screws, to avoid burning the screw threads). If the
starting motor operates, check the control system as
follows:

On the magnetic-switch system, put a jumper lead
from the heavy switch terminal connected to the battery to the nearest small magnetic-switch terminal. This
connects the magnetic switch directly to the battery,
eliminating the rest of the control circuit. If the magnetic switch does not operate, its winding is open. If it
and the starting motor operate, check the other control
devices in the system. By using a jumper lead and
connecting around each device in turn, you can find the
one that is not doing its job.

**2. Magnetic switch or solenoid operates but
starting motor does not** This is most commonly
caused by a low battery. The battery is strong enough
to operate the magnetic switch or solenoid but not the
starting motor. If the battery tests good (gravity or
open-circuit voltage up), then the cause is probably an
open circuit in the switch or the starting motor. If the
trouble is in the starting motor, it should be removed
for inspection and testing.

⚙ 6-4 Lights dim If the lights dim when the starting-
motor circuit is closed, it may help to try to find out
whether the lights dim only a little or whether they dim
a lot. If the lights dim only slightly with no cranking
action, there may be too much resistance or a partial
open in the starting motor. Since this condition would
prevent all but a small amount of current from flowing,
no cranking and only slight dimming of the lights would
result. If there is slight dimming along with the sound
of pinion engagement without cranking action, the
starting-motor solenoid is engaging the pinion, but the
overrunning clutch may be slipping. Also, the circuit
through the starting motor may be open.

If the lights dim considerably without cranking action, there could be mechanical trouble in the engine,
the battery could be run down, temperatures might be

very low, or there could be trouble in the starting motor
itself. The battery should be checked and recharged or
replaced as necessary. At very low temperatures, when
engine oil is stiff and cranking is hard, the battery is
much less able to maintain voltage under heavy load.
As a result, battery voltage will drop considerably and
lights will become very dim during cranking at very low
temperatures. The cold can be so severe that the starting motor cannot turn the engine over at all.

NOTE: Keep in mind that a driver may run the battery
down in a vain attempt to start the car. Then there is
no cranking action when you test the car, even though
the battery may still be in good enough condition to
light the lights. The cause of this failure is not in the
battery or starting motor but possibly in the ignition
system, fuel system, or engine.

⚙ 6-5 No lights, or lights go out If the lights burn
very dimly or not at all when the light switch is turned
on, then either the battery is completely discharged or
there is an open in the circuit. Test the battery and
check the wiring, connections, and switch.

If the lights come on when the light switch is turned
on but go off when the starting-motor circuit is closed,
chances are there is a bad connection between the
starting motor and battery. The bad connection is probably at one of the battery terminals. The poor connection will allow only a small current to get through.
There will be enough current for the lights, but when
the starting-motor circuit is closed, most of the current
that does get through then flows through the starting
motor. This is because the starting-motor resistance is
much lower than the resistance of the lights. However,
there will not be enough current to operate the starting
motor.

You can often tell whether there is a bad connection
at a battery terminal by keeping the starting-motor circuit closed for a few seconds while watching the battery-terminal connections. If there is a bad connection,
heat will develop (see ⚙ 1-21). You can feel this heat
by touching the cable clamp. Sometimes, there is so
much heat that the connection starts to smoke. Moving
the cable clamp around on the terminal a little may
improve the connection enough to get started. The
remedy is, however, to remove the cable clamp, clean
the clamp and terminal (see ⚙ 4-24), and replace the
clamp tightly.

NOTE: You can find almost any bad connection in a
circuit through which current is flowing by putting a
voltmeter across the connection (Fig. 6-2). If there is
resistance in the connection (which means a poor connection), there will be a voltage reading, or a voltage
drop, across the connection. Resistance causes a voltage drop (see ⚙ 1-19), since it takes voltage to push
current through a resistance. The higher the resistance,
the more the voltage drops overcoming the resistance.
See ⚙ 7-2 to 7-8 for discussions of how to locate excessive resistance in the starting-motor circuit with a
voltmeter.

✿ 6-6 Engine cranks slowly but does not start If the engine turns over slowly but does not start when the starting-motor switch is closed, there are several causes to consider. The battery may be run down, the temperature may be so low as to cause cranking difficulty, the starting motor may be defective, undersize cables may have been installed, or there may be mechanical trouble in the engine. It is also possible that the driver has run the battery down trying to start. In this case, the starting motor may crank normally with a fully charged battery but the engine will not start because of trouble in the ignition or fuel system or because of abnormal conditions in the engine.

Note what was said in ✿ 6-4 about the effects of low temperature on cranking difficulty.

✿ 6-7 Solenoid plunger chatters An open-circuit hold-in winding in the solenoid or magnetic switch will cause the plunger to pull in and release repeatedly when the control circuit is closed. With this defect, the pull-in winding pulls the plunger in and closes the circuit between the battery and starting motor. But as this happens, the switch contacts short out the pull-in winding. Since the hold-in winding is not operative, there is nothing to keep the plunger in and the plunger is released. The pull-in winding is again energized and pulls the plunger in once more. As a result, the plunger moves in and out of the solenoid or magnetic switch quite rapidly, and no cranking takes place.

The most common cause of solenoid chatter is a low battery. As soon as the circuit between the starting motor and battery is completed, the voltage of the battery drops (the lower the state of battery charge, the lower the voltage). Now the voltage of the discharged battery may drop too low to hold the solenoid plunger in. The plunger, therefore, is pulled back by the overrunning-clutch return spring. With the starting motor disconnected, the battery voltage goes up and the plunger is pulled in again. The action is rapidly repeated.

✿ 6-8 Pinion disengages slowly after starting Sometimes, the pinion will not release readily after the engine starts. Then, after engine speed increases, it may release with a loud "zooming" sound. This results from the overspeeding of the starting-motor armature. Such overspeeding may result in thrown armature windings and damage to the starting motor (✿ 7-21).

Possible causes are a sticky solenoid plunger, overrunning clutch sticking on the armature shaft, a defective clutch that will not allow the pinion to overrun normally, or a weak shift-lever return spring. If there is slow disengagement, prompt steps to eliminate the trouble should be taken before the armature is ruined by thrown windings. Remove the starting motor, if necessary, to check the freedom of the clutch on the armature shaft as well as clutch operation (✿ 7-19).

✿ 6-9 Unusual noises If you hear unusual noises during the start, there may be trouble in the starting

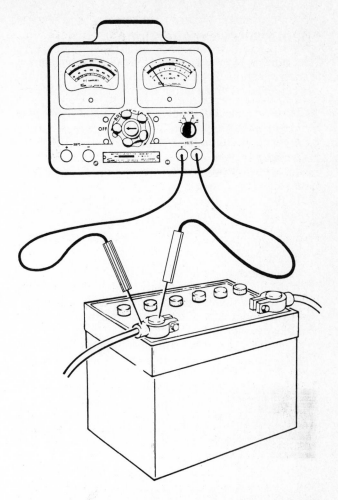

Fig. 6-2 Testing a connection for resistance with a voltmeter. With current flowing through the connection, put prods of the voltmeter on the terminal and on the clip, or clamp, as shown. A voltage reading indicates resistance at the connection.

motor. For example, a high-pitched whine during cranking and before the engine fires could be caused by excessive clearance between the clutch pinion and the flywheel. The high-pitched whine may be heard after the engine fires, just after the ignition key is released. This is probably due to the clearance between the pinion and flywheel being too small. (✿ 7-9 explains how to correct the distance between the pinion and flywheel.)

A loud whoop after the engine starts but while the pinion is still engaged with the flywheel is probably caused by a defective clutch. The starting motor must be removed from the engine so a new clutch can be installed. See ✿ 6-8.

Rumble, growl, or knock as the starting motor is coasting down to a stop after starting the engine is probably due to a bent armature shaft or unbalanced armature. The starting motor must be removed from the engine so a new armature can be installed.

Chapter 6 review questions

Select the *one* correct, best, or most probable answer to each question. Then check your answers against the correct answers given at the end of the book.

1. If the engine does not crank and the lights stay bright, the trouble could be:
   a. open circuit in the switch,
   b. open fusible link,
   c. open control circuit,
   d. all of the above.
2. If the engine does not crank and the lights dim heavily, the trouble is most likely:
   a. an open control circuit,
   b. a run-down battery,
   c. the drive slipping,
   d. a defect in the ignition system.
3. If the lights dim only slightly, and you can hear the sound of a running motor when trying to crank the engine, but the engine does not turn over, the probability is that the:
   a. starting-motor overrunning clutch is faulty,
   b. resistance in the starting circuit is excessive,
   c. battery is run down,
   d. there is a jammed condition in the engine.
4. If the lights burn normally when you turn them on, but they go out when you try to crank the engine, and the engine does not turn over, the trouble is probably:
   a. a run-down battery,
   b. poor connection at the battery,
   c. a defective ignition system,
   d. fuel system not delivering fuel to engine.
5. If the engine cranks at normal speed but does not start, the trouble could be:
   a. defects in the ignition system,
   b. defects in the fuel system,
   c. defects in the engine,
   d. all of the above.
6. If the engine cranks slowly but does not start, the trouble could be:
   a. a run-down battery,
   b. very low temperature,
   c. trouble in the engine,
   d. all of the above.
7. If you hear a loud whoop, buzzing, or siren sound after the engine fires but while the starter is still engaged, the cause is probably:
   a. a run-down battery,
   b. a defective starter clutch,
   c. a defective ignition system,
   d. excessive clearance between the pinion and fly-wheel.
8. If you hear a rumble, growl, or knock as the starter coasts down after a start, the probability is the trouble is due to:
   a. excessive clearance between the pinion and fly-wheel,
   b. a blown fusible link,
   c. a bent or unbalanced armature,
   d. engine trouble.
9. If the starting-motor-solenoid plunger chatters when a start is attempted, the trouble is probably:
   a. hold-in winding of solenoid open,
   b. battery overcharged,
   c. low temperature,
   d. an open in control circuit.
10. If you hear a high-pitched whine during cranking before the engine starts but the engine starts okay, the trouble is probably:
    a. too little clearance between the pinion and fly-wheel,
    b. battery run-down,
    c. ignition not firing properly,
    d. engine bearings worn.

STARTING-SYSTEM SERVICE

After studying this chapter, you should be able to:

1. Explain how to test starting-motor circuits and starting motors on the car.
2. Explain how to remove and replace starting motors.
3. Explain how to test starting motors off the car.
4. Explain how to disassemble, service, and reassemble a starting motor.
5. Under the supervision of the instructor, perform specific tests and services assigned to you.

7-1 Periodic maintenance Most starting motors require no maintenance between engine overhauls. Brushes are large enough, and the bushings have sufficient lubrication, to last until engine overhaul is required. Some starting motors, however, especially some larger heavy-duty units, do need periodic lubrication. Wiring circuits, mounting, and general condition of the starting motor should be checked periodically on all units.

1. **Lubrication** Most starting motors do not require lubrication except during overhaul. When a starting motor has been disassembled, any oil wicks and oil reservoirs should be saturated, or filled, with 10W engine oil. Coat bushings with a light grease such as Lubriplate. The roller-type overrunning clutch requires no lubrication since it is filled with lubricant during manufacture. It should not be washed or cleaned in a solvent tank as this would wash out the lubricant and cause clutch failure. After partial disassembly, sprag-type clutches should be lubricated with 5W-20 oil, as shown in Fig. 7-1. (A heavier grade of oil must not be used.) At the same time, the felt washer should be saturated with the same grade of oil. If there is a spiral spline on the shell assembly, it should be lubricated with 10W oil.

2. **Periodic inspection** During an engine tuneup or when checking under the hood for trouble, inspect the starting motor and the circuits. Most starting motors require no lubrication between engine overhauls. For this type the only checks would be for tight mounting, electric connections, and general condition of the unit as indicated by its operation.

3. **Neutral safety switch** The neutral safety switch is used on cars with automatic transmissions which do not have the steering-column ignition switch. If the neutral safety switch is not correctly adjusted, it will not close when the automatic-transmission selector lever is in neutral or park. Thus, cranking would not be possible. The switch is adjusted by shifting its position on the steering column. Refer to the applicable car shop manual for details.

Testing starting system

7-2 Variety of tests Different manufacturers have different testing procedures for checking starting motors and circuits on cars. These tests are changed occasionally by the manufacturer. For example, one manufacturer once recommended flooding the engine by pumping the accelerator pedal 10 times so the engine would not start during a cranking test. This is no longer recommended. It could damage the catalytic converter on the car. In the following sections, we outline tests that are recommended by various manufacturers. We suggest, however, that if you wish to check the starting motor and circuits on a car, you refer to the manufacturer's shop manual. Following are typical tests described here:

Cranking voltage test of starting system

Voltage-drop test of starting system

Current-draw test

7-3 Starting-system testers Three testing devices are needed to make starting-system tests, a voltmeter, an ammeter, and a variable resistance, or rheostat. These are usually combined into a single tester as shown in Fig. 7-2. The voltmeter measures voltage across a circuit or electric device. The ammeter measures current flow in a circuit. The variable resistance, or rheostat, can be adjusted from low resistance to high

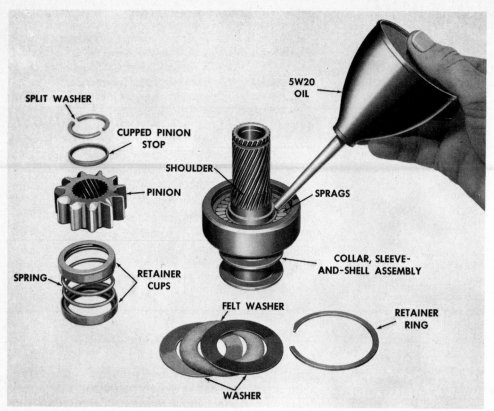

Fig. 7-1 Lubricating the sprags in the sprag overrunning clutch that can be disassembled. *(Delco-Remy Division of General Motors Corporation)*

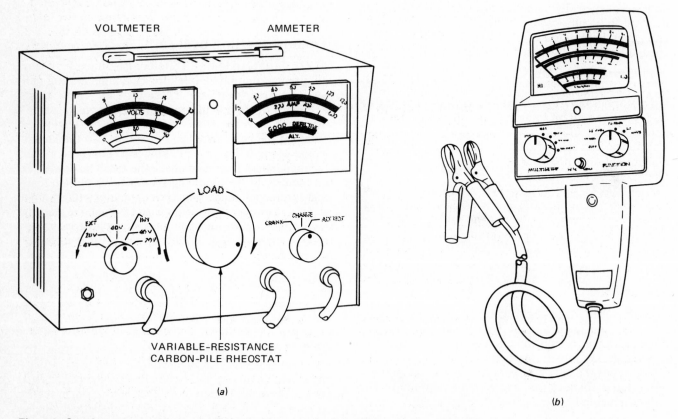

(a)

(b)

Fig. 7-2 Starting-system testers. *(a)* Tester with separate voltmeter and ammeter. *(b)* Tester with one meter which can be switched from an ammeter to a voltmeter by turning a knob. *(Ford Motor Company)*

resistance. The purpose of this device, when testing starting systems, is to connect a low resistance across the battery so as to get a high current draw. We described the use of the variable resistance in ☼ 4-18, explaining its use in making a high-discharge test of the battery. The variable resistance is used in a similar way when making certain starting-systems tests. The use of these instruments is explained below.

Careful: When using the ammeter, be sure to set it on the high-reading scale (0–400 or 0–600) to make the high-discharge test of the battery. If the ammeter is set on a low scale, and is connected across the battery, it would be like a direct short of the battery. A high current would flow and the ammeter would be damaged.

☼ 7-4 Preventing engine from starting during test
The engine must not start during the tests. To keep the engine from starting, deactivate the ignition system. There are several ways to do this. One way is to disconnect the lead that goes from the distributor to the ignition coil primary winding (contact-point system). Disconnecting this lead from the coil prevents any current flow through the ignition coil. On electronic ignition systems, disconnecting either primary terminal lead from the ignition coil, being careful not to ground it, will also deactivate the ignition system.

Ford offers a different idea; disconnect the leads (push-on connectors) from the S (switch) and I (ignition) terminals of the starter relay (magnetic switch). (Sometimes the I terminal is not used.) Connect a remote-control starter switch from the S terminal to the battery. Now, the starting motor can be operated without starting the engine, that is, with the ignition key turned to OFF.

NOTE: The General Motors high-energy ignition system, which has the ignition coil inside the distributor, cannot be deactivated by disconnecting the coil primary terminals. On these, disconnect, from the distributor, the lead connected to the BAT terminal. This is the feed wire from the ignition switch.

☼ 7-5 Cranking voltage test of starting system
This test is an overall efficiency check of the starting system. First, make sure the battery is in good condition and charged. Engine must be at operating temperature. With the ignition system deactivated and a voltmeter connected, as shown in Fig. 7-3, turn the ignition key to START. Quickly read the cranking voltage. Do not crank for more than a few seconds!

1. If the starting motor turns at normal cranking speed and the voltmeter reads 9 volts or more, the system is in normal condition.
2. If the cranking speed is low (battery charged) and the voltage is above 9 volts, the starting motor or circuit needs service.
3. If the cranking speed is low and the voltage is also low (below 9 volts), there is trouble in the starting motor. Also, it is possible that there is trouble in the engine. That is, the engine may lack oil or have the

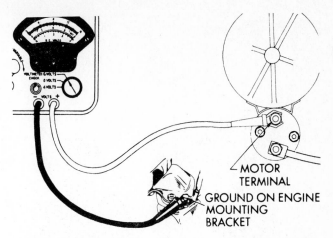

Fig. 7-3 Meter connections to make a cranking voltage test. *(Chevrolet Motor Division of General Motors Corporation)*

wrong oil. Or there could be excessive internal friction or binding due to worn or damaged parts.

☼ 7-6 Voltage-drop test of starting system
This test measures the voltage drop in the cranking circuit from the battery to the starting motor. You need a voltmeter that reads in the 0- to 2-volt range. With the ignition system deactivated, crank the engine with the starting motor. *Quickly* measure the voltage drop between the battery insulated terminal and the motor terminal on the starting motor. A voltage of more than 0.5 volt indicates (on most vehicles) a bad connection, defective wiring, or excessive resistance in the magnetic switch or solenoid contacts. You can locate the excessive resistance by checking the voltage across individual connections or as shown in Fig. 7-4. Ford gives the following maximum allowable voltages for the various connections shown:

Connections 1: 0.5 volt (as mentioned above)

Connections 2: 0.1 volt

Connections 3: 0.3 volt

Connections 4: 0.3 volt

If excessive voltage drop is found, correction should be made by cleaning and tightening connections and replacing defective wiring. If the excessive voltage drop is in the magnetic switch or solenoid, the internal contacts are burned. Replace the unit.

☼ 7-7 Current-draw test
This test measures the amount of current the starting motor is drawing when it is cranking the engine. The battery should be in good condition and charged. The engine should be at operating temperature.

Figure 7-5 shows the connections to be made to the starting motor to make the test. Be sure the rheostat is turned completely off. Crank the engine with the ignition system deactivated. Note the voltage reading.

Stop cranking the engine. Reduce the resistance of the rheostat until the voltage falls to the same reading as when cranking. Quickly note the current draw (am-

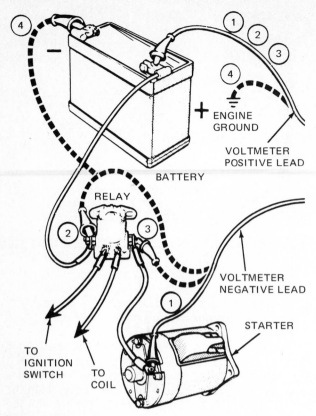

Fig. 7-4 Starting-motor-circuit test with voltmeter. *(Ford Motor Company)*

meter reading). Turn rheostat off and disconnect leads. If the reading is excessive (see manufacturer's specifications), there could be trouble in the starting motor or in the engine.

⚙ 7-8 Other tests Other tests have been suggested from time to time. For example, Chevrolet has recommended a voltage-drop test of the solenoid contacts and an amperage test of the solenoid windings. Both are made with the ignition system deactivated. The

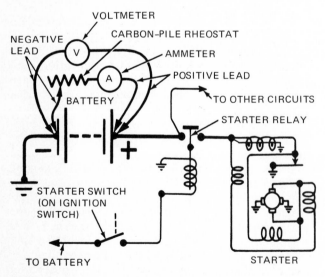

Fig. 7-5 Meter and carbon-pile connections to check starting-motor current draw. *(Ford Motor Company)*

connections to be made for the voltage-drop test are shown in Fig. 7-6.

⚙ 7-9 Adjusting starting motor on car to correct a noise problem In ⚙ 6-9 we described various abnormal noises during and after cranking and their possible causes. A high-pitched whine during cranking (before or after starting) is often due to an incorrect clearance between the motor pinion and the engine flywheel. To adjust the clearance, you need to shim between the starting motor and its mounting. Figure 7-7 shows various mounting arrangements and the shim locations. Checking and shimming procedures follow.

1. Remove lower flywheel housing cover and examine the flywheel ring-gear teeth for unusual wear patterns or out-of-alignment.
2. Start the engine. *Very carefully* touch the outside of the teeth of the flywheel ring gear with chalk or marking pen to determine maximum runout of teeth. Turn engine off. Rotate the flywheel so the marked teeth (with maximum runout) are in the area of the starting-motor drive pinion.
3. Disconnect the battery grounded terminal to prevent accidental operation of the starting motor.
4. Insert a screwdriver in the small hole in the bottom of the starting motor (see arrow in Fig. 7-8). Move the starting-motor drive pinion so it meshes with the flywheel teeth. You may need to rotate the flywheel slightly to secure meshing. Also, make sure a pinion tooth is exactly centered between two flywheel teeth, as shown in the upper left in Fig. 7-9.
5. You need a wire gauge, as shown at the bottom of Fig. 7-9, made from 0.020-inch [0.51 mm] diameter wire. Use the gauge, as shown to the upper right in Fig. 7-9. If the gauge does not fit between the top of the tooth and the bottom between the flywheel teeth, the clearance is less than the required minimum of 0.020 inch [0.51 mm]. Shim the starting motor away from the flywheel, as shown in Fig. 7-8. A shim 0.015 inch [0.38 mm] thick will move the starting motor out about 0.005 inch [0.13 mm].

If the gauge fits with clearance to spare, the starting motor is too far away from the flywheel. If the

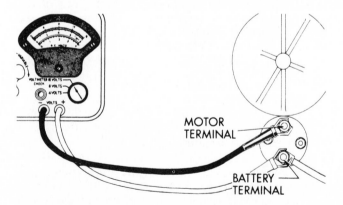

Fig. 7-6 Meter connections to check solenoid switch contacts. *(Chevrolet Motor Division of General Motors Corporation)*

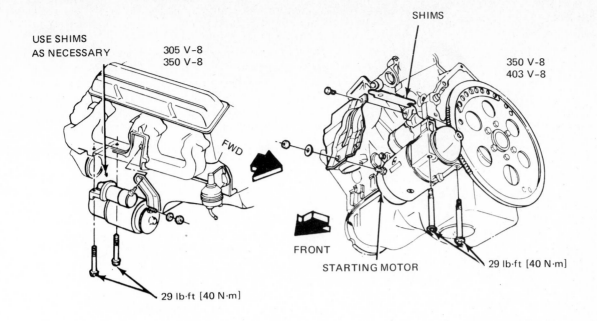

USE SHIMS
AS NECESSARY

305 V-8
350 V-8

FWD

29 lb·ft [40 N·m]

SHIMS

350 V-8
403 V-8

FRONT

STARTING MOTOR

29 lb·ft [40 N·m]

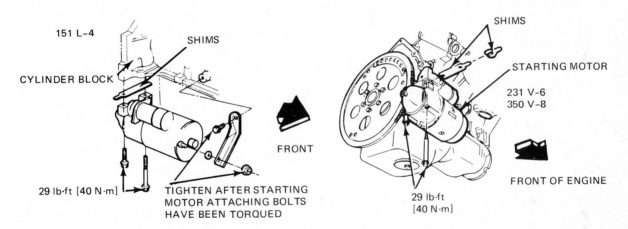

151 L-4

SHIMS

CYLINDER BLOCK

FRONT

29 lb·ft [40 N·m]

TIGHTEN AFTER STARTING
MOTOR ATTACHING BOLTS
HAVE BEEN TORQUED

SHIMS

STARTING MOTOR

231 V-6
350 V-8

FRONT OF ENGINE

29 lb·ft
[40 N·m]

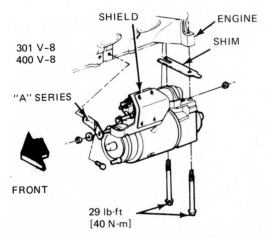

301 V-8
400 V-8

"A" SERIES

SHIELD

ENGINE

SHIM

FRONT

29 lb·ft
[40 N·m]

STARTER NOISE DIAGNOSTIC PROCEDURE
1. STARTER NOISE DURING CRANKING:
   REMOVE ONE 0.015 INCH [0.39 mm]
   DOUBLE SHIM OR ADD SINGLE 0.015
   INCH [0.39 mm] SHIM TO OUTER BOLT
   ONLY.
2. HIGH-PITCHED WHINE AFTER ENGINE
   FIRES: ADD 0.015 INCH [0.39 mm]
   DOUBLE SHIMS UNTIL NOISE
   DISAPPEARS.

Fig. 7-7 Shimming procedure to eliminate starter noises.
(Pontiac Motor Division of General Motors Corporation)

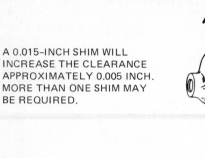

A 0.015-INCH SHIM WILL INCREASE THE CLEARANCE APPROXIMATELY 0.005 INCH. MORE THAN ONE SHIM MAY BE REQUIRED.

SCREWDRIVER

SHIM

Fig. 7-8 Using screwdriver to mesh starting-motor and flywheel teeth. *(Buick Motor Division of General Motors Corporation)*

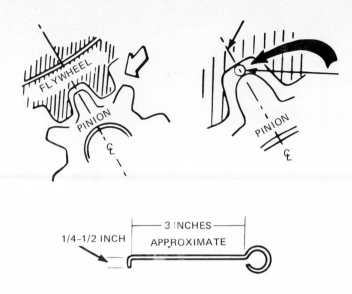

1/4–1/2 INCH

3 INCHES APPROXIMATE

SUGGESTED WIRE GAUGE

Fig. 7-9 Using wire gauge to check clearance between base of flywheel teeth and starting-motor drive-pinion teeth. *(Buick Motor Division of General Motors Corporation)*

clearance is greatly in excess of the normal 0.020 inch [0.51 mm], it may cause broken flywheel teeth and starter housing. To decrease the clearance, shim the starting motor toward the flywheel by shimming only the outer side of the mounting pad or removing shims from the inside of the pad. A shim at the outer side 0.015 inch [0.38 mm] thick decreases the clearance about 0.010 inch [0.26 mm].

The final test of the shim adjustment is to operate the starting motor and listen for noise. Add shims (or remove shims) until the noise goes away.

Bench-testing starting motor

Two tests of the detached starting motor can be made, no-load test and stall test. Some vehicle manufacturers no longer carry the stall-test procedure in their shop manuals. These tests are usually performed by starting-motor rebuilders or remanufacturers.

☼ 7-10 Removing starting motor First, disconnect the grounded battery cable from the battery. Raise the car. Remove starter braces, shields, shims, and other related parts that may be in the way. Remove the starting-motor mounting bolts. Disconnect the solenoid wires and battery cable and remove starting motor. Carefully note the locations of shims. Figure 7-7 shows various mounting arrangements.

☼ 7-11 No-load test Figure 7-10 shows a typical setup to no-load-test the starting motor. Refer to the specifications issued by the starting-motor manufacturer. Adjust the variable resistance to get the specified voltage. Then read the current draw and armature rpm.

☼ 7-12 Stall test The stall test is made with the starting motor off the car. The drive must be locked so the armature cannot turn. Then a specified voltage is applied to see what current the stalled motor will draw (Fig. 7-11). A high-reading ammeter is required for this test, as well as a high-capacity carbon-pile rheostat.

The starting-motor resistance can be determined at the same time that the stall test is made. With the rheostat adjusted to apply the specified voltage, the current is measured. Then the resistance is calculated by using Ohm's law (☼ 1-15).

☼ 7-13 Interpreting results of tests Even before making the no-load and stall tests, an experienced electrical service technician can get a good idea of the condition of the starting motor by operating it in the car. However, for an accurate analysis, the unit should be tested as described. Interpreting the results of these tests and further analysis with a test light to pinpoint causes of trouble are discussed below. Note the procedures to follow under the six conditions described.

1. Rated current draw and no-load speed indicate normal condition of the starting motor.
2. Low free speed and a high current draw may result from:
   a. Tight, dirty, or worn bearings; bent armature shaft; or loose field-pole screws, which allow the armature to drag on the pole shoes.
   b. Grounded armature or fields. To check for this, take off the end frame and test the field and armature separately.
   c. Shorted armature. Check the armature further on a growler (see ☼ 7-20).
3. Failure to operate at all, accompanied by a high current draw, may result from:
   a. Direct ground in the switch, terminal, or fields.
   b. Frozen shaft bearings, which prevent the armature from turning.
   c. Direct ground of armature windings—for example, due to thrown armature windings (☼ 7-21).
4. Failure to operate with no current draw may result from:

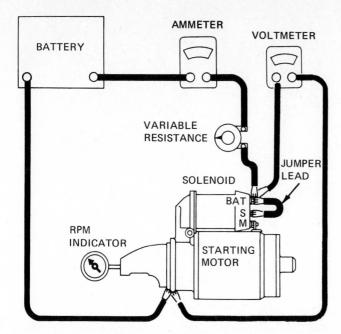

Fig. 7-10 No-load test of starting motor. A jumper lead must be used, as shown, to energize the solenoid so that it operates to connect the starting motor to the battery. *(Delco-Remy Division of General Motors Corporation)*

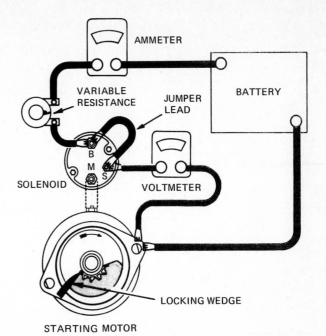

Fig. 7-11 Connections to check a starting motor on the stall test. The wedge is securely jammed into the drive-pinion teeth so the drive is locked and the armature cannot rotate. *(Delco-Remy Division of General Motors Corporation)*

a. Open field circuit. Inspect internal connections and trace the circuit with a test light, checking the brushes, armature, and fields.

b. Open armature coils. This condition causes badly burned commutator bars. There is a discussion of this condition in ☼ 7-21.

c. Broken or weak brush springs, worn brushes, high mica on the commutator, glazed or dirty commutator, or any other condition that would prevent good contact between the commutator and the brushes will prevent operation of the starting motor.

5. Low no-load speed with a low current draw indicates:

a. An open field winding.

b. High internal resistance due to poor connections, defective leads, dirty commutator, or any other condition listed under *4c,* above.

6. High free speed with a high current draw indicates shorted fields. Since the fields already have a very low resistance, there is no practical way to test for this condition. If shorted fields are suspected, install new fields and check the starting motor again. But before going to this trouble, check the other components of the starting motor.

Repair procedures

☼ **7-14 Disassembly** The disassembly procedure varies with different starting motors. The following sections describe methods of disassembling and reassembling various starting motors. As a rule, the disassembly should go only as far as is necessary to find and eliminate the defect or condition causing trouble. Inspection and repair of armatures are covered in ☼ 7-20. Inspection and replacement of bearings are outlined

in ☼ 7-23, while removal, repair, and installation of field coils are detailed in ☼ 7-25. Usually, it is not necessary to disassemble the field frame and remove the field coils unless the insulation is charred or damaged or the coils are grounded to the frame.

NOTE: On many starting motors today, the pole shoes and field coils are permanently attached to the field frame (pole shoes welded to frame). On these, the field coils are not separately serviced. If damaged, the field-frame assembly must be discarded and a new assembly installed.

Old-style armatures or fields must not be cleaned in solvent since this might dissolve the insulation or at least damage it. Most modern armatures and fields are plastic dipped and can be washed.

When a starting motor is being reassembled, the brush-spring tension should be checked with a spring scale. When the check is made, the armature and commutator end frame should be put together so that the brushes are resting on the commutator. Brushes should have full contact on the commutator and should be free in their holders so that good, firm contact will be maintained.

Careful: Do not allow the brushes or brush arms to snap down since this might cause the brushes to crack or chip.

☼ **7-15 Overrunning-clutch starting-motor service** Figures 5-14 and 7-12 show disassembled views of a solenoid-operated overrunning-clutch starting motor. To disassemble this type of motor, remove the solenoid assembly. Then take out the through bolts so

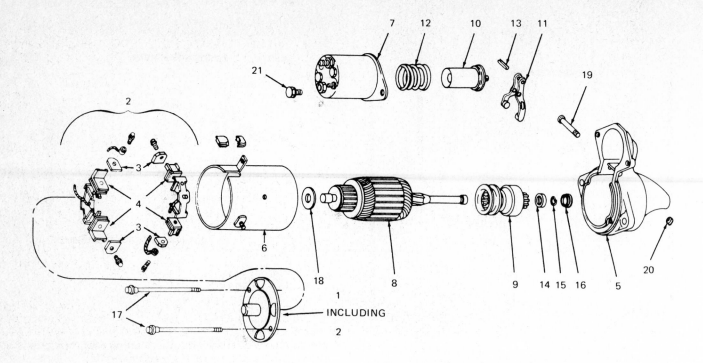

1. FRAME—COMMUTATOR END
2. BRUSH AND HOLDER
3. BRUSH
4. BRUSH HOLDER
5. HOUSING—DRIVE END
6. FRAME AND FIELD ASSEMBLY
7. SOLENOID SWITCH
8. ARMATURE
9. DRIVE ASSEMBLY
10. PLUNGER
11. SHIFT LEVER

12. PLUNGER RETURN SPRING
13. SHIFT LEVER PIN
14. PINION STOP
15. SNAP RING
16. BUSHING
17. THROUGH BOLT
18. WASHER
19. SHIFT-LEVER PIVOT BOLT
20. NUT
21. SOLENOID ATTACHING BOLT (TWO)

Fig. 7-12 Disassembled overrunning-clutch starting motor. *(Pontiac Motor Division of General Motors Corporation)*

the commutator end frame, field frame, and drive housing can be separated. Take the armature with the drive assembly from the drive housing. (If the starting motor has a center bearing, detach the bearing support from the drive housing before removing the armature from the housing.) The drive assembly is held on the armature shaft by a thrust collar, retainer, and snap ring. First remove the thrust collar. Then put a metal cylinder (such as a ½-inch [12.7 mm] pipe coupling) over the end of the armature shaft so it rests on the retainer. Tap the cylinder lightly with a hammer to force the retainer down off the snap ring. Remove the snap ring and slide the retainer and drive assembly from the armature shaft.

Armature service is covered in ☼ 7-20, while field-coil service is detailed in ☼ 7-25.

1. Overrunning clutch The overrunning clutch should be wiped clean but never cleaned by any degreasing or high-temperature cleaning method. This would remove the lubricant originally packed in the clutch, and the clutch would be ruined. If the pinion turns roughly or slips in the cranking direction, replace the drive assembly.

To install the overrunning clutch on the armature shaft (type using retainer and snap ring), first lubricate the end of the shaft with SAE 20W oil and install the drive assembly, pinion out. Slide the stop retainer down over the shaft, recessed side out. Put a new snap ring on the end of the armature shaft and slide it down into the groove in the shaft. If you have trouble starting the ring on the shaft, tap it down with a plastic hammer or rest a hardwood block on the ring and strike the block with a hammer (Fig. 7-13a). Install the thrust collar on the shaft. Use two pairs of pliers to squeeze the thrust collar and retainer on opposite sides so that the retainer is forced up over the snap ring (Fig. 7-13b).

NOTE: Using the special tool, shown in Fig. 7-14, simplifies snap-ring removal and replacement. This tool slips the ring from its channel and holds it in the tool ready for replacement.

2. Sprag-type clutch There are different types of sprag overrunning clutches. The one shown in Fig. 5-24 is called a heavy-duty type. An intermediate-duty type is illustrated in Fig. 7-15. You may need to disassemble these units. The intermediate-duty type is dis-

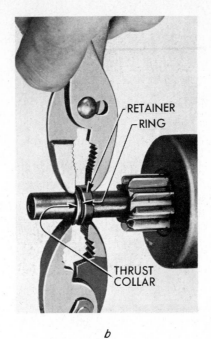

HARDWOOD BLOCK

SNAP RING
GROOVE IN ARMATURE SHAFT
RETAINER

DRIVE ASSEMBLY

a

RETAINER RING

THRUST COLLAR

b

Fig. 7-13 Installing the snap ring and retainer on the armature shaft after drive-assembly installation. *(Buick Motor Division of General Motors Corporation)*

assembled by removing the lockwire, the collar, the jump spring, the stop washer, and the second lockwire (Fig. 7-15). Reassemble by restoring parts in the order in which they were removed. To disassemble the heavy-duty unit (Fig. 5-24), remove the cupped pinion stop and split washer and slide other parts off the shaft as shown. Lubricate the sprags and the felt washer with 5W-20 oil (see Fig. 7-1) and reassemble. You will probably need a new pinion stop since the old stop will have been damaged during removal. Lubricate spiral splines with SAE 10W oil.

NOTE: Some earlier-model sprag clutches could be disassembled so the sprags could be lubricated. However, later models have lifetime lubrication built in and cannot be disassembled.

3. **Checking pinion clearance** Be sure that the clearance between the pinion and the thrust washer, retainer, or housing is correct. The clearance should be checked with the pinion in the cranking position. On solenoid-operated units, the solenoid should be connected to a battery and, with the pinion in the drive position, the check is made. However, since the clearance could not be checked if the pinion were rotating, the starting motor should be prevented from operating. One method of doing this is to disconnect the cable

between the solenoid and the starting motor. You cannot do this on units using a short connector strap between the solenoid motor terminal and the starting-motor terminal. On these units the connector must be disconnected from the terminal and carefully insulated. Then, a battery should be connected from the solenoid switch terminal to the solenoid frame (Fig. 7-16). Momentarily flash a jumper lead from the solenoid motor terminal to the solenoid frame or to the solenoid ground terminal. This will shift the pinion into cranking position. Push the pinion back and measure clearance.

Another method of checking the pinion clearance is to connect a 6-volt source between the solenoid terminal and ground. This voltage should be enough to make the solenoid work, but it probably will not operate the starting motor. As a further precaution, temporarily connect a jumper lead between the solenoid motor terminal and ground. Push the pinion back and check pinion clearance.

On Delco-Remy units without the retainer and snap ring on the armature shaft, the clearance between the pinion and housing should be $^3/_{16}$ inch [4.76 mm]. On Delco-Remy units using a retainer and snap ring on the armature shaft, clearance between the pinion and retainer—with the pinion pushed away from the retainer

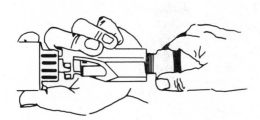

Fig. 7-14 This snap-ring tool simplifies snap-ring removal and replacement. *(Lisle Corporation)*

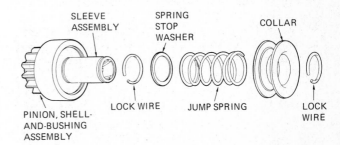

SLEEVE ASSEMBLY

SPRING STOP WASHER

COLLAR

PINION, SHELL-AND-BUSHING ASSEMBLY

LOCK WIRE

JUMP SPRING

LOCK WIRE

Fig. 7-15 Intermediate-duty sprag clutch. *(Delco-Remy Division of General Motors Corporation)*

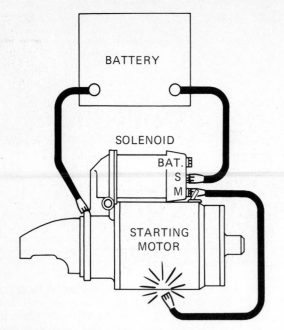

Fig. 7-16 Connections for checking pinion clearance. *(Delco-Remy Division of General Motors Corporation)*

as far as possible—should be 0.010 to 0.140 inch [0.254 to 3.56 mm].

On the late-model enclosed-shift-lever type of starting motor, there is no provision for adjustment. Incorrect clearance means that the motor has been incorrectly reassembled or that there are worn or damaged parts. On some earlier models, however, adjustment is possible. For example, the adjustment on some manual types is made by turning the switch button in or out. The adjustment on some solenoid types is made by turning the solenoid-plunger stud in or out. On other solenoid types, the stud is not adjustable. This means that the solenoid itself must be moved back or forth on the field frame. This is done by first loosening the four mounting screws and then moving the solenoid to get the proper clearance. A third arrangement has a serrated shift-lever linkage. On this arrangement, the adjustment is made by loosening the linkage screw.

NOTE: If the old rubber boot (where used) is breaking apart, it should be replaced. Otherwise, dirt or moisture will get into the solenoid and cause the plunger to work hard or jam.

⚙ 7-16 Gear-reduction starting-motor service The gear-reduction starting motor is shown in Fig. 5-28. A disassembled view is shown in Fig. 7-17. The disassembly–reassembly procedure for this unit is as follows.

Support the gear housing in the soft jaws of a vise but do not clamp it. Remove two through bolts, end head, armature, steel and fiber thrust washers. Lift the field and frame assembly up just enough to expose the brush-terminal screw and, supporting the assembly on blocks (Fig. 7-18), remove the screw. Unsolder the shunt field-coil lead from the brush terminal and lift off the frame assembly. Remove the brush-insulator-plate

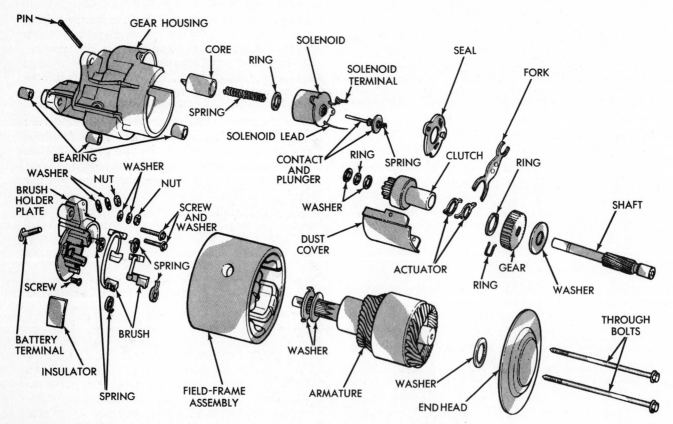

Fig. 7-17 Disassembled gear-reduction overrunning-clutch starting motor. *(Chrysler Corporation)*

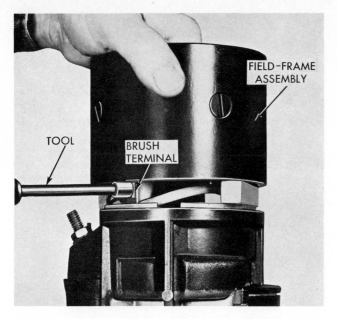

Fig. 7-18 Removing the brush-terminal screw. *(Chrysler Corporation)*

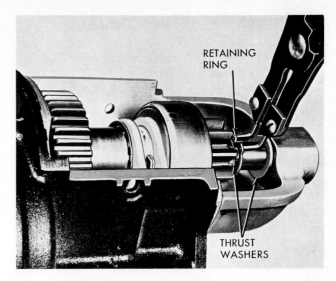

Fig. 7-19 Removing the pinion-shaft retaining ring. *(Chrysler Corporation)*

screw. Lift off the plate with brushes and solenoid as a unit. The overrunning clutch may be removed from the gear housing by removing the dust cover, releasing the snap ring that positions the driven gear on the pinion shaft, releasing the retainer ring at the clutch pinion (Fig. 7-19), and then pushing the shaft out through the rear of the housing. When releasing the snap ring, be sure to cover the area with a cloth to keep the snap ring from jumping out.

NOTE: There are several other special steps and measurements to be taken in disassembling and reassembling this unit. Refer to the manufacturer's shop manual for details before attempting to service this type of starting motor.

⚙ 7-17 Sliding pole-shoe starting-motor service
Figure 7-20 shows a sliding pole-shoe starting motor in disassembled view. To disassemble this unit, remove the cover screw, cover, through bolts, starter-drive end housing, and the lever return spring. Remove the pivot pin, lever, and armature. Remove other parts from the brush-end plate assembly as necessary. If the field coils require replacement, see ⚙ 7-25.

Examine the drive pinion and ring-gear teeth for damage and improper wear (Fig. 7-21). The pinion teeth must penetrate more than one-half of the ring-gear tooth depth. Replace the ring gear and overrunning-clutch assembly if necessary.

Reassembly is the reverse of disassembly. Figure 7-22 shows the assembly sequence of the contact assembly on the type of motor using a cover band.

⚙ 7-18 Diesel-engine starting-motor service
The starting motor used with the General Motors V-8 diesel engine (Fig. 5-30) is serviced in about the same way as other units previously discussed. Figures 7-23 and 7-24 show details of the components and how they go together. Note that this motor uses a center bearing.

⚙ 7-19 Checking an overrunning clutch
The pinion of an overrunning clutch in good condition should turn freely in the overrunning direction and should not slip in the opposite direction even under a load of 25 to 50 pound-feet [3.455 to 6.910 kg-m] of torque. To torque test the clutch, put it on an old armature that has been clamped in a vise. Apply torque with a torque wrench to the pinion. If the pinion slips when the specified torque is applied (see manufacturer's manual), discard the clutch.

If the pinion turns roughly in the overrunning direction, the rollers are chipped or worn and the clutch should be replaced. If the pinion slips in the cranking direction or if the pinion teeth are rough or broken, discard the clutch. Do not try to repair or relubricate a clutch.

⚙ 7-20 Armature inspection and repair
Check the armature both mechanically and electrically. As a first step, note the condition of the shaft, commutator, windings, and lamination. Look for such conditions as:

1. A bent or worn shaft
2. Thrown windings
3. Burned commutator bars
4. High commutator mica
5. Worn commutator
6. Scores or rub marks on the core lamination

If the lamination has scores on it, the armature has been rubbing on the pole shoes. This could be due to worn bearings, a bent armature shaft, or loose pole shoes.

The armature shaft as well as the commutator may be checked for an out-of-round condition with V blocks and an indicator, as shown in Fig. 7-25. Rotate the armature and note the "run-out," or out-of-round. An out-of-round, worn, or burned commutator on older-style armatures can usually be turned down in a lathe (⚙ 7-22) if the condition is not too bad. However, the modern lightweight starting-motor armature has com-

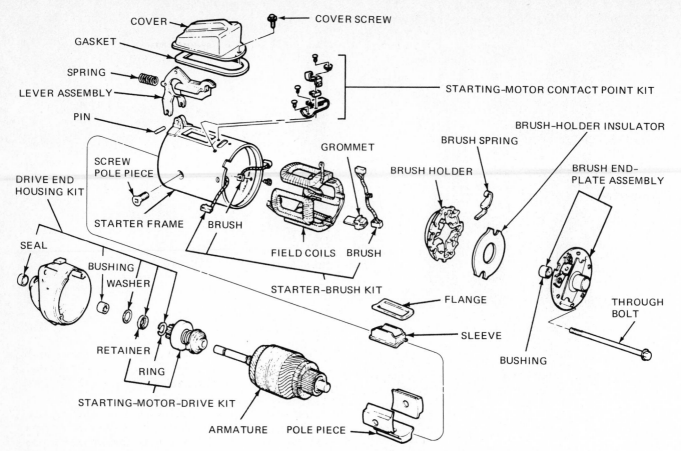

Fig. 7-20 Disassembled sliding-pole-shoe starting motor. *(Ford Motor Company)*

mutator segments too thin to be turned. On these, if the commutator is worn or burned, a new armature is required. If the armature shaft is bent, the armature should be discarded.

Thrown armature windings result from excessive armature speed, as explained in ✿ 7-21. Burned commutator bars are normally caused by open-circuited armature windings, as explained in ✿ 7-21.

1. Electrical tests The armature should be tested for grounds, shorts, and opens. It can be tested for grounds with a low-voltage test light. Place one test point on the core and another on the commutator (Fig. 7-26). Avoid touching the shaft bearing surface or brush-seating area on the commutator, since any arc would cause burning and roughening of the metal. If the light goes on, the armature has a ground and should be replaced. The armature may be tested on a growler for short circuits, as explained below.

Open circuits in a starting-motor armature most often occur at the commutator riser bars on the type where the coils are soldered to the bars. A poor connection or an open produces overheating and thus burning of the bars (see ✿ 7-21). As already explained, the motor will overheat if it is cranked too long. Then the solder will melt and be thrown out on the cover band. The armatures of many starting motors have the armature-coil leads welded to the commutator bars instead of soldered. This construction guards against damage due to opens at the connections.

2. Testing armature on growler The growler (Fig. 7-27) is an electromagnet that operates on alternating current. If the alternating current is 60-Hz, the current is reversing in direction 120 times a second. This means that the magnetic field in the electromagnet is changing directions 120 times a second. If an armature is placed in the growler, as shown in Fig. 7-27, the changing magnetism will exert a changing magnetic force on the armature, causing an actual growling noise.

To test the armature for short circuits, hold a hacksaw blade above each armature slot while the armature is slowly revolved by hand. If any winding is shorted, the blade will be alternately attracted to and repelled from the slot in which that winding is assembled. This is because the coil, being shorted, has a closed circuit, which permits current to flow (induced by the changing magnetic field). The flow of current in the shorted winding, alternating with the main magnetic field, sets up an alternating magnetic field of its own. This acts on the blade like a buzzer, causing the blade to vibrate against the core when it is held above the slot containing the shorted winding.

✿ 7-21 Burned commutator bars and thrown windings Burned commutator bars usually indicate an open-circuited armature coil. The open circuit is normally at the commutator riser bar; it is caused by overheating due to excessively long periods of cranking. Enough heat will develop to melt the solder at the riser

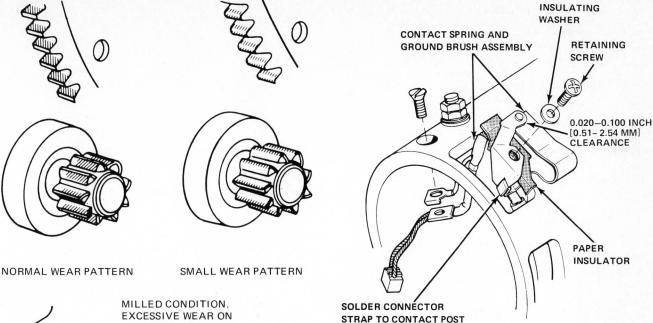

NORMAL WEAR PATTERN

SMALL WEAR PATTERN

MILLED CONDITION.
EXCESSIVE WEAR ON
2 OR 3 TEETH

MILLED TOOTH-METAL
BUILDUP WILL NOT
PERMIT ENGAGEMENT

MILLED GEARS

Fig. 7-21 Starting-motor drive pinion and flywheel ring-gear wear patterns. *(Ford Motor Company)*

INSULATING
WASHER

CONTACT SPRING AND
GROUND BRUSH ASSEMBLY

RETAINING
SCREW

0.020–0.100 INCH
[0.51– 2.54 MM]
CLEARANCE

PAPER
INSULATOR

SOLDER CONNECTOR
STRAP TO CONTACT POST

Fig. 7-22 Assembly of starting-motor contacts. These are the contacts that open when the pole shoe moves into the cranking position. *(American Motors Corporation)*

bars; this solder will be thrown and hence poor connections will occur. Because of these poor connections, arcing will take place every time the bar passes under the brushes; in a short time, the bar will be so badly burned that the starting motor will stop working. If the bars are not too badly burned, the leads may be resoldered in the riser bars—rosin, not acid, flux should be used. The commutator can then be turned down in a lathe (⚙ 7-22).

NOTE: Many starting-motor armatures now have welded connections at the commutator. These cannot be re-

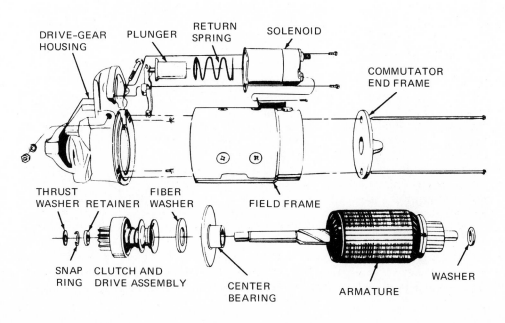

DRIVE-GEAR
HOUSING

PLUNGER

RETURN
SPRING

SOLENOID

COMMUTATOR
END FRAME

THRUST
WASHER

RETAINER

FIBER
WASHER

FIELD FRAME

SNAP
RING

CLUTCH AND
DRIVE ASSEMBLY

CENTER
BEARING

ARMATURE

WASHER

Fig. 7-23 Disassembled starting motor for diesel-engine application. *(Chevrolet Motor Division of General Motors Corporation)*

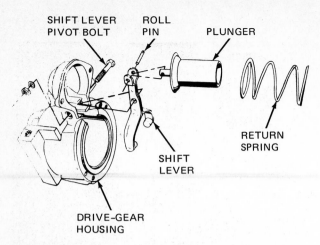

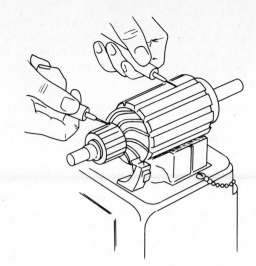

Fig. 7-24 Shift-lever and plunger attachment to the drive-gear housing. *(Chevrolet Motor Division of General Motors Corporation)*

Fig. 7-26 Checking an armature for grounds.

paired by soldering. However, the construction can withstand much greater stress. You will seldom find this type of armature with an open-circuited armature coil.

Thrown armature windings indicate that the armature has been spun at excessive speeds. This usually happens only to starting motors using the overrunning clutch. Several conditions can cause overspeeding of the armature. For example, if the solenoid plunger is sticky and releases slowly, if the overrunning clutch sticks on the armature shaft, or if the shift-lever return spring is weak, the pinion will disengage slowly after starting. Also, if the driver is slow to release the ignition key from the START position, the clutch overruns excessively.

Other evidence of excessive overrunning includes a blued or bronzed armature shaft where the pinion over-runs and a polished collar where rollers on the shift-lever yoke ride. Where you find thrown windings, you

will usually find evidence that the clutch has been excessively overrun. When replacing the armature, replace the clutch, too, since it may have been damaged. A defective clutch would soon ruin the new armature.

⚙ 7-22 Turning the commutator Only the older-style armature (with heavy commutator segments) and heavy-duty armatures should have the commutator turned. Modern lightweight starting motors have commutators too thin to be turned. When turning the commutator on a lathe, the cut should be smooth and as light as possible. Remove no more material than is necessary to eliminate the out-of-round, high-mica, rough, or worn conditions.

NOTE: Some starting motors use a molded armature commutator. The mica must not be undercut on these; this can damage the commutator. Undercutting can weaken the bonding between the molding material and

Fig. 7-25 Using V blocks and dial indicator to check commutator runout. *(Ford Motor Company)*

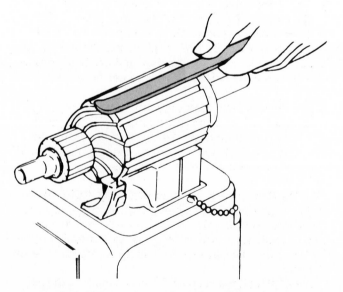

Fig. 7-27 Testing an armature for short circuit on a growler.

commutator bars. The molding material is softer than the copper, so it will wear away at the same rate as the copper. Generally, automotive manufacturers' shop manuals do not mention undercutting of mica on starting-motor armatures.

⚙ **7-23 Bearing inspection and replacement** Most starting motors use sleeve bearings, or bushings, although a few starting motors have been made with ball bearings. On the sleeve bearing, check for wear by noting the amount of side play the armature shaft has when inserted into the bearing. If it is excessive, replace the bearing. Usually, the wear will not be uniform but will be greatest on the side that sustains the thrust when cranking takes place. Another sign of bearing wear is rubbing of the armature core on the pole shoes. (This can also be caused by loose pole shoes or a bent armature shaft.)

To replace a bearing, drive out the old one and drive in a new one with the arbor press. The size of the arbor used should be such as to give the bearing the proper inside dimension when the job is finished. Some bearings cannot be replaced. On these, a new end frame is required. On some bearings, the new bearing will have to be reamed to size after it is installed.

⚙ **7-24 Field-frame inspection** The field frame from some motors should not be cleaned in a degreasing tank or by any grease-dissolving solution. The modern light-weight starting motor uses paper insulation on the field coils. The insulation will be damaged by solvents or other chemicals. Many field coils are plastic dipped and can be washed. Inspect the field windings and leads for poor insulation and note the tightness of the pole shoes. The windings can be checked for grounds with low-voltage test light. Place one point on the terminal stud or connector strap and the other on a clean spot on the frame. If the light goes on, the fields are grounded either at the terminal or in the windings. To find out which is at fault, remove the terminal stud from the field frame and let it hang free. Then try the test again. Grounded field windings may sometimes be repaired by removing and reinsulating them. However, it is important to avoid too much bulk. This might cause the pole shoes to cut through the new insulation and produce another ground when the pole-shoe screws are tightened.

NOTE: Some starting motors have the pole shoes permanently bonded to the field frame. On these, the field windings cannot be removed. If there is any trouble in the field windings such as a short or open, the field frame, with windings, must be replaced as an assembly.

⚙ **7-25 Removing and replacing field windings** Use a pole-shoe screwdriver (Fig. 7-28) to remove and replace pole shoes. You will need the arbor press to hold the screwdriver bit or socket tool in place in the screw. The wrench will apply enough torque to the screw.

A useful tool, particularly for reassembly, is the pole-shoe spreader (Fig. 7-29). When this device is in place, it forces the pole shoes against the frame, prevents

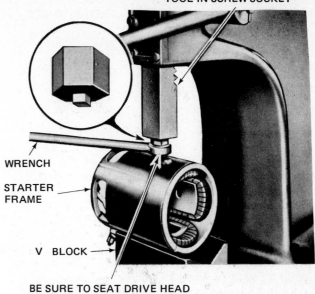

Fig. 7-28 Removing a pole-shoe screw with a special tool, wrench, and arbor press. *(Ford Motor Company)*

distortion of the frame as the screws are tightened, and makes the tightening job easier. While tightening the screws, strike the frame sharp blows with a plastic or rubber hammer. This helps to align the pole shoes. Apply a drop of Loctite to the screws before installation to seal them and prevent them from coming loose.

When installing the field windings, be sure to replace the insulating strips (where used) in their original positions. These strips are important. They guard against grounding of the leads or windings.

NOTE: Be sure to put the pole shoes back in the same places they originally occupied in the field frame. Also, be sure they are not turned around 180°. Some pole shoes have one long and one short lip. Turning this type of pole shoe around will reduce cranking performance.

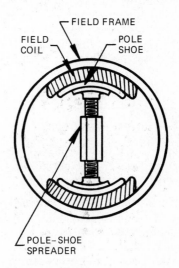

Fig. 7-29 Pole-shoe spreader.

CABLE SIZE, B & S GAUGE	FEET, 6 and 12 VOLTS	FEET, 24 VOLTS
0	10	20
00	12	24
000	16	32
0000	20	40

Fig. 7-30 Table of cable sizes for various lengths of starting-motor circuits.

☼ **7-26 Installing the starting motor** Before installing the starting motor, make sure the mounting surface is clean. The battery ground cable should be disconnected. Then the starting motor should be put into position, with the shims restored to their proper positions as you found them on motor removal (see ☼ 7-10). Install and tighten the mounting bolts to the correct specification. Install the braces, shields, and other parts that you removed when removing the starting motor. Connect the solenoid wires and battery cable. Finally, reattach the battery ground cable and try the starting motor to make sure it performs normally.

Wiring installation

☼ **7-27 Installation of wiring** When inspecting or installing starting-motor wiring, keep the following points in mind. Every precaution should be taken to guard against short circuits or grounds. All wires should be of sufficient size to carry the electric load without excessive voltage drop. Stranded wire or cable should be used since it is less apt to break from vibration. All joints and connections should be clean and tight.

All leads and cables should be supported at enough points to prevent them from moving and wearing the insulation. Special precautions should be taken to avoid grounds or shorts. Rubber boots, tape, or shellac should be used to protect exposed terminals. Recommended wire sizes are given in the table (Fig. 7-30). The lengths given include the distance from the battery to ground, from the battery to the starting-motor switch, and from the switch to the motor itself. Extra-long circuits should have two parallel cables to prevent excessive voltage drop. For example, two No. 0 cables, in parallel, should be used for a 20-ft 6- or 12-V circuit if larger cable is not available.

Chapter 7 review questions

Select the *one* correct, best, or most probable answer to each question. Then check your answers against the correct answers given at the end of the book.

1. To test the starting system, you need a voltmeter and:
   a. an ammeter and a rheostat,
   b. an ammeter and a dwell meter,
   c. a rheostat and a variable resistance,
   d. a jump-start battery and leads.

2. The overrunning clutch:
   a. should be lubricated with light engine oil,
   b. should be lubricated with grease,
   c. should be oiled every tuneup,
   d. does not require lubrication.

3. The sprag-type overrunning clutch:
   a. should be lubricated with light oil,
   b. should be lubricated with grease,
   c. does not require lubrication,
   d. should be oiled every tuneup.

4. The purpose of adjusting the distance between the starting-motor pinion and the flywheel is to:
   a. improve cranking speed,
   b. eliminate a whining noise,
   c. reduce wear on the overrunning clutch,
   d. reduce drain on the battery.

5. When making the cranking voltage test, you find the cranking speed is low (battery charged) and the voltage is above 9 volts. You conclude that the trouble is:
   a. a defective battery,
   b. defective cables or connections,
   c. in the engine,
   d. in the starting motor.

6. The starting-motor commutator end frame, field frame, and drive housing can be separated by removal of the:
   a. cover band,
   b. Bendix drive,
   c. through bolts,
   d. head-spring bolt.

7. The two methods of connecting the armature-coil leads to the commutator bars are:
   a. soldering and clamping,
   b. soldering and welding,
   c. riveting and welding,
   d. screw and solder.

8. The purpose of shims under the starting-motor mounting pads is to:
   a. assure a good ground,
   b. allow mounting bolts to be tightened properly,
   c. align the solenoid,
   d. secure correct alignment of pinion teeth and ring-gear teeth.

9. Snapping the brush or brush arm down may cause the:
   a. brush to crack or chip,
   b. commutator to dent,
   c. brush holder to distort,
   d. commutator segments to come loose.

10. On some starting motors, the drive assembly is held on the armature shaft by a thrust collar, retainer, and:
    a. thrust bolt,
    b. thrust washer,
    c. locking nut,
    d. snap ring.

11. The overrunning clutch:
    a. should be oiled,
    b. should be repacked with grease,
    c. cannot be relubricated,
    d. contains no lubricant.

12. If, when checking an overrunning clutch, it is found that the drive pinion slips in the driving direction, replace the:
    a. assembly,
    b. rollers and pinion,
    c. shell and rollers,
    d. drive pinion.
13. Open circuits in a starting-motor armature will probably produce:
    a. worn bearings,
    b. burned commutator bars,
    c. excessive armature speeds,
    d. a run-down battery.
14. The growler is used to test the armature for:
    a. short circuits,
    b. open circuits,
    c. excessive armature resistance,
    d. current.
15. Thrown armature windings indicate that the armature was:
    a. defectively made,
    b. subject to excessive torque,
    c. overloaded,
    d. spun at excessive speed.
16. When resoldering connections in the starting motor:
    a. use rosin flux,
    b. use acid flux,
    c. use no flux,
    d. use copper solder.
17. The no-load test procedure requires a battery, a high-reading ammeter, a high-reading voltmeter, and:
    a. a spring scale,
    b. a variable resistance,
    c. an rpm indicator,
    d. a growler.
18. When meter-testing the starting-motor circuit, a bad connection, frayed cable, or broken cable strands will be indicated by a voltage reading of more than:
    a. 0.001 volts,
    b. 0.01 volts,
    c. 1.0 volts,
    d. 0.1 volts.
19. On the voltage-drop test of the starting system, the system resistance is normal if the voltage drop is:
    a. 2.0 volts,
    b. 0.5 volts,
    c. 1.0 volts or less,
    d. 0.01 volts or less.
20. Three different methods of checking overrunning-clutch drive-pinion end clearance are specified, according to construction:
    a. between pinion and thrust washer, between pinion and housing, or between pinion and:
    a. retainer,
    b. adjusting nut,
    c. plunger link,
    d. shift collar.

AUTOMOTIVE CHARGING SYSTEMS

After studying this chapter, you should be able to:

1. Explain how the alternator is constructed.
2. Explain how the alternator works as part of the charging system.
3. Explain how the alternator voltage is regulated.
4. Describe three types of alternator regulators and explain how they work.

8-1 Purpose of the charging system The automobile needs electricity to run. The starting motor needs electricity to crank the engine for starting. The ignition system needs electricity to produce the sparks that ignite the air–fuel mixture in the engine cylinders and keep the engine running. The indicators and other electric devices also need electricity. There are two sources of electricity in the car, the battery and the charging system. The battery can furnish only a limited amount of electricity. After that, it is run down, or discharged. It needs recharging before it can supply additional electricity. However, the charging system can furnish electricity all the time the engine is running.

The charging system (Fig. 8-1) puts electric current back into the battery after the engine is started to keep it in a charged condition. The charging system also handles electric loads such as the ignition system, lights, radio, and dash indicators when the engine is running. The charging system includes the alternator, a regulator, and connecting wires. The regulator is shown as a separate unit in Fig. 8-1. In many systems, it is mounted inside the alternator.

8-2 Function of alternator The alternator (or electric generator) converts mechanical energy from the engine to electric energy. As already noted, it keeps the battery in a charged condition and handles electric loads when the engine is running. For many years, all cars used direct-current (dc) generators (Fig. 8-2). In the early 1960s, however, manufacturers switched to alternators, or alternating-current (ac) generators (Fig. 8-3).

NOTE: Direct current flows in one direction. Alternating current flows in one direction for a moment and then flows in the opposite direction. It alternates. The current in your home is alternating current. It alternates, or changes direction, 120 times per second. It is called 60-cycle [60 Hz] current. The electric devices on the car are all dc devices and require direct current. Because the alternator supplies alternating current, a device that converts this alternating to direct current is required. The device, called a *rectifier,* uses diodes, as we explain in a later section.

8-3 Generator You will seldom see a dc generator on anything except antique cars, some farm tractors, and in some small-engine applications. Figure 8-2 shows a generator. It is long and relatively small in diameter.

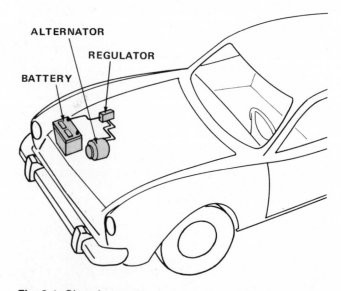

Fig. 8-1 Charging system on an automobile.

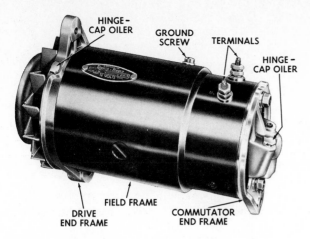

Fig. 8-2 A generator.

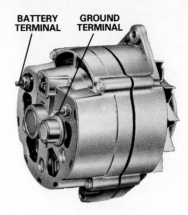

Fig. 8-3 An alternator.

☼ 8-4 Alternator The alternator (Fig. 8-3) is short and comparatively large in diameter. We show the two, generator and alternator (Figs. 8-2 and 8-3), so you can recognize them when you see them. The alternator has replaced the generator in automotive vehicles for several reasons. It is lighter in weight and simpler in construction. It has fewer wearing parts and is easier to service. The most important reason, however, is that in recent years inexpensive and small solid-state devices have become available. These solid-state devices include diodes and transistors, described in Chapter 2. Early alternators used rectifiers and regulators that were almost as big as the alternator itself (Fig. 8-4). The size was not particularly a problem because room to mount them under the hood could be found. But the cost and complexity of the system were the problem. A regulator is necessary to prevent the alternator from building up excessive voltage. High alternator voltage could damage all electric devices on the car. It could also cause the alternator to burn up from overload.

☼ 8-5 Rectifier and regulator With the development of the solid-state diode (☼ 2-6), it became possible to shrink the rectifier so much that it could be put inside the alternator (Fig. 8-5). Furthermore, mass production of these diodes brought the price down to a reasonable level.

The regulators for modern alternators are solid-state devices. They use diodes and transistors (☼ 2-6 to 2-8) to provide the necessary control of alternator voltage. At the same time that advances in solid-state technology produced the small and inexpensive diode rectifier, they also produced the transistors that could regulate the alternator. Here again, the price fell to reasonable levels so that manufacturers could adopt solid-state alternator regulators. These normally require no ad-

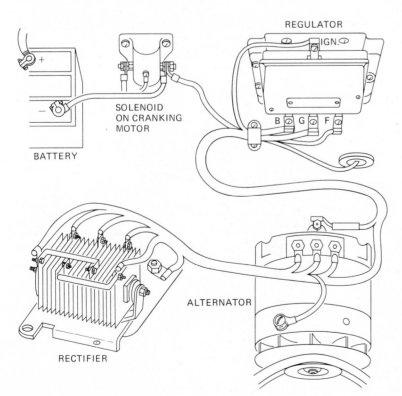

Fig. 8-4 An early alternator with an external rectifier and regulator. Note the size of the rectifier and regulator. Electronics has made it possible to reduce the size of these units and, in many installations, put them inside the alternator.

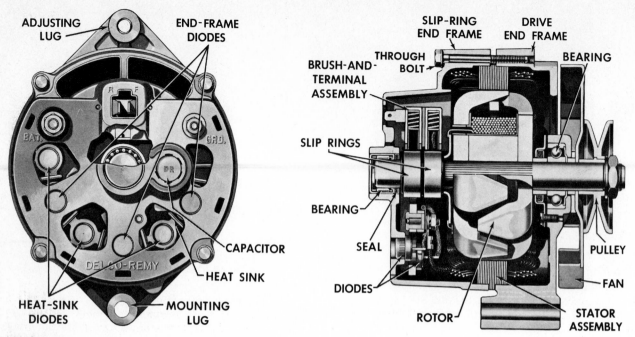

Fig. 8-5 End and side sectional views of an alternator with built-in diodes. The manufacturer calls this unit a *Delcotron*. *(Delco-Remy Division of General Motors Corporation)*

justment. In fact, no adjustment is possible for many of these regulators. Further development made it possible to construct the regulator so small (''miniaturize'' it) that it could be mounted inside the alternator (Fig. 8-6). Many modern alternators have both the rectifier and the regulator mounted inside them. This simplifies the installation and wiring system and also servicing. Solid-state rectifiers and regulators are go–no-go devices. They either work or do not work. If they fail, you discard them and install a new unit. We describe these devices and their application to alternators later in the chapter.

⚙ 8-6 Producing electricity Before we discuss the alternator, the rectifier, and the regulator, let us review what we have learned about electricity. In Chapter 1, we said that electric current is a flow of electrons. You can make electrons move by moving a wire through a magnetic field. This can be shown with a strong horseshoe magnet, a wire, and a sensitive ammeter, as in Fig. 8-7. As you move the wire through the magnetic field, the wire cuts magnetic lines of force. This causes the electrons (current) to move in the wire. Therefore, as you move the wire through the magnetic field, the meter needle registers the current flow. If you were to

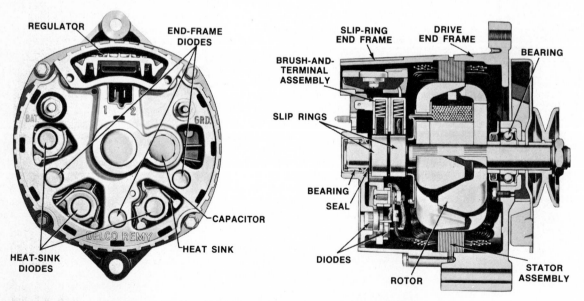

Fig. 8-6 End and side sectional views of an alternator with integral diodes and a built-in solid-state voltage regulator. *(Delco-Remy Division of General Motors Corporation)*

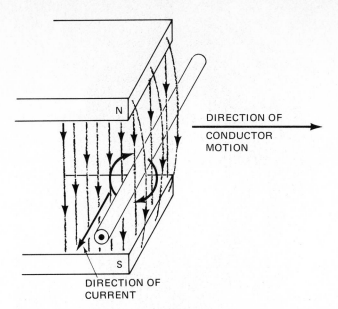

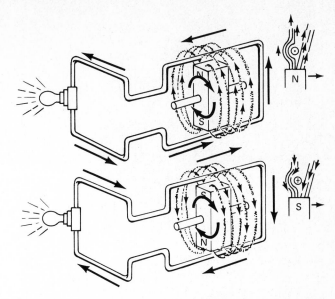

Fig. 8-7 A conductor, moving through a magnetic field, has a flow of current induced in it.

Fig. 8-8 Simplified alternator consisting of a single stationary loop of wire and a rotating bar magnet. The distortion of moving lines of force around the leg of the loop (conductor) and the direction of current (electron) flow are shown to the right.

move the wire back and forth, the needle would move first in one direction and then in the other. The same thing would happen if you held the wire stationary and moved the magnet back and forth. In either case, current flows in the wire. The key point here is that the wire is cutting through the magnetic field or lines of force. When it cuts the magnetic lines of force in one direction, the current flows one way. When it cuts them in the opposite direction, the current flows the other way in the wire.

☼ 8-7 Alternator principles In the alternator, the wires, or conductors, are held stationary, and a magnetic field is moved through them. Actually, the alternator rotates the magnetic field so that the stationary conductors cut the moving magnetic lines of force.

Let us look at a simple alternator (Fig. 8-8). In the simple one-loop unit shown, the rotating bar magnet furnishes the moving field. At the top, as the north pole of the bar magnet passes the upper leg of the loop and as the south pole passes the lower leg of the loop, current (electron flow) is induced in the loop in the direction shown by the arrows. At the bottom, the magnet has rotated half a turn so that its south pole is passing the upper leg of the loop and the north pole is passing the lower leg. Now, magnetic lines of force are cut by the two legs in the opposite direction. Thus, as the magnet spins and the two poles alternately pass the two legs of the loop, electrons are pushed first in one direction and then in the other in the loop. Alternating current flows.

Two things will increase the strength of the current (number of electrons) moving in the loop: increasing the strength of the magnetic field and increasing the speed with which the magnetic field moves past the two legs of the loop. Increasing the number of loops is a third method of increasing the current.

In the alternator, both the strength of the magnetic field and the number of loops are increased. Instead of

a simple bar magnet, the rotating part of the alternator is made up of two or more pole pieces assembled on a shaft over an electromagnetic winding (see ☼ 1-30). The electromagnet is made up of many turns of wire. When current flows in the electromagnet winding, a strong magnetic field is created so that the pointed ends of the two pole pieces become, alternately, north and south poles (Fig. 8-9). The winding is connected to the battery through a pair of insulated rings that rotate with the shaft and through a pair of stationary brushes that ride on the rings. The two ends of the winding are attached to the rings. The brushes make continuous sliding (or slipping) contact with the slip rings (Fig. 8-10).

Figure 8-11 shows the stationary loops of an alternator assembled into a frame. The assembly is called a *stator*. The loops are interconnected so that the current produced in all loops is added together. Since this current is alternating, it must be converted into direct current. The battery, ignition system, and other electric components in the automobile all use direct current.

NOTE: The current flow from the alternator is often called the *alternator output*. The maximum allowable output is called the *alternator rating*. The rating is often

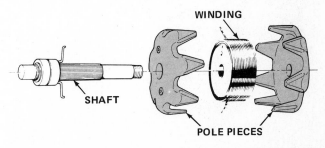

Fig. 8-9 Rotor of an alternator, partly disassembled. *(Delco-Remy Division of General Motors Corporation)*

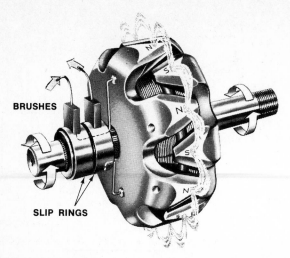

Fig. 8-10 Rotor of an alternator, showing brushes in place on slip rings. *(Delco-Remy Division of General Motors Corporation)*

stamped on the alternator nameplate, as for instance "50 amperes."

⚙ **8-8 Alternator operation** Some people call the alternator a *generator* or an *ac generator.* The modern term, however, is *alternator,* and we use that term in this book.

The alternator produces alternating current in the stator windings. This is changed to direct current by the diodes in the rectifier. The process is called *rectification.* We cover diode action in ⚙ 2-6. You might wish to review that section before proceeding with the following explanation of how the diodes work in the alternator.

The diode permits current to flow through it in one direction only. Figure 8-12 shows how four diodes can be used to change alternating to direct current. The four diodes are numbered 1 to 4 in the illustration. At the left, the current from the ac source follows the conductors shown in heavy, black lines. Diodes 1 and 3 permit the current to flow through, but diodes 2 and 4 will not permit the current to flow through them since the current is flowing in the wrong direction for them. However, when the direction of the current has re-

Fig. 8-11 Stator of an alternator. *(Delco-Remy Division of General Motors Corporation)*

versed, as shown to the right in Fig. 8-12, then diodes 2 and 4 will pass the current but diodes 1 and 3 will not. Since all the alternating current is changed to direct current, and none is lost, this is called *full-wave rectification.*

1. Three-phase The circuit shown in Fig. 8-12 is termed *single-phase* because there is only a single ac source. Such a source results in a pulsating current when it is rectified by the diodes. This can be compared with a single-cylinder engine which does not provide a smooth flow of power but rather a series of peaks between which no power is delivered. To provide a smooth flow of current, automotive alternators are *three-phase;* that is, they are built with three stator circuits which, in effect, give overlapping pulses of alternating current. When these pulses are rectified, a comparatively smooth flow of direct current is obtained.

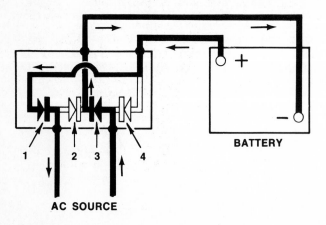

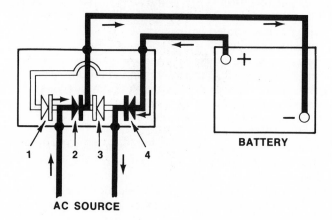

Fig. 8-12 Four diodes connected to an ac source. The diodes rectify the alternating current and change it to direct current to charge the battery.

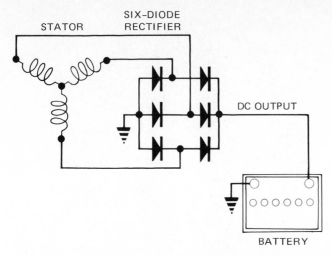

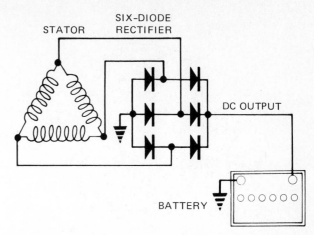

Fig. 8-13 Wiring circuit of an alternator with six-diode rectifier and a Y-connected stator.

Fig. 8-14 Wiring circuit of an alternator with a six-diode rectifier and a delta-connected stator.

2. Delta and Y stators The three stator circuits can be connected in two ways, with Y or with *delta* connections (Figs. 8-13 and 8-14). Both operate in a similar manner and are serviced in a similar way. The alternating current generated in the three legs of the stator circuit passes through the six diodes and is converted into direct current. Most automotive alternators use the Y-connected stator circuit.

3. Heat sinks Diodes are usually mounted in the slip-ring end of the alternator, as shown in Fig. 8-5. Note that three of the diodes are mounted in a metal bracket called a *heat sink*. In some units, all six diodes are mounted in the heat sink. The heat sink absorbs heat from the diodes, which can become rather hot in operation. The shape of the heat sink, with large radiating surfaces, allows this heat to radiate into the air

passing through the alternator. A fan, which rotates with the rotor, keeps air moving through.

4. Alternator drives Alternators are usually mounted directly on the engine and are driven by a belt from the engine-crankshaft pulley. Figure 8-15 shows two of many possible different drive arrangements for a V-8 and a six-cylinder engine. Not only the alternator, but also the water pump, power-steering pump, and other devices are driven by belts from the engine crankshaft. Figure 8-16 shows two of many possible alternator-mounting arrangements on a V-6 and a V-8 engine. The lower alternator mounting hole is attached by a long bolt that forms a swinging pivot. The upper mounting hole is attached to a brace which has a curved slot. This slot allows the alternator to be shifted outward, as necessary, to properly tighten the drive belt.

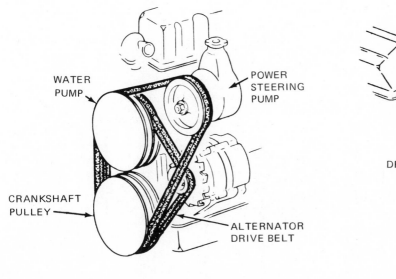

6-CYLINDER

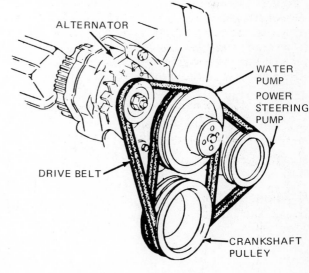

8-CYLINDER

Fig. 8-15 Alternator drive arrangements for a six-cylinder and a V-8 engine. *(Chevrolet Motor Division of General Motors Corporation)*

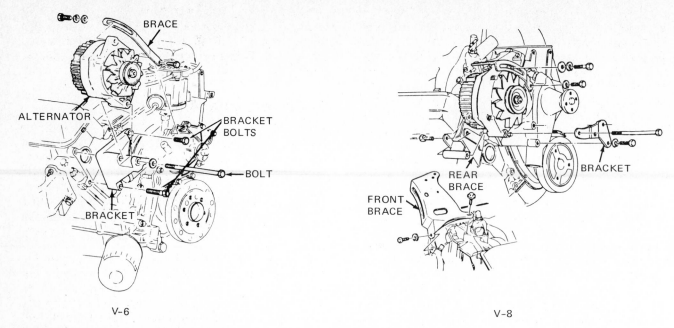

V-6

V-8

Fig. 8-16 Alternator mounting arrangements for a V-6 and a V-8 engine. *(Oldsmobile Division of General Motors Corporation)*

This adjusting operation is described in a following chapter.

⚙ 8-9 Types of alternators A variety of alternators have been made. Most have the diode rectifier built in (Fig. 8-5). Many also have the regulator built in (Fig. 8-6). Other alternators we look at now are those with stationary field coils and the oil-cooled alternator. At the end of the chapter, we describe a number of special-purpose alternators.

1. **Alternator with stationary field coils** Alternators described up to now have rotating field coils in the rotor assembly. The field coil is fed current through a pair of slip rings and two brushes. Some late-model alternators eliminate these parts by having stationary field coils. These alternators have, as moving parts, only the rotor and bearings. This construction eliminates the need for any periodic maintenance of the alternator. An alternator of this type is shown in Fig. 8-17. Although the field coil does not rotate, it produces

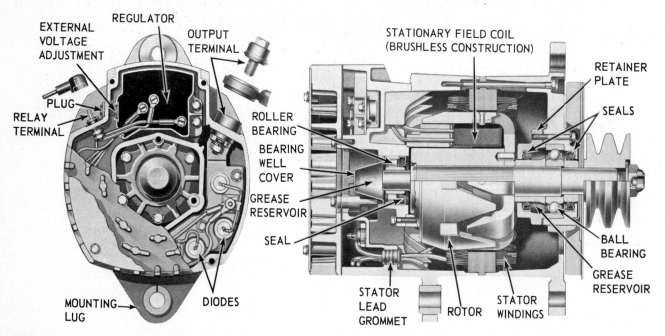

Fig. 8-17 End and side sectional views of an alternator with integral diodes and voltage regulator. The field coil is stationary. *(Delco-Remy Division of General Motors Corporation)*

a strong stationary magnetic field, just as in other alternators. In this alternator, however, the magnetic field is stationary. But when the rotor turns, it carries the permanent magnets in the rotor through this magnetic field. This action bends the magnetic lines of force first one way and then the other as the alternate north and south poles pass through. As a result, the lines of force move back and forth through the stator windings. This induces a flow of current in them, just as in other alternators.

This alternator has a built-in, or integral, solid-state regulator. A special feature of the alternator is that there is an external voltage adjustment. This is a large, heavy-duty alternator capable of producing a high output. The voltage at which the regulator holds the alternator, therefore, is especially important. Because the alternator is used in a variety of vehicles, it requires a means of tailoring the voltage setting to suit the installation.

Normally, no such adjustment is provided or required on the majority of regulators that are built into the alternator. The regulator is designed to provide good control through a varied temperature range. Figure 8-6 shows an alternator with a regulator of this type.

2. Oil-cooled alternator   The alternator illustrated in Fig. 8-18 has a stationary field-coil assembly and thus does not need brushes or slip rings. The unit is sealed, and cooling is provided by a flow of engine oil through it.

Regulators for alternators

⚙ 8-10 Need for regulation   The alternator requires voltage regulation. That is, there must be a means of preventing the voltage from rising above a safe maximum. If the voltage goes too high, the alternator will produce a high current output and overcharge the battery. Worse, the high voltage will damage electric equipment that is turned on. For example, it will greatly shorten the life of the headlights and could even burn them out.

The alternator does not need a current regulator because it is self-limiting so far as current output is concerned. Here is the reason. The current output increases with rotor speed. As current approaches a safe maximum, the rotor is turning so fast that the current pulses for each cycle do not have time to increase further. This limits the maximum current the alternator can produce.

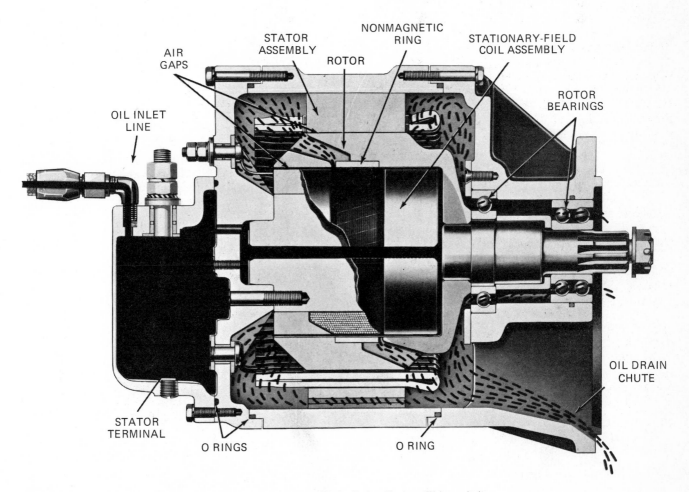

Fig. 8-18 Sectional view of a heavy-duty alternator with built-in diodes. This unit is cooled by circulation of engine oil through it. *(Delco-Remy Division of General Motors Corporation)*

☼ 8-11 Regulator operation The principle of alternator voltage regulation is simple. If the voltage begins to rise above the safe maximum, the regulator inserts resistance into the field circuit. This cuts down on the amount of current flowing in the field windings. As a result, the magnetic field is weakened. The stator windings cut by this weaker field cannot produce as much voltage. The voltage is held to a safe value.

A regulator that illustrates the principle is shown in Fig. 8-19. Figure 8-20 is the wiring diagram of the regulator and alternator. Regulators of this type, which have vibrating points, were used extensively in earlier years. They are often called *electromechanical regulators* and had one or two wire-wound relays in a metal case (Fig. 8-22) which mounted on the cover fender or radiator support. These regulators are no longer used on today's cars. But it is a good unit to use to explain regulator action. Follow the circuit in Fig. 8-20. Note that a wire runs from the rotor terminal (F) on the alternator to the F terminal on the regulator. Inside the regulator, this terminal is connected to contact points. When the voltage is below the value for which the regulator is set, the points connect the rotor windings to the battery (through the ignition switch when it is closed).

However, when the voltage rises to the value for which the regulator is set, the points separate. Note that the alternator voltage is applied to the regulator winding. The higher the voltage, the stronger the magnetic field of the winding. At the regulator-actuating voltage, the magnetic field is strong enough to pull the bottom contact point down. This point is on a flat plate (called the *armature*) which is spring loaded. The magnetic field overcomes the spring tension and pulls the armature down. The points separate. Now, the resistance is in the field circuit (from terminal 3 to F in the regulator). The resistance cuts down the amount of current flowing to the alternator rotor windings. The alternator voltage falls. When this happens, the magnetic field holding the armature down weakens. The armature is pulled up by spring tension. The points close, directly connecting the rotor windings to the battery again. Alternator voltage goes up. The cycle is

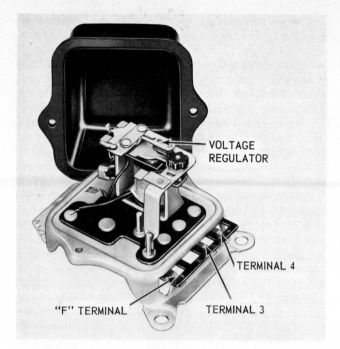

Fig. 8-19 An ac-voltage regulator with its cover off so that the unit can be seen. This unit has vibrating contact points and is often called an *electromechanical regulator*. (*Pontiac Motor Division of General Motors Corporation*)

repeated. The points vibrate very rapidly, holding the alternator voltage to a safe maximum.

The upper contact point comes into action when the alternator is turning at high speed with a minimum electric load turned on. With this condition, the alternator voltage can rise excessively even with the resistance in the rotor circuit. If the voltage does go up, this further increases the strength of the magnetic field of the regulator winding. Now, the magnetic field becomes so strong that it pulls the armature further down. This brings the top contact into touch with the middle contact. Notice that this connects the rotor windings to ground inside the regulator. With both ends of the field windings connected to ground, the magnetic field of the rotor drops off rapidly. As this happens, the

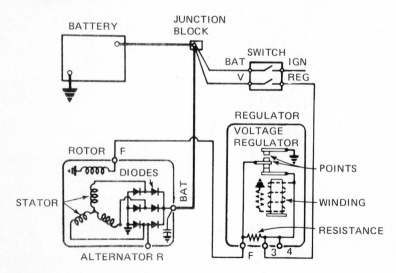

Fig. 8-20 Wiring circuit of ac regulator and alternator. The regulator is an electromechanical unit with vibrating contact points. (*Pontiac Motor Division of General Motors Corporation*)

alternator voltage drops and the magnetic field of the regulator winding weakens. The spring pulls the armature up. This allows the other contacts to close. This increases the alternator voltage once again, and the complete cycle is repeated. The points vibrate rapidly, preventing the voltage from rising above a safe maximum.

The major difference between the contact-point or electromechanical regulator we have just described and the modern solid-state regulator is this. In the solid-state regulator, transistors and diodes take over the job of inserting resistance into and removing it from the alternator field circuit. They do it much faster than vibrating contacts. They are very accurate and, theoretically at least, will never wear out. We describe these regulators in ✿ 8-13.

✿ **8-12 Regulators with field relay** A variety of alternator regulators have been used. The first alternator regulators were of the vibrating type, as described in ✿ 8-11. Some of these regulators include a field relay. The purpose of this field relay is to provide a positive means of disconnecting the alternator field (rotor) windings from the battery when the engine was turned off. Figure 8-21 shows the wiring system. Figure 8-22 shows what this two-unit regulator looks like with the cover removed. Note that Fig. 8-21 is practically the same as Fig. 8-20 except that a field relay has been added. When the engine first starts, the points of the field relay are open. The field windings are not connected to the battery. However, there is enough residual magnetism in the rotor iron core to produce some voltage in the stator windings. Residual magnetism is the magnetism that remains (or resides in the core) when the current flow stops. The voltage produced in the stator windings is picked off through the R (for relay) terminal. This voltage is impressed on the field-relay winding. The armature on which the upper point

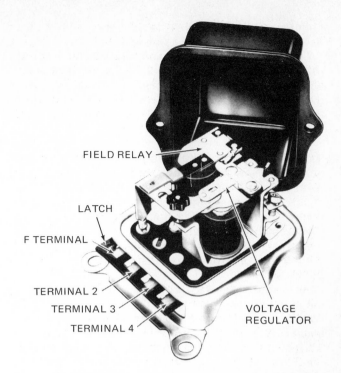

Fig. 8-22 An ac two-unit regulator with its cover off so the two units—the field relay and the regulator—can be seen. *(Delco-Remy Division of General Motors Corporation)*

is mounted is pulled down by the resulting electromagnetism in the winding. The points close. This connects the field windings directly to the battery. The rotor produces full magnetism, and alternator voltage rises. The voltage is now regulated (controlled) by the voltage regulator.

When the engine is turned off, the alternator rotor stops turning. The alternator voltage drops off to zero. Since there is no longer any voltage on the field-relay winding, the relay armature is released. The contact

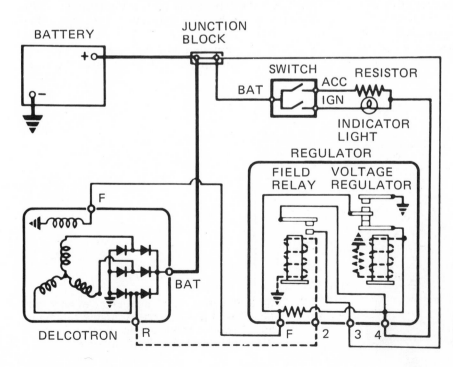

Fig. 8-21 Wiring circuit of a two-unit ac regulator and alternator. *(Delco-Remy Division of General Motors Corporation)*

points open to disconnect the rotor winding from the battery.

In later types of alternator and regulator, the function of the field relay is taken over by diodes (a diode trio). The three diodes, which are separate from the rectifier diodes, feed direct current to the field windings when the alternator is in operation. See Figs. 8-23, 8-25, and 8-40.

✿ 8-13 Alternator with integral regulator

Many alternators now have built-in, or integral, voltage regulators. Figures 8-6 and 8-17 show two of these. Figure 8-23 is the wiring diagram for the alternator with built-in regulator, shown in Fig. 8-6. The manufacturer calls the assembly an *integral charging system*. The external wiring circuit for this system is very simple (Fig. 8-24). As you read the explanation that follows, refer to Fig. 8-23.

As the rotor begins to turn, the permanent magnetism in the rotor induces voltage in the stator winding. This voltage sends current through the following in the regulator: diodes D1, D2, and D3 and resistors R1 and R4. Then it flows through the alternator diodes and back to the stator winding. The voltage turns on transistor TR1, and the battery now supplies current to the field coil through resistor R6 and TR1.

Current also flows through diodes D1, D2, and D3, resistor R2, transistor TR3, and the voltage-adjusting resistor R5, causing TR3 to turn on. Current now flows through R6, R3, TR3, and R5. With increasing speed and alternator buildup, voltage increases. The voltage across R5 is impressed across diodes D5 and D6, caused by current flow through R6, R3, TR3, and R5. When the preset voltage is reached, diodes D5 and D6 begin to conduct. This turns on TR2. TR1 turns off, and current flow through the field coil drops off. Alternator voltage, therefore, decreases. As this happens, diodes D5 and D6 and transistor TR2 all turn off. TR1, therefore, turns on again to permit field current and alternator voltage to increase. The whole cycle is repeated many times a second to limit the voltage to the value for which the voltage-adjusting resistor R5 is adjusted.

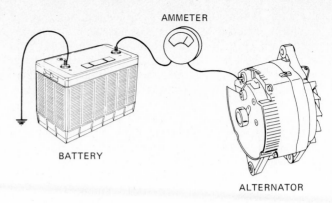

Fig. 8-24 Simplified wiring diagram of charging circuit and alternator with integral voltage regulator.

Capacitors C2 and C3 cause TR1 to turn on and off quickly. Diode D4 prevents high induced voltage in the field coil when TR1 turns off and the magnetic field in the field coil starts to collapse.

Capacitor C4 smooths out the voltage across R5. Resistor R6 raises the alternator voltage slightly as the output increases to maintain a more nearly constant voltage across the battery and thus compensate for line voltage drop. Capacitor C1 protects the alternator diodes from high transient, or surge, voltages and suppresses radio interference.

Figure 8-25 is the complete wiring diagram of an alternator with a built-in solid-state regulator. It is similar to the one shown in Fig. 8-23 and operates as follows. When the switch is turned on, current flows to alternator terminal 1, through resistor R1, diode D1, and the base-emitter of transistor TR1 to ground, and then back to the battery. This turns on TR1, and current flows through the alternator field and TR1 back to the battery. When the engine starts and the alternator rotor begins to turn, alternating voltage is built up in the stator windings. The six diodes in the rectifier bridge rectify the resulting current into direct current, which then flows to the battery. Some of the alternating current is rectified by the diode trio to feed the alternator field. (In other systems, a diode is not used, and field

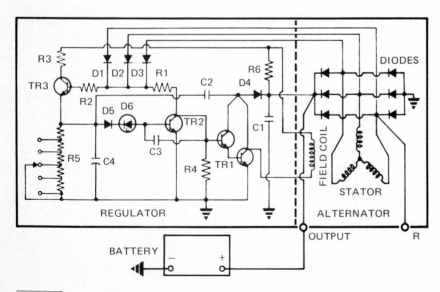

Fig. 8-23 Wiring circuit of an alternator with integral rectifier and voltage regulator. *(Delco-Remy Division of General Motors Corporation)*

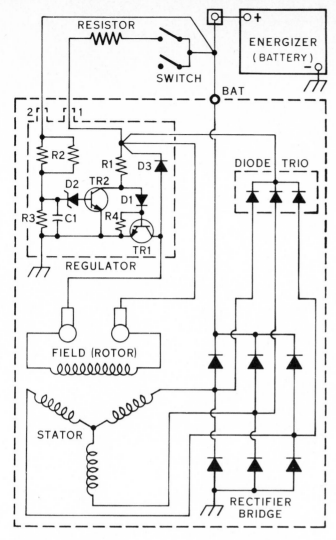

Fig. 8-25 Wiring diagram of an alternator with integral rectifier, solid-state regulator, and a diode trio to supply field current. *(Chevrolet Motor Division of General Motors Corporation)*

current is supplied through a field relay from the six diodes.)

As alternator speed and voltage increase, the voltage between R2 and R3 increases enough to force D2 to conduct. This turns TR2 on and TR1 off. With TR1 off, field current and alternator voltage are reduced and D2 then blocks current flow. This allows TR1 to turn back on again. Field current and alternator voltage once again increase, and the whole cycle is repeated many times a second to limit the alternator voltage to the preset value. Capacitor C1 smooths out the voltage across R3. R4 prevents excessive current through TR1 at high temperatures, and D3 prevents high induced voltages in the field winding when TR1 turns off.

The regulator has temperature compensation. This compensation increases the charging voltage as regulator temperature is reduced. The purpose of this increase is to provide a higher voltage to charge a cold battery. The compensation reduces the voltage as temperatures go up. This prevents overcharging at high temperatures.

✸ 8-14 Chrysler regulator In recent years, all Chrysler Corporation cars have used an externally mounted, solid-state alternator regulator (Fig. 8-26). It includes diodes, transistors, resistors, and capacitors, all interconnected to produce voltage regulation. Figure 8-27 is the wiring diagram for the system. The regulator operates in about the same manner as the solid-state regulators previously described (in ✸ 8-13). It limits the current to the field coils and thus prevents excessive alternator voltage. Note that one end of the field is connected through the regulator. The other end is connected through the ignition switch. If the voltage starts to rise above the specified maximum, the electronic circuitry cuts down the amount of field current. This weakens the magnetic field. The voltage is, therefore, prevented from rising any further. The regulator is not adjustable.

✸ 8-15 Ford regulators In recent years, Ford Motor Company cars have had three different types of voltage regulator: electromechanical, transistorized, and solid-state or electronic.

1. The electromechanical regulator has two mechanical units. These are a vibrating voltage regulator and a field relay. They work the same way as the units described in ✸ 8-12. When the voltage starts to go above the specified maximum, the points start to vibrate. This inserts resistance into the field circuit which cuts down the amount of current flowing. This reduces the strength of the rotor magnetic field and thus the voltage. The field relay is open until the engine starts and the alternator rotor begins to spin. This produces a voltage in the stator. The voltage causes the field relay to close, directly connecting the field to the battery.

2. The transistorized voltage regulator (Fig. 8-28) has

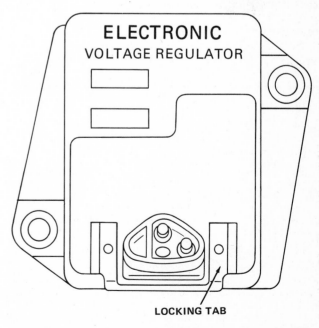

Fig. 8-26 Chrysler electronic voltage regulator. *(Chrysler Corporation)*

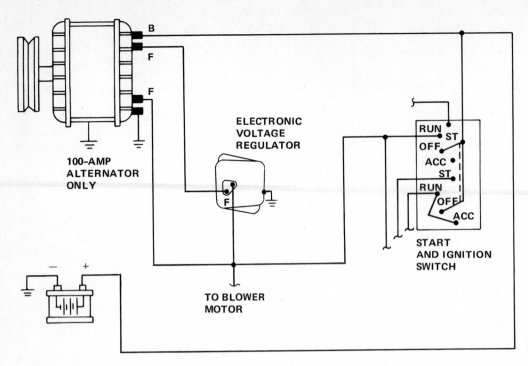

Fig. 8-27 Wiring diagram of Chrysler charging system. *(Chrysler Corporation)*

a solid-state voltage regulator with a field relay. The field relay is mechanical and works the same as the unit described previously. The voltage regulator, which includes transistors, diodes, and other electronic components, works the same way as the solid-state regulators described previously. The voltage at which this unit operates can be adjusted, as shown in Fig. 8-29, after removing the cover. A fiber rod, not a metal screwdriver, must be used to make this adjustment. This avoids the danger of shorting a transistor and damaging the system.

3. The electronic voltage regulator, now being installed on new-model cars, comes in two varieties, one for ammeter-equipped cars, the other for cars with indicator lamps. The circuits for these two are shown in Figs. 8-30 and 8-31. Note that none of the Ford

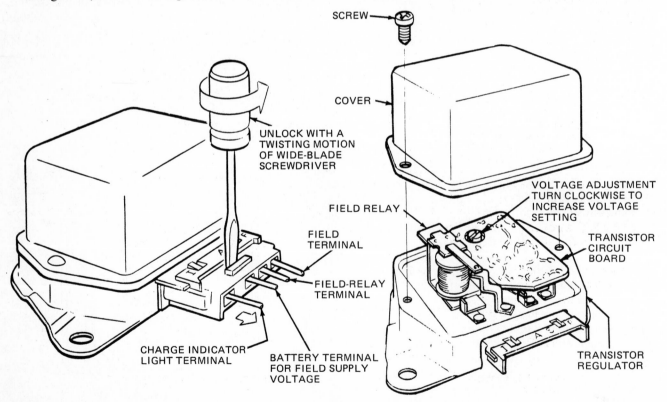

Fig. 8-28 Transistorized alternator regulator with field relay. The cover has been removed so that the voltage-adjustment screw can be seen. *(Ford Motor Company)*

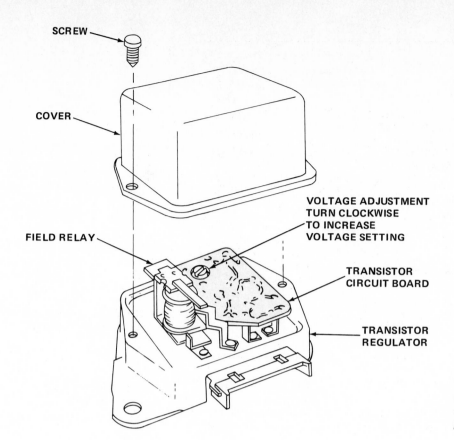

SCREW

COVER

FIELD RELAY

VOLTAGE ADJUSTMENT
TURN CLOCKWISE
TO INCREASE
VOLTAGE SETTING

TRANSISTOR
CIRCUIT BOARD

TRANSISTOR
REGULATOR

Fig. 8-29 Ford transistorized voltage regulator with cover removed and voltage being adjusted. *(Ford Motor Company)*

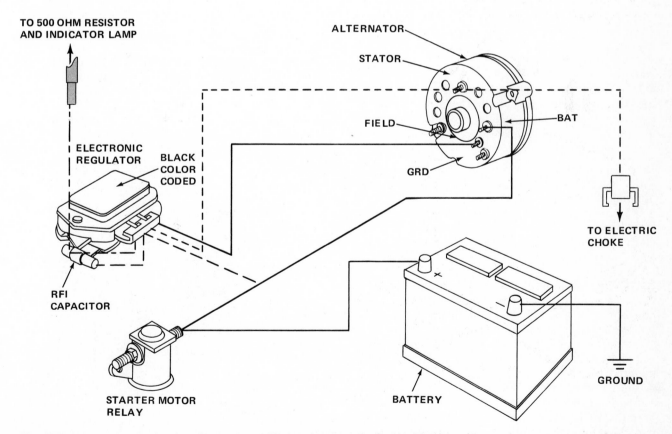

TO 500 OHM RESISTOR
AND INDICATOR LAMP

ALTERNATOR

STATOR

ELECTRONIC
REGULATOR

BLACK
COLOR
CODED

FIELD

BAT

GRD

TO ELECTRIC
CHOKE

RFI
CAPACITOR

STARTER MOTOR
RELAY

BATTERY

GROUND

Fig. 8-30 Wiring circuit of a charging system with warning-lamp indicator. *(Ford Motor Company)*

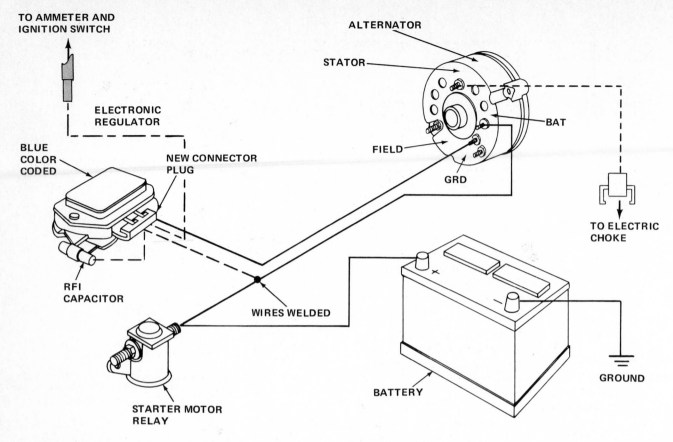

TO AMMETER AND IGNITION SWITCH

ELECTRONIC REGULATOR

BLUE COLOR CODED

NEW CONNECTOR PLUG

RFI CAPACITOR

WIRES WELDED

STARTER MOTOR RELAY

ALTERNATOR

STATOR

BAT

FIELD

GRD

TO ELECTRIC CHOKE

BATTERY

GROUND

Fig. 8-31 Wiring circuit of a charging system with ammeter. *(Ford Motor Company)*

regulators are interchangeable. That is, you cannot use the electronic voltage regulator in place of the other types. The alternators are also different for each type of regulator.

☼ 8-16 General Motors and American Motors regulators In recent years, both General Motors and American Motors have switched to alternators with built-in, integral, solid-state voltage regulators. We described these in ☼ 8-13.

NOTE: Some American Motors Corporation cars (recent V-8 types, for example) have continued to use the vibrating voltage regulator with field relay, as described in ☼ 8-12 and illustrated in Figs. 8-21 and 8-22. In 1979, some American Motors Corporation cars had Bosch alternators with the regulator bolted onto, but not inside, the alternator.

☼ 8-17 Charge indicators There are three types of charge indicator, the ammeter, the voltmeter, and the indicator light. The ammeter (Fig. 8-32) has a needle that swings across a dial to indicate whether current is going into, or coming out of, the battery. The needle also indicates how much current is flowing. It is mounted on a pivot. There is a small, oval-shaped piece of iron mounted on the same pivot. This is called the *armature*. A permanent magnet, round in shape, is placed so its two ends are close to the armature. The permanent magnet attracts the iron armature and holds it horizontal when no current is flowing. The needle

points to zero. If current starts to pass through the conductor, magnetism is produced. This acts on the armature and causes it to swing away from zero. If current is going from the alternator to the battery, the needle swings to the charge side, showing a charge. The stronger the current, the stronger the magnetic field and the farther the needle swings. If current is being taken out of the battery—for example, to light

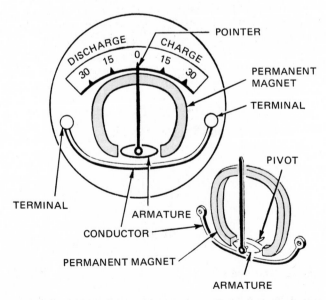

POINTER

PERMANENT MAGNET

TERMINAL

PIVOT

DISCHARGE CHARGE
30 15 0 15 30

TERMINAL

ARMATURE

CONDUCTOR

PERMANENT MAGNET

ARMATURE

Fig. 8-32 Simplified drawing of a car ammeter.

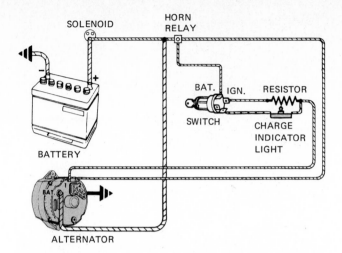

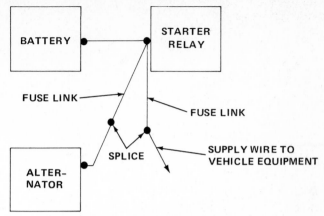

Fig. 8-33 Wiring diagram of a charging system using an alternator with an integral voltage regulator and a charge-indicator lamp. *(Delco-Remy Division of General Motors Corporation)*

FORD, MERCURY, LTD II, FAIRMONT,
ZEPHYR, GRANADA, MONARCH,
VERSAILLES, PINTO AND BOBCAT

the headlights when the engine is not running—the needle swings toward the discharge side. The ammeter is connected into the circuit from the alternator to the battery so the driver can see whether the battery is being charged or discharged.

The voltmeter has a very high resistance and is connected across the alternator so that it reads alternator voltage. ☼ 5-5 describes voltmeters and how they work. See also Fig. 24-1.

The charge indicator light has a different circuit (Fig. 8-33). When the ignition switch is turned on, current can flow through the resistor and the charge indicator light. This current comes from the battery. As soon as the engine starts and the alternator voltage builds up, the light goes out. When the alternator voltage builds up, the voltages on the two sides of the resistor and light become the same. There is no voltage on the resistor and light so the light goes out. This indicates that the alternator is working properly so it can charge the battery. If the alternator should fail for any reason, its voltage will drop and battery voltage will cause the light to come on to indicate the failure.

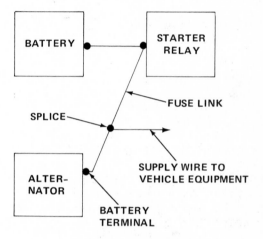

MUSTANG II AND COUGAR

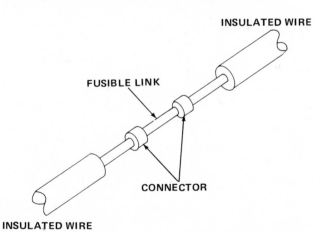

Fig. 8-34 Fusible link connected into a hot-wire circuit. Insulation has been removed so link can be seen.

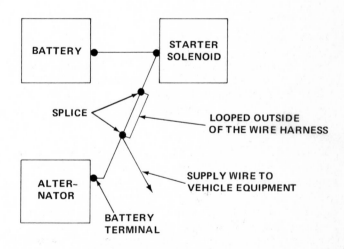

THUNDERBIRD, LINCOLN CONTINENTAL,
AND CONTINENTAL MARK V

Fig. 8-35 Locations of fusible links in various charging systems of Ford cars *(Ford Motor Company)*

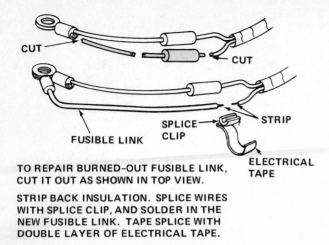

CUT

CUT

FUSIBLE LINK

SPLICE CLIP

STRIP

ELECTRICAL TAPE

TO REPAIR BURNED-OUT FUSIBLE LINK, CUT IT OUT AS SHOWN IN TOP VIEW.

STRIP BACK INSULATION. SPLICE WIRES WITH SPLICE CLIP, AND SOLDER IN THE NEW FUSIBLE LINK. TAPE SPLICE WITH DOUBLE LAYER OF ELECTRICAL TAPE.

Fig. 8-36 Repairing of burned-out fusible link. *(Buick Motor Division of General Motors Corporation)*

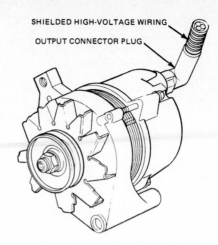

SHIELDED HIGH-VOLTAGE WIRING

OUTPUT CONNECTOR PLUG

Fig. 8-37 High-voltage alternator assembly. *(Ford Motor Company)*

⚙ 8-18 Fuse links The fuse link, or fusible link as it is also called, is a short length of insulated wire within the wiring harness. It is smaller than the circuit that it protects (Fig. 8-34). The illustration shows it uncovered. In the actual harness, it is covered with insulation. The fuse links are identified in the harness by a special tag or color code. On some cars, the fuse link is looped outside the wiring harness. Figure 8-35 shows the locations of fusible links in various charging systems. Their purpose is to burn or blow out if the current goes too high. This protects the rest of the system from damage. A blown fuse link is usually easy to spot. Bare wire may be sticking out of the insulation. Or the insulation may be bubbled or burned from the heat. Figure 8-36 shows a fusible link before and after it blew.

⚙ 8-19 Alternators for special purposes The alternator shown in Fig. 8-37 is a high-voltage unit which supplies the electric power to heat and defog the windshield and backlite (rear window) of the car. These windows are special. They have heating elements of metallic gold deposited in a thin film throughout the glass area. Thus almost the entire area of the glass is heated, and this quickly dispels any fog or ice.

Figure 8-38 shows the wiring circuit for the system. Note that there is no regulator. The alternator produces as much as 120 volts and can cause a severe shock. The alternator is completely isolated from the rest of the electric system, and all wire junctions have a warning tag. The alternator is driven by its own belt, independent of the charging-system alternator. Note also that

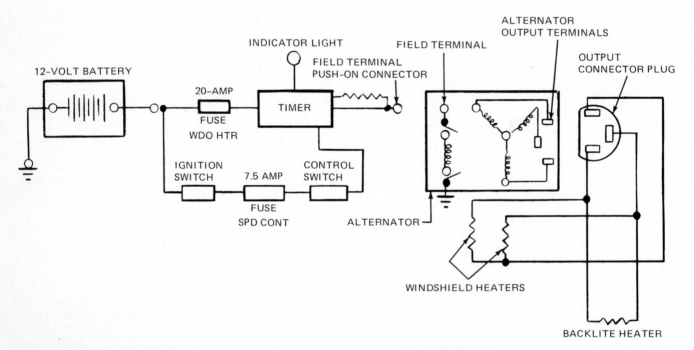

Fig. 8-38 Wiring circuit of the high-voltage alternator and heaters in the windshield and backlite. *(Ford Motor Company)*

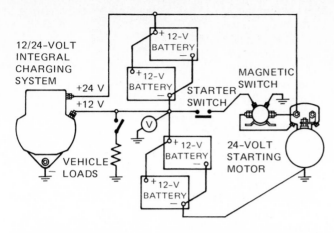

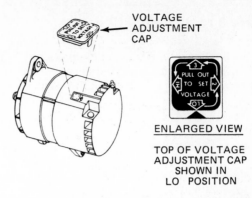

Fig. 8-39 The 12/24-volt system that uses an electronic transformer to supply 12 volts to the vehicle electric system. The batteries are in series to provide 24 volts for starting. *(Delco-Remy Division of General Motors Corporation)*

the field is supplied through a control system that includes the ignition switch, a control switch, and a timer. When everything is turned on, battery current feeds the alternator field. The alternator produces high voltage to heat the windshield and backlite.

NOTE: Most cars today with heated windshields and backlites no longer use the high-voltage system. Instead, they connect into the standard 12-volt system of the car (see ☸ 25-9).

The system shown in Fig. 8-39 includes a 24-volt starting system and a 12/24-volt charging system. The starting motor is a 24-volt unit. This higher voltage allows the starting motor to crank large engines that require a high cranking torque. To obtain this high voltage, two 12-volt batteries are connected in series.

Fig. 8-41 Voltage adjustment cap on a heavy-duty alternator. *(Cadillac Motor Car Division of General Motors Corporation)*

The alternator contains diodes and an integral voltage regulator, as with other alternators. In addition, it has a transformer that reduces the voltage to charge the two 12-volt batteries. This arrangement eliminates the need for a mechanical switching system such as described in ☸ 5-25.

Some heavy-duty Delco-Remy alternators have extra terminals to supply alternating current. Figure 8-40 shows the circuit. The alternating current, which can go above 110 volts, is obtained by tapping off the three legs of the delta stator, as shown. The integral voltage regulator in this alternator can be adjusted by removing the voltage adjustment cap (Fig. 8-41). You rotate the cap 90° to change the voltage setting. Note that there are four settings LO, 2, 3, and HI. The direction you turn the cap depends on whether the battery is being undercharged or overcharged. In the system described, there is an auxilliary transformer-rectifier combination (not shown) which is used to convert the alternating current into 110-volt direct current to operate special equipment.

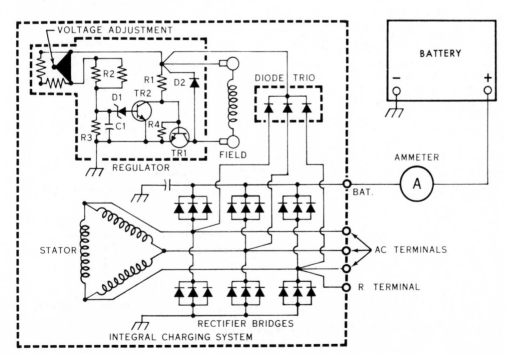

Fig. 8-40 Wiring diagram of a heavy-duty alternator with special terminals to supply alternating current. *(Cadillac Motor Car Division of General Motors Corporation)*

Chapter 8 review questions

Select the *one* correct, best, or most probable answer to each question. Then check your answers against the correct answers given at the end of the book.

1. In the alternator, the conductors in which current is induced:
   a. are in the armature,
   b. rotate,
   c. are series connected,
   d. are stationary.
2. In most alternators, the magnetic field is produced by:
   a. stationary field coils,
   b. the stator windings,
   c. field coils in the rotor,
   d. alternator magnets.
3. In the alternator, output regulation is achieved by varying:
   a. field current,
   b. speed,
   c. stator current,
   d. number of turns in stator.
4. The usual number of diodes in the alternator rectifier is:
   a. two,
   b. three,
   c. four,
   d. six.
5. The heat sink is located in the:
   a. rotor,
   b. stator,
   c. end frame,
   d. field frame.
6. The typical automotive alternator is:
   a. one-phase,
   b. two-phase,
   c. three-phase,
   d. four-phase.
7. In the alternator with stationary field coils, magnetic field movement is achieved by:
   a. the vibrating contacts,
   b. magnets in the rotor,
   c. stator action,
   d. windings in the rotor.

8. The alternator field is connected to the battery through the field relay or:
   a. the ignition switch,
   b. an indicator relay,
   c. the regulator,
   d. starter switch.
9. The ac vibrating voltage regulators described in the chapter have:
   a. one set of contacts,
   b. two sets of contacts,
   c. no contacts,
   d. three sets of contacts.
10. In the fully transistorized regulator, field current is controlled by:
    a. contact points,
    b. resistances,
    c. triodes,
    d. transistors.
11. In some charging systems with solid-state regulators, the field-relay function has been taken over by:
    a. a cutout relay,
    b. a magnetic switch,
    c. a diode trio,
    d. a triode.
12. Most integral or built-in voltage regulators:
    a. are adjustable,
    b. are not adjustable,
    c. are the contact-point type,
    d. do not use transistors.
13. In recent years, Chrysler Corp. cars have used:
    a. integral or built-in solid-state regulators,
    b. externally mounted vibrating voltage regulators,
    c. externally mounted solid-state regulators,
    d. no voltage regulators.
14. In recent years, Ford Motor Company cars have used three types of voltage regulator. The latest is:
    a. electromechanical,
    b. transistorized,
    c. full solid-state or electronic,
    d. vibrating contact.
15. The special high-voltage (up to 120 volts) alternator described in the chapter supplies electric power to:
    a. heat the windshield,
    b. heat the windshield and backlite,
    c. operate the television set,
    d. power the headlights.

CHARGING-SYSTEM TROUBLE DIAGNOSIS

After studying this chapter, you should be able to:

1. List and discuss the nine dos and don'ts of ac charging-system service.
2. List and explain the six alternator-regulator troubles discussed in the chapter and describe the procedures for each that point to causes and corrections.
3. Troubleshoot and find causes for any of the first five troubles in the chart.

9-1 Need for systematic procedure If trouble is suspected or reported, the cause is most easily found through a systematic approach. For example, a low battery might be caused by a low voltage setting, or a loose drive belt, or a number of other specific causes. These causes are listed, with the appropriate checks and corrections, in the charging-system trouble diagnosis chart.

You should pinpoint the cause of any problem before attempting to make a correction. Following sections describe various troubles, their causes, and their corrections.

9-2 Servicing charging systems There are a number of things to remember when servicing ac charging systems. The electrical technician should know these points:

1. Belt tension is more critical on alternators than on dc generators because of the greater inertia of the heavier rotor in the alternator. Check belt tension periodically.
2. Never install a battery backward. The reversed polarity can damage the alternator because a heavy current will flow through the diodes as soon as the battery is connected. This will burn out the diodes if the fusible link in the line does not burn out first. It will also burn out electronic ignition systems (if fusible link does not burn out first).
3. When charging a battery in the car, be sure to disconnect the battery ground strap from the grounded battery terminal. This protects the alternator diodes and the transistors (in transistor-type regulators) from the high charging voltage. The transistors in electronic ignition systems could also be damaged by the high charging voltage.

4. Be sure to connect the battery charger with the correct polarity to the battery. It is actually possible to reverse battery polarity by charging it backward. If this happens, then, when the battery ground strap is reconnected, the reversed polarity can ruin the alternator and alternator diodes, as mentioned in item 2 above.
5. If you have to use a booster battery to jump-start the engine, be sure to follow the instructions given in ✿ 4-27. Failure to follow the instructions can cause serious damage to equipment and possible personal injury.
6. Never operate the alternator on open circuit, that is, not connected to a battery. This will allow a ruinously high voltage to build up in the alternator. Make sure all connections in the system are tight before starting the engine.
7. Never short between or ground any of the terminals in the charging system. This could ruin diodes or transistors.
8. Never disconnect leads from the alternator or regulator without first disconnecting the ground strap from the battery's ground terminal. This guards against accidental grounds or shorts which could permit a high current to flow. This would probably ruin the alternator or other parts.

9-3 Checking out troubles in charging systems The basic complaints that will require the electrical technician to make some checks are:

1. Low battery—usually shows up as slow cranking.
2. Overcharged battery—usually shows up as frequent need of water. Also, since this condition can result from high charging voltage, frequent light replacement could be an added complaint.

3. Faulty indicator light or ammeter operation.
4. Noisy alternator.

NOTE: Always confirm the complaint. That is, check the battery, and note operation of the indicator light or alternator, before making further checks. In fact, this should be a standard diagnosis step in handling all complaints.

☼ **9-4 Trouble diagnosis of the charging system** The chart that follows lists the various trouble conditions that might be found in the system, together with their possible causes and corrections. The troubles are not listed in order of frequency.

NOTE: There are other ways of presenting troubles, their causes, and corrections, besides the one shown in the chart that follows. For example, we show, at the end of this chapter, charging-system diagnosis charts from American Motors, Chrysler, Ford, and General Motors shop manuals. Also, we show a diagnostic and repair simplification (DARS) chart from a General Motors shop manual. They give you procedures for locating causes of trouble. Also, they show the different ways that automotive manufacturers present trouble-diagnosis material in their manuals.

☼ **9-5 Charged battery and low charging rate** This is normal operation. Routine checks of the voltage setting and alternator output can be made, along with a check of the drive-belt condition and tension.

☼ **9-6 Charged battery and high charging rate** A charged battery with a high charging rate will show up as frequent need for watering the battery and also frequent light-bulb replacement. The cause is a high voltage setting, a defective regulator, loose connections, or a poorly grounded regulator base (separate regulator). In the vibrating-point regulator, such troubles as stuck contacts or an open voltage winding could prevent normal regulator operation, so the voltage would go too high. This could also result if the regulator base were poorly grounded; the excessive resistance introduced would prevent a good grounding of the field winding when the upper contacts were closed. Alternator voltage could therefore stay high. Checking and adjusting regulator voltage is detailed in Chapter 10.

NOTE: Alternator voltage cannot be adjusted on most of today's cars. It is preset in the electronic voltage regulator. Battery overcharge can occur if a non-maintenance-free battery (which has lead–antimony grids) is installed in a car having the Delcotron 10SI or similar alternator. These alternators have a higher voltage setting on their built-in voltage regulators. They are designed to be used with the Delco-Remy maintenance-free "Freedom" battery, which has a grid made of different elements. Mismatching the battery and alternator, as above, can cause the battery to be overcharged, even though the alternator voltage is normal.

☼ **9-7 Discharged battery and low or no charging rate** A discharged battery with low or no charging rate can be caused by frequent stops and starts, accessories or lights left on, loose drive belt, an old battery that will not accept a charge normally, or defects in the wiring or connections. Checking the belt tension is illustrated in Fig. 9-1. If everything else checks out

Charging-System Trouble Diagnosis Chart

(See ☼ 9-5 to 9-11 for detailed explanations of trouble causes and corrections listed in the chart.)

CONDITION	POSSIBLE CAUSE	CHECK OR CORRECTION
1. Charged battery and low charging rate (☼ 9-5)	This is normal operation	Check belt tension and voltage setting if desired
2. Charged battery and high charging rate (☼ 9-6)	a. High voltage setting b. Regulator defective c. Loose connections d. Regulator base poorly grounded	Reduce setting Replace regulator Correct Correct
3. Discharged battery and low or no charging rate (☼ 9-7)	a. Loose drive belt b. Bad connections in charging circuit c. Voltage setting low d. Regulator defective e. Alternator defective f. Field relay defective	Tighten, replace belt if necessary Clean, tighten Readjust Replace or repair Repair Repair or replace
4. Faulty indicator light or ammeter operation (☼ 9-8 and 9-9)	a. Indicator bulb burned out b. Defective wiring or connections c. Defective regulator	Replace Repair Replace
5. Noisy alternator (☼ 9-10)	a. Mounting loose b. Bad drive belt c. Internal defects	Tighten Replace Remove alternator for further checks
6. Discharged battery and high charging rate (☼ 9-11)	This is normal operation	Check for cause of low battery. Could be fuel system or engine trouble

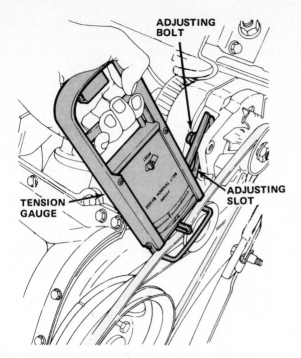

Fig. 9-1 Using a special gauge to check fan-belt tension. *(American Motors Corporation)*

okay, check the alternator output. Here is the procedure recommended by Chevrolet for an alternator with built-in voltage regulator.

1. Disconnect the battery ground cable. Connect an ammeter into the circuit at the BAT (battery) terminal of the alternator. Reconnect the ground cable.
2. Turn on accessories to load the battery. This includes the radio, high-beam headlights, windshield wipers, and heater motor at high speed. Add a carbon pile (a heavy variable resistance) across the battery.
3. Operate the engine at moderate speed. Adjust the carbon pile to get the maximum alternator output.
4. If the output is within 10 percent of the rated output stamped on the alternator, the alternator is okay. The trouble must be in the circuit connections, wiring, or drive belt.
5. If the output is not within 10 percent of rated value, ground the field winding by carefully inserting a screwdriver into the test hole of the alternator (Fig. 9-2). This bypasses the regulator. If the output now increases, the trouble is in the regulator. It must be replaced. If the output does not increase, the trouble is in the diodes, field winding, or stator. The alternator must be removed from the engine and disassembled in order to find the trouble.

NOTE: Other makes of alternators require different testing procedures. Also, alternators that use a separately mounted vibrating-contact type of regulator require a testing procedure that checks the regulator itself. See the manufacturer's shop manual when you work on a specific make and model of regulator and alternator. See also Chapter 10 on regulator checks and Chapter 11 on alternator service.

☼ 9-8 Faulty indicator light or ammeter operation If, before the engine starts, the indicator light does not come on when the ignition switch is turned on, it could be due to a burned-out bulb or fuse or to an open in the wiring, regulator, or field. It could also be due to a shorted diode in the alternator (this may also allow the light to burn even with the ignition switch off). Checks for these conditions are outlined in the following sections.

On systems equipped with an ammeter, or charge indicator, faulty ammeter action can be checked out by first turning the ignition switch to ACC (accessories) and then turning on an accessory. The ammeter should read "discharge." If it does not, check the ammeter circuit for an open or poor connection. If the ammeter reads "discharge," check further by starting the engine and watching the ammeter. If it fails to read "charge," the trouble could be that the alternator is not producing output (see ☼ 9-7) or the ammeter or ammeter circuit is faulty.

If the indicator light (on systems so equipped) fails to go off as the engine is started, the trouble could be low or no alternator output (☼ 9-7), a defective field relay, or a shorted diode in the alternator. Checking the relay is outlined in Chapter 10. Following is a checking procedure recommended by Chevrolet for testing the indicator-light circuit in the circuit using the alternator with the built-in voltage regulator.

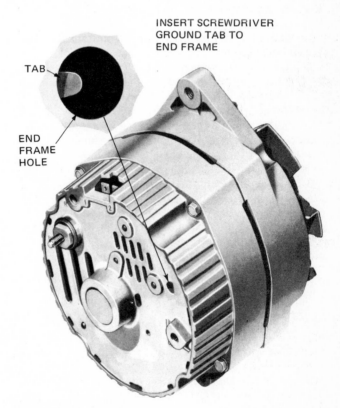

Fig. 9-2 Test hole in alternator. A screwdriver is inserted into the test hole to ground the field circuit. The screwdriver should be pushed in only far enough to touch the tab. If pushed in too far, it could damage the alternator. *(Chevrolet Motor Division of General Motors Corporation)*

⚙ 9-9 Indicator-light circuit check In normal operation, the light should come on when the engine is being cranked. It should go off when the engine starts. The light should be off when the ignition switch is off. There are three troubles that require checking.

1. **Switch off, light on** Disconnect the two leads from alternator terminals 1 and 2. If the light stays on, there is a short between these two leads. If the light goes off, the short is inside the alternator, in the diodes. Replace the rectifier bridge which carries the diodes. This requires disassembly of the alternator.

2. **Switch on, light off, engine stopped** This can be caused by diode defects, by a short between the leads to terminals 1 and 2, by reversal of the two leads to the terminals, or by an open in the circuit. An open can cause a run-down battery. To find the trouble if an open is suspected, proceed as follows:

1. Connect a voltmeter from terminal 2 to ground. If your reading is zero, there is an open between the terminal and the battery. If a reading is obtained, go to step 2.
2. With ignition switch on and terminal 1 and 2 leads disconnected, momentarily ground the terminal 1 lead.

CAUTION: Do not ground the terminal 2 lead! This directly grounds the positive terminal of the battery. It is a direct short across the battery terminals!

3. If the light does not go on with terminal 1 lead grounded, check for a blown fuse or fusible link, a burned-out bulb, or an open in the terminal 1 lead.
4. If the light comes on, unground the terminal 1 lead. Reconnect the two leads to terminals 1 and 2. Carefully insert a screwdriver into the test hole shown in Fig. 9-2. This grounds the field winding, and the light should come on.
5. If the light does not go on, check the connection between the wiring harness and terminal 1 of the alternator. Other possible troubles could be with the brushes, slip rings, and field winding in the rotor. Checking these requires removal and disassembly of the alternator.
6. If the light comes on and a voltmeter reading was obtained in step 1, replace the regulator in the alternator.

3. **Switch on, light on, engine running** There is a problem in the alternator. Check it out as outlined in Chapter 11.

⚙ 9-10 Noisy alternator A noisy alternator could be due to a loose or worn drive belt or loose alternator mounting; internal defects in the alternator such as worn bearings, open or shorted diodes, opens or shorts in the stator; or mechanical interference, for instance, between the alternator fan and frame.

⚙ 9-11 Discharged battery and high charging rate This is normal operation because when a battery is discharged, the alternator sends to it a high charging rate. When you find a discharged battery, you should always try to determine the cause. It could be that the driver ran the battery down trying to start and that a faulty fuel system or engine trouble is preventing normal starting.

⚙ 9-12 Chrysler charging-system diagnosis chart This chart (Fig. 9-3) covers the various steps to be taken if trouble occurs. If the drive belt is loose, it should be tightened by loosening the alternator mounting bolts and moving the alternator out. Use a belt tension gauge to check the belt tension (Fig. 9-1). Belt tension and belt condition are very important. If the belt is too loose, it will slip and wear rapidly. Also, the alternator will not be driven fast enough and the battery will not be charged. If the belt is too tight, it will cause rapid bearing wear.

⚙ 9-13 Ford trouble diagnosis and charging-system test chart Figure 9-4 shows the Ford trouble diagnosis chart from a late Ford shop manual. The diagnosis chart (Fig. 9-4) supplies very much the same information as the trouble diagnosis chart in ⚙ 9-4.

⚙ 9-14 General Motors charging-system diagnosis chart Figure 9-5 shows the charging-system diagnosis chart that is printed in many of the latest shop manuals for General Motors cars. It applies to systems using an indicator lamp. It starts with indicator-lamp operation (at top of chart) and shows the three conditions we discussed in ⚙ 9-9. Figure 9-6 is a DARS chart for this sequence. Compare the steps shown in the charts with the instructions discussed in ⚙ 9-9. You will see that the procedures are the same, with some small variations.

⚙ 9-15 DARS charts You will find DARS charts in American Motors and General Motors shop manuals. They provide a graphic method of diagnosing and correcting troubles. Figure 9-6 shows a DARS chart covering the indicator-lamp problems discussed in ⚙ 9-9 and also in ⚙ 9-14. The first problem is that the light stays on with the engine running. It should be off. Step 1 is to check the alternator belt. If the light now goes off, the trouble is fixed so you *stop*. If the light still stays on, you go to step 2. You follow the procedure there. If the light still stays on, you go to step 3, and so on, until you find the trouble and fix it.

NOTE: The charts from the shop manuals of the major automotive manufacturers in the United States are included here and in Chapter 10 so you can study and compare them. As you study and compare the charts, you become acquainted with the various troubleshooting procedures suggested by the different manufacturers. Studying them now will help you understand different kinds of troubleshooting charts when you go to work in an automotive shop.

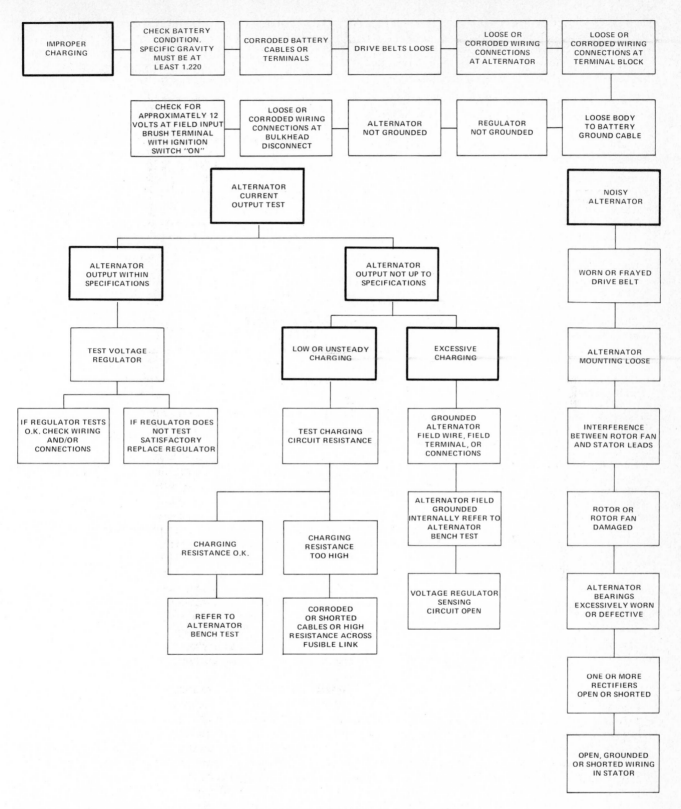

Fig. 9-3 The Chrysler alternator and voltage-regulator trouble diagnosis chart. *(Chrysler Corporation)*

CHARGING SYSTEM DIAGNOSIS

CONDITION	POSSIBLE CAUSE	RESOLUTION
• Battery does not stay charged—engine starts OK	• Battery • Loose or worn alternator belt • Damaged wiring or cables • Alternator • Regulator • Other vehicle electrical systems	• Test battery, replace if necessary • Adjust or replace belt • Service as required • Test, repair or replace as required • Test, replace if necessary • Check other systems for current draw. Repair as required
• Alternator noisy	• Loose or worn alternator belt • Bent pulley flanges • Alternator	• Adjust or replace belt • Replace pulley • Service or replace alternator
• Battery uses excessive water—lights and/or fuses burn out frequently	• Damaged wiring • Alternator regulator • Battery	• Service as required • Replace if necessary • Test, replace if necessary
• Charge indicator light stays on after engine starts	• Loose or worn alternator belt • Alternator • Regulator	• Adjust or replace • Service or replace • Replace
• Charge indicator light flickers while vehicle is being driven	• Loose or worn alternator belt • Loose or improper wiring connections • Alternator • Regulator	• Adjust or replace belt • Service as required • Service or replace • Service or replace
• Charge indicator gauge shows discharge (If constant high reading, see ''Battery uses excessive water'')	• Loose or worn alternator belt • Damaged wiring (Battery to alternator for ground or open) • Alternator • Regulator • Charge indicator gauge wiring and connections • Damaged gauge • Other vehicle electrical systems malfunction	• Adjust or replace belt • Service or replace wiring • Service or replace • Replace • Service as required • Replace gauge • Service as required

Fig. 9-4 Ford charging-system trouble diagnosis chart.

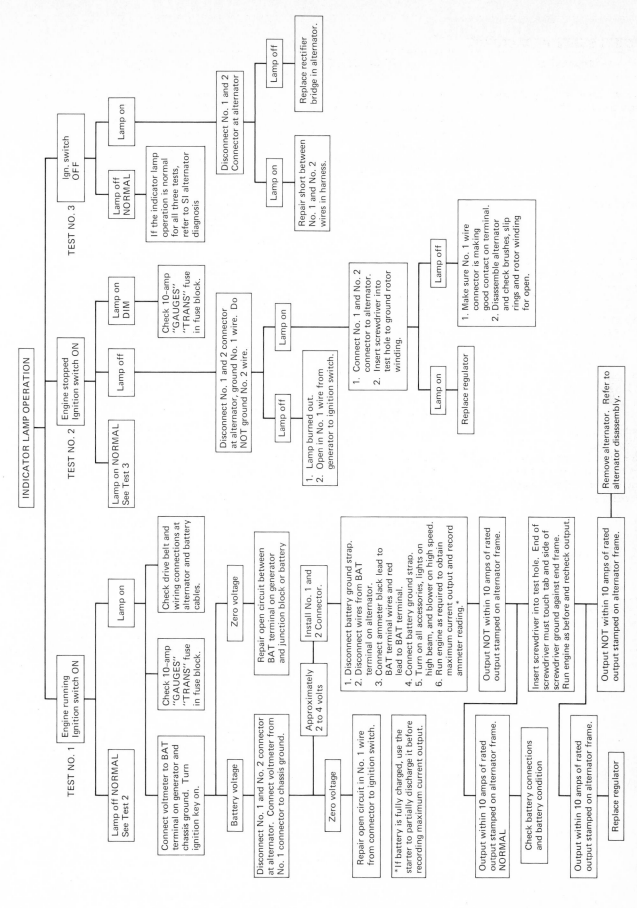

Fig. 9-5 Trouble diagnosis chart for tracking down causes of trouble with indicator-lamp operation. (*Pontiac Motor Division of General Motors Corporation*)

PROBLEM: ALTERNATOR LIGHT ON, ENGINE RUNNING

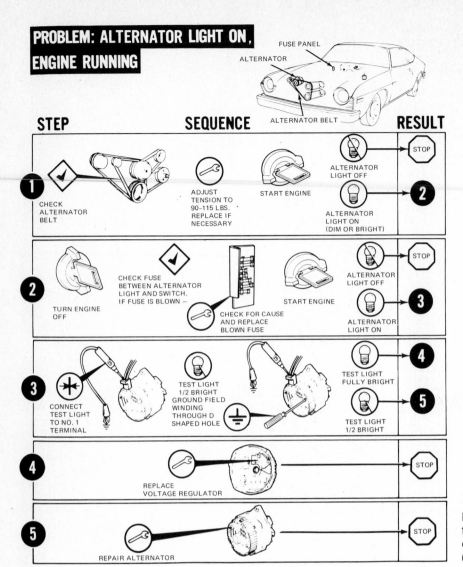

FUSE PANEL
ALTERNATOR
ALTERNATOR BELT

STEP **SEQUENCE** **RESULT**

1 CHECK ALTERNATOR BELT — ADJUST TENSION TO 90–115 LBS. REPLACE IF NECESSARY — START ENGINE — ALTERNATOR LIGHT OFF → STOP / ALTERNATOR LIGHT ON (DIM OR BRIGHT) → **2**

2 TURN ENGINE OFF — CHECK FUSE BETWEEN ALTERNATOR LIGHT AND SWITCH. IF FUSE IS BLOWN — CHECK FOR CAUSE AND REPLACE BLOWN FUSE — START ENGINE — ALTERNATOR LIGHT OFF → STOP / ALTERNATOR LIGHT ON → **3**

3 CONNECT TEST LIGHT TO NO. 1 TERMINAL — TEST LIGHT 1/2 BRIGHT GROUND FIELD WINDING THROUGH D SHAPED HOLE — TEST LIGHT FULLY BRIGHT → **4** / TEST LIGHT 1/2 BRIGHT → **5**

4 REPLACE VOLTAGE REGULATOR → STOP

5 REPAIR ALTERNATOR → STOP

Fig. 9-6 Diagnostic and repair simplification (DARS) chart for analysis and correction of indicator-lamp troubles. (*American Motors Corporation*)

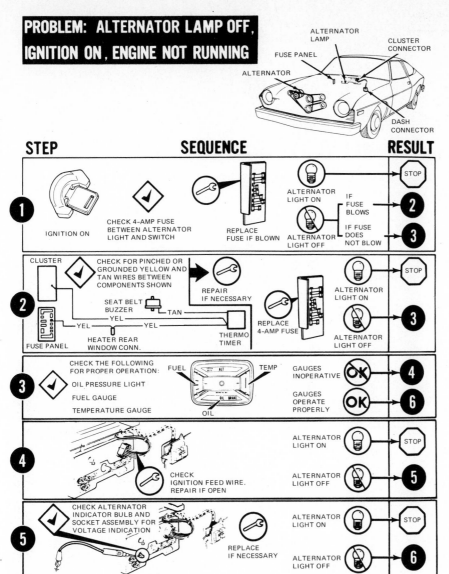

PROBLEM: ALTERNATOR LAMP OFF, IGNITION ON, ENGINE NOT RUNNING

ALTERNATOR LAMP
CLUSTER CONNECTOR
FUSE PANEL
ALTERNATOR
DASH CONNECTOR

STEP   **SEQUENCE**   **RESULT**

1   IGNITION ON   CHECK 4-AMP FUSE BETWEEN ALTERNATOR LIGHT AND SWITCH   REPLACE FUSE IF BLOWN   ALTERNATOR LIGHT ON → STOP   ALTERNATOR LIGHT OFF   IF FUSE BLOWS → **2**   IF FUSE DOES NOT BLOW → **3**

2   CLUSTER   CHECK FOR PINCHED OR GROUNDED YELLOW AND TAN WIRES BETWEEN COMPONENTS SHOWN   SEAT BELT BUZZER — TAN   YEL   YEL — YEL   FUSE PANEL   HEATER REAR WINDOW CONN.   THERMO TIMER   REPAIR IF NECESSARY   REPLACE 4-AMP FUSE   ALTERNATOR LIGHT ON → STOP   ALTERNATOR LIGHT OFF → **3**

3   CHECK THE FOLLOWING FOR PROPER OPERATION: OIL PRESSURE LIGHT, FUEL GAUGE, TEMPERATURE GAUGE   FUEL   ALT   TEMP   OIL   BRAKE   OIL   GAUGES INOPERATIVE OK → **4**   GAUGES OPERATE PROPERLY OK → **6**

4   CHECK IGNITION FEED WIRE. REPAIR IF OPEN   ALTERNATOR LIGHT ON → STOP   ALTERNATOR LIGHT OFF → **5**

5   CHECK ALTERNATOR INDICATOR BULB AND SOCKET ASSEMBLY FOR VOLTAGE INDICATION   REPLACE IF NECESSARY   ALTERNATOR LIGHT ON → STOP   ALTERNATOR LIGHT OFF → **6**

Fig. 9-6 (*Continued*)

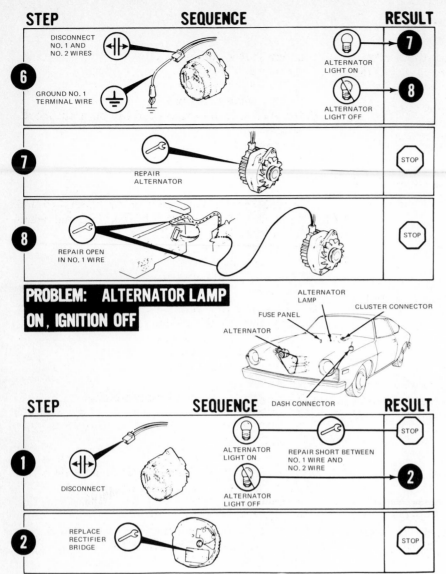

STEP	SEQUENCE	RESULT
6	DISCONNECT NO. 1 AND NO. 2 WIRES ・ GROUND NO. 1 TERMINAL WIRE	ALTERNATOR LIGHT ON → **7** ・ ALTERNATOR LIGHT OFF → **8**
7	REPAIR ALTERNATOR	STOP
8	REPAIR OPEN IN NO. 1 WIRE	STOP

PROBLEM: ALTERNATOR LAMP ON, IGNITION OFF

ALTERNATOR LAMP
CLUSTER CONNECTOR
FUSE PANEL
ALTERNATOR
DASH CONNECTOR

STEP	SEQUENCE	RESULT
1	DISCONNECT	ALTERNATOR LIGHT ON → REPAIR SHORT BETWEEN NO. 1 WIRE AND NO. 2 WIRE → STOP ・ ALTERNATOR LIGHT OFF → **2**
2	REPLACE RECTIFIER BRIDGE	STOP

Fig. 9-6 (*Continued*)

126

Chapter 9 review questions

Select the *one* correct, best, or most probable answer to each question. Then check your answers against the correct answers given at the end of the book.

1. A charged battery with a low charging rate:
   a. requires readjustment of the voltage setting,
   b. requires readjustment of the current setting,
   c. requires regulator replacement,
   d. is normal operation.
2. A charged battery with a high charging rate could be caused by a poor regulator ground, a defective regulator, or:
   a. a high voltage setting,
   b. a high current setting,
   c. a high relay setting,
   d. a loose belt.
3. A discharged battery with a low charging rate could be caused by a loose drive belt, poor connections, a defective unit, or:
   a. a low current setting,
   b. diodes connected backward,
   c. a low voltage setting,
   d. transistors missing.
4. Defects in the alternator that could cause a low or no charging rate include a grounded or open stator winding, defective diodes, an open field, worn brushes, or:
   a. burned commutator bars,
   b. defective slip rings,
   c. worn drive pinion,
   d. missing windings.
5. Defects in the vibrating contact regulator that could cause a low or no charging rate, aside from a low voltage setting, include a defective field relay, blown fusible wire, stuck or burned contacts, or:
   a. low current setting,
   b. open field circuit,
   c. low battery gravity,
   d. high voltage setting.
6. Installing a battery backward can burn out the alternator:
   a. stator,
   b. rotor,
   c. bearings,
   d. diodes.
7. The purpose in disconnecting the battery ground strap from the grounded battery terminal when booster-charging the battery is to:
   a. protect the alternator diodes,
   b. prevent overcharge,
   c. protect regulator contacts,
   d. protect the headlamps.
8. The alternator should never be operated on open circuit because this could:
   a. overcharge the battery,
   b. burn out light bulbs,
   c. damage the alternator,
   d. blow fuses.
9. A noisy alternator could be caused by:
   a. a loose drive belt,
   b. a shorted diode,
   c. a loose bolt,
   d. all of the above.
10. If the dashboard charge indicator light does not work, the first thing to check is:
    a. the battery cables,
    b. the ignition switch,
    c. the indicator light bulb,
    d. the S terminal of the alternator.

CHAPTER 10

CHARGING-SYSTEM AND AC REGULATOR SERVICE

After studying this chapter, you should be able to:

1. Use test instruments to check the charging circuits of automobiles, including voltage-regulator settings and alternator output.
2. Remove and replace regulators and alternators.

This chapter describes the procedures for checking charging system regulators and alternators. In the past, a great variety of regulators were used, as we explained in Chapter 8, Automotive Charging Systems. Today, almost all automobiles come equipped with solid-state regulators. Many of these are built into the alternator. None of these, with few exceptions, are adjustable. If they do not hold the voltage down to the specified value, they are replaced. However, some special heavy-duty regulators, used with high-output alternators, do have a method of adjustment. You find these on specialized applications, such as large trucks and buses and off-the-highway equipment.

⚙ 10-1 Cautions to observe when checking charging systems Always disconnect the ground cable from the battery ground terminal before disconnecting or connecting leads in the charging system. Then, after all connections are restored, reconnect the ground strap. This avoids accidental shorting of the battery through the regulator or alternator which could damage the equipment or cause a fire or explosion. Also, observe the dos and don'ts, as detailed in ⚙ 9-2. Turn back to that section and review these dos and don'ts.

⚙ 10-2 Removing and installing regulators and alternators If a regulator is found to be defective, it must be removed and a new unit installed. If an alternator has internal defects, it must be removed for service. The procedure of removing either of these is as follows.

1. Disconnect the battery ground cable to avoid accidental grounding of the insulated or "hot" side of the system.

2. Disconnect all wires from the regulator or alternator. Label any wires that are not in a multiple connector.
3. Remove screws or bolts attaching the unit and take the unit off. The alternator must be pushed in toward the engine to loosen the drive belt. This allows you to slip the belt over the drive pulley so the alternator can be lifted off the engine.

To install a regulator or alternator, bolt it in place and reconnect wires. Shift the alternator outward to tighten the drive belt. This belt is often called the *fan belt* because its major purpose is to drive the engine fan and water pump. Figure 9-1 shows one method of checking belt tension. Tension should be adjusted by moving the alternator out and then tightening the bolt that goes through the slotted brace and into the hole in the drive end of the alternator (Figs. 8-15 and 8-16). Start engine and check operation of alternator to make sure it is working properly.

⚙ 10-3 Specifications Before working on a charging system, make sure you know the specifications, that is, the rated voltage settings of the regulator and the current output of the alternator. Specifications can be found in the manufacturer's shop manuals and are sometimes stamped on the unit.

⚙ 10-4 Chrysler Corporation contact-point regulator service Modern Chrysler Corporation vehicles use an electronic voltage regulator that is not adjustable. It is checked, as explained in ⚙10-5. Before this regulator was introduced, Chrysler used a one-unit vibrating contact-point voltage regulator, shown in Fig. 10-1. On these, you make the electric connections, shown in Fig. 10-2, to check the alternator output and, as shown in Fig. 10-3, to check the voltage setting. If

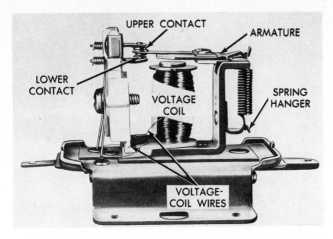

Fig. 10-1 Chrysler-built vibrating contact-point voltage regulator with cover removed. *(Chrysler Corporation)*

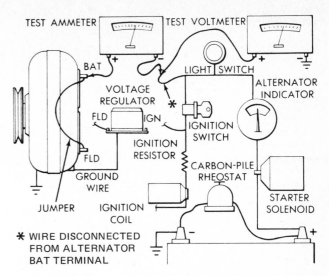

* WIRE DISCONNECTED FROM ALTERNATOR BAT TERMINAL

Fig. 10-2 Meter connections to check alternator output (vibrating contact-point regulator). *(Chrysler Corporation)*

the alternator output is too low, it must be removed and serviced. If the voltage setting is incorrect, it can be adjusted by bending the spring hanger down to increase the voltage setting. Bend it up to lower the voltage setting. This regulator also has means of adjusting the air gaps (which affect the voltage setting).

☼ 10-5 Chrysler Corporation electronic regulator service The charging system using the electronic voltage regulator is checked as follows for resistance, alternator output, and voltage setting. The electronic voltage regulator is not adjustable. If it does not hold the voltage to specifications, it should be replaced. Alternators, however, can be repaired if they do not perform as they should (Chapter 11).

1. **Charging-circuit-resistance test** See Fig. 10-4. Disconnect the battery ground cable and connect the test ammeter, voltmeter, and carbon-pile rheostat, as shown in Fig. 10-4. Note that the lead to the regulator F terminal has been disconnected from the alternator. A jumper wire has been connected from this terminal to ground. This eliminates regulator control of the field current that could influence the test. It can also permit the alternator voltage to go too high if you over-rev the engine. So do not increase engine speed any higher than necessary to make the test. Reconnect the battery ground cable.

Start the engine and immediately reduce engine speed to idle. Adjust engine speed and carbon pile to get a 20-ampere flow in the circuit. The voltage reading should not exceed 0.7 volt. If it does, there is excessive resistance in the system, and all connections and leads should be checked to find and eliminate the resistance.

2. **Current output test** This is a test of alternator output. Chrysler sets up the test as shown in Fig. 10-5. The connections are the same as for the circuit-resistance tests except that the test voltmeter is connected from the alternator hot terminal to ground. Disconnect the battery ground cable before making any connections and then reconnect it after all other connections have been made. Connect the tachometer to measure

engine speed. The tachometer is an electric meter that measures engine speed in rpm.

Run the engine at idle. Then slowly increase engine speed and readjust the carbon pile until the meter shows 1250 rpm and 15 volts (900 rpm and 13 volts if checking the 100-ampere alternator). Note the amperage output. It should be within the limits indicated by the alternator specification chart in the manufacturer's shop manual. If the alternator does not come up to rated output, it should be removed for further testing and servicing.

3. **Voltage regulator test** Chrysler supplies a special tester tool which, with an adaptor, can test any electronic voltage regulator installed on their cars. If this tester is not available, a voltmeter can be used, as shown in Fig. 10-6. First, check the battery gravity. If it is below 1.200, install a fully charged battery in its place. Then with the voltmeter connected, as shown in Fig. 10-6, operate the engine at 1250 rpm with all lights

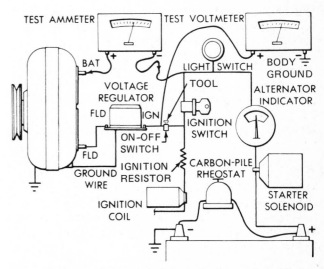

Fig. 10-3 Meter connections to check voltage setting (vibrating contact-point regulator). *(Chrysler Corporation)*

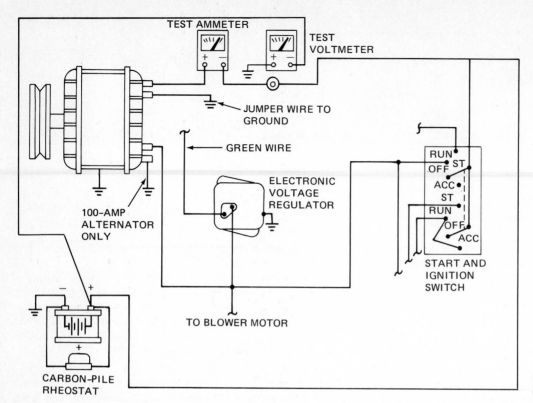

Fig. 10-4 Charging-circuit resistance test (electronic regulator). *(Chrysler Corporation)*

TEST AMMETER

TEST VOLTMETER

JUMPER WIRE TO GROUND

GREEN WIRE

ELECTRONIC VOLTAGE REGULATOR

100-AMP ALTERNATOR ONLY

RUN
OFF   ST
ACC
ST
RUN
OFF
ACC

START AND IGNITION SWITCH

TO BLOWER MOTOR

CARBON-PILE RHEOSTAT

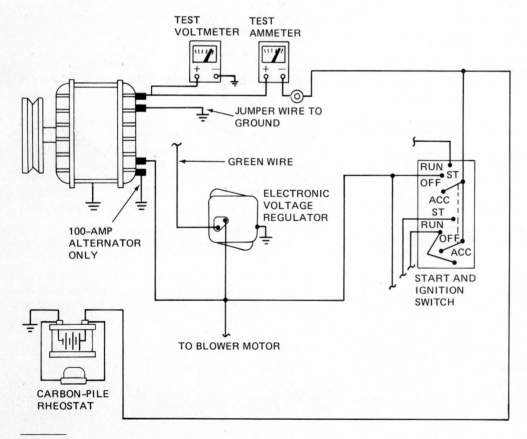

Fig. 10-5 Alternator output test (electronic regulator). *(Chrysler Corporation)*

TEST VOLTMETER

TEST AMMETER

JUMPER WIRE TO GROUND

GREEN WIRE

ELECTRONIC VOLTAGE REGULATOR

100-AMP ALTERNATOR ONLY

RUN
OFF   ST
ACC
ST
RUN
OFF
ACC

START AND IGNITION SWITCH

TO BLOWER MOTOR

CARBON-PILE RHEOSTAT

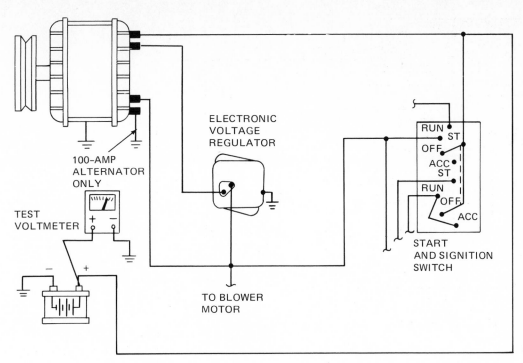

ELECTRONIC
VOLTAGE
REGULATOR

100–AMP
ALTERNATOR
ONLY

TEST
VOLTMETER

RUN
ST
OFF
ACC
ST
RUN
OFF
ACC

START
AND SIGNITION
SWITCH

TO BLOWER
MOTOR

Fig. 10-6 Voltage regulator operating-voltage test (electronic regulator). *(Chrysler Corporation)*

and accessories off. Voltmeter should read within the limits specified by the manufacturer. The voltage will go up as the temperature goes down. This is a built-in temperature compensation that helps to overcome the increasing battery resistance to charge as its temperature goes down. At low temperatures, a higher charging voltage is required. Note the following specifications for Chrysler voltage regulators.

Temperature near regulator	Voltage range
−20°F [−28.9°C]	14.9–15.9 volts
80°F [26.7°C]	13.9–14.6 volts
140°F [60.0°C]	13.3–13.9 volts
Above 140°F [60.0°C]	Less than 13.6 volts

If the regulator does not perform according to specifications, replace it.

NOTE: If the shop has the special tester designed to check Chrysler voltage regulators, follow the instructions in the operating manual for the tester. This tester is similar to the one Ford supplies for testing its charging systems. However, the testers are not necessarily interchangeable.

⚙ 10-6 Ford regulator service In ⚙ 8-15 we explained that Ford, in recent years, has used three different regulators: electromechanical, transistorized, and full solid-state or electronic. Prior to 1974, a Model ARE 27-38 tester was recommended for testing the charging system, regulator, and alternator. However, this tester must not be used on 1974 or later cars; it can damage the electronic ignition system and any other electronic device in the car. Instead, the charging systems in late-model cars can be tested with a voltmeter and ohmmeter.

⚙ 10-7 Ford regulator test with voltmeter and ohmmeter Here are the Ford shop manual instructions on how to test the charging system with a 0- to 20-volt voltmeter, an ohmmeter, a jumper wire, and a 12-volt test light. Before starting the charging-system tests, note the complaint. Refer to the diagnosis and testing charts (Figs. 9-4 and 10-7). The type of complaint will give you clues as to what needs to be checked out. As a first step in any testing procedure, give the system a visual inspection:

1. Visual inspection

1. Check the fuse link (Figs. 8-39 to 8-41). If it is burned out, determine the cause and correct it before proceeding. Replace fuse link.
2. Battery must be in a charged condition and have a specific gravity of at least 1.200. If not, replace it for the test. Check battery posts and cables. Clean them and tighten clamps (see ⚙ 4-7).
3. Check wiring and connections between alternator, regulator, and battery.
4. Check alternator belt tension (Fig. 9-1) and adjust it if necessary.

2. Battery drain test If the battery will not stay charged, there may be a slow drain (slow discharge) on it. Check this out as follows: Connect a 12-volt test light in series with the positive (ground) terminal of the battery. If the light glows, pull fuses, one at a time, to find out which circuit is causing the short or ground. When you locate the circuit, repair the wiring harness or components of the circuit.

3. Indicator-light test If the indicator light does not come on when the ignition key is turned to ON with the engine not running, the probable cause of trouble is this: There is an open circuit between the ignition

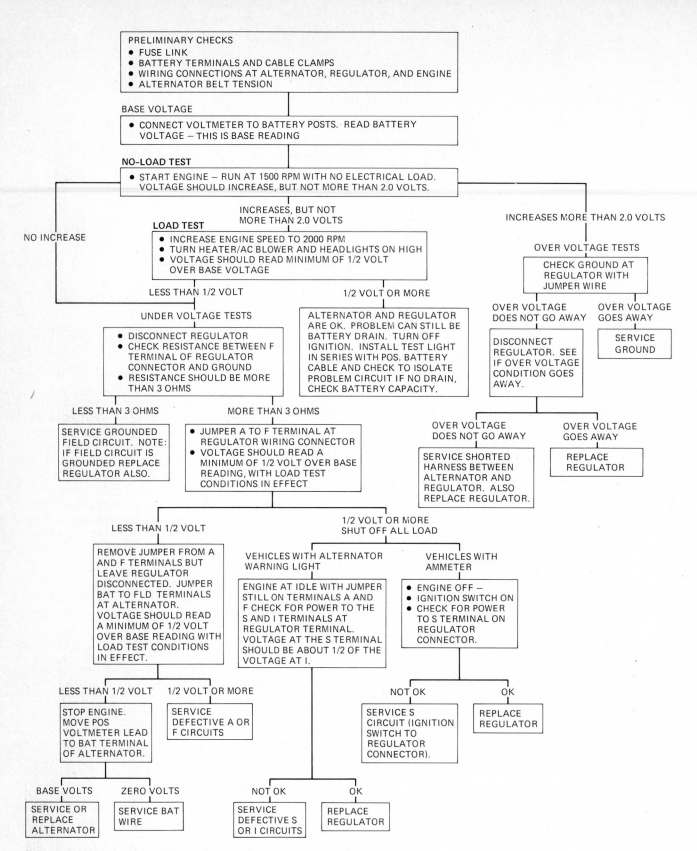

PRELIMINARY CHECKS
- FUSE LINK
- BATTERY TERMINALS AND CABLE CLAMPS
- WIRING CONNECTIONS AT ALTERNATOR, REGULATOR, AND ENGINE
- ALTERNATOR BELT TENSION

BASE VOLTAGE
- CONNECT VOLTMETER TO BATTERY POSTS. READ BATTERY VOLTAGE — THIS IS BASE READING

NO-LOAD TEST
- START ENGINE — RUN AT 1500 RPM WITH NO ELECTRICAL LOAD. VOLTAGE SHOULD INCREASE, BUT NOT MORE THAN 2.0 VOLTS.

NO INCREASE

INCREASES, BUT NOT MORE THAN 2.0 VOLTS

INCREASES MORE THAN 2.0 VOLTS

LOAD TEST
- INCREASE ENGINE SPEED TO 2000 RPM
- TURN HEATER/AC BLOWER AND HEADLIGHTS ON HIGH
- VOLTAGE SHOULD READ MINIMUM OF 1/2 VOLT OVER BASE VOLTAGE

OVER VOLTAGE TESTS

CHECK GROUND AT REGULATOR WITH JUMPER WIRE

LESS THAN 1/2 VOLT

1/2 VOLT OR MORE

OVER VOLTAGE DOES NOT GO AWAY

OVER VOLTAGE GOES AWAY

UNDER VOLTAGE TESTS
- DISCONNECT REGULATOR
- CHECK RESISTANCE BETWEEN F TERMINAL OF REGULATOR CONNECTOR AND GROUND
- RESISTANCE SHOULD BE MORE THAN 3 OHMS

ALTERNATOR AND REGULATOR ARE OK. PROBLEM CAN STILL BE BATTERY DRAIN. TURN OFF IGNITION. INSTALL TEST LIGHT IN SERIES WITH POS. BATTERY CABLE AND CHECK TO ISOLATE PROBLEM CIRCUIT IF NO DRAIN, CHECK BATTERY CAPACITY.

DISCONNECT REGULATOR. SEE IF OVER VOLTAGE CONDITION GOES AWAY.

SERVICE GROUND

LESS THAN 3 OHMS

MORE THAN 3 OHMS

OVER VOLTAGE DOES NOT GO AWAY

OVER VOLTAGE GOES AWAY

SERVICE GROUNDED FIELD CIRCUIT. NOTE: IF FIELD CIRCUIT IS GROUNDED REPLACE REGULATOR ALSO.

- JUMPER A TO F TERMINAL AT REGULATOR WIRING CONNECTOR
- VOLTAGE SHOULD READ A MINIMUM OF 1/2 VOLT OVER BASE READING, WITH LOAD TEST CONDITIONS IN EFFECT

SERVICE SHORTED HARNESS BETWEEN ALTERNATOR AND REGULATOR. ALSO REPLACE REGULATOR.

REPLACE REGULATOR

LESS THAN 1/2 VOLT

1/2 VOLT OR MORE SHUT OFF ALL LOAD

REMOVE JUMPER FROM A AND F TERMINALS BUT LEAVE REGULATOR DISCONNECTED. JUMPER BAT TO FLD TERMINALS AT ALTERNATOR. VOLTAGE SHOULD READ A MINIMUM OF 1/2 VOLT OVER BASE READING WITH LOAD TEST CONDITIONS IN EFFECT.

VEHICLES WITH ALTERNATOR WARNING LIGHT

ENGINE AT IDLE WITH JUMPER STILL ON TERMINALS A AND F CHECK FOR POWER TO THE S AND I TERMINALS AT REGULATOR TERMINAL. VOLTAGE AT THE S TERMINAL SHOULD BE ABOUT 1/2 OF THE VOLTAGE AT I.

VEHICLES WITH AMMETER

- ENGINE OFF —
- IGNITION SWITCH ON
- CHECK FOR POWER TO S TERMINAL ON REGULATOR CONNECTOR.

LESS THAN 1/2 VOLT

1/2 VOLT OR MORE

NOT OK

OK

STOP ENGINE. MOVE POS VOLTMETER LEAD TO BAT TERMINAL OF ALTERNATOR.

SERVICE DEFECTIVE A OR F CIRCUITS

SERVICE S CIRCUIT (IGNITION SWITCH TO REGULATOR CONNECTOR).

REPLACE REGULATOR

BASE VOLTS

ZERO VOLTS

NOT OK

OK

SERVICE OR REPLACE ALTERNATOR

SERVICE BAT WIRE

SERVICE DEFECTIVE S OR I CIRCUITS

REPLACE REGULATOR

Fig. 10-7 Chart of general charging-system tests. *(Ford Motor Company)*

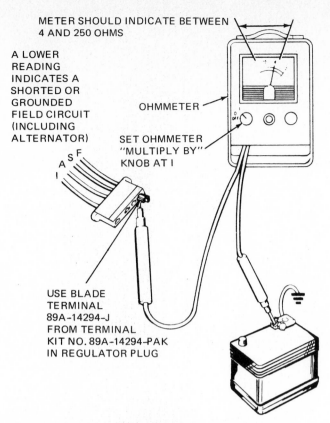

METER SHOULD INDICATE BETWEEN
4 AND 250 OHMS

A LOWER
READING
INDICATES A
SHORTED OR
GROUNDED
FIELD CIRCUIT
(INCLUDING
ALTERNATOR)

OHMMETER

SET OHMMETER
"MULTIPLY BY"
KNOB AT I

A S F
I

USE BLADE
TERMINAL
89A–14294–J
FROM TERMINAL
KIT NO. 89A–14294–PAK
IN REGULATOR PLUG

Fig. 10-8 Field circuit test. *(Ford Motor Company)*

switch and the regulator, or else a burned out indicator light. See also Figs. 9-5 and 9-6 which are indicator-light diagnosis charts for other manufacturers. These charts may give you some clues to the trouble.

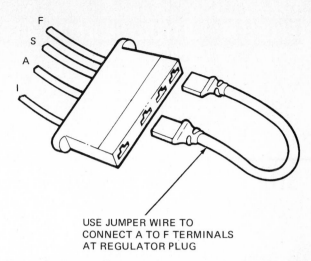

F
S
A
I

USE JUMPER WIRE TO
CONNECT A TO F TERMINALS
AT REGULATOR PLUG

Fig. 10-9 Connections for regulator plug–jumper wire. *(Ford Motor Company)*

4. Charging-system tests To make a complete test of the charging system, refer to the charging-system test chart (Fig. 10-7). It provides step-by-step procedures for checking the system with no-load and load tests. It tells you what to do if the part of the system being checked does not come up to specifications. Note Figures 10-8 to 10-10 which illustrate key steps in making connections to perform the tests. Figure 10-8 shows the procedure of checking the resistance between the F terminal of the regulator and ground. Figure 10-9 shows how to use a jumper wire to connect between the A and F terminals to isolate the trouble between the regulator or wiring and the alternator. Figure 10-10 shows jumper-wire connections between the BAT and

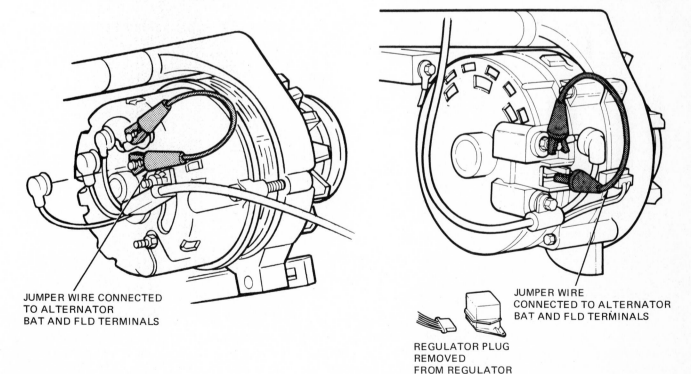

JUMPER WIRE CONNECTED
TO ALTERNATOR
BAT AND FLD TERMINALS

JUMPER WIRE
CONNECTED TO ALTERNATOR
BAT AND FLD TERMINALS

REGULATOR PLUG
REMOVED
FROM REGULATOR

Fig. 10-10 Jumper-wire connections on alternator. *(Ford Motor Company)*

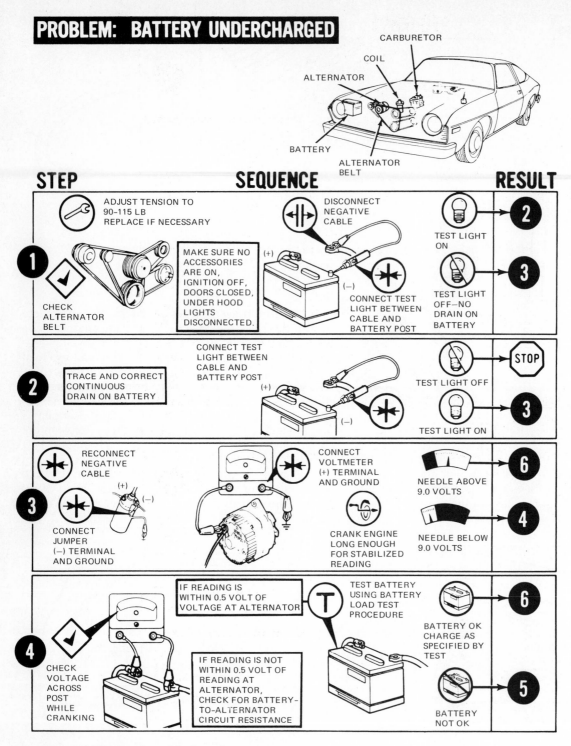

PROBLEM: BATTERY UNDERCHARGED

CARBURETOR

COIL

ALTERNATOR

BATTERY

ALTERNATOR BELT

STEP | SEQUENCE | RESULT

1 CHECK ALTERNATOR BELT

ADJUST TENSION TO 90-115 LB REPLACE IF NECESSARY

MAKE SURE NO ACCESSORIES ARE ON, IGNITION OFF, DOORS CLOSED, UNDER HOOD LIGHTS DISCONNECTED.

DISCONNECT NEGATIVE CABLE

CONNECT TEST LIGHT BETWEEN CABLE AND BATTERY POST

(+) (−)

TEST LIGHT ON → **2**

TEST LIGHT OFF—NO DRAIN ON BATTERY → **3**

2 TRACE AND CORRECT CONTINUOUS DRAIN ON BATTERY

CONNECT TEST LIGHT BETWEEN CABLE AND BATTERY POST

(+) (−)

TEST LIGHT OFF → STOP

TEST LIGHT ON → **3**

3 RECONNECT NEGATIVE CABLE

CONNECT JUMPER (−) TERMINAL AND GROUND

(+) (−)

CONNECT VOLTMETER (+) TERMINAL AND GROUND

CRANK ENGINE LONG ENOUGH FOR STABILIZED READING

NEEDLE ABOVE 9.0 VOLTS → **6**

NEEDLE BELOW 9.0 VOLTS → **4**

4 CHECK VOLTAGE ACROSS POST WHILE CRANKING

IF READING IS WITHIN 0.5 VOLT OF VOLTAGE AT ALTERNATOR

IF READING IS NOT WITHIN 0.5 VOLT OF READING AT ALTERNATOR, CHECK FOR BATTERY-TO-ALTERNATOR CIRCUIT RESISTANCE

TEST BATTERY USING BATTERY LOAD TEST PROCEDURE

BATTERY OK CHARGE AS SPECIFIED BY TEST → **6**

BATTERY NOT OK → **5**

Fig. 10-11 DARS chart for analysis and correction of charging-system troubles. *(American Motors Corporation)*

FLD terminals of the alternator to determine whether the trouble is in the alternator.

✿ 10-8 Delco-Remy alternator-regulator tests
Delco-Remy has produced a great variety of regulators and alternators, as described in previous chapters. For information on how to service the earlier, nonelectronic regulators and alternators, refer to older shop manuals

covering these older models. In this book, we concentrate on the modern electronic regulator and alternator. This type of alternator has the regulator built in. Figure 9-6 is a DARS chart covering the checking of an indicator light that is not working right. Figure 10-11 is a DARS chart covering, step-by-step, the procedures to follow if the battery is undercharged or overcharged. A careful study of this chart will explain to you the

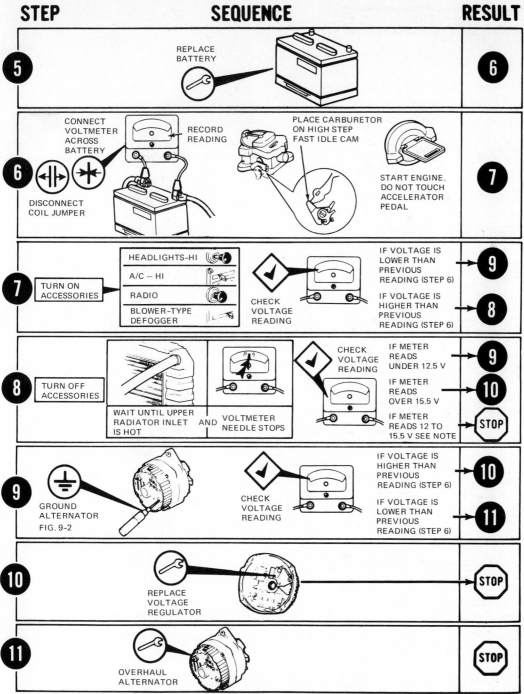

STEP	SEQUENCE	RESULT
5	REPLACE BATTERY	**6**
6	CONNECT VOLTMETER ACROSS BATTERY — RECORD READING — DISCONNECT COIL JUMPER — PLACE CARBURETOR ON HIGH STEP FAST IDLE CAM — START ENGINE. DO NOT TOUCH ACCELERATOR PEDAL	**7**
7	TURN ON ACCESSORIES — HEADLIGHTS–HI / A/C – HI / RADIO / BLOWER–TYPE DEFOGGER — CHECK VOLTAGE READING	IF VOLTAGE IS LOWER THAN PREVIOUS READING (STEP 6) → **9** / IF VOLTAGE IS HIGHER THAN PREVIOUS READING (STEP 6) → **8**
8	TURN OFF ACCESSORIES — WAIT UNTIL UPPER RADIATOR INLET IS HOT AND VOLTMETER NEEDLE STOPS — CHECK VOLTAGE READING	IF METER READS UNDER 12.5 V → **9** / IF METER READS OVER 15.5 V → **10** / IF METER READS 12 TO 15.5 V SEE NOTE → STOP
9	GROUND ALTERNATOR FIG. 9-2 — CHECK VOLTAGE READING	IF VOLTAGE IS HIGHER THAN PREVIOUS READING (STEP 6) → **10** / IF VOLTAGE IS LOWER THAN PREVIOUS READING (STEP 6) → **11**
10	REPLACE VOLTAGE REGULATOR	STOP
11	OVERHAUL ALTERNATOR	STOP

NOTE: IF NOTHING HAS BEEN FOUND, EXPLAIN TO OWNER THAT EXCESSIVE IDLING, AND SLOW OR SHORT DISTANCE DRIVING WITH ALL ACCESSORIES ON, MAY CAUSE HEAVY DRAIN ON BATTERY—RESULTING IN UNDERCHARGED CONDITION

Fig. 10-11 (Continued)

various steps to follow when you have to check out either of these two conditions.

Figure 10-12 shows a diagnostic tester developed by Delco-Remy to test their alternators with built-in voltage regulators. It is accurate and simple to use. You plug it in to the alternator as shown, and connect the ground lead-clip. Then you follow the instructions printed on the tester. With the engine off and then running at fast idle, note whether or not the light is on. This shows whether the alternator is operating properly or not.

⚙ **10-9 Test stand for alternators** Shops that rebuild alternators may have test stands, such as shown in Fig. 10-13. Alternators, as they come into the shop, can be installed on the stand and checked for output,

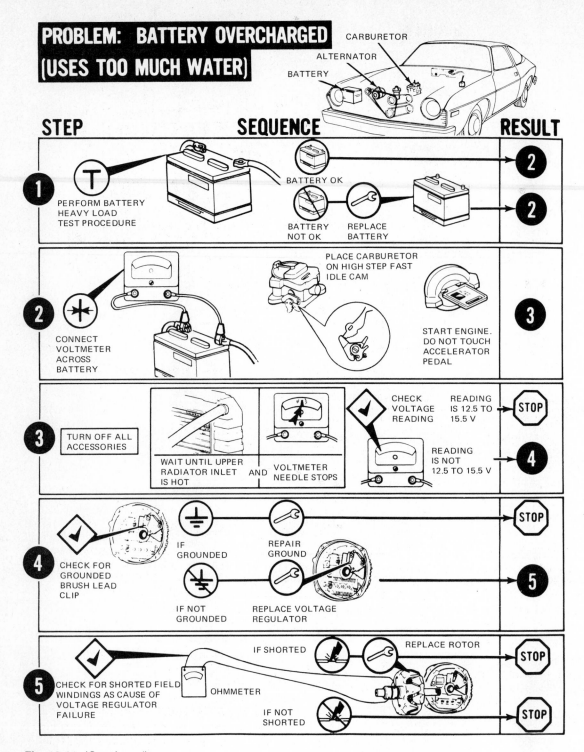

PROBLEM: BATTERY OVERCHARGED (USES TOO MUCH WATER)

CARBURETOR
ALTERNATOR
BATTERY

STEP   **SEQUENCE**   **RESULT**

1 — PERFORM BATTERY HEAVY LOAD TEST PROCEDURE

BATTERY OK → **2**

BATTERY NOT OK — REPLACE BATTERY → **2**

2 — CONNECT VOLTMETER ACROSS BATTERY

PLACE CARBURETOR ON HIGH STEP FAST IDLE CAM

START ENGINE. DO NOT TOUCH ACCELERATOR PEDAL → **3**

3 — TURN OFF ALL ACCESSORIES

WAIT UNTIL UPPER RADIATOR INLET IS HOT AND VOLTMETER NEEDLE STOPS

CHECK VOLTAGE READING — READING IS 12.5 TO 15.5 V → **STOP**

READING IS NOT 12.5 TO 15.5 V → **4**

4 — CHECK FOR GROUNDED BRUSH LEAD CLIP

IF GROUNDED — REPAIR GROUND → **STOP**

IF NOT GROUNDED — REPLACE VOLTAGE REGULATOR → **5**

5 — CHECK FOR SHORTED FIELD WINDINGS AS CAUSE OF VOLTAGE REGULATOR FAILURE

OHMMETER

IF SHORTED — REPLACE ROTOR → **STOP**

IF NOT SHORTED → **STOP**

Fig. 10-11 *(Continued)*

voltage, and internal conditions before any disassembly or repair operations are started. This pinpoints troubles and results in faster and more accurate repair and re- building of alternators. After rebuilding, the alternators can be rechecked on the test stand to make sure they operate properly.

Fig. 10-12 Special diagnostic alternator tester used to test the alternator with built-in voltage regulator. *(Kent-Moore)*

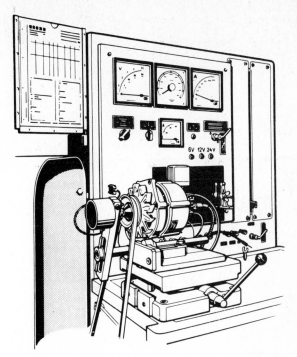

Fig. 10-13 Test stand for testing detached alternators. *(Robert Bosch GmbH)*

Chapter 10 review questions

Select the *one* correct, best, or most probable answer to each question. Then check your answers against the correct answers given at the end of the book.

1. Before you make or break connections in the electric circuit, you should:
   a. first disconnect the battery ground cable,
   b. first disconnect the battery insulated cable,
   c. be sure the ignition switch is turned off,
   d. be sure the engine is warmed up.

2. Voltage regulators are temperature compensated, which means that:
   a. the voltage goes up as temperature goes up,
   b. voltage goes down as the temperature goes up,
   c. voltage changes with load conditions,
   d. voltage remains constant when temperature changes.

3. The two major tests shown in the Ford charging-system test chart are:
   a. no-load test and load test,
   b. charging and discharging,
   c. current and voltage,
   d. idling and full power.

4. The DARS chart covers two basic problems:
   a. current and voltage readings,
   b. indicator light and circuit resistance,
   c. hard starting and stalling,
   d. battery undercharged and battery overcharged.

5. The sequence in the "battery overcharged" problem in the DARS chart determines whether the trouble is in the:
   a. battery or regulator,
   b. regulator or alternator,
   c. belt or indicator light,
   d. wiring or regulator.

ALTERNATOR SERVICE

After studying this chapter, you should be able to:

1. Test alternator performance
2. Disassemble, repair, and reassemble alternators
3. Identify parts of a disassembled alternator and explain their functions

11-1 Alternator checks This chapter discusses the checking and servicing of alternators. Chapter 9 described the best ways to diagnose charging-system troubles. The dos and don'ts listed in ✸ 9-2 are extremely important and should be reviewed. There are only three parts to check if an alternator fails to produce any output: the stator, the rotor windings and circuit, and the diodes and output circuit. Checking of alternator output was described in Chapter 10. A test stand for checking alternators is shown in Fig. 10-13. Checking alternator components and servicing procedures are detailed in following sections for the three major alternators in use today.

NOTE: Removing and installing regulators and alternators is described in ✸ 10-2. The parts that are most often replaced in alternators are the brushes, bearings, and diodes. Wear or damage to these parts is what you will most likely find as you service alternators.

✸ 11-2 Chrysler Corporation alternator service If the checks outlined in Chapters 9 and 10 point to alternator trouble, the alternator should be removed (✸ 10-2) for further checks and service. Figures 11-1 to 11-3 show an alternator of the type we discuss now.

CAREFUL: Always disconnect the battery ground strap from the battery terminal before disconnecting the leads from the alternator.

1. **Bench tests** Rotor field-coil draw, field-circuit ground check, and diode checks are three tests to be made with the alternator on the test bench.

a. Field-coil (rotor) draw Connect one terminal of a fully charged battery to one field terminal. Connect the other terminal of the battery to an ammeter. Connect the second terminal of the ammeter to the other field terminal. The rotor battery and the ammeter are now connected in series. Slowly turn the rotor by hand. The field coil should draw 4.5 to 6.5 amperes (for late-model units). A low current indicates high resistance in the field circuit. This could be due to poor brush seating, dirty or worn slip rings, or bad connections in the field coils. Excessive current draw indicates a shorted field coil.

b. Testing for grounds Use a test light and check with test prods from one field terminal to the end shield (end frame). Then switch the prod to the other field terminal, keeping the other prod on the end shield. If the light goes on, it indicates a ground.

NOTE: Earlier alternators had one of the brushes grounded. With this type, remove the grounded brush before making the test.

Check further by removing the brushes (Fig. 11-2). This is done by removing the brush screws and insulating washers, and lifting the brush assemblies from the end shield. Then remove the through bolts and pry between the stator and drive-end shield with the blade of a screwdriver (Fig. 11-3). Carefully separate the rectifier (diode) end shield and stator assembly from the pulley and rotor assembly with drive-end shield.

Use a self-powered test lamp to check between the two brush rings on the rotor. The light should come on. If it does not, the field is open. Test from one ring and then the other ring to the end of the rotor shaft. If the light comes on, the field coil is grounded. Discard an open or grounded rotor.

c. Testing diodes with C-3829 tester If the special Chrysler C-3829 tester is available, the diodes can be quickly and easily checked. Lay the end shield on an insulated surface.

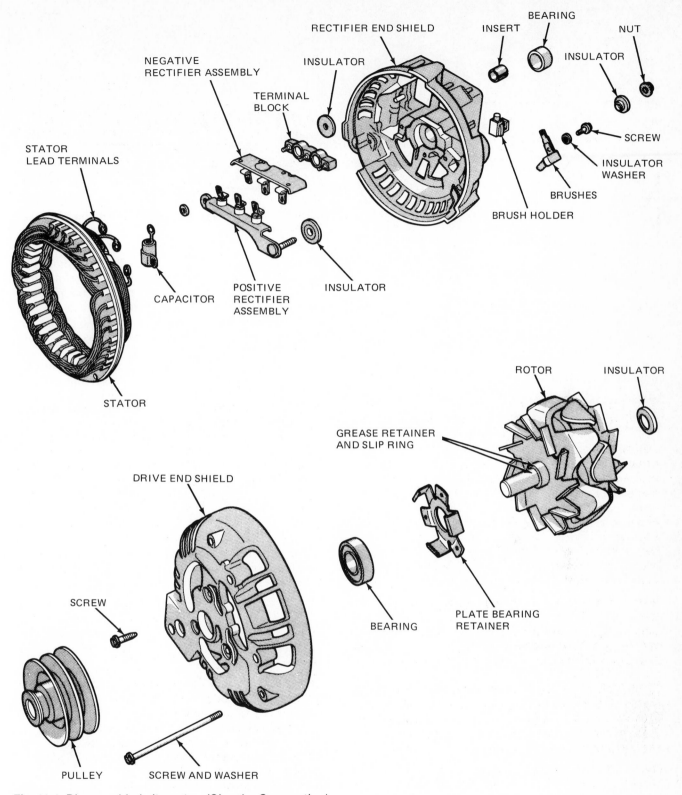

Fig. 11-1 Disassembled alternator. *(Chrysler Corporation)*

Positive diode test. Connect the test-lead clip to the alternator output (BAT) terminal. Touch the metal strap of each diode (Fig. 11-4) with the probe. Meter readings should be 1¾ amperes or more. Readings should be about the same for all diodes. Also, the needle should move in the same direction for each diode. If one diode is shorted and the other two are good, the good diodes will read low and the shorted diode will read zero. If one diode is open, it will read about one ampere and the two good diodes will read okay.

Negative diode test. Connect the test-lead clip to the end shield. Touch the metal strap of each diode with

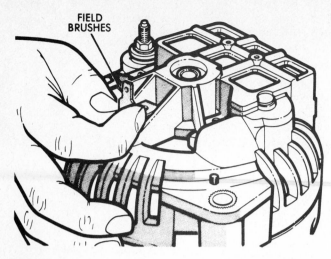

Fig. 11-2 Removing brushes from the alternator. *(Chrysler Corporation)*

the probe (Fig. 11-5). The test results are the same as for the positive diode test except that the meter will read in the opposite direction. If a negative diode shows shorted, isolate the stator from the rectifier end shield (see Fig. 11-6) and retest it. The bad reading could come from a grounded stator winding.

CAREFUL: Do not break the plastic cases of the rectifiers. The cases protect the diodes against corrosion. Always touch the metal strap close to the diode.

d. Testing diodes with test light If the C-3829 tester is not available, the diodes can be checked with a test light and battery. Note that the procedure is different for the earlier alternator and the later model used with the electronic voltage regulator. In the earlier model, the stator leads at the Y connections must be cut as

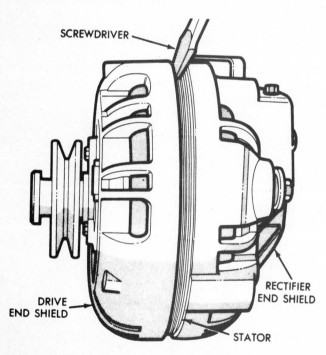

Fig. 11-3 Separating the drive-end shield from the stator. *(Chrysler Corporation)*

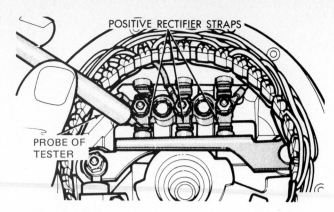

Fig. 11-4 Testing positive diodes with special tester. *(Chrysler Corporation)*

close to the Y as possible. This isolates the diodes so each is tested separately. The diodes can be isolated in the later model by removing the nuts on the terminal block attaching the stator windings and the positive and negative rectifier straps (see Fig. 11-6). Then lift the stator winding terminals and stator assembly from the end shield.

With the diodes isolated, check each first in one direction and then in the other by reversing the test probes (see Figs. 11-7 and 11-8). The light should go on in one direction but not in the other. If it lights in both directions, the diode is shorted. If it does not light in either direction, the diode is open. Replacement of diodes is explained in a following paragraph.

e. Testing stator Use a low-voltage test light, as shown in Fig. 11-9, and a 12-volt battery. Touch one probe to a pin in the frame, making sure that you touch bare metal and not varnish. Touch the other probe to each of the three stator leads in turn.

NOTE: On the earlier alternator, use a soldering gun to unsolder the diode leads. Do not blow off the melted solder with air. Particles could get into the diodes and short them out.

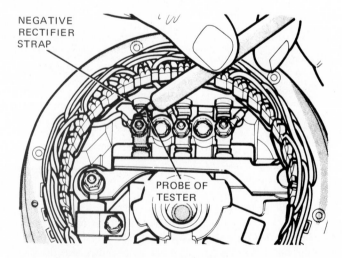

Fig. 11-5 Testing negative diodes with special tester. *(Chrysler Corporation)*

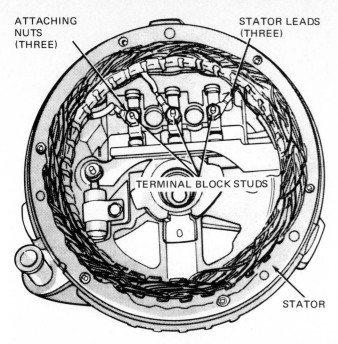

Fig. 11-6 Rectifier end shield and stator assembly. (Chrysler Corporation)

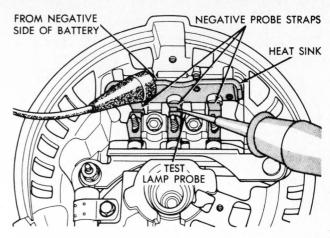

Fig. 11-8 Testing negative diodes with test light and battery. (Chrysler Corporation)

If the light goes on, the stator winding is grounded, and the stator assembly should be replaced.

Next, test for continuity by putting one test probe on one stator lead and the other to the Y connection. The light should go on. Try all three stator windings. If the light fails to go on, the winding is open and the stator should be replaced.

f. *Replacing diodes* In the earlier alternator, the diodes could be replaced individually with a special tool to push the defective diode out and the new diode in. Use care in resoldering the connection so you do not overheat the diode and ruin it. Use rosin-core solder.

On the late-model alternator, the two heat sinks, holding three diodes each, are removed as assemblies. New diode heat sinks are supplied as service items. Figures 11-10 to 11-12 show various steps in removing the heat sinks and the capacitor. The capacitor, shown

in Figs. 11-10 and 11-11, does not enter into the alternator or regulator action. Its function is to reduce radio noise by suppressing the high-frequency voltage surges from the stator.

2. **Alternator disassembly and reassembly** We have already described most of the steps required to disassemble the alternator. Additional steps include removing the pulley and bearings and replacing the old rotor slip rings with new ones, but this is seldom done.

a. *Disassembly* Further disassembly steps, after the rectifier end shield has been removed (Fig. 11-3), follow:

Remove the pulley with a puller (Fig. 11-13). Pry the drive-end-bearing spring retainer from the end shield with a screwdriver (Fig. 11-14). Support the end shield and tap the rotor shaft with a plastic hammer to remove the rotor. The drive-end bearing must be removed, if it is defective, with a puller.

The output terminal, capacitor, heat-sink insulator, and heat sink are held in place by the terminal nuts and washers. Remove these nuts to separate the parts.

If the needle bearing in the rectifier-end shield requires replacement, support the shield and press the bearing out with special tools.

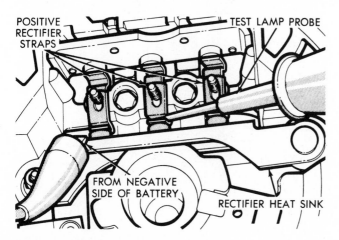

Fig. 11-7 Testing positive diodes with low-voltage test light and battery. (Chrysler Corporation)

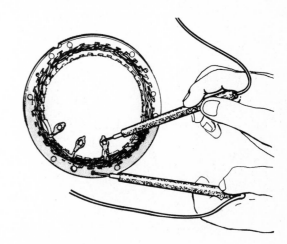

Fig. 11-9 Testing stator with low-voltage test light. (Chrysler Corporation)

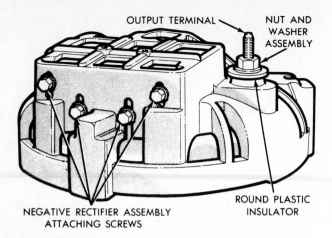

Fig. 11-10 Negative rectifier and heat-sink assembly attaching screws. *(Chrysler Corporation)*

b. Inspecting parts Electrical tests have already been covered. Inspect the parts for damage and wear. Worn bearings should be discarded. Check for burned insulation, poor soldering at connections, and cracked or damaged housings. Replace all damaged parts.

CAREFUL: Never clean the rotor, stator, bearings, or rectifier parts with solvent. This could damage them. Instead, wipe them with a clean cloth.

c. Slip rings Some years ago, Chrysler shop manuals carried instructions for replacing slip rings if they are too badly worn to clean up. Today, the shop manuals no longer carry this information. If the slip rings are slightly worn or pitted, they can be cleaned up with 400-grain polishing cloth held against the rings while the rotor is spun. Do not clean the rings with the rotor stationary. This can cause flat spots. If the rings are excessively worn, the rotor should be discarded.

d. Checking rotor (field windings) Test for ground with a low-voltage test light. Place one prod against a slip ring and the other against the rotor pole piece. If the light goes on, the rotor is grounded and must be discarded. Test the rotor for complete circuit by putting prods on the two rings. The light should go on. If it does not, the circuit is open. Check for broken leads. If the open is not evident and repairable, replace the rotor assembly.

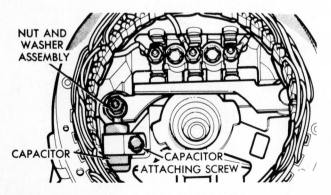

Fig. 11-11 Capacitor attaching nut and screw. *(Chrysler Corporation)*

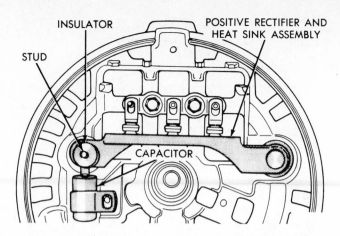

Fig. 11-12 With capacitor attaching nut and screw removed, the capacitor and positive diode and heat-sink assembly can be removed. *(Chrysler Corporation)*

e. Reassembly On reassembly, use bearing tools to install new bearings if required. After the drive-end shield—with bearing-spring retainer and bearing—has been installed on the rotor, press the pulley onto the rotor shaft. Support the lower end of the rotor shaft on the press table so pressure is applied to the shaft through the pulley and not through the end shield.

Install the heat-sink insulator, capacitor, and terminal screw with insulating washer, lock washers, and nuts. Put the stator and rectifier-end shield into place on the rotor and drive-end shield, pushing the rotor

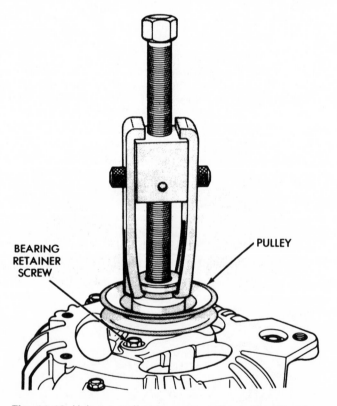

Fig. 11-13 Using a puller to remove the pulley. Turning the screw pulls the pulley off the shaft. *(Chrysler Corporation)*

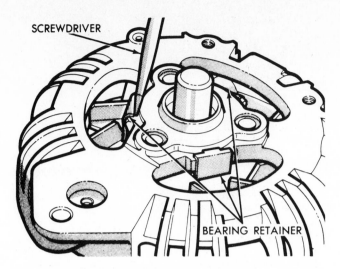

Fig. 11-14 Disengaging the bearing retainer from the end shield. *(Chrysler Corporation)*

shaft through the rectifier-end-shield bearing. Put the through bolts, washers, and nuts into place and tighten them evenly to the specified torque.

Install the insulated brush in the end shield, and put the bronze terminal on the plastic holder with the tab of the terminal in the holder recess. Put the nylon washer on the terminal and install the lock washer and attaching screw. Install the ground brush and the attaching screw.

Rotate the pulley slowly by hand to make sure the rotor poles do not hit the diodes, capacitor leads, or stator connections.

Install the alternator on the car, and connect the leads and ground wire. Reconnect the battery ground cable, start the engine, and check the alternator output as already described (✿ 10-5).

✿ 11-3 Ford alternator service
If the checks described in Chapters 9 and 10 indicate alternator trouble, the alternator should be removed for further checking.

NOTE: Always disconnect the battery ground strap from the battery before disconnecting the leads from the alternator.

1. Alternator disassembly Figure 11-15 is a disassembled view of the alternator discussed herein. Ford also supplies higher-output alternators. The alternator shown in Fig. 11-15 is disassembled as follows:

1. Mark both end housings with scribe marks so they can be properly realigned on reassembly. Remove the three through bolts. Then separate the front-end housing and rotor from the stator and rear-end housing.
2. Remove nuts and washers from the rear-end housing and separate the housing from the stator and rectifier assembly.
3. Remove brush-holder mounting screws and take off the holder, brushes, springs, insulator, and terminal.
4. If the bearing requires replacement, support the housing on the inner boss to press it out.
5. If the rectifier assembly is being replaced or the stator is being tested, unsolder the stator leads, using a small (100-watt) soldering gun. Avoid excessive heat.
6. If the rectifier has exposed diodes, remove the screws from the rectifier by rotating the bolt heads one-quarter turn clockwise to unlock them and then removing the screws (Fig. 11-16). On the type with built-in diodes, push the screws out.
7. Remove the drive pulley nut, lock washer, pulley, fan, spacer, rotor, and rotor stop (Fig. 11-17).
8. If the old front bearing is defective, remove the three screws that hold the retainer and remove the re-

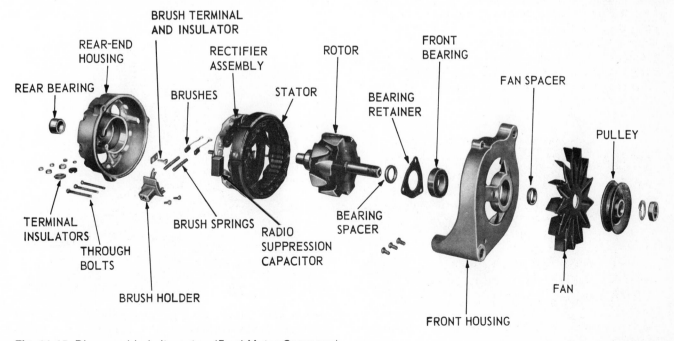

Fig. 11-15 Disassembled alternator. *(Ford Motor Company)*

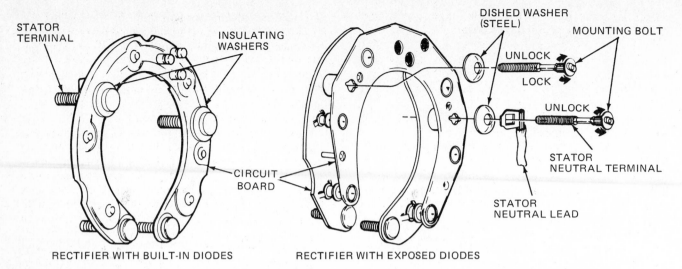

INSULATING WASHERS

DISHED WASHER (STEEL)

MOUNTING BOLT

UNLOCK

LOCK

UNLOCK

STATOR NEUTRAL TERMINAL

CIRCUIT BOARD

STATOR NEUTRAL LEAD

RECTIFIER WITH BUILT-IN DIODES

RECTIFIER WITH EXPOSED DIODES

Fig. 11-16 Rectifier assemblies. *(Ford Motor Company)*

tainer. Then support the housing near the boss and press the bearing out.

2. **Cleaning and inspecting parts** Never use solvent to clean the rotor, stator, bearings, and rectifier assembly. This could ruin them. Instead, wipe the parts with a clean cloth. Check bearings for wear or loss of lubricant, either of which would require bearing replacement.

Check rear of rotor shaft for roughness or chatter marks. These indicate slippage in the bearing, which would call for rotor replacement.

Replace the pulley if it is out of round or bent.

If the slip rings are rough or pitted, they can be turned down. But do not turn them down below 1.220 inch [31mm]. These slip rings are not replaceable. If they are damaged, the rotor must be replaced.

Check for stripped threads, poor soldered connections, burned insulation, and cracked housings. Replace defective parts. Resolder poor connections. Avoid excessive heat on diodes.

3. **Electrical checks** Both before and after the alternator is disassembled, the various components—diodes, rotor, and stator—should be electrically checked, as follows:

a. Rectifier-short or ground and stator-ground test Use an ohmmeter. Set the MULTIPLY BY knob at 10, and calibrate the ohmmeter as explained inside the instrument cover. Touch the probes to the BAT (battery) and STA (stator) terminals as shown in Fig. 11-18. Then reverse the probes and repeat the test. The ohmmeter should read about 60 ohms in one direction and infinity (no needle movement) in the other. A reading in both

SPECIAL TOOL

Fig. 11-17 Removing the pulley. *(Ford Motor Company)*

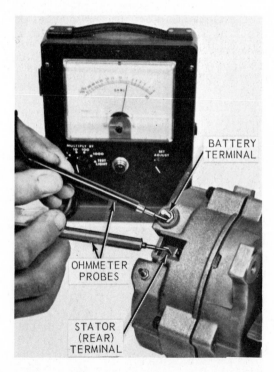

BATTERY TERMINAL

OHMMETER PROBES

STATOR (REAR) TERMINAL

Fig. 11-18 Testing with an ohmmeter for a shorted or grounded rectifier or a grounded stator. *(Ford Motor Company)*

directions indicates a bad positive diode, a grounded diode plate, or a grounded BAT terminal.

Perform the same test on the STA and GND (ground) terminals of the alternator. A reading in both directions indicates a bad negative diode, a grounded stator winding, a grounded positive diode plate, or a grounded BAT terminal.

Very high readings on all four tests indicate an open STA terminal lead inside the alternator.

b. Field-open or short-circuit test Use the ohmmeter with MULTIPLY BY knob set at 1. Calibrate. Probe the alternator field terminal and ground terminal (Fig. 11-19). Now, spin the alternator pulley. The ohmmeter reading should be between 2.4 and 25 ohms and should fluctuate while the pulley is turning. No needle movement indicates an open brush lead, worn or stuck brushes, or a bad rotor assembly. A reading of less than 2.4 ohms indicates a grounded brush assembly or field terminal or a bad rotor.

NOTE: The ohm readings given above are for one model alternator. Always check the manufacturer's shop manual for the alternator you are testing to make sure you have the right specifications.

c. Diode test on bench Disassemble the alternator and remove the rectifier assembly, as explained above. Set the ohmmeter MULTIPLY BY knob at 10 and calibrate the meter. Check each diode first in one direction and then in the other (Figs. 11-20 to 11-22). Diodes should show about 60 ohms in one direction and infinity in the other. If any diode does not, replace the rectifier assembly.

d. Stator-coil-open or ground test on bench Disassemble the alternator to separate the stator assembly. Set the ohmmeter MULTIPLY BY knob at 1000. Probe from one of the stator leads to the stator laminated core. Repeat for each of the stator leads. Reading should be infinite for each (no needle movement). Do not touch the metal probes or the stator leads with your hands. This will cause an incorrect reading.

e. Open-rotor or short-circuit test on bench Disassemble the alternator to separate the rotor. Set the ohmmeter MULTIPLY BY knob at 1. Touch the two probes to the two rotor slip rings. The meter should read 2.4 to 4.9 ohms. A higher reading indicates a bad connection at the slip ring or a broken wire. A lower reading indicates a shorted winding. If the defect is not obvious or not easily repairable, discard the rotor.

Touch one probe to the rotor shaft and the other to one ring and then the other. There should be no reading. If there is, the rotor winding is grounded to the shaft. Unless the ground can be easily fixed, replace the rotor.

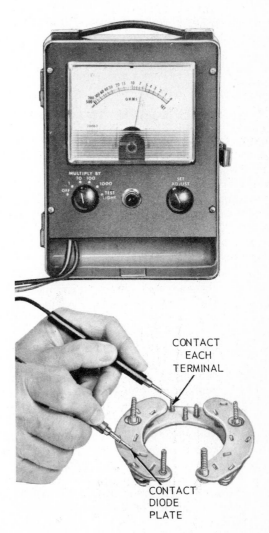

Fig. 11-20 Testing diodes in the assembly used in the rear-terminal alternator (except 60-ampere unit). *(Ford Motor Company)*

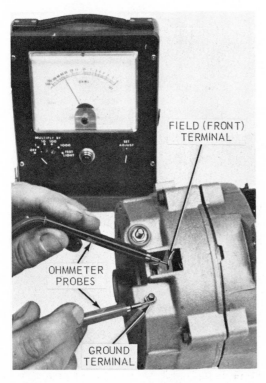

Fig. 11-19 Testing with an ohmmeter for an open or short-circuited field. *(Ford Motor Company)*

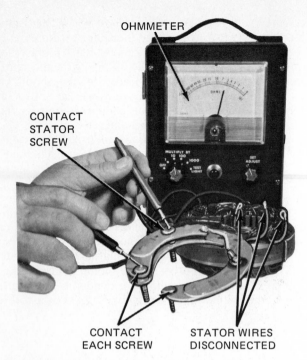

CONTACT STATOR SCREW

OHMMETER

CONTACT EACH SCREW   STATOR WIRES DISCONNECTED

Fig. 11-21 Testing diodes in the assembly used in the 60-ampere alternator. *(Ford Motor Company)*

4. Reassembly

1. Press in new bearings if the old have been removed. Support the housing at the boss.
2. If the stop ring on the rotor drive shaft is damaged, remove it. Install a new ring by pushing it onto the shaft and into the groove. Do not use snap-ring pliers, because this will damage the ring.
3. The rotor stop goes on the shaft with the recessed side against the stop ring. Put the front-end housing, fan spacer, fan, pulley, and lock washer on the shaft and install the retaining nut, tightening it to specifications (Fig. 11-17).
4. Use a piece of stiff wire, as shown in Fig. 11-23, to hold the brushes in position after placing the brushes, the springs, the terminal, and the insulator in the brush holder.
5. Install the brush-holder assembly in the rear-end housing and attach with mounting screws. Place the brush leads as shown in Fig. 11-24.
6. Wrap the three stator-winding leads around the printed-circuit-board terminals and solder them, using a low-heat (100-watt) gun and rosin-core solder. Avoid excessive heat on diodes. Position the stator neutral-lead eyelet on the stator terminal insulators (Fig. 11-25) and put the diode assembly in place as shown.
7. The molded-circuit-board rectifier with exposed diodes is attached with the mounting bolts (Fig. 11-16). Note the position of dished washers and stator neutral lead.
8. If the alternator uses a fiber circuit board built-in diodes, push the screws straight through into the holes.

CAUTION: Do not use the metal dished washers on the fiber circuit board. This will cause a short circuit.

9. Install the STA and BAT terminal insulators (Fig. 11-25). Put the stator and diode-plate assembly into the rear-end housing. Put insulators on the terminal bolts (black on STA, red on BAT, and white on FLD), and install five retaining nuts.
10. Position the rear-end housing and stator assembly over the rotor and align the scribe marks. Bring the housings together, seating the stator core in the steps in the housings. Install the through bolts. Remove the stiff wire holding the brushes (Fig. 11-23), and put a daub of waterproof cement over the hole to seal it.
11. Test the alternator for output on a test stand if available. If it tests okay, install it on the car (⚙ 10-2). Make a final check after installing the alternator by starting the engine and watching the indicator light or ammeter to see if the system is working correctly.

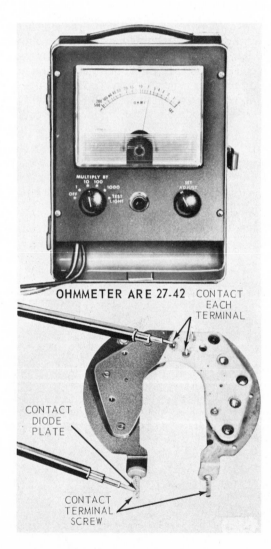

OHMMETER ARE 27-42   CONTACT EACH TERMINAL

CONTACT DIODE PLATE

CONTACT TERMINAL SCREW

Fig. 11-22 Testing diodes in the assembly used in the side-terminal alternator. *(Ford Motor Company)*

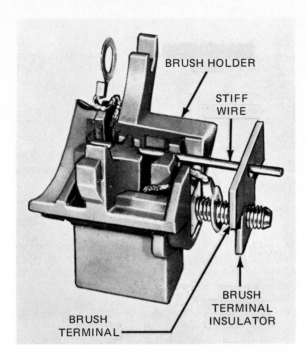

Fig. 11-23 Brush-holder assembly, showing a stiff wire being used to hold brushes in place during assembly of alternator. *(Ford Motor Company)*

✸ **11-4 General Motors (Delco-Remy) alternator service** The diodes and field may be checked with an ohmmeter as shown in Fig. 11-26. The alternator must be disconnected.

CAUTION: Always disconnect the ground strap from the battery before disconnecting alternator or regulator leads.

Tests A and B are diode tests (Fig. 11-26). Prods should be tried one way and then the other in each test. The meter should read high one way and low the other.

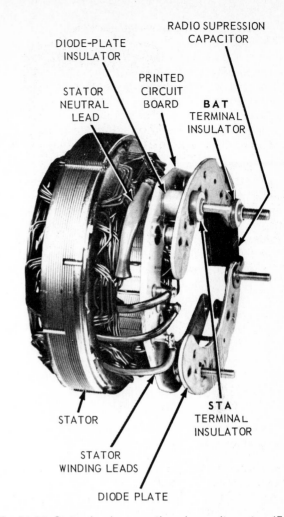

Fig. 11-25 Stator-lead connections in an alternator. *(Ford Motor Company)*

Fig. 11-24 Brush-lead positions in an alternator. *(Ford Motor Company)*

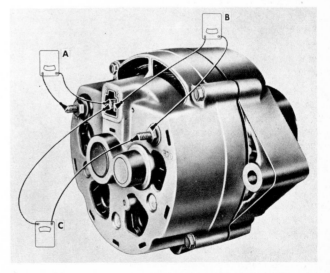

Fig. 11-26 Using an ohmmeter to check the diodes and field in an alternator. *(Delco-Remy Division of General Motors Corporation)*

If the meter reads the same in either direction (high or low), a diode is defective.

Test C is a field test for open. The meter should be connected between the field terminal and ground and should read within specifications. If it does not, the field is open or grounded.

1. Alternator disassembly If the tests in Chapters 9 and 10 or the checks above show the alternator to be defective, it must be disassembled as follows:

1. Clamp the alternator in a vise by the mounting flange and use box and allen wrenches (Fig. 11-27) to remove the pulley retaining nut. Then remove the washer, pulley, fan, and spacer from the shaft.
2. Remove four through bolts and loosen the end frames by prying at the bolt locations.
3. Remove the slip-ring end frame and stator, as an assembly, from the drive end and rotor assembly. Put a piece of electric or plastic tape (pressure-sensitive and not friction, which would leave a gummy deposit) over the slip-ring end-frame bearing to prevent dirt from entering.

NOTE: If the brushes drop onto the rotor shaft and become contaminated with bearing lubricant, they should be cleaned, prior to reinstallation, with an approved cleaner.

4. Remove the three stator-lead attaching nuts and separate the stator from the end frame.
5. Remove screws, brushes, and holder assembly.
6. Remove the heat sink from the end frame by removing BAT and GRD terminals and one attaching screw (Fig. 11-28).
7. Remove the slip-ring end bearing, if necessary, by removing the inner seal.
8. Take the rotor from the drive-end frame and take out the bearing, if necessary, by removing the retainer plate.

2. Cleaning and inspecting parts Clean all parts with a cloth, but do not wash the rotor, stator, diodes,

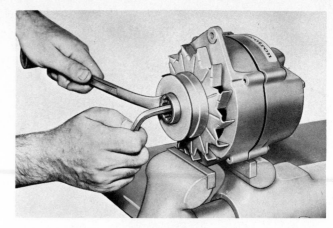

Fig. 11-27 Using box and allen wrenches to remove a pulley retaining nut. *(Delco-Remy Division of General Motors Corporation)*

or bearings in cleaning solvent. This could ruin them. If bearings are worn or rough, discard them.

Slip rings are not replaceable. If slightly worn, they may be cleaned up with 400-grain polishing cloth held against the rings while the rotor is spun in a lathe. Do not clean the rings with the rotor stationary. You will get flat spots which will cause brush noise. Rings should be true to 0.001 inch [0.0254 mm]. If excessive material must be removed or if rings are damaged, discard the rotor assembly.

If brushes are worn halfway (compare with a new brush), replace them. Make sure the brush springs have the proper tension and are not distorted. Brushes must move freely in the holders.

a. Rotor tests With an ohmmeter, check from either slip ring to the shaft and from one slip ring to the other to test for shorts or opens (Fig. 11-29). Check for grounded windings from one slip ring to the armature shaft. A grounded, open, or shorted rotor must be discarded.

b. Stator tests Connect an ohmmeter as shown in Fig.

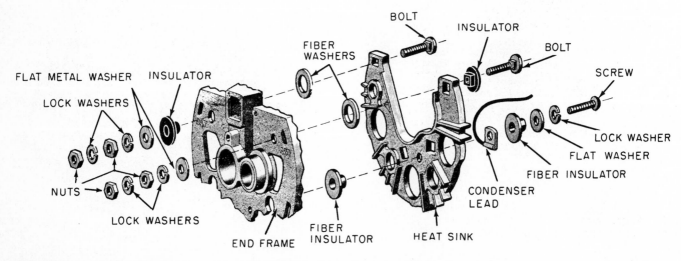

Fig. 11-28 Locations of heat-sink parts in a 5.5-inch Delcotron alternator. *(Delco-Remy Division of General Motors Corporation)*

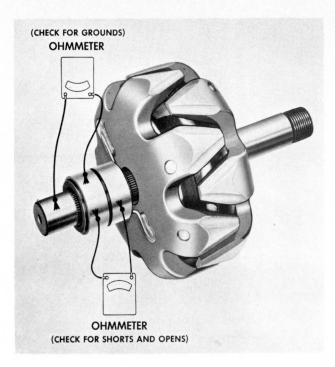

Fig. 11-29 Using an ohmmeter to check a rotor for grounds or opens. *(Chevrolet Motor Division of General Motors Corporation)*

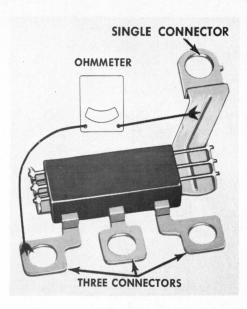

Fig. 11-31 Diode-trio checks. *(Chevrolet Motor Division of General Motors Corporation)*

11-30 to check for opens or grounds in the stator. Shorts are hard to find in the stator because of the low resistance of the winding. Usually, if all other tests are okay but the alternator does not supply rated output, the trouble is due to a shorted stator.

c. Diode checks The stator must be disconnected for a diode check. The diodes may be checked with an ohmmeter connected first in one direction and then in the other across each diode. If both readings are the same (high or low), the diode is defective and should be discarded.

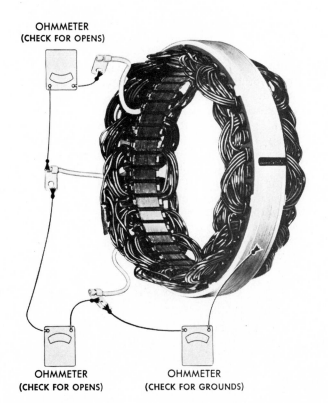

Fig. 11-30 Using an ohmmeter to check a stator for opens or grounds. *(Chevrolet Motor Division of General Motors Corporation)*

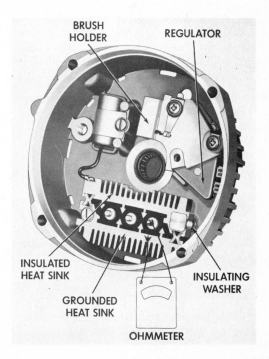

Fig. 11-32 Rectifier-bridge checks. *(Chevrolet Motor Division of General Motors Corporation)*

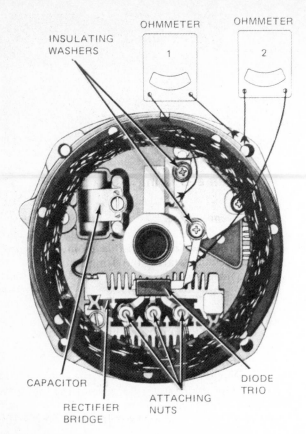

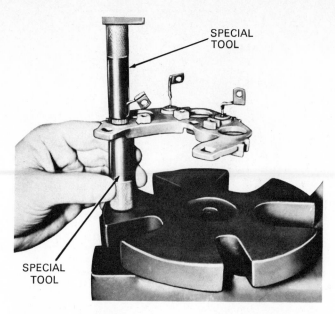

Fig. 11-34 Installing a diode with an arbor press and special tools. *(Chevrolet Motor Division of General Motors Corporation)*

Fig. 11-33 Brush-lead-clip checks. *(Chevrolet Motor Division of General Motors Corporation)*

On later models of this alternator, the diodes are permanently assembled into a diode trio (Fig. 11-31). On these, remove the diode trio from the slip-ring end frame and check each diode as shown.

NOTE: A 12-volt test light can also be used to check diodes. As the test prods are put across each diode, first in one direction and then in the other, the light should go on one way but not the other.

d. Rectifier-bridge check Later models require a rectifier-bridge check (Fig. 11-32). Connect the ohmmeter, as shown. Then reverse connections. If both readings are the same, replace the rectifier bridge. Repeat at each of the three terminals.

e. Voltage-regulator and brush-lead-clip check Connect an ohmmeter from the brush-lead clip to the end frame as shown in Fig. 11-33. Reverse the connections. If both readings are zero, either the brush-lead clip is grounded or the voltage regulator is defective. The brush-lead clip will be grounded if, on reassembly, the insulating sleeve or washer is omitted.

3. Alternator reassembly

1. If a diode requires replacement on the older-model alternator, support the heat sink with a diode support tool and press out the diode with a diode remover as shown in Fig. 11-34. Press in the new diode with a diode installer.

CAREFUL: Do not strike the diode, as any shock could ruin it. Also, do not bend the diode stem, as this could cause internal damage.

On the later-model alternator which uses a diode trio (Fig. 11-31), if one diode tests bad, discard the trio.

2. Replace the heat sink, noting proper relationship of parts as shown in Fig. 11-28. Before putting the heat sink in place, install the brush holder and brushes in the end frame (Fig. 11-35). Use a bent paper clip or stiff wire to hold the brushes down in place in the holder (Fig. 11-36). Then attach the holder to the end frame. (The paper clip or wire is removed after the alternator assembly is completed.) Finally, install the heat sink.

3. If a new bearing is installed in the drive-end frame, pack it about one-fourth full with bearing grease. Then press the bearing into the end frame and install a new retainer plate. Stake retainer-plate bolts to the plate so they will not loosen.

4. If the slip-ring end bearing requires replacement, press the old one out and press a new one in with a flat plate over the bearing so it is pressed down flush with the outside of the end frame. Support the end frame from the inside around the bearing boss to

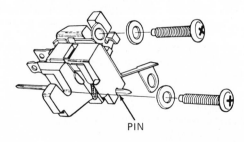

Fig. 11-35 Relation of parts in a brush-holder assembly. *(Chevrolet Motor Division of General Motors Corporation)*

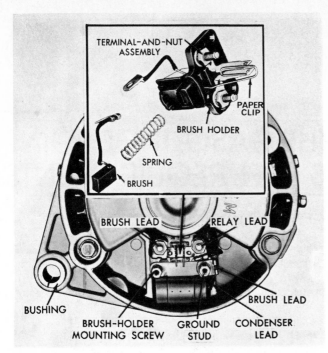

Fig. 11-36 Brush-holder assembly in an alternator, showing a paper clip being used to hold brushes in place during reassembly. *(Chevrolet Motor Division of General Motors Corporation)*

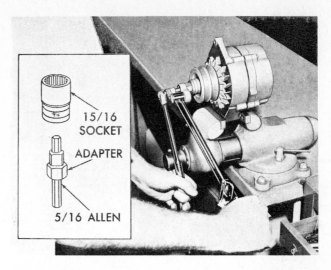

Fig. 11-37 Torquing a pulley nut to the proper tightness during reassembly. *(Chevrolet Motor Division of General Motors Corporation)*

avoid damage to the end frame. Saturate the felt seal with SAE 20 oil and install the seal and the retainer at the inner end of the bearing.

5. If a new bearing is not required, remove the protective tape you stuck on during disassembly.

6. To finish the reassembly, install the stator assembly in the slip-ring end frame and locate the diode connectors over the relay, diode, and stator leads, and tighten terminal nuts. Then install the rotor, fan, spacer, pulley, washer, and nut. Tighten with a torque wrench (Fig. 11-37).

7. Assemble the slip-ring end frame and stator assembly to the drive-end frame and rotor assembly. Secure with four through bolts. Remove the brush-holding wire to allow brushes to seat on the slip rings.

8. Check alternator operation after installation on car (✱ 10-2 and 10-5).

Chapter 11 review questions

Select the *one* correct, best, or most probable answer to each question. Then check your answers against the correct answers given at the end of the book.

1. Three alternator bench checks that Chrysler-Plymouth specify are field-circuit-ground check, diode check, and:
   a. commutator check,
   b. field-coil-draw check,
   c. voltage-setting check,
   d. current setting.

2. When using a test light to check a diode, the test light should go on:

a. in one direction only,
b. in both directions,
c. in neither direction,
d. none of the above.

3. If the field-coil draw is excessively high, the trouble is:
   a. worn slip rings,
   b. high field resistance,
   c. open stator,
   d. shorted field coil.

4. To start the disassembly of the Chrysler alternator remove the:
   a. brushes,
   b. rotor,
   c. stator,
   d. drive pulley.

5. If the slip rings on the Chrysler alternator are damaged, replace the:
   a. rotor,
   b. alternator,
   c. slip rings,
   d. brushes.

6. To clean the rotor, stator, or diodes, use:
   a. solvent,
   b. an oil-dampened cloth,
   c. a clean cloth,
   d. a steam bath.

7. If the light goes on when the test prods are touched to one slip ring and the shaft, the rotor:
   a. is okay,
   b. is grounded,
   c. is open,
   d. needs new slip rings.

8. On most alternators, if the slip rings are damaged, replace the:
   a. slip rings,
   b. stator,
   c. alternator,
   d. rotor.

THE GASOLINE ENGINE
AND ITS FUEL REQUIREMENTS

After studying this chapter, you should be able to:

1. Describe the construction and operation of a four-cycle engine.
2. Explain what happens during each of the four piston strokes.
3. Discuss compression ratio and explain what it means in terms of engine design and gasoline octane rating.
4. Explain the purpose of the ignition spark advance.
5. Explain how knocking, or detonation, is controlled.

12-1 Construction of a gasoline engine A gasoline engine is made up of one or more cylinders. Each cylinder is simply a cylindrical hole in the cylinder block. In one end, called the *combustion chamber,* are two valves and a spark plug. A tight-fitting piston works in and out of the opposite end of the cylinder (Fig. 12-1).

The piston is linked to a crank on the engine crankshaft by means of a connecting rod so that the up-and-down (reciprocating) motion of the piston is changed to the rotating motion of the crankshaft (Fig. 12-2). If each time the piston is "up" in the cylinder, pressure were exerted against it to push it "down," this straight-line pressure against the piston would create a turning or rotating pressure on the crankshaft. That is exactly what happens in the cylinder, except that in a four-cycle engine the pressure is exerted on the piston every *other* time it moves down in the cylinder.

12-2 Operation of a four-cycle engine Four-cycle[1] gasoline engines are by far the most common type used in cars, trucks, and buses. The cycle is made up of four piston strokes. These are the intake stroke, compression stroke, power stroke, and exhaust stroke.

On the *intake stroke* (Fig. 12-3), the intake valve has opened and the piston moves downward, causing a mixture of air and vaporized gasoline to enter the cylinder. The vaporized gasoline is mixed with the air in the carburetor, a device much like a spray gun or perfume atomizer (Fig. 12-4). As the air passes through the carburetor on its way to the cylinder, it rushes past

[1]Actually, a four-*stroke*-cycle engine (because four piston strokes make up the complete cycle of engine actions). However, in normal shop talk, the term is shortened to "four-cycle or four-stroke engine."

a nozzle through which liquid gasoline is being fed. In effect, the rapid movement of the air past the nozzle pulls liquid gasoline from the nozzle. The gasoline is broken up into a fine spray, or mist, and becomes vaporized. The amount of gasoline mixed with the air is varied by certain devices in the carburetor to meet different operating conditions, such as starting, acceleration, low speed, high speed, and so on. For normal running, every 15 pounds [6.80 kg] of air passing through the carburetor picks up about 1 pound [0.454 kg] of gasoline. During the whole time that the intake valve is open and the piston is moving down on the intake stroke, this mixture of air and gasoline is being delivered to the cylinder.

The ratio of air to gasoline in the previous paragraph is 15 to 1 (written 15:1). That is, there is 15 times as much air, by weight, as gasoline, by weight. This is a comparatively *lean* mixture. When a cold engine is started, the carburetor supplies a very rich mixture of about 9:1, that is, 9 pounds [4.08 kg] of air for each pound [0.45 kg] of gasoline. The carburetor supplies mixtures of various richness to suit operating conditions, from lean to rich, as the engine requires.

On the *compression stroke,* the piston is moving upward (Fig. 12-5). At the end of the intake stroke, as the piston reaches the limit of its downward travel (called *bottom dead center,* or BDC), the intake valve closes so that the combustion chamber is completely sealed. The piston starts upward on the compression stroke, compressing the mixture of air and gasoline.

As the piston nears the top of its travel (top dead center, or TDC) on the compression stroke, the ignition system produces and delivers a high-voltage surge to the spark plug in the cylinder. The spark plug consists of two electrodes which are insulated from each other, with a gap of up to 0.080 inch [2.03 mm] between them.

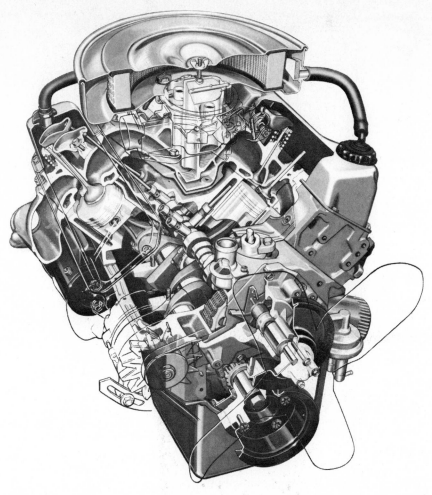

Fig. 12-1 Cutaway view of a 365-horsepower V-8 engine. *(Ford Motor Company)*

When the high-voltage surge is delivered to the spark plug, it jumps across this gap, creating an intensely hot electric spark. The spark sets fire to, or ignites, the mixture of compressed air and gasoline vapor in the cylinder. This mixture burns very rapidly, creating heat and a pressure of as much as 4000 pounds per square inch (psi) within the cylinder. This terrific pressure pushes the piston downward on the *firing,* or *power, stroke* (Fig. 12-6), causing a turning force to be transmitted to the engine crankshaft. This turning force, or torque, is transmitted to the rear wheels by gears, driveshaft, axle drive gears, and axles.

As soon as the piston reaches BDC, the exhaust valve opens and the piston starts to travel upward again on the *exhaust stroke* (Fig. 12-7). This forces the burned gases out of the cylinder. At the end of the exhaust stroke, when the piston has reached TDC, the exhaust valve closes and the intake valve opens. The intake stroke begins as the piston travels downward and air and gasoline vapor are delivered to the cylinder.

☼ 12-3 Meaning of compression ratio The compression ratio of an engine is the volume of air–fuel mixture in the cylinder when the piston is at BDC divided by the volume of air–fuel mixture in the cylinder when the piston is at TDC (Fig. 12-8). For example,

the engine of a popular car has a cylinder volume of 42.35 cubic inches [694 cm³] when the piston is at BDC (A in Fig. 12-8) and a volume of 4.45 cubic inches [73 cm³] (B in Fig. 12-8) when the piston is at TDC. The compression ratio is, therefore, 42.35 divided by 4.45 [694 ÷ 73], or $^{9.5}/_1$ (that is, 9.5:1). In this engine, a mixture of air and fuel in the cylinder would be compressed from 42.35 cubic inches [694 cm³] to 4.45 cubic inches [73 cm³], or to $^1/_{9.5}$ of its original volume, as the piston moved from BDC to TDC.

For many years, engine compression ratios went up as new and more powerful engines were introduced. Engineers found that increasing the compression ratio increases engine power and economy without increasing engine weight or size. A higher compression ratio means that the pressure on the piston is higher to begin with at the end of the compression stroke and at the beginning of the power stroke. Besides this, a higher compression ratio also means that the gases in the cylinder must expand to a greater volume during the power stroke. A larger percentage of the available power is thus utilized.

However, in recent years, the compression ratios have been lowered on the engines in new cars in order to reduce atmospheric pollution from the engines. See ☼ 12-14.

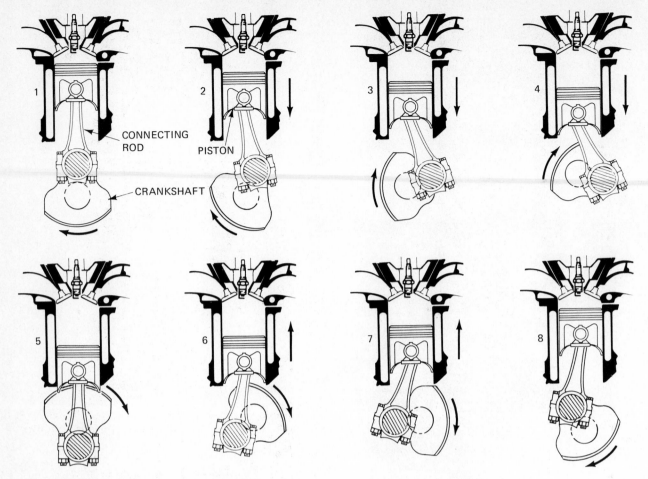

Fig. 12-2 Sequence of actions as the crankshaft completes one revolution and the piston moves from top to bottom to top again.

Igniting the mixture

⚙ 12-4 Heat of compression When air is compressed (in an engine cylinder, for example), its temperature increases. Air suddenly compressed to $1/16$ (16:1 compression ratio) of its original volume may reach a temperature of 1000°F [540°C]. In the gasoline engine, where the vaporized gasoline and air are first mixed and then compressed, such compression ratios as 16:1 are out of the question because the temperature reached would cause the mixture to ignite too early in the compression stroke. Diesel engines, however, can utilize such high compressions because they compress the air only; the fuel (usually oil) is sprayed into the cylinder at the end of the compression stroke. The heat of compression causes the fuel to ignite and burn as it is sprayed into the cylinder. The burning of the fuel creates the heat and pressure needed to drive the piston down and produce power from the engine.

⚙ 12-5 Need for electric ignition in gasoline engines Some early gasoline engines attempted to make use of the heat of compression to ignite the mixture that was being compressed. The mixture was drawn into the cylinder and compressed by the intake and compression strokes—and the theory being that at the top of the compression stroke the heat of compres-

sion would be sufficient to ignite the mixture. This did not work very well, however, because sometimes the heat of compression would ignite the mixture well before the piston reached TDC. When this happened, the piston, moving upward against the explosion, added still more pressure, so that the ultimate pressure reached was tremendously high. Sometimes it was enough to damage the engine. But even if this did not occur, the high pressures almost instantaneously attained in the cylinder often caused a very objectionable noise or knocking sound. It is easy to see how difficult it would be to control such an engine. Different fuels explode at different temperatures and burn at different rates; at different operating speeds the amounts of air and fuel drawn into the cylinder differ, so that the compression pressures vary.

To eliminate the troubles resulting from all these variables, the electric ignition system was developed. The system can be controlled so that the mixture can be ignited at the correct instant under every operating condition.

⚙ 12-6 Ignition spark advance Engine speed and throttle opening vary. Therefore the instant that the spark occurs in the cylinder (the "timing" of the spark) must also vary if maximum power and minimum emis-

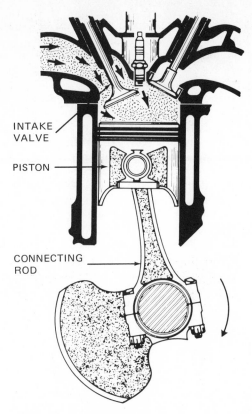

INTAKE
VALVE

PISTON

CONNECTING
ROD

Fig. 12-3 Intake stroke. The intake valve (to left) has opened. The piston is moving down, drawing a mixture of air and gasoline vapor into the cylinder.

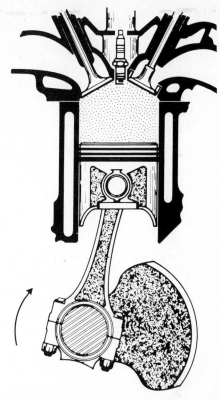

Fig. 12-5 Compression stroke. The intake valve has closed so that both valves are closed. The piston is moving upward, compressing the mixture.

sions are to be obtained. Each charge of air and vaporized gasoline taken into the cylinder must be ignited at the correct instant if it is to yield the maximum power available. When the engine is running at low speeds, the ignition system delivers the high-voltage surge with proper timing to produce the spark just before the piston reaches top dead center. At higher engine speeds,

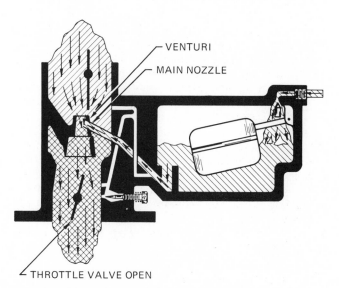

VENTURI

MAIN NOZZLE

THROTTLE VALVE OPEN

Fig. 12-4 Sectional view of a carburetor, showing the throttle valve open and fuel being delivered from the nozzle centered in the venturi.

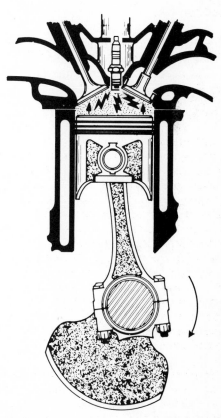

Fig. 12-6 Power stroke. The ignition system has delivered a spark to the spark plug that ignites the compressed mixture. As the mixture burns, high pressure is produced, and this high pressure pushes the piston down.

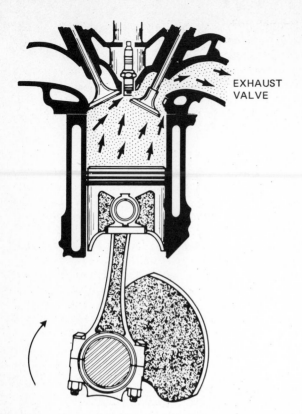

EXHAUST VALVE

Fig. 12-7 Exhaust stroke. The exhaust valve (to right) has opened. The piston is moving upward, forcing the burned gases out of the cylinder.

there is less time for the air–fuel mixture to burn because the piston is moving more rapidly.

To realize maximum power from the charge at higher speeds, it is necessary to ignite the air–fuel mixture earlier in the cycle, or well before the piston reaches TDC. At high speed, on some engines, the spark may occur before TDC by as many as 55° of crankshaft rotation. That is, the engine crankshaft may still have 55° to rotate on the compression stroke, pushing the piston upward, at the time the spark occurs and the mixture begins to burn. The speed of the piston is so great, however, that it is over TDC and moving downward on the power stroke before the burning of the

mixture and the pressure increase are well started. If the spark were not advanced at high speed, the piston would be moving downward so rapidly as the mixture began to burn that it would almost "keep step" with the pressure rise. Thus there would be little increase in pressure and most of the power would be lost.

⚙ 12-7 Determination of a spark-advance curve The graph in Fig. 12-9 illustrates a typical spark-advance curve. At idling speed, the spark is set at 5° before TDC. At higher speeds, the spark is advanced by a centrifugal device (see ⚙ 13-16) to produce a spark advance based on engine speed. At 2000 engine rpm, for instance, the spark will occur at 20° before TDC. The actual amount of spark advance for any engine speed is determined by operating the engine at that speed (with wide-open throttle) and gradually increasing the spark advance until maximum power is obtained. Since this amount of advance may cause some pinging (see ⚙ 12-10), a slight retarding of the spark can then be made. The engine is tested at all speeds, the best spark advance (considering power and pinging) is found for each speed, and then the centrifugal-advance device is built to provide that advance.

Fuels and their characteristics

⚙ 12-8 Rate of flame propagation in cylinder As compression ratios were increased, there was a greater tendency for the engine to ping. This ping was somewhat similar to that which occurred in the early engine discussed in ⚙ 12-5, and it was caused by similar conditions. Scientists seeking to find the cause of pinging used special engines with quartz-glass windows in the combustion chambers. Through the glass windows they took high-speed photographs during the instant of combustion. Thus it was learned that the air–fuel mixture does not explode instantly; an interval of time is required for the mixture to burn. The spark at the spark-plug gap starts the "fire" in the combustion chamber, and the flames spread out in all directions from the spark plug. The speed with which the flames spread through the air–fuel mixture is called the *rate of flame propagation*.

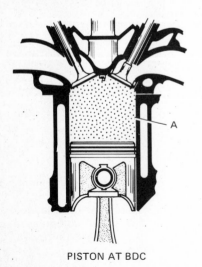

PISTON AT BDC

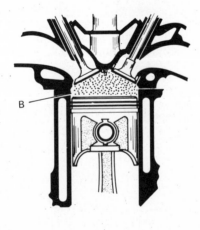

PISTON AT TDC

Fig. 12-8 The compression ratio is the volume in a cylinder with the piston at BDC divided by its volume with the piston at TDC, or A divided by B.

156

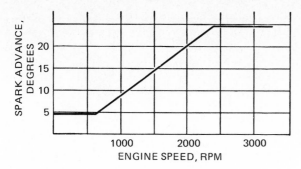

Fig. 12-9 Typical spark-advance curve. Not all advance curves are straight lines. Many bend, or "dogleg," to provide more rapid advance through some speed ranges than through others.

⚙ **12-9 Combustion** Let us take a closer look at the combustion process in the engine. Gasoline is a hydrocarbon, made up largely of hydrogen and carbon, and has the chemical formula HC. During complete combustion, all the carbon unites with oxygen in the air to form CO_2 or carbon dioxide. However, complete combustion does not take place in the engine. There is always some gasoline vapor (HC) left over. And some of the carbon does not get enough oxygen to make CO_2. Instead, it forms CO, or carbon monoxide.

HC and CO are two atmospheric pollutants coming out the tail pipe of automobiles. Various devices, called *emission controls,* are installed on modern cars to minimize these pollutants.

Carbon monoxide (CO) is a dangerous gas. It is colorless, odorless, and can be lethal. A ratio of only 15 parts of CO to 10,000 parts of air is dangerous to breathe. Higher concentrations can kill you. That is why you should never run an engine in a closed garage.

Enough carbon monoxide can be produced in 3 min by a running engine in a closed one-car garage to cause paralysis and death!

There is a third pollutant, nitrogen oxides (chemical formula NO_x) that the engine produces. These are caused by the high temperatures and pressures in the engine during combustion. Special devices have been installed on engines to reduce this pollutant.

⚙ **12-10 Cause of detonation** During the burning of the air–fuel mixture, it may happen that the piston cannot move downward fast enough to take advantage of the pressure rise or to prevent an excessive pressure increase. This pressure increase causes a further rise in the heat of compression, even at the far corners of the combustion chamber where no burning of the fuel is, as yet, taking place. But the pressure and heat of compression quickly increase enough to set off the fuel in the far corners, so that, almost instantly, the entire mixture goes off (Fig. 12-10). This is called *detonation.* The pressure increase resulting from detonation is almost instantaneous and goes so high that a distinct pinging sound is heard in the cylinder. This ping is believed to be due to the great stresses imposed on engine parts and to the hammering effect of the explosion on the piston.

When the compression ratio of an engine is increased, the engine is more subject to detonation. This is because, with a higher initial pressure as ignition begins, the pressure at which detonation takes place is reached sooner.

⚙ **12-11 Detonation and preignition** Detonation is caused by a secondary explosion that takes place after the spark at the spark-plug gap (Fig. 12-10). Preignition

NORMAL COMBUSTION

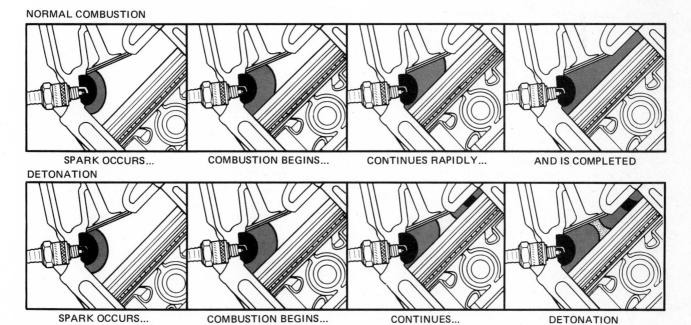

Fig. 12-10 Normal combustion without detonation is shown in the top row. The fuel charge burns smoothly from beginning to end. This provides an even, powerful thrust to the piston. In the bottom row, knocking, or detonation, is illustrated. The last part of the fuel explodes to produce detonation. *(Champion Spark Plugs)*

157

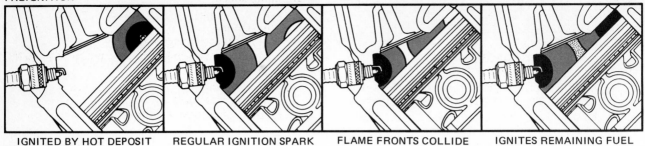

PREIGNITION

| IGNITED BY HOT DEPOSIT | REGULAR IGNITION SPARK | FLAME FRONTS COLLIDE | IGNITES REMAINING FUEL |

Fig. 12-11 One cause of preignition. The hot spot ignites the compressed mixture before the spark occurs at the spark-plug gap. *(Champion Spark Plugs)*

is the ignition of the air–fuel mixture before the spark occurs at the spark-plug gap. Preignition can be caused by hot spots in the combustion chamber (Fig. 12-11), hot exhaust valves, deposits on spark plugs, and so on. The hot spots act like spark plugs and cause the mixture to ignite before the spark occurs. The result can be engine rumble, ping, or irregular operation. Sometimes the hot spots act as substitutes for the spark plugs and keep the engine running even after the ignition is turned off. This condition is called *dieseling* and can cause serious engine damage.

Preignition is usually considered to be a service problem. It is normally caused by inadequate servicing of the engine, the wrong spark plugs, or the use of the wrong fuel or oil. The wrong oil or fuel can cause engine deposits that lead to preignition. Engine deposits also increase the compression ratio which can then cause detonation.

☼ 12-12 Measuring antiknock values of fuels Scientists wanted to step up compression ratios—for greater power and efficiency—without increasing engine size. The big problem, however, was detonation, and the scientists hoped to solve it by finding a no-knock fuel. In their research on this problem, they compounded and tried thousands of different chemical substances, some of which reduced and some of which increased detonation.

They had to develop a yardstick by which to compare the antiknock value of these various substances. They had to be able to say that one fuel knocked so many percentage points more than another, that a third fuel was so many percentage points worse. The measuring stick finally agreed upon was called *octane*. Octane is given as a number that expresses the antiknock quality of a fuel. A 96-octane gasoline, for example, is a certain percentage more knock-free than an 85-octane gasoline.

☼ 12-13 Chemically controlling detonation Substances were found which, when added to gasoline, reduce detonation. One of these is tetraethyl lead, and it has been so successfully used in stepping up the octane rating (or antiknock value) of gasoline that it has been widely adopted. This substance controls the rate of flame propagation so that excessive pressure and detonation are avoided. Gasoline containing te-

traethyl lead (commonly called "leaded" gasoline) has made it possible to increase compression ratios still further and to obtain still greater power and economy from gasoline engines without a corresponding increase in size or weight. Some emission controls, such as catalytic converters, are damaged by this lead. Therefore, the use of unleaded gasoline, which contains other octane-improving compounds, has become widespread. Many cars must, by law, use a fuel that does not contain tetraethyl lead, and are so labeled.

☼ 12-14 Compression-ratio reduction In recent years, compression ratios have been reduced to some extent. The reason for this is that federal laws require a reduction of atmospheric pollutants from automobile engines. This requirement could be met only by adding on certain emission controls and reducing compression ratios.

Chapter 12 review questions

Select the *one* correct, best, or most probable answer to each question. Then check your answers against the correct answers given at the end of the book.

1. The ignition spark occurs at the spark-plug gap in the cylinder as the piston approaches the end of the:
   a. intake stroke,
   b. compression stroke,
   c. power stroke,
   d. exhaust stroke.
2. Volume of air–fuel mixture with the piston at BDC divided by the volume with the piston at TDC is called:
   a. heat of compression,
   b. engine compression,
   c. the compression stroke,
   d. compression ratio.
3. In some engines, at high speed, the ignition spark may occur as many as:
   a. 55° before TDC,
   b. 55° before BDC,
   c. 90° before TDC,
   d. 60° before TDC.

4. When air is compressed, its:
   a. temperature goes down,
   b. volume goes up,
   c. temperature goes up,
   d. temperature holds steady.
5. One of the basic differences between the gasoline engine and the diesel engine is that in the gasoline engine, air and fuel are mixed and then compressed, but in the diesel engine:
   a. fuel alone is compressed,
   b. air and fuel are compressed,
   c. air and fuel are mixed before compression,
   d. air alone is compressed.
6. In the modern ignition system, as the engine speed increases, the spark is:
   a. advanced,
   b. retarded,
   c. also increased,
   d. vacuum controlled.
7. The speed with which the flame spreads through the air–fuel mixture in the engine cylinder is called:
   a. flame speed,
   b. rate of flaming,
   c. rate of burn,
   d. rate of flame propagation.
8. An engine's susceptibility to detonation or pinging increases as its:
   a. speed is increased,
   b. octane is increased,
   c. compression ratio is increased,
   d. speed is reduced.
9. The resistance of a gasoline to knocking is measured in terms of:
   a. heptane,
   b. butane,
   c. octane,
   d. propane.
10. Detonation in an engine can be reduced by:
   a. retarding the ignition timing,
   b. advancing the ignition timing,
   c. curving the ignition timing,
   d. increasing compression ratios.

IGNITION SYSTEM USING CONTACT POINTS

After studying this chapter, you should be able to:

1. Explain how the contact-point ignition system works.
2. Locate and identify the components of this system in automobiles.
3. Explain how mechanical centrifugal and vacuum-advance mechanisms work.

13-1 Function of the ignition system This chapter discusses the theory of contact-point ignition-system operation (Fig. 13-1). It explains how the ignition system produces, times, and delivers high-voltage surges to the spark plugs in the engine cylinders. It describes the mechanical spark advance devices that advance, or move ahead, the spark with increasing engine speed and during part-throttle operation. A later chapter (Chapter 16) describes the operation of electronic ignition systems. Both ignition systems do the same job. But they get the job done in a slightly different way. However, after you have studied these two chapters, you will see that the two systems are very similar, except for the way they open and close the circuit between the battery and the ignition coil. One uses contact points, the other uses solid-state electronic components.

Regardless of the type of system, the job of the ignition system is to supply high-voltage surges of up to 20,000 volts or more (contact-point system) to the spark plugs in the engine cylinders. These high-voltage surges must reach the spark plugs at the exact instant they are needed. This instant is when the piston nears TDC on the compression stroke. The high-voltage surge then produces the spark that ignites the compressed air–fuel mixture.

The ignition system includes a battery, ignition switch, ignition distributor, ignition coil, wiring, and spark plugs (Fig. 13-2). The distributor is two separate devices in one—a fast-acting switch and a high-voltage distributing mechanism. The distributor includes a shaft which is driven by gearing from the engine camshaft (Fig. 13-3). This gearing also drives the oil pump in most engines.

Briefly, here is how the contact-point ignition system works. The distributor shaft rotates. As it turns, a cam

on the upper end of the shaft causes contact points to open and close. When the points are closed, the ignition coil is connected to the battery. This loads the coil with electric (electromagnetic) energy. Then, when the points are opened, this energy is unloaded from the coil as a high-voltage surge. The surge is directed to the proper spark plug (in the cylinder completing the compression stroke) by the distributor cap and rotor. We describe these actions in detail in following sections.

13-2 Contact-point distributor The distributor using contact points (Figs. 13-4 and 13-5) consists of a

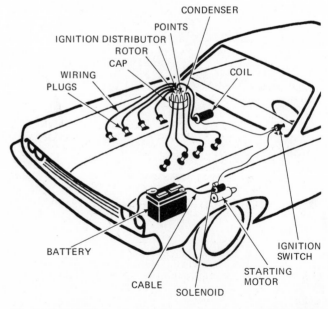

Fig. 13-1 Contact-point ignition system in an automobile.

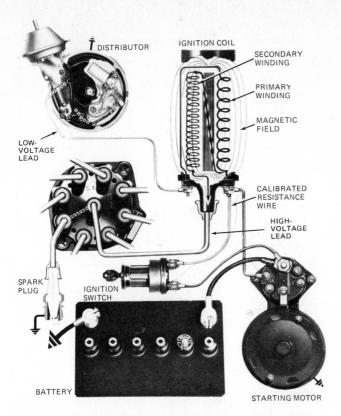

Fig. 13-2 Typical ignition system using contact points. It includes the battery (source of power), ignition switch, ignition coil (shown schematically), distributor (shown in top view wth its cap removed and placed below it), spark plugs (one shown in sectional view), and wiring. (Delco-Remy Division of General Motors Corporation)

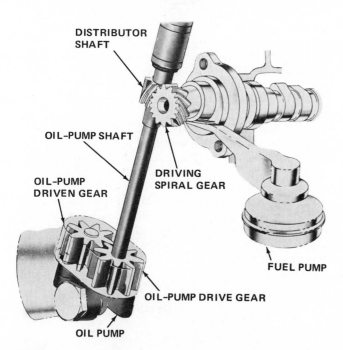

Fig. 13-3 Oil-pump, distributor, and fuel-pump drives. A gear on the end of the camshaft drives the distributor. An extension on the distributor shaft drives the oil pump. An eccentric on the camshaft drives the fuel pump. (Buick Motor Division of General Motors Corporation)

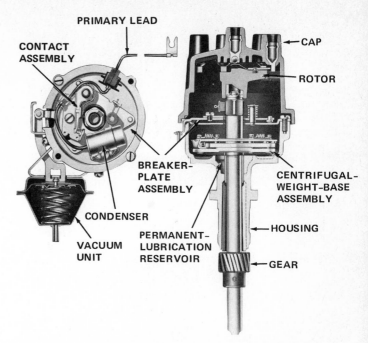

Fig. 13-4 Top and sectional views of an ignition distributor using contact points. In the top view (to left) the cap and rotor have been removed so the breaker plate can be seen. (Delco-Remy Division of General Motors Corporation)

housing, a drive shaft with a cam on top of it, an advance mechanism, a breaker plate with contact points and a condenser mounted on it, a rotor, and a cap. The contact points are in the primary circuit of the ignition system. The cap and rotor are in the secondary circuit of the system.

⚙ 13-3 Primary circuit The primary circuit of the system using contact points is shown in Fig. 13-6. It includes the contact points, the primary winding in the ignition coil, the ignition switch, and the battery. One of the contact points, the stationary point, is grounded through the distributor. That is, it is connected to the grounded terminal of the battery through the distributor housing, engine, and car frame.

The other contact point, the movable point, is insulated and is mounted on a movable contact arm (Fig. 13-7). The rubbing block of the contact arm rides on the cam. This cam has the same number of lobes, or high spots, as there are cylinders in the engine.[1]

When the engine is running, the cam is repeatedly causing the contact points to open and close. Every time a cam lobe comes up under the contact arm rubbing block, it pushes the arm out. This separates the contact points. Then, as the cam continues to rotate, the lobe moves out from under the rubbing block. Now, the spring on the contact arm pushes the arm in so the contact points come together again.

[1]On some distributors, there are two sets of contact points that close and open alternately. This "dual-point" arrangement produces the same switching effect as the breaker-cam and single-point-set arrangement.

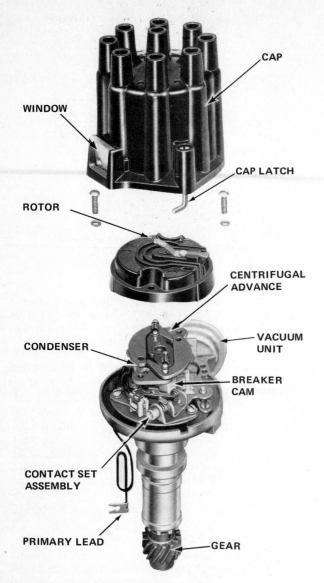

Fig. 13-5 Partly disassembled distributor using contact points. *(Delco-Remy Division of General Motors Corporation)*

How long the points stay closed before another cam lobe pushes them apart again is called *dwell*. Dwell is the number of degrees of distributor-cam rotation that the points stay closed.

The contact points are often called *breaker points*. They repeatedly *break* the circuit between the primary winding of the ignition coil and the battery. When the points are closed, current can flow from the battery through the ignition-coil primary winding and the points. The current, as it flows, causes a magnetic field to build up around the winding. Then, as the contact points are separated, the current stops flowing. The magnetic field collapses. As the magnetic field collapses, it produces a high voltage in the secondary winding of the ignition coil. This high voltage then surges out through the high-voltage wiring, distributor cap, and rotor, to a spark plug. The voltage jumps the gap in the spark plug and ignites the compressed air–fuel mixture. It burns. All these events are rapidly repeated in the running engine.

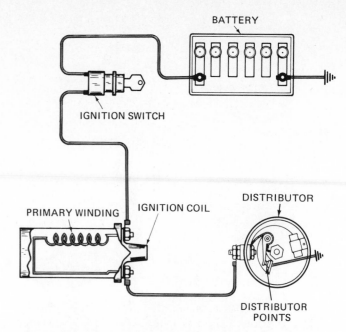

Fig. 13-6 Schematic diagram of the primary circuit of the ignition system using contact points.

All 12-volt contact-point ignition systems use a resistor or a resistance wire in the ignition-coil primary circuit (Fig. 13-2). This resistance is bypassed by the ignition switch when it is turned to START. Full battery voltage is applied to the ignition coil for good performance during cranking. After the engine is started and the ignition switch is turned to ON, the resistance is inserted in the ignition primary circuit, thus protecting the contact points from excessive current.

On some cars, the resistance consists of a separately mounted resistor unit. On most cars, the resistance consists of a length of resistance wire in the wiring harness. Most electronic ignition systems (Chapter 16) do not use a primary resistor. An exception is the Chrysler electronic ignition systems (Fig. 1-5).

⚙ 13-4 Secondary circuit The secondary circuit includes the secondary winding in the ignition coil, the secondary wiring, the distributor cap and rotor, and the spark plugs (Fig. 13-8). This circuit produces the high-voltage surges and distributes them to the spark plugs. Every time a piston nears TDC on the compression stroke, the secondary circuit delivers a high-voltage surge to the spark plug in that cylinder. A spark jumps the plug gap, the compressed mixture ignites, and a power stroke takes place.

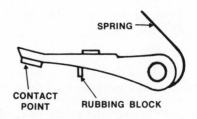

Fig. 13-7 Distributor contact arm.

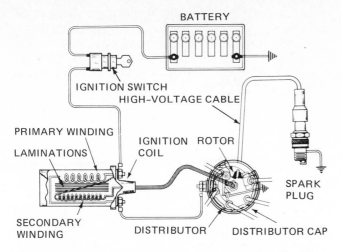

Fig. 13-8 Schematic diagram of the complete ignition system using contact points.

☸ 13-5 Distributor cap and rotor action   Rotors come in various sizes and shapes (Fig. 13-9). The rotor sits on top of the cam in the distributor, as shown in Fig. 13-10. As the distributor shaft rotates, the cam and rotor also rotate. The cap and rotor form a rotating switch. The rotor connects the center terminal of the distributor cap to the outside terminals of the cap, one after another as it rotates.

The terminals in the cap are insulated from each other and molded in place in the cap. You can see three of them cut away in Fig. 13-10. The center terminal of the cap has a carbon button on its lower end. A spring on the rotor rests on this button. This spring is attached to the metal blade of the rotor. Since the center terminal of the cap is connected to the secondary winding of the ignition coil, the rotor blade is also connected to the secondary winding. Whenever a high-voltage surge is produced by the secondary winding, it passes through the rotor blade. It jumps from the end of the blade to the outside cap terminal the blade is pointing to. This terminal is wired to the spark plug in the cylinder that is ready to fire (Fig. 13-11).

To summarize—the cam turns and a lobe opens the contact points. The magnetic field in the ignition coil collapses. This produces high voltage in the secondary winding. This high voltage surges from the coil, through

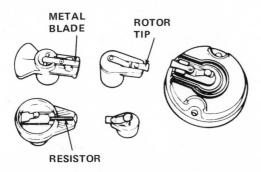

Fig. 13-9 Types of distributor rotors. The one at the lower left has a carbon resistor. The one at the right is attached to the advance mechanism with screws. (Delco-Remy Division of General Motors Corporation)

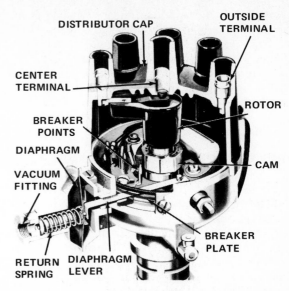

Fig. 13-10 A cutaway distributor using contact points, showing how the rotor is mounted on top of the cam. This picture also shows the construction of the vacuum-advance mechanism. (Ford Motor Company)

the high-voltage cable connected to the center terminal of the cap. From there, the rotor conducts this surge through the rotor to the outside terminal that is connected by a high-voltage cable to the spark plug in the cylinder where the compression stroke is ending.

☸ 13-6 Ignition coil   The ignition coil has two windings, a primary winding of a few hundred turns of rel-

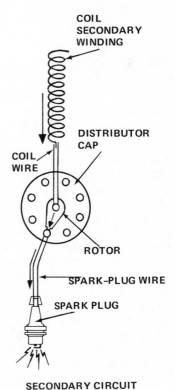

Fig. 13-11 Secondary circuit in simplified form. The coil secondary winding is connected through the distributor cap, rotor, and wiring to the spark plugs.

atively heavy wire and a secondary winding of many thousands of turns of very fine wire (Fig. 13-12). The secondary winding is on the inside, with the primary winding wrapped around it. The laminations, strips of iron, help to concentrate the magnetic lines of force. The center terminal is connected to one end of the secondary winding. We now look at the interactions of the two windings in the ignition coil to learn how the high-voltage surges are produced.

☼ 13-7 Mutual and self-induction When current starts to flow through a winding, a magnetic field builds up (see ☼ 1-30). And when the current stops flowing, the magnetic field collapses. The ignition coil uses this buildup and collapse of the magnetic field in the primary winding to induce high voltage in the secondary winding (as much as 40,000 volts in electronic ignition systems). This action—of the primary winding inducing a voltage in the secondary winding—is called *mutual induction*. The mutual magnetic actions of the two windings induce the voltage in the secondary winding.

As the magnetic field builds up or collapses, magnetic lines of force are moving in one way or the other. Any

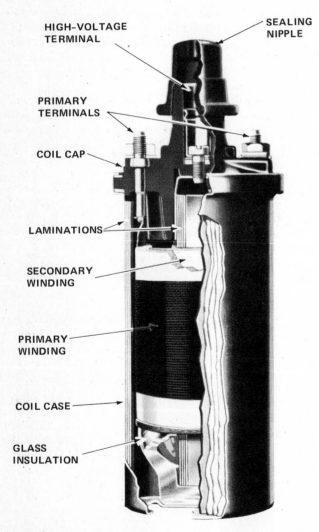

Fig. 13-12 Cutaway ignition coil. *(Delco-Remy Division of General Motors Corporaton)*

HIGH-VOLTAGE TERMINAL

SEALING NIPPLE

PRIMARY TERMINALS

COIL CAP

LAMINATIONS

SECONDARY WINDING

PRIMARY WINDING

COIL CASE

GLASS INSULATION

conductor that is held in the path of the moving magnetic field will have voltage induced in it. This voltage will force current through the conductor. Recall that, when there is a relative motion between a conductor and a magnetic field, voltage and current are induced in the conductor (see ☼ 8-6). It does not make any difference whether the magnetic field or the conductor is moved as long as one moves with respect to the other. The secondary winding is stationary, and the magnetic field, in building up and collapsing, moves through it to induce voltage in the secondary. The voltage induced during the buildup is not, however, very great. This is due to the *self-induction* of the primary winding.

All windings have self-induction. This means that as a magnetic field builds up in the winding, a voltage is induced in the winding. The voltage induced is always in the direction opposite to that of the voltage forcing current through the winding. For this reason, the self-induced voltage in the winding is known as the *countervoltage*. It opposes the flow of current that produces the magnetic field.

To understand this peculiar action of the coil, which "bites the hand that feeds it," we must go back to fundamentals for a moment. Figure 13-13 illustrates in end view two turns of wire in a winding. The current is flowing away from you (as indicated by the crosses), and the magnetic field circles the conductors as shown. When the current first starts to flow, the magnetic field begins to build up around each turn of wire. It does not, of course, reach its maximum instantly. Figure 13-14 shows what happens as the magnetic field begins to build up around the conductor to the left. Visualize the magnetic field, composed of circular lines of force, as moving outward from the conductor. As they move outward, they naturally cut across the conductor to the right. And this means that a flow of current toward you (indicated by the dot) is induced in the conductor to the right.

Actually, the current cannot flow that way, because the battery is already forcing current (or electrons) through the winding (and every turn of wire) in the opposite direction, as shown in Fig. 13-13. But there is a *tendency* for a flow of current to be induced in this reverse direction by the magnetic field as it builds up. (Or, you might say, this *tendency* makes it harder for the electrons from the battery to get through.) The magnetic field of every conductor produces this tendency on adjacent conductors. (And all conductors thereby resist letting additional electrons—or more current—through.)

Thus, at every point in the winding, a countervoltage is induced. This countervoltage opposes battery volt-

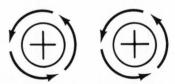

Fig. 13-13 Magnetic field around two adjacent conductors carrying current.

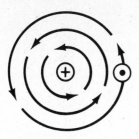

Fig. 13-14 Effects of an increasing magnetic field from one conductor on an adjacent conductor.

age. That is, it opposes any increase in the amount of current from the battery. A period of time is required for the battery to overcome this effect and increase the amount of current to the maximum as determined by the resistance of the winding. This period is called the *buildup time* (Fig. 13-15) and is only a small fraction of a second.

☼ 13-8 Action in the secondary winding during buildup

As the magnetic field strengthens, or builds up, in the primary winding, it induces a countervoltage in the primary winding. It also produces a voltage in the secondary side of the ignition system. In order for any activity to take place in the secondary, the voltage must increase to several thousand volts—enough to cause a spark to jump the spark-plug gap. During the buildup time, the secondary voltage does not reach a very high value. But when current stops flowing in the primary winding, a series of events begins that does produce a high voltage in the secondary winding.

☼ 13-9 Self-induction in the primary winding after current stops

During the time that current flows from the battery through the primary winding, the coil is being "loaded" with energy in the form of magnetic lines of force. When the current stops flowing, the magnetic field starts to collapse.

The magnetic field, in collapsing, cuts across the conductors as it did during buildup except that the motion is in the opposite direction. Consider Fig. 13-14 again. Now, instead of the magnetic field of the left-hand conductor expanding, it is collapsing back toward the conductor. This means that there is relative movement between the right-hand conductor and the magnetic field. This induces current in a direction opposite to that shown, that is, away from you. This is the actual direction in which the current from the battery was flowing through the primary winding.

In other words, when the battery is disconnected from the winding, the collapsing magnetism induces current in the same direction as that in which current originally flowed from the battery. This again is self-induction. Regardless of whether the magnetic field is building up or collapsing, it induces a voltage (or countervoltage) that opposes any change in the amount of current or magnetic strength. While the coil is being "loaded," the battery voltage has to overcome this countervoltage in order to start the current flow.

When the battery is disconnected, the self-induction of the winding attempts to keep the current flowing. In the system using distributor contact points, this is what could happen. The increasing voltage (due to magnetic field collapse) could quickly build up high enough to cause a severe arc to jump across the contact points as they separated. This would burn the points. But a condenser is used to prevent this from happening.

☼ 13-10 Condenser action

On ignition systems with distributor contact points, a *condenser* (also called a *capacitor*) is used to prevent arcing at the points. Thus the ignition coil can release its energy through the secondary winding in the form of a high-voltage surge. The condenser is made up of two plates which are electrically insulated from each other (Fig. 13-16). Each plate is connected to a lead. The plates in an automotive-ignition condenser are two long, narrow strips of lead or aluminum foil, insulated from each other with special condenser paper and wrapped on an arbor to form a winding. One plate is connected to the condenser case, the other to the condenser lead. The wind-

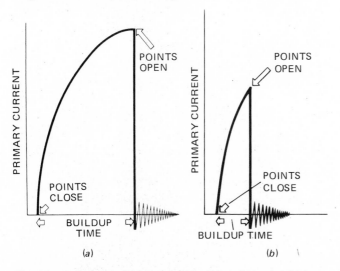

Fig. 13-15 Graphs showing coil buildup time. (a) At low speeds, the distributor contact points open as the primary current nears its maximum. At high speeds (b), the points remain closed a shorter time, so that buildup time, and primary current, are less.

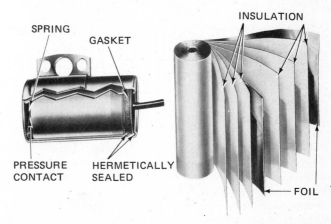

Fig. 13-16 Condenser assembled and with the winding partly unwound.

ing is impregnated in oily or waxy substances to improve the insulating properties of the condenser paper.

The condenser is connected in parallel with the contact points. When the points begin to open, the condenser momentarily provides a place for the current (or electrons) to flow. Current flows into the condenser, charging it, instead of jumping across the gap between the separating contact points.

The instant the points separate, even as little as one-millionth of an inch, current momentarily stops flowing in the primary winding. The magnetic field that is produced by the flow of current begins to collapse. A voltage is induced that attempts to keep the current moving. Without the condenser, the current would arc across the points. But with the condenser this does not happen, because the plates of the condenser provide ''room'' for the current (or electrons). The voltage, at first, does not have to be very high to push electrons into the condenser, and the condenser begins to become charged.

The induced voltage soon ''fills up,'' or charges, the condenser; the current in the primary winding stops flowing. The magnetic field further collapses, inducing a higher voltage, which further charges the condenser. This creates still more opposition in the condenser to a flow of current, which forces additional magnetic-field collapse, still higher voltage, and so on. The voltage in the primary winding may go as high as 250 volts. This must be thought of as a rapid and continuous process; the voltage constantly increases in an attempt to force current to flow. But as the voltage goes up, the contact points continue to get farther and farther apart, so that the voltage does not at any time reach a value that would cause an arc across the points. What does happen is that the increasing voltage continues to charge the condenser further.

NOTE: During the first few millionths of a second after the points separate, arcing does take place across the points, but this occurs *despite* condenser action, not because of it.

At the same time all this is happening in the primary winding, events are reaching a climax in the secondary winding—events that will produce a high-voltage surge of as much as 20,000 volts (in contact-point systems).

Instead of a winding as shown in Fig. 13-16, some condensers are wafers of ceramic mounted on the contact point set as shown in Fig. 15-12. Although it looks different, it acts the same as the wound condenser, as explained in the following paragraphs.

☼ 13-11 Action in the secondary winding during magnetic collapse

The secondary winding is connected to the spark-plug gap in the cylinder (Fig. 13-2). During the time that the primary winding is building up its magnetic field, the increasing magnetic field induces voltage in the secondary winding. We saw, however, that this voltage was not sufficient to cause any activity in the secondary winding (see ☼ 13-8). This is because the speed of the buildup is limited by the self-induction of the primary winding. If the buildup could take place very fast, the magnetic field would be moving rapidly enough across the secondary turns to induce a voltage sufficient to jump the spark-plug gap. But it is not easy to produce the high-voltage surge by this method. A high voltage can be induced, however, if the primary current flow can be stopped very quickly, since this causes a rapid collapse of the magnetic field.

The condenser action (in systems with contact points) causes the flow of current in the primary winding to be very rapidly stopped. Consequently, the magnetic field produced by the current flow quickly collapses also. We saw that as much as 250 volts is induced in the primary as the magnetic field collapses. The voltage continues to increase in an attempt to reach a value high enough to set the current flowing again in the primary.

The rapidly collapsing magnetic field also induces voltage in the secondary winding. Practically the same amount of voltage is induced in every turn of wire (primary or secondary) in the coil. There are about a hundred times as many turns of wire in the secondary winding as in the primary. Consequently the secondary voltage can go a hundred times higher. The voltage of the secondary winding quickly increases to a value sufficient to jump the gap at the spark plug, somewhere between 4000 and 20,000 volts (Fig. 13-17). Note that the firing voltage is attained in a few millionths of a second—a very short time indeed. The variation in voltage required is due to the width of the spark-plug gap, compression in the cylinder, temperature of spark-plug electrodes, and many other factors.

As soon as the plug fires, the energy in the ignition coil (stored momentarily in the form of magnetism) begins to be converted into a flow of current. This current flows through the secondary winding and across the spark-plug gap. Now, a reduction in voltage takes place. Here is the reason: The flow of current in the secondary winding produces a magnetic field. The magnetic field thus produced is in the same direction as that of the field already in existence (produced by the primary winding). The magnetic field, therefore, partially stops collapsing, and the induced voltage in the secondary drops to as low as 3000 volts—enough to sustain the arc after it has formed.

☼ 13-12 The complete voltage picture

We have described what happens in the ignition system to produce the high-voltage surges that make the spark plugs spark. Now let us draw a picture showing the complete voltages during the production of one spark (Fig. 13-18). To start with, the points open at A (and also F). When the points open, the secondary voltage jumps up to B. This is the voltage required to start the spark. A to B is called the *firing line*. After the spark has started, the voltage drops down to C. It takes much less voltage to keep the spark going after it is once started. The spark continues from C to D, on the *spark line*. This is also called the firing section of the complete voltage picture. C to D is a very short time, measured in hundred-thousandths of a second. But it is long enough to continue the spark through as many as 20° of crankshaft rotation. This is long enough to ignite the compressed air–fuel mixture in the cylinder.

After most of the magnetic energy in the coil has been converted into electricity to make the spark, the spark across the spark-plug gap dies as at D. However, there is still some energy left in the coil, and this produces the wavy line D to E—the intermediate section. This line is called the *coil-condenser oscillation line*. What this wavy line means is that the remaining energy is pushing electric current back and forth in the ignition secondary. The voltage alternates, but it is no longer high enough to produce a spark. After a very short time, the voltage dies out. Then, at E, the points close, sending current to the primary winding of the ignition coil. Now an alternating current is produced for a moment in the secondary winding. This is shown by the oscillations (wavy line) immediately after E. Shortly, however, the oscillations die out. The magnetic field builds up in the coil primary from E to F as the points remain closed. This is called the *dwell section*. Now, the points open at F and the whole process is repeated.

The voltage must go up high enough to fire the spark plug as shown in Fig. 13-18 (A to B). The wider the spark-plug gap, the higher the voltage must go. Also, the higher the compression ratio, the more compressed the mixture is, and the higher the voltage must go to push a spark through the denser mixture. In normal service, two factors work to increase the voltage required to fire the plug. One is that engine deposits can accumulate and increase the compression ratio. The other is that in normal service the spark-plug gap grows at the rate of about 0.001 inch [0.025 mm] per 1000 miles [1609.3 km]. The gap increases because of electrode erosion caused by the sparks. These two factors, engine deposits and plug-gap growth, mean that the required firing voltage goes up as the car is driven. Ultimately, new plugs and other service will be needed. The reason is that the engine begins to miss because

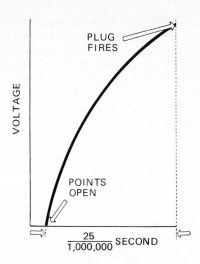

Fig. 13-17 Curve of secondary voltage, showing the approximate time between opening of the points and the instant the spark occurs across the spark-plug gap.

the ignition system can no longer supply the higher voltage required.

⚙ **13-13 Spark plugs** The spark plug (Fig. 13-19) consists of a metal shell to which are fastened a porcelain-like insulator and an electrode extending through the center of the insulator. The metal shell has a short electrode attached to one side; this is bent in toward the center electrode. There are threads on the metal shell that allow it to be screwed into a tapped hole in the cylinder head. The two electrodes are of special heavy wire, and there is a gap of up to 0.040 inch [1.02 mm] between them (or 0.080 inch [2.03 mm] for some electronic ignition systems). The electric spark jumps this gap to ignite the air–fuel mixture in the combustion

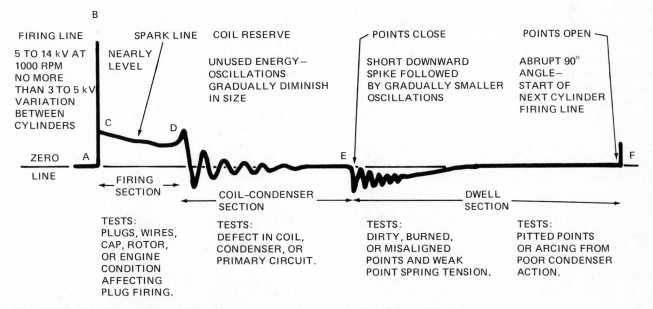

Fig. 13-18 Waveform, or trace, showing one complete spark-plug firing cycle for a contact-point ignition system. The *dwell section* is the period during which the contact points are closed. In the electronic system, it is the period during which the electronic control maintains a complete circuit between the battery and ignition coil.

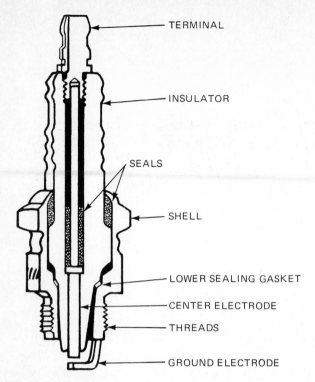

Fig. 13-19 Cutaway spark plug. *(Champion Spark Plugs)*

Labels on figure: TERMINAL, INSULATOR, SEALS, SHELL, LOWER SEALING GASKET, CENTER ELECTRODE, THREADS, GROUND ELECTRODE

chamber. The spark jumps from the center, or insulated, electrode to the grounded, or outer, electrode. The seals between the metal base, porcelain, and center electrode, as well as the porcelain itself, must be able to withstand the high pressure and temperature created in the combustion chamber during the power stroke.

The reason that the ignition system is designed so that the spark will jump from the center to the outer electrode, as mentioned above, is this. The center electrode is hotter and the spark can jump more easily from this electrode. That means that the voltage does not have to go as high. The ignition coil is wound and connected into the system so that the high-voltage surge from the coil secondary goes to the center electrode of the spark plug. If the connections in the ignition system are accidentally reversed, a higher voltage is required to fire the plugs. The spark must jump from the cooler ground electrode to the center electrode. More voltage is needed to jump the gap, and the engine may miss.

Some spark plugs have a built-in resistor which forms part of the center electrode (Fig. 13-20). The purpose of this resistor is to reduce radio and television interference from the ignition system. We have been talking of the high-voltage surge from the ignition-coil secondary as though it were a single powerful surge that caused the spark to jump instantaneously across the spark-plug gap. Actually, the action is more complex than that. There may be a whole series of preliminary surges and, at the end of the sparking cycle, the spark may be quenched and may re-form several times. The effect of all this is that the ignition wiring acts like a radio transmitting antenna; the surges of high voltage send out static that causes radio and television interference. However, the resistors in the spark plugs tend

to concentrate the surges in each sparking cycle, reduce their number, and thus reduce the interference.

Electronic ignition systems use high-resistance secondary wiring (high-voltage cables) and do not use spark plugs with built-in resistors.

⚙ **13-14 Spark-plug heat range and reach** Two important characteristics of spark plugs are their heat range and their reach. Heat range of the plug determines the temperature the spark plug will attain in the engine, that is, how hot the plug will get. This is controlled by the shape of the plug and the distance heat must travel from the center electrode of the plug to reach the cooler cylinder head (Fig. 13-21). If the path the heat must travel is long, the plug will run hot. If the path is short, the plug will run cooler.

If the plug runs too cold, it will not become hot enough to burn away sooty deposits that collect on the insulator around the center electrode. It can foul and miss. That is, the high-voltage surges will leak across the sooty deposit and not jump the spark gap. If the plug runs too hot, it will wear, or burn, the electrodes more rapidly. This also can lead to a miss because the gap becomes too wide for the spark to jump. There is more on this in ⚙ 14-14 which discusses the analysis of defective spark plugs.

Spark-plug reach is the depth the electrodes enter the combustion chamber. If a plug is too long, it can reach, or stick, into the combustion chamber too far. It could interfere with the turbulence, or movement, of the air–fuel mixture. Also, it could be struck by a valve or the piston. On the other hand, if the plug does not reach far enough, the spark will not be out far enough to effectively ignite the mixture. The ideal position is for the plug gap to be in the mainstream of the air–fuel mixture as it moves in the combustion chamber toward the end of compression.

⚙ **13-15 Secondary wiring** The secondary wiring consists of the high-voltage cables connected between the distributor cap, the spark plugs, and the high-voltage terminal of the ignition coil. These cables are heavily insulated because they carry the high-voltage surges that produce the sparks at the plug gaps. The insulation must be able to withstand the effects of high temperature and oil as well as the high voltage.

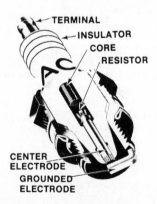

Fig. 13-20 Cutaway resistor-type spark plug. *(AC Spark Plug Division of General Motors Corporation)*

Labels on figure: TERMINAL, INSULATOR, CORE, RESISTOR, CENTER ELECTRODE, GROUNDED ELECTRODE

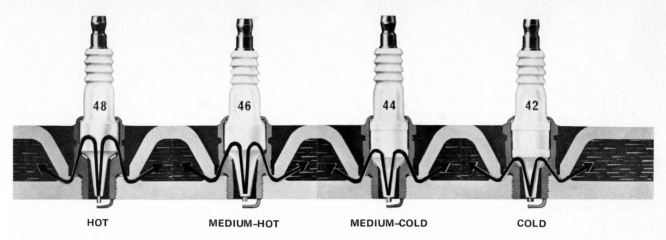

Fig. 13-21 Heat range of spark plugs. The longer the heat path (indicated by arrows), the hotter the plug runs. *(AC Spark Plug Division of General Motors Corporation)*

Before 1961, the cores of the cables were of copper or aluminum wire. However, in 1961, all automotive manufacturers in the United States began to install cables which had carbon-impregnated linen cores. The carbon-impregnated linen forms a resistance path for the high-voltage surges, producing the same effect as the resistors in the spark plugs (⚙ 13-13). These cables thus do an effective job of eliminating radio and television interference from ignition systems.

In 1963, many cars began using cables with graphite-saturated fiberglass cores. These operate in the same manner as the carbon-impregnated linen-core cables. However, it is claimed that the fiberglass cores are less likely to break when the cables are pulled off the spark plugs and have less tendency to char from the high temperatures that are caused by poor connections.

Today, spark-plug cables for electronic ignition systems are made of special string that is coated with carbon. A jacket of silicone is placed around the string; this is the insulation. Silicone cables are easily identified by their size. Older spark-plug wires are 7 mm [0.276 inch] in diameter. Silicone cables are 8 mm [0.315 inch] in diameter. You must handle silicone cables with extra care. They are more easily damaged than the older type of secondary cables. The General Motors HEI system (described in Chapter 16) uses these cables. Since 1977 all Ford and Lincoln-Mercury cars have used these cables. In addition to their larger size, you can identify them by color. The Ford cables are blue with longer silicone spark-plug boots which are red in color. The secondary cables used with the General Motors HEI systems are gray in color. Silicone cables must be handled with care, as we said. Ford states that they must be disconnected only when absolutely necessary, and then with a boot pliers. That is, they should be disconnected only when an obvious defect is seen, when necessary for diagnosis, or when spark plugs are to be replaced.

Spark advances

⚙ 13-16 Centrifugal spark advance Several things determine the correct instant for introducing the spark into the cylinder; one of the most important of these is engine speed. As has been already shown (see ⚙ 12-6), the spark has to be sent to the cylinder earlier in the compression stroke at high engine speeds so that the mixture can ignite and deliver its power to the piston. To obtain this advance of the spark timing based on engine speed, centrifugal-advance mechanisms of various types are used. One type is shown in Fig. 13-22. It consists of two weights, which are thrown out against spring tension as engine speed increases. This movement is transmitted through a toggle arrangement to the breaker cam. This causes the cam to move ahead or rotate with respect to the distributor drive shaft (Fig. 13-23).

NOTE: The weights, and centrifugal mechanism, may be located below the breaker plate (Fig. 13-4) or at the top of the distributor shaft, above the breaker cam (Fig. 13-5).

On the contact-point distributor, this centrifugal advance causes the cam to open and close the contact points earlier at high engine speeds. The timing of the spark to the cylinder consequently varies from no advance at low speed to full advance at high speed, when the weights have reached the outer limits of their travel. The contours of the toggle arrangement (advance cam and weights) and the strength of the springs are designed to suit the special requirements of the engine. They produce the spark advance at each engine speed that will give maximum power and best performance along with reduced emissions (see ⚙ 12-7).

⚙ 13-17 Intake-manifold vacuum spark advance There is another condition besides the engine speed that must be considered in determining the proper spark advance of an engine—and that is intake-manifold vacuum. The proper centrifugal-advance curve is developed with the engine operating at wide-open throttle. Under part throttle, additional spark advance could be used.

When the throttle is only partly opened, the admission of air into the intake manifold is restricted. A vacuum develops in the intake manifold. The speed of the engine and the amount of throttle opening determine the amount of vacuum. With vacuum in the intake

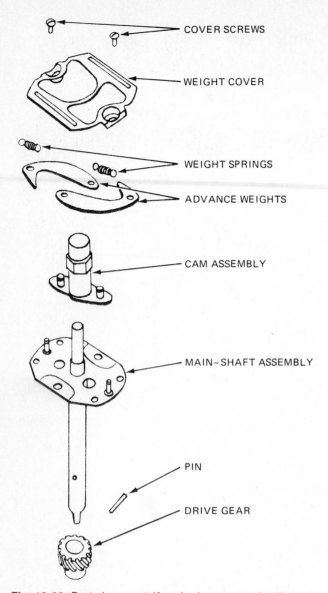

Fig. 13-22 Parts in a centrifugal advance mechanism.

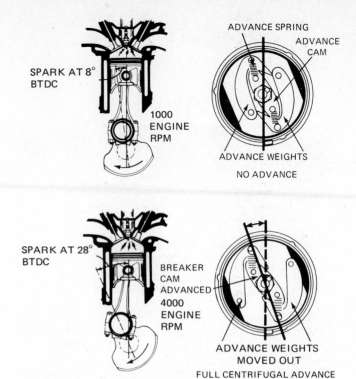

Fig. 13-23 Centrifugal-advance mechanism in a no-advance and full-advance position. In the example shown, the ignition is timed at 8° before TDC on idle. There is no centrifugal advance at 1000 rpm. But there is 28° total advance (20° centrifugal advance plus 8° original timing) at 4000 engine rpm. *(Delco-Remy Division of General Motors Corporation)*

manifold, less air and vaporized gasoline will be delivered to the cylinders. This means that the mixture that does get into the cylinder will not be compressed as much. There is less mixture to start with.

With lower compression, the rate of flame propagation will be slower as the mixture is ignited and burns. Unless there is an additional spark advance, the full power of the charge will not be realized because the piston will be moving downward before the mixture is well ignited. In order to provide this additional advance, most distributors have a vacuum-advance mechanism which produces a spark advance based on intake-manifold vacuum conditions. This spark advance is in addition to the centrifugal advance produced by the centrifugal-advance mechanism.

Figure 13-24 illustrates one type of vacuum-advance mechanism used on contact-point distributors. It contains a spring-loaded, airtight diaphragm connected by a linkage, or lever, to the breaker plate. The breaker plate is supported on a bearing or pivot so it can turn with respect to the distributor housing. The breaker

plate turns only a few degrees, since the linkage to the spring-loaded diaphragm prevents any greater rotation than this.

The spring-loaded side of the diaphragm is connected through a vacuum line to an opening in the carburetor (Figs. 13-24 to 13-27). This opening is called a *ported* vacuum source. It is on the atmospheric side of the throttle valve when the throttle is in the idling position. There is no vacuum advance in this position.

As soon as the throttle is opened, however, it swings past the opening of the vacuum passage. The intake-manifold vacuum can then draw air from the vacuum line and the airtight chamber in the vacuum-advance mechanism. This causes the diaphragm to move against the spring. The linkage to the breaker plate then rotates the breaker plate. This movement carries the contact points around so that the cam, as it rotates, closes and opens the points earlier in the cycle. The spark consequently appears at the spark-plug gap earlier in the compression stroke. As the throttle is opened wider, there will be less vacuum in the intake manifold and less vacuum advance. At wide-open throttle, there will be no vacuum advance at all. The spark advance under this condition will be provided entirely by the centrifugal-advance mechanism.

NOTE: Many vacuum-advance units are connected to a manifold-vacuum source that allows full vacuum advance at idle. This is necessary because of the very lean idle mixtures in emission-controlled engines.

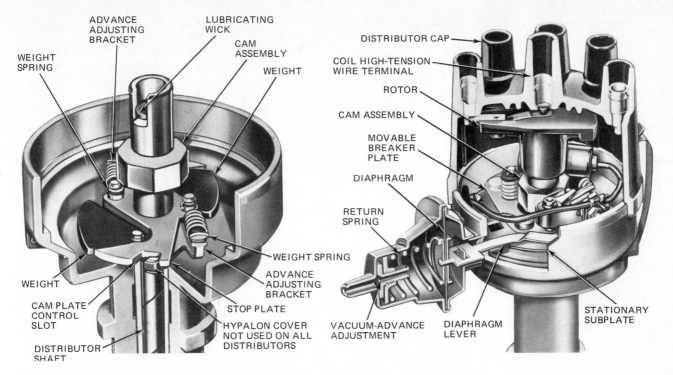

WEIGHT SPRING

ADVANCE ADJUSTING BRACKET

LUBRICATING WICK

CAM ASSEMBLY

WEIGHT

DISTRIBUTOR CAP

COIL HIGH-TENSION WIRE TERMINAL

ROTOR

CAM ASSEMBLY

MOVABLE BREAKER PLATE

DIAPHRAGM

RETURN SPRING

WEIGHT

CAM PLATE CONTROL SLOT

DISTRIBUTOR SHAFT

WEIGHT SPRING

ADVANCE ADJUSTING BRACKET

STOP PLATE

HYPALON COVER NOT USED ON ALL DISTRIBUTORS

VACUUM-ADVANCE ADJUSTMENT

DIAPHRAGM LEVER

STATIONARY SUBPLATE

Fig. 13-24 Cutaway views of a distributor, showing construction of the centrifugal- and vacuum-advance mechanisms. (Ford Motor Company)

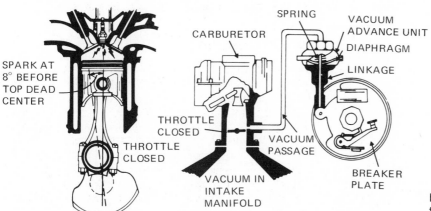

SPARK AT 8° BEFORE TOP DEAD CENTER

THROTTLE CLOSED

CARBURETOR

SPRING

VACUUM ADVANCE UNIT

DIAPHRAGM

LINKAGE

THROTTLE CLOSED

VACUUM PASSAGE

VACUUM IN INTAKE MANIFOLD

BREAKER PLATE

Fig. 13-25 When the throttle is closed, there is no vacuum advance.

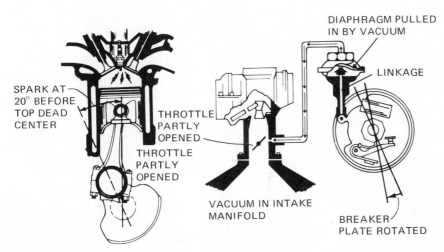

SPARK AT 20° BEFORE TOP DEAD CENTER

THROTTLE PARTLY OPENED

THROTTLE PARTLY OPENED

DIAPHRAGM PULLED IN BY VACUUM

LINKAGE

VACUUM IN INTAKE MANIFOLD

BREAKER PLATE ROTATED

Fig. 13-26 Operation of the vacuum-advance mechanism. When the throttle swings past the opening, a vacuum is admitted to the vacuum-advance mechanism on the distributor. The breaker plate, with the points, is rotated to advance the spark.

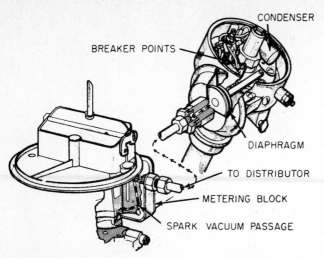

Fig. 13-27 Connection of the vacuum line between the carburetor and the vacuum-advance mechanism on the distributor. *(Ford Motor Company)*

⚙ **13-18 Combining centrifugal and vacuum advances** At any particular speed, there will be a certain definite centrifugal advance due to engine speed plus a possible additional spark advance resulting from vacuum conditions in the intake manifold. Figure 13-28 illustrates this. At 40 miles per hour (mph) [64.37 km/h], the centrifugal-advance mechanism provides 15° of spark advance on this particular application. The vacuum-advance mechanism will supply up to 15° additional advance under part-throttle conditions. However, if the engine is operated at wide-open throttle, this added vacuum advance will not be obtained. The advance, in the usual operating conditions, will vary somewhat between a straight line (centrifugal advance) and a curved line (centrifugal advance plus total possible vacuum advance) as the throttle is opened and closed and as engine speed changes.

The distributor illustrated in Fig. 13-29 does not contain a centrifugal-advance mechanism but utilizes vacuum from the carburetor venturi and the intake manifold to produce the proper advance. Full control by vacuum alone is possible because air speed through the carburetor air horn, and thus the vacuum in the venturi, are directly related to engine speed. Let us see how this system functions.

In the carburetor shown in Fig. 13-29 there are two vacuum openings in the air horn, one at the venturi and the other just above the throttle when it is closed. The lower, or throttle, bore vacuum takeoff opening may have two ports on some models as shown in Fig. 13-29. These openings are connected by vacuum passages to each other and to the distributor vacuum-advance mechanism by a vacuum line. Vacuum imposed on the diaphragm in the vacuum-advance mechanism causes the breaker-plate assembly to rotate. This is very similar to other vacuum-advance devices discussed above. Rotation of the breaker plate causes a spark advance.

As engine speed increases, the vacuum at the venturi in the carburetor increases because the air speed through the venturi increases. This causes an increasing spark advance that is related to engine speed. At the same time, under part-throttle operating conditions, there will be a vacuum in the intake manifold, and this acts at the throttle vacuum ports in the carburetor to produce a further vacuum advance. Thus, the interrelation of the vacuum conditions at the two points in the carburetor produces, in effect, a speed advance (as with a centrifugal-advance device) combined with a vacuum advance.

A variation of this design for V-8 engines with four-barrel carburetors uses a spark-control valve in the

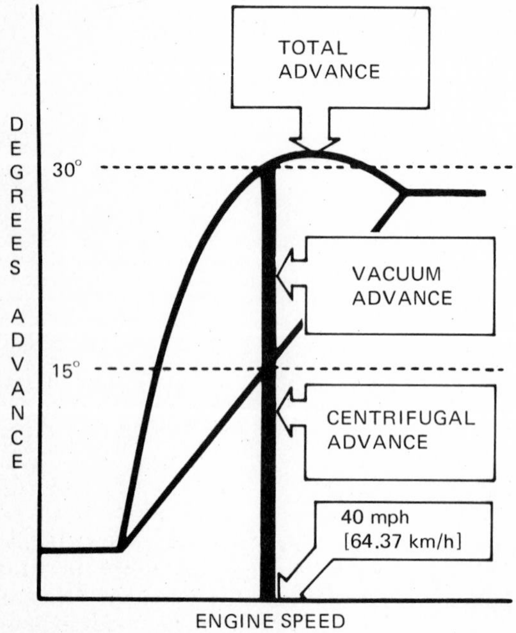

Fig. 13-28 Centrifugal- and vacuum-advance curves for one application.

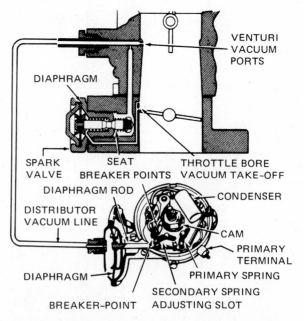

Fig. 13-29 Vacuum-line connections between the carburetor and distributor having full vacuum control. *(Ford Motor Company)*

carburetor. The complete arrangement is shown in Fig. 13-30, and the valve details are shown in Fig. 13-31. The spark-control-valve device momentarily retards the spark during acceleration to prevent excessive ping (engine knock). When the throttle is held steady in a partly opened position, manifold vacuum is sufficient to hold the spark-control valve open. The vacuum, acting through the vacuum opening D (Fig. 13-31), causes diaphragm A to be pulled in so that valve B is open. Now, intake-manifold vacuum can act through valve B and the additional vacuum passage (shown dotted in Fig. 13-31). This provides the part-throttle vacuum advance discussed in previous paragraphs. However, when the throttle is opened further for acceleration, manifold vacuum drops. Now, the vacuum against the diaphragm is reduced so much that the diaphragm spring can move the spark-control valve to the closed position. As the valve closes, there is a rapid spark retard; this reduces the chances of ping during acceleration. When the accelerator is again moved toward the closed position, or as engine speed builds up so that intake-manifold vacuum increases, then the spark-control valve will open again. This again produces the part-throttle vacuum advance.

On the distributor shown in Fig. 13-30, there are two spark-control diaphragms. The secondary spark-control diaphragm (G in Fig. 13-30) has the purpose of reducing or eliminating ping on sudden acceleration. When the throttle is opened suddenly, the intake-manifold vacuum falls sharply. This permits the spring in the secondary spark-control chamber to push the diaphragm inward. This pushes air into the primary spark-control chamber so that, for a moment, the primary spark-control diaphragm is pushed inward slightly. This action forces a momentary spark retard while the distributor-vacuum line, carburetor-vacuum passages,

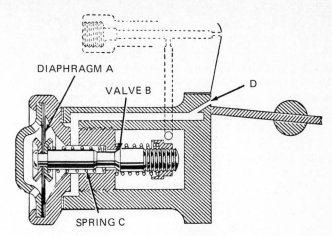

Fig. 13-31 Sectional view of a spark-control valve. *(Ford Motor Company)*

and primary spark-control diaphragm are becoming adjusted to the new pressure conditions which have developed. Thus the engine ping that could otherwise develop on quick acceleration is reduced or eliminated.

NOTE: Vacuum-advance disconnect devices, installed (retrofitted) on older cars to provide exhaust emission control, should not be installed on engines with distributors having full vacuum control, such as we have just discussed.

⚙ 13-19 Distributor for exhaust-emission control The internal-combustion engine does not completely burn all the fuel entering the engine cylinder; some unburned fuel escapes in the exhaust gases. As operating conditions change, the amount of unburned fuel also changes. This unburned fuel is bad because it helps create smog, which is a health hazard. Therefore

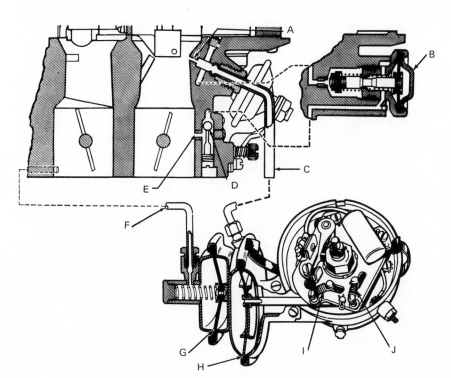

Fig. 13-30 Vacuum-line connections between a four-barrel carburetor for a V-8 engine and a distributor with full vacuum control. A, primary venturi-vacuum passage. B, spark-control valve. C, distributor-vacuum line. D, vacuum-passage check ball. E, manifold-vacuum passage. F, manifold-vacuum line. G, secondary spark-control diaphragm. H, primary spark-control diaphragm. I, secondary breaker-plate spring. J, primary breaker-plate spring. *(Ford Motor Company)*

the government has set limits to the amount of unburned fuel that may remain in the exhaust gases. In order to comply with these restrictions, automobile manufacturers have made numerous changes to the engine and accessory systems. Some engines have air pumps that force air into the exhaust manifolds; this added air burns up much of the unburned fuel exiting from the engine cylinders.

Many late-model cars have a catalytic converter to change unburned and partly burned fuel in the exhaust gases into harmless products. In addition, combustion chambers have been redesigned and carburetor settings have been made leaner (to deliver less fuel). Also, ignition timing has been changed and special devices have been installed in ignition systems to improve combustion in the engine cylinders.

⚙ 13-20 Idle vacuum retard

Figure 13-32 shows one distributor that has a special dual-diaphragm vacuum advance. One diaphragm provides vacuum advance in the same manner as other units previously described. The second diaphragm provides a spark retard during idle. This assures better combustion when the engine idles, so that less unburned fuel escapes from the engine.

Figure 13-33 shows sectional views of the dual-diaphragm vacuum-advance unit and illustrates the different positions of the diaphragms during different operating conditions. The outer, or advance, diaphragm, which provides vacuum advance, is coupled to the movable breaker plate, just as in other vacuum advance

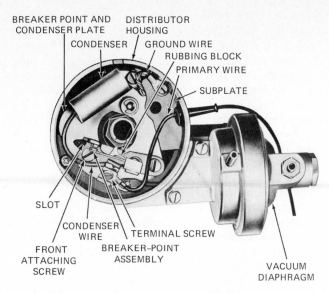

Fig. 13-32 Distributor with dual-diaphragm vacuum advance. *(Ford Motor Company)*

distributors. As vacuum increases in the carburetor venturi, this diaphragm produces a vacuum advance. The illustration to the left in Fig. 13-33 shows the position of the advance diaphragm during full vacuum advance.

When the throttle is closed so the engine idles, intake-manifold vacuum is applied to the inner, or retard, diaphragm. This moves the retard diaphragm in toward the distributor so that ignition timing is retarded. The

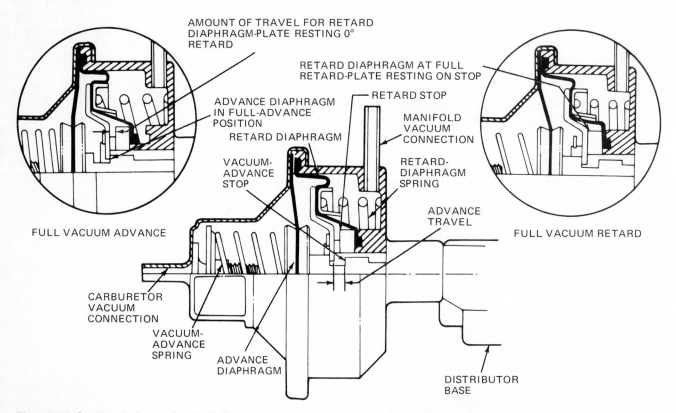

Fig. 13-33 Sectional views of a dual-diaphragm vacuum-advance unit showing positions of the diaphragms during full vacuum advance and full vacuum retard. *(Ford Motor Company)*

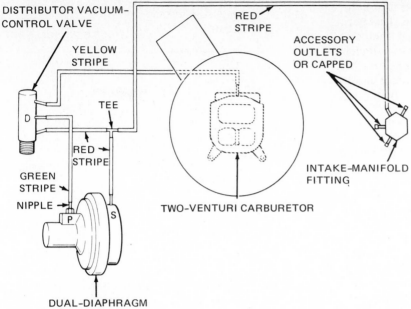

DISTRIBUTOR VACUUM-
CONTROL VALVE

YELLOW
STRIPE

RED
STRIPE

ACCESSORY
OUTLETS
OR CAPPED

TEE

RED
STRIPE

GREEN
STRIPE

NIPPLE

INTAKE-MANIFOLD
FITTING

TWO-VENTURI CARBURETOR

DUAL-DIAPHRAGM
DISTRIBUTOR

Fig. 13-34 Vacuum-line connections to the distributor vacuum-control valve and the dual-diaphragm distributor. *(Ford Motor Company)*

illustration to the right in Fig. 13-33 shows the position of the retard diaphragm during full retard.

⚙ 13-21 Temperature-controlled vacuum advance The dual-diaphragm vacuum-advance system also includes a distributor vacuum-control valve which is a temperature-sensing device. It is incorporated in the distributor vacuum-advance line to provide ignition-timing advance under certain operating conditions. This valve is installed in the engine cooling system so that it is subjected to cooling-system temperatures. Normally, the valve connects the vacuum line from the carburetor ported vacuum source to the vacuum line going to the outer, or advance, diaphragm in the vacuum-advance unit (Fig. 13-34). However, during periods of prolonged idle, engine temperatures may rise above normal. This causes the valve to op-

erate. When this happens, the vacuum line to the carburetor is closed off and the line to the intake manifold is opened, thus applying full manifold vacuum to the outer diaphragm. This produces a timing advance and an increase in engine speed. This increased speed continues until engine temperatures return to normal.

⚙ 13-22 Deceleration valve Some Ford engines use a deceleration valve that functions during hard deceleration to prevent afterburning, or popping, in the engine exhaust system. This valve is connected into the system as shown in Fig. 13-35. It is used with a dual-diaphragm distributor. Normally, the outer, or advance, diaphragm is connected to a vacuum port on the carburetor. But, during fast deceleration, when the intake-manifold vacuum rises excessively, the deceleration valve closes off the carburetor vacuum and pro-

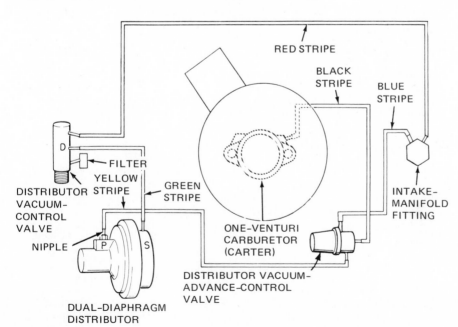

RED STRIPE

BLACK
STRIPE

BLUE
STRIPE

FILTER

YELLOW
STRIPE

GREEN
STRIPE

DISTRIBUTOR
VACUUM-
CONTROL
VALVE

NIPPLE

ONE-VENTURI
CARBURETOR
(CARTER)

INTAKE-
MANIFOLD
FITTING

DISTRIBUTOR VACUUM-
ADVANCE-CONTROL
VALVE

DUAL-DIAPHRAGM
DISTRIBUTOR

Fig. 13-35 Ignition vacuum-advance control system for a six-cylinder engine. *(Ford Motor Company)*

vides a direct connection between intake-manifold vacuum and the distributor outer diaphragm. This permits maximum ignition-timing advance, so that the air–fuel mixture has ample time to burn in the cylinder and does not cause afterburning, or popping, in the exhaust system. The reason the mixture needs more time to burn is this: With high-manifold-vacuum conditions, much less air–fuel mixture enters the cylinder. The mixture is, therefore, much less highly compressed. As a result, it burns much more slowly (rate of flame propagation is lower—see ⚙ 12-8). Advancing the ignition provides the additional time that is needed for the air–fuel mixture to burn.

⚙ **13-23 TCS control of vacuum advance** During part-throttle operation, the distributor vacuum advance operates. This provides more time for the leaner air–fuel mixture to burn. However, this added time also allows more NO_x to develop. Thus a variety of controls have been used to prevent vacuum advance under certain conditions. For example, a transmission-controlled spark (TCS) system is used on some cars. The TCS system prevents vacuum advance when the car is operated in reverse, neutral, or low forward gears. Under these special conditions, vacuum advance could greatly increase the formation of NO_x.

Figure 13-36 shows the TCS system for a six-cylinder engine in a manual-transmission car. The diagram also shows the engine temperature switch (*lower left*) and the idle-stop solenoid. Figure 13-37 shows the situation during starting. Turning on the ignition switch energizes the idle-stop solenoid. The plunger extends to contact the throttle lever. This prevents the throttle from closing completely, so that the engine idles normally. When the engine is turned off, the idle-stop solenoid allows the throttle to close almost completely. This prevents "dieseling," or the engine running with the ignition off.

Now refer to Fig. 13-37 again. Note that turning on the ignition switch completes the circuit through the

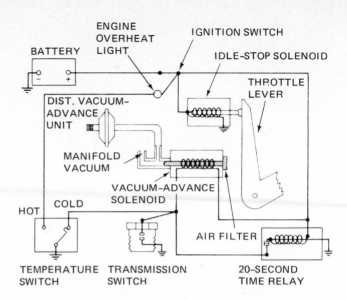

Fig. 13-37 TCS system with cold engine running. (*Chevrolet Motor Division of General Motors Corporation*)

vacuum-advance solenoid and temperature-switch cold terminal. At the same time, the circuit to the 20-second time relay is completed. With either of these circuits complete, the vacuum-advance solenoid is energized. Vacuum is admitted to the distributor vacuum-advance mechanism so that vacuum advance is obtained.

Figure 13-38 shows the system in low-gear operation. If the engine temperature has gone up enough, the temperature-switch cold points have opened. Also, after 20 seconds, the time-relay switch points open. Thus the circuit to the vacuum-advance solenoid is opened by either of these conditions. The solenoid plunger moves to block vacuum to the distributor vacuum advance. No vacuum advance results.

Figure 13-39 shows the system in high gear. The transmission switch closes its points when the transmission is shifted into high. This energizes the vacuum-advance solenoid so that vacuum is admitted to the

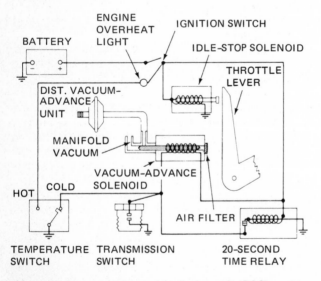

Fig. 13-36 Transmission-controlled spark (TCS) system with engine off. (*Chevrolet Motor Division of General Motors Corporation*)

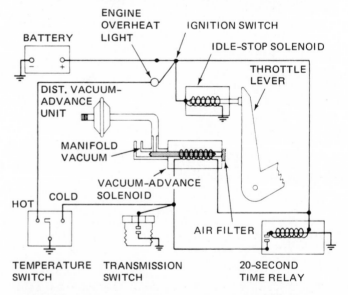

Fig. 13-38 TCS system during low-gear operation. (*Chevrolet Motor Division of General Motors Corporation*)

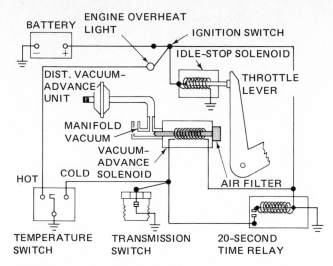

Fig. 13-39 TCS system during operation in high gear. *(Chevrolet Motor Division of General Motors Corporation)*

distributor vacuum-advance mechanism. Vacuum advance can then result.

Some systems have a temperature override switch. This switch causes the system to provide vacuum advance under any condition if the engine begins to overheat. This system is shown in Fig. 13-40. If the engine becomes too hot, the hot points in the temperature override switch close. This energizes the solenoid so that vacuum is admitted to the distributor vacuum advance. With vacuum advance, engine speed increases and improved cooling results.

☼ 13-24 TRS control of vacuum advance A Ford transmission-regulated spark (TRS) system is shown in Fig. 13-41. It is for both manual and automatic transmissions. The system works in about the same way as the Chevrolet TCS system described in ☼ 13-23. The solenoid valve is normally open, allowing vacuum ad-

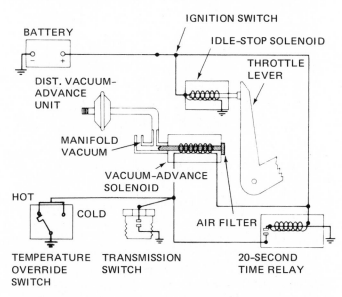

Fig. 13-40 Schematic view of the TCS system which uses a thermostatic temperature override switch. *(Chevrolet Motor Division of General Motors Corporation)*

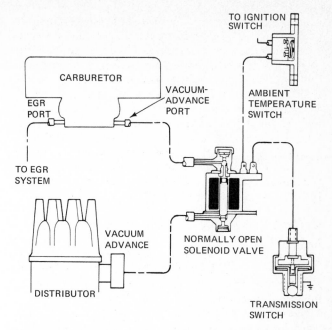

Fig. 13-41 Transmission-regulated spark (TRS) system. *(Ford Motor Company)*

vance when the transmission is in high gear. In the lower gears, the transmission switch is closed. This closes the solenoid valve. With the solenoid valve closed, vacuum is shut off from the distributor vacuum advance. Thus there is no vacuum advance.

☼ 13-25 Other vacuum-advance control systems There are other vacuum-advance controls. Most are especially tailored for the engines and vehicles with which they are used. Recent cars produced by Chrysler Corporation use an orifice spark-advance control (OSAC). The valve has a very small hole, or orifice. This delays any change in the application of vacuum to the distributor by about 17 seconds, when going from idle to part throttle. Therefore there is a delay in vacuum advance until acceleration is well under way. This is a critical time, during which vacuum advance could produce high NO_x.

Ford has used a similar device called the *spark-delay valve device* (Fig. 13-42). It delays vacuum advance during some vehicle-acceleration conditions. The spark-delay valve is connected in series with the vacuum supply from the vacuum-advance port in the carburetor and the distributor vacuum advance. During mild acceleration, the vacuum signal to the distributor can increase only gradually. This is because the spark-delay valve only allows the vacuum to pass through slowly. During deceleration or heavy acceleration, the change in vacuum is great enough to open a check valve. This valve allows the vacuum to bypass the spark-delay valve. This action produces vacuum advance and better engine performance during these critical times. If engine temperatures are low, the temperature switch actuates the solenoid valve. The actuated valve then passes vacuum directly to the distributor vacuum advance (through the check valve). This action provides vacuum advance when the engine is cold.

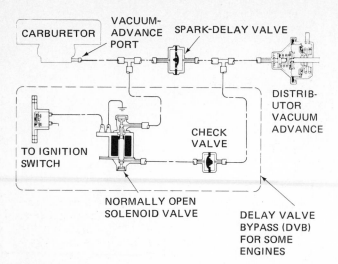

Fig. 13-42 Spark-delay valve device. *(Ford Motor Company)*

☼ 13-26 Radio-frequency-interference shield
Some contact-point distributors, used on cars with radio antennas concealed in the windshield, have a metal shield that covers the distributor contact points. This shield prevents the antenna from picking up interference—static—from the opening and closing of the contact points. The shield is in two parts and is held in place by two screws. Figure 13-43 shows the shield in the installed position. It is removed by taking out the two screws. The half of the shield that covers the contact points has insulation on the inside to prevent accidental grounding of the points to the shield.

☼ 13-27 Ignition switch Originally, the ignition switch had one job to do—turn the ignition primary circuit on and off. However, in recent years, the ignition switch has been given several other jobs. In most cars, there is a START position on the ignition switch that actuates the starting-motor circuit. Also, the alternator field is connected to the battery through the ignition switch. A steering-wheel lock can be built into the ignition switch. An accessory circuit is included to operate a buzzer if the ignition key is left in the lock and a door is opened. An electric fuel pump can be connected to the battery through the ignition switch. Such accessories as the radio and heater are also connected through the ignition switch to the battery.

Several of these systems have already been discussed. Following chapters discuss the others except for the steering-wheel lock, which is described below. Figures 13-44 and 13-45 show the combination ignition switch and steering-wheel lock. The ignition switch is mounted on the steering column, as shown, and it has a gear attached to the cylinder in the lock. When the ignition key is inserted and the ignition switch is turned to ON, the gear rotates and pulls the rack and plunger out of the notch in the disk. The disk is mounted on the steering shaft. This frees the steering shaft and wheel so that the car can be steered. When the ignition switch is turned to OFF, the rotation of the gear moves the rack and plunger toward the locked position. If the plunger is lined up with a notch in the disk, it will enter the notch and lock the steering wheel. However, if the wheel and disk happen to be in a position where the plunger cannot enter a notch in the disk, the plunger will be spring-loaded against the side of the disk. Now, a slight turn of the wheel will turn the disk enough so that the plunger will enter a notch and thereby lock the steering wheel.

Fig. 13-43 Ignition distributor with cap and rotor removed to show the radio-frequency-interference shield. Left, one of the two attaching screws being removed. Right, shield being removed. *(Delco-Remy Division of General Motors Corporation)*

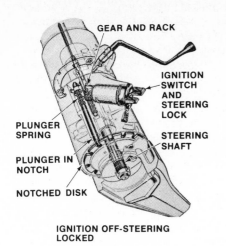

IGNITION OFF-STEERING
LOCKED

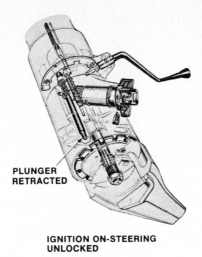

IGNITION ON-STEERING
UNLOCKED

Fig. 13-44 Combination ignition switch and steering lock in phantom views, showing the two positions of the lock. *(General Motors Corporation)*

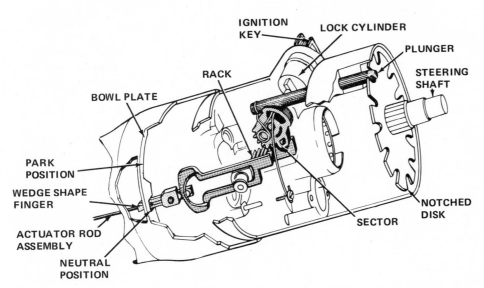

Fig. 13-45 A line drawing giving a more detailed look at the internal mechanism in the combination ignition switch and steering lock. *(Oldsmobile Division of General Motors Corporation)*

Chapter 13 review questions

Select the *one* correct, best, or most probable answer to each question. Then check your answers against the correct answers given at the end of the book.

1. The ignition coil has:
   a. one winding,
   b. two windings,
   c. three windings,
   d. four windings.
2. The primary winding of the ignition coil is connected to the battery through the:
   a. spark-plug wiring,
   b. distributor cap and rotor,
   c. distributor gearing,
   d. distributor contact points.
3. The voltage induced in a winding by self-induction is called:
   a. reverse voltage,
   b. reduced voltage,
   c. countervoltage,
   d. maximum voltage.

4. The spark-producing high voltage is produced in the secondary winding during:
   a. magnetic buildup,
   b. magnetic collapse,
   c. the time points are closed,
   d. the moment before the points open.
5. The ignition condenser is connected:
   a. across points,
   b. in series with points,
   c. in the secondary circuit,
   d. in the primary circuit.
6. The main function of the ignition condenser is to protect the contact points and produce:
   a. quick magnetic collapse,
   b. slow magnetic collapse,
   c. high voltage on points,
   d. minimum primary voltage.
7. The rotating switch that connects the various spark plugs to the ignition-coil secondary in regular firing order is formed by the distributor:
   a. points and condenser,
   b. cap and rotor,
   c. switch and contact points,
   d. cap and wiring.

8. The device in many distributors that pushes the breaker cam ahead as engine speed increases is called the:
   a. vacuum-advance mechanism,
   b. centrifugal-advance mechanism,
   c. full-advance mechanism,
   d. vacuum-brake mechanism.

9. The device in many distributors that shifts the position of the breaker plate to produce a change in the timing of the spark is actuated by:
   a. intake-manifold vacuum,
   b. engine speed,
   c. centrifugal advance,
   d. throttle opening.

10. With the throttle wide open, vacuum advance will be:
   a. at a maximum,
   b. part to full,
   c. at a minimum,
   d. more than the centrifugal advance.

CONTACT-POINT IGNITION-SYSTEM TROUBLE DIAGNOSIS

After studying this chapter, you should be able to:

1. List the 11 trouble conditions in the trouble-diagnosis chart.
2. Explain possible causes and checks or corrections to be made for each trouble.
3. List the various ignition-testing instruments described in the chapter.
4. Use each available testing instrument in the shop to make ignition-system tests.

14-1 Causes of ignition failure This chapter lists ignition failures in contact-point systems, their possible causes, and checks or corrections to be made. The latter part of the chapter describes the various testing instruments used to check the components of the ignition system as well as the complete system. Chapter 15 describes contact-point distributor service. In Chapter 16 we discuss electronic ignition systems, and in Chapter 17 the servicing of these electronic systems.

Ignition-system failures can be grouped into three categories, as follows:

1. Loss of energy in the primary circuit. This, in turn, may be caused by several conditions.
   a. Resistance in the primary circuit due to defective leads, bad connections, burned distributor contact points or switch, or open coil primary
   b. Points not properly set
   c. Discharged battery or defective charging system
   d. Defective condenser (shorted, low insulation resistance, or high series resistance)
   e. Grounded primary circuit in coil, wiring, or distributor
   f. Defective electronic amplifier unit or pickup-coil circuit
2. Loss of energy in the secondary circuit.
   a. Plugs fouled, broken, or out of adjustment
   b. Defective secondary wiring which allows high-voltage leaks
   c. High-voltage leakage across coil head, distributor cap, or rotor
   d. Defective connections in high-voltage circuits
3. Out of time.
   a. Timing not set properly
   b. Distributor bearing or shaft worn, or shaft bent

   c. Centrifugal or vacuum advance defective
   d. Preignition, due to plugs or wrong heat range, fouled plugs, etc.

14-2 Contact-point ignition-system trouble diagnosis chart The chart that follows lists (1) various ignition-system troubles and possible engine troubles that might originate in the contact-point ignition system, (2) possible causes of these various troubles, and (3) checks or corrections to be made.

NOTE: The chart covers only conditions that might arise from troubles in the ignition system. Many of these conditions could result from troubles in other components and systems of the engine.

14-3 Quick checks to locate trouble There are several quick checks that can be made when certain types of troubles are reported. These quick checks often immediately indicate the cause of trouble. On the other hand, it may be necessary to use special testing instruments (as explained on following pages) to find the cause. Often, the first step will be to recharge or replace the battery, since the driver may have run it down in a vain attempt to start. Quick checks to be made, as well as causes and corrections of various ignition troubles, are described below.

NOTE: If an oscilloscope is available (see 14-19) and the engine can be started, the oscilloscope can pinpoint many trouble causes in the ignition system.

14-4 Engine cranks normally but will not start If the starting motor cranks the engine at normal cranking speed but the engine will not start, the trouble is probably in the ignition system or the fuel system. First,

Ignition-System Trouble Diagnosis Chart

(See ☀ 14-3 to 14-14 for detailed explanations of trouble causes and checks or corrections listed below.)

CONDITION	POSSIBLE CAUSE	CHECK OR CORRECTION
1. Engine cranks normally but will not start (☀ 14-4)	a. Open primary circuit	Check connections, coil, contact points, and switch for open
	b. Coil primary grounded	Replace coil
	c. Points not opening	Adjust
	d. Points burned	Clean or replace
	e. Out of time	Check and adjust timing
	f. Condenser defective	Replace
	g. Coil secondary open or grounded	Replace coil
	h. High-voltage leakage	Check coil head, distributor cap and rotor, and leads
	i. Spark plugs fouled	Clean and adjust or replace
	j. Fuel system faulty	
	k. Engine faulty	
2. Engine runs but misses—one cylinder (☀ 14-5)	a. Defective spark plug	Clean or replace
	b. Distributor cap, rotor, or lead defective	Replace
	c. Engine defects such as stuck valve, defective rings, piston, gasket	
3. Engine runs but misses—different cylinders (☀ 14-6)	a. Points dirty, worn, or out of adjustment	Clean, replace or adjust as necessary
	b. Condenser defective	Replace
	c. Advance mechanisms defective	Repair or replace distributor
	d. Defective high-voltage wiring	Replace
	e. Defective (weak) coil	Replace
	f. Bad connections	Clean and tighten connections
	g. High-voltage leakage	Check coil head, distributor cap and rotor, and leads
	h. Defective spark plugs	Clean, adjust or replace
	i. Defective fuel system	
	j. Defects in engine such as loss of compression or faulty valve action	
4. Engine lacks power (☀ 14-7)	a. Timing off	Retime ignition
	b. Exhaust system clogged	Clear
	c. Excessive rolling resistance	Check tires, brakes, wheel bearings, and alignment
	d. Heavy engine oil	Use correct oil
	e. Wrong fuel	Use correct fuel
	f. Engine overheats	See item 5
	g. Other defects listed under item 3	
5. Engine overheats (☀ 14-8)	a. Late ignition timing	Retime ignition
	b. Lack of coolant or other trouble in cooling system	
	c. Late valve timing or other engine conditions	
6. Engine backfires (☀ 14-9)	a. Ignition timing off	Retime ignition
	b. Ignition crossfiring	Check high-voltage wiring, cap, and rotor for leakage paths
	c. Spark plugs of wrong heat range	Install correct plugs
	d. Engine overheating	See item 5
	e. Fuel system not supplying proper air–fuel ratio	
	f. Engine defects such as hot valves or carbon	
	g. Defective air-injection system	Check system
7. Engine knocks or pings (☀ 14-10)	a. Improper timing	Retime ignition
	b. Advance mechanisms faulty	Rebuild or replace distributor
	c. Points out of adjustment	Readjust
	d. Distributor bearing worn or shaft bent	Rebuild or replace distributor

(See ☼ 14-3 to 14-14 for detailed explanations of trouble causes and checks or corrections listed below.)

CONDITION	POSSIBLE CAUSE	CHECK OR CORRECTION
	e. Spark plugs of wrong heat range	Replace with correct plugs
	f. Low-octane fuel	Use fuel of proper octane
	g. Conditions listed under item 6	
8. Rapid wear of centrifugal-advance mechanism (☼ 14-11)	a. Loose or worn valve-timing gears b. Worn oil pump	
9. Pitted contact points (☼ 14-12)	a. Transfer of point material	Buildup on positive points: install new condenser with higher capacity; separate leads or move closer to ground; shorten condenser lead Buildup on negative points: install new condenser with lower capacity; move leads closer together or away from ground; lengthen condenser lead
10. Burned or oxidized contact points (☼ 14-13)	a. Excessive resistance in condenser circuit b. High voltage c. Excessive dwell d. Weak spring tension	Tighten condenser mounting and connection; replace condenser if bad Readjust or replace voltage regulator Reset point opening Adjust contact-spring tension
11. Spark plugs defective (☼ 14-14)	a. Cracked insulator b. Plug sooty c. Plug white or gray, with blistered insulator	Careless installation; install new plug Install hotter plug; correct condition in fuel system or engine causing oil burning or high fuel consumption Install cooler plug

test the ignition system by trying the spark test, as follows: Disconnect the lead from the center terminal of the distributor cap. Use insulated pliers to hold the lead clip about ¼ inch [6.35 mm] from the engine block while cranking the engine. If a good spark repeatedly jumps to the block, the chances are the primary and secondary circuits are in good condition. These circuits must be more or less normal to produce a good spark.

If you get a good spark, then failure to start could be due to fouled spark plugs or out-of-time ignition. More probably, the trouble is in the fuel system. However, it should be remembered that many other conditions—malfunctioning valves, loss of engine compression, and so on—could prevent normal starting.

One condition that sometimes prevents starting of older cars on humid or rainy days is moisture collecting on the spark-plug insulators. The moisture allows the high voltage to leak to the ground instead of jumping the spark gap. Thus, no ignition occurs and the engine will not start. However, if the moisture is wiped from the spark-plug insulators, a normal start can be made. Today's cars have molded insulating boots which cover the spark plug. Their tight fit prevents moisture from collecting on the spark plugs.

NOTE: Another way of checking for a spark is to remove the distributor cap and snap the contact points open and closed. The ignition switch should be on, and the lead from the coil high-voltage terminal should be held close to the engine block. This check does not, of course, test the distributor drive or the secondary wiring.

If a spark does not occur when the spark test is made, it means the ignition system is not doing its job of producing high voltage. Check further by connecting a test ammeter in series or test light in parallel with the ignition primary circuit.

1. If there is a small reading which fluctuates somewhat during cranking, or if the test light blinks on and off, then the primary circuit is probably okay. The trouble is most likely in the secondary and is due to a defective coil secondary, defective secondary connections or leads, or high-voltage leakage across the coil head, cap, or rotor. See Figs. 14-1 and 14-2. Also, an open or "weak" condenser could be preventing high-voltage buildup in the secondary.
2. If the ammeter shows a fairly high and steady discharge reading with no fluctuations during cranking, or if the test light glows brightly and steadily, then the trouble is probably in the primary circuit. Either the points are not opening because they are out of adjustment or the condenser is grounded, or else the primary circuit is grounded in the coil or primary wiring.
3. If there is no ammeter reading, or if the test light does not glow, the primary circuit is open. The open could be due to a loose connection, defective wiring or switch, distributor contact points out of adjust-

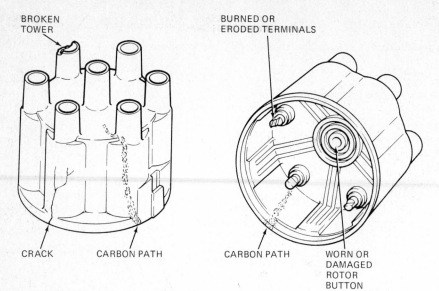

Fig. 14-1 Defects in distributor caps that require them to be discarded. *(American Motors Corporation)*

Labels in figure: BROKEN TOWER; BURNED OR ERODED TERMINALS; CRACK; CARBON PATH; CARBON PATH; WORN OR DAMAGED ROTOR BUTTON

ment or burned, or an open coil primary. A voltmeter or test light can be used to find the open by checking from various terminals in the primary to ground to see where voltage is available. First, check from the distributor primary-lead terminal on the coil to ground. If there is voltage here, the trouble is inside the distributor. If there is no voltage at the distributor primary-lead terminal on the coil, check from the other ignition-coil primary terminal to ground. If you now get a reading, the trouble is in the coil primary winding. If you get no reading, the trouble is in the wiring or the switch.

⚙ 14-5 Engine runs but misses—one cylinder   The quick way to locate the cause of engine missing is to check the ignition system with an oscilloscope as explained in ⚙ 14-19 to 14-22. The way technicians used to do it was to short out each cylinder spark plug one by one with a screwdriver. Here is how that was done.

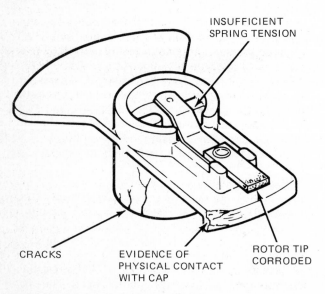

Fig. 14-2 Rotor defects such as these mean the rotor must be discarded. *(American Motors Corporation)*

Labels in figure: INSUFFICIENT SPRING TENSION; CRACKS; EVIDENCE OF PHYSICAL CONTACT WITH CAP; ROTOR TIP CORRODED

You use an insulated-handle screwdriver and put the metal bit from the spark-plug terminal to the cylinder block. This prevents a spark from occurring and causes the cylinder to miss. If the engine rhythm or speed changes, the cylinder was delivering power before the plug was shorted out. If no change occurs, the cylinder was not delivering power.

Shorting out the plugs one by one used to be an easy way to locate a missing cylinder. It is not so easy today. The spark plugs have neoprene boots to protect the insulation from moisture and dirt. You cannot short these out without pulling off the boots. Furthermore, many of the new ignition systems (General Motors HEI and Ford Dura-Spark) deliver very high voltages of up to 40,000 volts or more. This high voltage can jump a considerable distance and can give you a nasty shock. For these reasons, it is much better to use an oscilloscope. It provides a quick and accurate check of the system. Most oscilloscopes have a built-in device that can be operated to short out any spark plug (⚙ 14-19 to 14-22).

NOTE: General Motors and Chrysler still supply procedures for using the spark test. See ⚙ 17-5.

⚙ 14-6 Engine runs but misses—different cylinders   If the miss seems to jump around and you cannot pin it down to any particular cylinder, then the trouble could be due to any of several conditions in the ignition system, fuel system, or engine. The distributor contact points could be worn, dirty, or out of adjustment. The condenser or ignition coil could be "weak," so that the spark would not be uniform, and erratic missing would occur. The advance mechanisms might be erratic in action and thus cause uneven timing and missing. Distributors with the breaker plate supported by balls running in a ball track in the distributor housing may have the following troubles: The ball track wears, or the balls get dirty or worn; this causes the breaker plate to hang up or tilt when the vacuum-advance mechanism operates. This then causes a momentary erratic miss.

Bad ignition-circuit connections or defective wiring

can also cause missing. If high-voltage leakage occurs across the coil head, distributor cap, or rotor, or if there is leakage through secondary-wiring insulation, missing may occur. Long-continued leakage across the coil head or the rotor will etch a visible path (Fig. 14-1). If this occurs, the part will require replacement. Otherwise, wiping dirt from the part and keeping it clean and dry will prevent such leakage. If the insulation on the secondary wiring has deteriorated (is cracked, pierced, or hardened), it may allow high-voltage leakage. This condition requires replacement of the wiring.

Installing a coil with incorrect connections so that the secondary polarity is reversed could increase the voltage requirements so much that missing would result. The coil terminals are usually marked to prevent reversed connections. Reversed connections mean that the electrons must jump from the relatively cool outer electrode to the center electrode. This requires a considerably higher secondary voltage and increases the possibility of engine missing, especially at high speeds. Normally, the coil is connected so as to cause the electrons to jump from the hot center electrode to the outer electrode. With the emitting electrode hot, voltage requirements are considerably lower. The oscilloscope will show reversed polarity because the secondary pattern will appear upside down on the scope.

Worn or fouled spark plugs will miss, especially during a hard pull or on acceleration. By ''wear'' we mean that the plug gap has increased. In normal service the gap increases about 0.001 inch [0.025 mm] per 1000 miles [1609.3 km]. See ⚙ 13-12.

Remember also that many other conditions in the engine and fuel system could cause missing. If the fuel system fails to deliver an air–fuel mixture of the proper proportions or if the engine has faulty valve action or loss of compression, missing will occur.

⚙ 14-7 Engine lacks power
Many conditions can cause lack of power. With the timing off or with any of the conditions discussed in ⚙ 14-6, the engine will not deliver normal power. In addition, if the exhaust system is restricted, if heavy engine oil or the wrong fuel is being used, or if there is excessive rolling resistance due to underinflated tires, dragging brakes, and so on, then the engine will seem sluggish and lacking in power.

⚙ 14-8 Engine overheats
Engine overheating may be caused by many conditions in the engine cooling system or in the engine itself. It can also be caused by late ignition timing or troubles in the emission control systems.

⚙ 14-9 Engine backfires
Backfiring is a ''pop'' or ''bang'' in the exhaust system or intake manifold. It can be caused by several conditions in the ignition system. If the ignition timing is considerably off or if ignition crossfiring occurs (due to spark jumpover from one terminal or lead to another), ignition may result before the intake valve closes. This causes a backfire; there will be a ''pop'' back through the carburetor.

If a spark plug runs too hot, it may glow enough to ignite the air–fuel mixture before the intake valve closes. Here, the remedy is to use a cooler-running plug.

Preignition, and possibly backfiring, will also occur if valves run red hot or if carbon in the combustion chambers gets so hot it glows. Incorrect air–fuel ratio may also cause backfiring. A lean air–fuel mixture tends to cause backfire through the carburetor. A rich mixture can cause backfire in the exhaust system. A defective air-injection system can also cause backfiring in the exhaust system.

⚙ 14-10 Engine detonates or pings
Detonation, or pinging, is often blamed on the ignition system (it is often called a *spark knock*). But there are many other conditions that will cause detonation. In the ignition system, detonation may result from such conditions as excessively advanced timing, faulty advance mechanisms (which cause excessive advance), out-of-adjustment points, distributor bearing worn or shaft bent (which causes erratic point opening and possible excessive advance to some cylinders), spark plugs of wrong heat range (which glow and cause preignition), and so on. Other causes of detonation include fuel with an octane rating too low for the engine and the type of operation, excessive carbon in the engine combustion chambers, and conditions listed in ⚙ 14-9. Actually, of all these conditions, the most usual causes of pinging are excessive ignition advance and gasoline with an octane rating too low for the engine and operating conditions.

⚙ 14-11 Rapid wear of centrifugal-advance mechanism
Rapid wear of the centrifugal-advance mechanism will occur on certain engines as a result of loose or worn valve-timing gears or a worn oil pump. Either of these causes backlash and torsional vibration in the distributor drive. This, in turn, wears the centrifugal-advance mechanism rapidly.

⚙ 14-12 Pitted contact points
Some arcing across the contact points will occur in spite of condenser action. Under some conditions, this arcing may cause point pitting. Pitting is due to the transfer of point material from one contact to the other; a pit is left in one contact and there is a matching buildup of material on the other contact. Normally, the system is balanced, so pitting is at a minimum. But under certain unusual conditions, it will occur. To correct point pitting, note the following.

If the negative point loses material, with the buildup on the positive points, then one, two, or all three of the following steps should be taken.

1. Install a new condenser with a higher capacity.
2. Separate the low- and high-voltage leads or move these leads closer to ground. This reduces the capacity effect between these leads.
3. Shorten the condenser lead if possible.

If the positive point loses material and the buildup is on the negative point, install a new condenser with a lower capacity, move the leads closer together or away from ground, or lengthen the condenser lead.

☼ 14-13 Burned or oxidized contact points
Burning or oxidizing of contact points can be caused by several conditions, as follows:

1. Excessive resistance in the condenser circuit. This is detectable with a condenser tester and is corrected by either tightening the condenser mounting and connections or replacing the condenser, according to where the resistance is.
2. High voltage, which causes excessive current flow through the points. This can be detected by making a voltmeter check with the engine operating at medium speed. Correction normally requires readjustment of the voltage-regulator setting or replacement of the regulator.
3. Dwell angle too large (point opening too small). Points remain closed too long, so they burn rapidly. This requires checking of the dwell angle or point opening and readjustment as necessary.
4. Weak spring tension, which causes the points to flutter, bounce, and arc at high speeds. Measure the spring tension, readjust; or replace points.
5. Oil or crankcase vapors entering the distributor housing and depositing on the point surfaces, causing them to burn rapidly. A glance at the breaker plate usually discloses this condition, since the oil on the point surfaces, in burning, causes a black smudge on the breaker plate under the point (Fig. 14-3). A clogged engine crankcase ventilating system, which forces oil into the distributor, excessive oiling of the distributor, or worn distributor bearings will produce this trouble.

☼ 14-14 Analyzing defective spark plugs
Spark plugs fail for two basic reasons, from fouling so they cannot spark, and from gap growth (see ☼ 13-12). The

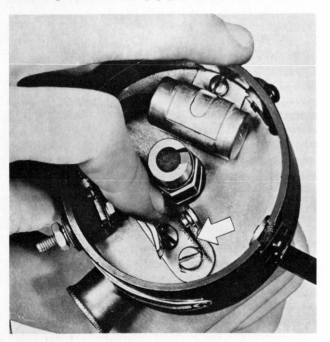

Fig. 14-3 A smudgy line under the contact points indicates that oil or crankcase vapor is getting between the contact points, causing them to burn rapidly.

appearance of a plug as you examine it can tell you a great deal about what condition caused the failure. This is sometimes called "reading" the plug. When removing the plugs from an engine, lay them out in proper order so you can tell which plug came from which cylinder.

Figure 14-4 illustrates several spark-plug conditions and explains their causes. Plug heat range is an important factor in plug fouling. Recall from ☼ 13-14 that spark-plug heat range is a measure of how hot a plug will run in an engine. If it does not become hot enough, it will foul. It will not get hot enough to burn away oil and fuel soot that deposits on it. When enough of these materials accumulate, the high-voltage surges will leak to ground through the deposits instead of jumping the spark gap. The plug will not fire and the engine will miss.

On the other hand, if the plug runs too hot, it will wear rapidly and may burn.

Conditions that encourage plug fouling include:

1. Excessive amounts of oil entering the combustion chamber owing to worn piston rings or cylinder, or to defective valve-stem oil seals.
2. Excessively rich air–fuel mixture from choking, worn carburetor jets, carburetor leaks, and so on. Overchoking can wet the end of the plug with fuel which cannot then fire across the plug.

If there is excessive plug fouling due to any of the causes listed above, installing a hotter plug can give some relief (see ☼ 13-14). But this would not, of course, cure the basic trouble.

If the plug runs too hot, a white or grayish cast will appear on the insulator, and the insulator may also appear blistered. A plug that runs hot will wear more rapidly; the electrodes will burn away more rapidly. One cause of high plug temperature, aside from improper heat range, is incorrect installation of the plug in the engine. If the plug is not tightened to the correct tension, the plug gasket will not be sufficiently compressed. In such a case, the heat path is apt to be somewhat restricted; the plug will, therefore, run hotter. This may also result if the plug seat in the cylinder head is not cleaned before the plug is installed. Dirt could block off the heat path and cause a hot-running plug. In some engines, the plugs do not use gaskets. On these, the seating faces (on plug and head) must be clean and smooth to form a good seal and heat path.

Cracked insulators are caused, as a rule, by careless installation or by improper adjustment of the plug gap.

☼ 14-15 Ignition-coil testers
Two general types of ignition-coil testers are widely used: the oscilloscope and the type that uses a spark gap or neon tube. On the latter, the coil to be tested is connected to the spark gap, and the spark it can produce is measured. Variations may creep in and distort the conclusions on this type of test unless great care is taken in making connections and adjusting the gap. Then, too, this type of coil tester will not always detect such defects as a shorted primary winding in a coil.

Most shops use an oscilloscope (called a "scope")

NORMAL

Brown to grayish tan color and slight electrode wear. Correct heat range for engine and operating conditions.

RECOMMENDATION: Properly service and reinstall. Replace if over 10,000 miles of service.

SPLASHED DEPOSITS

Spotted deposits. Occurs shortly after long-delayed tune-up. After a long period of misfiring, deposits may be loosened when normal combustion temperatures are restored by tune-up. During a high-speed run, these materials shed off the piston and head and are thrown against the hot insulator.

RECOMMENDATION: Clean and service the plugs properly and reinstall.

CARBON DEPOSITS

Dry soot.

RECOMMENDATION: Dry deposits indicate rich mixture or weak ignition. Check for clogged air cleaner, high float level, sticky choke, or worn breaker contacts. Hotter plugs will temporarily provide additional fouling protection.

HIGH-SPEED GLAZING

Insulator has yellowish, varnish-like color. Indicates combustion chamber temperatures have risen suddenly during hard, fast acceleration. Normal deposits do not get a chance to blow off, instead they melt to form a conductive coating.

RECOMMENDATION: If condition recurs, use plug type one step colder.

OIL DEPOSITS

Oily coating.

RECOMMENDATION: Caused by poor oil control. Oil is leaking past worn valve guides or piston rings into the combustion chamber. Hotter spark plug may temporarily relieve problem, but positive cure is to correct the condition with necessary repairs.

MODIFIER DEPOSITS

Powdery white or yellow deposits that build up on shell, insulator, and electrodes. This is a normal appearance with certain branded fuels. These materials are used to modify the chemical nature of the deposits to lessen misfire tendencies.

RECOMMENDATION: Plugs can be cleaned or, if replaced, use same heat range.

TOO HOT

Blistered, white insulator, eroded electrodes and absence of deposits.

RECOMMENDATION: Check for correct plug heat range, overadvanced ignition timing, cooling system level and/or stoppages, lean air-fuel mixtures, leaking intake manifold, sticking valves, and if car is driven at high speeds most of the time.

PREIGNITION

Melted electrodes. Center electrode generally melts first and ground electrode follows. Normally, insulators are white, but may be dirty due to misfiring or flying debris in combustion chamber

RECOMMENDATION: Check for correct plug heat range, overadvanced ignition timing, lean fuel mixtures, clogged cooling system, leaking intake manifold, and lack of lubrication.

Fig. 14-4 Appearance of spark plugs related to causes. *(Ford Motor Company)*

or a scope-type coil tester (Figs. 14-5 and 14-6). This type of tester measures coil performance and gives an accurate picture of coil conditions.

✿ 14-16 Ignition-condenser testers Ignition condensers are relatively inexpensive, and technicians often replace the condenser on any ignition job. Yet it is sometimes desirable to test the condenser, particularly where trouble is being traced. Four conditions may cause ignition-condenser troubles. These are:

1. Grounding or shorting of the condenser, caused by a breakdown of the insulation between the two condenser plates. This condition prevents any condenser action. It can be detected with a test light.
2. Low insulation resistance, which prevents the condenser from holding a charge, so that the condenser is said to be "weak." The insulation permits the charge to leak from one plate to the other. Moisture weakens the insulation and is one cause of low insulation resistance or condenser leakage.

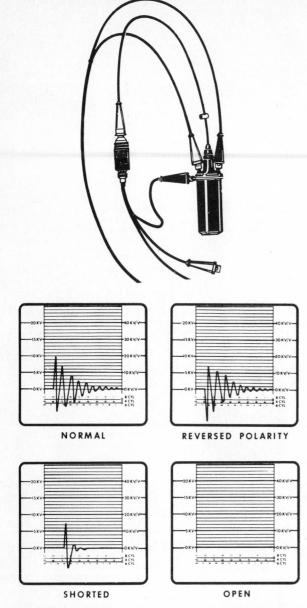

Fig. 14-6 Combination coil and condenser tester. *(Sun Electric Corporation)*

Fig. 14-5 Top, leads from scope to test coil. Bottom, scope patterns for various coil conditions. *(Sun Electric Company)*

3. High series resistance, which results from a defective condenser lead or poor connection within the condenser.

4. Capacity, which determines the amount of charge that the condenser can take. The capacity of any condenser depends on the area of the plates and on insulating and impregnating materials. It will not normally change in service.

Condenser testers that can check all these conditions should be used (Fig. 14-6).

⚙ **14-17 Distributor testers** Distributor testers, or synchroscopes, are variable-speed devices into which the distributor is clamped for checking (Fig. 14-7). As the distributor speed is increased, the synchroscope indicates the distributor rpm and the amount of cen-

trifugal advance. These testers incorporate vacuum-advance testers, wherein a source of vacuum is applied to the vacuum-advance mechanism on the distributor. The degree of vacuum advance and the amount of vacuum required to secure it can be checked. These testers will also detect shaft eccentricity caused by worn bearings and bent shafts. The tester usually has a dwell meter for measuring contact-point opening, or dwell.

NOTE: To test electronic distributors on some testers, a special *distributor pulse amplifier* must be fitted to the tester. This takes the place of the pulse amplifier (electronic control unit) which is left on the car.

⚙ **14-18 Checking contact-point opening** In normal service, the rubbing block on the movable point arm gradually wears away. This allows the contact-point opening to decrease (and the dwell to increase). This is one reason that the contact points should be checked periodically and, if necessary, adjusted. The other reason is to see if the points are worn or burned and need replacement.

There are two ways to check point opening, or dwell. One is with a round feeler gauge, and the other is with a dwell meter.

1. **Feeler gauge** Tuneup kits usually have a round feeler gauge which can be inserted between the points when the rubbing block on the movable point arm is on a cam lobe. If the point opening is not correct, the stationary point is adjusted. This adjustment moves the stationary point closer to, or farther from, the movable point. The adjusting procedure is explained in detail in

Fig. 14-7 Ignition-distributor tester. *(Sun Electric Corporation)*

⚙ 15-8. You may not be able to get an accurate setting if the points are worn. On used points that have become rough, the feeler gauge measures from high point to high point on the contacts (Fig. 14-8). The actual setting would then be excessively wide.

2. **Dwell meter** The dwell meter is an electric meter that measures the number of degrees of cam rotation that the points are closed (or dwell). See Fig. 14-9. As the point opening is increased, the dwell angle is reduced. If the point opening is reduced, the dwell angle is increased. The dwell meter is connected into the ignition primary circuit to read the average dwell angle. Using the dwell meter and adjusting the points is described in ⚙ 15-8. An oscilloscope can also be used to check dwell (⚙ 14-19).

⚙ 14-19 Oscilloscope testers The oscilloscope is a high-speed voltmeter that uses a televisionlike picture tube to show ignition voltages. Figure 14-10 shows an electronic engine tester which includes an oscilloscope. The oscilloscope, or "scope," is to the upper left in the picture.

The oscilloscope draws a picture of the ignition voltages on the face of the tube. The picture shows what is happening in the ignition system. If something is wrong, the picture will show where the trouble is.

To understand the pictures, let us review the ignition system. When the ignition-coil primary circuit is opened (either by opening of the contact points or by the electronic control), the voltage in the secondary winding jumps up. This high voltage surges to a spark plug and produces a spark. That is, the high voltage jumps the gap between the insulated and grounded electrodes of the spark plug. It takes a high voltage to start the spark. But after the spark is established, much less voltage is needed to keep the spark going. The scope can, among other things, draw a picture of how and when this voltage goes up and then drops down.

The picture is drawn on the face of the tube by a

Fig. 14-8 Why a feeler gauge may not accurately measure the point opening of used and roughened points. Roughness of points shown exaggerated.

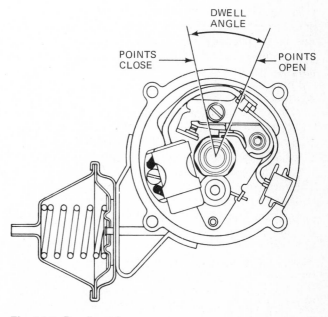

Fig. 14-9 Dwell angle.

189

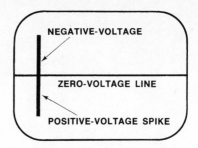

Fig. 14-11 The oscilloscope draws a horizontal zero-voltage line until a negative or positive voltage pulse enters. This causes the trace to kick up or down, as shown. The sharp up-and-down movements of the trace are called *spikes*.

After most of the magnetic energy in the coil has been converted into electricity to make the spark, the spark across the spark-plug gap dies. However, there is still some energy left in the coil, and this produces a wavy line, from D to E. This line is called the *coil-condenser oscillation line*. This wavy line means that the remaining energy is pushing electricity back and forth in the ignition secondary circuit. The voltage alternates, but it is no longer high enough to produce a spark. After a very short time, the voltage dies out. Then, at E, the points close. This sends current to the primary winding of the ignition coil. Now an alternating voltage is momentarily produced in the secondary. This is the result of the buildup of current in the coil primary winding. It is shown by the oscillations following E. The section from E to F is called the *dwell section*. This is the time during which the contact points are closed. (Or, in the electronic system, the time during which the electronic control permits current to flow to the ignition coil primary winding.) During this time, the magnetic field is building up in the ignition-coil primary. Then, when the points open at F (or the electronic control opens the primary circuit), we are back at A again. The magnetic field collapses, and the whole process is repeated.

NOTE: As you have probably noticed, this is the same picture we showed and described in Fig. 13-18 and ☼ 13-12. It is the complete secondary voltage pattern for one cylinder in a normally operating ignition system. The basic pattern is somewhat different in the electronic ignition system from that shown in Fig. 14-12, as we will learn in Chapter 17.

☼ 14-20 Oscilloscope patterns The curves that the scope draws on the tube face are called *patterns*. The patterns can be drawn on the tube face in different ways. For example, the scope can be adjusted to draw a *parade pattern*, as shown in Fig. 14-13. It is called a parade pattern because the traces for the separate cylinders follow one another across the tube face, like marchers in a parade. Note that they follow from left to right across the screen, in normal firing order, with No. 1 cylinder on the left.

By adjusting the scope in a different way, the traces can be stacked one above the other, as shown in Fig. 14-

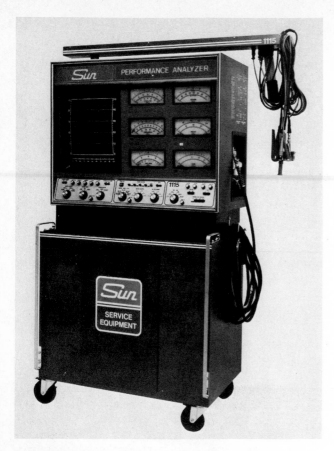

Fig. 14-10 An electronic engine tester with oscilloscope. *(Sun Electric Company)*

stream of electrons. This is exactly the way the picture tube in a television works. In the scope, however, the stream of electrons draws a picture of just one thing—the ignition-system voltages feeding into the scope. Figure 14-11 shows the face of the picture tube and helps to explain what we mean.

When a voltage, such as the voltage that fires a spark plug, is detected by the scope, a "spike," or vertical line, appears on the face of the tube. This is shown in Fig. 14-11. The higher the spike, the higher the voltage. If the voltage spike points down, it indicates that the ignition coil or the battery is connected backward, or the polarity switch on the oscilloscope is in the wrong position.

To see how the scope picks up the voltages and what the pictures that the scope draws mean, let us first study what is called the basic pattern (see Fig. 14-12). The basic pattern is what the scope would show if it were drawing the voltage pattern for one spark plug. To start with, the contact points have opened. The high-voltage surge from the coil has arrived at the spark plug. The voltage goes up, from A to B, as shown. This is called the *firing line*. After the spark is established, the voltage drops off considerably and holds fairly steady, from C to D. Of course, this is a very short time, measured in hundred-thousandths of a second. But the spark lasts for as long as 20° of crankshaft rotation. This is long enough to ignite the compressed air–fuel mixture in the cylinder.

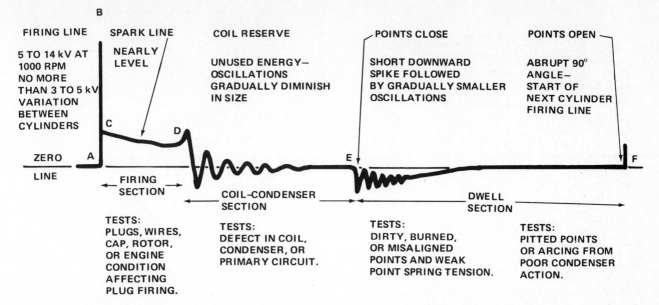

FIRING LINE 5 TO 14 kV AT 1000 RPM NO MORE THAN 3 TO 5 kV VARIATION BETWEEN CYLINDERS	**SPARK LINE** NEARLY LEVEL	**COIL RESERVE** UNUSED ENERGY—OSCILLATIONS GRADUALLY DIMINISH IN SIZE	**POINTS CLOSE** SHORT DOWNWARD SPIKE FOLLOWED BY GRADUALLY SMALLER OSCILLATIONS	**POINTS OPEN** ABRUPT 90° ANGLE—START OF NEXT CYLINDER FIRING LINE

ZERO LINE

FIRING SECTION

COIL–CONDENSER SECTION

DWELL SECTION

TESTS: PLUGS, WIRES, CAP, ROTOR, OR ENGINE CONDITION AFFECTING PLUG FIRING.

TESTS: DEFECT IN COIL, CONDENSER, OR PRIMARY CIRCUIT.

TESTS: DIRTY, BURNED, OR MISALIGNED POINTS AND WEAK POINT SPRING TENSION.

TESTS: PITTED POINTS OR ARCING FROM POOR CONDENSER ACTION.

Fig. 14-12 A waveform, or trace, showing one complete spark-plug firing cycle. Note that the "dwell section" is the period during which the points are closed, or the electronic control unit is maintaining a complete circuit between the battery and the ignition coil. *(Sun Electric Company)*

14. Stacking the traces this way is called a *raster pattern*. It lets you compare the traces, so you can see whether something is wrong in a cylinder. The pattern is usually read from the bottom up in the firing order, with No. 1 cylinder at the bottom.

A third way to display the traces is to superimpose them (Fig. 14-15), that is, put them one on top of another. This gives a quick comparison and shows whether the voltage pattern from any one cylinder differs from those of the others. If everything is okay in the cylinders, only one curve would appear on the tube face, because all the curves would fall on top of one another.

☼ **14-21 Using the scope** There are many makes of oscilloscopes. Some are combined in consoles with other test instruments for testing the separate ignition components, engine rpm, intake-manifold vacuum, and so on. Figure 14-16 shows a complete tester of this

type. Figure 14-10 shows the face of a similar tester. Scopes have pickup sensors that can be clamped onto the ignition wires, as shown in Fig. 14-17. Thus it is not necessary to disconnect and reconnect the ignition circuits. The pattern-pickup sensor is clamped onto the wire that goes from the ignition coil to the distributor-cap center terminal. The pickup senses the high-voltage surges going to all the spark plugs. The trigger-pickup sensor is clamped onto the wire that goes to the plug in the No. 1 cylinder. The trigger pickup senses when the plug fires. This is the signal to the scope to start another round of traces.

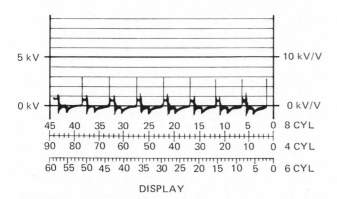

DISPLAY

Fig. 14-13 A parade or display pattern of the secondary voltages in an eight-cylinder engine. *(Sun Electric Corporation)*

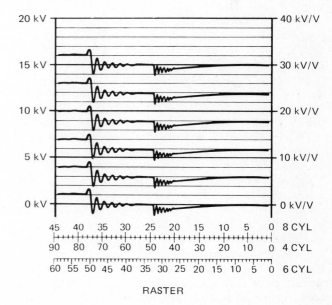

RASTER

Fig. 14-14 A stacked or raster pattern of the ignition secondary voltages in a six-cylinder engine. *(Sun Electric Corporation)*

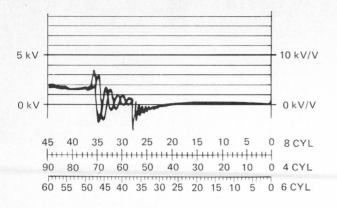

SUPERIMPOSED

Fig. 14-15 A superimposed pattern of the ignition secondary voltages in a six-cylinder engine.

⚙ **14-22 Reading the patterns** The patterns in Fig. 14-18 show different troubles that occur in the ignition system. The pattern that the scope draws of any cylinder's ignition-circuit voltage shows what voltages are occurring in that circuit. The way that the voltage varies from normal shows you where the electrical problem exists. For example, the scope can detect wide or nar-

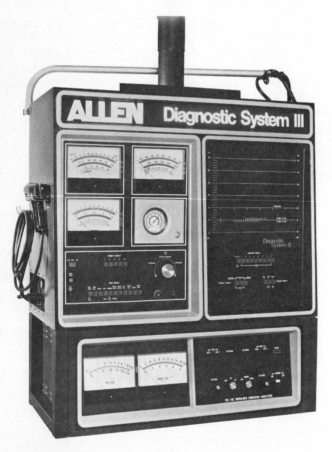

Fig. 14-16 An electronic-diagnosis engine tester. This tester includes an oscilloscope (top center) and other testing devices to check the condenser, distributor contact-point dwell, engine speed, and so on. *(Sun Electric Company)*

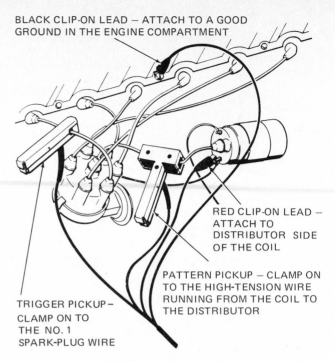

BLACK CLIP-ON LEAD — ATTACH TO A GOOD GROUND IN THE ENGINE COMPARTMENT

RED CLIP-ON LEAD — ATTACH TO DISTRIBUTOR SIDE OF THE COIL

PATTERN PICKUP — CLAMP ON TO THE HIGH-TENSION WIRE RUNNING FROM THE COIL TO THE DISTRIBUTOR

TRIGGER PICKUP — CLAMP ON TO THE NO. 1 SPARK-PLUG WIRE

Fig. 14-17 Test leads are clipped to terminals, and pickup sensors are clamped on high-voltage leads, to test an ignition system. The tester uses an oscilloscope. *(Autoscan, Inc.)*

row spark-plug gaps, open spark-plug wires, shorted coils or condensers, arcing contact points, improper contact-point dwell, and so on. Many abnormal engine conditions change the voltage required to fire the plug. This, too, shows up on the scope.

⚙ **14-23 Ignition timing** The spark must occur at the spark-plug gap as the piston reaches some definite position in the compression stroke. Adjusting the distributor on the engine so the spark occurs at this correct instant is called *setting the ignition timing*. The ignition timing is checked with the engine idling at a specified speed. For example, Chrysler specifies an engine idle speed of 1000 rpm. On engines equipped with idle-speed solenoids, the solenoid must be energized. Also, the vacuum hose from the intake manifold should be disconnected at the vacuum-advance unit so the vacuum advance will not work. Plug this hose to prevent air leakage into the intake manifold which could affect timing adjustments. (A wooden golf tee makes a handy plug.) Adjustment is made by turning the entire distributor in its mounting. If you rotate the distributor in the direction opposite to normal distributor shaft rotation, you move the timing ahead. That is, the contact points will open earlier (or the voltage pulse from the pickup coil will occur earlier). This advances the spark so the sparks will appear at the spark plugs earlier. Turning the distributor in the opposite direction, or in the direction of distributor shaft rotation, will retard the sparks. The sparks appear at the plugs later.

NOTE: The reason that ignition timing on contact-point systems should be checked periodically is this: As contact points and the contact arm rubbing block wear, the

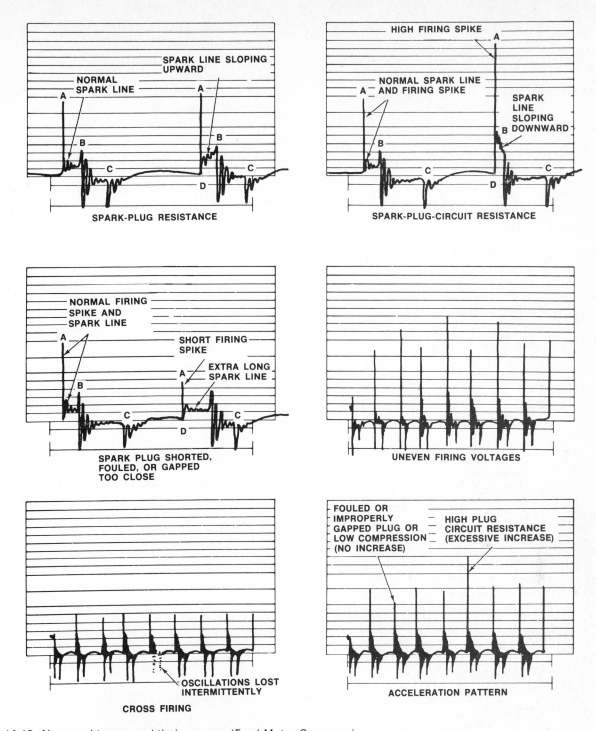

Fig. 14-18 Abnormal traces and their causes. *(Ford Motor Company)*

ignition timing and the dwell angle change. Adjustments have to be made to restore the original specifications. However, with the electronic ignition systems which have no contact points, once the ignition timing is set, it should not ever require any adjustment.

Timing with a timing light To time the ignition, check the markings on the crankshaft pulley with the engine idling. Since the pulley turns rapidly, you cannot see the markings in normal light. But by using a timing light, you can make the pulley appear to stand still. The timing light is a *stroboscopic* light. You use it by connecting the timing-light lead to the No. 1 spark plug, as shown in Fig. 14-19, or by clamping an inductive pickup around the No. 1 spark-plug cable. Until recently, timing lights used an adaptor inserted in series in the No. 1 spark-plug circuit (Fig. 14-19). Later-model timing lights have been made more sensitive by electronic devices so that the timing procedure is simpler. You just clamp an inductive pickup such as shown in Fig. 14-17 around the cable to No. 1 spark plug.

By either method, every time the plug fires, the tim-

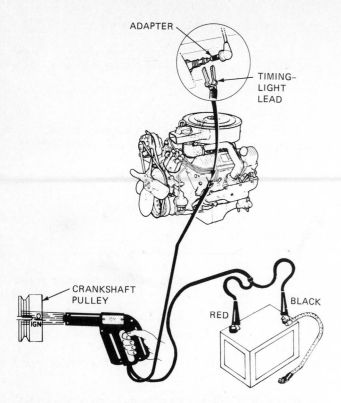

Fig. 14-19 Using a timing light to check ignition timing.

ing light gives off a flash of light (Fig. 14-20). The light lasts only a fraction of a second. The repeated flashes of light make the pulley seem to stand still.

Careful: Never use ice picks, pins, or wires pushed through the insulation in order to connect the timing light. Holes left in the insulation will probably result in a high-voltage leak and an engine miss.

CAUTION: Keep hands and timing light leads out of the engine fan. Your hand could be seriously cut if hit by a blade of the revolving fan. Also, if the leads got tangled with the fan, the timing light could be pulled

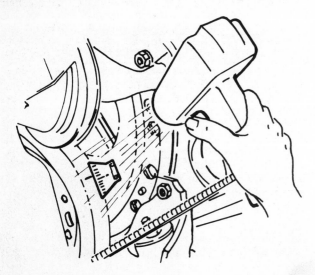

Fig. 14-20 The timing light flashes every time the No. 1 spark plug fires.

into the fan. It could be destroyed, and flying pieces could hurt you or anyone else standing nearby.

CAUTION: Never stand in line with the engine fan when the engine is running. There have been serious injuries resulting from fan blades breaking off and hitting someone standing nearby.

To set the ignition timing, loosen the clamp screw that holds the distributor in its mounting. Then turn the distributor one way or the other. As you turn the distributor, the marking on the pulley will move ahead or back. When the ignition timing is correct, the markings will align with a timing pointer, or timing mark, as shown in Fig. 14-21. Tighten the distributor clamp.

Careful: Do not try to turn the distributor by putting pressure on the vacuum-advance unit. Excessive pressure can damage it.

☀ **14-24 Timing diagnostic computer** Chrysler recently introduced a timing light that does not only the timing-light job, as just described, but also gives you a digital (in numbers) readout of the engine rpm and the dwell. It has a series of buttons plus a small viewing screen, as shown in Fig. 14-22. When the TEST button is pressed, it performs like other timing lights. When the RPM button is pressed, it reports the engine speed on the screen. Pressing the DW button gives you, on the screen, the dwell (the time the points are closed) for each cylinder. This allows you to check the dwell for each cylinder and detect a worn distributor cam, for example. The instrument also gives you a readout on the spark advance as engine speed and intake-manifold change.

☀ **14-25 Magnetic or monolithic timing** This is a relatively new timing method. It uses an electronic timing tester that reports the timing on a meter face. The tester is triggered by a location indicator on the crankshaft such as shown in Fig. 14-23. A magnetic probe is inserted into a hole in the cylinder block or next to the crankshaft pulley (Figs. 14-24, 14-25, 18-6, and 18-7). Every time the indicator passes the probe, it induces a voltage pulse in the probe. This triggers the electronic timing tester. The tester puts this pulse to-

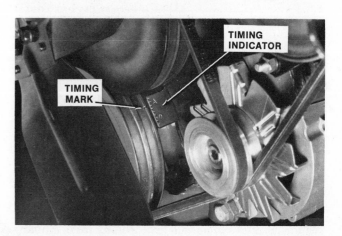

Fig. 14-21 Ignition timing mark on the crankshaft pulley.

Fig. 14-22 Diagnostic timing computer. With this instrument, you not only check timing, but also get readouts on engine rpm, dwell, and spark advance. (Chrysler Corporation)

gether with the pulse from the ignition secondary wire and reports on the meter face the number of degrees of spark advance. Adjustment is made as already explained.

⚙ **14-26 Spark-plug service** Spark plugs will foul or the electrodes will wear rapidly if their heat range is wrong for the engine. See Fig. 13-21, which illustrates spark-plug heat range. Figure 14-4 relates spark-plug appearance to various conditions in the engine. Figure 14-26 shows a spark-plug cleaner. The spark plug is put

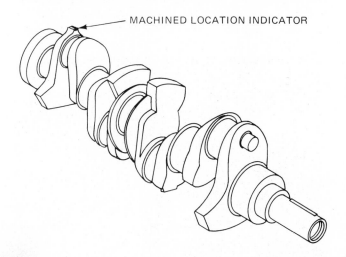

Fig. 14-23 Crankshaft with location indicator for magnetic or monolithic timing.

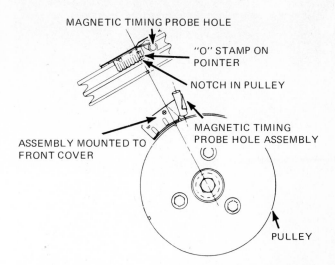

Fig. 14-24 Magnetic timing probe hole and timing marks. (Chevrolet Motor Division of General Motors Corporation)

into the cleaner. The cleaner sends a blast of grit against the electrodes and insulator, to clean them. After the cleaning, the spark-plug electrodes should be filed flat with an ignition file. Then a special tool is used to adjust the plug gap (Fig. 14-27).

NOTE: The cost of labor is high, and the cost of spark plugs is relatively low. Thus many service experts insist that it is cheaper and more efficient to install new plugs than to clean and regap the old ones. One manufacturer (of small engines) strongly opposes the use of cleaned and regapped plugs in the engines it makes. It says that if the plug is not perfectly cleaned, particles of grit will be introduced into the engine. This can severely damage pistons, rings, and cylinder. Also, sandblasting can roughen the porcelain insulator so that carbon sticks to it. This can set up a leakage path which causes the plug to misfire. That is, the high voltage leaks across the insulator rather than producing a spark at the gap.

When selecting a new set of spark plugs to install in an engine, always pick the type specified for the engine. The plugs will then have the right reach and heat range

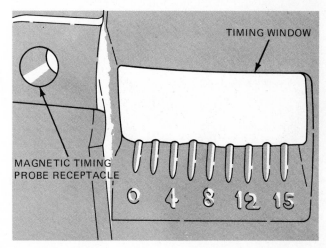

Fig. 14-25 Magnetic timing probe hole and timing marks on a front-drive car. (Chrysler Corporation)

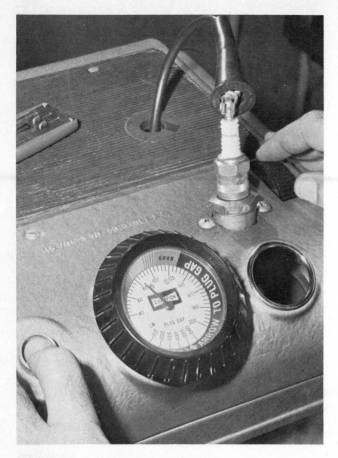

Fig. 14-26 Spark-plug cleaner. (*Champion Spark Plug Company*)

(🌣 13-14) for the engine. The only variation would be if examination of the old plugs shows that the engine needs plugs of a different heat range. You would then select a set of plugs of the heat range you think would work better over the long haul in the engine.

🌣 **14-27 Removing spark plugs from the engine** Spark-plug manufacturers recommend installing new spark plugs at periodic intervals. The mileage at which replacement should take place varies with different manufacturers. One recommendation has been to replace plugs every 10,000 miles [16,093 km].

Refer to the shop manual of the car you are servicing for specific time periods. Replacement of the plugs periodically avoids loss of engine operating economy and atmospheric pollution, which are caused by worn plugs. Before the plugs are removed, the area surrounding them should be cleaned thoroughly so that dirt will not fall into the cylinders. One method of doing this is to blow the dirt away with a compressed-air hose. Another is to loosen the plugs a little and then start the engine. Running the engine for a few moments will allow the leakage of compression to blow dirt away from around the plugs.

NOTE: See 🌣 14-28 on the proper way to disconnect and connect the spark-plug cables. This must be done properly to avoid damaging the cables.

Some engines have the spark plugs mounted in wells. On these, the spark-plug covers must first be pulled out, with the cables. Then, a spark-plug socket must be used to reach down into the wells to loosen and remove the plugs. This socket has a rubber boot which grips the insulator and makes lifting out the plug easier after it is unscrewed.

🌣 **14-28 Ignition wiring** An important part of ignition service is to inspect the wiring to make sure it is in good condition. Cracks or punctures in the secondary-wiring insulation can allow high-voltage leakage and engine miss, particularly under heavy load.

Visually inspect the secondary wiring for cracks, burned spots caused by being too close to the exhaust manifold, and brittleness. Feel the wiring to see if it is hard or crumbly. You can make a secondary-insulation check with the oscilloscope. If you do not have an oscilloscope, you can check secondary-wiring insulation as follows: With the engine not running, connect one end of a test probe to a good ground such as the engine block. The other end is left with the test point free to probe. Disconnect the cable from a spark plug, and insulate the clip end from ground. Figure 14-28 shows the use of a special Ford tool and the Ford-recommended way to remove spark-plug wires. Now start the engine, and move the test probe along the entire length of the wire. If there are punctures or cracks, a spark will jump through the insulation to the end of the test point.

Here is one recommended way to install new cable assemblies: Grasp the boot and clip end of the cable,

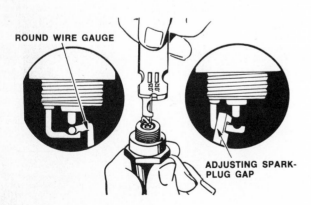

Fig. 14-27 Using a special gauge and adjusting tool to adjust the spark-plug gap.

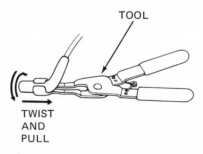

Fig. 14-28 Using cable pliers to remove a cable from a spark plug. (*Ford Motor Company*)

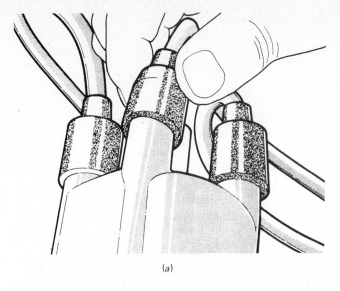

(a)

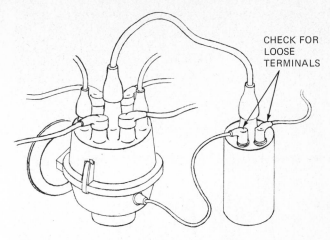

Fig. 14-31 Check the terminals for loose connections. *(Ford Motor Company)*

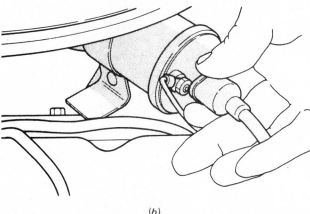

(b)

Fig. 14-29 Installing a cable and boot on *(a)* a distributor cap and *(b)* a coil tower. *(Chrysler Corporation)*

as shown in Fig. 14-29. Gently push the cable clip into the cap or coil tower. Pinch the larger diameter of the boot to release trapped air. Then push the cable and boot until the cable clip is fully entered into the cap terminal and the boot is all the way down around the tower. If a connector is loose on the spark-plug terminal, the fit can be improved by squeezing the connector as shown in Fig. 14-30. Check the coil terminals for loose connections (Fig. 14-31).

NOTE: If you are replacing a set of ignition cables or a

distributor cap, replace one cable at a time. (See Fig. 14-32.) This avoids getting mixed up and connecting a cable from the distributor cap to the wrong spark plug. If all cables have been removed, first determine which direction the rotor turns and the firing order. From these, you will be able to figure out how the cables are to be connected.

Careful: Never remove cable and boot assemblies from the distributor or coil towers unless (1) the boots are damaged or (2) cable testing shows the cables are bad and must be replaced. You can ruin a cable by careless removal and installation.

Careful: Do not puncture cables or boots with test probes. Puncturing cable insulation or a boot can ruin the cable. The probe can separate the conductor and cause high resistance. Also, breaking the insulation can result in high-voltage leakage to ground. Either of these can cause engine miss.

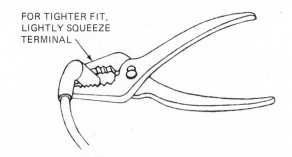

FOR TIGHTER FIT, LIGHTLY SQUEEZE TERMINAL

Fig. 14-30 Squeezing the clip together to improve the fit. *(Ford Motor Company)*

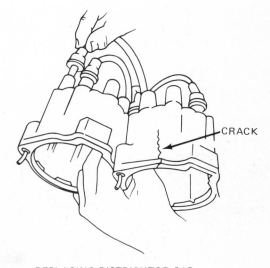

CRACK

REPLACING DISTRIBUTOR CAP

Fig. 14-32 Changing the cables from an old cap to a new cap.

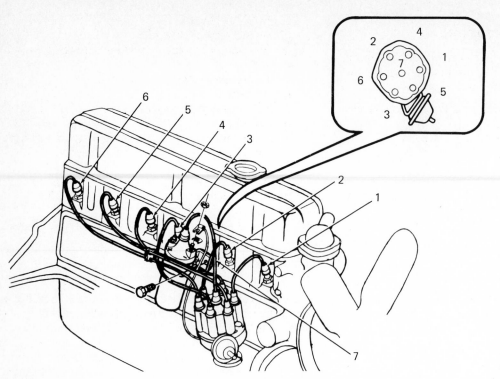

Fig. 14-33 Spark-plug cable locations on a six-cylinder engine. *(Chevrolet Motor Division of General Motors Corporation)*

⚙ **14-29 Location of secondary wiring** The high-voltage cables, or secondary wiring, must be connected correctly between the distributor cap and the spark plugs. Also, the secondary wiring must be positioned correctly and held apart by the plastic looms provided (see Figs. 14-33 and 14-34). Note how the cables are positioned and separated. Improper placement or the bundling of cables together can cause crossfiring. That is, the high-voltage surge leaks from one cable to another, causing the wrong spark plug to fire. When this happens it can cause engine missing or backfire (see ⚙ 14-9).

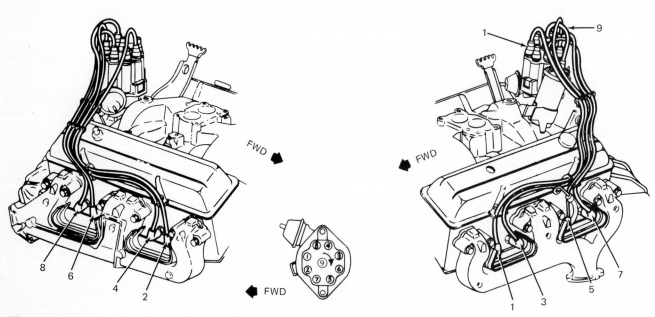

Fig. 14-34 Spark-plug locations on a V-8 engine. *(Chevrolet Motor Division of General Motors Corporation)*

Chapter 14 review questions

Select the *one* correct, best, or most probable answer to each question. Then check your answers against the correct answers given at the end of the book.

1. Failure to start with normal cranking is usually due to troubles in the:
   a. ignition or starting system,
   b. ignition or engine,
   c. ignition or fuel system,
   d. battery or fuel system.

2. If you cannot get a spark during the spark test, chances are the trouble is in the:
   a. engine,
   b. fuel system,
   c. ignition system,
   d. spark plugs.

3. If no spark occurs during the spark test and the ammeter shows a small fluctuating reading, chances are the trouble is in the:
   a. secondary circuit,
   b. primary circuit,
   c. ignition switch,
   d. starting system.

4. If no spark occurs during the spark test and the ammeter shows a fairly high and steady reading, chances are the trouble is in the:
   a. secondary circuit,
   b. primary circuit,
   c. spark plugs,
   d. wiring.

5. If no spark occurs during the spark test and the ammeter shows no reading, the trouble is in the:
   a. secondary circuit,
   b. primary circuit,
   c. alternator,
   d. battery.

6. If no change in the operation of the engine is noted when a spark plug is shorted out, then that:
   a. spark plug is okay,
   b. cylinder is delivering power,
   c. means everything is okay,
   d. cylinder is missing.

7. Ignition crossfiring or hot plugs or valves are apt to cause:
   a. late ignition timing,
   b. burned contact points,
   c. engine backfiring,
   d. burned engine valves.

8. Excessively advanced ignition timing is apt to cause:
   a. burned contacts,
   b. pinging,
   c. loss of energy in primary,
   d. crossfiring.

9. Excessive resistance in the condenser circuit, high voltage or large dwell angle can cause:
   a. pitted contact points,
   b. ignition crossfiring,
   c. burned plugs,
   d. burned contact points.

10. In regard to heat range of spark plugs, the longer the heat path, the:
    a. hotter the plug,
    b. colder the plug,
    c. shorter the reach,
    d. longer the reach.

11. A plug that runs too cold is apt to be:
    a. blistered,
    b. sooty,
    c. blue,
    d. burned.

12. The oscilloscope reacts to the high-voltage surges from the:
    a. coil primary terminal,
    b. coil high-voltage terminal,
    c. contact points closing,
    d. condenser action.

13. If the firing voltage for one cylinder is considerably higher than for the others, the probability is that:
    a. the plug gap is excessive,
    b. there is a short in the circuit,
    c. voltage is leaking from the high-tension lead,
    d. piston rings are bad.

14. A dwell meter is used for setting the distributor:
    a. vacuum advance,
    b. contact-point opening,
    c. ignition timing,
    d. centrifugal advance.

15. On many distributors, contact-point opening is adjusted by:
    a. shifting the stationary point,
    b. moving the breaker cam,
    c. changing the spring tension,
    d. turning distributor in its mounting.

CONTACT-POINT IGNITION DISTRIBUTOR SERVICE

After studying this chapter, you should be able to:

1. Service the components of the distributor, including points, cap, rotor, condenser, advance mechanisms, and shaft.
2. Remove a distributor from an engine, replace it, and time it.

15-1 Servicing contact-point distributors In Chapters 13 and 14, we explained how the contact-point ignition system works, various causes of ignition-system trouble, and ignition-system testing instruments. Also, we described servicing procedures for all ignition-system components except distributors and electronic systems. In this chapter, we cover contact-point distributor service. Chapter 16 covers electronic ignition systems. Chapter 17 covers servicing of electronic ignition, and Chapter 18 covers servicing of ignition systems which have electronic spark-advance control.

We have discussed, in previous chapters, testing of the battery, cables, ignition coil, condenser, and complete ignition system. Now, we shall look at the various checks and services required for contact-point distributors.

The contact-point distributor requires installation and adjustment of the contact points. It also requires checking of the centrifugal and vacuum-advance mechanisms, the bearings, and the cap and rotor.

☼ 15-2 Checking cap and rotor The cap with the spring-loaded screw clamps (Fig. 15-1) is removed by pressing down on the screw and then turning the screw either way. The cap with spring clamps (Fig. 15-2) is removed by prying the clamps with a screwdriver. Do not apply pressure to this cap, as it might break. Check the cap and rotor as shown in Fig. 15-3. Wipe the cap out with a cloth dampened with solvent. Discard the cap if it is cracked, broken, or has carbonized paths inside or out that could permit high-voltage leakage. You should also replace the cap if the rotor button is worn or broken. To replace a defective cap, hold the old and new caps side-by-side (Fig. 15-3, *upper right*) and change the leads one by one from the old cap to

the new cap. In this way, you will not get the leads mixed up. When removing a lead, grasp it through the rubber boot, as close to the tower as possible. Twist slightly to break the seal of the boot on the tower and then pull straight out. When inserting the lead, be sure to push it all the way down into the high-tension towers. On the type which enters the towers vertically (Fig. 15-3), push the lead down first and then slip the rubber boot down snugly over the tower. On the type which has a right-angle bend (Fig. 14-27), push the terminal clip down into place through the rubber boot. Before pushing the boot all the way down into place, pinch the larger part of the boot to squeeze out the trapped air. Then push the boot all the way down into place. Dis-

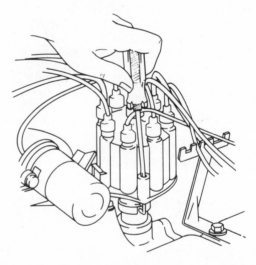

Fig. 15-1 Removing a distributor cap which has spring-loaded screw clamps. *(Delco-Remy Division of General Motors Corporation)*

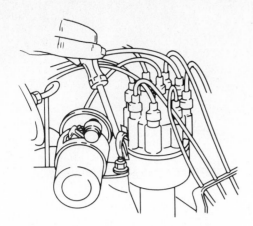

Fig. 15-2 Removing a distributor cap which has spring clamps. *(Delco-Remy Division of General Motors Corporation)*

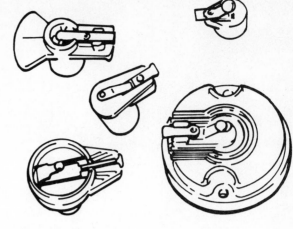

Fig. 15-4 Types of rotors.

tributor caps have a locating lug that registers with a slot in the distributor housing. When replacing the cap, be sure to turn the cap so the lug drops into the slot. This assures proper positioning of the cap on the distributor housing. If the cap is not properly positioned, the rotor will strike the cap when the engine is cranked, breaking the rotor.

NOTE: See also ☸ 14-28 on ignition wiring inspection and replacement.

Various types of rotors are shown in Fig. 15-4. Most of these rotors will slip off the breaker cam. The one at the lower right in the illustration, however, is attached

to the advance mechanism with screws (see also Fig. 13-5). Examine the rotor for wear or erosion of the metal segment and for cracks or carbonized paths that could permit high-tension leakage. Discard rotors in doubtful condition. If the rotor has a carbon resistor (Fig. 15-4), discard the rotor if the resistor is damaged.

☸ **15-3 Checking the advance mechanisms** On some distributors, the centrifugal- and vacuum-advance mechanisms can be checked for freedom of movement. The centrifugal-advance mechanism advances the breaker cam. The vacuum-advance mechanism advances the breaker plate. Thus if the advance

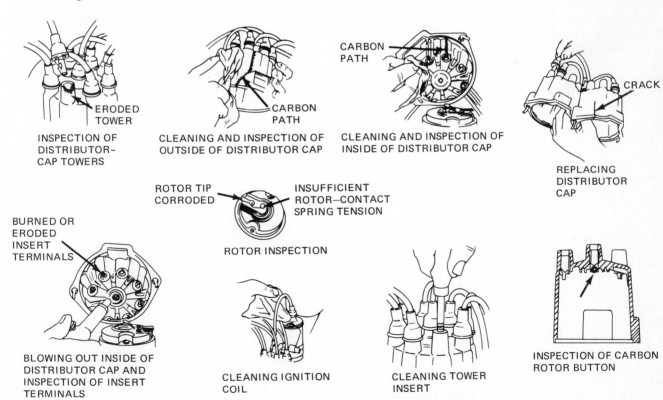

Fig. 15-3 Checking and servicing a distributor cap and rotor. *(Chevrolet Motor Division of General Motors Corporation)*

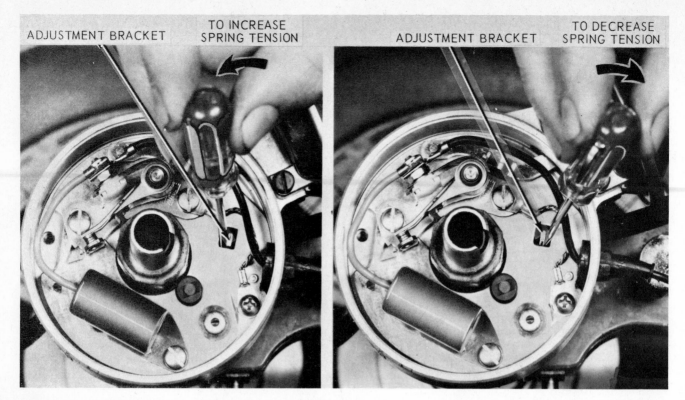

ADJUSTMENT BRACKET   TO INCREASE SPRING TENSION   ADJUSTMENT BRACKET   TO DECREASE SPRING TENSION

Fig. 15-5 Adjusting centrifugal advance. *(Ford Motor Company)*

springs are not too strong, it is possible to turn the cam or reluctor to see whether the centrifugal advance is free. Likewise, on some distributors, it is possible to turn the breaker plate to check the freeness of the vacuum advance.

Careful: Do not put too much pressure on the parts to turn them! Also, do not try to turn the breaker cam or reluctor by putting pressure on the rotor. You can break it.

An accurate way to check the advance mechanism is to remove the distributor from the engine and put it in a distributor tester (Fig. 14-7). You can then drive the distributor in the direction of its rotation and check out the advance curve. That is, you start out at low speed and gradually increase speed, noting when the advance starts and how the advance increases with speed. On some distributors, the centrifugal advance can be adjusted (☸ 15-4). On others, if the advance is not within specifications, the distributor must be disassembled for replacement of the advance springs and other parts.

Vacuum advance is checked with the distributor being driven at a specified speed. Vacuum is then applied to the vacuum-advance mechanism, and the amount of advance obtained is noted. Some distributors have provision for adjusting vacuum advance (☸ 15-5). On others, failure to provide the proper advance requires replacement of the advance unit.

☸ 15-4 Adjusting centrifugal advance
Some distributors have provision for adjusting centrifugal advance. Figure 15-5 shows how to adjust the centrifugal

advance on some Ford six- and eight-cylinder distributors. Bend the adjustment bracket out to increase the spring tension and thus *decrease* centrifugal advance. Bend the adjustment bracket in to decrease the spring tension and thus *increase* centrifugal advance.

Other distributors have different adjustment procedures. Refer to the manufacturer's shop manual for the specifications and procedures.

☸ 15-5 Adjusting vacuum advance
Some distributors have provision for adjusting vacuum advance.

Fig. 15-6 Adjusting vacuum advance. *(Ford Motor Company)*

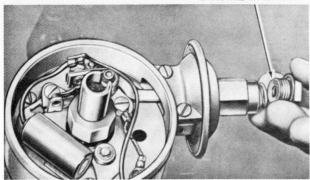

Fig. 15-7 Vacuum advance can be adjusted on some distributors by installing or removing spacing washers. *(Ford Motor Company)*

Figure 15-6 shows how it is done on some late-model Ford distributors. Use an allen wrench of the proper size to turn the socket-head screw in the vacuum-advance mechanism. Turn it clockwise to increase the vacuum advance, or counterclockwise to decrease it. On some earlier distributors, adjustment was made by installing or removing spacing washers under the plug in the vacuum-advance unit (Fig. 15-7).

✿ **15-6 Inspecting contact points** Use a screwdriver to carefully separate the contact points. Note their color and roughness. Points should be uniform and gray in color. If they are blue or burned, it may mean excessive current in the primary, possibly due to a high voltage-regulator setting. Points get rather rough in service. Actually, rough points may have a greater contact area than new contacts. However, if the contacts are burned or heavily pitted, they should be replaced. For example, if the contact-material transfer has produced a buildup on one point of 0.020 inch [0.51 mm] (see Fig. 15-8), the contact set should be replaced. See ✿ 14-12 and 14-13 for causes of contact-point pitting and burning.

✿ **15-7 Replacing contact points** Most contact points are supplied as assembled sets. On these, the stationary contact and the movable contact are replaced as a unit. On others, the breaker arm and then the stationary-contact base are removed. The removal of a contact-point set is shown in Figs. 15-9 and 15-10.

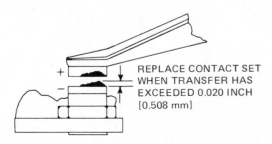

Fig. 15-8 If contact-material transfer exceeds 0.020 inch [0.51 mm], the contact points should be replaced. *(Delco-Remy Division of General Motors Corporation)*

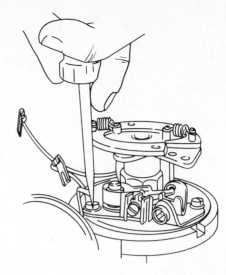

Fig. 15-9 Loosening a screw to remove the contact-point set. *(Delco-Remy Division of General Motors Corporation)*

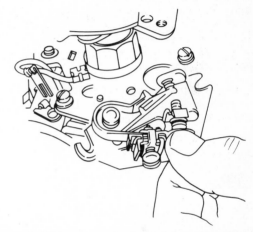

Fig. 15-10 Lifting a contact set from a breaker plate. *(Delco-Remy Division of General Motors Corporation)*

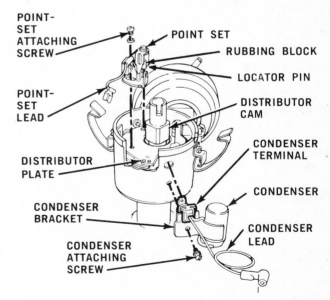

Fig. 15-11 Partly disassembled distributor showing proper locations of contact-point set and condenser. *(Ford Motor Company)*

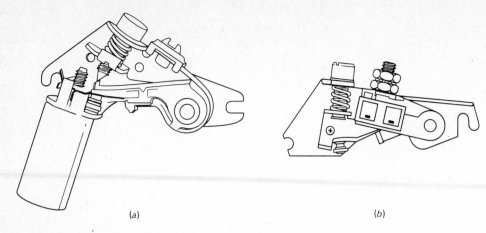

(a)   (b)

Fig. 15-12 *(a)* Contact set with attached condenser, called a *Uniset*. *(b)* Contact set with a wafer-type condenser, called a *Sure-set. (Delco-Remy Division of General Motors Corporation and Chrysler Corporation)*

After the lead screw is loosened and the leads are detached, the two screws holding the contact set to the breaker plate are loosened. The contact set will then slip out from under the screws. Figure 15-11 shows a contact-point set removed from a distributor.

To replace the set, first wipe the breaker plate clean. If the distributor does not have a cam lubricator, apply a trace of cam lubricant to the cam. Install the new contact set, attach leads, and adjust the contacts as explained in ☼ 15-8.

NOTE: Many contact sets are now supplied with the condenser as part of the assembly (Fig. 15-12). These are called *Unisets* by Delco-Remy and *Sure-Set* by Chrysler. The installation procedure is the same as for other sets except that it is not necessary to bother with a separately installed condenser. Many automotive technicians normally replace the condenser when new points are installed.

The separately mounted movable point and stationary point are removed by loosening the lever-spring attaching nut. Then the screw that holds the stationary point to the breaker plate is removed. The lever and stationary point can then be lifted off separately (see

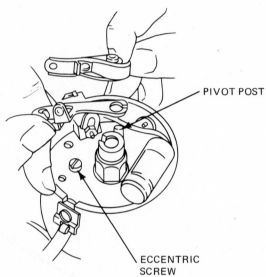

PIVOT POST

ECCENTRIC SCREW

Fig. 15-14 Removing the lever and stationary point. *(Delco-Remy Division of General Motors Corporation)*

Figs. 15-13 and 15-14). Adjust the new contacts after they have been installed (☼ 15-8).

☼ 15-8 Adjusting contact-point opening Before adjusting the point opening or dwell angle, align the points. Figures 15-15 and 15-16 show right and wrong ways of aligning points. Figure 15-17 shows an align-

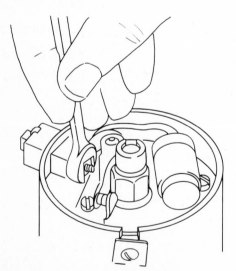

Fig. 15-13 Loosening the nut that attaches the spring of the contact arm. *(Delco-Remy Division of General Motors Corporation)*

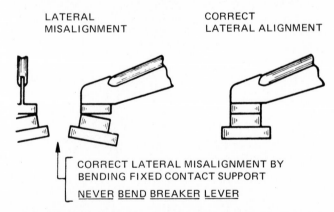

LATERAL MISALIGNMENT   CORRECT LATERAL ALIGNMENT

CORRECT LATERAL MISALIGNMENT BY BENDING FIXED CONTACT SUPPORT

NEVER BEND BREAKER LEVER

Fig. 15-15 Correct and incorrect lateral adjustment of flat contact points.

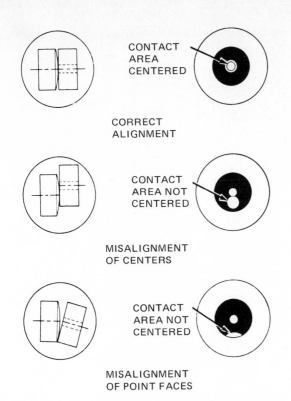

CONTACT AREA CENTERED

CORRECT ALIGNMENT

CONTACT AREA NOT CENTERED

MISALIGNMENT OF CENTERS

CONTACT AREA NOT CENTERED

MISALIGNMENT OF POINT FACES

Fig. 15-16 Correct and incorrect alignment of contact points.

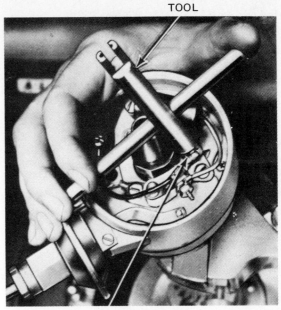

TOOL

BEND STATIONARY BRACKET

Fig. 15-18 Aligning contact points with alignment tool. Note that the bracket with the stationary contact point is being bent to get alignment. *(Ford Motor Company)*

ment tool recommended by Ford. Note that twisting the tool one way or the other bends the stationary point support. See also Fig. 15-18. NEVER BEND THE LEVER ARM! This can break it. After the points are aligned, adjust the point opening or dwell angle.

New contact points can be adjusted with a feeler gauge. Turn the distributor shaft until the peak of a cam lobe is under the center of the lever rubbing block (Fig. 15-19). If the distributor is on the engine, rotate the distributor in its mounting. With the rubbing block as shown in Fig. 15-19, measure the gap between the lever point and the stationary point (Fig. 15-20). Figures 15-20 to 15-22 show how to adjust the contact-point opening on different distributors. The stationary-contact

support is moved to make the adjustment. Then, the lock screw is tightened.

Some tuneup kits come with special disposable tools. For example, Fig. 15-23 shows a special plastic tool for contact-point and spark-plug gap adjustment. It is used as shown in Fig. 15-24. First, you break off the feeler gauge (see the break-off point in Fig. 15-23). Then, you slip the sleeve over the cam as shown in Fig. 15-24. Note that with the sleeve in place the position of the cam lobes makes no difference. The sleeve and the special feeler gauge used together will provide the proper spacing for the contact points. Insert the feeler gauge as shown (Fig. 15-24) and adjust the points. Figure 15-25 shows how the round feeler gauges are used to check spark-plug gaps. (See ☼ 14-26.)

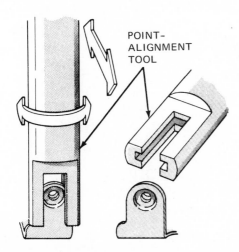

POINT-ALIGNMENT TOOL

Fig. 15-17 Point alignment tool. *(Ford Motor Company)*

Fig. 15-19 Cam lobe must be under the rubbing block to check point opening. *(Delco-Remy Division of General Motors Corporation)*

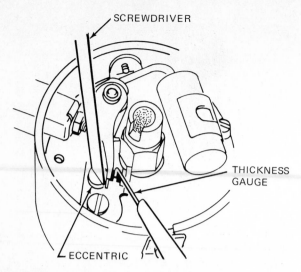

Fig. 15-20 On some distributors, the eccentric is turned with a screwdriver to adjust the point opening. *(Delco-Remy Division of General Motors Corporation)*

Figure 14-8 shows you why it is difficult to get an accurate setting with a feeler gauge on used points. The roughness of the contact surfaces makes it impossible to set the points to the specified opening. You may need to make a preliminary setting on used points with a feeler gauge so you can start the engine. Then a dwell meter can be used to final-set the points (✿ 14-18). The dwell meter also permits you to make adjustments of the contact points in distributors with the cap window (Fig. 15-26) without removing the cap.

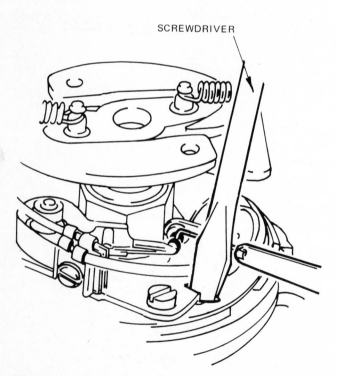

Fig. 15-21 On some distributors the stationary point base is pried back and forth with a screwdriver to adjust point opening. *(Delco-Remy Division of General Motors Corporation)*

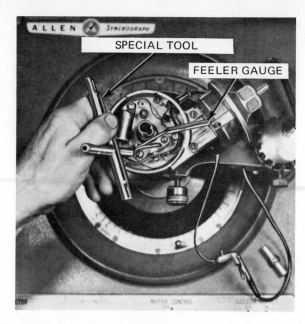

Fig. 15-22 Adjusting contact point gap. *(Ford Motor Company)*

✿ **15-9 Adjusting contact-point spring tension** The preassembled contact set (Fig. 15-12) has the spring tension checked at the factory and does not require adjustment. On other contact sets, the spring tension must be measured as shown in Figs. 15-27 and 15-28. Figure 15-29 shows how to make the adjustment. First, disconnect the primary lead wire and the condenser lead. Loosen the nut holding the spring in position. Move the spring toward the breaker-arm pivot to decrease tension. Move it in the opposite direction to increase tension. Tighten the locknut and recheck the tension. Repeat the procedure until the tension is right. Then reconnect the primary lead wire and condenser lead.

✿ **15-10 Distributor lubrication** Most distributors now have built-in oil reservoirs to lubricate the shaft bushings. Also, some contact-point types have a cam lubricator. These distributors may require no lubrication except during overhaul. However, the cam lubri-

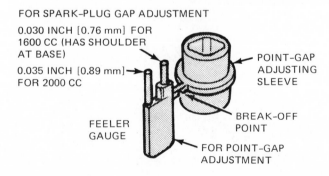

Fig. 15-23 Plastic throwaway tool included in some tuneup kits. The tool is used to adjust the contact-point opening and also the spark-plug gap. *(Ford Motor Company)*

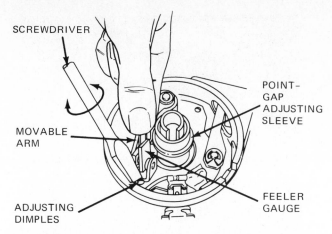

Fig. 15-24 Using the special plastic tool to adjust contact-point opening. The sleeve is placed over the breaker cam. Then the feeler gauge is used to gauge the opening while the stationary point is adjusted to get the proper gap. *(Ford Motor Company)*

cator requires turning or replacement at periodic intervals if it is of the type shown in Fig. 15-31. Also, some distributors should have the cam lightly lubricated periodically or during overhaul. See the manufacturer's shop manual for specific recommendations.

☼ **15-11 Distributor disassembly** The procedure of disassembling a distributor varies somewhat because distributors are constructed differently (see Figs. 15-30 to 15-32). On the typical ignition distributor, after the cap, rotor, and dust seal or radio-frequency-interference shield (Fig. 13-43) are off, the terminal (where present) is disassembled and the breaker plate taken out. Then the coupling or gear is removed by grinding or filing off the peened-over head of the pin and driving out the pin. Next, the shaft and advance-mechanism assembly can be lifted out of the distributor housing.

Careful: Before attempting to take out the shaft, be sure that there are no burrs around the pinhole. Burrs might damage the distributor bushing when the shaft is removed from the housing. File down any burrs before removing the shaft.

The advance mechanism can be disassembled by taking off the nuts or screws holding the weight hold-

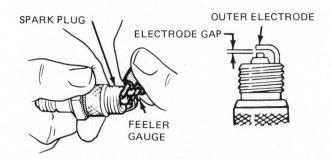

Fig. 15-25 Using the feeler gauge from the plastic throwaway tool to check the spark-plug gap. *(Ford Motor Company)*

Fig. 15-26 The contact points of the distributor which has a metal window in the cap can be adjusted by raising the window and using a box wrench. *(Delco-Remy Division of General Motors Corporation)*

Fig. 15-27 Places where the spring gauge should be hooked on breaker arms to measure contact-point spring pressure. Exert pull in the direction of the arrows.

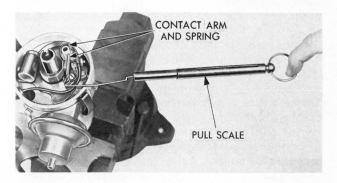

Fig. 15-28 Using spring gauge to check contact-point pressure.

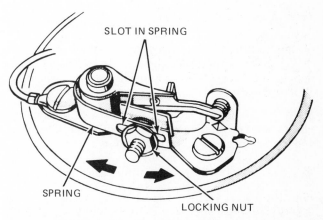

Fig. 15-29 Adjusting contact-point spring tension *(Ford Motor Company)*

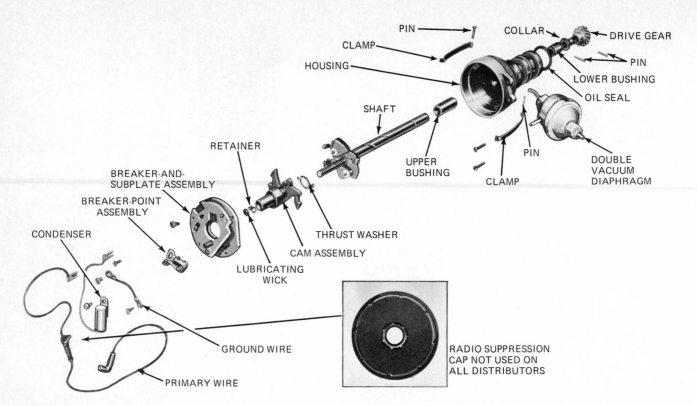

Fig. 15-30 Disassembled distributor used on a V-8 engine. *(Ford Motor Company)*

down plate in place. Note the condition of the bearing in the distributor housing, and replace it if it is excessively worn (see ☼ 15-12).

During disassembly, check for bearing wear. Note condition of the bushing in the distributor housing, and replace it if it is worn. A worn bushing will cause variations in contact-point opening, sometimes to such an extent that engine missing will occur. The bushing can be checked for wear by placing the shaft in its normal position in the bushing and then attempting to move the shaft sideways. A dial indicator can be attached to the housing so that the actual side movement of the shaft in thousandths of an inch can be checked. One manufacturer recommends that if the side play is more than 0.006 inch [0.152 mm] with 5 pounds [2.268 kg] of side pull applied with a spring gauge, the bushing is sufficiently worn to require replacement (see Fig. 15-33). An arbor press should be used to press out the old bushing and to press in a new one. To install the new bushing, a special arbor is required. The extension on the special arbor is of the right length and diameter to maintain the proper bushing inside diameter when the bushing is pressed into the housing.

NOTE: On some distributors, the bushings are not replaceable. If bushings are worn, the distributor housing and the bushing should be replaced as a unit.

☼ 15-12 Distributor reassembly During reassembly, the following should be kept in mind.

1. **Installing the shaft** When installing the gear or the coupling, be sure that the shaft end play is correct,

since it varies with different distributors. (See the manufacturer's specifications.) On some distributors, end play is adjusted by adding or removing shims on the lower end of the shaft between the coupling, or gear, and the distributor housing. On other distributors, end play is established by drilling a new hole through the shaft if necessary. During reassembly, the shaft is put into position in the distributor housing or base and pushed down as far as it will go. Then the gear or coupling is slipped onto the shaft and up against a feeler gauge held between the gear and housing (or washer if used). Finally, a hole is drilled through the gear and shaft, and the pin is installed. A check of the end play can be made after the gear, or coupling, pin has been put into place but before it has been peened over. The end play should be rechecked after peening to make sure that it is still within specifications.

2. **Ball-supported breaker-plate installation** On distributors in which the breaker plate is supported by three balls, place a small amount of petroleum jelly in the ball seats in the breaker plate and then put the balls in the seats. The jelly will keep the balls in place while the plate is being installed. Then align the balls with the vertical grooves in the housing. The spring seat should be on the plate next to the vacuum-control-link slot in the housing. Finally, push the plate down and turn it slightly to bring it into position.

3. **Bearing-supported breaker-plate installation** The bearing arrangement to support the breaker plate in some Delco-Remy external-adjustment distributors is shown in Fig. 15-34.

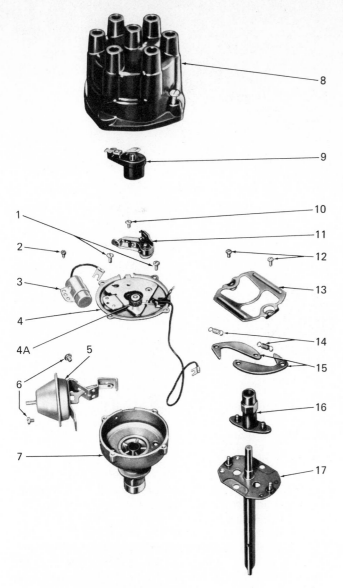

1. Breaker-plate attaching screws
2. Condenser attaching screw
3. Condenser
4. Breaker-plate assembly
4A. Cam lubricator
5. Vacuum-control assembly
6. Vacuum-control attaching screws
7. Housing
8. Cap
9. Rotor
10. Contact-point attaching screw
11. Contact-point assembly
12. Weight-cover attaching screws
13. Weight cover
14. Weight springs
15. Advance weights
16. Cam assembly
17. Main-shaft assembly

Fig. 15-31 Disassembled distributor for a six-cylinder engine. (*Chevrolet Motor Division of General Motors Corporation*)

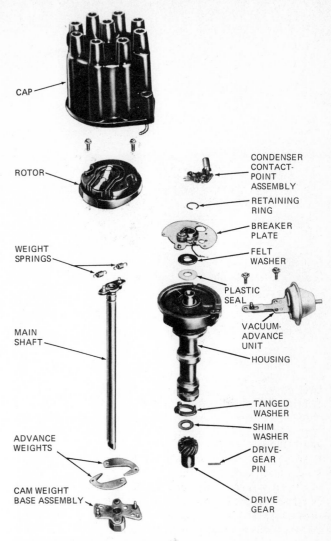

Fig. 15-32 Disassembled distributor for a V-8 engine. (*Chevrolet Motor Division of General Motors Corporation*)

4. **Contact-point adjustment**   Installation and adjustment of the contact points has already been described (✱ 15-6 to 15-9).

5. **Adjustment of advances**   In some models, adjustment of the advance mechanisms is possible, as already explained (✱ 15-4 and 15-5).

6. **Lubrication**   During reassembly, lubricate the distributor as required. (See ✱ 15-10.)

✱ **15-13 Distributor removal and installation**
Distributor removal and installation is simple if the engine is left undisturbed while the distributor is out. However, if the engine is cranked so that the crankshaft and camshaft are turned with the distributor out, installation is a little more complicated.

1. **Distributor removal**   Remove the air cleaner and disconnect the vacuum hose or hoses from the distributor. Disconnect the primary lead running from the ignition coil to the distributor. Remove the distributor cap, and push the cap-and-cable assembly aside.

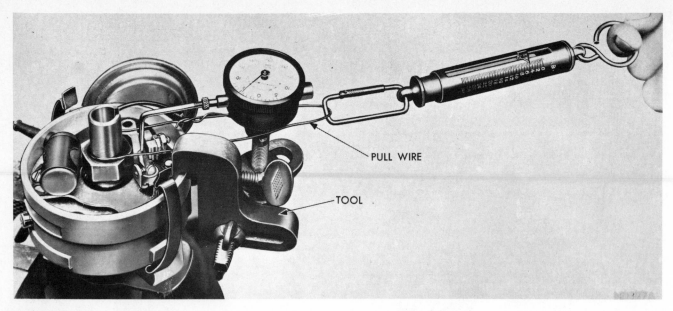

Fig. 15-33 Using a dial indicator and spring gauge to check the side movement of the shaft and determine how much the bearing has worn. *(Chrysler Corporation)*

Scratch a mark on the distributor housing. Scratch another mark on the engine block, lining it up with the first mark. These marks locate the position of the distributor housing in the block (Fig. 15-35). Scratch a third mark on the distributor housing exactly under the rotor tip. This mark locates the position of the rotor in the housing.

Remove the distributor hold-down bolt and clamp. Lift the distributor out of the block.

DISTRIBUTOR INSTALLATION NOTE: If the engine is not cranked while the distributor is out, the distributor can be installed in the correct position as follows. Align the marks on the distributor housing and cylinder block. Note, however, that as you push the distributor down in place, the shaft and rotor will turn as the spiral gears

mesh. Therefore, you will have to start with the rotor turned back from the installed position so that when you install the distributor, the rotor will turn to the correct position. That is, the tip will line up with the mark on the distributor housing. When correctly installed, the tip will point to the cap terminal connected to the spark plug in No. 1 cylinder.

2. Distributor installation If the engine has been cranked with the distributor out, timing has been lost. The ignition must be retimed. This is necessary to establish the proper relationship between the distributor rotor and the No. 1 piston.

Remove No. 1 spark plug from the cylinder head. Place a shop towel over your fingers and cover the spark-plug hole. Crank the engine until you feel compression pressure on your finger.

Fig. 15-34 Detached breaker-plate support used in an externally adjustable distributor. *(Delco-Remy Division of General Motors Corporation)*

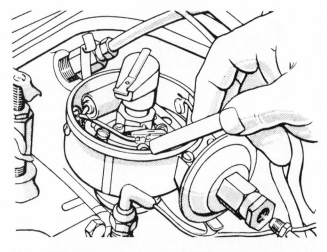

Fig. 15-35 Marking the location of the distributor housing in the engine block. If the rotor does not line up with the marks, make an extra mark in the distributor housing to show the location of its tip. *(Ford Motor Company)*

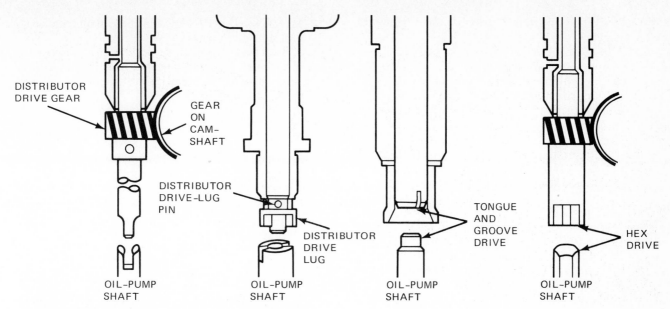

Fig. 15-36 Distributor drive and installation methods.

Bump the engine with the starting motor until the timing marks on the crankshaft pulley and timing cover are aligned. This means that No. 1 piston is in firing position.

Now, the distributor can be installed in the cylinder block. Make sure to align the marks you made on the distributor housing and cylinder block. Check to make sure that the distributor gasket or rubber O ring is in place when you install the distributor.

Four different distributor drives are shown in Fig. 15-36. You may have to turn the rotor slightly to engage the drive. Also, when the distributor goes down into place on the spiral-gear drive, the rotor will turn. So you must start with the rotor back of the proper position. Then it will turn into the correct position as the distributor goes down into place.

Make sure the distributor housing is fully seated against the cylinder block. If it is not, the oil-pump shaft is not engaging. Hold the distributor down firmly and bump the engine a few times until the distributor housing drops into place. Then bump the engine again to realign the timing marks.

Install, but do not tighten, the distributor clamp and bolt. Rotate the distributor until the contact points just start to open to fire No. 1 cylinder. Hold the distributor cap in place above the distributor. Make sure that the rotor tip lines up with the No. 1 terminal on the cap. Install the cap, with wires. Connect the primary wire from the ignition coil to the distributor.

Start the engine. Set the ignition timing (⚙ 14-23). Connect the vacuum hose or hoses to the distributor. Replace the air cleaner.

Chapter 15 review questions

Select the *one* correct, best, or most probable answer to each question. Then check your answers against the correct answers given at the end of the book.

1. The distributor cap held on with spring clamps is removed by:
   a. removing spring screws,
   b. rotating cap on distributor,
   c. unclamping the clamps with pliers,
   d. unclamping the clamps with a screwdriver.
2. Some rotors will slip off the breaker cam. Others are attached with:
   a. clamps,
   b. snap rings,
   c. screws,
   d. locating lugs.
3. Some distributors have provision for adjusting the centrifugal advance by:
   a. turning the adjusting screw,
   b. bending the adjustment bracket,
   c. using an allen wrench,
   d. replacing weights.
4. Some distributors have provision for adjusting the vacuum advance by:
   a. bending the adjustment bracket,
   b. turning the adjustment screw,
   c. installing or removing spacing washers,
   d. both *(b.)* and *(c.)*.
5. As the point opening increases, the dwell:
   a. increases,
   b. decreases,
   c. does not change,
   d. requires bending the lever arm to correct.
6. When adjusting point opening or dwell:
   a. bend the lever arm,
   b. bend the stationary point support,
   c. move the lever-arm support,
   d. move the stationary point support.
7. To adjust the point opening of used and rough points, use:
   a. a dwell meter,
   b. a flat feeler gauge,
   c. a round feeler gauge,
   d. none of these.

8. Before removing the distributor shaft from the housing:
   a. disassemble the centrifugal advance,
   b. remove burrs around the pinhole,
   c. mark position of breaker cam in housing,
   d. mark position of advance cam in housing.
9. To make it easier to reinstall the distributor, scratch marks on the:
   a. engine block,
   b. distributor housing aligning it with the block mark,
   c. distributor housing under the rotor tip,
   d. all of these.
10. If the engine has been cranked with the distributor out, timing has been lost. The first thing to be done before reinstalling the distributor is to:
   a. install the distributor with the marks aligned,
   b. position No. 1 piston in firing position,
   c. position No. 1 piston at TDC,
   d. position piston No. 1 at BDC.
11. In servicing the contact-point distributor, the following operations are required:
   a. checking advance mechanisms,
   b. installing and adjusting points,
   c. checking cap and rotor,
   d. all of the above.
12. To assure proper location of the cap on the distributor housing, there is a:
   a. stud that enters a hole in the cap,
   b. a screw to fasten the cap down,
   c. locating lug in the cap that registers with a slot in the housing,
   d. window through which the points can be adjusted.
13. The terms "Uniset" and "Sure-Set" refer to:
   a. contact-point sets with condenser,
   b. the procedure for adjusting the points,
   c. methods of adjusting the timing,
   d. preset ignition distributors.
14. Before removing the distributor shaft:
   a. remove the coupling or gear pin,
   b. remove the coupling or gear,
   c. remove the burrs on the shaft,
   d. all of the above.
15. To permit proper alignment of the distributor housing and rotor when reinstalling the distributor in the engine, you make:
   a. one mark,
   b. two marks,
   c. three marks,
   d. four marks.

ELECTRONIC IGNITION SYSTEMS

After studying this chapter, you should be able to:

1. Explain the difference between contact-point and electronic ignition systems.
2. Explain how the electronic ignition systems work.
3. Explain how the General Motors HEI and the Ford Dura-Spark I and Dura-Spark II work.
4. Explain how the electronic spark-advance systems work.
5. Locate and identify the components of these systems on automobiles.

16-1 Electronic ignition systems This chapter discusses the various electronic ignition systems used on modern vehicles. The basic difference between the electronic systems and the systems using contact points is the way they close and open the circuit between the ignition coil and the battery. In the contact-point system, the points do this job. In the electronic system, solid-state electronic devices open and close the circuit. Other components in the two systems are about the same. The ignition coil and the distributing system (distributor cap and rotor) work the same way as we described in the previous chapter. Also, the mechanical centrifugal and vacuum-advance mechanisms are the same for both systems and work the same way. However, some of the newer electronic ignition systems use electronic controls and sensing devices to produce more accurate control of spark advance. Chapter 17 covers the diagnosis of electronic ignition troubles plus testing and servicing of all electronic ignition-system components except distributors and electronic spark-advance systems. Chapter 18 covers servicing of ignition systems with electronic spark advance, such as the Chrysler Lean-Burn, the Ford Electronic Engine Control (EEC), and the General Motors EST or MISAR systems.

16-2 Comparing contact-point and electronic ignition systems As we mentioned, the basic difference between the two ignition systems (electronic and contact-point) is in the primary circuit. The secondary circuits are practically the same. Figure 16-1 shows in simplified form the primary circuits of the two systems. The difference is on the right-hand side. In the contact-point system, contact points close and open the circuit to the primary winding of the ignition coil. In the electronic ignition system, the circuit is opened and closed by the electronic control unit (ECU) on command from a magnetic pickup sensor coil in the distributor.

The sensor responds to a moving magnetic field produced by an armature on the distributor shaft that takes the place of the breaker cam. Figure 16-2 is a top view of a distributor with the cap off to show these two parts (armature and pickup coil). Figure 16-3 is a disassembled view of the distributor in which you can see the shapes of the parts we are referring to. As the armature (rotor) rotates, its tips carry a magnetic field through the coil in the pickup assembly (sensor). This produces a voltage pulse—a sudden voltage rise—that signals the ECU. Upon receiving the signal, the ECU almost instantly opens the circuit of the primary winding of the ignition coil. The effect is the same as when the contact points open. The ignition coil magnetic field collapses, and a high-voltage surge is produced in the ignition coil secondary winding. The high-voltage surge is led through the wiring, distributor rotor and cap, to the spark plug in the cylinder that is ready to fire (piston nearing TDC on the compression stroke).

Manufacturers have different names for some of the parts in the electronic ignition system. For example, Ford calls the rotor an *armature* and Chrysler calls it a *reluctor*. Figure 16-4 is a chart showing the various names.

16-3 Chrysler electronic ignition system An electronic ignition system has been used in all Chrysler Corporation cars made in the United States since 1973. In this system, the distributor has a metal rotor with a series of tips on it. This rotor, called the *reluctor*, is shown in Fig. 16-5. The reluctor takes the place of the breaker cam in the contact-point distributor. Notice that the reluctor in Fig. 16-5 has six tips. It is for a six-cylinder engine, so there is one tip for each cylinder.

213

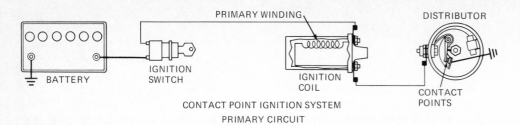

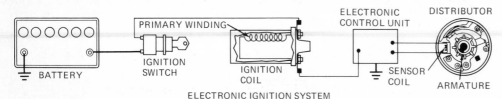

PRIMARY WINDING

DISTRIBUTOR

BATTERY

IGNITION SWITCH

IGNITION COIL

CONTACT POINTS

CONTACT POINT IGNITION SYSTEM
PRIMARY CIRCUIT

PRIMARY WINDING

ELECTRONIC CONTROL UNIT

DISTRIBUTOR

BATTERY

IGNITION SWITCH

IGNITION COIL

SENSOR COIL

ARMATURE

ELECTRONIC IGNITION SYSTEM
PRIMARY CIRCUIT

Fig. 16-1 Comparison of the primary circuits of a contact-point ignition system with an electronic ignition system.

The distributor for a four-cylinder engine would have four tips. The distributor for an eight-cylinder engine would have eight tips. This compares with the number of lobes on a breaker cam in a contact-point distributor. There are the same number of lobes as there are cylinders. Likewise, in the electronic distributor, there are the same number of tips in the reluctor as there are cylinders in the engine.

Notice also that the distributor has a pickup coil assembly which includes a coil and a permanent magnet (to the right of the coil in Fig. 16-5). The pickup coil has many turns of wire. The distributor is mounted and driven in the same manner as contact-point distributors (Fig. 13-3). When the engine is running and the distributor shaft is rotating, the tips of the reluctor sweep past the pickup coil assembly. As each tip passes the pickup coil, it carries magnetic lines of force through the coil. This produces a voltage pulse in the pickup coil which signals the ECU that it is time to cut off the ignition coil primary winding current flow.

The ECU uses electronic devices—diodes and transistors—to control the flow of current to the ignition coil primary winding. As the voltage pulse from the pickup coil arrives at the ECU, the ECU stops the flow

of current to the ignition-coil primary winding. The magnetic field in the ignition coil collapses, and the secondary winding of the ignition coil produces a high-voltage surge. This high-voltage surge is carried through the wiring, distributor rotor and cap, to the spark plug in the cylinder ready to fire.

Let us look in more detail at an ECU and the way it operates. Figure 16-6 shows the internal circuit of an ECU that is similar to those used by Chrysler and others. Figure 16-6 shows the conditions in the ECU before the voltage pulse from the pickup coil arrives.

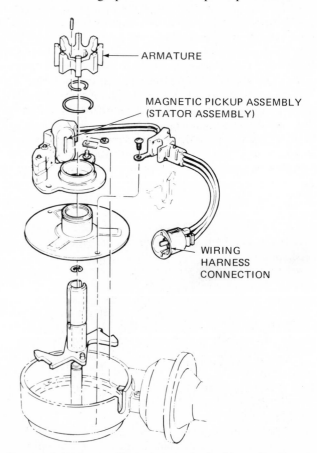

ARMATURE

MAGNETIC PICKUP ASSEMBLY (STATOR ASSEMBLY)

WIRING HARNESS CONNECTION

Fig. 16-3 Disassembled electronic ignition distributor, showing the shapes of the magnetic pickup assembly and the armature. *(Ford Motor Company)*

MAGNETIC PICKUP ASSEMBLY

ARMATURE

Fig. 16-2 Top view of an electronic ignition distributor, showing the magnetic pickup assembly which includes the sensor coil, and the armature. *(Ford Motor Company)*

PART NAME			
AMC	Trigger wheel	Sensor	Electronic control unit (ECU)
Chrysler	Reluctor	Pickup coil	Electronic control unit (ECU)
Ford	Armature	Magnetic pickup or stator	Ignition or amplifier module
General Motors	Timer core	Magnetic pickup	Electronic module

Fig. 16-4 Different names used by automobile manufacturers for the essential parts of the electronic ignition distributor.

Current is flowing from the battery, through resistor R7, and through the control unit (via R1 and transistor TR1) to the ignition coil primary winding.

But when the signal (voltage pulse) from the pickup coil arrives at the ECU, it causes transistor TR3 to become conductive. The reason for this is that the voltage pulse from the pickup coil supplies the TR3 transistor base with current carriers. When this happens, current flows as shown in Fig. 16-7. (Review ☼ 2-5 to 2-8 if the transistor action is not clear.) With TR3 conductive, current carriers are drained away from the base of TR2 so that TR2 becomes a nonconductor. With no current flowing through TR2, there is a reduced voltage drop across resistor R1, and the base of TR1 becomes about the same voltage as the lower TR1 connection. Thus, there are no current carriers at the TR1 base. Transistor TR1 now becomes, in effect, a diode. Current stops flowing from the battery through TR1 to the ignition coil primary winding. The magnetic field in the ignition coil collapses, and the ignition coil produces a high-voltage surge.

Figure 16-8 shows the wiring for the Chrysler electronic ignition system. The dual ballast is a double-resistor unit that protects both the ECU and the coil primary from overload but allows maximum current to flow during cranking. This assures a strong spark for good starting performance.

☼ 16-4 Ford electronic ignition system The Ford electronic ignition system, which went into 1974 and later Ford vehicles, is similar to the Chrysler system (☼ 16-3). Figures 16-9 and 16-10 show top and disassembled views of the distributor used in the Ford system. Note that the rotor (or *armature* as Ford calls it) has eight tips, so the distributor is for an eight-cylinder engine. In Fig. 16-10, you can see what the pickup coil looks like. Ford calls this the *stator*. The core of the stator is iron around which the coil is assembled. The voltage pulse reaches its maximum in the pickup coil at the instant that a tip aligns fully with the core of the pickup coil, as shown in Fig. 16-11. Note that a one-half–tooth error in alignment means a 7¾° timing error. (We shall discuss timing later.)

The amplifier module or ECU for the Ford electronic ignition system is shown in Fig. 16-12. It works the same as the ECU covered in ☼ 16-3.

☼ 16-5 Ford Dura-Spark electronic ignition systems Ford has two Dura-Spark systems, Dura-Spark I and Dura-Spark II. Basically, they work the same

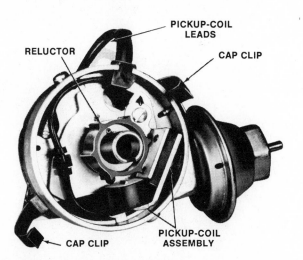

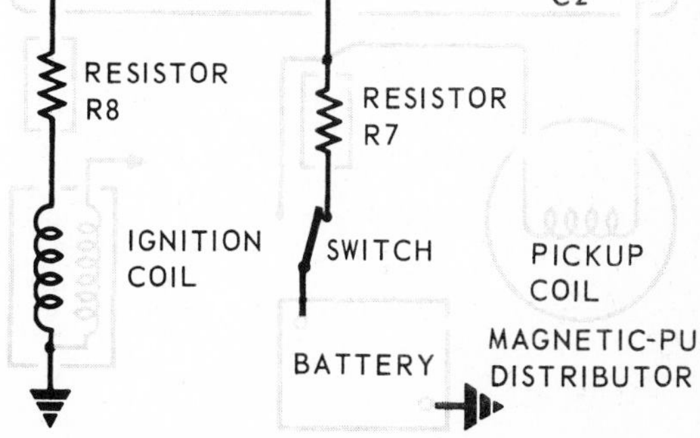

Fig. 16-5 Top view of the Chrysler electronic ignition distributor. The cap and rotor have been removed to show the reluctor and pickup coil. (*Chrysler Corporation*)

IGNITION-PULSE AMPLIFIER

Fig. 16-6 Current flow (heavy lines) through the ignition-pulse amplifier when the ignition-coil primary is being fed current from the battery. (*Delco-Remy Division of General Motors Corporation*)

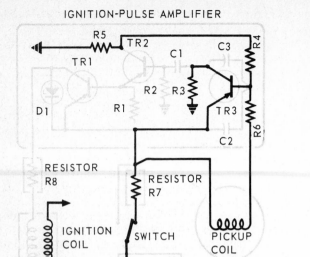

IGNITION-PULSE AMPLIFIER

Fig. 16-7 Current flow (heavy lines) through the ignition-pulse amplifier when the pickup coil in the distributor sends a signal (a voltage pulse) to the control unit. Transistors TR1 and TR2 have "turned off" to interrupt the flow of current to the ignition-coil primary. The secondary winding, therefore, discharges a high-voltage surge. (Delco-Remy Division of General Motors Corporation)

way as the systems described previously. However, they do produce higher secondary voltages of up to 40,000 volts and use the silicone secondary wiring previously described in ⚙ 13-15. Figure 16-13 is a wiring diagram of the Ford system, and Fig. 16-14 is a top view of the distributor with the cap and rotor removed. Notice that the distributor has the same general structure as the other electronic distributors previously discussed. Note also that the rotating element with spokes is called the *armature* and the sensor is called a *magnetic pickup assembly*. Figure 16-15 is an external view

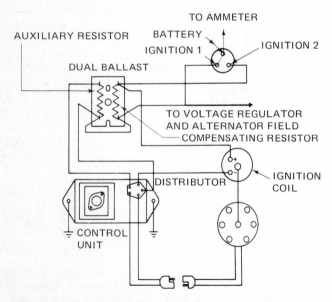

Fig. 16-8 Wiring diagram of the Chrysler electronic ignition system. (Chrysler Corporation)

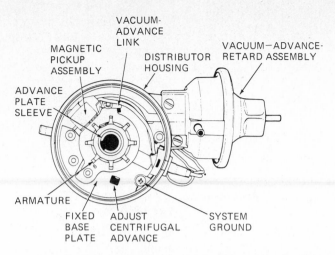

Fig. 16-9 Ignition distributor for an electronic ignition system. Note that Ford calls the rotating part an armature. Chrysler calls it a *reluctor*. (Ford Motor Company)

of the distributor which emphasizes another difference. The cap has solid-spark-plug-type terminals instead of the push-in type used in many other distributor caps (such as shown in Fig. 13-5).

Some Dura-Spark electronic modules have altitude and load compensation. That is, the module provides a change in spark advance as altitude and atmospheric pressure change. The module includes an atmospheric-pressure switch which signals the electronic control

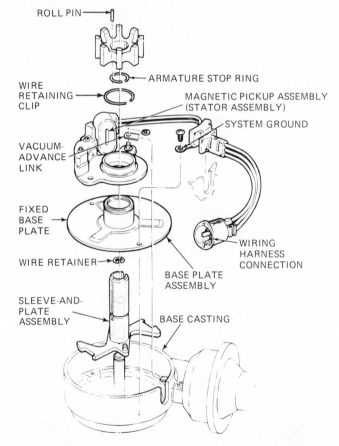

Fig. 16-10 Disassembled electronic distributor. (Ford Motor Company)

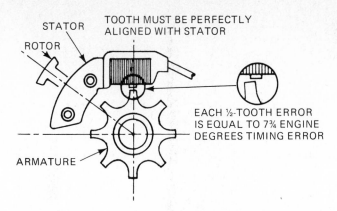

Fig. 16-11 Proper relationship between the tooth on the armature and the core of the stator with the distributor rotor at the No. 1 firing position. *(Ford Motor Company)*

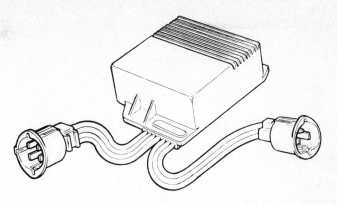

Fig. 16-12 Amplifier module for the electronic ignition system. *(Ford Motor Company)*

module as pressure changes. The module then changes the ignition spark advance. For example, as the car is driven to higher altitudes—going up a mountain, for instance—the system produces additional spark timing to compensate for the thinner mixture. It then retards the spark as the car goes down to lower altitudes and higher atmospheric pressures to prevent spark knock (detonation).

The system also includes a vacuum switch which senses intake-manifold vacuum. The signals from this switch cause the module to change the spark advance as manifold vacuum changes. Thus, when the throttle is open and the engine is under heavy load, the module retards the spark to prevent spark knock. At light loads and part throttle, the module advances the spark.

Because of the high voltage this system can produce, extra precautions have been taken to prevent high-voltage leakage inside the distributor cap and inside the

spark-plug boots. The inner surfaces of the cap, and the rotor—everywhere leakage could occur—are coated with a special silicone grease. As this compound ages, it looks like a contaminant. But this residue is normal and must not be removed. The insides of the spark-plug boots are also coated with silicone grease. The grease helps prevent high-voltage leakage to ground through insulated parts carrying high voltage. It also serves to block radio interference from the high-voltage surges passing through the rotor segment and cap.

⚙ 16-6 General Motors High-Energy Ignition (HEI) System In 1973, General Motors introduced an ignition system that produces high voltage of up to 35,000 volts. They named it the High-Energy Ignition (HEI) System. The ignition coil is assembled into the distributor (Fig. 16-16). With this assembly, the wiring is greatly simplified, as shown in Fig. 16-17. Note that there is one lead from the battery (which Delco-Remy

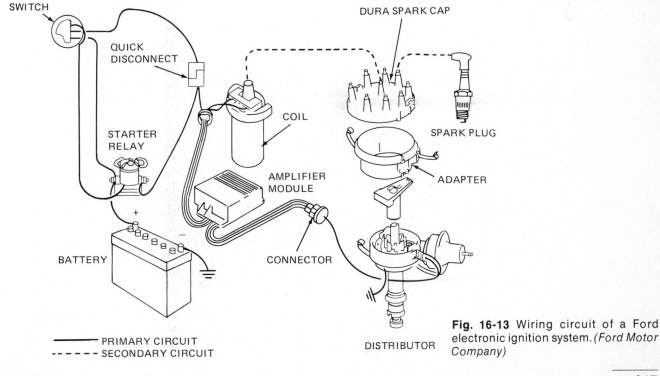

Fig. 16-13 Wiring circuit of a Ford electronic ignition system. *(Ford Motor Company)*

— PRIMARY CIRCUIT
----- SECONDARY CIRCUIT

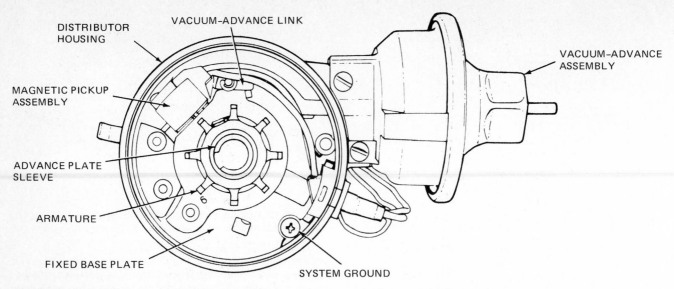

Fig. 16-14 Top view, with cap and rotor removed, of a Ford electronic distributor. *(Ford Motor Company)*

calls an *energizer*). This lead goes through the ignition switch to the distributor. No primary resistance is used. The only other leads are the high-voltage cables to the spark plugs. Because of the higher voltage, special silicone insulation spark-plug cables are used. These cables have a larger diameter 0.32 inch [8 mm], than standard spark-plug cables, as explained in ☼ 13-15. The silicone insulation is soft and must not be mishandled or allowed to rub against other parts. Special retainers are used to hold the spark-plug cables securely in place (Fig. 16-18).

Some HEI systems for in-line engines had the ignition coil separately mounted, as shown in Fig. 16-19. This requires additional wiring between the coil and the distributor.

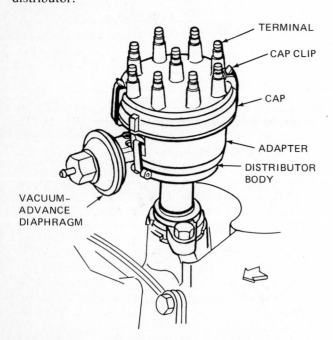

Fig. 16-15 Ford electronic distributor. Note the spark-plug-type terminals in the cap. *(Ford Motor Company)*

Both distributors have the electronic amplifier or *electronic module* as General Motors calls it, mounted inside the distributor. Figure 16-20 shows a top view of the distributor with the cap and rotor removed. The electronic module has also been removed and set to one side, with dashed lines indicating its location inside the distributor. The capacitor (condenser) in the distributor is for control of radio noise. It has no function in the HEI system. This system uses the magnetic-pulse or voltage-pulse principle, as do all the other electronic ignition systems (see ☼ 14-2). The special procedures to test the HEI system are described in Chapter 17. Figure 16-21 is an assembled view of the HEI distributor which includes the ignition coil. Note the tachometer connections to the distributor.

For a short time prior to the introduction of the HEI system, General Motors installed a unit distributor on some cars. This was an early version of the HEI distributor which included the ignition coil and had the electronic module attached to the distributor housing. The unit distributor and the HEI distributor shared many features. However, the unit distributor did not have the higher secondary voltage that the HEI system can deliver.

NOTE: The HEI system uses spark plugs with a wider gap—as much as 0.080 inch [2.03 mm]. Actually, this was one purpose of designing the HEI system, to produce a higher voltage that could jump a wider gap at the spark plugs. The longer spark can ignite leaner mixtures in the engine cylinders. Because of the increasingly stringent fuel-mileage requirements mandated by the federal government, carburetors are set to deliver leaner mixtures. The older-style ignition systems and smaller spark gaps have less chance to ignite these leaner mixtures.

Careful: Do not install standard spark plugs in an engine with the HEI system. To get the required wider gap, you would have to bend the side electrode at a

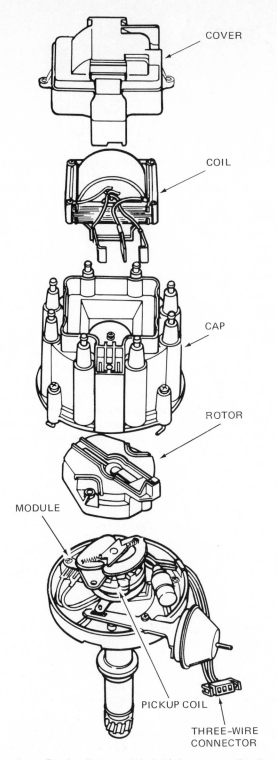

Fig. 16-16 Partly disassembled high-energy distributor. *(Delco-Remy Division of General Motors Corporation)*

severe angle, and it would not work satisfactorily. Instead, use spark plugs made for the HEI system.

⚙ 16-7 Electronic spark control (ESC)

This system was developed to provide a safeguard against detonation in engines using turbochargers. The turbocharger is a device that pushes more air–fuel mixture into the engine cylinders. It uses the pressure of the exhaust

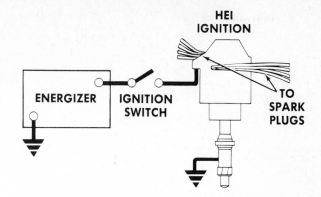

Fig. 16-17 Basic wiring diagram for the High-Energy Ignition (HEI) System. *(Delco-Remy Division of General Motors Corporation)*

gases to spin a turbine rotor (Fig. 16-22). The turbine is mounted on the same shaft as a compressor. When the turbine spins, the compressor also spins. This compresses air and sends it through the air cleaner and carburetor. The compressed air picks up additional fuel so that more fuel enters the engine cylinders. The turbocharger comes into operation only when high performance or power is required from the engine.

As we learned in Chapter 12, if you compress the air–fuel mixture too much, it will tend to detonate. That is, the last part of the mixture will ignite before the flame front reaches it (see ⚙ 12-10). Forcing more mixture into the cylinders (by turbocharging) means there is more mixture to be compressed each compression stroke. This can, under some conditions, cause an excessive compression or pressure rise so that detonation occurs near the end of the compression stroke.

On the other hand, it is desirable to push as much mixture into the cylinders as possible without causing detonation. The reason is that more mixture per power stroke means more power from each power stroke. Using a turbocharger can increase the power output from an engine 30 percent or more. But too much turbocharging leads to detonation and the possibility of a ruined engine.

It was these ideas that led engineers at Buick, Delco-Remy, and Delco Electronics to develop the ESC system for the Buick V-6 turbocharged engine (Fig. 16-23). What this system does is back off, or retard, the ignition timing if detonation starts to occur. It allows full centrifugal or vacuum advance (from the mechanical advance mechanisms in the distributor) until the engine is starting to detonate. At this point, a sensor picks up the resulting vibration and signals an electronic controller. The controller instantly signals the distributor and, in effect, "tells" it to back off, or retard, the ignition. What the system does is allow the engine to produce maximum power when called for, right up to the point of detonation. But it prevents severe detonation. The arrangement allows the engine to operate at maximum efficiency when it is called on for maximum power.

Figure 16-24 shows schematically the electronic logic system of the ESC. The detonator sensor is mounted on the intake manifold at the thermostat housing. This

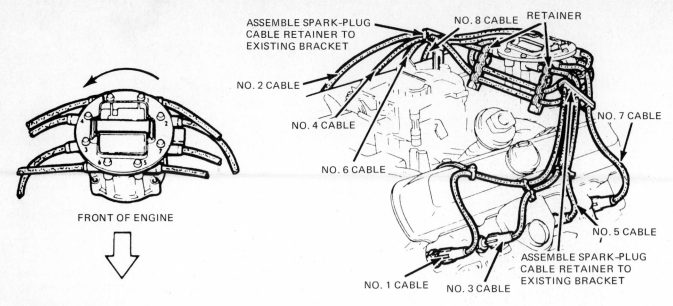

Fig. 16-18 HEI system cable routing on a V-8 engine. Cable retainers hold the silicone spark-plug cables securely in place. *(Oldsmobile Division of General Motors Corporation)*

point is the most sensitive spot on the engine to detect detonation as it starts to occur. When detonation starts, the signal from the sensor activates the electronic controller. The signal goes to both the detonation filter and to a part of the controller that continuously monitors background noise (noise of a normally running engine). The signal comparator continuously compares the signals from the detonator filter and the background-noise monitor. When the detonation-filter signal gets too loud, indicating that detonation is on the verge of occurring, the signal comparator instantly sends a signal to the retard command. The retard command responds by sending a signal to the distributor so it, in effect, overrides the distributor advance mechanisms and causes the spark to retard. Figure 16-25 is a layout of the system. Note that an HEI distributor is used. The signal goes to the electronic module in the distributor and causes it to delay its signal so the spark is retarded. Refer to ☼ 16-6 and Figs. 16-16 to 16-21 which describe and illustrate the HEI system.

Electronic ignition systems with electronic spark-advance controls

All the electronic ignition systems described so far are very similar in operation. A pickup coil senses the rotation of a trigger wheel or armature. The pickup coil sends voltage pulses to the electronic module. These pulses cause the module to close and open the battery-to-coil circuit (just like the contact points in the contact-point system). This causes the coil to produce the high-voltage surges which are carried by the secondary wiring, distributor cap, and rotor to the spark plugs.

We now look at a further advance in the use of electronics in ignition systems—electronic control of spark advance. These new systems are the same as the electronic systems previously described with one major exception. They have no mechanical centrifugal or vac-

uum-advance controls. Instead, various sensors feed information to a central computer which then produces the proper advance for the operating conditions. We describe three variations of this system, the Chrysler Lean-Burn System, the General Motors Electronic Spark Timing (EST) or MISAR System, and the Ford Electronic Engine Control (EEC) System.

☼ 16-8 Chrysler Electronic Lean-Burn (ELB) System This system (Fig. 16-26) includes a spark-control computer, several engine sensors, and a lean calibration carburetor. The air–fuel ratio for normal highway driving is about 15:1 (15 parts air, by weight, to 1 part gasoline, by weight). The Lean-Burn System uses ratios of 17:1 to 18:1. The leaner mixture reduces emissions and also improves fuel mileage. The system is designed to provide voltage surges of sufficient strength and duration to burn lean air–fuel mixtures. Also, the system electronically times the sparks so they occur at the spark plugs at the ideal instant. That is, it varies ignition timing to suit the operating condition—engine speed, engine temperature, throttle position, intake-manifold vacuum, and in-going air temperature. Before we discuss the operation of the system, we look at the computer and the sensors.

1. **Spark-control computer** The spark-control computer, which is mounted on the air cleaner (Fig. 16-26), includes two interrelated modules, the program-schedule module and the ignition-spark-advance control module. The program-schedule module continuously receives signals from the sensors and almost instantly computes the correct spark advance for the operating condition. It then "tells" the ignition-control module exactly how much to advance or retard the spark for that particular operating condition. The system is much more accurate and faster acting than the mechanical centrifugal and vacuum-advance units used on other distributors.

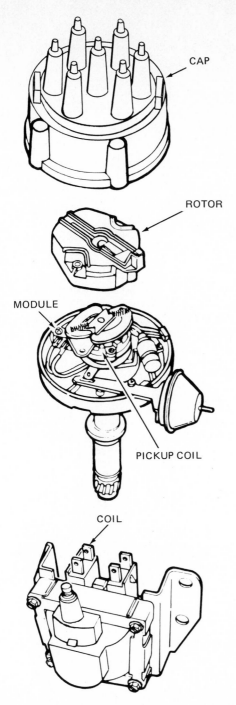

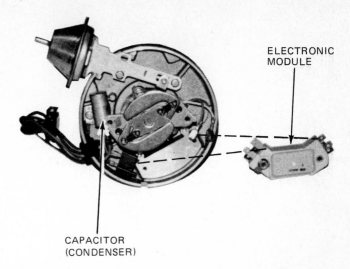

Fig. 16-20 HEI distributor with the electronic module removed. *(Delco-Remy Division of General Motors Corporation)*

3. **Sensors** There are seven sensors that send information to the spark-control computer. Some of these are transducers. A *transducer* is a device that converts an input signal of one form into an output signal of another form. For example, the automobile horn converts an electric signal to sound. Another example is the throttle-position sensor used in the Lean-Burn System. It sends an electric signal to the computer which results from the position and the movement of the throt-

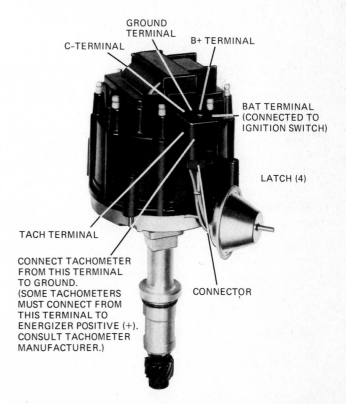

Fig. 16-21 Distributor for the HEI system which includes the ignition coil. *(Delco-Remy Division of General Motors Corporation)*

Fig. 16-19 HEI system distributor with separate ignition coil. *(Delco-Remy Division of General Motors Corporation)*

2. **Ignition distributor** Figure 16-27 shows the distributor used with the Lean-Burn System. The cap and rotor have been removed so you can see the pickup sensors. The RUN PICKUP sensor is the same sensor used with the Chrysler electronic ignition system discussed in ✿ 16-3. This is the sensor that sends voltage pulses to the electronic control unit when the engine is running. The other sensor, the START PICKUP sensor, overrides the RUN PICKUP when the engine is being started. That is, it provides the correct advance for starting.

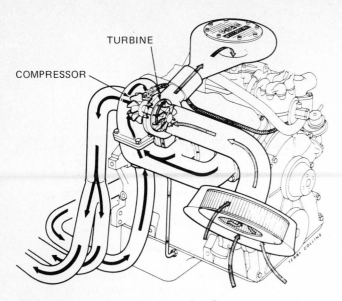

COMPRESSOR

TURBINE

Fig. 16-22 Ford 182-cubic inch [3-L] V-6 engine with turbocharger. *(Ford Motor Company)*

tle valves in the carburetor. We now look at the seven sensors in the Lean-Burn System.

a. Coolant temperature sensor This sensor is located in the water-pump housing. Its function is to signal the computer when the engine cooling temperature is below 150°F [65.6°C].

b. Air temperature sensor This sensor is located in the computer, and it supplies a signal based on the temperature of the air entering the air cleaner. The signal also affects the amount of additional spark advance produced by the computer as related to the throttle-position transducer.

c. Throttle-position transducer This transducer (Fig. 16-28) is located in the carburetor. It signals to the

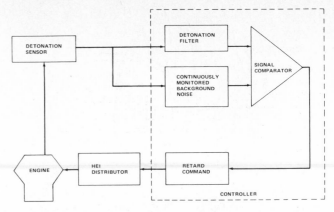

Fig. 16-24 Block diagram of the electronic logic system for the ESC system which works to prevent detonation. *(Buick Motor Division of General motors Corporation)*

computer the position and rate of change of the throttle valves. As the throttle valves start to open, the transducer signals the computer and the computer provides additional advance. The amount the throttle opens determines the amount of additional advance. The speed with which the throttle is opened also affects the amount of advance. For example, if the throttle is opened quickly, maximum advance is provided for about one second. However, the air-temperature-sensor signal controls the amount of this maximum advance that will be allowed. If the air temperature is high, it will allow less advance. If cold, it allows more advance.

d. Carburetor-idle-stop-switch sensor This sensor (Fig. 16-28) is located on the right side of the carburetor. It tells the computer whether the engine is operating at idle or off-idle.

e. Vacuum transducer This transducer is located on

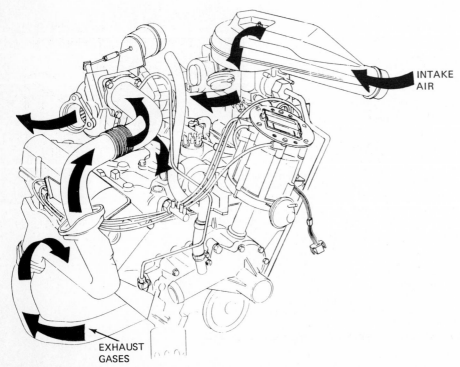

INTAKE AIR

EXHAUST GASES

Fig. 16-23 V-6 turbocharged engine of type equipped with electronic spark control (ESC) which guards against detonation. Arrows show flow of air and exhaust gas in the system. *(Buick Motor Division of General Motors Corporation)*

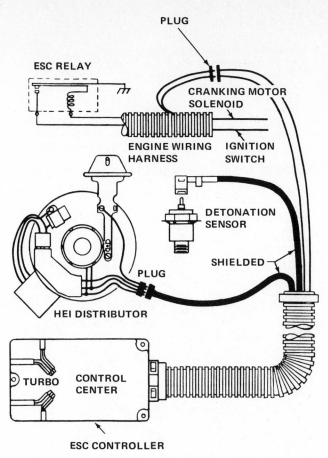

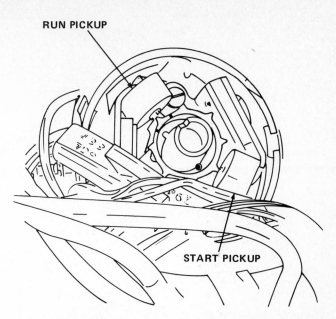

Fig. 16-27 Locations of START PICKUP and RUN PICKUP sensors in the distributor. *(Chrysler Corporation)*

the computer and is connected to a port in the carburetor so it senses intake-manifold vacuum. As vacuum increases, its signal to the computer produces more advance. With less vacuum, there is less spark advance. You can see that the vacuum transducer works about the same as the diaphragm type of vacuum-advance unit on the earlier distributors.

f. Start pickup This is one of two sensors located inside the distributor (Fig. 16-27). During cranking, this sen-

Fig. 16-25 Layout of the ESC system. *(Buick Motor Division of General Motors Corporation)*

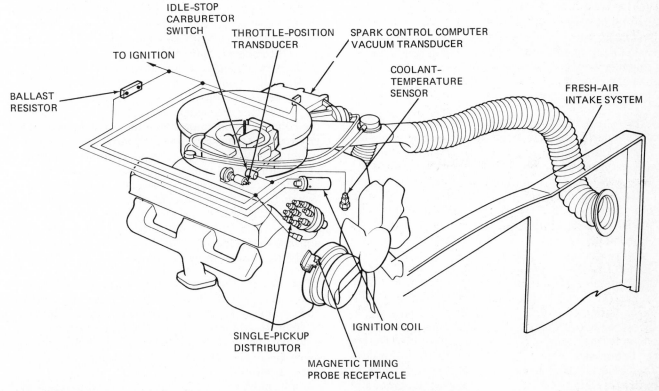

Fig. 16-26 Chrysler Lean-Burn System, showing locations of components. *(Chrysler Corporation)*

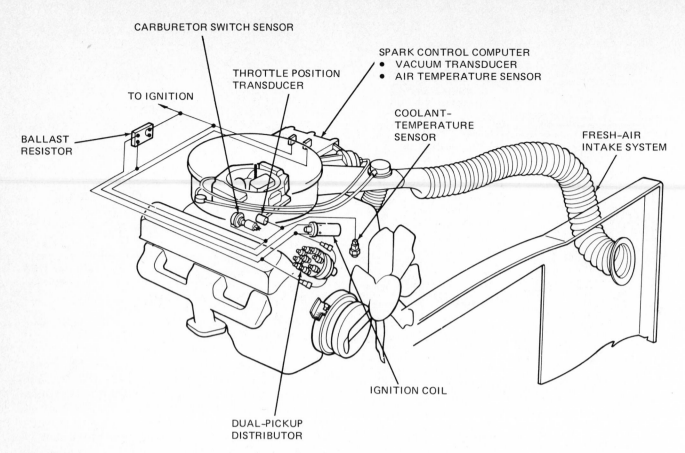

CARBURETOR SWITCH SENSOR

SPARK CONTROL COMPUTER
• VACUUM TRANSDUCER
• AIR TEMPERATURE SENSOR

THROTTLE POSITION
TRANSDUCER

TO IGNITION

COOLANT-
TEMPERATURE
SENSOR

BALLAST
RESISTOR

FRESH–AIR
INTAKE SYSTEM

IGNITION COIL

DUAL–PICKUP
DISTRIBUTOR

Fig. 16-28 Location of the throttle-position transducer in the carburetor. *(Chrysler Corporation)*

sor supplies a signal to the computer that causes it to provide a fixed spark advance. All other advance possibilities are cancelled out.

g. Run pickup This sensor (Fig. 16-27) supplies the basic timing signal to the computer. The signal tells the computer how fast the engine is running. It also tells the computer when the pistons are moving up on their compression strokes.

NOTE: The description of the Chrysler Lean-Burn System you have just read applies to one particular model. You will find some variations in this basic design from year to year. However, all these variations work the same way to control the spark advance as determined by the engine and operating conditions. Be aware that there are these year-by-year differences. When you are checking a Lean-Burn System, try to have the correct shop manual available for your reference.

⚙ **16-9 Operation of Chrysler ELB system** When the ignition key is turned to START, the START PICKUP signals the computer to supply additional spark advance during cranking. Then, when the engine starts, the RUN PICKUP takes over, and it pulses to tell the computer the engine speed and piston locations. During the first minute of running, the computer also supplies additional advance to give the cold mixture time to burn. This additional advance is phased out gradually over the first minute of operation.

If the engine coolant temperature is below 150°F

[65.6°C], the coolant temperature sensor supplies a signal that prevents additional spark advance asked for by the vacuum-transducer signal. This prevents excessive spark advance with a high intake-manifold vacuum when the engine is cold. Such spark advance during the cold-operating mode could cause engine stumble.

After the engine gets up to operating temperature, the warm-engine operating mode is reached. The RUN PICKUP signals the engine speed and piston positions to the computer so it can provide the correct advance for any speed. At the same time, the input signals from the air-temperature sensor, throttle position transducer, carburetor switch sensor, and vacuum transducer are all entering the computer. The computer puts all these signals together and computes the exact spark advance required for best engine operation, based on all these signals. This is a continuous process with the computer constantly making spark-advance changes in response to changes in operating conditions.

⚙ **16-10 Ford Electronic Engine Control (EEC) System** This system (Fig. 16-29) also uses a computer and is similar in many ways to the Chrysler Lean-Burn System. In addition to controlling the spark advance, however the Ford EEC system also controls the exhaust-gas recirculation (EGR) and the air-injection systems, as we will explain.

First, however, we discuss these two systems that the EEC system controls: the exhaust-gas recirculation system and the air-injection system.

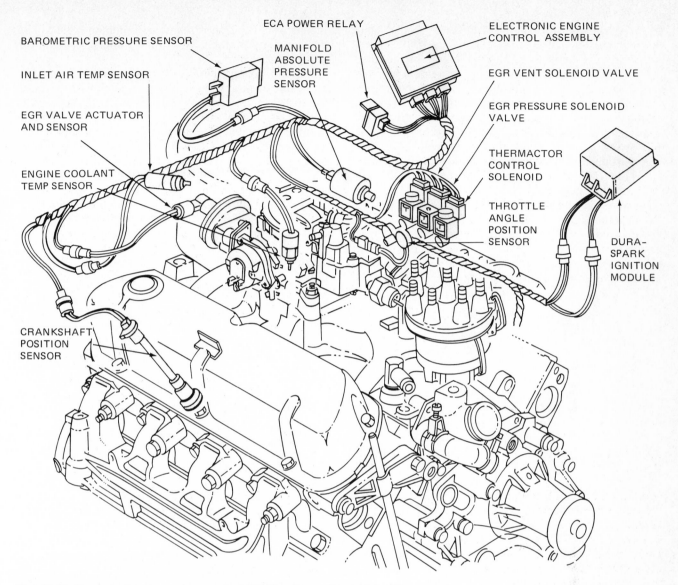

Fig. 16-29 Ford electronic engine control (EEC) system. *(Ford Motor Company)*

☼ 16-11 Exhaust-gas recirculation The exhaust-gas recirculation (EGR) system (Fig. 16-30) sends some exhaust gas back through the engine during some phases of engine operation. The purpose of this is to lower the peak combustion temperatures somewhat and thereby reduce the amount of nitrogen oxides formed during combustion. Nitrogen oxide (NO_x is the general chemical formula) is an atmospheric pollutant, and federal law mandates the maximum allowable amount of NO_x in the exhaust gas. The EGR valve, which is located between the exhaust and intake manifolds (Fig. 16-30), opens or closes on signals to allow exhaust-gas flow into the intake manifold or to shut it off.

The Ford EEC system controls the operation of the EGR valve. It uses two solenoid valves to produce the control. The purpose of the control is to allow the EGR system to work only when the engine temperature and operating conditions can tolerate the exhaust gas. That is, it allows the exhaust gas to enter the intake manifold only when it will not reduce engine performance.

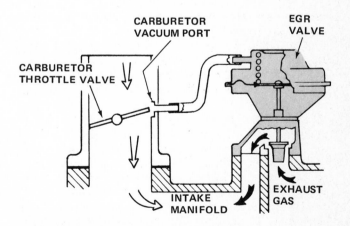

Fig. 16-30 Schematic diagram of an exhaust-gas recirculation (EGR) system. *(Chevrolet Motor Division of General Motors Corporation)*

⚙ 16-12 Air-injection or thermactor system This system (Fig. 16-31) treats the exhaust gas as it leaves the engine cylinders to reduce pollutants in the gas. The pollutants treated by this system are unburned and partly burned gasoline. Gasoline is mainly hydrogen and carbon and has the chemical formula HC. During combustion, the hydrogen and carbon break apart and combine with oxygen. The hydrogen and oxygen form H_2O, which is water. The carbon unites with oxygen to form carbon dioxide which has the chemical formula CO_2—provided there is enough oxygen available and combustion is perfect.

However, combustion is never perfect in the engine, and so some HC is left in the exhaust gas. Also, some of the carbon only partly unites with oxygen to form carbon monoxide or CO. Carbon monoxide is a deadly poisonous gas. That is the reason you are warned never to operate an engine in an enclosed space without some means of ventilation. Enough carbon monoxide can be produced in 3 minutes by a running engine in a one-car garage to kill you!

Federal law mandates the maximum HC and CO allowable in exhaust gas. The air-injection or thermactor system helps reduce the HC and CO in this way. It has an air pump, driven by a belt from the engine crankshaft pulley. The air pump sends air through an air manifold into a series of air-injection tubes. These tubes are located close to the engine exhaust valves. The oxygen in the air helps burn the HC or CO in the exhaust gas and form harmless H_2O and CO_2. The Ford EEC system controls the airflow from the air pump. It cuts off the airflow to the exhaust manifold when it could cause reduced engine performance.

⚙ 16-13 Ford EEC system components We have noted that the Ford EEC system (Fig. 16-29) has a

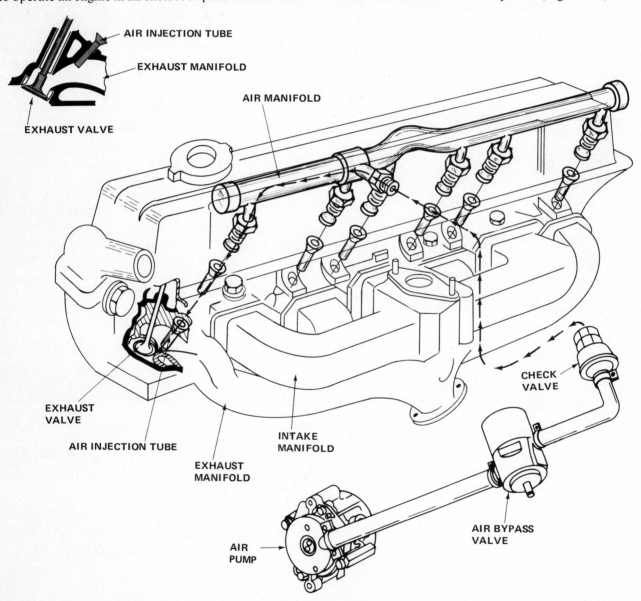

Fig. 16-31 Air-injection system. Air manifold and other parts have been shown detached so they can be seen better. The cylinder head has been cut away at the front to show how the air-injection tube fits into the head.

computer which controls the spark advance, just as the Chrysler Lean-Burn System does. The Ford EEC system also controls the EGR and air-injection systems, as we have said. The control computer is fed information from sensors that sense the following:

1. Inlet air temperature entering the air cleaner.
2. Throttle movement and position.
3. Engine coolant temperature.
4. Air pressure which changes as altitude changes.
5. Intake-manifold vacuum.
6. Crankshaft and thus piston position. This signal originates at a disk or pulse ring with four teeth 90° apart on the rear of the crankshaft (Fig. 16-32). When a tooth lines up with the sensor, it produces a voltage pulse that signals the computer the crankshaft position.
7. Engine speed. The signal from the crankshaft pulse ring and sensor also tells the computer how fast the crankshaft is turning.

As you can see, these sensing devices are similar to those we have discussed previously when we described the Chrysler Lean-Burn System. In a continuous process, it monitors various aspects of the engine operating condition. It then calculates the ideal spark advance for the condition, continuously changing the advance as operating conditions change. The Ford EEC system also controls the operation of the EGR valve as previously noted (✹ 16-10 and 16-11). In addition, it controls the air-injection or thermactor system (✹ 16-12), cutting off the airflow to the exhaust manifold when it could cause reduced engine performance.

✹ 16-14 General Motors electronic spark timing (EST) ignition system

This system is similar in many ways to the two systems previously described. It is called the Microprocessed Sensing and Automatic Regulation (MISAR) system. The system controls spark advance electronically, on the basis of information fed to the electronic control unit by four engine sensors. These sensors are:

1. Crankshaft sensor in the first year the system was used (1977 Oldsmobiles). In later years, the sensor was located inside the distributor, as in the electronic ignition distributors described earlier in the chapter. The sensor senses engine speed and piston positions.
2. Engine coolant sensor.
3. Manifold-vacuum sensor.
4. Atmospheric-pressure sensor.

The 1977 version has a crankshaft sensor mounted to the front engine-mounting brackets (Fig. 16-33). A disk with teeth is mounted between the pulley and harmonic balancer on the front of the crankshaft (Fig. 16-34). As the engine runs and the disk rotates, the disk causes the crankshaft sensor to send voltage signals to the electronic control unit. These signals tell the control unit how fast the engine is running and the position of the crankshaft (and thus the locations of the pistons on the compression strokes). Using this information and information from the other sensors, the control unit adjusts the spark advance to suit engine speed and load.

The later version of the system places the speed and piston position sensor in the distributor. In this location, it provides the same information as the disk on the crankshaft and its sensor.

NOTE: The timing of the 1977 version is adjusted by moving the crankshaft sensor (Fig. 16-34). The later version is adjusted by shifting the distributor in its mounting.

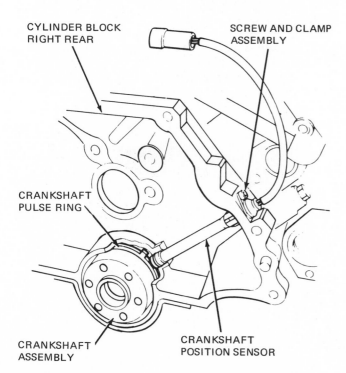

Fig. 16-32 Location of crankshaft pulse ring. As part of the timing procedure, a crankshaft position sensor is installed, as shown. *(Ford Motor Company)*

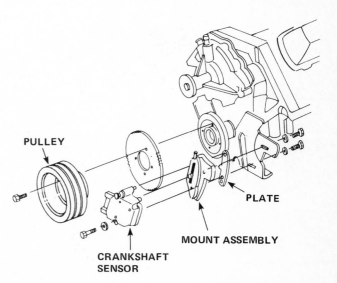

Fig. 16-33 Crankshaft sensor mounting for the 1977 MISAR ignition system. *(Oldsmobile Division of General Motors Corporation)*

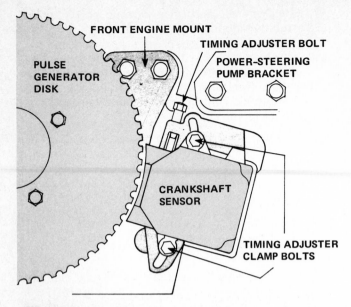

Fig. 16-34 Relationship of crankshaft sensor to the pulse-generator disk on the engine crankshaft. *(Oldsmobile Division of General Motors Corporation)*

The engine coolant sensor is located in the engine cooling system and senses engine coolant temperature. It sends a continuous voltage signal to the electronic control unit to tell it the engine temperature. The control unit takes this information into account as it adjusts spark timing.

The manifold-vacuum sensor reacts to intake-manifold vacuum, providing a continuous voltage signal to the control unit. This causes the control unit to make whatever adjustment to the spark advance is required by vacuum conditions. For example, when the throttle is partly closed and there is high intake-manifold vacuum, the control advances the spark. This gives the leaner air–fuel mixture more time to burn. This is the same thing that the vacuum-advance unit on the mechanical distributor does.

The atmospheric-pressure sensor adjusts the spark advance to take into account atmospheric pressure. For example, at higher altitudes, where the pressure is lower, the sensor tells the electronic control to advance the spark. Less air–fuel mixture is getting into the cylinders when the atmospheric pressure is lowered. The spark advance gives this less dense mixture enough time to burn. When the car moves down to a lower altitude, where the atmospheric pressure is higher, the control reduces the spark advance to prevent knocking or pinging.

⚙ 16-15 Bosch electronic vehicle control system The Robert Bosch Corporation has developed an electronic control system that includes an electronic ignition system. It also controls ignition spark advance and has the built-in design capability of controlling other variables such as fuel injection, automatic transmission shifts, and antilock braking systems. Antilock braking is covered in Chapter 25. Figure 16-35 is a block diagram of the system. It uses a speed sensor and toothed wheel and a reference mark sensor, as shown. The reference marker informs the ECU of the positions of the pistons in the cylinders.

Figure 16-36 shows one arrangement for the system, with various sensors feeding information to the ECU so that it can determine when high-voltage surges should be generated.

⚙ 16-16 Hall-effect ignition system The Hall-effect ignition system depends on the reaction of a semiconductor (like a diode) to a magnetic field that is alternately applied and cut off. When the magnetic field is applied, a voltage appears across the semiconductor. When the magnetic field is cut off, the voltage disappears.

This effect is put to work in some electronic ignition distributors. The distributor has a rotor with a series of steel shutters which pass through an air gap between a permanent magnet and the semiconductor sensor. Let us take a Hall-effect distributor apart to see how it

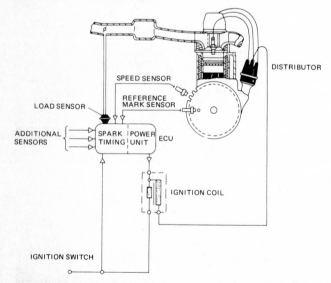

Fig. 16-35 Bosch electronic control system for spark-advance control plus control of other operating variables. *(Robert Bosch GmbH)*

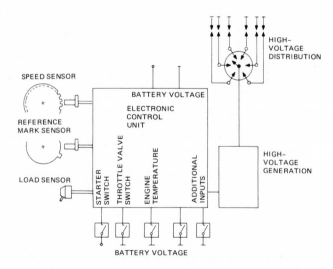

Fig. 16-36 Schematic layout of Bosch electronic control system. *(Robert Bosch GmbH)*

works. The distributor we look at is for a four-cylinder engine.

Figure 16-37 shows the cap being removed from the distributor. The rotor is a little different from the rotors for other distributors. Figure 16-38 shows the rotor being removed from the distributor. In this picture, you can see the shutters and the air gap they pass through as the rotor rotates. Note that there are four shutters, one for each cylinder in the engine. Take another look at the top of the rotor which shows in Fig. 16-37. Here you can see the spring and segment that connect the center terminal of the cap to the four outside cap terminals. This is the same arrangement found in all other distributors. This rotor has a small counterweight opposite the tower on which the segment and spring mount.

Figure 16-39 shows the Hall-effect pickup assembly being removed from the distributor housing. By studying these three illustrations, Figs. 16-37 to 16-39, you can see how the arrangement works. A signal is produced in the sensor by the magnetic field when a shutter is not in the way. This signal is in the form of a voltage. The voltage signal goes to the electronic control unit (which the manufacturer calls the *spark control computer*). The signal "tells" the control unit to cut off the flow of current to the ignition coil primary winding. The ignition coil magnetic field then collapses, and the secondary winding produces a high-voltage surge. This is carried through the high-voltage cables to the center terminal of the distributor cap. From there, it passes through the rotor segment to the outer cap terminal connected to the spark plug in the cylinder that is ready to fire (piston nearing end of compression stroke).

As you can see, the secondary side of the system works the same as do all other ignition systems described so far. Now let us go back to the Hall-effect

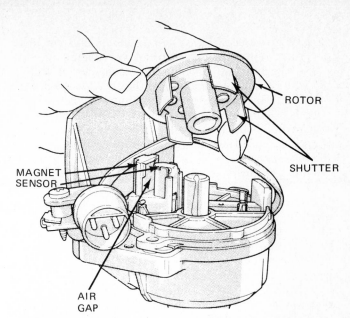

Fig. 16-38 Removing rotor from a Hall-effect distributor. *(Chrysler Corporation)*

device. The instant a shutter on the rotor starts to pass through the air gap between the permanent magnet and the sensor, the magnetic field is cut off. With no magnetic field on the sensor, the sensor voltage drops to zero. This is almost instantaneous. As the voltage drops to zero, the electronic control unit instantly reestablishes the circuit to the ignition-coil primary winding. The magnetic field builds up, ready to produce another high-voltage surge. This next surge occurs the instant the rotor shutter moves out of the air gap between the magnet and the sensor.

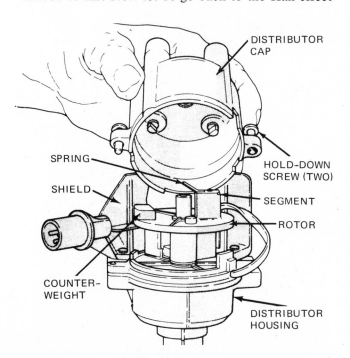

Fig. 16-37 Hall-effect distributor with cap removed. *(Chrysler Corporation)*

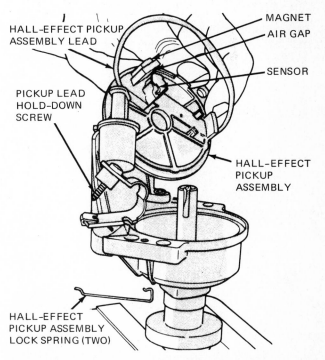

Fig. 16-39 Removing the Hall-effect pickup assembly from distributor. *(Chrysler Corporation)*

As you can see, this system is very similar to the electronic ignition systems we have covered previously. The basic differences are in the manner in which the voltage signal originates and the speed with which it is cut off. In the other electronic ignition systems, the voltage originates in a coil of wire, the sensor coil. This voltage builds up as a tip of the reluctor swings up to the sensor coil. Then the voltage drops off as the tip of the reluctor moves on past the coil. Note that this is a buildup and drop-off of the voltage. In contrast, the Hall effect provides an almost instantaneous starting and stopping of the voltage signal. The Hall effect has another advantage. The length of each voltage pulse, and the frequency of the voltage pulses, are so accurate that they can be used to provide a spark advance related to engine speed. In other words, this takes the place of a centrifugal advance mechanism.

Vacuum advance is achieved by a vacuum transducer in the spark-control computer (the ECU). Figure 16-40 shows the spark-control computer for the system. It includes solid-state devices that are similar to those already described for other electronic ignition systems. The computer receives signals from the Hall-effect distributor, from the intake-manifold vacuum, the engine coolant temperature, and from the carburetor which signals whether the engine is idling or running off-idle. The computer puts all these together and instantly calculates the proper spark advance for the operating condition.

In summary, then, the basic difference between the Hall-effect distributor and the other electronic distributors is in the way the signal voltage is produced, either by a sensor coil or by a semiconductor that produces voltage when a magnetic field is applied to it.

A "no-distributor" ignition system

Ford engineers have been working on an ignition system for a four-cylinder engine that has no distributor. Instead, the system fires two plugs at once, one in a cylinder during its exhaust stroke, and the other in another cylinder near the end of the compression stroke. The system is not in production now, but it may be in the near future.

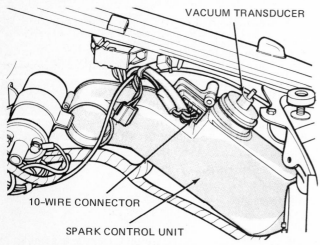

Fig. 16-40 Spark-control unit (ECU) for a Hall-effect ignition system. (Chrysler Corporation)

230

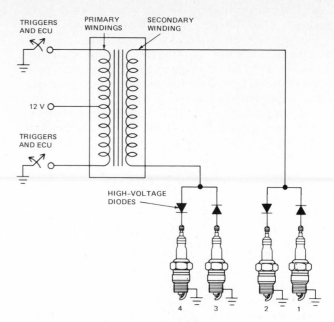

Fig. 16-41 Schematic wiring diagram of a "no-distributor" ignition system for a four-cylinder engine with a firing order of 1-3-4-2. (Ford Motor Company)

16-17 Ford "no-distributor" ignition system This system is shown schematically in Fig. 16-41. There are two primary windings and one secondary winding in the ignition coil (Fig. 16-42). The action is controlled by a rotating sensor on the crankshaft, similar to the 1977 Oldsmobile MISAR system (16-14) or the Ford EEC system (16-13). The trigger has two triggering points, one for one of the primary windings and the other for the other primary winding in the coil. Each triggering point operates an ECU which stops the flow of current through one of the primary windings. When this happens, the magnetic field of the primary winding collapses and a high voltage is produced in the secondary winding. The polarity of this high voltage, as well as the bias of the high-voltage diodes, determines which two plugs fire. For instance, suppose the upper end of the secondary winding (in Fig. 16-41) is negative. The high-voltage surge (electrons) can, therefore, flow to ground through plug 2. From ground it flows through plug 3 and back to the other end of the secondary winding. It cannot flow through plug 1 because the bias of the high-voltage diode for plug 1 prevents it.

Now let us assume that the compression stroke is near its end in cylinder 2. The high-voltage surge causes a spark, and the power stroke starts. At the same time, cylinder 3 is on its exhaust stroke. The spark in plug 3 takes place in relatively low-pressure exhaust gases. It takes much less voltage to jump the spark-plug gap. Thus, there is ample voltage available at plug 2 gap to make a good spark.

At the same time, current is flowing in the lower primary winding (Fig. 16-41). But it is flowing in the opposite direction from the direction it flowed in the upper winding. Therefore, when the trigger stops the flow of current, the magnetic field collapses in the opposite direction. This means the lower end of the sec-

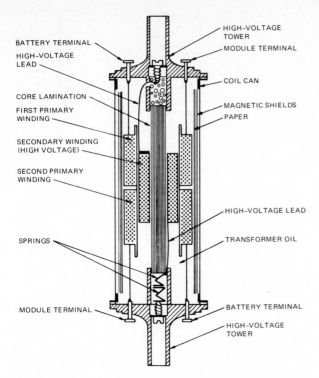

Fig. 16-42 Sectional view of the "double-ended" ignition coil used in the "no-distributor" ignition system. *(Ford Motor Company)*

Labels on figure:
BATTERY TERMINAL
HIGH-VOLTAGE LEAD
CORE LAMINATION
FIRST PRIMARY WINDING
SECONDARY WINDING (HIGH VOLTAGE)
SECOND PRIMARY WINDING
SPRINGS
MODULE TERMINAL

HIGH-VOLTAGE TOWER
MODULE TERMINAL
COIL CAN
MAGNETIC SHIELDS
PAPER
HIGH-VOLTAGE LEAD
TRANSFORMER OIL
BATTERY TERMINAL
HIGH-VOLTAGE TOWER

ondary winding is negative. Now, the high-voltage surge can flow only to plug 4 and produce a spark. It then flows to plug 1 and back to the secondary winding.

A key to the successful operation of the system is in the action of the high-voltage diodes. They permit the high-voltage surges to flow in one direction only, and not the other. For example, when the upper end of the secondary winding is negative, the high-voltage surge flows toward plugs 1 and 2. It cannot flow into plug 1, however, because the diode prevents it. But the diode for plug 2 permits the high-voltage surge to flow into plug 2.

Although this system is not in use on any car now in production, it has been experimentally installed and tested on cars. It can also be adapted for V-8 engines. In this book, we like to look as far ahead as possible so that you will be prepared to handle not only present electrical and electronic equipment, but new developments you will see in the future.

Chapter 16 review questions

Select the *one* correct, best, or most probable answer to each question. Then check your answers against the correct answers given at the end of the book.

1. In the electronic ignition system, the circuit between the battery and ignition-coil primary winding is closed and opened by:
   a. a field relay,
   b. contact points,
   c. a switch,
   d. solid-state devices.
2. The timer core, reluctor, and armature are:
   a. different components on different systems,
   b. different names for the same component,
   c. seldom used in electronic ignition systems,
   d. distributor drives.
3. Rotation of the timer core or reluctor:
   a. carries magnetic lines of force through the sensor or pickup coil,
   b. trips the contacts in the distributor,
   c. causes the spark to advance as engine speed increases,
   d. provides vacuum and centrifugal advance.
4. The timer core or reluctor rotates:
   a. at half crankshaft speed,
   b. at crankshaft speed,
   c. at twice crankshaft speed,
   d. clockwise.
5. The Dura-Spark altitude compensation:
   a. retards the spark as the car is driven to a higher altitude,
   b. advances the spark as the car is driven to a higher altitude,
   c. operates on intake-manifold vacuum,
   d. operates on centrifugal advance.
6. The distributor for the General Motors HEI system used on V-8 engines:
   a. does not require an ignition coil,
   b. includes the ignition coil,
   c. has the ignition coil separately mounted,
   d. uses a pair of ignition coils.
7. High-energy ignition systems require spark plugs:
   a. with silicone insulation,
   b. with wider gaps,
   c. with narrower gaps,
   d. with less reach.
8. Ignition systems with electronic spark-advance control include a computer that:
   a. controls engine speed,
   b. decides how much the spark should be advanced,
   c. feeds information to a series of sensors,
   d. controls the centrifugal advance.
9. A transducer:
   a. converts an input signal of one form into an output signal of another form,
   b. is a special sort of transistor,
   c. has at least three diodes,
   d. induces a change.
10. The Ford EEC system controls not only the spark advance but also:
    a. engine speed,
    b. manifold vacuum,
    c. fuel and exhaust systems,
    d. EGR and air-injection systems.

SERVICING ELECTRONIC IGNITION SYSTEMS

After studying this chapter, you should be able to:

1. List the nine abnormal operating conditions in the trouble diagnosis chart and explain possible causes and corrections for each trouble.
2. Explain and demonstrate how to safely make the spark test.
3. Explain in what basic way the oscilloscope patterns for electronic ignition systems differ from those for contact-point systems.
4. Explain and demonstrate the testing procedures described in the chapter for Chrysler, Ford, and General Motors electronic ignition systems.

17-1 Electronic ignition-system service In many ways, the servicing of electronic ignition systems and of contact-point ignition systems are similar. Chapter 14 covered contact-point ignition-system troubleshooting. Chapter 15 covered contact-point distributor service. Much of what we discussed in those chapters also applies to electronic ignition-system service. However, in this chapter, on servicing electronic ignition systems, we cover the complete trouble shooting and servicing procedure as it applies to these systems. We cover each of the systems separately—Chrysler, Ford, and General Motors.

First, however, we look at the troubles that may be common to all these systems and list possible causes.

✿ 17-2 Possible causes of electronic ignition-system failure Ignition-system failures can be grouped into three categories, as follows:

1. Loss of energy in the primary circuit. This could result from:
   a. Resistance in the primary circuit due to defective leads, bad connections or ignition switch, or open ignition-coil primary.
   b. Discharged battery or defective alternator
   c. Grounded primary circuit in ignition coil, wiring, or distributor
   d. Defective electronic control unit (ECU) or sensor-coil circuit to ECU
2. Loss of energy in the secondary circuit, due to:
   a. Plugs fouled, defective, or out of adjustment
   b. Defective high-voltage wiring which allows high-voltage leakage
   c. High-voltage leakage across ignition-coil head, distributor cap, or rotor
   d. Defective connections in high-voltage circuits

3. Out-of-time ignition, due to:
   a. Timing not set properly
   b. Centrifugal or vacuum advance defective
   c. Preignition from plugs of wrong heat range, fouled plugs, carbon in combustion chambers, and so on

✿ 17-3 Electronic ignition-system trouble diagnosis chart The chart that follows covers, in general, various possible troubles that might be caused by conditions in the ignition system. Keep in mind, however, that many of these conditions could result from troubles in other components and systems of the engine.

✿ 17-4 Quick checks to locate trouble Several checks have been used in the past to help locate the cause of various troubles. For example, one test is to remove a cable from a spark plug, insert a plug extender into the cable end, and hold the extender about ⅜ inch [9.53 mm] from the engine block. Crank the engine and check for sparking (Fig. 17-1). Use insulated pliers. If no sparking occurs, there is trouble in the ignition system.

If there is a good spark, the failure to start is probably in the fuel system. This test must be used with caution today because of the high voltages the modern electronic ignition systems are capable of producing.

Today, most shops have an oscilloscope (✿ 14-19 to 14-22), and using the oscilloscope is a quick way to analyze ignition systems and help the technician pinpoint trouble causes.

Often, the first step in analysis will be to recharge or replace the battery since the driver may have run it down in a vain attempt to get the engine started.

Following sections discuss in detail the various trou-

Electronic Ignition-System Trouble Diagnosis Chart

Refer to ☼ 17-4 to 17-13 for detailed explanations of trouble causes and checks or corrections to be made.

CONDITION	POSSIBLE CAUSE	CHECK OR CORRECTION
1. Engine cranks normally but fails to start (☼ 17-5)	a. No voltage to ignition system	Check battery, ignition switch, wiring
	b. ECU ground lead open, loose, or corroded	Repair as needed.
	c. Primary wiring connectors not fully engaged	Clean, firmly seat connectors
	d. Ignition coil open or shorted	Test coil, replace if defective
	e. Damaged armature (trigger wheel, reluctor) or sensor	Replace damaged part
	f. ECU faulty	Replace
	g. Defective distributor cap or rotor	Replace defective part
	h. Fuel system faulty	
	i. Engine faulty	
2. Engine backfires but fails to start (☼ 17-6)	a. Incorrect timing	Check and adjust timing
	b. Moisture in distributor cap	Dry cap
	c. Cap faulty—voltage leakage across carbon paths	Replace cap
	d. High-voltage cables not connected in firing order	Reconnect cables correctly
3. Engine runs but misses—does not run smoothly (☼ 17-7)	a. Spark plugs fouled or faulty	Clean and regap, or replace
	b. Distributor cap or rotor faulty	Replace
	c. High-voltage cables defective	Replace
	d. Defective (weak) coil	Replace
	e. Bad connections	Clean, tighten
	f. High-voltage leakage	Check distributor cap, rotor, cables
	g. Advance mechanisms defective	Check advances, repair or replace distributor
	h. Defective fuel system	
	i. Defects in engine such as loss of compression or faulty valve action	
4. Engine runs but backfires	a. Ignition timing off	Retime
	b. Ignition crossfiring	Check high-voltage cables, distributor cap, and rotor for leakage paths
	c. Faulty antibackfire valve	Replace valve
	d. Spark plugs of wrong heat range	Install correct plugs
	e. Defective air-injection system	Check system
	f. Engine overheating	See Item 5
	g. Fuel system not supplying proper air–fuel ratio	
	h. Engine defects such as hot valves, carbon, etc.	
5. Engine overheats (☼ 17-9)	a. Late ignition timing	Retime
	b. Lack of coolant or other trouble in cooling system	
	c. Late valve timing or other engine conditions	
6. Engine lacks power (☼ 17-10)	a. Ignition timing off	Retime
	b. Troubles listed in Item 3	
	c. Exhaust system restricted	Clear
	d. Heavy engine oil	Use correct viscosity oil
	e. Wrong fuel	Use correct fuel
	f. Excessive rolling resistance	Check tires, brakes, wheel bearings, alignment
	g. Engine overheats	See Item 5
7. Engine detonates or pings (☼ 17-11)	a. Improper timing	Time ignition
	b. Wrong fuel	Use correct fuel
	c. Spark plugs of wrong heat range	Install correct plugs
	d. Advance mechanism faulty	Rebuild or replace distributor
	e. Carbon buildup in cylinders	Service engine
8. Spark plugs defective (☼ 17-12)	a. Cracked insulator	Careless installation, install new plug
	b. Plug sooty	Install hotter plug, correct condition in engine causing oil burning or high fuel consumption

Electronic Ignition-System Trouble Diagnosis Chart (*Continued*)

Refer to ✿ 17-4 to 17-13 for detailed explanations of trouble causes and checks or corrections to be made.

CONDITION	POSSIBLE CAUSE	CHECK OR CORRECTION
	c. Plug white or gray, with blistered insulator	Install cooler plug
	d. See also detailed discussion of analyzing defective spark plugs in ✿ 14-14.	
9. Engine runs on or diesels (✿ 17-13)	a. Idle-stop solenoid out of adjustment or defective	Readjust, replace as necessary
	b. Hot spots in combustion chambers	Service engine
	c. Engine overheating	See Item 5
	d. Advanced timing	Retime ignition

bles and possible causes as listed in the trouble diagnosis chart.

✿ 17-5 Engine cranks normally but fails to start If there is no spark during the spark test, or if the oscilloscope fails to show a secondary-voltage pattern, then there are several possible causes. See item 1 in the trouble diagnosis chart (✿ 17-3).

If you get a good spark, chances are the ignition primary and secondary circuits are okay. The failure to start could be due to fouled spark plugs or out-of-time ignition. More likely, however, the failure to start with a good spark is due to trouble in the fuel system. The fuel system is not delivering the correct amount or ratio of air–fuel mixture. There are other conditions that could prevent starting, however—malfunctioning valves, loss of engine compression, and other engine troubles.

General Motors offers a different procedure for making the spark test. They supply a special tester (Fig. 17-2) which is inserted between the end of the cable clip and the spark-plug terminal. See also Fig. 17-24.

CAUTION: The electronic ignition systems can deliver a very high voltage, so proceed with care when making the spark test. Use rubber gloves or insulated pliers. The 40,000 volts some of these systems can produce can give you a very painful and dangerous shock!

Later in the chapter, we describe the servicing procedures for Chrysler, Ford, and General Motors electronic ignition systems. We discuss additional ignition-system checks.

✿ 17-6 Engine backfires but fails to start This can be caused by ignition timing that is considerably off, by a faulty or wet distributor cap or rotor that allows high-voltage leakage across from one terminal to another, or by the high-voltage cables being incorrectly connected.

✿ 17-7 Engine runs but misses An engine that misses runs unevenly and does not develop full power. It is sometimes difficult to tell, by listening, whether one cylinder is missing, or whether the miss is inter-

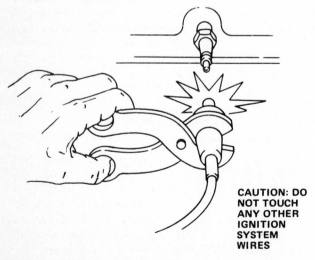

CAUTION: DO NOT TOUCH ANY OTHER IGNITION SYSTEM WIRES

Fig. 17-1 Checking for spark from spark-plug cable clip to engine block. (*American Motors Corporation*)

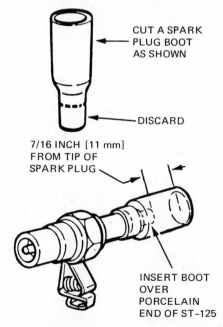

CUT A SPARK PLUG BOOT AS SHOWN

DISCARD

7/16 INCH [11 mm] FROM TIP OF SPARK PLUG

INSERT BOOT OVER PORCELAIN END OF ST-125

Fig. 17-2 How to prepare a spark-plug boot to fit over the end of the ST-125 spark-test tool. (*Pontiac Motor Division of General Motors Corporation*)

mittent and jumping around from one cylinder to another. If one cylinder is missing, the cause could be a defective spark plug or high-voltage cable, a bad connection, or high-voltage leakage across the distributor cam or through the cable insulation. In the engine, the miss could be due to a stuck or burned valve or loss of compression resulting from broken piston rings.

If the miss jumps around, the cause could be defects in the electronic part of the system—the ECU and the sensor coil in the distributor. This requires checking out as explained later when we get to specific systems.

Another cause of a jump-around miss is the advance mechanisms not working properly so the advance provided is erratic. Also, a defective fuel system that is delivering too-rich or too-lean a mixture can cause missing. An excessively lean mixture will not fire. An excessively rich mixture can wet or foul the plugs, causing them to misfire.

☼ 17-8 Engine runs but backfires

Backfiring is a "pop" or "bang" in the exhaust manifold or intake manifold. It can be caused by several conditions in the ignition system. If the ignition timing is considerably off, or if ignition cross-firing occurs, ignition may result before the intake valve closes. This produces a backfire. There will be a "pop" back through the carburetor. Cross-firing is spark jumpover from one terminal to another, or from one high-voltage cable to another. Cracked or damaged cable insulation can allow spark jumpover.

If a spark plug runs too hot, it may glow enough to ignite the air–fuel mixture before the intake valve closes. This produces a backfire, or pop back through the carburetor. This action is called *preignition* (☼ 12-11) and can also be caused by excessively hot valves or carbon deposits in the combustion chamber.

Incorrect air–fuel ratios can also cause backfiring. A lean mixture tends to cause backfiring through the carburetor. A rich mixture can cause backfire in the exhaust system. A defective air-injection system can also cause backfiring in the exhaust system.

☼ 17-9 Engine overheats

Most engine overheating is caused by loss of coolant through leaks in the cooling system. Other causes include a loose or broken fan belt, a defective water pump, clogged water jackets in the engine, a defective radiator hose, and a defective thermostat or fan clutch.

Late ignition or valve timing, lack of engine oil, overloading the engine, or high-speed, high-altitude, or hot-climate operation can cause engine overheating. Freezing of the coolant can cause lack of coolant circulation, resulting in local hot spots and boiling. Also, if a faulty TCS system prevents vacuum advance in any gear, or if the distributor vacuum advance is defective, overheating may result.

☼ 17-10 Engine lacks power

Many conditions can cause the engine to lose power. The wrong ignition timing, or any of the conditions discussed in ☼ 17-7 which cause the engine to miss, will reduce engine power. Also, a restricted exhaust system can create excessive back pressure which will prevent normal exhaust flow from the engine. The cylinders will retain pressure and will not be able to take in a full air–fuel charge during the intake strokes. Heavy engine oil, the wrong fuel, or excessive rolling resistance can also give the impression of low engine power.

☼ 17-11 Engine detonates or pings

Detonation, or pinging, is often blamed on the ignition system (it is often called a *spark knock*). But there are many other possible causes. In the ignition system, detonation may be caused by excessively advanced ignition timing, faulty advance mechanisms (which can cause excessive advances), and spark plugs of the wrong heat range. Fuel with an octane rating too low for the engine can cause pinging or detonation. Carbon buildup in the engine combustion chambers can result in detonation in two ways. First, the carbon may glow or become so hot that it can cause preignition, and this can result in ping. Second, the carbon buildup increases the compression ratio. This can also cause detonation.

☼ 17-12 Spark plugs defective

☼ 14-14 describes in some detail possible defects in spark plugs and their causes. Basically, plugs that run too cold will foul up. Plugs that run too hot will wear rapidly and even burn. By rapid wear, we mean the plug gap increases rapidly due to the eroding effect of the spark combined with the excessive temperature of the electrodes.

☼ 17-13 Engine diesels, or runs on

Modern engines, with their emission controls, require a fairly high, hot, idle for best operation. This makes run-on, or dieseling, possible. Hot spots in the combustion chambers, along with enough air–fuel mixture getting past a slightly opened throttle can keep the engine running. The hot spots act as the spark plugs, igniting the mixture in the combustion chambers. These hot spots, as we have mentioned previously, could be from hot plugs or exhaust valves, or from carbon deposits in the combustion chambers. Dieseling can damage an engine.

To prevent dieseling, modern engines have an idle-stop solenoid to close the throttle completely when the ignition switch is turned off. If an engine runs on, or diesels, first check the idle-stop solenoid. Make sure it is releasing when the ignition switch is turned off to allow the throttle to close completely. Make sure the engine idle is not set too high. Engine run-on could also be caused by advanced ignition timing.

Servicing specific electronic ignition systems

Although all electronic ignition systems operate in a similar manner, they require somewhat different checking and servicing procedures. The General Motors HEI system, with its coil mounted in the distributor, requires its own special procedure. Likewise, the Ford Dura-Spark Systems and the Chrysler electronic system require their own individual testing and servicing procedures. We cover these three systems in the remainder of this chapter. Also, we discuss the servicing of the Hall-effect ignition system described in ✪16-16.

✪ 17-14 Oscilloscope patterns One important point to note in servicing electronic ignition systems is that the oscilloscope patterns for the various systems are not always the same. However, all have the common characteristic of increasing the dwell with speed. The term *dwell* is a carryover from the contact-point system. In that system, you recall, dwell is the number of degrees that the contact points are closed. That is, it is the number of degrees of distributor shaft rotation that the primary winding of the ignition coil remains connected to the battery. In the electronic ignition system, it means the same thing—the number of degrees of distributor shaft rotation that the ignition-coil primary winding remains connected to the battery. Dwell in the electronic ignition system increases with engine (and distributor shaft) speed. Figure 17-3 illustrates this for the General Motors HEI system. Figure 17-4 shows how, in this system, the dwell can vary considerably from cylinder to cylinder. This is considered normal in the HEI system.

In late-model HEI ignition systems, the rotor air gap (gap between the rotor tip and cap inserts) has been increased to 0.120 inch [3.1 mm]. This was done to reduce radio noise. When testing these systems with the oscilloscope, you will note an increase in the voltage pattern when you check for cap-rotor wear.

NOTE: Always follow the oscilloscope maker's instructions when checking electronic ignition systems. Their instruction booklets illustrate the various patterns for the different ignition systems.

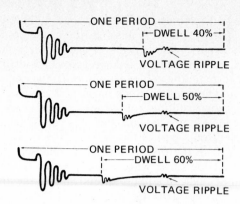

SECONDARY VOLTAGE PATTERNS:
IT IS NORMAL IF DWELL TIME VARIES FROM CYLINDER TO CYLINDER. A 40 TO 60% VARIATION IS SHOWN; IT COULD BE MORE OR LESS. THE VOLTAGE RIPPLE SHOWN MAY OR MAY NOT BE SEEN; EITHER IS NORMAL. VARIATION IN DWELL TIME OR VOLTAGE RIPPLE AS SHOWN DOES NOT INDICATE A BAD MODULE.

Fig. 17-4 Typical scope patterns for different cylinders in a running engine. Note that the dwell varies considerably from cylinder to cylinder. This is normal. *(Oldsmobile Division of General Motors Corporation)*

✪ 17-15 Special points to watch when servicing electronic ignition systems Many of the service procedures required for servicing electronic ignition systems are similar to those used in servicing contact-point ignition systems. However, there are some special points to watch when working on electronic ignition systems. Let us look at the similarities and differences.

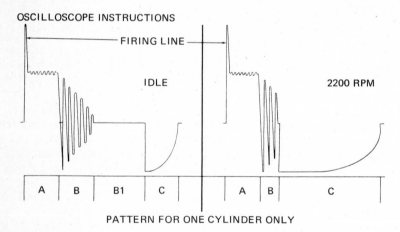

SCOPE INSTRUCTIONS:
1. SCOPE SECONDARY PICKUP CANNOT BE CONNECTED SINCE CENTER COIL TERMINAL IS INSIDE DISTRIBUTOR.
2. CONNECT PICKUP TO NO. 1 SPARK PLUG AS USUAL.
3. CONNECT PRIMARY PICKUP TO TACH TERMINAL OF DISTRIBUTOR.

THIS WILL DISPLAY PRIMARY PATTERN IN PARADE ONLY.
(NOTE: A SPECIAL ADAPTER PLACED ON TOP OF THE COIL–CAP ASSEMBLY MAY BE USED WITH SOME SCOPES TO VIEW THE SECONDARY PATTERN. THE OUTPUT VOLTAGE WILL READ LOW WITH THE ADAPTER; THIS IS NORMAL.)

SCOPE PATTERN:
A.   SPARK ZONE – SPARK PLUG ARCING
B.   COIL – CONDENSER ZONE
B1. FIRING ZONE – NO PLUG ARC
C.   DWELL ZONE – MODULE ON, CURRENT THROUGH COIL PRIMARY

Fig. 17-3 Scope pattern for one cylinder, showing how the dwell increases with engine speed. *(Oldsmobile Division of General Motors Corporation)*

236

1. **Spark plugs** We covered in detail, in ☼ 14-14, how to analyze, or "read," defective spark plugs. The general instructions there apply to the plugs used in the electronic ignition system. However, if unleaded fuel has been used you would not find lead fouling. Automobiles with catalytic converters are required by law to use unleaded fuel. Engineers agree, in general, that spark plugs in modern engines using electronic ignition systems and unleaded fuel last longer.

2. **Timing** The timing procedure for electronic ignition systems is similar to that for timing contact-point ignition systems (see ☼ 14-23 to 14-25). Modern cars have decals or labels in the engine compartment which outline, step by step, the approved procedure for adjusting ignition timing. These instructions must be followed.

3. **High-voltage cables** These cables should be handled with care. While the insulation is electrically strong to contain the 40,000 volts the electronic systems can produce, it is relatively soft. These cables should never be punctured or bent sharply so the insulation is damaged. Any pinhole or other damage will allow the high voltage to leak and jump to the nearest ground so the plug will not fire. The cables should be disconnected only if they are suspected of being faulty or if other tests of the system must be made. Figure 14-28 shows the use of cable pliers to disconnect a cable, with boot, from a spark plug. Figure 14-29 shows how to install a cable and boot on a distributor cap and the coil tower.

4. **Silicone grease** Silicone grease is used to coat the brass rotor segment and cap electrodes on many distributors. A similar grease is used to coat the insides of the spark-plug boots. It is also used in harness connectors. The purpose of the grease in the distributor is to reduce radio interference from the high-voltage surges as they pass through the rotor segment to the cap electrodes. The grease greatly reduces this effect. The grease also serves as added insulation against high-voltage leakage. It protects the connectors against corrosion.

5. **Visual checks** Before proceeding with actual tests of the system, always make visual checks. You should look over all wiring and cables, distributor cap, coil, and the retainers that hold the cables in place. Check all connections for tightness. If there are no obvious defects, you should then proceed with tests. Following sections cover testing and servicing procedures on Chrysler, Ford, and General Motors electronic ignition systems. The procedures are different because the various systems are different, although all work in about the same way.

6. **Oscilloscope** When using an oscilloscope, remember that the patterns are different from those for contact-point systems. Also, the patterns for the various electronic ignition systems may differ. Always follow the oscilloscope maker's instructions; they illustrate the patterns, normal and abnormal, for the different systems.

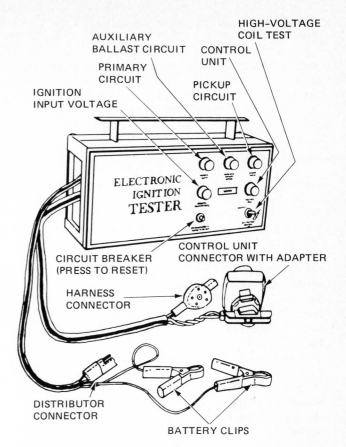

Fig. 17-5 Electronic ignition-system taster. *(Chrysler Corporation)*

☼ 17-16 Chrysler ignition tests Chrysler recommends the use of a special electronic ignition tester (Fig. 17-5) to test their electronic ignition systems. If this tester is not available, the following procedure can be used. It requires a voltmeter with a 20,000-ohm/volt rating and an ohmmeter which uses a 1½-volt battery for its operation. Both meters must be in calibration. Figure 17-6 is a wiring diagram of the system.

Careful: Using other types of voltmeter or ohmmeter can damage the ignition system.

To make a complete check of the system, proceed as follows. Correct any abnormal condition found as you proceed.

1. Visually inspect all high-voltage cables for cracks and proper connections. They can be tested as explained in Item 12, below. Check primary wire for good connections at the ignition coil and ballast resistor. Replace cables and tighten connections as required.
2. Check battery voltage. It should be 12 volts or more. If not, charge the battery or install a charged battery.
3. Turn off ignition and disconnect the multiwiring connector from the electronic control unit.
4. Turn ignition switch to ON. Connect the negative lead of the voltmeter to a good ground. Connect the positive lead of the voltmeter to connector cav-

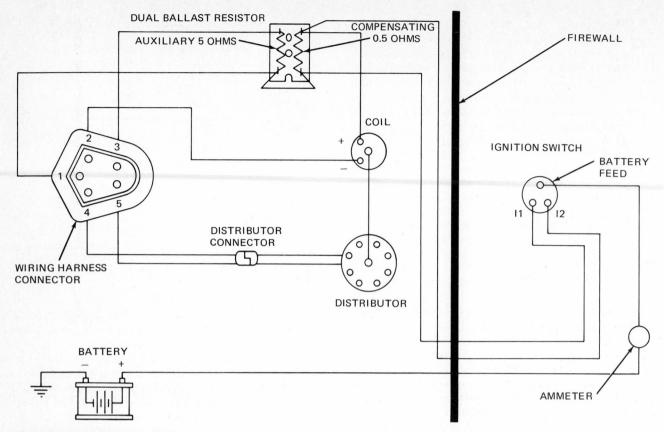

Fig. 17-6 Schematic wiring diagram of the Chrysler electronic ignition system. *(Chrysler Corporation)*

ity No. 1 (Fig. 17-7). Voltage should read within a volt of the battery voltage (all accessories turned off). If there is a greater voltage difference, there is excessive resistance in the circuit (Fig. 17-7).

5. Now connect the positive voltmeter lead to cavity No. 2 (Fig. 17-8). If voltage is not within a volt of battery voltage, check the circuit (Fig. 17-8) for bad connections, leads, or other possible causes of excessive resistance.

6. Now connect the positive voltmeter lead to cavity

No. 3 (Fig. 17-9). Again, the voltage should be within a volt of battery voltage. If it is not, check the circuit for excessive resistance.

7. Turn ignition switch OFF. Connect the ohmmeter to connector cavities Nos. 4 and 5 as shown in Fig. 17-10 to check the pickup coil in the distributor. If the ohmmeter does not read between 150 and 900 ohms, disconnect the dual-lead connector that runs from the distributor. Check the resistance at the distributor side of the connector (Fig. 17-11). If the

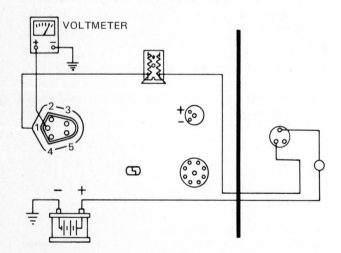

Fig. 17-7 Testing cavity 1 which should be near battery voltage. *(Chrysler Corporation)*

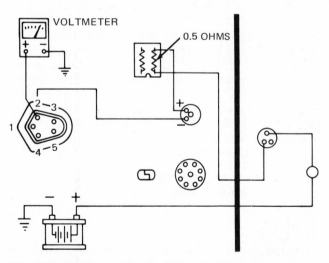

Fig. 17-8 Testing cavity 2 which should be near battery voltage. *(Chrysler Corporation)*

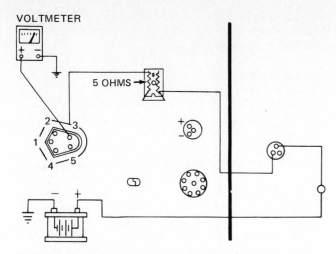

Fig. 17-9 Testing cavity 3 which should be near battery voltage. *(Chrysler Corporation)*

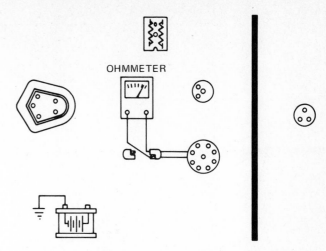

Fig. 17-11 Testing the pickup coil at the distributor-lead connector. *(Chrysler Corporation)*

resistance still does not read within the 150- to 900-ohm range, replace the pickup assembly in the distributor.

8. If the pickup coil tests okay (150 to 900 ohms), check it for ground with the positive ohmmeter lead connected to cavity No. 5 (and with the negative lead still grounded). If the ohmmeter shows a reading, the pickup coil is grounded and should be replaced.

9. Next, check the electronic control unit ground circuit. Connect one ohmmeter lead to ground and the other to connector pin 5 on the control unit (Fig. 17-12). If the control unit is not grounded properly (ohmmeter shows no circuit), tighten the bolts attaching the control unit to the fire wall. Then recheck. If continuity still does not exist, replace the control unit.

10. Reconnect wiring harness at the control unit. *Ignition switch must be* OFF! Check air gap between a reluctor tooth and the pickup coil (Fig. 17-13). Align one reluctor tooth with the pickup-coil tooth, as shown. Loosen the pickup coil hold-down screw. Insert a 0.006-inch [0.15-mm] *nonmagnetic*

feeler gauge in the air gap. Adjust the air gap if necessary so that the feeler gauge is a slip fit in the air gap. Tighten the hold-down screw.

11. Check the ignition secondary. Remove the high-voltage cable from the center terminal of the distributor cap. With insulated pliers, hold the cable clip $^3/_{16}$ inch [4.76 mm] from the engine block (Fig. 17-1). Crank the engine.

   If there is no spark, replace the control unit. Then crank the engine again. If there is still no spark, replace the ignition coil.

12. The high-voltage cables can be checked for punctures or cracks, as follows. With engine not running, connect one end of a test probe to ground on the engine block, leaving the other end free for probing. Disconnect a cable from one spark plug. Insulate the clip or hang it well away from ground. Start the engine, and move the test probe along the entire length of the cable. If the insulation is defective, you will see a spark jump to the test probe. Stop the engine, reconnect the cable (if good), and repeat with the next spark-plug cable. Any defective cables should be replaced. Figure 14-29 shows the proper way to install a cable and boot. See also ✹ 14-28.

Careful: Do not run the engine with cables disconnected any longer than absolutely necessary. The

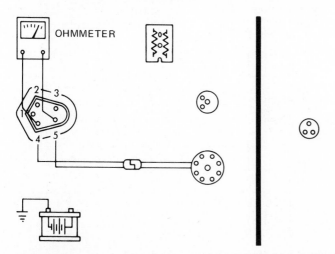

Fig. 17-10 Testing the pickup coil at the wiring harness connector cavities 4 and 5. *(Chrysler Corporation)*

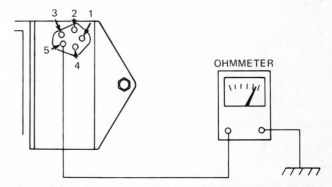

Fig. 17-12 Testing the electronic control unit ground circuit. *(Chrysler Corporation)*

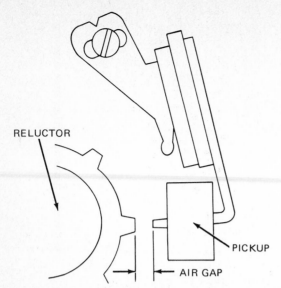

RELUCTOR

PICKUP

AIR GAP

Fig. 17-13 Place at which to check the air gap. Note that the reluctor tooth is exactly opposite the pickup coil core. Use a nonmagnetic feeler to make the check. *(Chrysler Corporation)*

whole testing procedure must be completed in less than 10 min. Otherwise, the catalytic converter may overheat and be damaged.

13. High-voltage cables can also be checked for resistance if they are of the high-resistance type. These are identified by the words "electronic suppression" printed on the cable insulation. To check for resistance, remove the cable from a spark plug. Take off the distributor cap. Do not remove the cables from the cap. Use a high-reading ohmmeter connected between the plug end clip and the corresponding electrode inside the distributor cap. The resistance should read less than 50,000 ohms. If it reads more, remove the cable from the distributor cap and test the cable again by itself. If it is still high, replace the cable. Test all cables the same way. Test the coil-to-distributor high-voltage cable by checking from the center electrode in the cap to either primary terminal at the ignition coil. If the resistance is more than 25,000 ohms, remove the cable from the coil tower and check again. If the

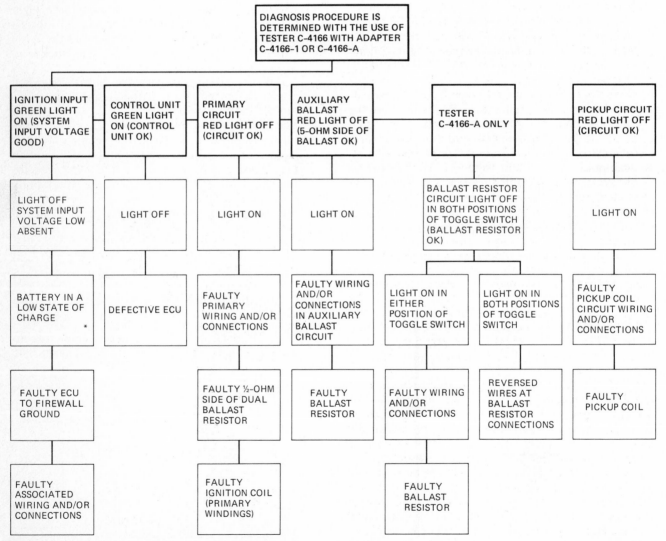

Fig. 17-14 Chart showing testing procedures of the ignition primary circuit using the special Chrysler electronic ignition system tester. *(Chrysler Corporation)*

resistance is more than 15,000 ohms, replace the cable.

☼ 17-17 Chrysler ignition tests with electronic ignition tester

Figure 17-5 shows the electronic ignition tester Chrysler recommends for testing their electronic ignition systems. Figure 17-14 shows, in chart form, how to use the tester to check the system on the vehicle. To make the test, first make sure the battery is charged (12.0 volts at least and 1.220 gravity or higher). Then, with the ignition switch turned off, connect the control-unit connector into the system at the control unit. Do not connect the battery clips or the distributor connector. These are to be used only to test components when they are removed from the vehicle. Turn ignition switch on.

CAUTION: Do not touch the control unit now. You will get a strong electric shock if you do!

If the green ignition input-voltage light comes on, proceed with the test. If it does not, check the battery, ignition switch, wiring, and control-unit ground to find the trouble. Make correction and then proceed after the green light has come on.

Next, make sure the green control-unit light is on. If the light does not come on, check the connector pins on the control unit to make sure they are making good contact with the control-unit connector. Then check the control unit for a good ground. If everything else appears in good condition, the control unit is defective and must be replaced.

If both green lights are on, check the ignition coil. Disconnect the ignition coil high-voltage cable from the distributor cap. Use insulated pliers to hold the clip about ¼ inch [6.35 mm] from the engine block (Fig. 17-1). Operate the high-voltage coil test switch. A good spark should jump to the block. While still holding the test switch closed, pull the clip away from the engine until the spark stops. Look at the coil tower while you are doing this to see if arcing occurs. If it does, the coil tower may have carbon paths that allow high-voltage leakage, and the coil must be replaced.

The primary circuit red light and the auxiliary ballast circuit red lights must be off. If either is on, check the circuits for opens or shorts. The pickup circuit red light must also be off. If it is on, check the wiring and connections for opens or shorts. If everything seems in order, the pickup coil is defective and must be replaced.

☼ 17-18 Chrysler distributor service

Figure 17-15 is a disassembled view of a Chrysler six-cylinder distributor. Removal of the gear pin allows the shaft assembly to be withdrawn from the housing. Make sure there are no burrs around the pin hole in the shaft. If there are, they must be filed off before the shaft is pulled out. Otherwise, the burrs will damage the bearing. Normally, you would not disassemble the distributor unless you determined that the shaft or bushing was worn (0.006 inch [0.15 mm] side play). The check is made with a spring scale as shown in Fig. 15-33.

If you do remove the shaft assembly, first make a scribe mark half-way across the end of the shaft that is

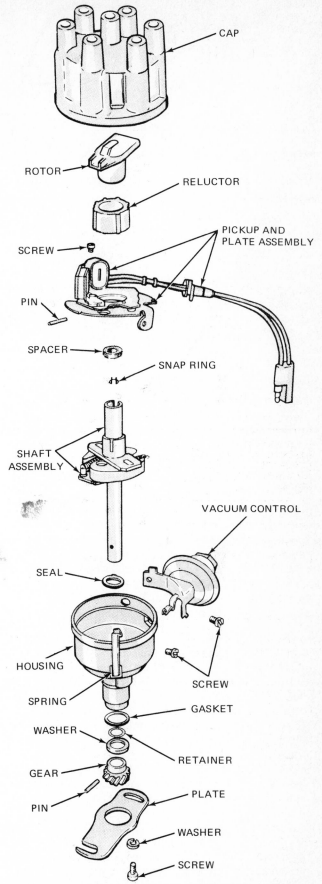

Fig. 17-15 Electronic ignition distributor for a six-cylinder engine, disassembled. *(Chrysler Corporation)*

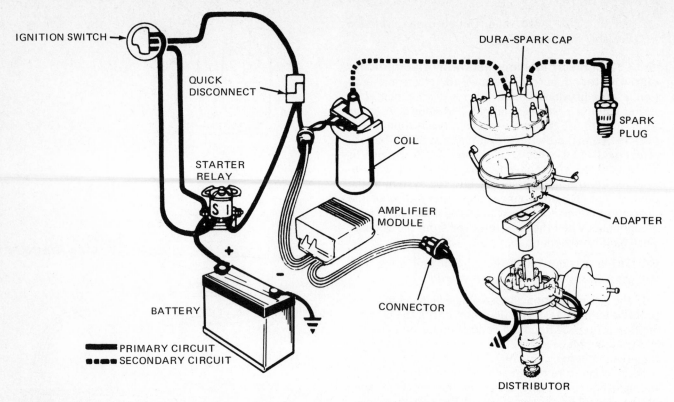

Fig. 17-16 Typical Ford Dura-Spark electronic ignition system. *(Ford Motor Company)*

in line with the gear pin and the center of the rotor segment. This enables you to realign the gear and rotor on reassembly. Also, when removing the reluctor, use two screwdrivers, one on each side, and gently pry up on the reluctor.

NOTE: When removing a distributor, scribe a mark on the edge of the distributor housing and on the engine block to indicate the position of the rotor. Then you can line up the marks on reinstallation to get approximately correct timing. See ☀ 15-13 on distributor removal and installation. See ☀ 14-23 to 14-25 for timing instructions. Also, refer to the decal or label in the engine compartment which has timing information.

The pickup coil can be tested in a detached distributor with the electronic ignition tester. This is the same procedure as covered in ☀ 17-17. The electronic control unit can also be checked off the vehicle with the electronic ignition tester.

☀ 17-19 Ford electronic ignition service Figure 17-16 shows a typical Ford Dura-Spark electronic ignition system. Figure 17-17 is a disassembled view of a Dura-Spark distributor. The procedure for checking the system is very similar to that for the Chrysler electronic ignition system. That is, you make a visual check of the system. Then you make sure the battery is charged and in good condition. You make a spark test. Then with a voltmeter and ohmmeter you check out the circuits and the components. The resistance of the pickup coil should be between 400 and 1000 ohms.

Ford recommends the use of an oscilloscope to check the system, particularly the secondary circuit. When using an oscilloscope, refer to the scope manufacturer's special instructions for electronic ignition systems. The patterns for electronic ignition systems are different from those for contact-point systems (Figs. 17-3 and 17-4). Figure 17-18 shows in chart form the procedure for checking the system to determine whether the ignition primary circuit is okay.

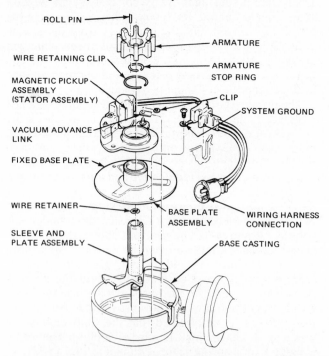

Fig. 17-17 Disassembled Dura-Spark distributor for an eight-cylinder engine. *(Ford Motor Company)*

242

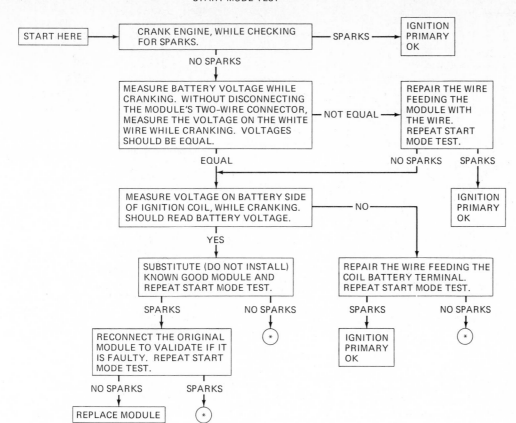

START HERE → CRANK ENGINE, WHILE CHECKING FOR SPARKS. — SPARKS → IGNITION PRIMARY OK

NO SPARKS

MEASURE BATTERY VOLTAGE WHILE CRANKING. WITHOUT DISCONNECTING THE MODULE'S TWO-WIRE CONNECTOR, MEASURE THE VOLTAGE ON THE WHITE WIRE WHILE CRANKING. VOLTAGES SHOULD BE EQUAL. — NOT EQUAL → REPAIR THE WIRE FEEDING THE MODULE WITH THE WIRE. REPEAT START MODE TEST.

EQUAL / NO SPARKS / SPARKS

MEASURE VOLTAGE ON BATTERY SIDE OF IGNITION COIL, WHILE CRANKING. SHOULD READ BATTERY VOLTAGE. — NO → IGNITION PRIMARY OK

YES

SUBSTITUTE (DO NOT INSTALL) KNOWN GOOD MODULE AND REPEAT START MODE TEST. — SPARKS / NO SPARKS (*)

REPAIR THE WIRE FEEDING THE COIL BATTERY TERMINAL. REPEAT START MODE TEST. — SPARKS → IGNITION PRIMARY OK / NO SPARKS (*)

RECONNECT THE ORIGINAL MODULE TO VALIDATE IF IT IS FAULTY. REPEAT START MODE TEST. — NO SPARKS → REPLACE MODULE / SPARKS (*)

Fig. 17-18 Chart showing start-mode test to determine whether the ignition primary circuit is okay. *(Ford Motor Company)*

Special points to watch when checking the Ford Dura-Spark system follow.

Use the cable pliers as shown in Fig. 14-28 when disconnecting the cables from the spark plugs. One test is to measure the resistance of the high-voltage cables, and this is done as explained in the Chrysler story (☼ 17-16, item 13). Ford specifies that the resistance of a cable should not exceed 5000 ohms per inch (25.4 mm). They do not recommend using a probe passed along a cable as explained in ☼ 17-16, item 12, however.

To use a tachometer, connect the tachometer lead to the ignition coil as shown in Fig. 17-19.

When it is necessary to replace only a boot on a spark-plug cable, cut off the old boot. Apply silicone lubricant to that part of the old wire that will be under the new boot. Use the special tool shown in Fig. 17-20 to install the new boot. Push the tool through the new boot and into the cable clip. Slide the boot onto the wire and remove the tool.

Ford electronic ignition systems are timed the same as other systems. Refer to the decal or label in the

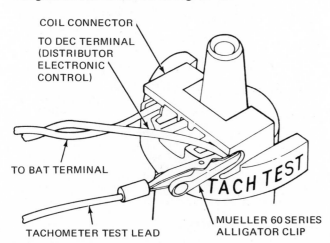

Fig. 17-19 How to attach a tachometer test lead. *(Ford Motor Company)*

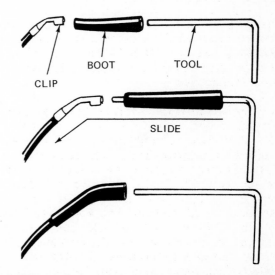

Fig. 17-20 Using a special tool to install a boot on a cable. *(Ford Motor Company)*

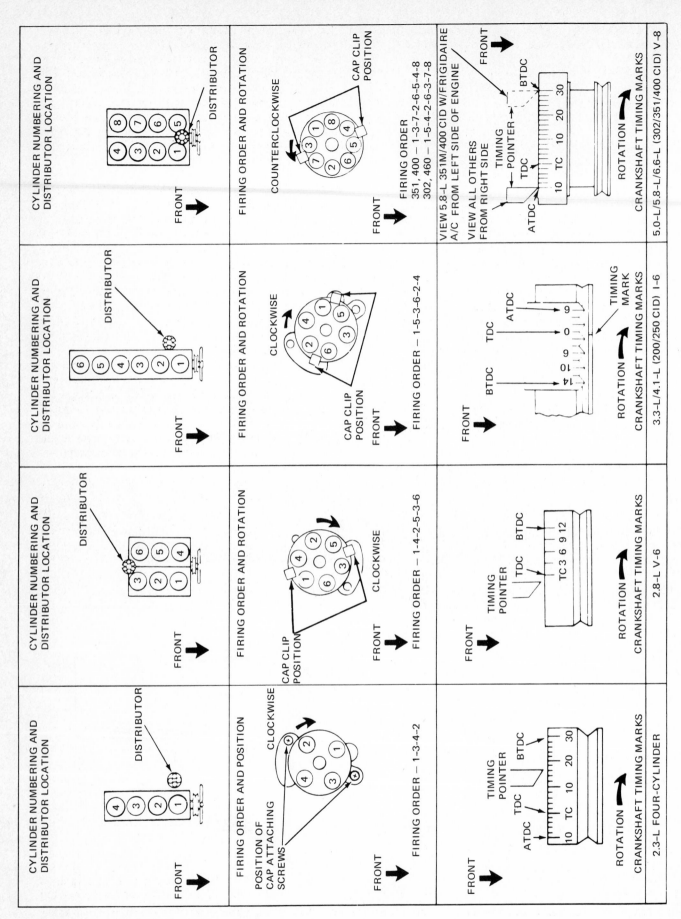

Fig. 17-21 Engine timing and cylinder firing order for Ford engines. (*Ford Motor Company*)

engine compartment for details. Figure 17-21 shows timing marks and firing orders for Ford engines.

☼ 17-20 General Motors HEI systems service

This system is described in detail in ☼ 16-6 and illustrated in Figs. 16-16 to 16-21. Figure 17-22 is a schematic wiring diagram of the ECU, or module. Figure 17-23 is a chart showing the complete procedure for checking the system if the engine cranks but will not start. The references to View A and View B in the chart are to Fig. 17-24, which show the use of the special tool (ST-125) in making the checks described in the chart (Fig. 17-23). This tool is illustrated in Fig. 17-2.

Figure 17-25 is a chart which shows how to proceed if the engine operates intermittently or misses.

Figures 17-26 and 17-27 show how to test the ignition coil and the pickup coil and vacuum advance. To check the ignition-coil primary winding, connect the ohmmeter, on the low scale, to the primary terminals as shown at 1 in Fig. 17-26. Resistance should be less than an ohm. If it is more, replace the ignition coil. To test the ignition-coil secondary winding, make the connections as shown at 2 in Fig. 17-26. Ohmmeter should be on the high scale. Resistance should be between 6000 and 30,000 ohms. If it is not within this range, replace the ignition coil.

Figure 17-27 shows how to test the pickup. With the ohmmeter set on the middle scale, connect it as shown in 1 in Fig. 17-27. Connect the vacuum-advance unit to a vacuum source. The ohmmeter should show an open circuit. If the ohmmeter shows a reading, replace the pickup coil. If the vacuum advance does not operate, replace it.

Next, connect the ohmmeter as shown in 2 in Fig. 17-27. Pull on the wires and move them around to check for broken wires. Resistance should read between 500 and 1500 ohms. Do not operate the vacuum advance

when making this check. Operating the advance will move the pickup coil and cause a voltage impulse which will move the ohmmeter pointer. If the pickup coil does not read within the 500- to 1500-ohm range, replace it.

The ECU, or module, requires a special tester (J-24642) to check it. If the tester is not available, the ignition coil and pickup coil can be tested as explained above. Then, if these test okay and there is still trouble in the ignition system, the defect is in the module, and it should be replaced.

☼ 17-21 Servicing the General Motors HEI distributor

The distributor is shown in Fig. 17-28. Removal and installation of this distributor are essentially the same as for other distributors (see ☼ 15-13). One special suggestion that General Motors makes about this procedure is to first note the position of the rotor after removing the distributor cap. Then as you pull the distributor up, note its position after it stops turning. This is the point at which the spiral gears have disengaged. If you reinstall the distributor with the rotor in this same exact position, the rotor will turn back to the fully installed position.

Figure 17-29 shows the spark-plug cable retainer and how to release the cables from this retainer. As previously mentioned, these cables have a very good but soft insulation that can be easily damaged by rough treatment, cuts, and abrasion from rubbing against each other or against engine parts. This is the reason the cables are carefully cradled in retainers and supports to hold them in position.

Figure 17-30 shows the latch release for the cables. It is not necessary to disconnect the cables from the cap in order to check the ignition coil. However, if the cap or any of the cables are defective, the cables must be removed.

Figure 17-31 shows the ignition-coil mounting. To

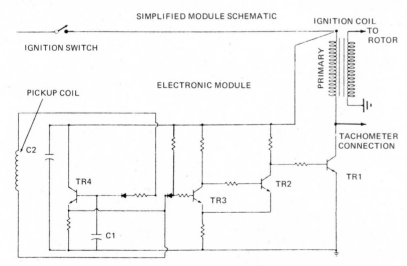

DWELL MODE — TR1-ON; TR2 -OFF; TR3 -ON. SIGNAL AT PICKUP COIL TURNS TR3 OFF. CHARGES C1 AND TURNS ON TR4. THIS RESULTS IN FIRING MODE: TR2 -OFF; TR2 -ON; AND TR3 -OFF. THE REDUCED PRIMARY CURRENT INDUCES A HIGH VOLTAGE IN THE SECONDARY WINDINGS FIRING THE SPARK PLUG.

TR4 STAYS ON UNTIL C1 IS DISCHARGED. WHEN C1 IS DISCHARGED TR3 TURNS ON RETURNING TO DWELL MODE. AT HIGHER ENGINE SPEEDS, C1 CHARGES LESS AND LESS, RESULTING IN REDUCED FIRING TIMES, AND THUS LONGER DWELL PERIODS. THIS IS HOW THE DWELL ZONE EXPANDS. C2 IS CAPACITOR IN DISTRIBUTOR FOR RADIO SUPPRESSION.

Fig. 17-22 Schematic wiring diagram of the ECU, or module, for the General Motors HEI system. *(Oldsmobile Division of General Motors Corporation)*

NOTE: IF A TACHOMETER IS CONNECTED TO THE TACHOMETER TERMINAL, DISCONNECT IT BEFORE PROCEEDING WITH THE TEST.

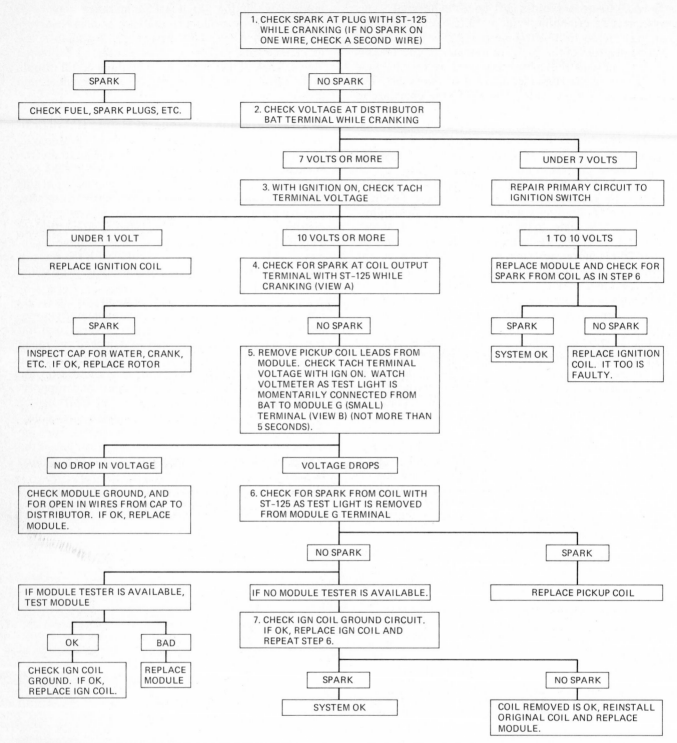

Fig. 17-23 Chart showing procedure to follow if the engine cranks but will not start. *(Oldsmobile Division of General Motors Corporation)*

remove the ignition coil from the cap, first remove the secondary cable retainer from the distributor cap by moving the two latch releases (Fig. 17-30). Then remove the coil cover and the four coil-attaching screws and lift the coil with leads from the cap. Remove the ignition-coil arc seal (Fig. 17-32).

Mark the distributor shaft, gear, and housing so they can be reassembled in the same positions. Put the distributor in the soft jaws of a vise and drive out the roll pin (Fig. 17-33). Remove the gear. File off any burrs left so they will not damage the bearing. Remove the shaft assembly from the housing. Disconnect the

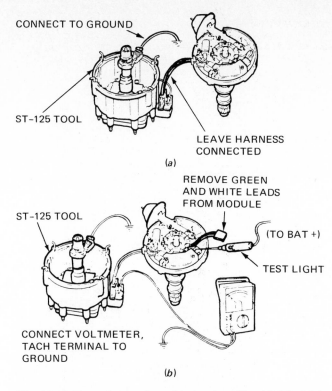

CONNECT TO GROUND

ST-125 TOOL

LEAVE HARNESS
CONNECTED

(a)

ST-125 TOOL

REMOVE GREEN
AND WHITE LEADS
FROM MODULE

(TO BAT +)

TEST LIGHT

CONNECT VOLTMETER,
TACH TERMINAL TO
GROUND

(b)

Fig. 17-24 Two views referred to in chart Fig. 17-23 which show how to use the special ST-125 tool to check for a spark at the ignition coil output terminal *(a)*, and to check the pickup coil. *(Oldsmobile Division of General Motors Corporation)*

INTERMITTENT OPERATION OR MISS

CHECK SPARK AT TWO PLUG
WIRES WITH ST-125

SPARK ON ONE OR BOTH — NO SPARK

CHECK FOR DWELL INCREASE
FROM LOW TO HIGH RPM — SEE NO START
PROCEDURE

CHECK PICKUP COIL
WITH OHMMETER

BAD — GOOD

REPLACE

DWELL
INCREASED — DWELL DIDN'T
INCREASE

TROUBLE
NOT FOUND — REPLACE
MODULE

CHECK FUEL, PLUG
WIRES, CAP AND PLUGS

Fig. 17-25 Chart showing procedure to use if the engine operates intermittently or misses. *(Oldsmobile Division of General Motors Corporation)*

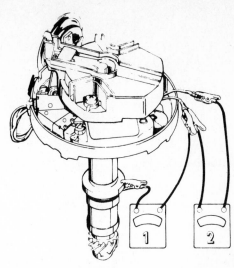

Fig. 17-26 Ohmeter connections to check the ignition-coil primary and secondary winding. *(Oldsmobile Division of General Motors Corporation)*

pickup coil leads from the electronic module (Fig. 17-34). Remove retainer ring and the pickup coil and magnet. (Figure 17-34 shows the arrangement for a V-8 engine, Figure 17-35 shows it for a four-cylinder engine.)

Now, the vacuum advance can be removed by taking out three attaching screws (Fig. 17-37). The module, harness, and capacitor can now come out after the removal of the three attaching screws.

Reassembly is the reverse of disassembly. Follow the pictures (Figs. 17-28 to 17-37) and the instructions above.

☼ 17-22 Servicing the Hall-effect ignition system This system is described in **☼** 16-16. While it works in much the same way as the other electronic ignition systems we have been discussing, the servicing

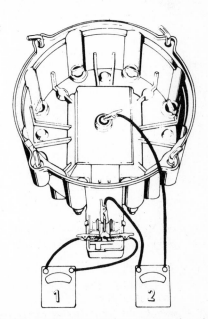

Fig. 17-27 Ohmmeter connections to test the pickup coil. *(Oldsmobile Division of General Motors Corporation)*

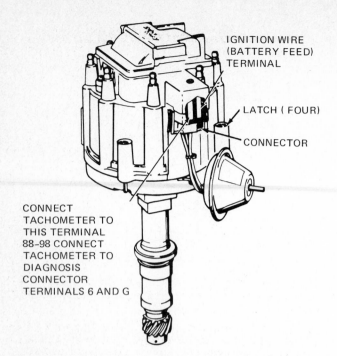

Fig. 17-28 HEI distributor. (Oldsmobile Division of General Motors Corporation)

IGNITION WIRE (BATTERY FEED) TERMINAL

LATCH (FOUR)

CONNECTOR

CONNECT TACHOMETER TO THIS TERMINAL 88-98 CONNECT TACHOMETER TO DIAGNOSIS CONNECTOR TERMINALS 6 AND G

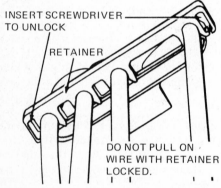

INSERT SCREWDRIVER TO UNLOCK

RETAINER

DO NOT PULL ON WIRE WITH RETAINER LOCKED.

Fig. 17-29 Spark-plug cable retainer, showing where to use a screwdrive to unlock it. (Oldsmobile Division of General Motors Corporation)

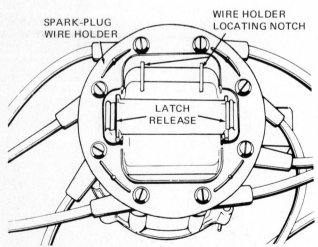

SPARK-PLUG WIRE HOLDER

WIRE HOLDER LOCATING NOTCH

LATCH RELEASE

Fig. 17-30 High-voltage cable holder and the latch release. (Oldsmobile Division of General Motors Corporation)

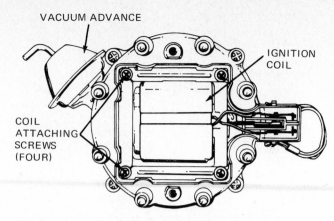

VACUUM ADVANCE

IGNITION COIL

COIL ATTACHING SCREWS (FOUR)

Fig. 17-31 Ignition-coil mounting. It is attached with four screws. (Oldsmobile Division of General Motors Corporation)

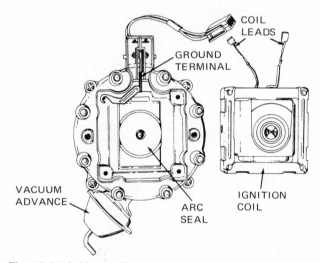

COIL LEADS

GROUND TERMINAL

VACUUM ADVANCE

ARC SEAL

IGNITION COIL

Fig. 17-32 Igition coil and arc seal. (Oldsmobile Division of General Motors Corporation)

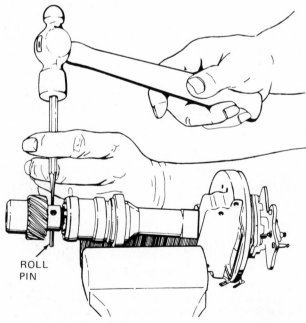

ROLL PIN

Fig. 17-33 Removing the gear roll pin. (Oldsmobile Division of General Motors Corporation)

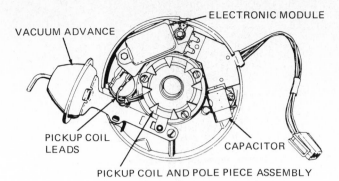

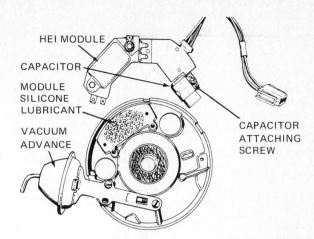

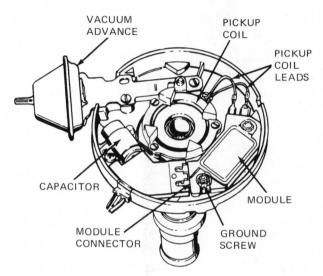

Fig. 17-34 Top view of distributor for a V-8 engine with shaft removed. *(Oldsmobile Division of General Motors Corporation)*

Fig. 17-35 Top view of distributor for a four-cylinder engine with shaft removed. *(Oldsmobile Division of General Motors Corporation)*

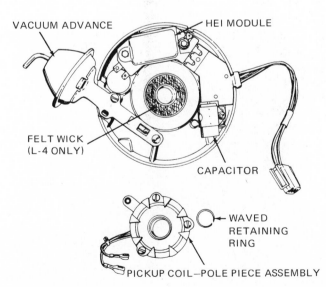

Fig. 17-36 Location of felt wick in the distributor for the four-cylinder engine. *(Oldsmobile Division of General Motors Corporation)*

Fig. 17-37 The HEI module, with capacitor, and the vacuum-advance unit can be removed by taking out the attaching screws. *(Oldsmobile Division of General Motors Corporation)*

procedure is somewhat different. Here is the procedure recommended by Chrysler Corporation.

1. If the engine cranks normally but does not start, make the spark test, using the high-voltage cable removed from the center terminal of the distributor cap. With the engine cranking, hold the clip of the cable about ¼ inch [6.35 mm] from the engine block. Use insulated pliers to hold the cable (Fig. 17-1). If a good spark occurs, the ignition system is probably okay. Look at the fuel system and elsewhere for the failure to start.

2. If the spark is weak or there is no spark, proceed as follows. Make sure the battery is charged. Measure battery voltage and specific gravity. With ignition OFF, disconnect wire from the negative terminal of the coil (Fig. 17-38). Disconnect cable from center terminal of the distributor cap. This is the cable that runs from the coil tower to the distributor. Connect a jumper wire from the coil negative terminal. Turn ignition ON and touch the other end of the jumper wire to ground while holding the coil high-voltage cable clip ¼ inch [6.35 mm] from ground. You should get a spark. If you do not, disconnect the

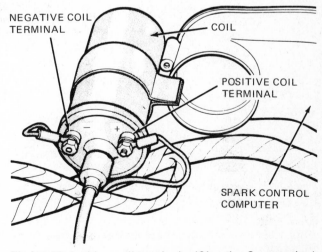

Fig. 17-38 Ignition coil terminals. *(Chrysler Corporation)*

jumper lead from the negative coil terminal. Measure the voltage between the coil positive terminal and ground with the ignition ON. You should get at least 9 volts. If you do, the coil is defective and should be replaced. If you do not, check the ballast resistor, wiring, and connections.

3. If everything looks okay and the car still will not start, turn ignition OFF. Reconnect the lead to the coil negative terminal. Disconnect the distributor three-wire harness (Fig. 17-39). Turn ignition ON and check voltage between pin B and ground. It should read battery voltage. If it does not, turn ignition OFF and disconnect the 10-wire harness going into the spark control computer (Fig. 17-40).

NOTE: Do not remove the grease from the connector or connector cavity. This grease protects the terminals from corrosion. If there is not at least ¼ inch [6.35 mm] of grease in the bottom of the cavity, add a liberal amount of the special grease recommended by Chrysler to the entire end of the connector plug before reconnecting it. See Item 4 in ☼ 17-15.

4. Check for continuity with a test lamp or ohmmeter between pin B (Fig. 17-39) and pin 3 of the harness connector (Fig. 17-40). If the circuit is open, the wire or connections are bad and should be repaired. If the circuit is complete, make the next test.

5. Turn ignition ON and check voltage between pin 2 and pin 10 of the 10-wire connector. If you do not get battery voltage, check wiring and connections. If you do get voltage, replace the spark control computer.

6. Check the Hall-effect pickup as follows. Turn ignition ON and hold the clip of the cable removed from the distributor cap center terminal ¼ inch [6.35 mm] from ground. Momentarily jump between pins A and C (Fig. 17-39). If you get a spark, the Hall-effect pickup is defective and should be replaced. If you do not get a spark, make the next test.

7. Turn ignition OFF. Check continuity with a test lamp or ohmmeter between pin C of the three-wire harness connector and pin 9 of the disconnected 10-wire

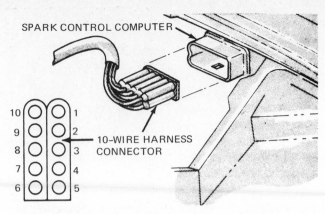

Fig. 17-40 Disconnecting the 10-wire harness from the spark control computer. *(Chrysler Corporation)*

harness connector. Also check between pin A and pin 5. If continuity exists, replace the spark control computer.

☼ **17-23 Servicing the Hall-effect ignition distributor** Figures 16-37 to 16-39 show various steps in disassembling the distributor. As you can see, this is a very simple distributor to service. There is no need to remove the distributor shaft unless the bearing is worn. Then, the drive gear must come off by removing the pin (Fig. 17-33). File off any burrs before sliding the shaft out.

☼ **17-24 Universal electronic ignition tester** Figure 17-41 shows an electronic ignition tester that the maker claims will test most of the electronic ignition systems on domestic cars. With the special adaptors supplied, it can make the various tests shown in Fig. 17-42.

☼ **17-25 Retrofitting electronic ignition system** *Retrofit* means fitting something new on an older unit. Manufacturers have made available retrofit kits which can be used to install electronic ignition in place of the contact points. For example, a recent Ford (Motorcraft) retrofit kit has the following parts in it:

Electronic control unit

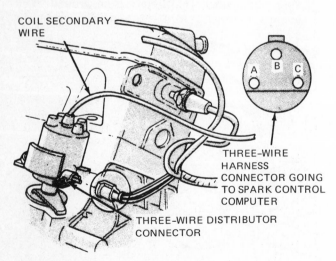

Fig. 17-39 Disconnecting the three-wire harness from the distributor. *(Chrysler Corporation)*

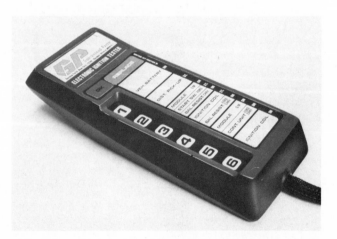

Fig. 17-41 Electronic ignition tester. *(Guaranteed Parts Company)*

GENERAL MOTORS HIGH ENERGY IGNITION
(Except MISAR)

MODELS WITH COIL IN CAP:

1. Remove Red battery feed wire and 3 wire connector from distributor cap.
2. Remove cap and rotor from distributor. (leave spark plug wires in cap and all leads attached to module).
3. Connect Green adapter clip to module terminal "G".
4. Connect White adapter clip to module terminal "W". (position clips so distributor shaft turns freely).
5. Install adapter 3 wire connectors between distributor and cap.
6. Connect adapter Red jumper wire to cap terminal "BAT".
7. Connect Red battery feed wire to adapter.
8. Connect adapter to tester.
9. Test system (always press number switches in order).

MODELS WITH EXTERNAL COIL:

1. Remove connector from coil and install adapter between coil and harness.
2. Connect Black clip (ground) to engine block.
3. Remove distributor cap and rotor. (leave spark plug wires in cap and all leads attached to module).
4. Position cap to clear advance weights.
5. Connect Green clip to module terminal "G".
6. Connect adapter White clip to module terminal "W". (position clips so distributor shaft turns freely).
7. Connect adapter to tester.
8. Test system (always press number switches in order).

CHRYSLER ELECTRONIC IGNITION
(Except LEAN BURN)

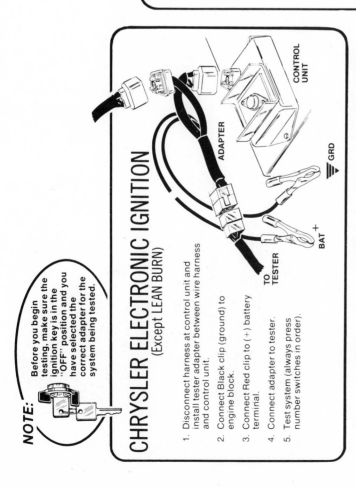

1. Disconnect harness at control unit and install tester adapter between wire harness and control unit.
2. Connect Black clip (ground) to engine block.
3. Connect Red clip to (+) battery terminal.
4. Connect adapter to tester.
5. Test system (always press number switches in order).

FORD SOLID STATE IGNITION and DURA SPARK SYSTEMS
(Including AMC with Ford Ignition System)

1. Disconnect harness at control unit and install tester adapter between wire harness and control unit.
2. Connect adapter to tester.
3. Test system (always press number switches in order).

Fig. 17-42 Special adaptors and procedures for testing different electronic ignition systems. (*Guaranteed Parts Company*)

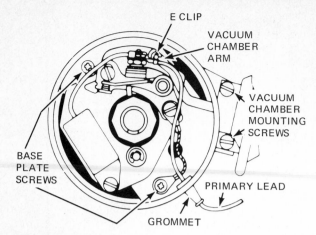

Fig. 17-43 A typical contact-point distributor, viewed from the top with the cap and rotor removed. *(Ford Motor Company)*

Trigger wheel and sensor assembly

Wiring harness

Package of hardware parts.

Figure 17-43 shows a typical contact-point distributor. To make the changeover, first disconnect the battery ground cable to prevent shorting the battery during the installation procedure.

NOTE: The conversion can be made either with the distributor on the engine or with the distributor removed. You use the original distributor cap, rotor, spark-plug wires, and spark plugs, provided they are all in good condition. If they are not, replace them with new parts.

Remove the distributor cap, with wires attached, and move it to one side. Remove the rotor. Disconnect the distributor primary lead at the coil terminal marked DIST or (−). Pull wire and grommet to the inside of the distributor (Fig. 17-43). Remove the vacuum chamber by taking off two mounting screws and disengaging the arm from the breaker plate (Fig. 17-43). Remove the two base-plate screws and lift out the complete assembly with points, condenser, and lead. Reinstall the screws as hole plugs.

Before installing new parts, lubricate the advance mechanism and oil wick. Check the distributor housing and remove any foreign material. Remove cam lubricant.

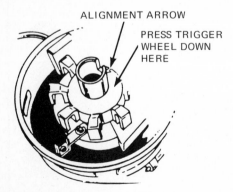

Fig. 17-44 Positioning the trigger wheel. *(Ford Motor Company)*

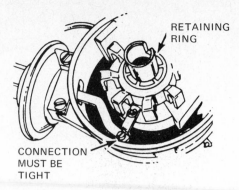

Fig. 17-45 Installing the vacuum-advance unit and retaining ring. *(Ford Motor Company)*

Thread the sensor leads through the distributor housing primary lead hole. Seat the grommet in place. The leads should enter the side of the grommet and follow the contour of the distributor housing.

Install the new trigger wheel sensor assembly on the cam. If there is an arrow on the trigger wheel, line it up with the shaft rotor slot. Gently press the assembly down until it seats on the cam. Press on the hub of the new trigger wheel and not on the trigger wheel teeth (Fig. 17-44).

Careful: Do not press on the trigger-wheel teeth! You could bend or damage them and ruin the wheel.

Put the retaining ring (tabs pointing up) on the distributor shaft. Push the ring down until it holds the assembly firmly in place. If a deep socket is available, use it to push the ring down into place.

Reinstall the vacuum chamber with the original mounting screws. Fasten the vacuum-chamber arm to the vacuum-arm bracket with the self-locking screw in the kit. This connection (Fig. 17-45) must be tight.

Carefully draw the leads through the grommet one at a time to take up the slack. Allow only enough slack for movement of the vacuum advance.

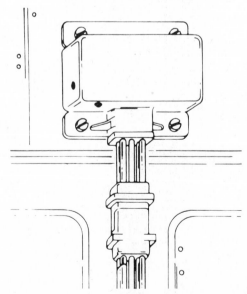

Fig. 17-46 Installing the electronic control unit. *(Ford Motor Company)*

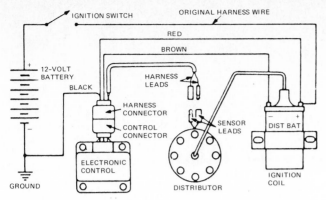

Fig. 17-47 Electric circuit for the electronic ignition system. *(Ford Motor Company)*

Install the rotor and cap. Find a good place for the electronic control unit, using the four metal screws in the kit (Fig. 17-46). The fender well, fire wall, or radiator support are good places. NEVER INSTALL IT ON THE ENGINE. The unit can be ruined by excessive heat and vibration.

Make the electric connections as follows (Fig. 17-47). Avoid sharp bends and keep the wiring harness away from sharp objects that could cut the insulation. Also, keep the wires away from hot surfaces such as the exhaust manifold. There must be some slack to provide for engine movement.

Connect the black (ground) lead to ground at a coil-bracket mounting screw or similar ground connection. Connect the red wire to the coil primary terminal marked BAT (+). Cut off and discard the "push-on" connector at the coil BAT or (+) terminal. If the vehicle harness has a ring or eye terminal, this step is not necessary. Replace with the eye connector provided in the kit. In some cases, you may have to use both eye terminals in the kit. Reconnect to the coil BAT or (+) terminal. Connect the brown coil wire to the terminal marked DIST or (−). Use the nuts and lock washers in the kit.

Tightly connect the harness sensor leads to the distributor leads using the molded connectors in the kit. DO NOT CUT LEADS! If a lead is longer than required, fold and tape it clear of any obstruction.

Connect the electronic control connector to the mating harness connector. Reconnect the battery cable. Start the engine and adjust the timing.

Chapter 17 review questions

Select the *one* correct, best, or most probable answer to each question. Then check your answers against the correct answers given at the end of the book.

1. Failure of the engine to start although it cranks normally could be due to:
   a. no voltage to the ignition system,
   b. ignition coil open,
   c. ECU faulty,
   d. all these.
2. An engine can overheat due to:
   a. low battery,
   b. early ignition timing,
   c. late ignition timing,
   d. high voltage setting.
3. One cause of engine run-on or dieseling is:
   a. low battery,
   b. idle-stop solenoid defective,
   c. defective ECU unit,
   d. defective EGR.
4. The reason you must be careful in making the spark test on electronic ignition systems is that these systems can produce:
   a. 400 volts,
   b. 4000 volts,
   c. 40,000 volts,
   d. 400,000 volts.
5. Backfire can take place in:
   a. both the intake and exhaust manifold,
   b. only the intake manifold,
   c. only the exhaust manifold,
   d. only through the carburetor.
6. When comparing the oscilloscope patterns between contact-point and electronic ignition systems, we find that dwell:
   a. is the same for both,
   b. increases with speed in the electronic system,
   c. decreases with speed in the electronic system,
   d. does not apply to electronic systems.
7. The Chrysler ignition tests where the special electronic tester is not available require a:
   a. voltmeter and an ammeter,
   b. voltmeter and an ohmmeter,
   c. voltmeter and a test light,
   d. battery and variable resistor.
8. The high-voltage cables in the Chrysler electronic ignition system should have a resistance not exceeding:
   a. 500 ohms,
   b. 5000 ohms,
   c. 50,000 ohms,
   d. 500,000 ohms.
9. In the procedure described in the chapter, the ignition coil in the General Motors HEI system is checked with the:
   a. coil removed from the distributor cap,
   b. coil in the distributor cap,
   c. cap on the distributor housing,
   d. engine running.
10. The instructions on the decals or labels in the engine compartment are:
    a. for reference only,
    b. to be followed only for the first tuneup,
    c. to be followed at all times,
    d. for the customer to follow.

SERVICING ELECTRONIC SPARK-ADVANCE SYSTEMS

After studying this chapter, you should be able to:

1. Explain the fundamentals of servicing the three electronic spark-advance systems covered in the chapter.
2. Under the supervision of the instructor, and with the correct testing equipment and tools, perform servicing operations on the three systems.

18-1 Three electronic spark-advance systems Previous chapters describe troubleshooting and servicing procedures for the older types of ignition systems—those using contact points and also the electronic ignition systems. In this chapter, we take a look at the servicing procedures for the three electronic ignition systems using electronic spark-advance controls. These are described in Chapter 16 (✿ 16-8 to 16-14). They are:

1. Chrysler Lean-Burn System
2. Ford Electronic Engine Control (EEC) System
3. General Motors Electronic Spark Timing (EST) or MISAR System

✿ 18-2 Chrysler Lean-Burn System service This system, described in ✿ 16-8 and 16-9, uses a series of sensors to feed information to the spark-control computer. On the basis of this information, the computer decides how much spark advance the system requires. Figure 18-1 is a schematic wiring diagram of the system. One analysis procedure requires a special analyzer, built specifically for the Chrysler Lean-Burn System. This analyzer is shown in Fig. 18-2. It is a programmed tester. You dial the test code for the engine system being tested. The analyzer then checks the ignition coil, ballast resistor, ignition switch contacts, battery voltage, basic ignition timing, and idle speed. It also checks out the spark-control computer (SCC) and associated sensors.

A second way to check the system, if the special analyzer is not available, uses a voltmeter and an ohmmeter. We describe this procedure first, and then find out how to use the analyzer.

✿ 18-3 Voltmeter-ohmmeter check of lean-burn system If the computer should fail while on the high-

way, the system goes into the "limp-in" mode. The system will still operate, but only well enough to get the car in for repair. However, if the pickup coil or start mode fails, the engine will not start or run. Now, let us see how to check the system with a voltmeter and ohmmeter if the engine cranks but does not start. First, you make sure the battery is in a charged condition and that all the wiring and high-voltage cables are in good condition. Then you perform the spark test (✿ 17-5). If you get a good spark but the engine will not start, proceed as follows:

1. Disconnect wiring harness connector from the coolant switch.
2. If the curb idle adjustment screw is touching the carburetor idle-stop switch, put a piece of insulating paper between them.
3. Connect voltmeter negative lead to a good ground on the engine. Turn ignition switch ON and check voltage at the carburetor idle-stop switch terminal. If the voltage is greater than 5 volts but less than 10 volts, proceed to step 5. If voltage is greater than 10 volts, check for proper ground at terminal 10 of the connector (Fig. 18-3).

   If the voltage is not at least 5 volts, turn ignition switch OFF and disconnect the connector from the bottom of the spark control computer. Turn ignition switch back to ON and check voltage at terminal 2 of connector (Fig. 18-3). Voltage should be within one volt of battery voltage. If voltage is correct, proceed to step 4. If it is not, check the wiring between terminal 2 and the ignition switch for opens, shorts, or poor connections.
4. Turn ignition switch OFF and disconnect connector from the computer. Check with ohmmeter between terminal 7 and the carburetor idle-stop switch terminal. There should be continuity between these

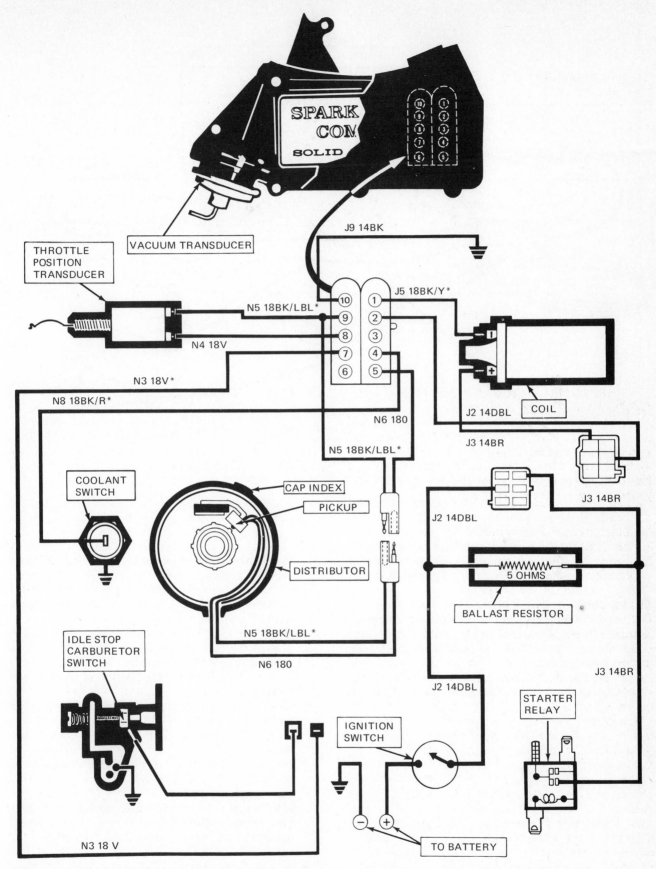

Fig. 18-1 Chrysler Lean-Burn wiring system. There are several variations of this basic system. Always have the servicing information that covers the specific model you are working on. *(Chrysler Corporation)*

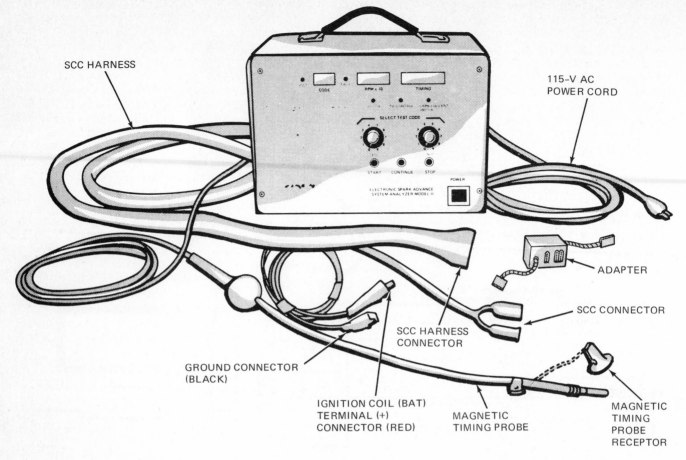

Fig. 18-2 Special analyzer to test the lean burn system. *(Chrysler Corporation)*

two points. If not, check wire between them for opens, shorts, or poor connections. If there is continuity, check for continuity between terminal 10 of connector and ground. If there is, replace the computer. If there is not, check for opens and poor connections and proceed to step 5 only if the engine fails to start.

5. Turn ignition switch ON and check voltage at terminal 1. Voltage should be within 1 volt of battery voltage. If it is, proceed to step 6. If it is not, check wiring and connections between the connector and the ignition switch.

6. With ignition switch ON, measure resistance with an ohmmeter between terminals 5 and 9 (Fig. 18-

3). Resistance should be between 150 and 900 ohms. If it is, proceed to step 7. If it is not, disconnect pickup coil leads from the distributor and measure the resistance at the lead going into the distributor. If it is now between 150 and 900 ohms, there is an open, short, or poor connection between the distributor connector and terminals 5 and 9. If resistance is still incorrect, the pickup coil is defective.

7. With one lead of the ohmmeter connected to ground, check for continuity at each terminal of the lead going into the distributor. There should be no continuity. Reconnect the distributor lead and proceed to step 8.

8. Remove distributor cap and check air gap at the pickup coil (see Fig. 17-13). If it is not right, adjust it (⚙ 17-16, item 10). If the air gap is correct, proceed to step 9.

9. Install distributor cap, reconnect all wiring, and try to start. If engine still fails to start, replace the computer.

10. If the engine still fails to start, reinstall the original computer and repeat the test procedure. Chances are one of the tests was not done correctly.

⚙ **18-4 Poor performance of lean-burn system** Besides the usual checks you make for poor engine performance (see chart in ⚙ 17-3), check the timing using an adjustable timing light (Fig. 14-19).

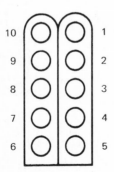

Fig. 18-3 Numbering of terminals in wiring-harness connector.

Connect a ground lead to the carburetor idle-stop switch. With timing light connected, start engine and immediately note timing mark on the crankshaft damper. Adjust timing light so the basic timing signal is seen at the timing plate. The meter on the timing light should show the specified advance (see factory manual for specifications). Continue to note the timing while continuing to adjust timing light to maintain the basic timing signal. The additional advance should slowly reduce to the basic signal after about a minute. If timing does not increase and return to basic, replace the computer. If timing checks out okay, proceed to check speed advance.

Leave the jumper lead and timing light connected. Make sure the throttle-position transducer is properly adjusted by gauging the distance between the outer part of the transducer and the mounting bracket with a special gauge. If it is not correct, turn the transducer in or out to adjust.

1. With ignition OFF, disconnect the connector from the computer. Check resistance between terminals 8 and 9 (Fig. 18-3) with an ohmmeter. Resistance should be 60 to 90 ohms. If it is, reconnect the connector and proceed to step 2. If it is not, remove connector from the transducer and measure the resistance at the transducer terminals. If it is 50 to 90 ohms, there is an open, short, or poor connection in the circuit between terminals 8 and 9 and the transducer. If the resistance is not between 50 and 90 ohms, replace the transducer.

2. Disconnect the connector from the transducer and connect it to another transducer known to be good. Throttle linkage should be on the fast-idle cam. With the jumper lead still grounding the carburetor idle-stop switch, start engine and run it for 90 seconds. Then, holding the test transducer in your hand, slowly move the core out. Adjust the timing light so the basic timing signal is seen at the timing plate. The meter on the timing light should show additional advance. If it is within specifications, move the core back into the transducer. Timing should return to basic setting. If timing does not advance or return within specifications, replace the computer. Then recheck the throttle position transducer.

☼ 18-5 Checking lean-burn system with electronic analyzer
Figure 18-2 shows this analyzer. Figure 18-4 shows it connected into the system in preparation for running the tests. Figure 18-5 is a close-up of the analyzer face with the various controls and readouts named. Note that the face also contains step-by-step instructions for running the tests. Figures 18-6 and 18-7 show the magnetic-timing-probe receptacles on six- and eight-cylinder engines. Briefly, here is how a complete test of the system is made.

1. Make sure the battery is fully charged.
2. Inspect all electric wiring and connections to make sure they are in good condition. Also, make sure the vacuum hoses are in good condition and are properly connected. Any defects found in the wir-

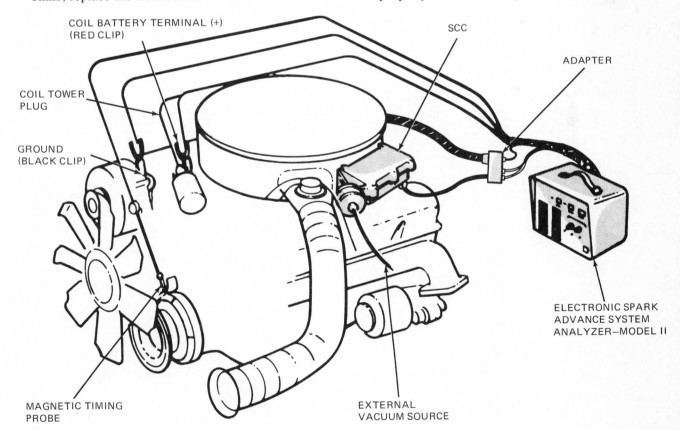

Fig. 18-4 Connections from the analyzer to the components of the Lean-Burn System. *(Chrysler Corporation)*

257

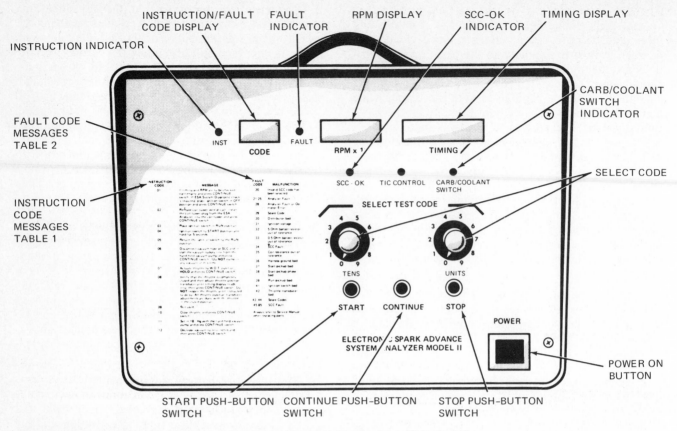

Fig. 18-5 Front panel of the analyzer, showing controls and indicators. Note that the panel carries instructions on how to use the analyzer. *(Chrysler Corporation)*

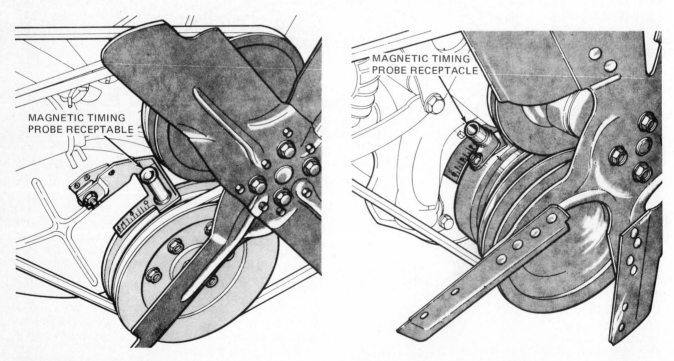

Fig. 18-6 Magnetic timing probe receptacle for a six-cylinder engine. *(Chrysler Corporation)*

Fig. 18-7 Magnetic timing probe receptacle for a V-8 engine. *(Chrysler Corporation)*

INSTRUCTION CODE LISTING AND MESSAGE

INSTRUCTION CODE	MESSAGE
01	If timing and RPM are to be checked, start engine and press CONTINUE switch. If ESA system diagnostic check is required, place ignition switch in OFF position and press CONTINUE switch.
02	Remove coil tower wire at coil, install the coil tower plug from the ESA analyzer into the coil tower and press CONTINUE switch.
03	Place ignition switch in RUN position.
04	Ignition switch to START position and hold for 5 seconds.
05	Return the ignition switch to the RUN position.
06	Disconnect vacuum hose at SCC and install the vacuum supply line from the hand-held vacuum pump and press CONTINUE switch. (Do NOT pump in any vacuum at this time.)
07	Actuate throttle to W.O.T. position, HOLD and press CONTINUE switch.
08	Verify that the throttle is completely closed and then adjust throttle position transducer until timing display reads zero, then press CONTINUE switch. Do NOT reopen the throttle until instructed to do so. All throttle position transducer adjustments are done with the throttle in the closed position.
09	Not used.
10	Close throttle and press CONTINUE switch.
11	Set in 18 inches Hg with the hand held vacuum pump and press CONTINUE switch.
12	Decrease vacuum to zero inches and then press CONTINUE switch.

Fig. 18-8. Instruction code listing and instructions. (*Chrysler Corporation*)

ing or hoses should be corrected before the testing proceeds.
3. Ignition switch should be OFF.
4. Connect the adapter to the analyzer.
5. Disconnect wiring harness 10-way connector from underneath the SCC.
6. Connect female 10-way connector from the analyzer to the SCC. Connect the male 10-way connector from the analyzer to the harness 10-way connector you disconnected from the SCC. The analyzer is now plugged into the system.
7. Connect the analyzer *red* alligator clip lead to the BAT (+) terminal of the ignition coil, NOT to the NEG (−) terminal. DOING THIS COULD DAMAGE THE ANALYZER.
8. Connect the analyzer *black* ground lead clip to a suitable ground on the engine or alternator.
9. Install the magnetic timing probe in the receptacle (Figs. 18-6 and 18-7). Use the receptor to hold the probe in position.
10. Do not connect the analyzer coil-tower plug yet. Wait until instructed to do so.
11. Plug the analyzer into a 115-volt 60-Hz outlet.

CAUTION: In making all the connections, be sure to keep all leads out of the way of the engine fan, pulleys, and belts. If a lead were caught in the fan or pulley, it could pull the analyzer into the fan or belt pulley. You could be hurt by the flying pieces.

Figure 18-8 is a copy of the instructions that appear on the face of the analyzer, giving step-by-step instructions on how to carry out the complete analysis. Figure 18-9 is a copy of the fault code listing and troubleshooting guide that appears on the face of the analyzer.

☀ 18-6 Ford EEC system This system, described in ☀ 16-10 to 16-13, controls not only the spark advance, but also the exhaust gas recirculation (EGR) and air-

injection or thermactor systems. See Figs. 16-29 to 16-32. An EEC tester is required to check out the system. Other special tools are also required. Here is the complete list of test equipment needed:

1. Meter—a digital volt/ohm meter (DVOM)
2. EEC tester including these test fixtures:
   a. Three sensors (blue, yellow, and brown)
   b. One ignition module
3. Tachometer
4. Timing light with built-in advance meter

NOTE: If the special testing equipment is not available, you can perform the spark test (☀ 17-5) and make checks with a voltmeter and ohmmeter, similar to those outlined previously for Chrysler Lean-Burn Systems. You can also use the "replace-and-try" method. That is, replace the components of the system, one by one, and then check for improvement in performance. Of course, you would first consider the possible troubles that could occur in the standard electronic ignition system (see chart in ☀ 17-3). Also, remember that many troubles such as failure to start, backfiring, missing, poor performance, and so on, can result from troubles in the fuel system or engine as well as in the ignition system.

Figure 18-10 shows the test equipment hookup to run a test of the system. Before making the test, inspect all electric wiring to make sure it is in good condition and that all connections are okay. Also, inspect all vacuum and pressure hoses for their condition and to make sure that they are properly connected. Any defects found in the wiring or hoses should be corrected before the test starts. Figure 18-11 is the complete wiring diagram of the system. It also shows the various sensors that feed the control module.

Ford outlines two tests in their shop manual, one if the engine will not start and the other to check out all

FAULT CODE	MALFUNCTION	REMARKS
20	Invalid SCC code has been selected	Test code is stamped on side of SCC.
21–25	Analyzer fault	Rerun the test; if fault code continues, contact authorized service center.
28	Analyzer fault or operator error	Code 28 appears if the RED clip is not making proper contact at coil BAT (+) terminal.
29	Spare code	
30	Distributor bad	The relationship between the start and run pickups is incorrect. Replace pickup coils assembly.
31	Ignition voltage	Check all harness connections, battery, ignition switch, and wiring.
32	5-ohm ballast resistor out of tolerance	Check for continuity from ballast resistor to SCC connector. If okay replace the ballast resistor.
33	0.5-ohm ballast resistor out of tolerance	Check for continuity from ballast resistor to coil (+). If okay replace the ballast resistor.
34	SCC fault	Power or ground connections, SCC open, or SCC bad.
35	Coil resistance out of tolerance	Check connections to coil and wiring. If okay replace the coil.
36	Harness ground bad	Engine harness connector not grounded properly.
37	Start pickup bad	Check the pickup gap, wiring, and connections. If okay replace the pickup.
38	Start pickup phase bad	Wiring is reversed to start pickup. Check the wiring.
39	Run pickup bad	Check the pickup gap, wiring, and connections. If okay replace the pickup.
40	Run pickup phase bad	Wiring to run pickup is reversed; correct the wiring.
41	Ignition switch bad	Ignition switch is bad in the START position. Check the ignition bypass circuit wiring. If okay replace the switch.
42	Throttle transducer bad	Check wiring to transducer; if okay replace the transducer.
43, 44	Spare codes	
45–85	SCC fault	Record this code and attach to failed SCC.

Fig. 18-9. Fault code listing and troubleshooting guide. (*Chrysler Corporation*)

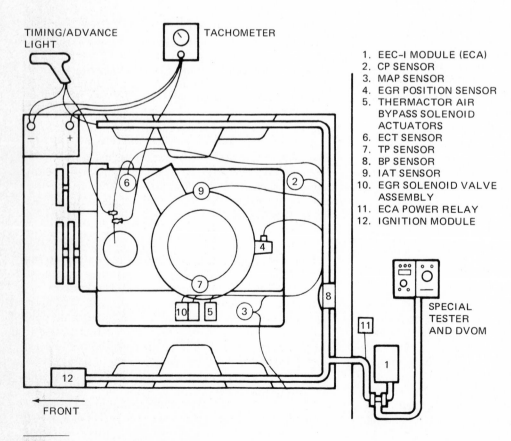

1. EEC–I MODULE (ECA)
2. CP SENSOR
3. MAP SENSOR
4. EGR POSITION SENSOR
5. THERMACTOR AIR BYPASS SOLENOID ACTUATORS
6. ECT SENSOR
7. TP SENSOR
8. BP SENSOR
9. IAT SENSOR
10. EGR SOLENOID VALVE ASSEMBLY
11. ECA POWER RELAY
12. IGNITION MODULE

TIMING/ADVANCE LIGHT

TACHOMETER

SPECIAL TESTER AND DVOM

FRONT

Fig. 18-10 Test equipment hookup and component locations of Ford EEC system. (*Ford Motor Company*)

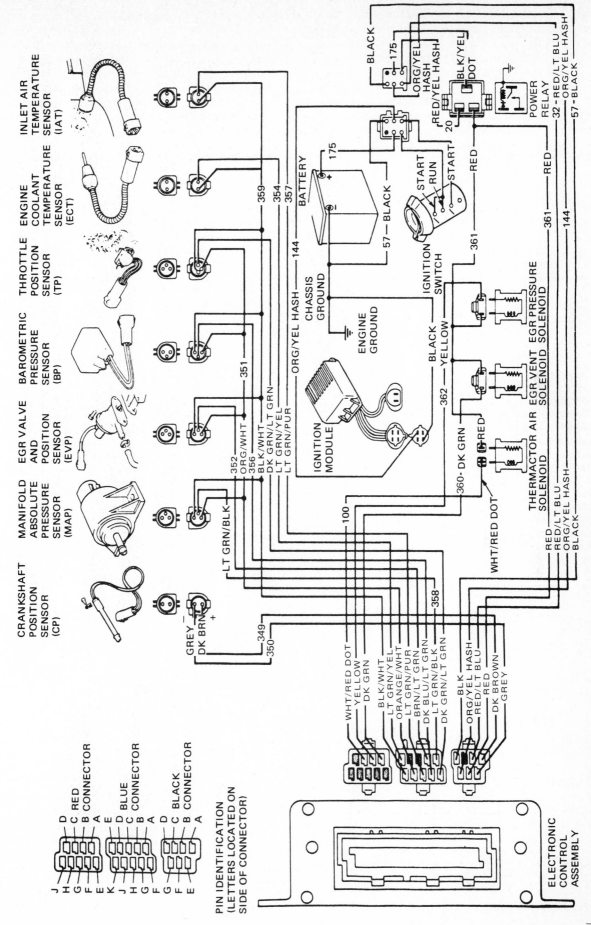

Fig. 18-11 Complete wiring circuit of the Ford EEC system. *(Ford Motor Company)*

ELECTRONIC CONTROL ASSEMBLY

PIN IDENTIFICATION
(LETTERS LOCATED ON SIDE OF CONNECTOR)

D   RED
C   CONNECTOR
B
A

E   BLUE
D   CONNECTOR
C
B
A

K   BLACK
J   CONNECTOR
H
G
F

INLET AIR TEMPERATURE SENSOR (IAT)

ENGINE COOLANT TEMPERATURE SENSOR (ECT)

THROTTLE POSITION SENSOR (TP)

BAROMETRIC PRESSURE SENSOR (BP)

EGR VALVE AND POSITION SENSOR (EVP)

MANIFOLD ABSOLUTE PRESSURE SENSOR (MAP)

CRANKSHAFT POSITION SENSOR (CP)

BATTERY

CHASSIS GROUND

ENGINE GROUND

IGNITION MODULE

IGNITION SWITCH

START
RUN
START

POWER RELAY

EGR PRESSURE SOLENOID

EGR VENT SOLENOID

THERMACTOR AIR SOLENOID

BLACK

175

ORG/YEL HASH

BLK/YEL DOT

RED/LT BLU

20

32 — RED/LT BLU
ORG/YEL HASH
57 — BLACK

361

144

RED

RED

175

57 — BLACK

144 — ORG/YEL HASH

BLACK

YELLOW

362

361

360 — DK GRN

RED

RED
RED/LT BLU
ORG/YEL HASH
BLACK

WHT/RED DOT

100

358

359
354
357

351

352
356
BLK/WHT
DK GRN/LT GRN
LT GRN/YEL
LT GRN/PUR

LT GRN/BLK

350

349

GREY
DK BRN

ORG/WHT

WHT/RED DOT
YELLOW
DK GRN
BLK/WHT
LT GRN/YEL
ORANGE/WHT
LT GRN/PUR
BRN/LT GRN
DK BLU/LT GRN
LT GRN/BLK
DK GRN/LT GRN
BLK
ORG/YEL HASH
RED/LT BLU
RED
DK BROWN
GREY

261

components if the engine does start and run. Figure 18-12 is the diagnostic data chart that Ford states should be filled out as the tests are run. For details of how to run the tests, refer to the Ford shop manual covering the model and year of the car you are checking.

⚙ 18-7 General Motors electronic spark timing (EST) system Figure 18-13 is the wiring diagram of the later version of this system. Recall, from ⚙ 16-14, that the earlier version has the crankshaft sensor mounted to the front engine mounting bracket (Fig. 16-33) with a disk on the crankshaft (Fig. 16-34). The later version has the sensor pickup coil mounted inside the distributor, the same as in other electronic ignition distributors (Fig. 18-14). The distributor is similar to the HEI distributors except that it does not have centrifugal or vacuum advance. The electronic module is mounted inside the distributor. This is the electronic device that works with the pickup coil to close and open the circuit to the ignition coil. In this version, the

Vehicle Condition	Test Selector Switch Position								Spark advance (degrees)
	1 Vref	2 MAP	3 TP	4 BP	5 ECT	6 IAT	7 TAB	8 EVP	
TEST SEQUENCE I									
1. Parking brakes on	Limits	Limits	Limits	Limits	Limits	Limits	Limits	Limits	
2. Engine, off & hot, key run	8.5 – 9.5 V **	table A	1.65 – 2.14 V	table A	1.9 – 3.7 V	4.1 – 6.3 V	Greater Than 10.5 V	1.09 – 1.61 V	
3. All accessories off									
4. Crank signal checked	Reading ___V	Reading ___V	Reading ___V	Reading ___V	Reading ___V	Reading ___V	Reading ___V	Reading ___V	
TEST SEQUENCE II									
1. Parking brakes on		Limits 4				Limits 4	Limits 5	Refer 6 to en-	Refer 6 to engine
2. Install test fixtures: MAP (yellow), IAT (brown)		3.5 – 5.5 V**				5.2 – 7.2 V**	Less than 1.6 V	gine emis-	emission label
3. Engine hot and running in park at curb idle. All accessories off.		Reading ___V				Reading ___V	chang- ing to	sion label	Reading ___V
4. Observe MAP and IAT data.							greater than	Reading ___V	
5. Raise rpm to 1600–1800. Start timing TAB when throttle returns to curb idle.							10.5 V within 60 ± 5		
6. Set engine to 1600 ± 50 rpm. Observe EVP and spark advance.							seconds yes no		
DATA ANALYSIS									
	If out of limits** Step VI.D.1.	If out of limits* Step VI.D.2.	If out of limits* Step VI.D.3.	If out of limits* Step VI.D.4.	If out of limits* Step VI.D.5.	If our of limits* Step VI.D.6.	If out of limits* Step VI.D.7.	If out of limits* Step VI.D.8.	If out of limits* Step VI.D.10.

TABLE A

Service location elevation (feet)	MAP and BP limits
0 – 1000	6.7 – 7.8V
1000 – 2000	6.5 – 7.4V
2000 – 3000	6.2 – 7.3V
3000 – 4000	6.0 – 7.0V
4000 – 5000	5.8 – 6.8V
5000 – 6000	5.5 – 6.6V
6000 – 7000	5.3 – 6.4V

*Complete all data gathering per Test Sequences I and II prior to performing any diagnostic subroutine except as noted with **.
**If reading is out of limits, perform indicated diagnostic step prior to continuing Test Sequence.
BP   Barometric (atmospheric) pressure
ECT   Engine coolant temperature
EVP   EGR valve position
IAT   Inlet air temperature
MAP   Manifold absolute pressure (vacuum)
TAB   Thermactor air bypass
TP   Throttle position

Fig. 18-12. Diagnostic data for EEC used on the 302-cubic-inch-displacement 5.0-L engine. (*Ford Motor Company*)

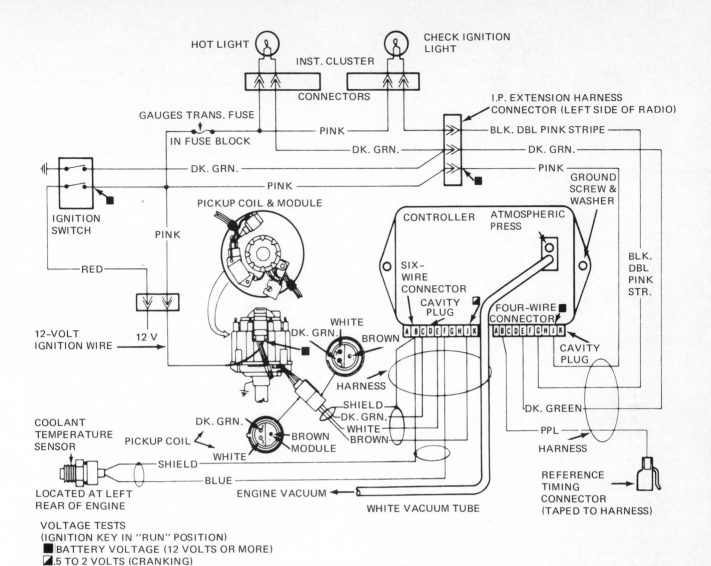

Fig. 18-13 EST wiring system. *(Oldsmobile Division of General Motors Corporation)*

ignition coil is mounted on top of the distributor (Fig. 18-15).

The controller (to right in Fig. 18-13) is the electronic device that adjusts the spark timing to suit the operating conditions. It receives signals from the distributor pickup coil, engine vacuum, atmospheric pressure, and coolant temperature (from sensor, Fig. 18-16). From these signals it decides how much spark advance to provide.

The system has a CHECK IGNITION light on the instrument panel. This light comes on under the following conditions:

1. Ignition switch is turned to START.
2. If electric system voltage is low due to a low battery

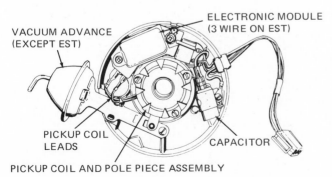

Fig. 18-14 Top view of distributor with cap, rotor, and shaft removed. *(Oldsmobile Division of General Motors Corporation)*

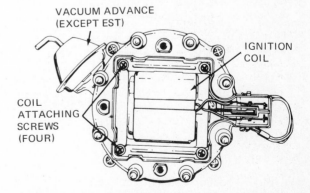

Fig. 18-15 Ignition coil mounting. *(Oldsmobile Division of General Motors Corporation)*

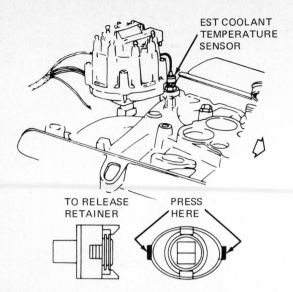

Fig. 18-16 Location of EST coolant-temperature sensor. *(Oldsmobile Division of General Motors Corporation)*

and a heavy electric load. (The light will go off if the electric load is turned off and the voltage returns to normal.)

3. When checking reference timing and the reference-timing connector is grounded.

4. If the controller fails so there is no electronic spark advance.

The only services required, aside from trouble diagnosis, include setting the reference timing, removing and replacing the components of the system, and disassembly and reassembly of the distributor.

1. **Setting reference timing** The magnetic-probe timing method is preferred. This method uses a probe that is inserted into the receptacle on the timer bracket (Fig. 18-17). To check and set the reference timing, refer to Fig. 18-18. Use a jumper lead about 2 ft long [0.61 m] to ground the reference timing connector.

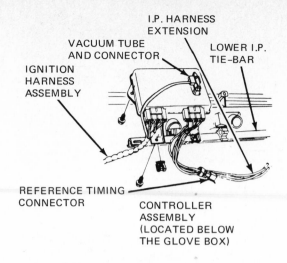

TO SET REFERENCE TIMING

1. CONNECT OPEN REFERENCE TIMING CONNECTOR (TAPED TO HARNESS) TO GROUND USING ABOUT A 2-FOOT JUMPER WIRE.
2. CONNECT TIMING LIGHT OR METER AND TACHOMETER THEN START ENGINE. "CHECK IGNITION" LIGHT WILL BE ON IF GROUND WIRE WAS PROPERLY INSTALLED.
3. TIMING SHOULD BE 20° AT 1100 RPM (CALIFORNIA 22°) AT 1100 RPM).
4. IF TIMING IS INCORRECT, LOOSEN DISTRIBUTOR CLAMP BOLT AND TURN DISTRIBUTOR TO ADJUST TIMING.
5. TIGHTEN DISTRIBUTOR CLAMP BOLT. REMOVE JUMPER WIRE. "CHECK IGNITION" LIGHT WILL GO OUT.

Fig. 18-18 Reference timing connector. *(Oldsmobile Division of General Motors Corporation)*

With the transmission in PARK, drive wheels blocked, and parking brake applied, start the engine and run it at the specified speed. One specification for a recent model year calls for 1100 rpm at which timing should be 20° (or 22 ° for California).

If the timing is not correct, loosen the distributor clamp bolt. Turn the distributor to set the timing correctly. Turning it clockwise advances the timing, counterclockwise retards the timing. When timing is correct, tighten clamp bolt and remove the jumper lead.

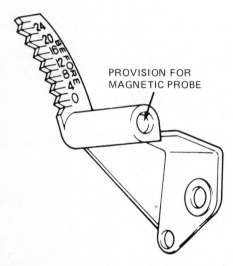

Fig. 18-17 Location of timing hole for magnetic timing probe. *(Oldsmobile Division of General Motors Corporation)*

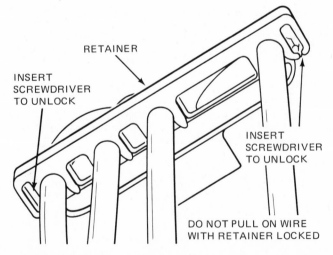

Fig. 18-19 Spark-plug cable retainer. *(Oldsmobile Division of General Motors Corporation)*

264

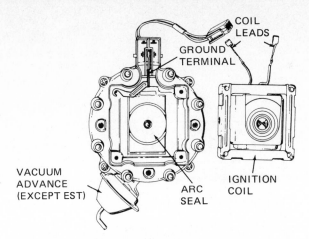

COIL LEADS

GROUND TERMINAL

VACUUM ADVANCE (EXCEPT EST)

ARC SEAL

IGNITION COIL

Fig. 18-20 Location of arc seal. *(Oldsmobile Division of General Motors Corporation)*

2. Removing and replacing components The controller, the temperature sensor, and the distributor are the only items unique to this system to be removed and replaced. Other components which are common to all ignition systems are the ignition switch, cables, and spark plugs. Service to these has been covered previously. The high-voltage cables have silicone insulation which is soft and requires special care to avoid damaging them. They are held in place by retainers (Fig. 18-19). Use a small screwdriver in the slots at the ends of the retainer to unlock it.

3. Distributor service This distributor requires very little in the way of service because it has no centrifugal or vacuum-advance mechanisms. The procedures covered in Chapter 16 apply to this unit. This distributor does have one special feature, an arc shield, as shown in Fig. 18-20. The arc shield protects the electronic components below it from false impulses that might come from the arcing between the rotor blade and terminal inserts in the distributor cap.

Figure 18-20 shows the ignition coil removed from the distributor. It is held in place by four attaching screws.

NOTE: When disassembling and assembling the distributor, do not wipe the silicone lubricant from the electronic module or the base of the distributor. This lubricant is necessary because it helps to transfer heat from the module and keep it cool.

Chapter 18 review questions

Select the *one* correct, best, or most probable answer to each question. Then check your answers against the correct answers given at the end of the book.

1. To check the Chrysler Lean-Burn System, if you do not have the special analyzer, you can use:
   a. a voltmeter and an ammeter,
   b. an ohmmeter and an ammeter,
   c. a voltmeter and an ohmmeter,
   d. a high-discharge resistor and a voltmeter.
2. To check the Chrysler Lean-Burn System with a voltmeter and ohmmeter, first check the battery and cables, and then:
   a. perform the spark test,
   b. check the starting system,
   c. test the charging system,
   d. adjust idle speed.
3. When using the analyzer to check the Chrysler Lean-Burn System:
   a. also use a voltmeter,
   b. also use an ammeter,
   c. also use a rheostat,
   d. use none of these.
4. To check the Ford EEC system, you need:
   a. a voltmeter and ammeter,
   b. the EEC tester,
   c. to remove it from the engine,
   d. a voltmeter, ammeter, and rheostat.
5. The distributor used in the General Motors EST system:
   a. has vacuum advance,
   b. has centrifugal advance,
   c. has both vacuum and centrifugal advance,
   d. has none of these.
6. The controller in the General Motors EST system receives signals from the distributor pickup coil, engine vacuum, atmospheric pressure, and:
   a. exhaust gas oxygen,
   b. mixture richness,
   c. coolant temperature,
   d. charging-system voltage.
7. The three items special to the General Motors EST system are the distributor, controller, and the:
   a. oxygen sensor,
   b. mixture-richness sensor,
   c. temperature sensor,
   d. pressure sensor.
8. The first check of the lean-burn system is:
   a. perform the spark test,
   b. make sure battery is charged,
   c. test the centrifugal and vacuum advance,
   d. remove and test the ignition coil.
9. The Ford electronic engine control system controls not only the spark advance, but also the:
   a. EGR system,
   b. air-injection system,
   c. thermactor system,
   d. all of the above.
10. The only services the General Motors electronic spark-timing system requires, aside from trouble diagnosis, is:
   a. setting the reference timing,
   b. removing and replacing system components,
   c. servicing the distributor,
   d. all of the above.

ELECTRONIC CARBURETED FUEL SYSTEMS

After studying this chapter, you should be able to:

1. List the six systems of the carburetor and explain how each works.
2. Explain how the General Motors Electronic Fuel Control (EFC) and the Ford Feedback Carburetor Systems work.
3. Describe the checking and servicing procedures for the two systems. Under the supervision of the instructor and with the correct testers and service tools, follow various diagnostic procedures to find trouble causes and then fix the troubles.

19-1 Electronic fuel systems Electronics is playing an important part in the new fuel systems now appearing on late-model cars. The purpose of the fuel system is to supply the engine with a combustible mixture of air and gasoline vapor. Putting electronics to work in fuel systems improves the accuracy of the fuel metering. That is, the system can more accurately tailor the air–fuel mixture to suit operating conditions. This improves fuel mileage (more miles per gallon) and also reduces atmospheric pollutants coming out of the tail pipe.

19-2 Two fuel systems for gasoline engines For many years, the gasoline engines used in automobiles have had carburetors in their fuel systems (Fig. 19-1). The carburetor is a mixing device which combines air and gasoline vapor in the proper proportions to produce a combustible mixture. Figure 19-2 shows a simplified version of carburetor action. Air moving down through the carburetor air horn picks up gasoline being sprayed into the air. The mixture flows down through the carburetor, into the intake manifold, and from there into the engine cylinders as the intake valves open.

In recent years, several cars have been equipped with a different kind of fuel system. This is the gasoline fuel-injection system. Figure 19-3 is a simplified drawing of one design. The gasoline is sprayed into the intake manifold by a series of fuel injectors. There is a fuel injector for each cylinder. Each injector is positioned just opposite an intake valve. The fuel sprays into the air in the intake manifold. When the intake valve opens, the fuel and air enter the cylinder. This arrangement is usually called *a port-injection system* because the fuel is injected into the intake-valve ports. Note that the major difference between the carbureted system and the fuel-injection system is the point at

which the gasoline enters the air going into the cylinders. In the carbureted system, the gasoline enters the air passing through the carburetor. In the fuel-injection system, the gasoline enters the air in the intake manifold.

In this chapter, we describe the carbureted fuel system which has an electronic control that continuously readjusts the air–fuel ratio, which is the ratio of the air to fuel by weight. The ideal ratio, which provides about the right amount of air to burn all the fuel, is 14.5 to 1 (usually shown as 14.5:1). That is, there is 14.5 times as much air, by weight, as there is gasoline, by weight. This is called the *stoichiometric (ideal)* air–fuel ratio. If the ratio is reduced, say, to 13:1 or 14:1, the mixture is said to be rich. There is too much gasoline for the amount of air in the mixture. This means that not all the gasoline will burn and some will come out the tail pipe as unburned gasoline (HC) and partly burned gas-

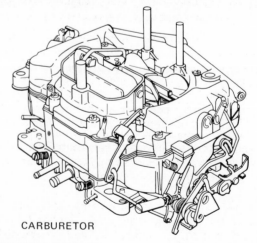

CARBURETOR

Fig. 19-1 A carburetor.

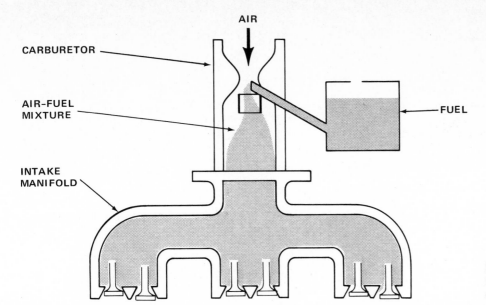

CARBURETOR

AIR

AIR–FUEL
MIXTURE

FUEL

INTAKE
MANIFOLD

Fig. 19-2 Simplified view of a carbureted fuel system, showing flow of fuel and air through the system.

oline (carbon monoxide, or CO). If the mixture is too lean—say, 17:1 or 18:1—the engine will not run well because these lean mixtures are harder to ignite in the engine. The gasoline fuel-injection systems are described in the following chapter.

☼ 19-3 Gasoline and combustion

Before we discuss electronic control of the air–fuel ratio, we look into the way gasoline burns in the engine. Gasoline is a hydrocarbon—made up largely of hydrogen and carbon with the chemical formula HC. During combustion, the hydrogen unites with oxygen in the air to form H_2O, or water. The carbon unites with oxygen in the air to form CO_2, or carbon dioxide. As we explained in ☼ 16-12, when we examined the operation of the air-injection or thermactor system, combustion is never quite complete so that some HC and some CO remain in the exhaust gas. These are pollutants that must be kept down to a minimum in order to meet the allowable limits set by federal law. Recall, from ☼ 16-12, that the air-injection system sends air into the engine exhaust manifold. This air enters through air-injection tubes positioned close to the engine exhaust valves (Fig. 16-31). The oxygen in the air helps burn up any HC or CO in the exhaust gas coming out past the exhaust valves.

CAUTION: CO is carbon monoxide, a deadly poisonous gas, as we have warned previously. Enough carbon monoxide is produced in three minutes by a normally running engine in a one-car garage to kill you!

In order to achieve as nearly ideal combustion as possible, the electronic air–fuel-ratio control system continuously adjusts the ratio to suit operating conditions and maintain the stoichiometric mixture (14.5:1). Before we describe this system, however, we review carburetor action.

☼ 19-4 Carburetor fundamentals

A simple carburetor could be made from a round cylinder with a squeezed-in section, a fuel nozzle, and a round disk, or valve (Fig. 19-4). The round cylinder is called the *air*

horn, the squeezed-in section the *venturi*, and the valve the *throttle valve*. The throttle valve can be tilted more or less to open or close the air horn (Fig. 19-5). In the horizontal position it shuts off, or *throttles*, the airflow through the air horn. When the throttle is turned away from this position, air can flow through the air horn.

☼ 19-5 Venturi effect

As air flows through the venturi, a partial vacuum is produced in the venturi. This is just where the end of the fuel nozzle is located. The lower end of the fuel nozzle is in a fuel reservoir, the float bowl, as shown in Fig. 19-6. Atmospheric pressure from the air cleaner acts through a vent in the float bowl. It pushes on the fuel in the float bowl. Since there is a vacuum at the upper end of the fuel nozzle, the atmospheric pressure pushes fuel up through the nozzle. It sprays out into the air passing through the venturi and quickly turns to vapor. The more air that flows through the venturi, the greater the vacuum in the venturi. And the greater the vacuum, the more fuel flows. This means that, in a properly calibrated carburetor, a fairly constant air–fuel ratio is maintained.

☼ 19-6 Throttle-valve control

The throttle valve is controlled by linkage to the accelerator pedal in the

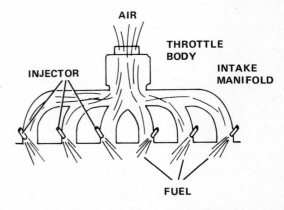

AIR

THROTTLE
BODY

INJECTOR

INTAKE
MANIFOLD

FUEL

Fig. 19-3 Simplified view of a fuel-injection system.

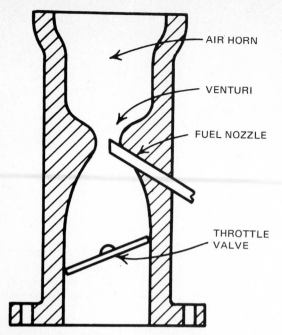

Fig. 19-4 Simple carburetor consisting of a round air horn, a fuel nozzle, and a throttle valve.

driver's compartment (Fig. 19-7). When the driver "steps on the gas"—pushes down on the accelerator pedal—the linkage tilts the throttle valve so that more air–fuel mixture can pass through the carburetor. The engine gets more air–fuel mixture and can produce more power.

⚙ **19-7 Air–fuel ratio requirements** The fuel system must vary the air–fuel ratio to suit different oper-

Fig. 19-5 Throttle valve in the air horn of a carburetor. When the throttle is closed, as shown, little air can pass through. But when the throttle is opened, as shown in dashed lines, there is little throttling effect.

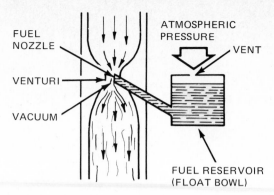

Fig. 19-6 The venturi, or constriction, causes a vacuum to develop in the air stream just below the constriction. Then atmospheric pressure pushes fuel up and out the fuel nozzle.

ating conditions. The mixture must be rich (have a high proportion of fuel) for starting and running a cold engine. It must be leaner (have a lower proportion of fuel) for medium-speed operation. It must be enriched for quick acceleration and for high-speed operation. Figure 19-8 shows typical air–fuel ratios as related to various car operating conditions.

The reason the mixture must be rich for cold-engine starts is that the fuel vaporizes poorly when it and the engine are cold. Therefore, extra amounts of fuel must be fed to the engine so that enough will vaporize to get the car started. Likewise, when the throttle is suddenly opened, a sudden inrush of air results. At this moment, extra fuel must be delivered so the mixture does not lean out too much. The following sections describe the various systems in carburetors that change the air–fuel ratios as required to assure easy starting and smooth engine operation under varying conditions.

⚙ **19-8 Carburetor systems** The systems in the carburetor are:

1. Float system
2. Idle and low-speed system
3. Main metering system
4. Power system
5. Accelerator-pump system
6. Choke system

⚙ **19-9 Float system** The float system includes a float bowl, a float, and a needle valve. Figure 19-9 is a simplified drawing of a float system. The system keeps the fuel in the bowl at a constant level. If the level is too high, too much fuel will feed through the nozzle and the mixture will be too rich. If the level is too low, not enough fuel will feed through the nozzle. The mixture will be too lean.

As fuel is withdrawn from the float bowl through the fuel nozzle, the float will move down. This releases the needle. That is, the needle can move off its seat. This allows the fuel pump to push fuel into the float bowl. The fuel pump takes fuel from the fuel tank and sends it to the float bowl. As the fuel level in the bowl rises, the float also rises. This pushes the needle back into its seat so the flow of fuel into the bowl is stopped. In

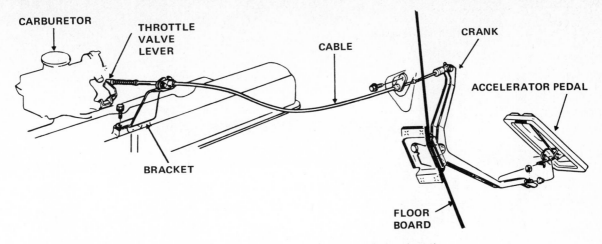

Fig. 19-7 One linkage arrangement between the accelerator pedal and the throttle valve in the carburetor.

actual practice, the float tends to hold the needle valve partly closed so that the incoming fuel just balances the fuel being withdrawn.

Figure 19-11 shows a carburetor partly cut away so you can see the float bowl and the two floats. The float bowl partly surrounds the carburetor air horn. The two floats are attached by a U-shaped lever and operate a needle valve.

☼ 19-10 Idle system
When the throttle is closed or only slightly open, only a small amount of air can pass through the air horn. There is not enough air going through the venturi to create a vacuum. This means that the fuel nozzle will not deliver any fuel. However, during this time the idle system takes over (Fig. 19-10). It has passages through which air and fuel can flow. When the throttle is closed, there is a high vacuum in the intake manifold below the throttle plate. This causes the idle system to discharge a rich air–fuel mixture through the idle port in the lower part of the carburetor. The mixture flows past the tapered point of the idle air–fuel-mixture adjustment screw. It leans out somewhat as it mixes with the small amount of air getting past the throttle valve. But it is still rich enough for good engine idling.

NOTE: Carburetors have a number of special features in the idle system to assure smooth operation. Some of the electronically controlled carburetors have a special valve that can change the mixture ratio if it is too rich or too lean. We describe it later in this chapter.

☼ 19-11 Low-speed or off-idle operation
When the throttle is opened slightly, as shown in Fig. 19-11, the edge of the throttle valve moves past the low-speed port in the side of the air horn. The port is a vertical slot or series of holes, one above the other. As the edge of the throttle valve moves past this port, intake manifold vacuum can act on it. That is, the vacuum causes this port—the low-speed port—to deliver fuel. This compensates for the lowered vacuum (due to more air passing the throttle) which reduces the amount of air–fuel mixture the idle system is delivering.

☼ 19-12 Main metering system
As the throttle moves toward the wide-open position, more air can pass through. Intake-manifold vacuum is reduced, and less air–fuel mixture flows through the idle and low-speed systems. However, the increased airflow creates a vacuum in the venturi so that the main nozzle begins to deliver fuel. Therefore, the main metering system (main nozzle) takes over as the throttle moves toward the open position (Fig. 19-12).

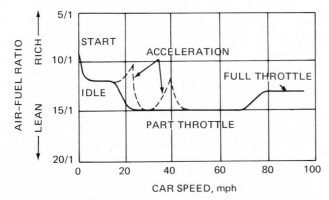

Fig. 19-8 Graph of air–fuel ratios for different car speeds. The graph is typical. Car speeds at which the various ratios are obtained may vary with different cars and engines. Also, there will be variations in the ratios.

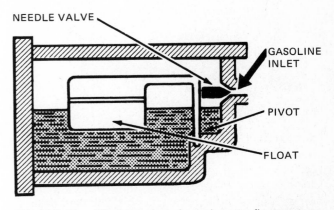

Fig. 19-9 Simplified drawing of a carburetor float system.

269

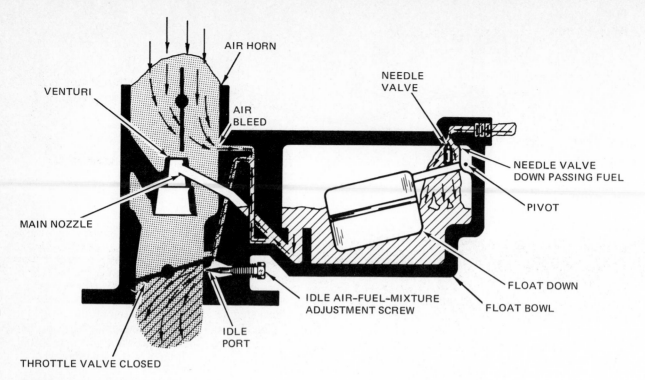

Fig. 19-10 Idle system in a carburetor. The throttle valve is closed so that only a small amount of air can get past it. All fuel is being fed past the idle adjustment screw. Arrows show the flow of air and fuel.

⚙ 19-13 Power system For high-speed, full-power, wide-open throttle operation, the air–fuel mixture must be enriched (see Fig. 19-8). Additional devices are built into the carburetor to take care of this.

One system includes a metering-rod jet (a calibrated orifice or hole) and a metering rod (Fig. 19-13). The metering rod has two or more steps of different diameters, or else it is tapered. The metering rod is attached to the throttle linkage (Fig. 19-14). When the throttle is partly closed, the metering rod is down. The larger diameter of the metering rod is centered in the metering-rod jet. This partly restricts the flow of fuel to the main nozzle. However, enough fuel does flow to provide the proper air–fuel ratio for part-throttle operation. When the throttle is opened further, the metering rod is lifted. Now, a smaller diameter of the rod is centered in the metering-rod jet. This is just the same as providing a larger hole. More fuel can flow. The main nozzle is, therefore, supplied with more fuel, and the resulting air–fuel mixture is richer.

Another power system is operated by intake-manifold vacuum. It has a vacuum piston or diaphragm linked to a valve or metering rod similar to the one shown in Fig. 19-13. One arrangement is shown in Fig. 19-15. During part-throttle operation, the piston is held down by intake-manifold vacuum. But when the throttle is opened wide, manifold vacuum is reduced. This allows the spring under the vacuum piston to push the

Fig. 19-11 Low-speed operation. The throttle valve is slightly open, and fuel is being fed through the low-speed port as well as through the idle port. The dark color is fuel; the light color is air.

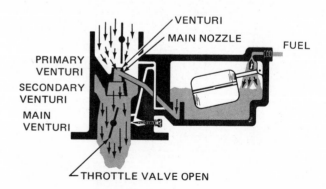

Fig. 19-12 Main metering system in a carburetor. The throttle is open, and fuel is being fed through the high-speed, or main, nozzle. The dark color is fuel; the light color is air.

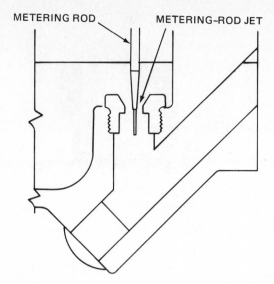

Fig. 19-13 Metering rod and metering-rod jet for better performance at full throttle.

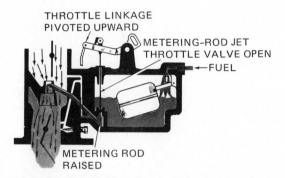

Fig. 19-14 Mechanically operated power system. When the throttle is open, as shown, the metering rod is raised so the smaller diameter of the rod clears the jet. This allows additional fuel to flow.

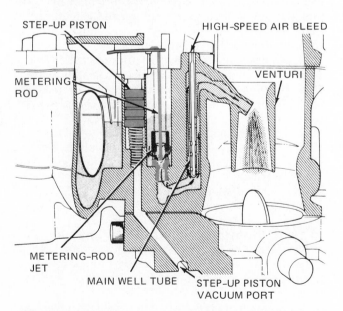

Fig. 19-15 Sectional view of a carburetor using a power or step-up piston, operated by intake-manifold vacuum, to control the position of the metering rod. *(Chrysler Corporation)*

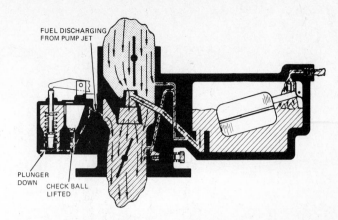

Fig. 19-16 Accelerator-pump system of type using a pump plunger. When the throttle is opened, the pump lever pushes the pump plunger down. This forces fuel to flow through the accelerator-pump system and out the jet.

piston up. The motion raises the metering rod so that a smaller diameter of the rod clears the jet. Now, more fuel can feed to the fuel nozzle, producing a richer mixture for full-power operation.

⚙ **19-14 Accelerator-pump system** For acceleration, the carburetor must deliver additional fuel (Fig. 19-8). Rapid opening of the throttle lets in a rush of air. This happens so fast that the fuel nozzle cannot instantly increase its fuel flow. Therefore, for a moment, the mixture is too lean to support combustion. Without some additional fuel, the engine would stumble and even stall.

The system that takes care of this is the accelerator-pump system (Fig. 19-16). It includes a pump plunger which is forced down by a pump lever that is linked to the throttle. When the throttle is opened, the pump lever pushes the plunger down. This pushes fuel through the accelerator-pump system and out the pump jet (Fig. 19-16). This fuel enters the air passing through the carburetor and provides the additional fuel needed for smooth acceleration.

⚙ **19-15 Choke system** When a cold engine is started, a very rich mixture is required. This is because

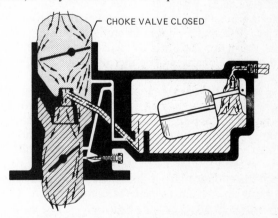

Fig. 19-17 With the choke closed, intake-manifold vacuum is introduced into the carburetor air horn. This causes the main nozzle to discharge fuel.

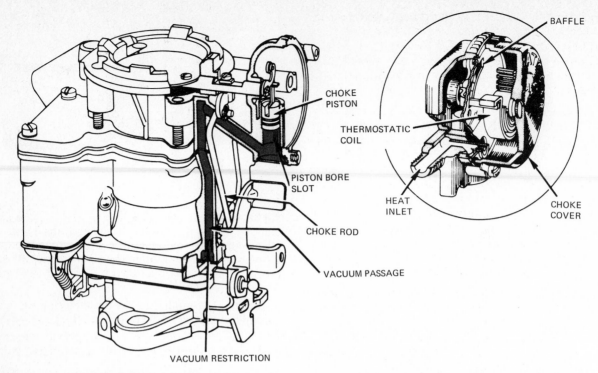

Fig. 19-18 Automatic choke system on a carburetor. *(America Motors Corporation)*

the gasoline does not vaporize very well, and so extra gasoline must be supplied to make sure enough does vaporize to get the engine started. The choke system causes this enrichment (Fig. 19-17). It includes a round valve, shaped like the throttle valve, located in the top of the air horn. It is controlled, in most engines, by an automatic device. When the choke is closed, it is almost horizontal and "chokes off" the airflow. Only a small amount of air can get through. This means that a high vacuum develops in the carburetor and intake manifold. The high vacuum causes the main nozzle to discharge a heavy stream of fuel. This mixes with the air passing through to produce the very rich mixture needed to start the cold engine.

Chokes are controlled by automatic devices in most vehicles. Figure 19-18 shows the automatic choke on a carburetor. It includes a thermostatic coil or spring and a vacuum piston, both linked to the choke valve. The thermostatic coil is made of two different metal strips. The metals have different expansion rates as they warm up. Thus, the coil will wind up or unwind as temperature changes. The thermostatic spring may be heated by an electric element, hot coolant, hot air (heated by the exhaust manifold), or a combination of these. When the engine is cold, the coil is wound up enough to close the choke valve. Therefore, a rich mixture is delivered to the engine. As the engine starts, a high vacuum develops in the intake manifold. This acts on the vacuum piston, tending to move it so as to open the choke valve. It does succeed to some extent, working against the thermostatic-coil tension. This allows enough air to get through so that the mixture is leaned out somewhat. This prevents the carburetor from delivering too rich a mixture. An excessively rich mixture could cause the engine to stall.

As the engine warms up, the thermostatic coil begins to unwind. This moves the choke toward the open position. A mixture not quite as rich is needed by the engine as it starts to warm up. By the time the engine has reached operating temperature, the thermostatic coil has unwound and has opened the choke wide. The choke has done its job. Figure 19-19 shows a carburetor partly cut away so you can see the construction of the choke.

Many engines use a vacuum-operated diaphragm instead of a piston. The diaphragm is airtight on one side, and that side is connected by a tube to the intake manifold. The diaphragm is linked to the choke and does the same job as the vacuum piston.

Many late-model cars have electric automatic chokes. This type of choke includes an electric heating element (Fig. 19-19). The purpose of the heater is to make the choke open fast. As we mentioned, the choking action produces a rich mixture. This rich mixture does not burn well (although it is necessary to start a cold engine). Poor combustion means high pollution (HC and CO) in the exhaust gases. Therefore, the quicker the choke valve can be made to open, the better—so long as the quick opening does not cause engine stall or stumble.

✿ 19-16 Electronic control of the air–fuel ratio With this review of carburetor action and carburetor systems, we are now ready to look into electronic control of the air–fuel ratio that the carburetor delivers.

We have noted previously that some late-model cars have electronic control of the spark advance (Chapter 16). These systems provide a more accurate delivery of the spark to the spark plugs so that the compressed air–fuel mixture is ignited at the exact right moment. The accuracy improves engine performance and reduces pollutants in the exhaust gases.

The electronic control of the air–fuel ratio has the same aim—to improve engine performance and reduce pollutants in the exhaust gas.

NOTE: Engine performance is usually considered in terms of drivability, that is, how well the car drives. An engine that tends to stall, hesitate, or stumble does not give good drivability. The term *drivability* is used to indicate how well an engine performs under various operating conditions. An engine that responds quickly when called upon to accelerate the car, starts easily, idles well, and runs smoothly at all speeds makes a car very "drivable." An engine that hesitates or stumbles when the accelerator pedal is pushed down, is hard to start, is logy or slow on acceleration, tends to miss, and is noisy has very poor drivability.

What these air–fuel-ratio-control systems do is monitor the exhaust gas in the exhaust manifold. If the exhaust gas is too low in oxygen, the air–fuel mixture going into the engine is too rich. If it is high in oxygen, the air–fuel mixture is lean. By continuous measurement of the oxygen content in the exhaust gases, the system determines whether the air–fuel ratio needs adjustment. If adjustment is needed, and the mixture is rich, for example (less oxygen in the exhaust gas), the system automatically reduces the amount of fuel entering the air going through the carburetor. This leans out the mixture. If the mixture becomes too lean (more oxygen in the exhaust gas), the electronic system al-

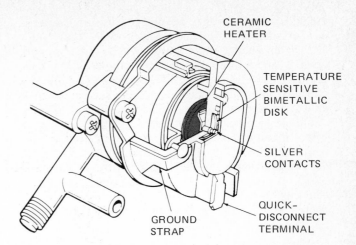

Fig. 19-19 Cutaway view of an electric-assist choke. At low temperature, the ceramic heater turns on, adding heat to the choke so it opens more quickly. *(Ford Motor Company)*

lows more fuel to flow, and so the mixture is enriched. What the system does, then, is to provide the engine with the best mixture ratio for every operating condition.

We now discuss two systems that control air–fuel ratios electronically, the General Motors Electronic Fuel Control System and the Ford Feedback-Carburetor Electronic Engine Control System.

⚙ 19-17 General Motors Electronic Fuel Control (EFC) System This system is shown in Fig. 19-20. It

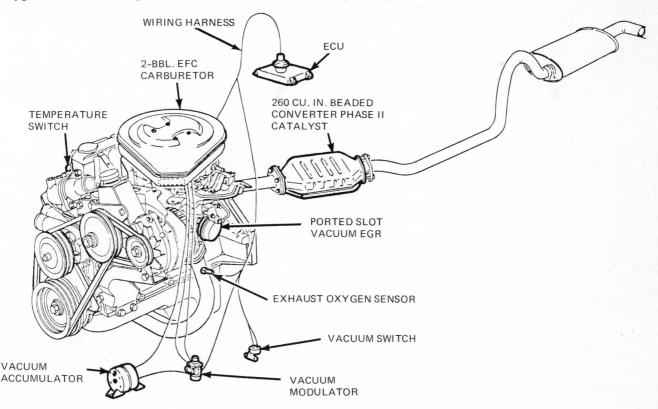

Fig. 19-20 Electronic fuel control (EFC) system. *(Pontiac Motor Division of General Motors Corporation)*

includes an exhaust-gas oxygen sensor (or "sniffer," as it is sometimes called), an electronic control unit (ECU), an engine temperature switch, three vacuum devices, and a three-way catalytic converter that handles NO$_x$ as well as CO and HC. The catalytic converter changes these pollutants into harmless substances such as water, carbon dioxide, free nitrogen, and oxygen.

The oxygen sensor is installed in the exhaust pipe where it can sample exhaust gas flowing from the exhaust manifold (Fig. 19-21). The sensor generates a voltage that varies as the oxygen in the exhaust gas varies. As the oxygen content increases, indicating a lean mixture, the voltage falls. As the oxygen content decreases, indicating a richer mixture, the voltage goes up. The sensor sends this varying voltage signal to the ECU.

NOTE: The oxygen sensor gradually loses its ability to "sniff" oxygen. For this reason, it should be replaced every 15,000 miles. Many cars have a sensor-replacement reminder on the instrument panel that reminds the driver when the sensor should be replaced.

The ECU produces a cycling (off-on) current signal that is controlled by the voltage signal from the oxygen sensor. When the voltage signal is high, the current "on" time is greater than the "off" time. The average current is higher. When the voltage signal is low, the average current is low. This cycling current signal goes to the vacuum modulator. Figure 19-22 shows the location of the vacuum modulator in one model car. The

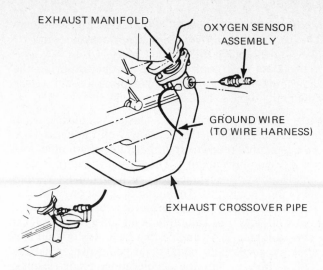

Fig. 19-21 Location of oxygen sensor. *(Pontiac Motor Division of General Motors Corporation)*

vacuum modulator is connected to a vacuum accumulator which serves as a high-vacuum source. The accumulator gets this high vacuum from the intake manifold.

The vacuum modulator sends a portion of this high vacuum to the carburetor control. The carburetor control then adjusts the air–fuel ratio. If the voltage signal from the oxygen sensor is high, indicating a rich mixture, the carburetor control leans out the mixture. If the oxygen-sensor voltage is low, indicating a lean mix-

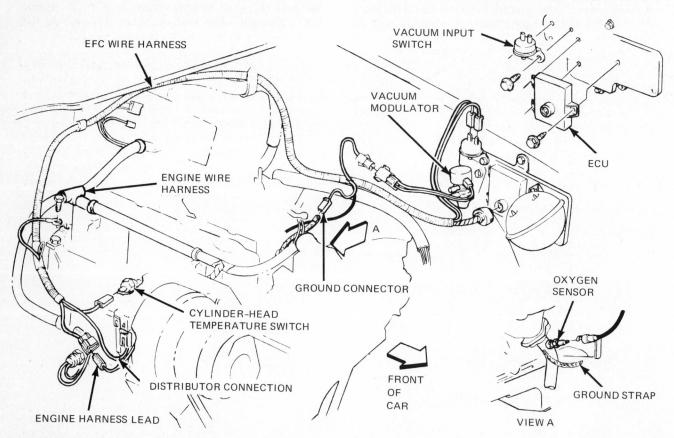

Fig. 19-22 Wiring system for an electronic fuel control (EFC) system. *(Pontiac Motor Division of General Motors Corporation)*

ture, the carburetor control allows more fuel to flow so the mixture is enriched. Before we discuss the carburetor control, let us take a further look at the vacuum modulator.

The vacuum modulator has a solenoid valve which cycles on and off. When the ECU signal is ON, current flows and the valve is open, passing vacuum. When the ECU signal is OFF, the valve closes, preventing any vacuum from passing. When the signal is on more than it is off, more vacuum passes through.

Let us review the action. When the oxygen content in the exhaust gas is low, indicating a rich mixture, the voltage signal from the oxygen sensor is high. This causes the ECU to send a high average current (on more than off) to the vacuum modulator. The modulator, therefore, passes more vacuum. This increased vacuum operates the carburetor control so that the air–fuel mixture is leaned out.

⚙ 19-18 Carburetor control

The carburetor control in the General Motors EFC system has two feedback diaphragms. One diaphragm controls the idle system, the other the main metering system (Figs. 19-23 and 19-24).

The idle system diaphragm (Fig. 19-23) operates an idle needle in the carburetor which allows more or less air to bleed into the idle system. If the vacuum coming from the vacuum modulator is high enough, it causes the diaphragm to pull the needle back. This allows more air to bleed into the idle system so the idle mixture is leaned out.

The main-metering-system diaphragm (Fig. 19-24) operates a tapered needle which is centered in the main metering orifice. If the vacuum coming from the vacuum modulator is high enough, the diaphragm will lift the needle. This reduces the amount of fuel that can flow to the main metering system. The mixture being delivered by the main metering system is leaned out.

In operation, then, when the mixture is rich, the oxygen content in the exhaust gas is low. The oxygen-sensor voltage, therefore, is high. The average current from the ECU is also high. This keeps the vacuum-modulator solenoid valve open a greater part of the

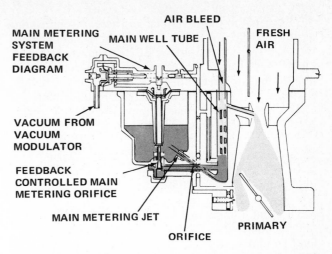

Fig. 19-24 Sectional view of the carburetor for the EFC system, showing the main metering system with feedback diaphragm. *(Pontiac Motor Division of General Motors Corporation)*

time. More vacuum passes to the feedback diaphragms. If the engine is idling, the idling mixture is leaned out. If the engine is operating at higher speed, the main-metering-system mixture is leaned out. Result—the mixture is leaned out, the oxygen content increases, and the oxygen sensor voltage drops.

When the mixture leans out too much, the oxygen content increases. The oxygen sensor voltage drops off. The average current from the ECU also drops off. The vacuum modulator passes less vacuum. Less vacuum gets to the feedback diaphragms. The idle and main-metering-system mixtures are enriched.

⚙ 19-19 Control during unstable engine operating conditions

During engine warm-up, the engine's requirements are different. That is, it requires a rich mixture, and any variation from this enrichment may upset engine operation, causing stumble or even stall. A cylinder-head temperature switch is, therefore, used. This switch is mounted on the cylinder head (left, Fig. 19-22) and senses engine temperature. When the coolant temperature is low, the switch is closed. This sup-

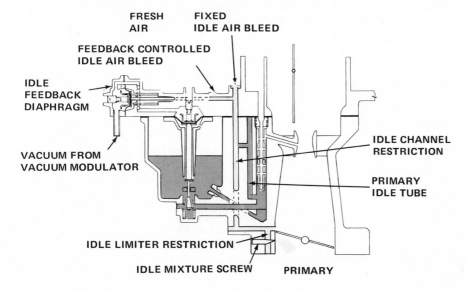

Fig. 19-23 Sectional view of the carburetor for the EFC system, showing the idle system and idle feedback diaphragm. *(Pontiac Motor Division of General Motors Corporation)*

275

plies a signal to the ECU that restricts it from leaning out the mixture too much. That is, this signal modifies the average current from the ECU to the vacuum modulator. The vacuum modulator, therefore, reduces vacuum to the carburetor feedback diaphragms. The mixture stays enriched. When the engine reaches operating temperature, the engine temperature switch opens. Now, the ECU operates in the hot-engine mode.

⚙ **19-20 Control during full throttle** During full-throttle, high-load conditions, the intake-manifold vacuum is low. If the mixture is too lean, the amount of NO_x in the exhaust goes up. To prevent this, the system has a vacuum-input switch which senses intake-manifold vacuum. When the vacuum drops down to the full-load condition, the vacuum-input switch closes contacts. This provides a signal to the ECU. The ECU, therefore, reduces its average current flow to the vacuum modulator. The modulator reduces the vacuum to the feedback diaphragms in the carburetor. This prevents the air–fuel mixture from leaning out too much.

⚙ **19-21 Self-diagnosing capability** The 1980 version of the General Motors electronic fuel control (EFC) system has an added feature. It possesses the ability to analyze itself and report where a fault lies if the system malfunctions. When the system is triggered, a two-digit fault-code number is flashed on a dashboard readout. The technician then checks this code number against the code reference to determine exactly where the trouble lies, if it is in the system.

⚙ **19-22 Ford Feedback-Carburetor Electronic-Engine-Control (FCEEC) System** The Ford system for air–fuel-mixture control is somewhat more complex than the General Motors EFC system. It is tied in with the thermactor or air-injection system and the catalytic converter. We have discussed the thermactor or air-injection system (⚙ 16-12). Recall that the air-injection system blows fresh air into the exhaust manifold to help burn any unburned gasoline (HC) or partly burned gasoline (CO).

The system consists of three subsystems:

1. Dual catalytic converter
2. Thermactor air control
3. Electronic feedback carburetor

The electronic feedback carburetor is very similar to the General Motors unit (Figs. 19-23 and 19-24). However, it has only one feedback diaphragm, and this controls the main metering system (Fig. 19-25). The system uses a similar oxygen sensor (sniffer) in the exhaust manifold. When the oxygen content of the exhaust gas goes down, indicating a rich mixture, the sensor reports this to the ECU. The ECU then signals the vacuum switch system to send more vacuum to the feedback diaphragm. The diaphragm then lifts the metering rod to restrict the flow of fuel. Less fuel gets to the main fuel nozzle, and so the mixture is leaned out.

The thermactor system has two operating modes (Figs. 19-26 and 19-27). When the engine is cold (Fig.

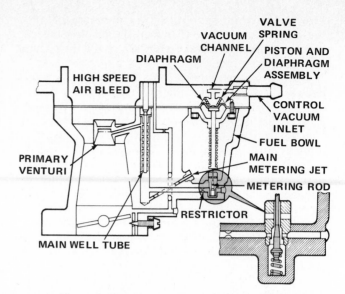

Fig. 19-25 Sectional view of the feedback carburetor for an electronic engine control system with diaphragm control of the main metering system. *(Ford Motor Company)*

19-26), the fuel system is feeding a rich mixture to the engine. This is due to the choke action, as explained earlier (⚙ 19-15). The exhaust gas is, therefore, rich in unburned and partly burned fuel (HC and CO). With these conditions, the thermactor sends air into the exhaust manifold to help complete the combustion of these pollutants. The additional oxygen in the air helps turn the HC into H_2O and CO_2. It helps turn the CO into CO_2. In doing this, it guards the catalytic converter from overload. That is, excessive amounts of these pollutants going into the converter can cause it to overheat. Overheating might ruin it.

When the engine warms up (Fig. 19-27), the vacuum switch, which senses engine coolant temperature, shuts off the vacuum to the air-control valve. As a result, the thermactor system now starts sending the air it pumps to the catalytic converter. Here, it aids the converter in changing the pollutants into harmless gases, as we mentioned in ⚙ 19-17.

Servicing carbureted fuel-system electronic controls

We now look at the diagnostic and servicing procedures recommended for the General Motors EFC system and the Ford FCEEC system. Here, we consider the electric and vacuum part of the complete control system.

⚙ **19-23 Servicing the General Motors EFC system** Listed below are engine troubles that might be caused by some malfunctions in the EFC system. However, there are many other conditions in the engine, fuel, or ignition system that could cause these troubles.

1. Detonation
2. Stalls or idles roughly (engine cold)
3. Stalls or idles roughly (engine hot)
4. Engine misses
5. Engine hesitates or stumbles
6. Engine surges or rolls

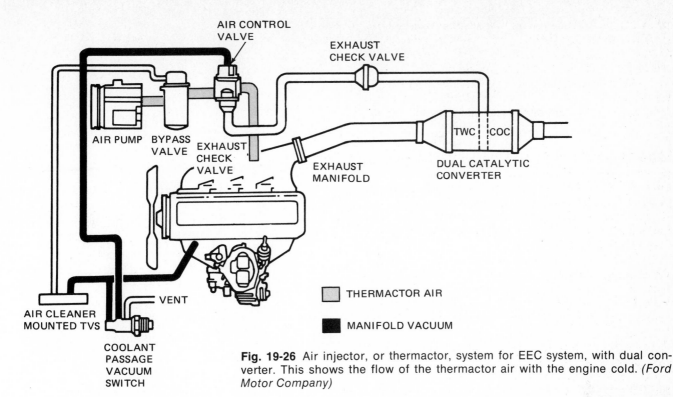

Fig. 19-26 Air injector, or thermactor, system for EEC system, with dual converter. This shows the flow of the thermactor air with the engine cold. *(Ford Motor Company)*

7. Engine sluggish or spongy—slow to respond
8. Poor gasoline mileage
9. Hard starting (engine cold)
10. Hard starting (engine hot)
11. Exhaust odor
12. Engine cuts out

The diagnosis chart (Fig. 19-28) outlines how to check out the system. With Figs. 19-29 and 19-30, this covers the complete procedure, including the ECU wiring harness continuity check (Fig. 19-30).

CAUTION: When electrical tests are being made, use extreme care to avoid short-circuiting the battery hot

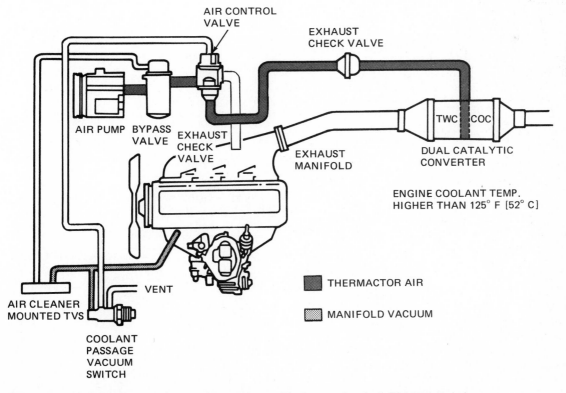

Fig. 19-27 Air injection, or thermactor, system with the engine hot. Thermactor air flows to the dual catalytic converter. *(Ford Motor Company)*

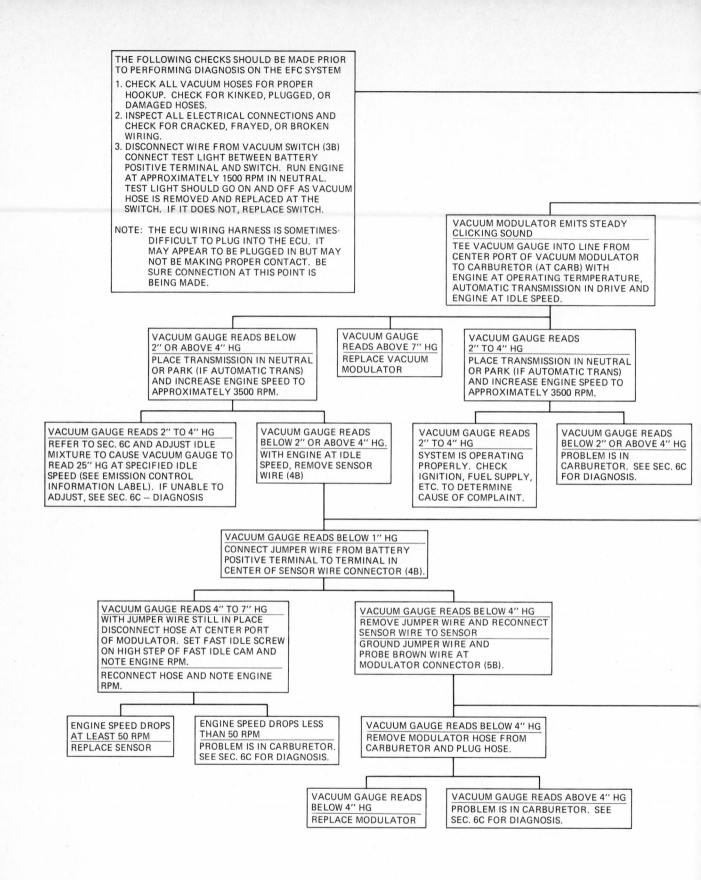

THE FOLLOWING CHECKS SHOULD BE MADE PRIOR
TO PERFORMING DIAGNOSIS ON THE EFC SYSTEM

1. CHECK ALL VACUUM HOSES FOR PROPER
   HOOKUP. CHECK FOR KINKED, PLUGGED, OR
   DAMAGED HOSES.
2. INSPECT ALL ELECTRICAL CONNECTIONS AND
   CHECK FOR CRACKED, FRAYED, OR BROKEN
   WIRING.
3. DISCONNECT WIRE FROM VACUUM SWITCH (3B)
   CONNECT TEST LIGHT BETWEEN BATTERY
   POSITIVE TERMINAL AND SWITCH. RUN ENGINE
   AT APPROXIMATELY 1500 RPM IN NEUTRAL.
   TEST LIGHT SHOULD GO ON AND OFF AS VACUUM
   HOSE IS REMOVED AND REPLACED AT THE
   SWITCH. IF IT DOES NOT, REPLACE SWITCH.

NOTE: THE ECU WIRING HARNESS IS SOMETIMES·
   DIFFICULT TO PLUG INTO THE ECU. IT
   MAY APPEAR TO BE PLUGGED IN BUT MAY
   NOT BE MAKING PROPER CONTACT. BE
   SURE CONNECTION AT THIS POINT IS
   BEING MADE.

VACUUM MODULATOR EMITS STEADY
CLICKING SOUND
TEE VACUUM GAUGE INTO LINE FROM
CENTER PORT OF VACUUM MODULATOR
TO CARBURETOR (AT CARB) WITH
ENGINE AT OPERATING TERMPERATURE,
AUTOMATIC TRANSMISSION IN DRIVE AND
ENGINE AT IDLE SPEED.

VACUUM GAUGE READS BELOW
2" OR ABOVE 4" HG
PLACE TRANSMISSION IN NEUTRAL
OR PARK (IF AUTOMATIC TRANS)
AND INCREASE ENGINE SPEED TO
APPROXIMATELY 3500 RPM.

VACUUM GAUGE
READS ABOVE 7" HG
REPLACE VACUUM
MODULATOR

VACUUM GAUGE READS
2" TO 4" HG
PLACE TRANSMISSION IN NEUTRAL
OR PARK (IF AUTOMATIC TRANS)
AND INCREASE ENGINE SPEED TO
APPROXIMATELY 3500 RPM.

VACUUM GAUGE READS 2" TO 4" HG
REFER TO SEC. 6C AND ADJUST IDLE
MIXTURE TO CAUSE VACUUM GAUGE TO
READ 25" HG AT SPECIFIED IDLE
SPEED (SEE EMISSION CONTROL
INFORMATION LABEL). IF UNABLE TO
ADJUST, SEE SEC. 6C – DIAGNOSIS

VACUUM GAUGE READS
BELOW 2" OR ABOVE 4" HG.
WITH ENGINE AT IDLE
SPEED, REMOVE SENSOR
WIRE (4B)

VACUUM GAUGE READS
2" TO 4" HG
SYSTEM IS OPERATING
PROPERLY. CHECK
IGNITION, FUEL SUPPLY,
ETC. TO DETERMINE
CAUSE OF COMPLAINT.

VACUUM GAUGE READS
BELOW 2" OR ABOVE 4" HG
PROBLEM IS IN
CARBURETOR. SEE SEC. 6C
FOR DIAGNOSIS.

VACUUM GAUGE READS BELOW 1" HG
CONNECT JUMPER WIRE FROM BATTERY
POSITIVE TERMINAL TO TERMINAL IN
CENTER OF SENSOR WIRE CONNECTOR (4B).

VACUUM GAUGE READS 4" TO 7" HG
WITH JUMPER WIRE STILL IN PLACE
DISCONNECT HOSE AT CENTER PORT
OF MODULATOR. SET FAST IDLE SCREW
ON HIGH STEP OF FAST IDLE CAM AND
NOTE ENGINE RPM.
RECONNECT HOSE AND NOTE ENGINE
RPM.

VACUUM GAUGE READS BELOW 4" HG
REMOVE JUMPER WIRE AND RECONNECT
SENSOR WIRE TO SENSOR
GROUND JUMPER WIRE AND
PROBE BROWN WIRE AT
MODULATOR CONNECTOR (5B).

ENGINE SPEED DROPS
AT LEAST 50 RPM
REPLACE SENSOR

ENGINE SPEED DROPS LESS
THAN 50 RPM
PROBLEM IS IN CARBURETOR.
SEE SEC. 6C FOR DIAGNOSIS.

VACUUM GAUGE READS BELOW 4" HG
REMOVE MODULATOR HOSE FROM
CARBURETOR AND PLUG HOSE.

VACUUM GAUGE READS
BELOW 4" HG
REPLACE MODULATOR

VACUUM GAUGE READS ABOVE 4" HG
PROBLEM IS IN CARBURETOR. SEE
SEC. 6C FOR DIAGNOSIS.

Fig. 19-28 EFC diagnosis chart. The references to Sec.
6C in the chart are to the manufacturer's shop manual.
(Pontiac Motor Division of General Motors Corporation)

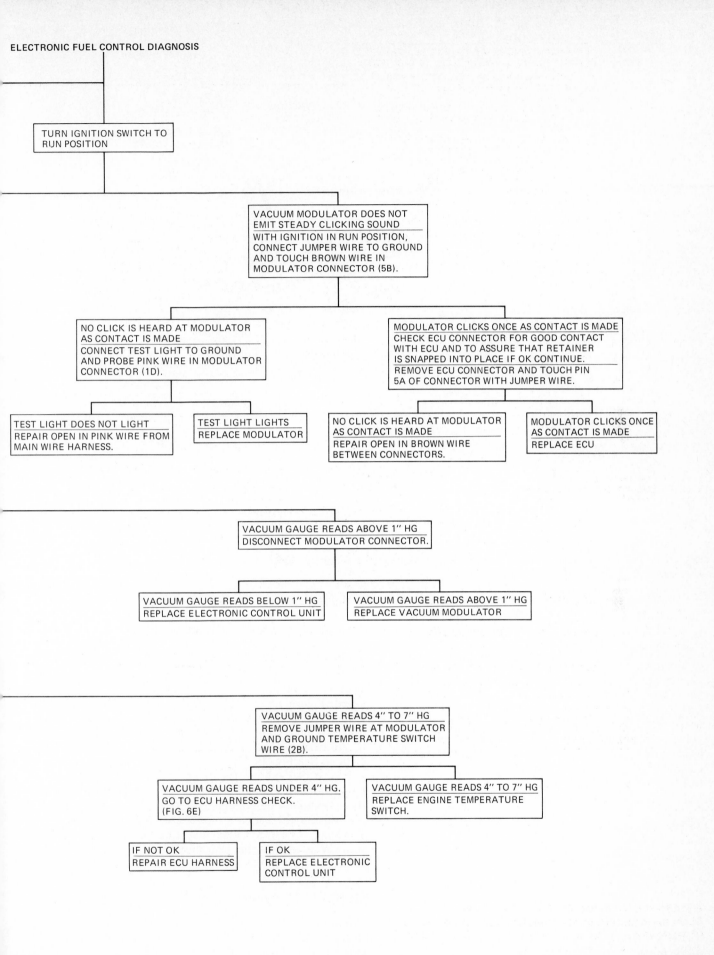

TURN IGNITION SWITCH TO
RUN POSITION

VACUUM MODULATOR DOES NOT
EMIT STEADY CLICKING SOUND
WITH IGNITION IN RUN POSITION,
CONNECT JUMPER WIRE TO GROUND
AND TOUCH BROWN WIRE IN
MODULATOR CONNECTOR (5B).

NO CLICK IS HEARD AT MODULATOR
AS CONTACT IS MADE
CONNECT TEST LIGHT TO GROUND
AND PROBE PINK WIRE IN MODULATOR
CONNECTOR (1D).

MODULATOR CLICKS ONCE AS CONTACT IS MADE
CHECK ECU CONNECTOR FOR GOOD CONTACT
WITH ECU AND TO ASSURE THAT RETAINER
IS SNAPPED INTO PLACE IF OK CONTINUE.
REMOVE ECU CONNECTOR AND TOUCH PIN
5A OF CONNECTOR WITH JUMPER WIRE.

TEST LIGHT DOES NOT LIGHT
REPAIR OPEN IN PINK WIRE FROM
MAIN WIRE HARNESS.

TEST LIGHT LIGHTS
REPLACE MODULATOR

NO CLICK IS HEARD AT MODULATOR
AS CONTACT IS MADE
REPAIR OPEN IN BROWN WIRE
BETWEEN CONNECTORS.

MODULATOR CLICKS ONCE
AS CONTACT IS MADE
REPLACE ECU

VACUUM GAUGE READS ABOVE 1" HG
DISCONNECT MODULATOR CONNECTOR.

VACUUM GAUGE READS BELOW 1" HG
REPLACE ELECTRONIC CONTROL UNIT

VACUUM GAUGE READS ABOVE 1" HG
REPLACE VACUUM MODULATOR

VACUUM GAUGE READS 4" TO 7" HG
REMOVE JUMPER WIRE AT MODULATOR
AND GROUND TEMPERATURE SWITCH
WIRE (2B).

VACUUM GAUGE READS UNDER 4" HG.
GO TO ECU HARNESS CHECK.
(FIG. 6E)

VACUUM GAUGE READS 4" TO 7" HG
REPLACE ENGINE TEMPERATURE
SWITCH.

IF NOT OK
REPAIR ECU HARNESS

IF OK
REPLACE ELECTRONIC
CONTROL UNIT

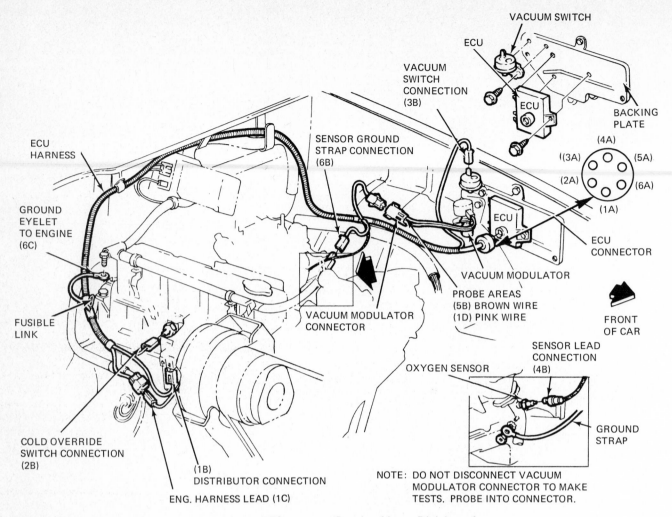

Fig. 19-29 Electric system and wiring for the EFC system. *(Pontiac Motor Division of General Motors Corporation)*

cable and terminal. A short circuit will allow a very high current to flow which will not only damage the system but could also give you severe burns and even eye damage from sparks.

Replacing any defective unit in the system is usually simple and straightforward. One that might cause you trouble is the oxygen sensor. It may be difficult to remove this unit if the engine is cold. You will find it easier if the engine is warmed up. Spray some heat-valve lubricant or similar lubricant on the threads and allow it to soak for a while. When installing the sensor, coat the threads with antiseize compound and tighten to 18 lb·ft [24 N·m].

⚙ **19-24 Servicing the Ford FCEEC system** To service this system, Ford recommends the following equipment:

1. Digital volt-ohm meter, Ford no. T78L-50-DVOM
2. Tester T78L-50-FBC-1
3. Snap-On vacuum gauge MT-14F or equivalent
4. Vacuum tester model 21-0014 or equivalent
5. Tachometer
6. Speed-control tool Snap-On GA-437 or equivalent

Before starting the tests, look over the system, hoses, electric wiring, and components to make sure everything is in order. Leaky, broken, cracked, or pinched vacuum lines will cause trouble. Likewise, damaged wiring or electric connections can give trouble. Refer to Fig. 19-31 which shows a complete system with all vacuum and air lines and electric wiring indicated. Figure 19-32 shows the system with the testers connected. Before making any electric connections, make sure the ignition switch is off. Note that the hose length between the vacuum gauge and the test setup is critical. See Fig. 19-32.

Figure 19-33 shows the diagnostic chart for the system. To make a complete test of the system, including the individual components, refer to the shop manual that covers the specific model and year car you are servicing. These systems may change from year to year. What applies this year might have to be modified for next year's model.

Chapter 19 review questions

Select the *one* correct, best, or most probable answer to each question. Then check your answers against the correct answers given at the end of the book.

ECU WIRE HARNESS CONTINUITY CHECK

1. ENGINE AT NORMAL OPERATING TEMPERATURE.
2. KEY IN "ON" POSITION.
3. ENGINE NOT RUNNING.
4. REMOVE MAIN WIRE HARNESS AT ECU AND TEST AS FOLLOWS.

TEST LIGHT CLIP LEAD	PROBE	RESULT	ACTION
GROUND	1A	LIGHTS	OK
		NO LIGHT	CHECK WIRING, CONNECTIONS FUSIBLE LINK, ETC. REPAIR
POSITIVE BATTERY TERMINAL	2A	LIGHTS	OK
		NO LIGHT	UNPLUG CONNECTOR WIRE AT COLD OVERRIDE SWITCH AND GROUND CONNECTOR WIRE. LIGHTS—WIRE OK, REPLACE SWITCH. NO LIGHT—WIRING PROBLEM, REPAIR.
POSITIVE BATTERY TERMINAL	3A	LIGHTS	OK
		NO LIGHT	UNPLUG WIRE CONNECTOR AT VACUUM SWITCH AND GROUND CONNECTOR WIRE. LIGHT—WIRE OK, REPLACE SWITCH. NO LIGHT—WIRING PROBLEM, REPAIR.
CAUTION: BEFORE CHECKING TEST POINT 4A, REMOVE WIRE CONNECTOR AT 02 SENSOR AND GROUND THE WIRE CONNECTOR. APPLYING 12 VOLTS TO THE SENSOR MAY DAMAGE THE SENSOR.			
POSITIVE BATTERY TERMINAL	4A	LIGHTS	OK
		NO LIGHT	CHECK WIRING, REPAIR.
GROUND	5A	LIGHTS	OK
		NO LIGHT	1. IF 1A WAS OK, WIRING PROBLEM OP DEFECTIVE VACUUM MODULATOR. 2. IF 1A WAS NOT OK, CORRECT 1A PROBLEM AND THEN RECHECK 5A.
POSITIVE BATTERY TERMINAL	6A	LIGHTS	OK
		NO LIGHT	CHECK WIRING, GROUND EYELET AT ENGINE BLOCK, REPAIR.

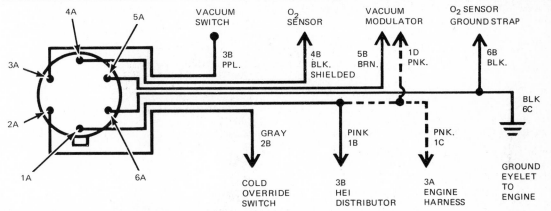

Fig. 19-30 Schematic layout of the EFC wiring system and the procedure for checking out the ECU continuity. *(Pontiac Motor Division of General Motors Corporation)*

1. For highway cruising, an air–fuel ratio of 12:1 is:
   a. rich,
   b. about right,
   c. lean,
   d. very lean.
2. Three pollutants in exhaust gas are:
   a. HC, CC, and CO,
   b. CO, NO_x, and HC,
   c. H_2O, CO_2, and NO_x,
   d. H_2, H_2O, and NO_x.
3. To achieve as nearly ideal combustion as possible, the electronic air–fuel-ratio control system continuously adjusts:
   a. the air–fuel ratio,
   b. the spark advance,
   c. both,
   d. neither.

4. The maximum vacuum in the carburetor is:
   a. in the float bowl,
   b. at the throttle valve,
   c. in the manifold,
   d. in the venturi.
5. The General Motors EFC system controls the:
   a. idle system,
   b. main metering system,
   c. both,
   d. neither.
6. The EFC system uses an oxygen sensor to sense the amount of oxygen in the:
   a. air–fuel mixture,
   b. exhaust gas,
   c. combustion chambers,
   d. intake manifold.

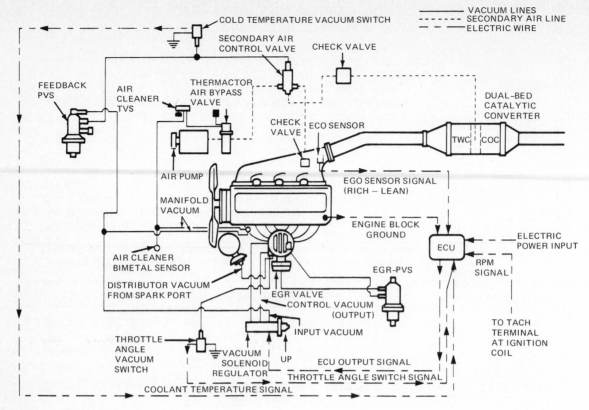

Fig. 19-31 Ford EEC system. *(Ford Motor Company)*

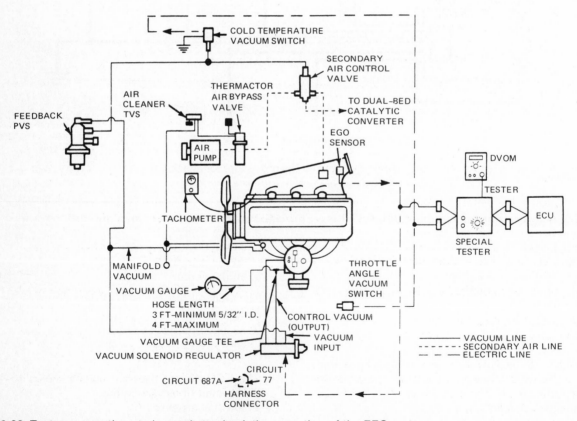

Fig. 19-32 Tester connections to be made to check the operation of the EEC system. Note that the tester has been connected between the ECU and the rest of the system. *(Ford Motor Company)*

Test sequence	Vehicle condition	No. 1 vehicle battery voltage	No. 2 Cold temperature switch and throttle angle switch	EGO sensor indicator	Vacuum regulator light	Feedback vacuum control
I Step V.D.1	1. Front wheels blocked 2. Parking brake ON 3. Engine Hot in neutral 4. rpm = 2200–2800	Limits 11.5–18.0	Limits 11.5–18.0	Limits Alternating between lean and rich	Limits "Blinking"	Limits See performance specifications book
II Step V.D.2	1. Remove the carburetor feedback vacuum control line from TEE and immediately cover the TEE opening. 2. rpm = 2200–2800				Limits From "Blinking" to ON in ** seconds or less	Limits See performance specifications book
III Step V.D.3	1. Replace carburetor feedback vacuum control line. rpm = 2200–2800 2. Apply 5 inches vacuum to cold temperature switch	Limits Condition 2: 0.3 (V) max			Limits Condition 2: Blinking	Limits See performance specifications book
	3. While covering carburetor idle air bleed hole, remove vacuum from cold temperature switch.	Condition 3: 11.5 (V) min			Condition 3: ON	
	4. Uncover idle air bleed hole.	Condition 4: 11.5 (V) min			Condition 4: Blinking	
	5. Return to curb idle	Condition 5: 0.3 (V) max				
		If out of limits, stop sequence and proceed to V.I.A	If out of limits* See VI-B	If out of limits* See VI-C	If out of limits* See VI-D	If out of limits* See VI-E

*Complete all data gathering per test sequences I, II, and III prior to performing any diagnostic subroutines, except as noted.
**See performance specifications book.

Fig. 19-33. Test sequence and the meaning of various results of the tests. (*Ford Motor Company*)

7. As the oxygen content in the exhaust gas increases, it indicates:
   a. an increasingly lean mixture,
   b. an increasingly rich mixture,
   c. loss of power,
   d. increasing power.
8. In the General Motors EFC system, the vacuum modulator sends varying amounts of vacuum to:
   a. a feedback diaphragm,
   b. two feedback diaphragms,
   c. the temperature control,
   d. the ECU.
9. The cylinder-head temperature switch in the General Motors EFC system signals the ECU to maintain a richer mixture when:
   a. engine speed increases,
   b. the engine is cold,
   c. the engine is warmed up,
   d. the engine is idling.
10. The Ford FCEEC system controls the air–fuel mixture richness and also the:
   a. catalytic converter,
   b. carburetor,
   c. engine idle,
   d. thermactor system.

ELECTRONIC FUEL INJECTION

After studying this chapter, you should be able to:

1. Explain how electronic fuel-injection systems work.
2. Describe the components in an electronic fuel-injection system and explain how each works.
3. Under the supervision of the instructor, and with the proper testing equipment and tools, check out an electronic fuel-injection system.

20-1 Electronically controlled fuel systems As we mentioned at the beginning of the previous chapter, electronics is helping fuel systems do a better and more accurate job. That is, electronics increases the accuracy with which the fuel system operates. The fuel system supplies a more exact air–fuel ratio to meet the operating conditions, thus improving gasoline mileage and reducing pollutants from the exhaust system. The previous chapter covered electronically controlled carbureted fuel systems. This chapter looks into electronically controlled fuel-injection systems. Recall, from 19-2, that the gasoline fuel-injection system (Fig. 19-3) injects, or sprays, fuel into the intake manifold at the intake-valve ports. When an intake valve opens, a charge of air–fuel mixture is waiting for it. The downward movement of the piston after the intake valve opens produces a vacuum. Atmospheric pressure then pushes the charge of air–fuel mixture into the cylinder.

20-2 Fuel injection In the fuel-injection system, the carburetor is replaced by a throttle body which has only one job. That job is to control the amount of air flowing into the intake manifold. The manifold has a series of fuel injectors assembled into it, one per cylinder. The injector is a spraying device that, at the proper moment, sprays a metered amount of gasoline into the intake manifold, opposite the intake valve (Fig. 20-1). When the intake valve opens, this atomized gasoline and air enters the cylinder. This type of fuel injection is called *indirect injection* because the fuel is sprayed into the intake manifold instead of into the cylinder.

This system is called a *pulsed*, or *timed, injection system*. That is, the instant for the injection to occur, and the length of time that injection continues, are determined by an electronic control. Injection starts at some specific instant prior to the opening of the intake valve.

Another and simpler fuel-injection system does not use the pulsed or timed injection process. Instead, the fuel injectors spray continuously, varying the amount of fuel sprayed to suit operating conditions.

The basic difference between the carbureted system and the fuel-injection system is the point at which the gasoline enters the air going to the cylinders. In the carburetor, the gasoline enters the air passing through the carburetor. In the fuel-injection system, the gasoline is sprayed into the air after it enters the intake manifold. The key point we emphasize here is that

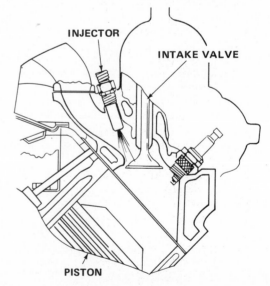

Fig. 20-1 Simplified view showing the method of injecting fuel into the intake manifold just back of the intake valve.

some versions of the two systems use electronics extensively to get better control of the amount of fuel entering the air and the engine cylinders.

On some 1980 cars with V-8 engines, the point of injection has been located in the carburetor throttle body. The system uses a two-barrel throttle body. Each barrel has an injection valve. The system is similar to that described above except for the point of injection. That is, it is a pulsed, or timed, injection system. The amount of fuel injected is determined by how long the valves are held open. Each injection valve feeds four of the cylinders in the eight-cylinder engine.

NOTE: A different kind of fuel-injection system is used in diesel engines. This system sprays the fuel directly into the combustion chambers (Fig. 20-2) and is called *direct injection*. There, the heat of compression ignites the fuel. As you compress air, it becomes hot. In the diesel engine, the air is compressed so much that its temperature goes up to 1000°F [537.8°C] or more. This high temperature ignites the fuel. The diesel engine, therefore, needs no ignition system as is required on gasoline engines.

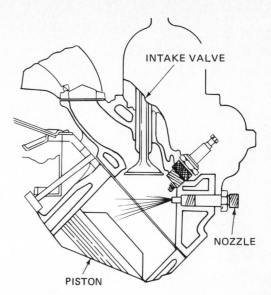

Fig. 20-2 Simplified view showing the method of injecting fuel directly into the combustion chamber of an engine.

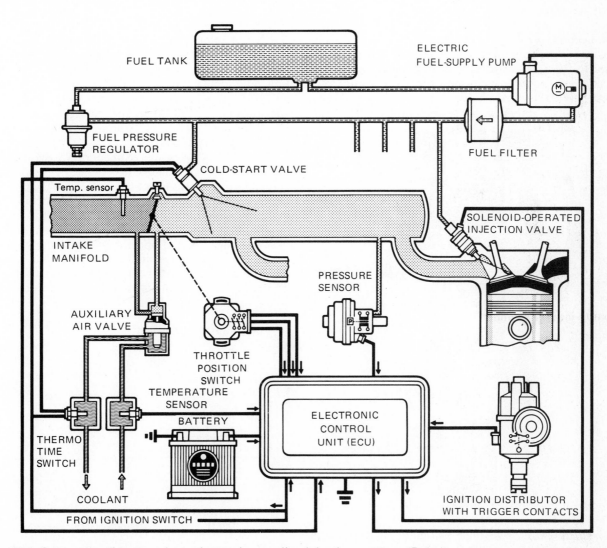

Fig. 20-3 Schematic diagram of an electronic gasoline-injection system. *(Robert Bosch GmbH)*

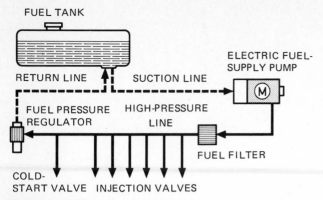

Fig. 20-4 Schematic diagram of the fuel supply. *(Robert Bosch GmbH)*

⚙ **20-3 Electronic fuel injection** Now let us look at an electronic fuel-injection system for gasoline engines (Fig. 20-3). The electronic fuel-supply pump maintains a high pressure in the fuel line to the solenoid injection valves in the intake manifold (Fig. 20-4). At the proper instant, trigger contact points in the ignition distributor close. Figure 20-5 shows the distributor, cut away so that the trigger contacts and cam can be seen. This cam is very different from the cam that opens and closes the ignition contact points.

When the trigger contacts close, they send an electric signal to the ECU. The ECU then connects half the solenoid injection valves to the battery. In a four-cylinder engine, this would be two valves. In a six, three

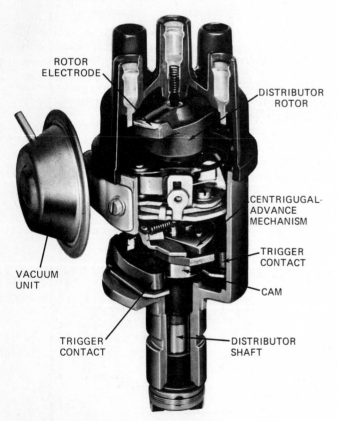

Fig. 20-5 Cutaway view of the distributor, showing the trigger contacts which activate the electronic control. *(Robert Bosch GmbH)*

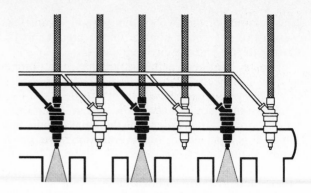

Fig. 20-6 Injection valve grouping. *(Robert Bosch GmbH)*

valves. In an eight, four valves. Note that half of the solenoid valves are activated at a time. Figure 20-6 shows three of the valves of a six-cylinder engine in operation, spraying fuel into the intake manifold.

The fuel enters just opposite the intake valves, as shown in Fig. 20-3. Figure 20-7 is the injection timing chart for a six-cylinder engine. Note that the individual intake valves open at varying times (crankshaft degrees) after injection. For example, look at the top line, which is for the No. 1 cylinder. Injection takes place at 300° of crankshaft rotation. Almost 60° later (near 360°), the No. 1 intake valve opens and the intake stroke starts. Cylinder No. 5 is next in the firing order. Its intake valve opens near 480°, or about 180° after injection. The intake valve for No. 3 cylinder opens about 300° of crankshaft rotation after injection. During these varying intervals between fuel injection and intake-valve opening, the fuel is "stored" in the intake ports, opposite the intake valves.

Having only two groups of injection valves simplifies the system. No appreciable loss of engine performance results from this storage of the fuel. Also, the timing of injection in these indirect systems is not critical. Remember, the whole action takes place in a small fraction of a second. At highway speed, for example, the time between injection and opening of the intake valve averages only about one-hundredth of a second.

The fuel pressure at the injectors remains constant. Therefore, the amount of fuel injected is determined solely by the length of time that the injection valve is

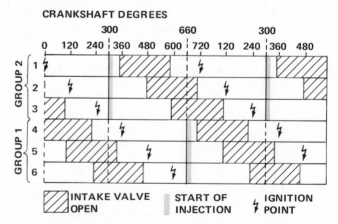

Fig. 20-7 Injection timing chart for a six-cylinder engine. *(Robert Bosch GmbH)*

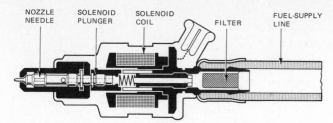

Fig. 20-8 Sectional view of the solenoid-operated injection valve. *(Robert Bosch GmbH)*

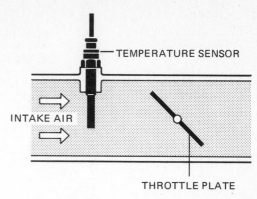

Fig. 20-9 Temperature sensor in the intake manifold. *(Robert Bosch GmbH)*

open. And this valve-open time is determined by the ECU. The fuel pump and pressure regulator maintain a constant pressure to the injection valves. When the ECU signals the solenoid in an injection valve to open, it is energized and spraying starts. When the ECU signal to the injection valve stops, it closes and spraying stops. If the engine is operating under load, for example, it needs more fuel. The ECU responds by holding the valves open longer.

A solenoid injection valve is shown in sectional view in Fig. 20-8. When the solenoid is connected to the battery, the winding produces a magnetic field. The magnetism pulls the plunger and needle valve away from the valve seat in the nozzle. The fuel can then spray through the nozzle into the intake manifold. The longer the needle is off its seat, the more fuel is sprayed. When the solenoid is disconnected from the battery, the needle reseats and cuts off the flow of fuel.

☼ 20-4 Electronic controls for fuel injection

Several factors determine how long an injection valve remains open, delivering fuel to the intake manifold. They include throttle position, intake-manifold vacuum, ingoing-air temperature, and coolant (or engine) temperature. See Fig. 20-3. Sensing devices continuously monitor these factors and send changing voltage signals to the ECU. The ECU puts the varying signals together and then decides how long the injector valves should stay open.

For example, the intake-air-temperature sensor (Fig. 20-9) constantly measures the temperature of the air entering the intake manifold. The intake-air-temperature sensor contains an element that passes varying amounts of electric current as the temperature changes. At low temperature, for example, it passes more current. It thus sends more current or a stronger signal to the ECU. The ECU then increases the time during which the fuel-injection valves are open. More fuel is delivered to compensate for the colder and denser air.

In a similar way, the coolant temperature sensor sends varying amounts of current to the ECU, depending on the temperature of the engine coolant—and thus engine temperature. When the engine is cold, the engine must receive more fuel so that the mixture will be rich enough. The ECU, therefore, increases the injection time when the coolant temperature sensor reports that the engine is cold. As the engine warms up, the ECU decreases the injection time.

The intake-manifold-pressure (vacuum) sensor (Fig. 20-10) measures intake-manifold pressure or vacuum and compares it with atmospheric pressure. It contains

a pair of *aneroids*. These are flat, hollow disks. In many models, both aneroids are evacuated. That is, they hold a vacuum. As the outside pressure changes, the sides of the aneroid bulge out or in, depending on whether the outside pressure is relatively low or high.

Intake-manifold vacuum enters the end of the pressure sensor. This vacuum acts on the aneroids. For example, if the throttle valve is open and there is little vacuum in the intake manifold, the aneroids are collapsed (Fig. 20-10). But if intake-manifold vacuum is high, the aneroids bulge out. This repositions the plunger in the coils. Changing the position of the plunger changes the magnetic strength of the coil and the strength of the electric signal to the ECU. The ECU then changes the injection time so that the correct amount of fuel is injected to meet intake-manifold-vacuum conditions. For example, the manifold vacuum is high when the throttle is closed or nearly closed. This means that only a little air is getting through to the cylinders. Therefore, only a little fuel should be injected. As a result, the ECU shortens the injection time. This is the same as the carburetor feeding fuel to the air through the carburetor idle system.

When the throttle is opened, the vacuum in the intake manifold is reduced. The aneroids collapse somewhat (see Fig. 20-10). They pull the plunger into the coils. This changes the electric signal from the coils. The ECU, therefore, increases the injection time. More fuel

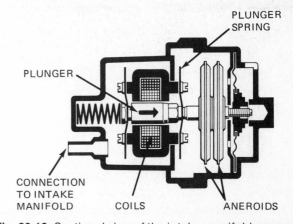

Fig. 20-10 Sectional view of the intake-manifold pressure sensor with the throttle valve open. The aneroid disks are compressed. *(Robert Bosch GmbH)*

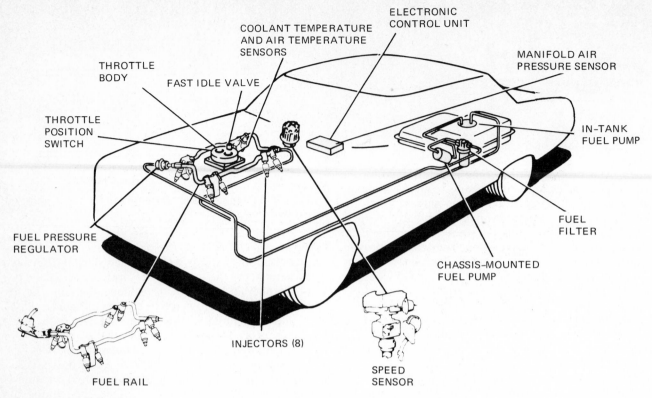

Fig. 20-11 Components of the Cadillac electronic fuel-injection system. *(Cadillac Motor Car Division of General Motors Corporation)*

is injected to match the increased airflow so that the air–fuel ratio remains constant.

There are other controls in the electronic system. One is the cold-start valve. This valve is located in the intake manifold (Fig. 20-3). It is normally closed when the engine is running or if it is warm when starting is attempted. However, when the engine temperature sensor and the air-temperature sensor tell the ECU that the engine and air are cold, the ECU triggers the cold-start valve. Now, when cranking is attempted, the so-

lenoid in the cold-start valve opens the valve so additional fuel is sprayed into the air entering the intake manifold. This enriches the ingoing air–fuel mixture for a good cold-engine start.

The throttle-position switch also influences the length of the injection time. As the throttle opens, the switch sends a changing signal to the ECU. For example, when the throttle is wide open, the signal tells the ECU to increase the injection time so that a richer, full-power mixture enters the engine cylinders.

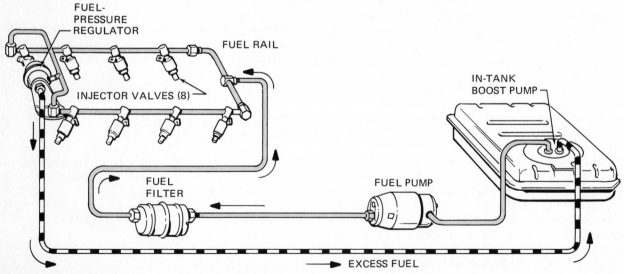

Fig. 20-12 Schematic view of the fuel system used on the Cadillac fuel-injected engine. *(Cadillac Motor Car Division of General Motors Corporation)*

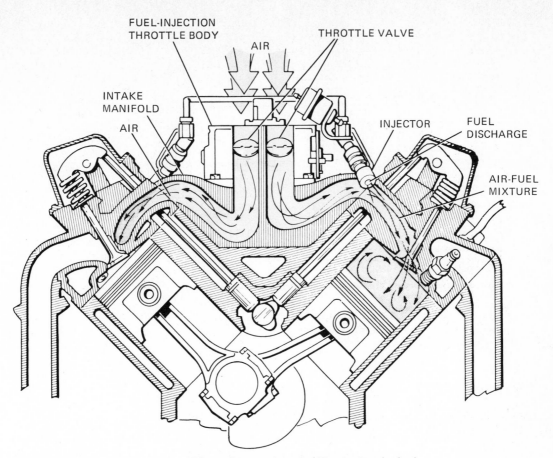

Fig. 20-13 Sectional view of the Cadillac V-8 engine equipped with electronic fuel injection. *(Cadillac Motor Car Division of General Motors Corporation)*

The image shows labels: FUEL-INJECTION THROTTLE BODY, AIR, THROTTLE VALVE, INTAKE MANIFOLD, AIR, INJECTOR, FUEL DISCHARGE, AIR-FUEL MIXTURE

✿ 20-5 Cadillac electronic fuel-injection system

Now let us look at an electronic fuel-injection system on a V-8 engine (Fig. 20-11). This system has separate fuel-injector valves for each cylinder (Fig. 20-12), just as in the system previously discussed. The eight injectors are connected to a fuel rail. They are divided into two groups of four injectors each. Each group of injectors is alternately turned on and off by the ECU. The injectors are turned on once for each two revolutions of the crankshaft. Figure 20-13 is a sectional view of the Cadillac V-8 engine with electronic fuel injection.

Figure 20-14 is a wiring diagram of the complete system. The block diagram in Fig. 20-15 shows, on the left, the sensors that send information to the ECU. With this and other previously programmed information, the ECU computes the amount of fuel the engine requires for every operating condition. It then sends control signals to the injectors and other parts of the system (on the right in Fig. 20-15).

The timing of the injections (the instant the injection valves open) is controlled by two reed switches installed in a plastic housing on the distributor housing. These switches are positioned outside a rotor on the distributor shaft which has two magnets. As the shaft rotates, the magnets open and close the reed switches. As the switches close and then open, they signal the ECU which then activates either one or the other group of injectors.

The ECU is a preprogrammed computer which is installed above the glove box within the passenger compartment. It converts the input information from the sensors into an electric signal which opens the injectors for the proper duration at the proper time. When a malfunction is traced to the ECU, it is removed from the car and a new ECU unit is installed. This unit is not adjustable or repairable. Proper diagnosis of the system requires a special tester.

✿ 20-6 Cadillac electronic throttle-body injection

This latest version of the Cadillac electronic fuel injection does not have the two fuel rails and eight injectors. Instead, the system uses only two injectors, which are located in the throttle body. Each supplies half of the cylinders. This is a considerably simplified system although it uses the same type of electronic control unit. The ECU also has a self-diagnosis feature. If trouble develops in the fuel-injection system, the diagnostic system, when triggered, flashes two numbers on the dashboard readout. The numbers tell the technician what the trouble is. That is, the technician can check the number on a code reference list, which tabulates the possible causes of the trouble.

✿ 20-7 Servicing electronic fuel-injection systems

There is a considerable variety among electronic fuel-injection systems. Servicing procedures for these systems also vary to some extent. Therefore, we

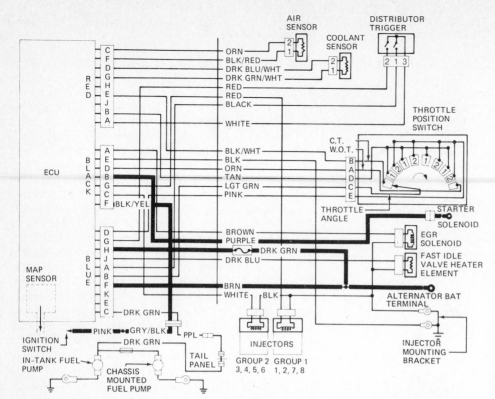

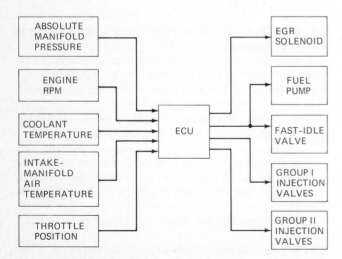

Fig. 20-14 Wiring diagram of the fuel-injection system. *(Cadillac Motor Car Division of General Motors Corporation)*

select for our discussion here the Cadillac system which we described earlier in the chapter. It requires a special analyzer (J-25400) as shown in Fig. 20-16. This analyzer has a series of 20 switches. It also has a series of overlays, each of which pertains to a specific model of electronic fuel-injection system. When starting to analyze a system, you select the appropriate overlay and place it on the analyzer panel.

Before using the analyzer, first give the entire system, its components, the wiring harnesses, connections, and vacuum lines and connections a careful visual inspection. All these must be in good condition

before the tests start. Figure 20-17 shows vacuum-hose routings on one model using electronic fuel injection.

Connect the analyzer so that it is part of the system. Then operate switches 1 to 20, one after the other, to check out the various components of the electronic system and its operating phases. As you operate a switch, you are required to go through a series of steps to check a component or operating condition. Switch 2, for example, checks the battery voltage and also permits calibration of the analyzer so that the test can proceed. Switch 3 tests the injectors in group 1 (for cylinders 1, 2, 7, and 8). Switch 4 tests the injectors in

Fig. 20-15 Block diagram showing the sensors (left) that provide information to the ECU. *(Cadillac Motor Car Division of General Motors Corporation)*

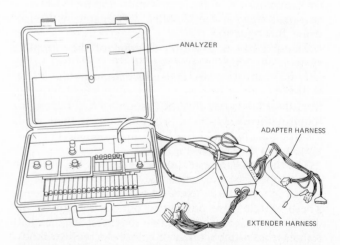

Fig. 20-16 Special analyzer to check injection system. *(Cadillac Motor Car Division of General Motors Corporation)*

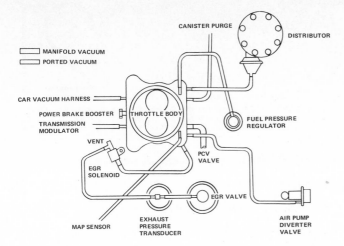

MANIFOLD VACUUM
PORTED VACUUM
CANISTER PURGE
DISTRIBUTOR
CAR VACUUM HARNESS
THROTTLE BODY
POWER BRAKE BOOSTER
TRANSMISSION MODULATOR
FUEL PRESSURE REGULATOR
VENT
PCV VALVE
EGR SOLENOID
EGR VALVE
MAP SENSOR
EXHAUST PRESSURE TRANSDUCER
AIR PUMP DIVERTER VALVE

Fig. 20-17 Vacuum routings for one Cadillac model with electronic fuel injection. *(Cadillac Motor Car Division of General Motors Corporation)*

group 2 (for cylinders 3, 4, 5, and 6). Switch 5 tests the fast-idle valve and circuit.

The other switches check the other components and the operating phases of the system. Refer to the man-

ufacturer's shop manual or the operating instructions for the analyzer for details.

CAUTION: There is one caution you must observe when working with fuel-injection systems. Pressure exists in the fuel-injection lines to the injection valves at all times, even when the engine is not running. This pressure is much higher than that of the fuel pump in a carbureted fuel system. If you should loosen a fuel-line connection without relieving the pressure, a large quantity of gasoline can spurt all over the place. This can be especially dangerous if the engine is hot. The gasoline can ignite from heated metal or from sparks caused by loosening electric connections or metal tools striking metal parts. To avoid the danger of a fire or explosion, relieve the pressure as follows. Find the Schrader fitting for the fuel system. This is a valve that looks much like a tire valve. On some cars it is located on one of the fuel rails, on other cars near the fuel inlet. Remove the protective cap from the fitting. Loosely install a valve depressor. Wrap a shop towel around the fitting or hold a container to catch any gasoline that comes out. Slowly tighten the valve depressor so the gasoline dribbles out gradually to relieve the pressure. Dispose of the gasoline properly. Put the wet shop towel outside in a safe place for it to dry out. Remove the valve depressor and install the protective cap.

Chapter 20 review questions

Select the *one* correct, best, or most probable answer to each question. Then check your answers against the correct answers given at the end of the book.

1. The basic difference between carbureted systems and most fuel-injection systems is:
   a. in the kind of fuel used,
   b. the point at which the fuel enters the air,
   c. the type of engine with which they are used,
   d. the type of ignition they use.
2. In most fuel-injection systems, the fuel is sprayed:
   a. into the intake manifold, just under the carburetor,
   b. directly into the carburetor,
   c. into the intake manifold, just opposite the intake valves,
   d. into the cylinders.
3. In the diesel engine, the fuel is injected directly into the:
   a. combustion chambers,
   b. intake manifold,
   c. exhaust manifold,
   d. carburetor.
4. The injection valves are:
   a. divided into two groups,
   b. divided into three groups,
   c. one for each cylinder,
   d. on the cylinder head.
5. The longest time, in terms of degrees of crankshaft rotation, between fuel injection and intake-valve opening (six-cylinder engine) is:
   a. 60°,
   b. 180°,
   c. 220°,
   d. 300°.
6. The amount of fuel injected is determined by the:
   a. pressure on the fuel,
   b. speed of the engine,
   c. length of time the injection valve is open,
   d. all these.
7. As intake-manifold pressure increases, the ECU:
   a. shortens injection time,
   b. lengthens injection time,
   c. increases engine speed,
   d. advances injection time.
8. The purpose of the cold-start valve is to:
   a. reduce the amount of fuel being injected to avoid overchoking,
   b. increase the amount of fuel being injected,
   c. connect the starting motor with the battery,
   d. relieve cylinder pressure for easier cranking.
9. The purpose of the aneroids (in the Bosch system) is to:
   a. vary the intake manifold vacuum,
   b. advance ignition timing as speed increases,
   c. vary the injection time as intake-manifold vacuum varies,
   d. increase the pressure on the fuel as speed increases.
10. The latest version of the Cadillac electronic fuel injection
   a. uses only four injectors,
   b. uses only two fuel injectors,
   c. uses two injectors per cylinder,
   d. has only one fuel injector.

INTERIOR AND EXTERIOR LIGHTS

After studying this chapter, you should be able to:

1. Trace out the various lighting circuits and harnesses on cars.
2. Explain how to adjust headlights. Perform this job.

21-1 Lights The lighting system in a typical automobile includes both exterior and interior lights. The chart, Fig. 21-1, lists the light bulbs used by an automotive manufacturer for one line of their cars. This chart was taken directly from the manufacturer's service manual and is typical of the lists you will be referring to. The bulb numbers indicate the type and size of bulb. Figure 21-2 is the wiring diagram for the head- and taillamps of some car models. The wires are numbered and their colors are named to indicate where the wires go and how they can be identified. Notice the use of harness connectors which join several circuits at once. Figure 21-3 shows the forward wiring for one late-model car.

Figure 21-4 is the wiring diagram for some models for the car interior lights, including the dome lights, courtesy lights, and deck-lid or trunk light.

⚙ 21-2 Headlamps When the light switch is pulled out, the circuit from the battery to the headlamps is completed. This circuit goes through the beam selector (dimmer) switch. This switch has two positions: passing beam (called *low beam*) and driving beam (called *high beam*). The selector switch is located on the floor convenient to the driver's left foot on many cars. On other cars, the selector switch is on the steering column and is operated with the left hand by a lever.

Figure 21-5 shows a headlamp. It has a reflector and a filament at the back, and a lens at the front. When the filament is connected to the battery through the light switch, current flows through the filament. It glows white hot. The light is concentrated by the reflector into a forward beam and is focused by the lens.

Headlamps are made in two types and four sizes—two round and two rectangular (Fig. 21-6). The round sizes are 5¾ inches [146 mm] in diameter and 7 inches

[178 mm] in diameter. The rectangular sizes are 6.5 by 4 inches [165 by 100 mm] and 7.9 by 5.6 inches [200 by 142 mm]. All are identified by the number 1 or 2 molded into the glass at the top of the lens. Type 1 has only one filament. Type 2 has two filaments, one for the high beam and the other for the low beam (or driving beam and passing beam as they are also called). The low beam is for city driving and for passing a car coming in the opposite direction. The use of the low beam in passing prevents the oncoming driver from being temporarily blinded by the high beam.

The driver uses the dimmer, or beam selector, switch to select the filaments that will glow. On a car having only one pair of headlamps (type 2), the driver operates the switch to select either the high or the low beam. This headlamp has two filaments in two different positions. When the high-beam filament comes on, it throws light far down the road. The low-beam filament is differently positioned in the headlamp so that it throws the light downward.

On a car with two sets of headlamps (one set of type 1 and one set of type 2), the arrangement is different. When the driver operates the dimmer switch for low-beam driving, one of the filaments in the type 2 lights comes on. When the switch is operated to select high beam, the other filament of the type 2 light comes on. At the same time, the single filament of the type 1 lights comes on. Figure 21-7 shows the method of mounting and adjusting the headlamps on an older model of car. See also Fig. 21-8 for rectangular headlamps.

NOTE: Many cars are now equipped with halogen or quartz headlamps. These lamps provide considerably more light. The headlamps are interchangeable with the standard type. However, cars with these headlamps should not have the standard headlamps installed if

WHERE USED	BULB NO.	NO. USED	CANDLE POWER	MODEL
FRONT				
HEADLAMP - 142.0 X 200.0 2B	6052	2	55/65	ALL
PARK & DIRECTIONAL SIGNAL LAMP & SIDE MARKER	1157NA	2	32&3	ALL
HEADLAMP - 142.0 X 200.0 EXPORT		2	55/60	ALL T 85
HEADLAMP - 142.0 X 200.0 EXPORT		2	55/60	ALL T 84
HEADLAMP - 142.0 X 200.0 EXPORT		2	55/60	ALL T 72
REAR				
TAIL - STOP & DIRECTIONAL SIGNAL LAMP	1157	2	32&3	CENTURY
TAIL - STOP & DIRECTIONAL SIGNAL LAMP	1157	4	32&3	WAGONS ONLY
BACK-UP LAMP	1157	2	32&3	REGAL
LICENSE LAMP	194	1	2	CENTURY
SIDE MARKER LAMP	194	2	2	ALL
LUGGAGE COMPARTMENT LAMP	1003	1	15	ALL LESS WAGON
BACK-UP LAMP	1156	2	32	WAGON & CENTURY
TAIL - STOP & DIRECTIONAL	1157	4	32&3	REGAL
TAIL	194	2	2	CENTURY
SIDE REFLEX	194	2	2	CENTURY
TURN	1156	2	32	CENTURY
TAIL & SIDE REFLEX	194	6	2	REGAL
INSTRUMENT PANEL				
INDIRECT LAMP (SPEEDO)	168	1	3	ALL
INDIRECT LAMP, (FUEL GAGE & INDIRECT LAMP	168	1	3	ALL
INDIRECT LAMP (GAGES)	194	2	3	ALL
CLOCK	1816	1	3	ALL
"WIPER" ILLUMINATION	168	1	3	ALL
INDICATORS				
HEADLAMP HI BEAM	194	1	2	ALL
DIRECTIONAL SIGNAL	194	1	2	ALL
OIL PRESSURE	194	1	1	ALL
WATER TEMPERATURE	194	1	1	ALL - GAGES
GENERATOR CHARGE	194	1	2	ALL
BRAKE WARNING	194	1	1	ALL
CRUISE CONTROL	161	1	1	ALL
FASTEN SEAT BELT	194	1	1	ALL
REAR WINDOW DEFOGGER (HEATED GLASS)	194	1	2	ALL
TURBO LIGHTS	161	2	1	ALL -UR4
FUEL ECONOMY	161	2	1	ALL - UR1
SERVICE ILLUMINATION				
GLOVE COMPARTMENT LAMP	1891	1	2	ALL
RADIO DIAL (ALL)	1893	1	2	ALL
ASH TRAY ASSEMBLY	1445	1	.5	ALL
HEATER OR AIR CONDITIONING CONTROL	194	1	2	ALL
HEADERMAP LAMP	211-2	1	12	ALL
STEREO INDICATOR LIGHT (AM-FM STEREO)	66	1	.1	ALL
INTERIOR ILLUMINATION				
QUARTER COURTESY LAMP	562	2	6	4AJ47
TAILGATE COURTESY LAMP	562	1	6	WAGON
DOME	561	1	12	ALL
COURTESY LAMP	906	2	6	ALL
FLASHER-DIRECTIONAL SIGNAL 2 LAMP				AE87-09 G87 AH87-09 L87-09
FLASHER-DIRECTIONAL SIGNAL 3 LAMP		1		AE35-J47 AH35-M47
FLASHER-HAZARD		1		ALL
DOME WITH READING LAMP	212	1	6	ALL
READING LAMP	1004	2	15	* ALL

Fig. 21-1 Chart showing locations and types of light bulbs used on late-model Buick Series A cars. *(Buick Motor Division of General Motors Corporation)*

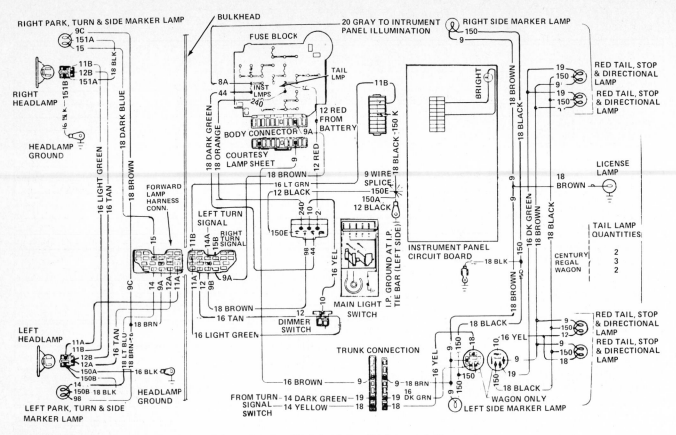

Fig. 21-2 Headlamp and taillight wiring circuits. *(Buick Motor Division of General Motors Corporation)*

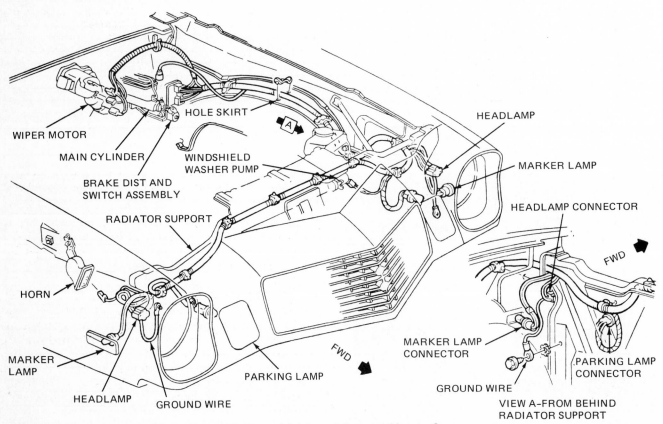

Fig. 21-3 Forward lamp wiring. *(Chevrolet Motor Division of General Motors Corporation)*

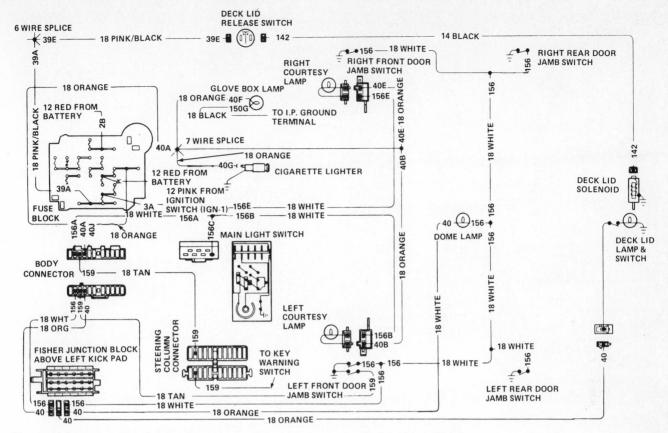

Fig. 21-4 Courtesy, dome, and other interior-light wiring system. *(Buick Motor Division of General Motors Corporation)*

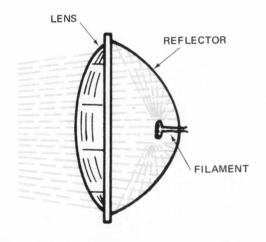

Fig. 21-5 Parts of a headlamp.

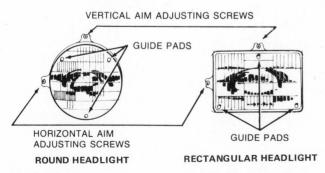

ROUND HEADLIGHT

RECTANGULAR HEADLIGHT

Fig. 21-6 Shapes of round and rectanglar headlamps.

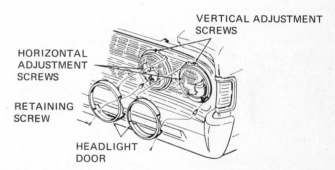

Fig. 21-7 Left front headlamps with bezels (doors) removed so the adjustment screws can be seen. *(Ford Motor Company)*

replacement is necessary. Standard headlamps on a car originally equipped with the halogen or quartz headlamp will not have the same appearance and light and customers could be dissatisfied.

⚙ **21-3 Headlamp covers** Some cars have headlamp covers or doors that move upward or downward when the headlamps are turned on. This exposes the headlamps. When the headlamps are turned off, the covers move back up or down to cover them. This protects the headlamps from mud, rain, or flying stones. Some cars use vacuum from the engine intake manifold to operate the covers. Other cars use electric motors.

Figure 21-9 shows the front sheet metal of a car that uses an electric motor to operate the headlamp doors

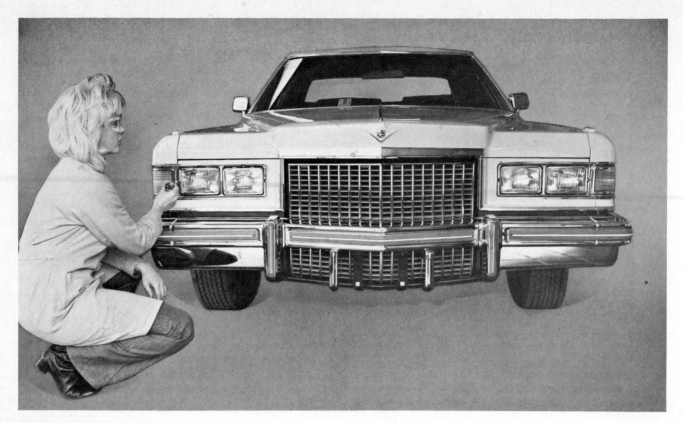

Fig. 21-8 Adjusting rectangular headlamps. *(Cadillac Motor Car Division of General Motors Corporation)*

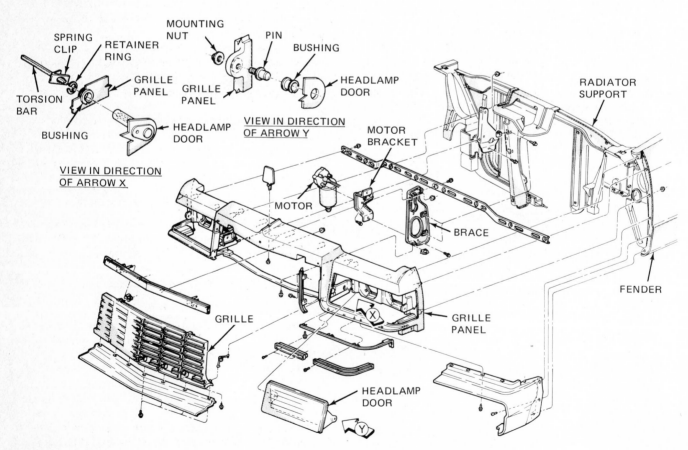

Fig. 21-9 Headlamp door, actuated by an electric motor. *(Chrysler Corporation)*

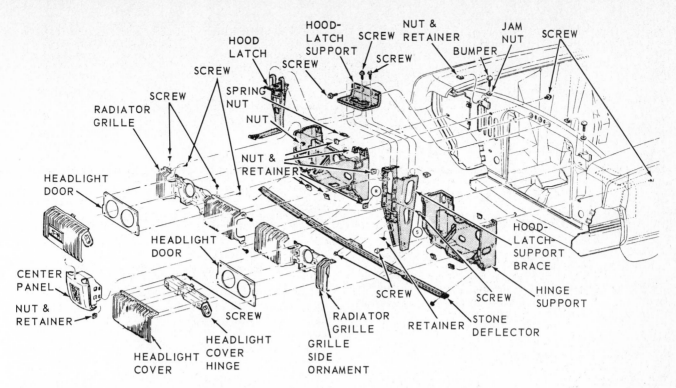

Fig. 21-10 Grill on car disassembled to show locations of the various parts, including the headlamp covers (to left). *(Ford Motor Company)*

(covers). View Y at the top shows how the door is hinged so the electric motor can swing it out of the way.

Figure 21-10 shows the front sheet metal of a car using vacuum motors to operate the headlamp covers (doors). Figure 21-11 shows how a vacuum motor is connected to the cover. In operation, the light switch is pulled out all the way to turn on the headlamps. This action operates a distribution valve that is mounted on the back end of the light switch. This valve then directs vacuum to the two vacuum motors. Vacuum thus applied to the diaphragms in the motors causes them to

move and thus lift the headlamp covers. The distribution valve also has an opening through which the atmosphere side of the motor diaphragms is vented. Thus atmospheric pressure is always applied to this side of the diaphragm.

When the headlamps are turned off, the distribution valve allows atmospheric pressure to enter the vacuum side of the vacuum motors. Now, springs on the headlamp covers cause them to drop down to cover the headlamps.

There is a vacuum reservoir which holds sufficient vacuum for several cover operations if the headlamps are turned on and off when the engine is not running. Also, the headlamp covers can be operated manually

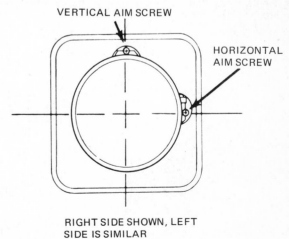

Fig. 21-11 Headlamp cover actuator (vacuum motor) on a car. *(Ford Motor Company)*

Fig. 21-12 Locations of the two aiming screws on a round headlamp (two-headlamp system). *Chevrolet Motor Division of General Motors Corporation*

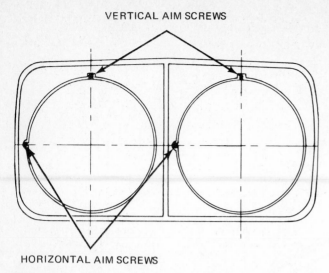

Fig. 21-13 Locations of the aiming screws on the round headlamps of a four-headlamp system. (*Chevrolet Motor Division of General Motors Corporation*)

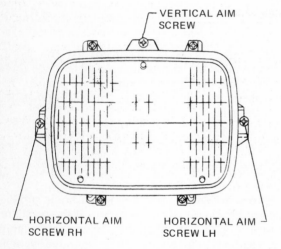

Fig. 21-14 Location of aiming screws on a rectangular headlamp. (*Chevrolet Motor Division of General Motors Corporation*)

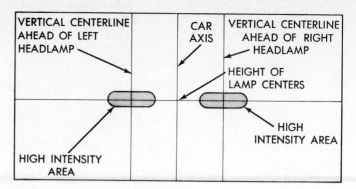

Fig. 21-16 High beams when adjustments are correct. (*Chrysler Corporation*)

in case the vacuum system fails. This is done by turning on the headlamps and then lifting the covers by hand.

NOTE: In some cars, the entire headlamp module rotates to swing the headlamps up into position when the light switch is turned on.

☼ 21-4 Headlamp aiming It is important for the headlamps to be aimed correctly. If they are aimed too high or too far to the left, they could blind an oncoming driver and cause a serious accident. Incorrect aim can also reduce the driver's ability to see the road properly, and this could also lead to an accident.

Headlamp adjustments are made by turning spring-loaded screws. There is one spring-loaded screw at the top for up-and-down adjustment and one at the side for left-to-right adjustment (Figs. 21-12 to 21-14).

A variety of headlamp aiming instruments are in use in shops. You should learn to use as many different kinds of instruments as possible. The simplest uses a screen set 25 feet [7.62 m] in front of the vehicle and a perfectly level floor (Fig. 21-15). With the car aligned perpendicular to the screen, the low beam and high beam are checked separately. Figures 21-16 and 21-17 show the proper patterns when the headlamps are correctly adjusted.

NOTE: Some manufacturers, in their aiming instructions, call for a full fuel tank and an empty car. Others call for a partly full tank and two people in the front

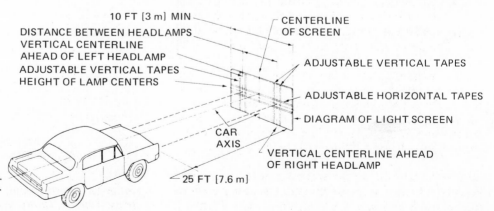

Fig. 21-15 Aiming-screen setup. (*Society of Automotive Engineers*)

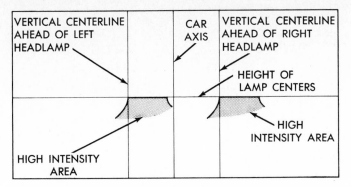

Fig. 21-17 Low beams when adjustments are correct. *(Chrysler Corporation)*

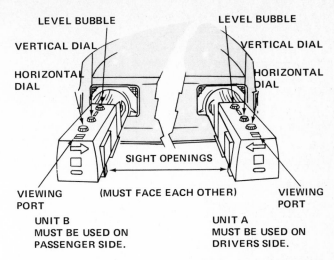

Fig. 21-18 Headlamp aimers in position on the two headlamps. *(Chrysler Corporation)*

seat. Tires must be inflated to the specified pressure. Just before checking the aim, after the car has been positioned, bounce each corner of the car a couple of times to equalize the suspension system.

Another type of aiming instrument is moved into position in front of the headlamp and centered on the lens. With the headlamp turned on, lenses in the aiming instrument throw a small picture of the lighting pattern on a screen which the technician can read. This tells the technician whether adjustment is needed and in which direction adjustments should be made. Another type of instrument, recommended by Chrysler, is shown in Fig. 21-18. Note that two are required. They are installed by vacuum cups onto the two front headlamps. Adaptors must be used to install them on the two different-size round headlamps and the rectangular headlamps (Fig. 21-19). The instruments shown are attached, leveled, and then sighted through to determine the aim of the headlamps. Adjustments are made as shown in Figs. 21-12 to 21-14.

☼ 21-5 Automatic headlamp dimmer This is a system which electronically selects the proper headlamp beam for country driving. It holds the lights on upper or high beam until a car approaches from the other direction. Then, the headlamps of the approaching car trigger the system so that it shifts the headlamps to the lower beam. When the other car has passed, the system electronically shifts the headlamps back to the upper beam.

Figure 21-20 is the wiring diagram of the system. The sensor amplifier combines a light-sensing optical device and a transistorized amplifier. It is located at the front of the car where it can sense the headlights of oncoming cars. The driver has a sensitivity control (center in Fig. 21-20) which allows adjustment of the system to the surrounding light. The foot-dimmer switch is an override switch which allows the driver to manually control the system. This might be used, for example, if an oncoming car does not dim and the driver needs more light to see by. Operating the foot-dimmer switch returns the headlamps to the upper beam.

☼ 21-6 Automatic on-off and time-delay headlamp control This is a device that electronically controls the on-off operation of the headlamps and taillights. It

has various names such as Twilight Sentinel and Safeguard Sentinel. Figure 21-21 shows a typical installation. It is mounted under the instrument-panel grille, facing upward so it is exposed to direct outside light through the windshield (see Fig. 21-22). The internal resistance of the photocell varies according to the amount of light striking it. As the amount of light is reduced, the internal resistance of the photocell increases until it finally causes the amplifier to turn the lights on. It turns the lights off if the amount of external light increases enough.

The amplifier contains a transistorized amplifier unit, a sensitive relay, a power relay, and a transistorized time-delay unit. The time-delay unit delays the turning on or off of the lights. For example, it delays the turning on of the lights anywhere from 10 to 60 seconds. This keeps the lights from coming on in the daytime when the car is passing under a viaduct or trees. The time

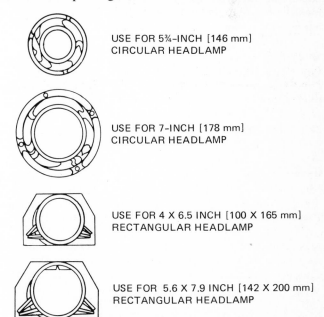

USE FOR 5¾-INCH [146 mm] CIRCULAR HEADLAMP

USE FOR 7-INCH [178 mm] CIRCULAR HEADLAMP

USE FOR 4 X 6.5 INCH [100 X 165 mm] RECTANGULAR HEADLAMP

USE FOR 5.6 X 7.9 INCH [142 X 200 mm] RECTANGULAR HEADLAMP

Fig. 21-19 Adaptors to fit headlamp aimers on the headlamps. *(Chrysler Corporation)*

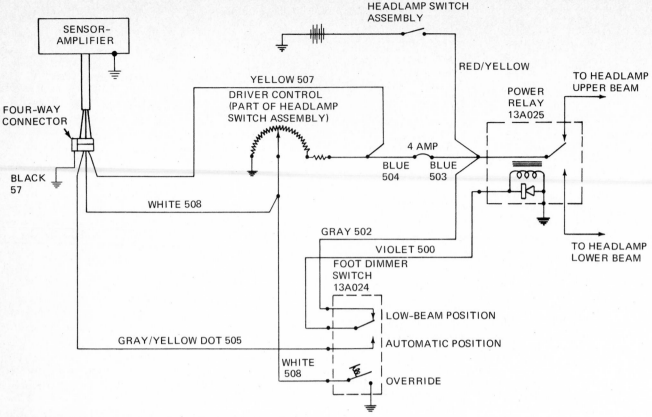

Fig. 21-20 Wiring diagram of an electronic headlamp dimmer system. *(Ford Motor Company)*

delay for turning off the lights is adjustable; there is a control lever on the light switch which can be swung in one direction or the other to change the delay period from a few seconds to 4½ minutes. This permits the driver to drive into the garage, leave the lights on, get out of the car, lock the garage, enter the house, and lock the house door, all in the light from the car headlamps before they are turned off automatically.

⚙ 21-7 Headlamps-on warning buzzer This system (Fig. 21-23) is usually combined with the open-door warning-buzzer system. When the headlamps are on and the driver's door is opened, a warning buzzer sounds. This warns the driver to turn off the headlamps before leaving the car.

⚙ 21-8 Headlamp replacement Headlamps are installed in a variety of ways. The assembly includes an adjustment ring in back of the headlamp and a retaining ring in front of the headlamp. Figure 21-24 shows one arrangement for headlamps, cornering lamps, and parking lamps. Note that springs are used to hold the headlamp-adjusting rings in adjustment after the adjuster screws have been adjusted for proper headlamp aiming. To replace a headlamp, remove the headlamp door, retainer ring, and headlamp bulb. Be sure to replace the old bulb with a new one of the proper type. Replacing a halogen bulb with a standard bulb reduces illumination and can cause customer dissatisfaction. After installation, aim the headlamps (⚙ 21-4).

⚙ 21-9 Headlamp switch The headlamp switch (Figs. 21-25 to 21-27) controls not only the headlamps but also the parking lamps, marker lamps, taillamps, license-plate lamp, courtesy lamps, instrument panel lamps, and ashtray lamps. Figure 21-25 shows typical headlamp switches without the switch knob. The knob-release button holds the switch in position in the instrument panel. When pushed down, it releases the switch for removal. Figure 21-26 shows one mounting arrangement.

Many headlamp covers are actuated by vacuum (⚙ 21-3). The vacuum is directed to vacuum motors by a distribution valve on the back of the headlamp switch (Fig. 21-27).

The headlamp switch has three positions (see Fig. 21-28):

1. All lamps off when knob is pushed all the way in.
2. Parking, side marker, and instrument panel lamps on when the knob is pulled out to the first position.
3. All lamps in no. 2 above and also headlamps on when the knob is pulled out all the way.

The instrument-panel circuit is routed through a rheostat in the switch. When the switch knob is rotated, the instrument-panel lights are dimmed or made lighter. If the switch knob is turned all the way counterclockwise, it turns on the dome light.

⚙ 21-10 Stoplight switch Until the introduction of the dual-brake system, stoplight switches were hy-

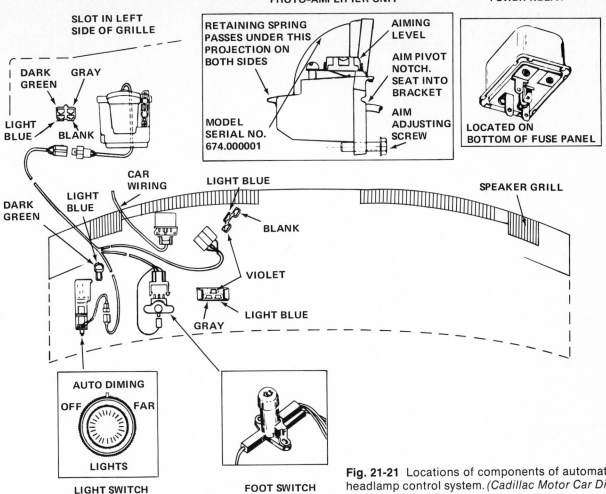

SLOT IN LEFT SIDE OF GRILLE

DARK GREEN

GRAY

LIGHT BLUE

BLANK

RETAINING SPRING PASSES UNDER THIS PROJECTION ON BOTH SIDES

MODEL SERIAL NO. 674.000001

AIMING LEVEL

AIM PIVOT NOTCH. SEAT INTO BRACKET

AIM ADJUSTING SCREW

LOCATED ON BOTTOM OF FUSE PANEL

CAR WIRING

LIGHT BLUE

LIGHT BLUE

DARK GREEN

BLANK

VIOLET

LIGHT BLUE

GRAY

SPEAKER GRILL

AUTO DIMING

OFF

FAR

LIGHTS

LIGHT SWITCH CONTROL

FOOT SWITCH

Fig. 21-21 Locations of components of automatic on-off headlamp control system. *(Cadillac Motor Car Division of General Motors Corporation)*

draulic. They contained a small diaphragm that was moved by hydraulic pressure when the brakes were applied. This action closed a switch which connected the stoplights to the battery.

When the dual-brake system came on the scene, however, the hydraulic switch could no longer be used. With this system, there are two separate hydraulic systems, one for each set of two wheels. If the hydraulic switch were connected into one system and it failed, then the car would have no stoplights even though the other system was still working and stopping the car.

Thus the mechanical switch came into use. Figures 21-29 and 21-30 illustrate one design. When the pedal is pushed for braking, it carries the switch contacts with it (to left in Fig. 21-30). This brings the switch contacts together so the stoplights come on.

⚙ 21-11 Turn signals Turn signals permit the driver to signal an intention to turn right or left (Fig. 21-31). They are operated by a switch on the steering column. When the switch lever is moved (up for a right turn, down for a left turn), circuits are completed between the battery and the appropriate lights. There is a flasher in the circuit which intermittently closes and opens contacts. This causes the turn-indicator lights to flash

on and off. This intermittent flashing makes the lights more noticeable.

The flasher contains a thermostatic blade and a heater. The heater carries the circuit current and heats up. This heating causes the blade to bend, opening the contacts. Now, current stops flowing, and the blade cools, straightens, and closes the circuit. The cycle is repeated as long as the turn-signal switch is closed. If

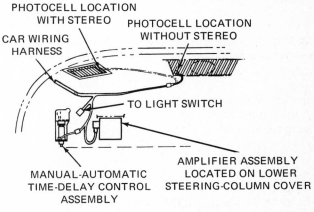

PHOTOCELL LOCATION WITH STEREO

PHOTOCELL LOCATION WITHOUT STEREO

CAR WIRING HARNESS

TO LIGHT SWITCH

MANUAL-AUTOMATIC TIME-DELAY CONTROL ASSEMBLY

AMPLIFIER ASSEMBLY LOCATED ON LOWER STEERING-COLUMN COVER

Fig. 21-22 Locations of the photocell. *(Cadillac Motor Car Division of General Motors Corporation)*

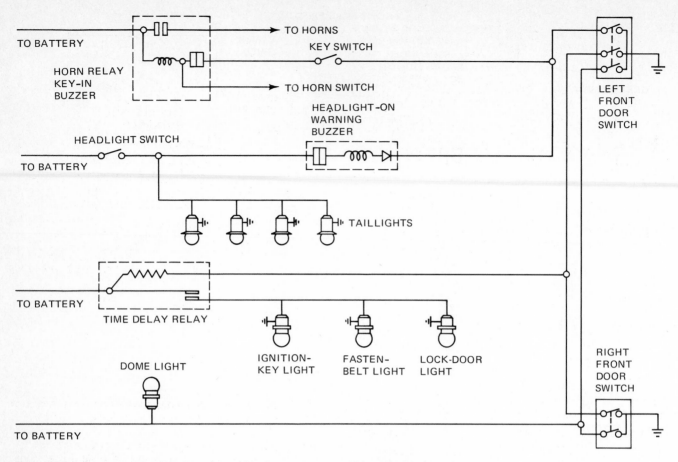

Fig. 21-23 Open-door headlamps-on warning-buzzer system. *(Chrysler Corporation)*

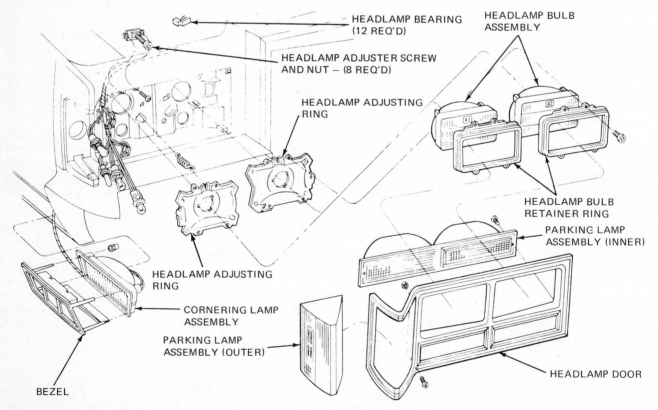

Fig. 21-24 Headlamps, cornering lamp, and parking lamp removed from the right front of a car. *(Ford Motor Company)*

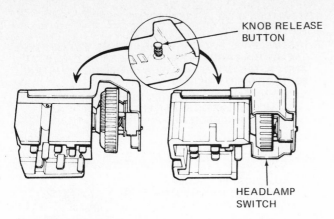

Fig. 21-25 Headlamp switches. *(Ford Motor Company)*

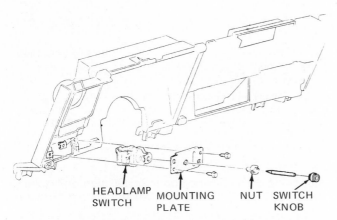

Fig. 21-26 Headlamp switch and attaching parts. *(Oldsmobile Division of General Motors Corporation)*

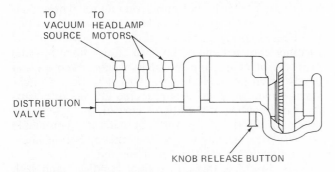

Fig. 21-27 Headlamp switch with distribution valve which controls headlamp covers. *(Ford Motor Company)*

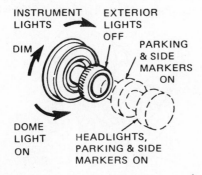

Fig. 21-28 Positions of a headlamp switch and the lamps it controls. *(Ford Motor Company)*

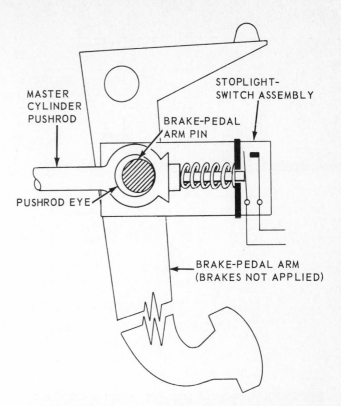

Fig. 21-29 Mechanical stoplight switch shown open, with brakes not applied. *(Ford Motor Company)*

the stoplight switch is closed by operation of the brakes, it overrides the turn-signal system so that both rear signal lights stay on steadily to signal that the driver is braking the car.

✸ 21-12 Backup lights The backup lights come on when the driver shifts into reverse. Figure 21-32 shows the backup-light switch and how to adjust it for one model of car. The switch contacts are closed when the shift lever is moved to R (reverse). This connects the backup lights at the rear of the vehicle with the battery.

✸ 21-13 Emergency or hazard flasher The emergency-flasher, or hazard-warning system, is designed to signal following cars that a car has stopped or stalled or has pulled up to the side of the road. When the driver operates the flasher switch, it causes all four turn signal lights to flash on and off every few seconds. The system includes a flasher similar to the one used for turn signals. The system is operated by a switch usually located on the side of the steering column (Fig. 21-33).

✸ 21-14 Courtesy lights Courtesy lights come on when the car doors are opened so passengers or driver can see to get in or out of the car. The courtesy lights are operated by switches in the doors. When a door is opened, the switch closes to connect the internal lights in the dome or side to the battery.

✸ 21-15 Fiber optic monitor systems In many cars, the instrument panel requires lights at many places—to illuminate the speedometer, the indicating gauges, and the various controls. Because of the small

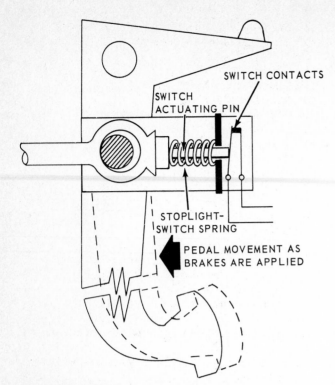

Fig. 21-30 Mechanical stoplight switch shown closed, with brakes applied. *(Ford Motor Company)*

SWITCH CONTACTS

SWITCH ACTUATING PIN

STOPLIGHT-SWITCH SPRING

PEDAL MOVEMENT AS BRAKES ARE APPLIED

FRONT PARKING LAMPS

TO POWER DISTRIBUTION PANEL

MAJOR FILAMENT

MAJOR FILAMENT

MINOR FILAMENT

MINOR FILAMENT

TO TURN SIGNAL SWITCH

LEFT REAR SIDE MARKER *

RIGHT FRONT SIDE MARKER *

INDICATOR LAMPS

LH CORNERING LAMP RELAY

HEADLIGHT SWITCH

RH CORNERING LAMP RELAY

LEFT FRONT SIDE MARKER

RIGHT REAR SIDE MARKER

TO TURN SIGNAL SWITCH FOR STOP LAMP FEED

REAR LAMPS

*ADD CORNERING LAMPS INTO CIRCUIT TO FUNCTION WITH PARK & TURN LAMPS WHEN TURN SIGNAL IS ACTIVATED.

NOTE: IF PARKING LAMP OR TAILLAMP HAS A THREE-WIRE SOCKET, THE BLACK WIRE IS THE GROUND. IF PARKING LAMP OR TAILLAMP HAS A TWO-WIRE SOCKET, THE BULB IS GROUNDED THROUGH THE LAMP ASSEMBLY.

Fig. 21-31 Side-marker, cornering lamp, and turn-signal circuits. *(Ford Motor Company)*

NEW SWITCH INSTALLATION PROCEDURE
1. POSITION SHIFT LEVER IN NEUTRAL
2. ASSEMBLE THE SWITCH TO THE COLUMN BY INSERTING THE SWITCH CARRIER TANG IN THE SHIFT TUBE SLOT AND FASTEN IN POSITION BY ASSEMBLING MOUNTING SCREWS TO RETAINERS.
   NOTE: NEW SWITCH IS PINNED IN NEUTRAL POSITION WITH PLASTIC SHEAR PIN (NO ADDITIONAL PINNING REQUIRED FOR INSTALLATION)

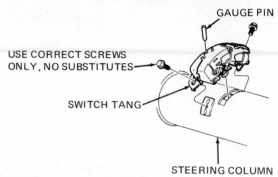

GAUGE PIN

USE CORRECT SCREWS ONLY, NO SUBSTITUTES

SWITCH TANG

STEERING COLUMN

RESET INSTALLATION PROCEDURE
1. POSITION SHIFT LEVER IN NEUTRAL
2. LOOSEN ATTACHING SCREWS.
3. ROTATE SWITCH ON COLUMN AND INSERT .096 DIA GAUGE PIN INTO NEUTRAL GAUGE HOLE TO DEPTH OF 3/8 INCH.
4. TIGHTEN ATTACHING SCREWS.
5. REMOVE .096 DIA GAUGE PIN.

Fig. 21-32 Backup-lamp-switch installation and adjustment. *(Oldsmobile Division of General Motors Corporation)*

spaces available, it becomes a problem to locate light bulbs where they are needed. To eliminate this problem, some cars use fiber optic conductors. These conductors are made up of a very large number of very fine and flexible threads or fibers of glass, which are bound together into a bundle, or cord. Each fiber has the property of being able to conduct light, even around bends or corners. Here is the way it works: As light starts down the fiber, it is reflected off the outer surfaces of the fiber. If the fiber is curved, the light keeps bouncing off the outer surfaces without appreciable loss. By the time it comes out the other end of the fiber, it is almost as strong as when it entered.

Now, to utilize this effect, fiber bundles (each with many fibers) are run from a central light source to the various outlets on the instrument panel where light is needed. Thus only one light bulb is needed to provide light at many places. Installation and servicing prob-

KEY RELEASE BUTTON

HAZARD FLASHER

Fig. 21-33 Location of hazard flasher switch. *(Ford Motor Company)*

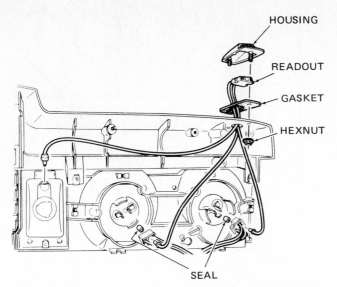

HOUSING

READOUT

GASKET

HEXNUT

SEAL

Fig. 21-34 Fiber optic monitoring system for headlamps. *(Cadillac Motor Car Division of General Motors Corporation)*

lems are made easier to solve by the use of the fiber bundles. Only one light bulb needs to be replaced if a burnout occurs, and the fiber bundles can be bent almost any way without damaging them.

Fiber optics are also used in a "lights-out" warning system. This allows the driver to check the operation of the exterior lights without leaving the car. Fiber optic conductors are connected at one end to the headlamps, at the other to a readout mounted in a housing on the top of the fenders (Fig. 21-34). If a headlight is on, light from it passes through the fiber optic conductor to the readout. The high-beam headlamp readout is blue (on one automobile series) which matches the high-beam indicator in the speedometer face. The low-beam readout is clear and has no color.

The taillamp monitor system has fiber optic conductors running from the taillights to a readout in a housing in the headliner or roof of the car, just above the rear window. When the taillights are on, the spots of light in the readout tell the driver that they are on.

Chapter 21 review questions

Select the *one* correct, best, or most probable answer to each question. Then check your answers against the correct answers given at the end of the book.

1. When a light bulb burns out, determine what type and size of replacement bulb to install by:
   a. looking at the burned-out bulb,
   b. referring to the car manufacturer's shop manual,
   c. referring to the bulb manufacturer's catalog,
   d. any of these.
2. The headlamp beam selector has:
   a. two positions, city and country,
   b. two positions, high beam and low beam,
   c. three positions, high beam, center beam, and low beam,
   d. only one position.
3. Headlamps come in four sizes:
   a. three square and one round,
   b. three round and one rectangular,
   c. two round and two rectangular,
   d. all rectangular.
4. A car with two sets of headlamps has:
   a. one pair of type 1 and one pair of type 2,
   b. one round pair and one rectangular pair,
   c. four headlamps each with one filament,
   d. four headlamps each with two filaments.
5. Headlamp aiming is made by:
   a. moving the light bulb back of the lens,
   b. turning spring-loaded adjustment screws,
   c. rotating the headlamps in their sockets,
   d. bending adjustment brackets.
6. The automatic on-off and time-delay headlamp control:
   a. turns the headlamps off as the driver gets out of the car,
   b. times the flashing of the lights when the hazard system is energized,
   c. turns the headlamps off after a preset time delay following the turning off of the engine,
   d. turns the headlamps off 3 minutes after the driver leaves the car.
7. The typical headlamp switch has:
   a. two positions,
   b. three positions,
   c. four positions,
   d. five positions.
8. The device that includes a thermostatic blade which works to open and close the turn-signal indicator light is called a:
   a. lighter,
   b. signaler,
   c. circuit breaker,
   d. flasher.
9. When properly adjusted, the high-intensity areas of the low beams will be:
   a. to the right of the vertical centerline of the left headlamp,
   b. to the right of the vertical centerline of the right headlamp,
   c. below the centerline of the lamp centers,
   d. all of these.
10. When properly adjusted, the high-intensity areas of the high beams will be:
    a. to the right of the vertical centerline of the left beam,
    b. to the right of the vertical centerline of the right beam,
    c. centered on the vertical and horizontal centerlines of the lamps,
    d. below the horizontal centerlines of the lamps.

HORNS AND HORN RELAYS

After studying this chapter, you should be able to:

1. Explain how horns and horn relays work.
2. Explain how a security-alarm system works.
3. Adjust a horn.

22-1 Horn operation Today, practically all horns of the automotive type are the vibrating kind. They employ a winding that is connected in series with a pair of points within the horn itself. The points are closed when the horn is not operating. When the external circuit to the battery is closed (by the horn pushbutton or horn relay), current can flow through the points and winding. This causes a magnetic field, which attracts a heavy iron armature toward the winding core. The armature is mounted to the horn diaphragm so that the movement of the armature causes a distortion of the diaphragm. The armature movement also causes the horn points to open so that the horn winding circuit is opened. The magnetic field of the winding collapses, and the armature is released and returns to its original position as the distortion of the diaphragm is relieved. As soon as the armature moves back to its original position, however, the points close, the winding again becomes energized, and the armature is once more attracted. This cycle is repeated many times a second; the repeated distortion of the diaphragm causes the diaphragm to vibrate and produce the warning signal. The number of times a second that the diaphragm is vibrated determines the pitch of the signal. The diaphragm vibrates more rapidly on higher-note signals. To reduce arcing at the points, most horns have a condenser or resistor connected across the points (Fig. 22-1).

22-2 Horn checks and adjustments Horns are often used in matched pairs (high and low note) so that a blended and more resonant signal is produced. On matched pairs of horns, the horn with the shorter projector is adjusted to produce the higher note.

1. If the horn produces a weak signal, check the voltage at the horn while it is operated. It should be at least 11 volts for a 12-volt horn (5.25 volts for a 6-volt horn). If it is less than this, test the battery and the connections and wiring in the horn circuit. Use a jumper lead and connect around the horn pushbutton (or the horn relay) to determine if this is the cause of the excessive voltage drop. Check also the ground connections and mounting of the horn.

2. If the horn signal is raspy, check the horn for loose back shell or other parts, cracked diaphragm, or broken parts. On matched pairs of horns, poor horn tone sometimes results if the projectors are not assembled with their matching power plants.

3. If no sound at all is obtained, use a set of test lights and check the horn for an open circuit. (Also check for ground on the type of horn with two terminals.) If an open is found, remove the back shell and inspect the contact points. If they are burned or oxidized, they may not be making good contact and should be dressed with a few strokes of a clean contact file. If the points have been worn down in service, an open will result. This may be corrected by loosening the locknut and turning the current-draw adjusting nut (Fig. 22-1). If the points appear in good condition and are making contact without any horn operation, the winding may be open. This means that the winding or complete horn must be replaced.

4. If the tone is still poor and the trouble cannot be attributed to any of the above, the horn can be readjusted. Two adjustments can be made: current draw and air gap. It is rare that a horn air gap will need to be reset, so this procedure will not be considered here. Refer to the manufacturer's specifications if air-gap readjustment of a horn is required. For readjustment of the current draw, connect an ammeter into the horn circuit and check the current draw. Readjust by loosening the locknut and turning the

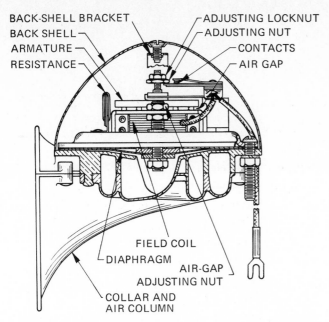

Fig. 22-1 Sectional view of a "sea-shell" type electric horn.

LABELS (Fig. 22-1):
BACK-SHELL BRACKET · BACK SHELL · ARMATURE · RESISTANCE · ADJUSTING LOCKNUT · ADJUSTING NUT · CONTACTS · AIR GAP · FIELD COIL · DIAPHRAGM · AIR-GAP ADJUSTING NUT · COLLAR AND AIR COLUMN

adjusting nut or screw, according to the type of horn. Tighten the locknut before rechecking. Turn the adjusting nut only one-tenth of a turn each time, as this adjustment is very sensitive.

5. Many horns are now manufactured with an adjusting screw which protrudes through the back case (Fig. 22-2). This screw can be adjusted without removing the back shell.

6. When adjusting a set of horns on the car, disconnect one of the horns so that only one horn will blow at a time. Then run a wire from the horn-relay terminal connected to the horn switch. The other end of this lead can then be touched to ground during the horn test. This procedure will cause the horn relay to operate and the horn to sound; it is a handy way of operating the horn while it is being adjusted on the vehicle. If the horn cannot conveniently be checked on the car, remove it for a bench check.

NOTE: Adjustment of the horn will only clear up the sound. It cannot change the frequency of the tone. That is, it cannot raise or lower the tone.

✿ 22-3 Adjusting horns with removable back shell
There are two methods of making the current adjustment on these horns. Both begin with the removal of the back shell. Then the procedures are as follows:

1. Method A Loosen the current locknut without turning the current-adjusting nut, using two wrenches (see Fig. 22-3). Then rotate the current-adjusting nut one-tenth of a turn at a time, tighten the locknut, and test the horn. Rotate counterclockwise to increase the current or clockwise to decrease the current. Adjust current within specifications.

2. Method B Insert a feeler gauge 0.007 inch [0.178 mm] thick (not more than ¼ inch [6.35 mm] wide) between the adjusting nut and the contact-blade

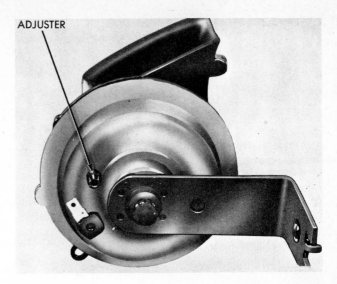

Fig. 22-2 Adjuster on horn. (Chrysler Corporation)

insulator (Fig. 22-3). Do not allow the gauge to touch the contact points. Loosen the locknut, and turn the adjusting nut to a position that will allow the horn to just operate. Lock the nut in position, remove the feeler gauge, and check horn performance.

After adjustments are made, replace the back shell, making sure the insulator is in place around the horn terminal.

NOTE: This type of horn is grounded internally and must have a good ground connection to the frame through the horn bracket. Make sure the bracket is making good clean contact with the car frame. A loose mounting or poor ground connection will affect horn tone.

✿ 22-4 Horn relay
Most horn circuits use a horn relay (Fig. 22-4). With the horn relay, it is not necessary to run a heavy wire up to the horn switch on the steering

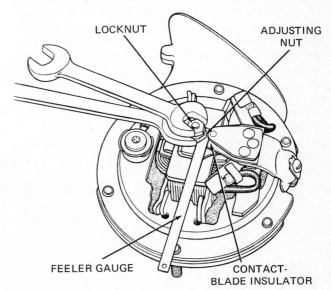

LOCKNUT · ADJUSTING NUT · FEELER GAUGE · CONTACT-BLADE INSULATOR

Fig. 22-3 Adjusting horn of the type with a removable back shell. (Delco-Remy Division of General Motors Corporation)

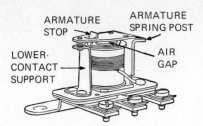

Fig. 22-4 Horn relay with cover removed, showing the checks and adjustments.

wheel or column. Instead, only a small wire is sufficient to carry the low current needed to operate the relay (Fig. 22-5). The relay has a single winding which is energized when the horn switch is closed. This connects the winding to the battery. The winding electromagnetism then pulls down the armature and closes the relay contacts. This action connects the horns to the battery so they operate.

The closing voltage of the relay can be checked by connecting the relay to a source of variable voltage such as a battery and variable resistor in series (Fig. 22-6). A voltmeter connected across the winding, as shown, will then measure the closing voltage. Start with the full resistance in the circuit and turn the resistance knob to decrease the resistance and increase the voltage on the relay winding. Note the voltage at which the relay points close. Adjust, if necessary, by bending the armature-spring post to change the spring tension (Fig. 22-4). Increasing the spring tension increases the closing voltage.

⚙ 22-5 Open-door warning buzzer

The horn relay serves a second purpose—as a warning that the ignition key has been left in the ignition switch when a car door is opened. Figure 22-7 shows the circuit. When the ignition key is in the ignition switch, a special set of contacts is closed. Now, if a car door is opened, the door switch will complete the circuit through the buzzer (upper) contacts and winding of the relay to the battery. The winding becomes energized and pulls the armature down. This opens the contacts and the winding loses its magnetism, so the spring closes the contacts again. This cycle is repeated rapidly so that the relay emits a

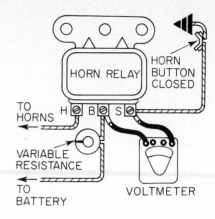

Fig. 22-6 Connections with variable resistance and voltmeter to check closing voltage of the horn-relay.

buzzing sound to warn the driver that he or she has forgotten the ignition key. Many of the car thefts in this country are caused by the driver leaving the ignition key in the switch. Therefore this warning system serves as a deterrent to car theft.

Some cars have a warning "lights-on" system that is tied in with the "ignition-key" system. That is, if the driver leaves the lights on and removes the ignition key, the buzzer will sound if the driver then opens the car door. This warns the driver that the lights have been left on. The buzzer will stop if the lights are then turned off.

⚙ 22-6 Security alarm system

The security alarm system, shown in one version in Figs. 22-8 and 22-9, sounds an alarm if a thief tries to force entry to any

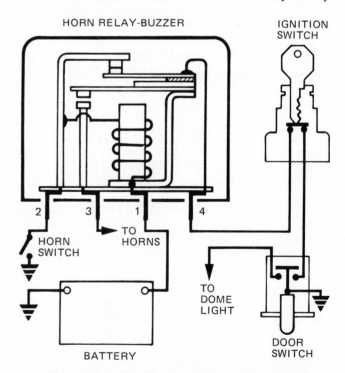

Fig. 22-7 Horn-relay-wiring system which includes a buzzer reminder that the ignition key is still in the ignition switch when the car door is opened. (Chevrolet Motor Division of General Motors Corporation)

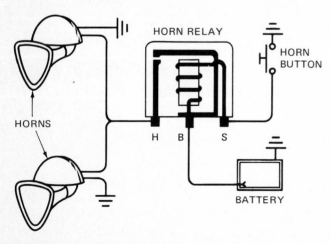

Fig. 22-5 Horn relay and horn circuit.

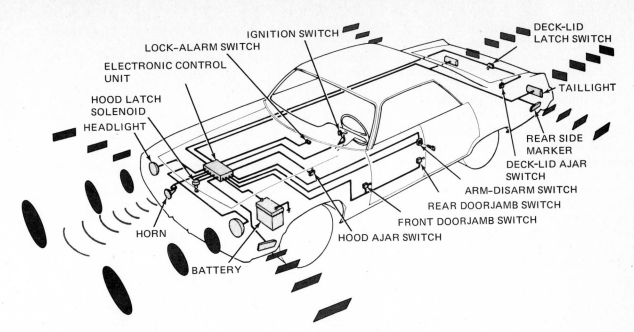

Fig. 22-8 Locations of components of a security alarm system. The circles and rectangles represent the flashing lights when the system is in action. The arcs represent the blowing of the horn. *(Chrysler Corporation)*

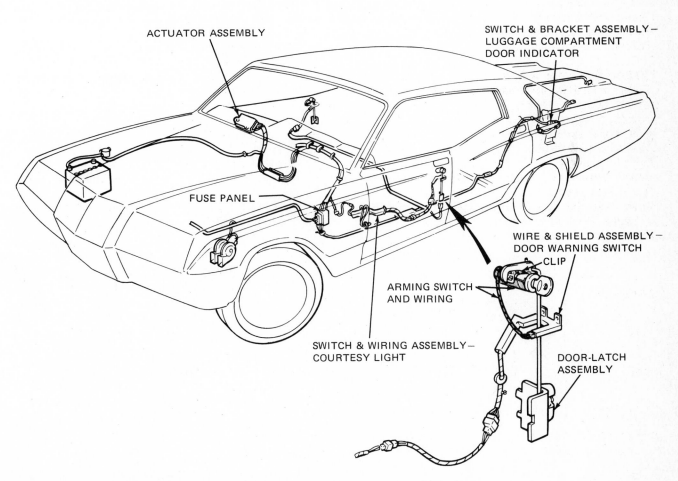

Fig. 22-9 Locations of components and wiring circuit of a security, or antithief, alarm system. *(Ford Motor Company)*

door, the hood, the trunk, or the tailgate. The alarm consists of the horn sounding at about 90 cycles per minute for 3 to 5 minutes. At the same time, the headlights, taillights, and side-marker lights flash on and off at the same rate.

When either front door is locked with the key, the system shown is armed. That is, it is ready to sound the alarm if any attempt is made to force entry into the car. The system can be turned off by using the door key to unlock the door.

Security alarm systems can also be installed in the field. One field-installed system has the arming lock mounted in the side of the right-front fender. It is wired to the courtesy lights and also to the trunk and hood lights. If the arming lock has been turned on (a special key is required) and if a door, the hood, or trunk is opened, the circuit to a siren is completed. The siren will then sound.

Chapter 22 review questions

Select the *one* correct, best, or most probable answer to each question. Then check your answers against the correct answers given at the end of the book.

1. The horn has:
   a. vibrating contact points,
   b. a vibrating diaphragm,
   c. an electromagnet,
   d. all these.
2. The horn relay is connected between the battery and the:
   a. ignition switch,
   b. horn,
   c. charging system,
   d. headlamps.
3. The purpose of the open-door warning buzzer is to sound the buzzer:
   a. when the door is opened with the key in the ignition switch,

b. when the door is opened when the headlights are on,
   c. to warn the driver the lights are on or that the key should be removed,
   d. all these.
4. The security alarm system sounds the alarm if it is armed when someone tries to force entry to:
   a. any door,
   b. hood,
   c. trunk,
   d. any of these.
5. A raspy horn sound could be caused by:
   a. mismatched projectors and power plants,
   b. loose back shell,
   c. cracked diaphragm,
   d. all of these.
6. Adjustment of the horn can:
   a. lower the tone,
   b. raise the tone,
   c. clear up the sound,
   d. all of these.
7. In some cars, the horn relay:
   a. serves as an open-door buzzer,
   b. serves as a lights-on buzzer,
   c. completes the circuit to the horns,
   d. all of these.
8. The security alarm system operates, when armed, whenever:
   a. the lights are turned on,
   b. the engine is started,
   c. whenever a door, trunklid, or hood is opened,
   d. all of these.
9. One type of security alarm is armed when:
   a. the ignition switch is turned off,
   b. the driver's weight is not on the front seat,
   c. either front door is locked with the key,
   d. none of the above.
10. If the horn sound is weak,
    a. check the size of the projector,
    b. check the voltage of the horn while it is operating,
    c. check for a cracked diaphragm,
    d. all of the above.

SAFETY-BELT ELECTRIC CONTROLS

After studying this chapter, you should be able to:

1. Explain why everyone should wear safety belts.
2. Describe the two types of safety belts—lap and shoulder.
3. Explain how the safety-belt starter interlock system worked.

23-1 Safety belts The purpose of safety belts is to restrain the driver and passengers if there is an accident. During a front-end crash, for example, the car is brought to a sudden stop. But everything inside the car continues to move forward until it hits some solid object. An unrestrained passenger would continue to move forward until he or she hit the windshield or the instrument panel. It is these so-called second collisions that hurt and kill people. However, if the passengers and driver are wearing safety belts, they will be restrained. They will not continue to move forward until they hit some solid object in the car.

There are two kinds of safety belts, *lap belts* and *shoulder belts* (Fig. 23-1). The lap belt has been credited with saving many lives and preventing many injuries. The lap belt and shoulder belt together are even more effective. The lap belt prevents the passenger or driver from being thrown forward. The shoulder belt keeps the passenger or driver from jackknifing; that is, the upper body is kept from bending at the waist and moving forward. The driver who jackknifed would be thrown into the steering shaft. A passenger who jackknifed would strike the instrument panel with his or her head.

The safety belts installed on earlier-model cars were optional; that is, the driver and passengers did not have to use them. Then, on later-model cars, a warning buzzer was incorporated which buzzed if the safety belts were not fastened. Another arrangement that lasted only a few months was called the *safety-belt starter interlock system*. This system required the driver and any front-seat passengers to buckle their safety belts before the engine could be started. The purpose of these devices was to force the driver and front-seat passengers to use their safety belts and thus

protect themselves from injury or death if there was an accident.

23-2 Front-seat safety-belt warning system The front-seat safety-belt warning system includes a buzzer and a red warning light which remind the driver and

Fig. 23-1 Safety belts consist of a lap belt and a shoulder belt.

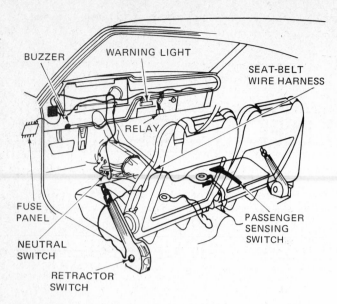

Fig. 23-2 Seat-belt warning system. *(American Motors Corporation)*

passengers to buckle their safety belts. Figure 23-2 is a schematic drawing of the system. Figure 23-3 is a wiring diagram of the system. The reminder signals (light and buzzer or chimes) come on if the belts are not buckled and the driver starts the engine and then releases the parking brake (manual transmission) or shifts into gear (automatic transmission).

The outboard safety-belt retractors have switches which are closed when the belts are retracted. When the belts are pulled out and buckled, the retractor switches open, thus preventing the buzzer and light from coming on.

There is a sensing switch under the passenger side of the front seat. This switch is interconnected with the right-hand safety-belt-retractor switch. The sensing switch closes when a weight of more than a few pounds (a passenger) is placed on the seat. Then, if the passenger fails to buckle up, the retractor switch, also closed, completes the circuit to the buzzer and light. Now, when the driver releases the parking brake (manual transmission) or shifts into gear (automatic transmission), the reminders come on.

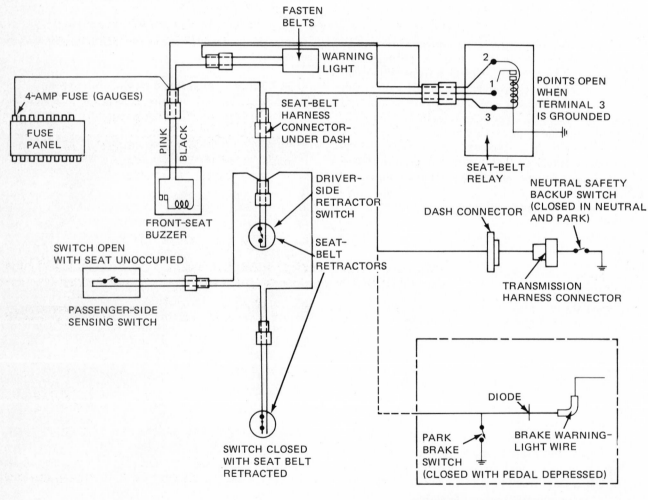

Fig. 23-3 Seat-belt warning-system wiring diagram. *(American Motors Corporation)*

Some manufacturers supply adjusting information for the passenger sensing switch such as: "If the switch is too sensitive, apply your full weight on one knee directly above the sensing switch. When the cushion bottoms, the switch contacts will be bent. This should increase the amount of weight necessary to actuate the switch." Other manufacturers state that the switch should be replaced if it does not work satisfactorily.

☼ **23-3 Safety-belt starter interlock system** The safety-belt starter interlock system made it necessary to buckle the front safety belts before the engine could be started. The sequence required of the driver was as follows:

1. Get in the car; sit down.
2. Buckle the safety belt. If a passenger gets in, the passenger must also buckle up.
3. Insert the ignition key and turn the switch to START.

This is the only sequence that would get the engine started.

Because many people objected to this system, the federal government has eliminated the regulation requiring manufacturers to install it. Furthermore, it is now legal for the system to be deactivated on cars now in operation. The approved procedure allows the interlock to be bypassed and the buzzer to be disconnected. However, the safety-belt warning light must remain operative. Procedures for making the disconnect are available from the vehicle manufacturer.

Chapter 23 review questions

Select the *one* correct, best, or most probable answer to each question. Then check your answers against the correct answers given at the end of the book.

1. There are two types of safety belts:
   a. seat and lap,
   b. seat and shoulder,
   c. lap and shoulder,
   d. overlapping and lapping.

2. The seat-belt starter interlock system:
   a. lasted only a few months,
   b. was eliminated because many people objected to it,
   c. required proper seat-belt coupling before the car would start,
   d. all of these.

3. The front-seat-belt warning system has:
   a. a sensing switch under the passenger side of the seat,
   b. a sensing switch under the driver's side of the seat,
   c. an interlock with the starter system,
   d. all of these.

4. The front-seat-belt warning system has:
   a. a retractor switch on the passenger side,
   b. a retractor switch on the driver side,
   c. a sensing switch under the passenger side of the seat,
   d. all of these.

5. In the front seat safety-belt warning system, the pressure- or weight-sensing switch is located:
   a. under the driver's seat,
   b. under the front-seat passenger's seat,
   c. in the left-hand front door,
   d. in the right-hand front door.

INDICATING DEVICES

After studying this chapter, you should be able to:

1. List and explain how the various indicating devices used on cars work.
2. Explain how to check out gauge circuits and what to do if a gauge does not work.
3. Under the supervision of the instructor, check gauge systems and remove and install gauges.

24-1 Automotive indicating devices Most automobiles have four electrically operated indicating devices on the instrument panel. Their purpose is to keep the driver informed on the operating condition of the engine and the charging system, and the amount of fuel in the tank. If some abnormal condition shows up, an indicator will register this fact. The driver can then seek service before serious damage is done.

The four indicating devices are the fuel gauge, the engine oil-pressure indicator, the engine temperature indicator, and the charging system indicator light, ammeter, or voltmeter.

Figure 24-1 is the instrument panel wiring diagram for the indicating devices. Note that this system has a voltmeter and also a tachometer (tach). The tachometer reports the speed with which the engine is turning in revolutions per minute.

Figure 24-2 shows the printed circuit that includes the circuits in Fig. 24-1. We described printed circuits in ☼ 1-34.

Automotive vehicles also have other indicating devices—speedometer and odometer (which registers the distance traveled), brake-malfunction light, turn-indicating lights, and tail-ajar light (for station wagons), for instance. Some cars also have other indicating devices to signal when the coolant is low or the brake system needs fluid. These and other indicators are described in this chapter.

☼ 24-2 Fuel gauges Electrically operated fuel gauges are of either the balancing coil or the thermostatic type (Figs. 24-3 and 24-4).

1. Balancing-coil type In the balancing-coil system (Fig. 24-3), there are two separate units, the tank unit (Fig. 24-4) and the instrument-panel unit (the dash unit). these are connected in series by a wire to the battery (through the ignition switch). When the ignition is turned on, current from the battery flows through both the tank unit and the instrument-panel unit. The tank unit consists of a variable resistance and a sliding contact that is positioned by a float lever. The float lever, in turn, moves up or down as the level of gasoline changes in the tank. When the gasoline level is low, the sliding contact has moved up to cut out most of the resistance. Therefore most of the current passing through the left-hand coil in the instrument-panel unit flows through the resistance. Little of it flows through the right-hand coil. Consequently, the left-hand coil is stronger magnetically than the right-hand coil. The armature, and thus the pointer, are swung to the left, so that the low fuel level is indicated. On the other hand, when the fuel level is high, the float is up, and the sliding contact has cut most of the resistance into the circuit. Therefore most of the current that goes through the left-hand coil also goes through the right-hand coil. The right-hand coil is, therefore, relatively stronger and causes the armature and pointer to swing to the right to indicate the high fuel level.

2. Thermostatic type Two types of thermostatic fuel gauges have been used. The earlier type had thermostatic blades in both the tank unit and the instrument-panel unit. The later type uses a thermostatic blade in the instrument-panel unit but uses variable resistance in the tank unit. This variable resistance is similar to the one used in the balancing-coil fuel gauge, described in the preceding paragraph and illustrated in Fig. 24-5. We will look at the earlier type first—the type using two thermostatic blades.

In this earlier type, shown in Fig. 24-5, the tank float

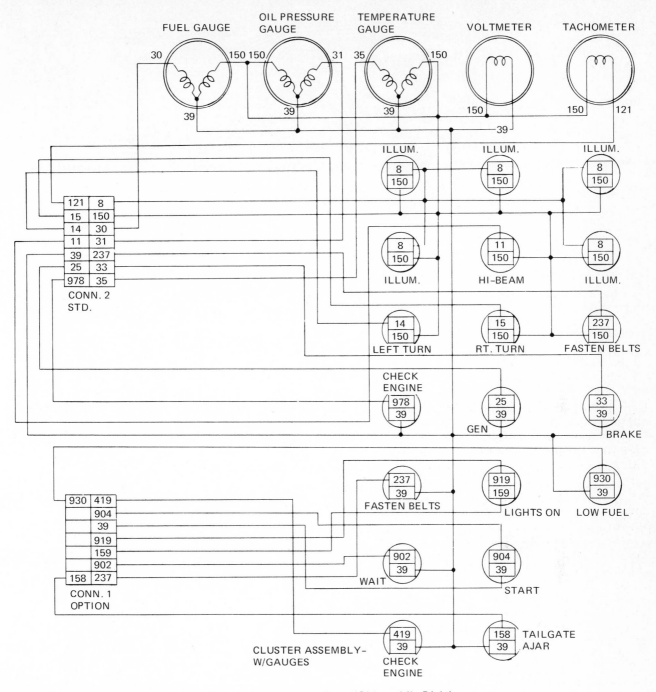

Fig. 24-1 Instrument panel wiring circuits for indicating devices. *(Oldsmobile Division of General Motors Corporation)*

actuates a cam that, in turn, causes more or less warping of a thermostatic blade. The thermostatic blade has a heating coil wrapped around it, and this coil is connected through a similar heating coil in the instrument-panel unit to the battery (through the ignition switch). When the ignition is turned on, current flows through both coils and causes heating of the thermostatic blades in both the instrument-panel unit and the tank unit. As a result, both blades begin to warp. In the instrument-panel unit, this movement is carried by linkage to the dash pointer, causing it to move across the indicator face. In the tank unit, the warping of the blade ultimately causes a set of contacts to open. If the fuel level is low, the original warping produced by the cam is slight. Under such circumstances, only a small amount of warping (by the heating-coil effect) will cause the contacts to open. As soon as they open, the heating effect stops in both the instrument-panel and the tank units. Therefore the thermostatic blades begin to straighten. In the tank unit this causes the contacts to close, and the heating effect takes place once again. The contacts, therefore, continue to open and close. The amount of warpage produced in the tank thermostatic blade is, therefore, approximately reproduced in the instrument-panel unit. This causes the instrument-panel unit to indicate the fuel level in the tank.

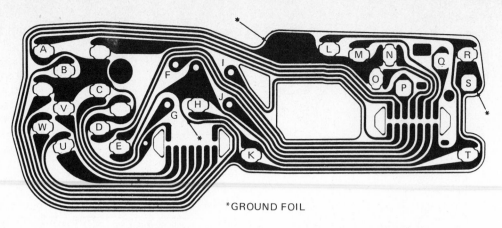

*GROUND FOIL

A = GENERATOR
B = LOW FUEL
C = FASTEN SEAT BELTS
D = BRAKE
E = FASTEN SEAT BELTS
F = OIL PRESSURE GAUGE
G = VOLTMETER
H, K, L, R, T = PANEL LIGHT
I = TEMPERATURE GAUGE
J = FUEL GAUGE

M = RIGHT TURN INDICATOR
N = LEFT TURN INDICATOR
O = HI–BEAM INDICATOR
P = 12 V (IGN)
Q = TACHOMETER
S = GROUND
U = LIGHTS ON
V = WAIT
W = START

Fig. 24-2 Printed circuit for instrument-panel indicating devices. *(Oldsmobile Division of General Motors Corporation)*

Figure 24-6 illustrates the later type of thermostatic fuel gauge which uses a variable resistance in the tank unit and a thermostat in the instrument-panel unit. The illustration also shows the circuit for a low-fuel-level indicator which is used with some fuel-gauge systems. The thermostatic fuel gauge and low-fuel-level indicator are described in following paragraphs.

3. **Low-fuel-level indicator**   Some systems have a special indicator system which turns on a warning light when the fuel tank is nearly empty. This gives the driver an additional warning that the fuel supply is getting low. Figure 24-6 shows one such system. First note that the fuel gauge is of the thermostatic type. The fuel sender unit, in the fuel tank, has a resistance and a sliding contact that slides up and down as the float moves up and down. When it is up, indicating a full tank, the resistance is at a minimum, allowing maxi-

mum current to flow. This heats the thermostatic unit in the fuel gauge to its maximum, causing it to warp and move the needle to F (indicating a full tank). Note that this system does not use contact points that open and close.

The system includes an instrument voltage regulator which is also thermostatic and has a pair of contact points. When the coil in the regulator is connected to the battery, it heats up, causing the thermostatic blade to warp. As the blade warps, it opens the contact points, disconnecting the coil from the battery. The coil cools, the thermostatic blade straightens, and the contact points close. The whole process is repeated. This action continues and keeps the voltage to the fuel-gauge system from increasing beyond the designed

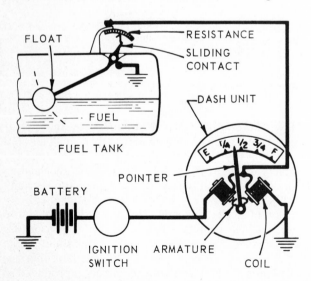

Fig. 24-3 Schematic wiring circuit of a balancing-coil fuel-gauge indicating system.

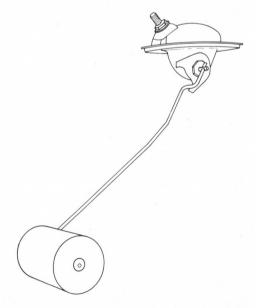

Fig. 24-4 Tank unit for a balancing-coil fuel-gauge indicating system.

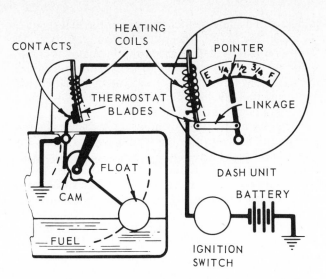

Fig. 24-5 Schematic wiring circuit of a thermostatic fuel gauge indicating system.

value. Notice also that the system includes a radio choke and a resistor. The voltage surges that are produced when the contact points open and close could cause radio interference. However, the choke, which is a coil of wire, prevents this from happening because it, in effect, smooths out the voltage surges.

Now, let us look at the low-fuel-level indicator. This system includes a thermistor assembly in the tank, a relay, and a warning light, as shown in Fig. 24-6. As long as there are more than a few gallons of fuel in the tank, the thermistor is submerged in the fuel and is kept cool. However, when the fuel level is low, the thermistor is exposed to vapors and gets hotter. The thermistor is a special sort of resistor that loses resistance as it heats up. This is just the reverse of resistors made of wire. Copper, as you know, increases in resistance as it heats up. But the thermistor, as it heats up, loses resistance (see ☼ 1-22), and this allows more current to flow from the battery through the warning relay winding. The increasing current produces an increasing

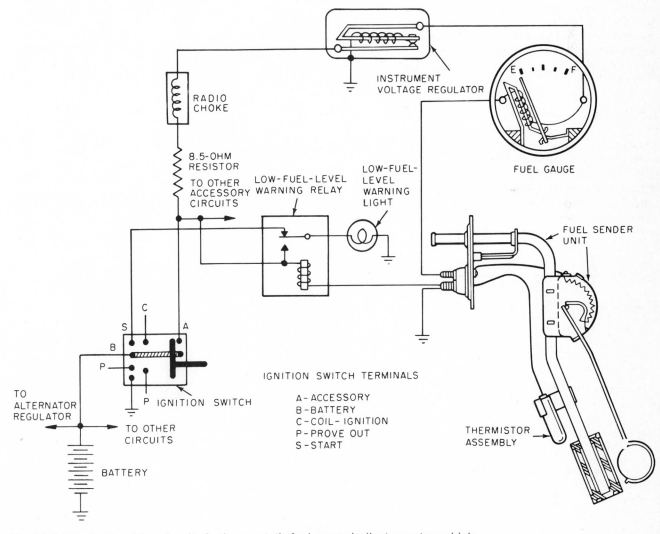

Fig. 24-6 Schematic wiring circuit of a thermostatic fuel-gauge indicator system which uses a variable-resistance tank unit. The system also includes a low-fuel-level warning light. *(Ford Motor Company)*

magnetic field. This magnetic field becomes strong enough to pull the relay contact points together, thereby completing the circuit from the battery to the warning light. The warning light comes on to signal the driver that the fuel supply is getting low.

The system also includes a "prove out" circuit. When the ignition switch is turned to START for cranking the engine, special contacts in the ignition switch connect the warning light to the battery. Thus, during cranking, this light comes on. The purpose of this special circuit is to prove out the system every time the engine is cranked. When the light comes on during cranking, the driver is reassured that the system is working. If the light should not come on, then the driver would know something was wrong—that the light was probably burned out or the relay was defective. In any case, it would be clear that the warning system was no longer working and that it needed checking.

Some more recent cars use an electronic low-fuel-level warning system (Fig. 24-7). This system also includes the fuel-level indicator. The low-fuel-level warning system works off the voltage difference between the two terminals of the fuel gauge. As the needle moves toward E (empty), the voltage increases. When the tank is about one-eighth full, the voltage is great enough to trigger the low-fuel-level switch. It then turns the low-fuel-level warning on.

⚙ 24-3 Miles-to-empty fuel indicator
This system allows the driver to find out how many more miles the car can be driven before it runs out of gasoline. The indicator is usually located just under the fuel gauge on the dash (Fig. 24-8). When the button is pressed, the MILES TO EMPTY will flash on the indicator for a few seconds. If there is less than 50 miles of fuel remaining, the mileage will remain on. This system is used instead of the low-fuel-level warning system. Figure 24-9 shows the components of the system.

The system continuously adjusts for changes in driving conditions as well as the way the car is used. That is, if the car is used around town, where gasoline mileage is relatively poor, the system will adjust to this increased consumption. However, if the car is generally used on the highway, where gasoline mileage is better, the system will adjust to this rate of fuel usage. Note that the system measures car speed and mileage traveled as well as the rate at which the fuel is being taken out of the fuel tank.

⚙ 24-4 Oil-pressure indicators
The oil-pressure indicator tells the driver what the engine oil pressure is. This gives warning if some defect occurs in the lubricating system that prevents delivery of oil to vital engine parts. Oil-pressure indicators are of three types: pressure-expansion, electric-resistance, and indicator-light. The last two are the more commonly used.

1. **Pressure expansion** The pressure-expansion indicator uses a hollow Bourdon (curved) tube that is fastened at one end and free at the other. The oil pressure is applied to the curved tube through an oil line from the engine; as this pressure increases, it causes

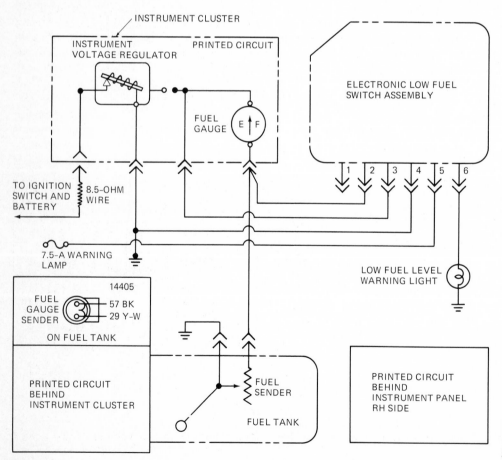

Fig. 24-7 Electronic low-fuel-level warning system wiring diagram. (Ford Motor Company)

Fig. 24-8 Fuel gauge and miles-to-empty indicator. *(Ford Motor Company)*

the tube to straighten out somewhat. This movement is transmitted to a needle by linkage and gears from the end of the tube. The needle moves across the face of a dial to register the amount of oil pressure.

2. **Electric** Electrically operated oil-pressure indicators are of two types, balancing-coil (Fig. 24-10) and thermostatic, as with fuel gauges. In fact, the actions are very similar. In the balancing-coil type, there is a variable resistance in the engine unit. Increasing oil pressure causes the diaphragm to be pushed upward. This moves the sliding contact along the resistance so that the amount of resistance in the circuit is increased. As a result, the right-hand coil in the instrument-panel unit becomes relatively stronger than the left-hand coil.

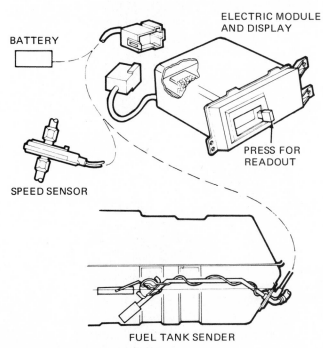

Fig. 24-9 Components in the miles-to-empty indicator system. *(Ford Motor Company)*

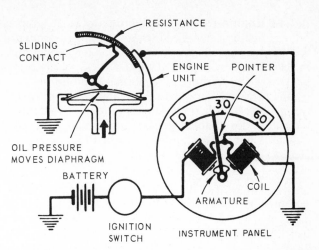

Fig. 24-10 Schematic wiring circuit of a balancing-coil oil-pressure indicating system.

Therefore, the armature and pointer swing to the right to indicate the higher oil pressure. In the thermostatic-blade type, the diaphragm movement warps the thermostatic blade in the engine unit. This action is similar to that of the thermostatic fuel gauge.

3. **Indicator light** Instead of a gauge, many vehicles use an oil-pressure indicator light (Fig. 24-11). The light comes on when the ignition is turned on and the oil pressure is low. Normally, after the engine has started and the oil pressure has built up, the light goes off. If it does not, then the engine and lubricating system should be checked at once to find the cause of low oil pressure. The light is connected to a pressure switch in the engine, and this switch is closed except when oil pressure increases to normal operating values. The indicator light and the pressure switch are connected in series to the battery through the ignition switch. When the ignition is turned on, the indicator light comes on and stays on until the engine starts and the oil pressure builds up enough to open the pressure switch.

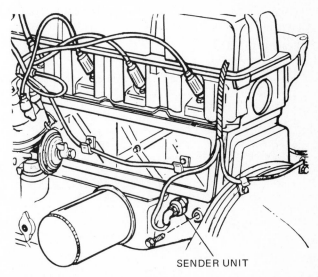

Fig. 24-11 Oil-pressure sender unit for an indicator light on an in-line engine. *(Ford Motor Company)*

⚙ 24-5 Engine-temperature indicators A temperature indicator is installed in the car so that the operator will know at all times whether the water temperature in the cooling system is at a safe level. An abnormal heat rise is a warning of abnormal conditions in the engine. The indicator thus warns the operator to stop the engine before serious damage is done. Temperature indicators are of three general types: vapor-pressure (which is nonelectric and will not be discussed here), electric-gauge, and indicator-light.

1. Electric   Electrically operated temperature indicators are of two types: balancing-coil and bimetal-thermostat. The balancing-coil-type oil-pressure indicator, fuel gauge, and temperature indicator all operate in a similar manner. The instrument-panel indicating units are, in fact, practically identical, consisting of two coils and an armature to which a needle is attached, as shown in Fig. 24-12. The engine unit is a type of thermistor. It loses resistance as its temperature increases. This is characteristic of thermistors and is the reverse of what happens to the wiring used in most electric circuits, which increases in resistance with an increase in temperature (see ⚙ 1-22 for an explanation of thermistors and resistance). Thus the engine unit will lose resistance and pass more current as engine temperature increases. As this happens, more current passes through the right-hand coil in the indicating unit, so that the armature and needle swing to the right and the needle thus indicates the higher temperature.

The bimetal-thermostat-type temperature indicator is similar to the bimetal-thermostat fuel gauge. The dash, or instrument-panel, units are practically identical. The engine unit of the temperature indicator is of the thermistor type, and the temperature of the coolant in the cooling system is directly imposed on it. When the temperature is low, the thermistor resistance is high. Thus it passes only a small current, and the thermostatic blade in the instrument-panel unit distorts only a little to indicate the low temperature. As engine temperature increases, the thermistor resistance goes down and it passes more current. This increasing current heats the instrument-panel thermostatic blade more. It distorts more, causing the needle to move over to show the higher temperature.

2. Indicator light   One indicator-light system is shown in Fig. 24-13. This system has a coolant-temperature sending unit mounted on the engine, so it is exposed to the cooling-system coolant. The sending unit is connected to two light bulbs and the battery through the ignition switch. When the ignition switch is first turned on to start the cold engine, the sending-unit thermostatic blade is in the proper position to connect the COLD light to the battery. The COLD light, which appears in blue on the instrument panel, comes on and remains on until the engine approaches operating temperature. As this happens, the thermostatic blade in the sending unit is bent by the increasing temperature. The blade, therefore, moves off the cold terminal, disconnecting the COLD light so it is turned off. If the engine should overheat, the thermostatic blade will warp further so that it moves under the hot terminal. This connects the HOT bulb on the instrument panel to the battery so that it glows red. This is a signal to the driver that the engine has overheated and should be stopped before serious damage results.

⚙ 24-6 Ammeter, or charge indicator The ammeter, or charge indicator, which is used on many cars, is connected between the alternator and the battery. It tells the driver whether the alternator is working properly and charging the battery when the engine is running. Electric-meter principles were discussed in ⚙ 5-5. However, the car ammeter is somewhat simpler than the meters described in that section. Figure 24-14 shows a car ammeter. It contains a steel armature mounted on the same shaft as the pointer. A permanent

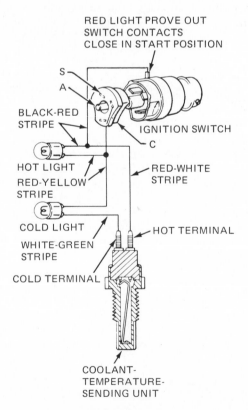

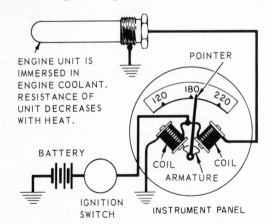

Fig. 24-12 Schematic wiring circuit of a balancing-coil engine-temperature indicating system.

Fig. 24-13 Temperature indicating system using COLD and HOT indicating lights. *(Ford Motor Company)*

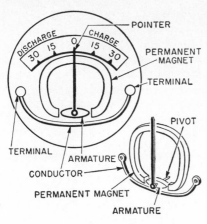

Fig. 24-14 Simplified drawing of a car ammeter, or charge indicator.

horseshoe magnet holds the armature in such a position that the pointer indicates zero when no current is flowing through the ammeter. When current does flow through, it passes through a conductor connected between the ammeter terminals. This current flow produces a secondary magnetic field that bucks the magnetic field from the permanent magnet. The secondary magnetic field therefore acts on the steel armature on the pointer shaft, causing it to swing around so the pointer moves away from zero. The amount of the swing is determined by the strength of the secondary magnetic field, which is, in turn, determined by the strength of the current flow. When the current flows in one direction—for instance, from the alternator to the battery—the armature and pointer move around to indicate on the charge side. However, when the battery is delivering current to, say, the lights, the pointer moves around on the other side of the scale to indicate discharge.

⚙ 24-7 Voltmeter   Many cars now have a voltmeter instead of an ammeter (Fig. 24-1). The voltmeter gives a continuous reading of the voltage in the charging system. Since the voltage provides a good measure of the battery condition and the charging action, many consider the voltmeter a better instrument than the ammeter. ⚙ 5-5 describes the operation of dc ammeters and voltmeters.

⚙ 24-8 Charge-indicator light   The charge-indicator light is used in many cars instead of an ammeter. It is connected between the alternator or alternator regulator and the battery through the ignition switch. The indicator light is connected in parallel with a resistance. Current flows through the resistance and the indicator light on its way to the alternator field. The voltage drop through the resistance provides enough voltage to the indicator light to make the light glow. It glows until the engine starts and the alternator begins to charge the battery. When this happens, the voltage is the same on both sides of the resistance and the light. The light, therefore, goes off, indicating that the alternator is charging the battery.

⚙ 24-9 Gauge service   If faulty gauge action is sus-

pected, a new engine unit (or tank unit in fuel gauge) can be temporarily substituted for the old. If the gauge then indicates normally, the old engine (or tank) unit was defective. If the gauge still does not register properly, the instrument-panel unit or wiring is at fault. On the fuel gauge, it is not necessary to actually install the substitute tank unit in the tank. Instead, disconnect the lead from the old tank unit and reconnect it to the terminal of a new tank unit. Then connect a grounding wire from the tank unit case to the car frame. Now, the float of the substitute unit can be moved up or down by hand and the action of the instrument-panel unit noted.

NOTE: On the thermostatic type of gauge, it takes a minute or so for the thermostats to heat up and cause the instrument-panel unit to start indicating.

There is little in the way of service that gauges require. If a unit is found to be defective, it should be replaced with a new unit. On some fuel gauges, the float or float arm can be shifted so as to recalibrate the tank unit and correct the gauge reading. Also, on some units, it is possible to shift the winding poles toward or away from the armature so as to recalibrate the gauge. On the type of gauge that has vibrating thermostatic blades, dirty contact points (which cause needle fluctuation) can be cleaned by pulling a strip of clean bond paper between them. Be sure that no particles of paper are left between the points. Never use emery cloth to clean the points. Particles of emery will be embedded in the points and cause erratic gauge action.

⚙ 24-10 Sensor panel   A recent innovation in indicating devices is the sensor panel introduced by Toyota in 1974 (Fig. 24-15). This panel is installed on the roof of the car above the driver (Fig. 24-16). It is connected to sensors in the light circuits, brakes, windshield washer, battery, cooling-system radiator, and engine crankcase (see Fig. 24-15). The sensor panel has eleven warning lights which come on if something needs attention. For example, if any of the four lights at the top of the panel (LICENSE, BRAKE, TAIL, HEAD) come on, it indicates trouble in that light circuit. If one headlight burns out, HEAD would come on to warn the driver of the trouble. The four FLUID LEVEL lights (W-WASHER, BATTERY, RADIATOR, ENGINE OIL), indicate low fluid level in any of these four areas. That is, if the engine oil drops to a low level, the ENGINE OIL light would come on. The BRAKE section of the panel warns of low brake fluid, loss of vacuum in the power-brake unit, or excessive brake-lining wear. Figure 24-17 shows how the eleven warning lights are connected by sensors to the service areas.

Figure 24-18 shows how the brake-fluid-level sensor is installed on the brake-master-cylinder cap. Figure 24-19 shows a similar monitoring system. It has the indicator lights mounted on the instrument panel. When the test button (1) is pressed, all the lights will go on if everything is okay. If a light does not go on, something is wrong with the system which that light monitors.

⚙ 24-11 Trip computer   On command from the driver, the trip computer (Fig. 24-20) supplies a series

Fig. 24-15 Sensor panel, called an *Electro Sensor Panel,* or *ESP,* by the manufacturer. *(Toyota Motor Sales, Limited)*

of figures relating to the engine, fuel, average speed, and more. Actually, there are 12 buttons that, when pressed, provide the following:

Miles per gallon of fuel

Average speed

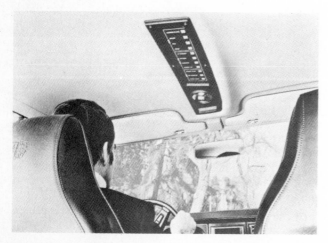

Fig. 24-16 Location of the sensor panel in a car. *(Toyota Motor Sales, Limited)*

Fig. 24-17 Connections from the sensor panel to the eleven service areas. *(Toyota Motor Sales, Limited)*

Time of day

Elapsed time since starting

Driving range in miles on remaining fuel supply

Miles to predetermined destination

Estimated arrival time

Engine rpm

Engine temperature

System voltage

The heart of the system is an electronic computer. It is fed information from a series of sensors. These report all the data listed above. The computer then makes calculations as necessary to supply any information the driver asks for. When the driver presses a button, the computer displays on the dash the numbers asked for. For example, the upper part of Fig. 24-20 shows the driver pressing the miles-per-gallon button. Instantly, the numeral 16 flashes on the display. This tells the driver that at the speed the car is traveling, it is getting 16 miles to a gallon of gasoline.

Fig. 24-18 Brake fluid-level sensor installed on a master cylinder. *(Ford Motor Company)*

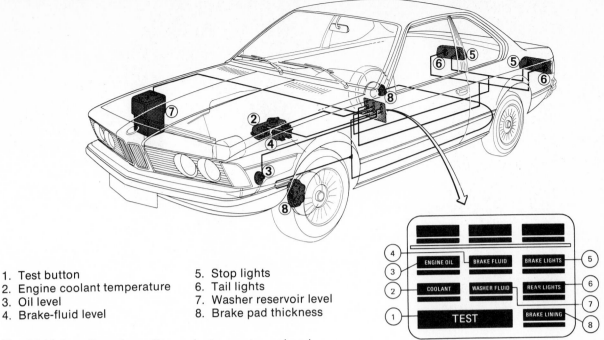

1. Test button
2. Engine coolant temperature
3. Oil level
4. Brake-fluid level
5. Stop lights
6. Tail lights
7. Washer reservoir level
8. Brake pad thickness

Fig. 24-19 Location of monitor on instrument panel and the components it monitors. *(BMW)*

Fig. 24-20 Cadillac trip computer. At top, the driver is touching the MPG button. The display indicates that the car is getting 16 miles per gallon. At bottom, the 12 buttons of the system are shown. *(Cadillac Motor Car Division of General Motors Corporation)*

Chapter 24 review questions

Select the *one* correct, best, or most probable answer to each question. Then check your answers against the correct answers given at the end of the book.

1. In the balancing-coil-type fuel gauge, filling the tank causes the resistance of the tank unit to be:
   a. increased,
   b. reduced,
   c. held steady,
   d. cut off.

2. In the balancing-coil type of fuel gauge, all the current flows through the:
   a. left-hand coil,
   b. right-hand coil,
   c. tank-unit resistance,
   d. tank itself.

3. In the balancing-coil type of fuel gauge, as the tank is filled, the amount of current flowing through the right-hand coil:
   a. increases,
   b. is reduced,
   c. holds steady,
   d. drops to zero.

4. In the electric oil-pressure gauge, changing oil pressure causes movement of a:
   a. diaphragm,
   b. float,
   c. Bourdon tube,
   d. resistance.

5. As the engine temperature goes up, the resistance of the engine unit in the engine-temperature gauge:
   a. goes up,
   b. goes down,
   c. holds steady,
   d. goes to zero.

OTHER ELECTRIC AND ELECTRONIC EQUIPMENT

After you have studied this chapter, you should be able to:

1. Explain the purpose and operation of all the devices described in the chapter.

25-1 Other electronic and electric devices This chapter describes several electric and electronic items not previously covered in the book. These include such electric devices as seat adjusters, window regulators, windshield wipers, and radios. Electronic equipment covered in the chapter includes electronic level controls, cruise control, antilock braking system, and anticollision radar.

25-2 Seat adjusters Electric seat adjusters are used on front seats to adjust the seat height, position, and tilt (on some models). The adjuster that moves the seat up and down, and from front to rear, is called a *four-way adjuster*. This can also include a tilt feature which will provide tilt forward and tilt backward. The latter arrangement is called a *six-way adjuster* (Fig. 25-1). The adjuster includes a drive motor, a transmission, drive cables, jack screws, slides, tracks, and supports.

In operation, the closing of one of the switches starts the motor and also, in the transmission, operates one of the solenoids. A four-way adjuster has two solenoids; a six-way adjuster has three solenoids. Let us take a typical four-way adjuster, for example, and see what happens when the up-down switch is pushed up to raise the seat. The motor starts to turn and, at the same time, the up-down solenoid is actuated to throw the up-down gears into mesh. (Actually not mesh—the solenoid pushes a driving dog—a type of clutch—into the side of the up-down gears.) The up-down gear turns in the proper direction to raise the seat. (If the switch were pushed down, the motor—and gear—would turn in the opposite direction.)

The drive is carried through drive cables to screw jacks on the lifting mechanism at the two sides of the seat. The screw jacks turn to raise the seat.

To move the seat back or forward, the back-or-for-

ward switch is operated. This actuates the horizontal-movement solenoid so that it causes the horizontal-movement gear to turn. This carries the drive through drive cables to drive pinions to move the seat forward or back. The drive pinions turn on horizontal racks to produce the movement.

The six-way adjuster has a third solenoid, gear, and drive cables to produce the forward or backward tilt.

25-3 Window regulators A power window regulator has an electric motor which is mounted in the lower part of the door (Fig. 25-2). It drives a rack and lever, or levers, which raise or lower the window. Figure 25-2 shows one type which uses a single lever. The type using a pair of levers (one an equalizer arm) is shown in Fig. 25-3.

25-4 Windshield washers and wipers Windshield wipers move rubber blades back and forth across the windshield to wipe away rain, snow, or other ma-

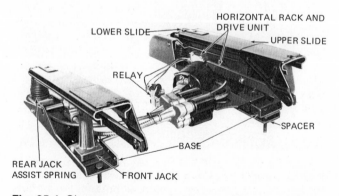

Fig. 25-1 Six-way power seat adjuster. *(Chrysler Corporation)*

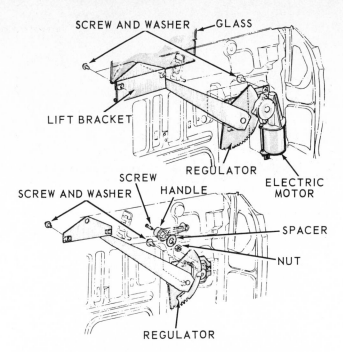

Fig. 25-2 Window regulators, mechanical (at bottom) and electric (at top). *Chrysler Corporation*

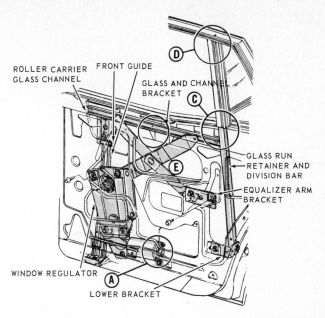

Fig. 25-3 Electric window regulator using a pair of levers. *(Ford Motor Company)*

terial that could prevent a clear view of the road ahead (Fig. 25-4). The windshield washer squirts a solution of water and windshield cleaner on the windshield when necessary to help the blades do a good job.

The system requires two electric motors. One, a two-speed unit (on most cars), drives the windshield wipers across the windshield. The other drives the pump that squirts cleaning fluid on the windshield.

The wiper motor is mounted on the engine side of the cowl. It is connected through reduction gears to linkage which is attached to the wiper-blade shafts. Figure 25-5 is a disassembled two-speed wiper motor. Figure 25-6 is the wiring circuit for the motor. Note that the motor has three brushes. One is a common brush. The other two are the low-speed and the high-speed brushes. The difference, besides their locations, is that the low-speed brush has a resistor in its circuit. This reduces the torque that the motor can develop and thus its speed. This system includes a connection that allows the motor to move the blades down into the concealed position when the wipers are turned off.

1. Intermittent operation   Many windshield wipers have a provision for intermediate operation. That is, when the control is set to intermediate, the windshield wiper will take a swipe, pause, and repeat the wiping operation. The length of the pause can be adjusted. The adjustment is made by turning a rheostat which is part of the control knob. This changes the amount of current being fed to the electronic governor which responds by changing the length of the pause between swipes.

2. Windshield washer   The windshield washer (Fig. 25-7) sends a squirt of washing fluid through rubber tubes to the wiper arms. In some models, the rubber tubes end in two or more nozzles on the arms. When

they squirt, they cover the essential parts of the windshield (Fig. 25-8). Other systems have a single nozzle, aimed to dispense the cleaning fluid over the windshield.

3. Controls   Some controls are mounted on the instrument panel (Fig. 25-9). When the knob is turned to the first position, the windshield wipers move across the windshield at the slower speed. Turning the knob further to the right (clockwise) sets the wipers moving at high speed. To set the wipers on the interval mode (on cars so equipped), the knob is turned to the left (counterclockwise). The farther it is turned, the longer the pauses between swipes. You push the knob in momentarily to cause the windshield washer to deliver a squirt of cleaning fluid. This action also starts the windshield wipers, and they continue for an interval and then shut off.

Some cars have the controls on an arm which is mounted on the steering shaft (Fig. 25-10). You move the arm and turn it to control the wipers and washer.

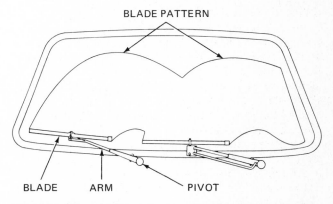

Fig. 25-4 Wiper-blade pattern on windshield. *(Ford Motor Company)*

325

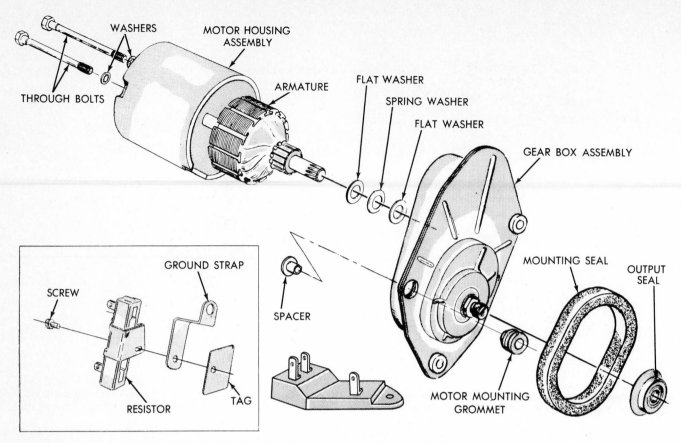

Fig. 25-5 Disassembled two-speed wiper motor. *(Chrysler Corporation)*

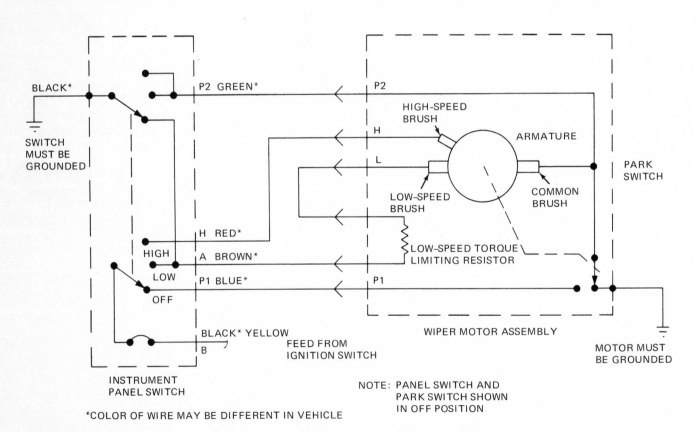

Fig. 25-6 Wiring diagram of wiper system with two-speed motor. *(Chrysler Corporation)*

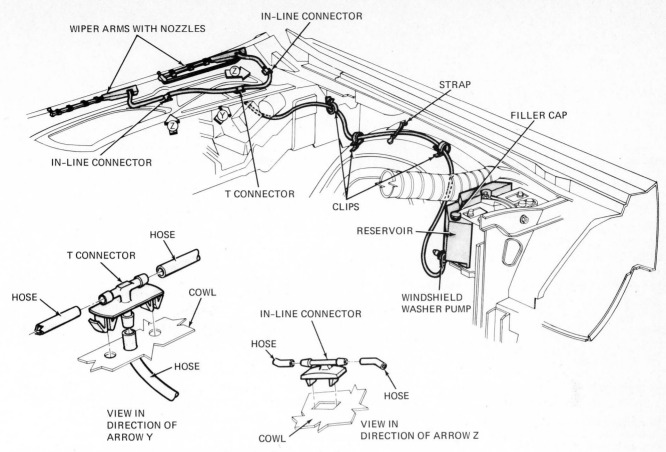

Fig. 25-7 Windshield-washer system. *(Chrysler Corporation)*

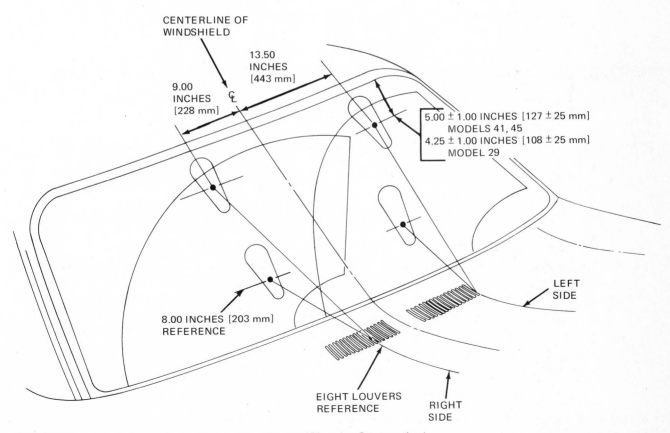

Fig. 25-8 Washer aiming pattern for one line of cars. *(Chrysler Corporation)*

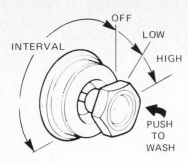

Fig. 25-9 Windshield washer-wiper control knob on instrument panel. *(Ford Motor Company)*

4. **Replacing wiper blades** The most common service required on the washer-wiper system, aside from keeping the washer reservoir filled, is replacement of the wiper blades. Over a period of time, they tend to harden and become brittle. A variety of attachments are used. Figure 25-11 shows three and the methods of releasing the old blades.

⚙ **25-5 Electric-fuel-pump control system** The tank-mounted electric fuel pump (Fig. 25-12) is connected through an oil-pressure switch to the ignition switch. The hydraulic switch is operated by pressure in the engine lubricating system. This switch has two pairs of contacts. During engine cranking, the first set of contacts is closed, and current is fed through these contacts from the solenoid on the starting motor. This current flows to the fuel pump, so that it operates. These connections continue as long as the engine is

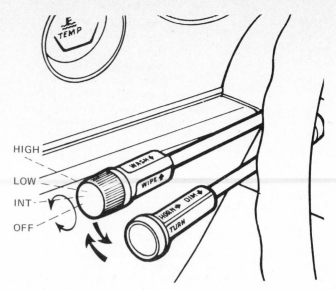

Fig. 25-10 Windshield washer-wiper control on arm mounted on steering column. *(Ford Motor Company)*

being cranked. As soon as the engine starts, the solenoid is disconnected from the battery, so this source of current is cut off. However, since the oil pressure builds up as soon as the engine starts, this causes the control switch to open the first set of contacts and close the second set of contacts. Now, current is fed to the fuel pump through the ignition switch and the second set of contacts in the control switch.

If the engine should stall during operation, the pressure will become too low to keep the second set of

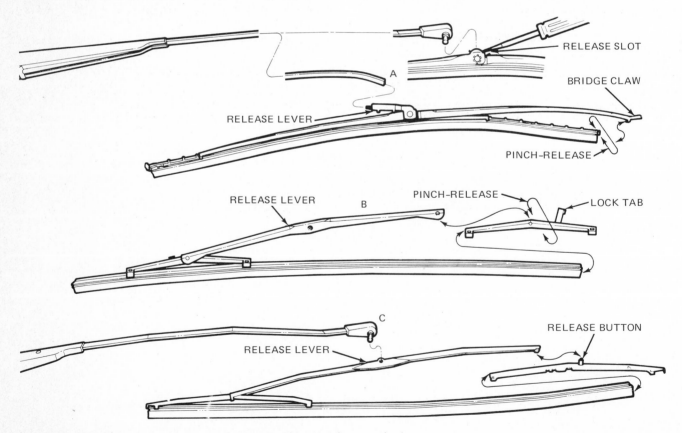

Fig. 25-11 Windshield wiper blade replacement. *(Chrysler Corporation)*

contacts in the control switch closed. They will open and the fuel pump will stop. If the engine should suddenly lose oil pressure, the second set of contacts in the control switch will open and the fuel pump will stop. Now the engine will run only until the fuel in the carburetor float bowl is used up. This protects the engine against serious damage from operating without oil pressure. The fuel pump will also stop when the ignition switch is turned off.

The electric-pump circuit also has a roll-over switch that opens the circuit if the car is in an accident and is rolled over. This prevents continued fuel pumping which could spew out fuel and cause a disastrous fire.

⚙ 25-6 Door locks Many cars are equipped with electric door-locking devices. The typical device includes a small solenoid in the door (Fig. 25-13) which actuates the lock when a switch is closed. If the switch is moved in one direction, the lock comes on; if in the other direction, the door is unlocked. Usually, there is a master control in the driver's position so that he or she can lock and unlock all doors simultaneously.

⚙ 25-7 Radios Radio service is a specialized business that requires special testing equipment and training. Thus radio servicing procedures are beyond the scope of this book. Nevertheless, there are some quick checks that an electrical technician can make that might pinpoint the cause of trouble as being either in the radio, in the electric circuit to the radio, or in the antenna circuit. A typical trouble-diagnosis procedure follows on the next page.

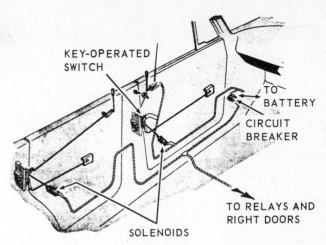

Fig. 25-13 Electric door-lock system. *(Chrysler Corporation)*

⚙ 25-8 Heaters and defrosters Heaters are, in a sense, part of the engine cooling system since they circulate the cooling liquid from the engine through the heater radiator. The heater has an electrically driven fan which circulates air through the radiator so that the air is warmed.

The defroster operates like the heater, often deriving heat from the same heater radiator. The defroster, however, directs the flow of warm air against the windshield to prevent condensation or freezing of moisture.

Normally, the only service the heater will require is a periodic flushing out when the engine radiator is flushed out. If the heater or defroster motor does not

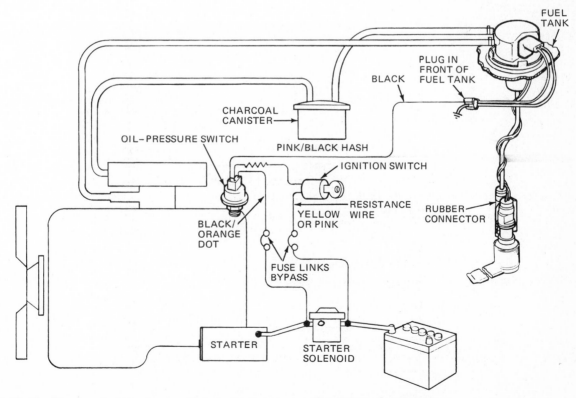

Fig. 25-12 Electric circuit of a tank-mounted electric fuel pump. *(Ford Motor Company)*

Radio Trouble Diagnosis Chart

CONDITION	POSSIBLE CAUSE	CORRECTION
1. Radio inoperative	a. Blown fuse	Replace fuse; check for short or open in wiring harness. Test voltage of fuse and tighten all connections.
	b. Antenna open or shorted	Test with an auxiliary antenna with lead-in plugged into receiver set and test antenna head outside of car. If radio plays with test antenna, use original antenna and check antenna for shorts to ground while rocking antenna slightly. Unplug antenna lead from radio and use ohmmeter to check from center contact of antenna to outside case. If reading on ohmmeter is less than 500,000 ohms, replace antenna.
	c. Receiver or speaker connections loose or faulty	With speaker control turned to either stop, rotate control to other stop. If radio plays, replace faulty speaker. If radio does not play, remove radio receiver for servicing.
2. Radio reception weak	a. Unbalanced antenna trimmer	Carefully adjust antenna trimmer. See "Service Procedures" in factory manual.
	b. Shorted antenna lead-in	Turn on radio and wiggle antenna. If speaker static is heard, check for antenna mounting tightness. If speaker static is still heard after tightening, disassemble antenna and test for faulty insulators or presence of moisture. Make an ohmmeter check step, as in item 1b. If no static is heard, test for faulty or loose receiver or antenna connections at receiver. Also check antenna lead-in at antenna. If antenna checks okay, remove radio receiver for servicing.
3. Radio noisy (engine running)	a. Outside electrical interferences	Move car or eliminate interference.
	b. Insufficient or faulty interference suppression	Install effective capacitor in ignition system.
4. Radio noisy (engine not running)	Faulty antenna	Turn on radio and wiggle antenna lead and listen for speaker static. If static is heard, disassemble antenna and check for faulty insulators or presence of moisture. Make an ohmmeter test, as in item 1b. If no static is heard, check for a loose or faulty capacitor. If capacitor is okay, remove antenna plug from radio receiver and bump receiver with heel of hand. If no static is heard, start engine, turn on headlights, and slowly accelerate engine speed. If whining noise is heard, turn off headlights, and if whining noise is still present, recheck ignition-coil capacitor; if capacitor is okay, remove radio receiver for servicing.
5. Radio reception distorted	a. Speaker voice-coil leads rubbing on speaker cone	Install an auxiliary speaker and compare. Replace if improved.
	b. Torn speaker cone	Replace speaker.
	c. Faulty radio	Send radio to authorized radio service station for repair.
	d. Foreign material in speaker	Clean or replace speaker.
6. Intermittent reception	a. Broken or shorted antenna lead-in wire	Test with a substitute antenna and replace if necessary.
	b. Faulty radio	Send radio to authorized radio service station for repair.

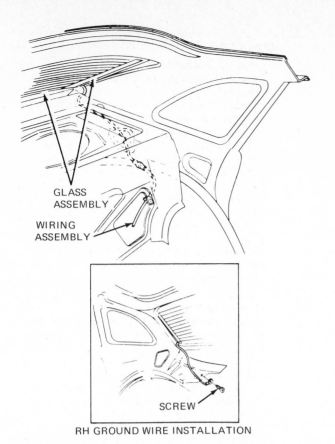

Fig. 25-14 Heated rear window (backlite and wiring assemblies. *(Ford Motor Company)*

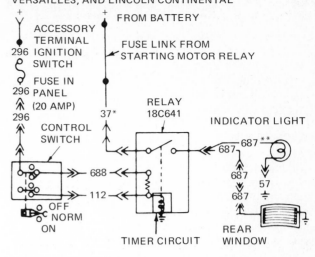

FAIRMONT, ZEPHYR, MUSTANG, CAPRI, LTD II, THUNDERBIRD, COUGAR, CONTINENTAL MARK V, VERSAILLES, AND LINCOLN CONTINENTAL

* 37 IS 686 FOR LINCOLN CONTINENTAL
** 687 IS 186 FOR LINCOLN CONTINENTAL

Fig. 25-15 Wiring diagram for heated backlite system. *(Ford Motor Company)*

operate properly and the electric circuit to it is in good condition, the motor should be replaced. As a rule, these motors are serviced by complete replacement, although it is possible, on some motors, to replace bearings, armature, brushes, and other small parts.

⚙ **25-9 Heated rear window (backlight)** In this system, the rear window or backlight has a grid of resistance wire baked onto the inside surface of the back window (Fig. 25-14). When the grid is connected to the battery, the wire gets hot and heats the window, thus preventing the buildup of fog, ice, or snow. Figure 25-15 shows the wiring diagram for the system. When the control switch is moved to ON, it connects the timer relay coil to the battery. The relay closes its points to connect the indicator light and the rear-window grid to the battery. The control switch is spring loaded to re-

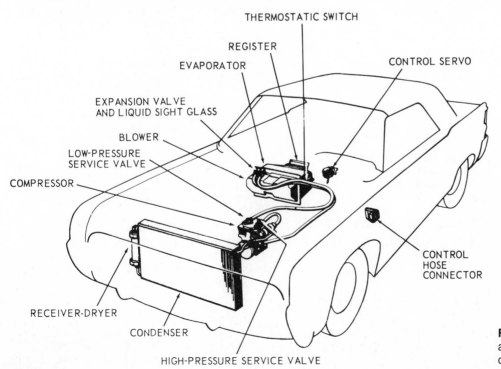

Fig. 25-16 Installation of an air conditioner in a passenger car. *(Ford Motor Company)*

turn to its center or NORMAL position. As soon as the driver releases the switch lever, it returns to NORMAL. However, the timer relay still holds its points closed. The relay includes a timer circuit which is a thermostatic device. It heats up, and after about ten minutes it opens the relay so the indicator light goes off and the window grid is disconnected from the battery.

If the rear window needs additional heat, the system can be reactivated by again turning the control switch momentarily to ON.

⚙ 25-10 Air conditioners

Automotive air conditioners are operated by the engine; a special pulley on the engine crankshaft drives the air-conditioner compressor through a V belt. The air conditioner both cools the air and removes moisture from it. Figure 25-16 shows a typical system. Air conditioners have electric controls to operate the system. The control circuit for one system is shown in Figure 25-17. This system has three switches: a push-button switch to turn the air conditioner on or off, a fan switch to turn the blower on or off, and a temperature-control switch.

Air-conditioning service is a specialized business, and only a technician trained in this field, and having the necessary equipment and tools, should attempt to service air conditioners.

⚙ 25-11 Diesel-engine glow plugs

In diesel engines, ignition of the air–fuel mixture results from the high temperature of the air compressed in the cylinder. When air is compressed, it gets hot. In the diesel engine, the air is so highly compressed that it reaches temperatures of 1000°F [538°C]. Fuel is then sprayed into this superheated air, and it ignites.

When a cold diesel engine is being started, the heat of compression can escape from the compressed air so fast that the air is not hot enough to ignite the fuel being sprayed in. Therefore, help is needed to start the cold diesel engine. In many engines, the help comes from glow plugs installed in the combustion chambers. These are small electric heaters. Figures 25-18 and 25-19 show the wiring harness to the glow plugs in a V-8 engine. Before a cold diesel engine is cranked, the driver turns on the glow plugs. They heat rapidly and warm up the combustion chambers in the engine. After a short time (half a minute or less), enough heat has been added. This is indicated by a light on the instrument panel that tells the driver it is time to crank the engine.

⚙ 25-12 Automatic level control

The automatic-level-control system takes care of changes in the load at the rear of the car. In a car without automatic level control, adding weight at the rear will make the rear

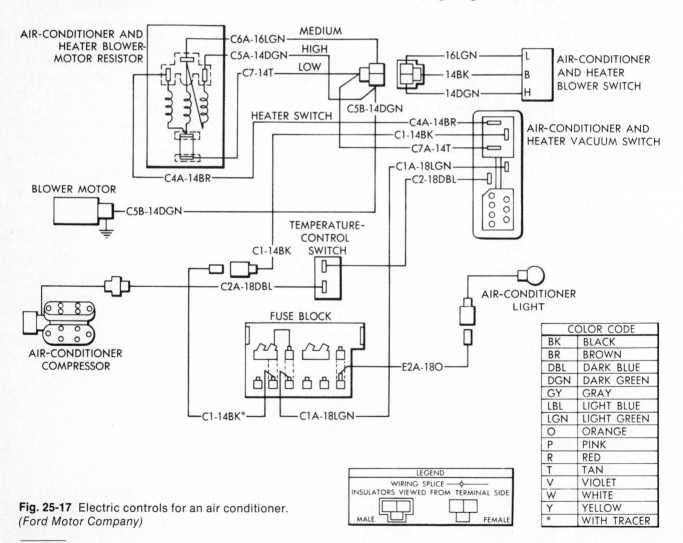

Fig. 25-17 Electric controls for an air conditioner. *(Ford Motor Company)*

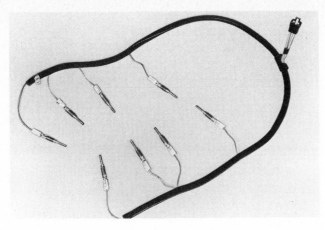

Fig. 25-18 Glow plugs with wiring harness for a V-8 diesel engine. *(Oldsmobile Division of General Motors Corporation)*

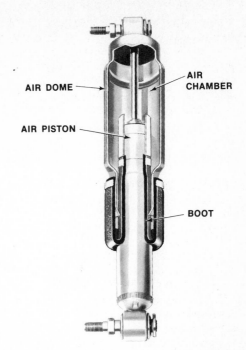

Fig. 25-20 Cutaway view of a special shock absorber (called a Superlift) used in an automatic level control.

end of the car squat. This changes the handling characteristics and also causes the headlights to point upward. The automatic level control prevents this by automatically raising the rear end of the car up to level when a load is added. The system also automatically lowers the rear end of the car to level when the load is removed.

The system includes a compressor which supplies compressed air, an air-reserve tank, two special shock absorbers with built-in chambers (Fig. 25-20), and a control. In the earlier mechanical system, a mechanical valve served as the control. More accurate control is achieved by electronic means. Figure 25-21 shows one system. The electronic height sensor has a shutter connected to the control arm. The control arm is connected to a suspension arm so that it moves as the height of the car rear end changes. The shutter can interrupt a beam of light inside the height sensor if the height is not correct. This triggers either the compressor relay or the solenoid exhaust valve. If the height is low, it triggers the compressor relay. The relay connects the compressor to the battery. The compressor runs and supplies air to the rear shock absorbers. They raise the rear of the car to level.

If the height is too great, the sensor triggers the solenoid exhaust valve. The solenoid opens the valve to allow some of the air in the shock absorbers to escape. This lowers the car rear end to level.

Figure 25-22 shows another electronic level control. The major difference between this and the previously described system is that this system has the electronic control installed inside one of the rear shock absorbers. An electric eye (photo-optic sensor) is built into the shock absorber. The sensor tells the electronic control module either to send air to the shock absorbers or to release air from them to adjust the height to the correct level.

All electronic level controls have a time delay of from about 8 to 14 seconds. This keeps normal ride motions from triggering the system. Also, the operating time is limited in the electronic system to 3 or 4 minutes.

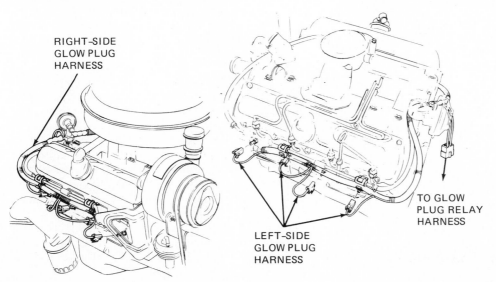

Fig. 25-19 Glow plugs and wiring harness mounted on a V-8 diesel engine. *(Oldsmobile Division of General Motors Corporation)*

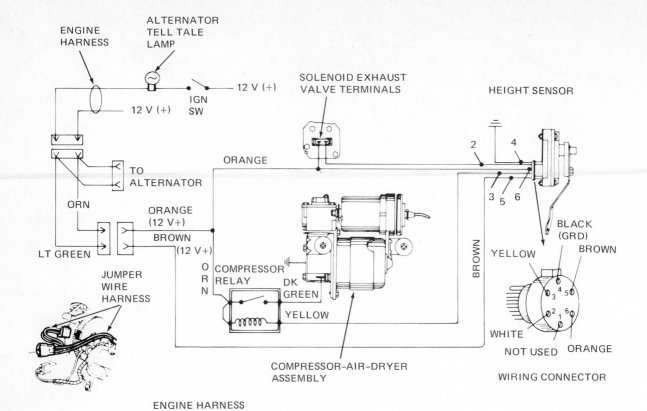

Fig. 25-21 Schematic wiring diagram of an electronic automatic level control using an electronic height sensor. *(General Motors Corporation)*

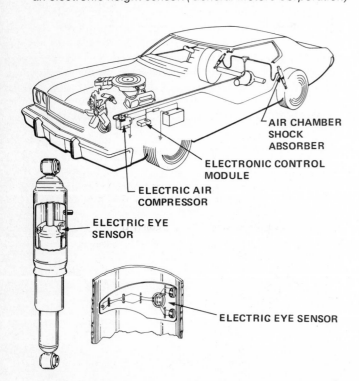

Fig. 25-22 Electronic automatic-level-control system. An electric eye is built into one of the shock absorbers. It signals the electronic control module if the rear of the car is too high or too low. The air shocks are then either bled of air to lower the rear, or air is admitted from the air compressor to raise the car. *(Monroe Auto Equipment Company)*

This prevents continued operation in case there is some trouble in the system such as leakage of air.

⚙ 25-13 Speed (cruise) control system This system allows the driver to pick a speed (anything above about 30 mph), set a control, and take his or her foot off the accelerator pedal. This system will then hold the car to the speed set. If the car starts to slow down when going up a hill, the throttle automatically opens. If the car starts to speed up coasting down a hill, the throttle automatically closes.

The system includes two switches—OFF-ON, and SET-ACC and SET-COAST—a throttle actuator, a speed sensor, an amplifier, wires, check-valve assembly, vacuum reserve tank, and vacuum hoses. See Fig. 25-23.

The speed sensor is located in back of the speedometer (Fig. 25-24). An electronic device "reads" the car speed by noting how fast the speed indicator in the speedometer is rotating. This information is fed to the electronic controller. The controller then compares this with the speed the driver has picked. If car speed is too low, the controller signals the vacuum control valve. The valve then admits more air to the power unit. This causes the diaphragm in the power unit to move. The motion carries to the throttle through linkage, and the throttle opens to increase engine power so car speed goes up. When the preset car speed is reached, the power unit eases off to prevent any further increase in car speed. The system also senses brake operation. When the brakes are applied, the system is automatically turned off.

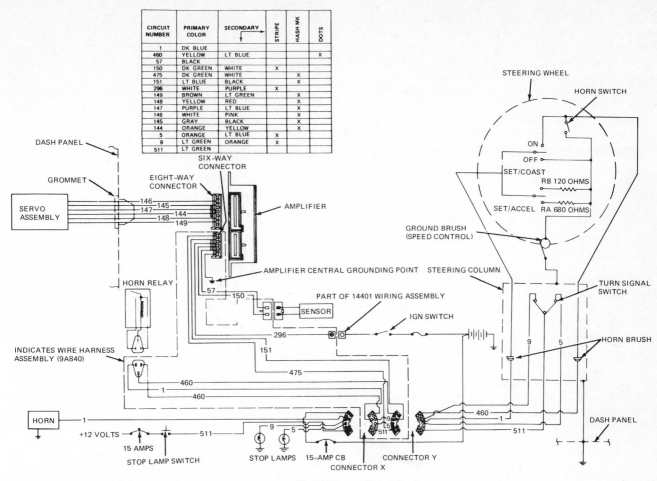

CIRCUIT NUMBER	PRIMARY COLOR	SECONDARY	STRIPE	HASH MK	DOTS
1	DK BLUE				
460	YELLOW	LT BLUE			X
57	BLACK				
150	DK GREEN	WHITE	X		
475	DK GREEN	WHITE		X	
151	LT BLUE	BLACK		X	
296	WHITE	PURPLE	X		
149	BROWN	LT GREEN		X	
148	YELLOW	RED		X	
147	PURPLE	LT BLUE		X	
146	WHITE	PINK		X	
145	GRAY	BLACK		X	
144	ORANGE	YELLOW		X	
5	ORANGE	LT BLUE	X		
9	LT GREEN	ORANGE	X		
511	LT GREEN				

Fig. 25-23 Wiring diagram of speed control system. *(Ford Motor Company)*

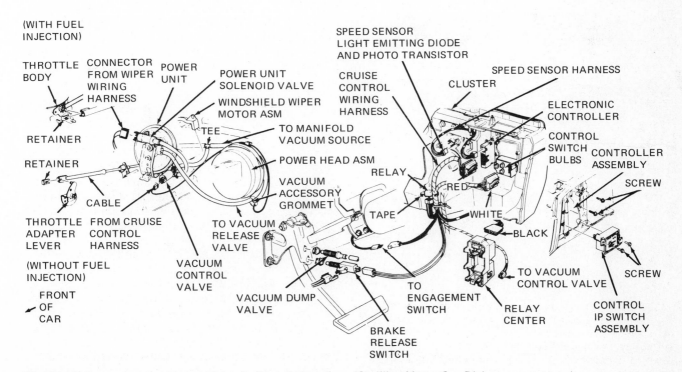

Fig. 25-24 Components of a speed (cruise) control system. *(Cadillac Motor Car Division of General Motors Corporation)*

The controlling switches are mounted either in the spokes of the steering wheel or on the instrument panel and on the turn-signal lever. When the OFF-ON switch is ON, the system is ready to accept a speed value set by the driver. When the driver then accelerates to the desired speed and momentarily presses the SET-ACC switch, the system takes over and holds that speed. The speed may be decreased by momentarily braking and then allowing the car to slow to the desired speed. At that point, the driver presses the SET-ACC switch again, and this speed is automatically maintained.

To increase speed, press down on the accelerator until the desired new speed is attained. Then momentarily press the SET-ACC switch to set the new speed. Or you can hold the SET-ACC switch down, and the car speed will increase. When the desired speed is attained, release the switch.

☀ 25-14 Antilock braking system The most efficient braking takes place when the wheels are still revolving. If the wheels lock and the tires skid, braking is much less effective. Antilock systems relieve hydraulic pressure at wheels that are about to lock. This reduces the braking effort on the wheel that is about to lock.

Figure 25-25 shows the antilock mechanism at a front wheel. Figure 25-26 shows the antilock mechanism at a rear wheel. The action is the same at either wheel. A magnetic wheel is attached to the brake disk. As the wheel revolves, the magnetic wheel produces an alternating current in a sensor located close to the magnetic wheel. This is the same action taking place in alternators (Chapter 8). The alternating current is fed to an electronic control (called the *logic control unit* by Chrysler). The electronic control continuously compares the alternating current coming from all wheels. If the frequency of the alternating current is about the same, it means that all wheels are turning at about the same speed. However, if the frequency drops rapidly at any wheel, it means that wheel is about to lock and skid. Sensing this, the electronic control signals the modulator that controls the brake at that wheel (Fig. 25-27). The modulator then reduces the hydraulic pressure to that brake so the braking action eases up enough to prevent lockup and skid.

☀ 25-15 Transmission electronic control Automatic transmissions automatically shift up or down as operating conditions change. In present-day automatic transmissions, control results from the interplay of car speed, throttle position, and intake-manifold vacuum. However, electronics is beginning to be applied to automatic transmission control. One of the first electronic controls is that developed for the Renault 5 hatchback. This is a small car and needs a small, simple, and lightweight transmission. The electronic control in this transmission signals a pair of electrically operated valves which then "order" the hydraulic system to provide the shift called for.

The basic signal starts at a small alternator that is mounted in one side of the transmission. The voltage of this alternator goes up with speed. The alternator stationary windings (stator) can be shifted. They are linked to the throttle. Thus, the final voltage the alternator produces results from car speed and throttle position. This voltage provides the basic signal to the electronic control.

☀ 25-16 Air-bag controls Air bags are designed to protect the driver and passenger in case of a front-end

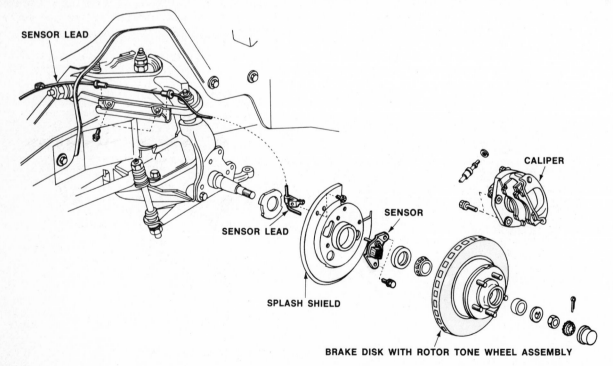

SENSOR LEAD

SENSOR LEAD

SENSOR

CALIPER

SPLASH SHIELD

BRAKE DISK WITH ROTOR TONE WHEEL ASSEMBLY

Fig. 25-25 Antilock components for the Chrysler Sure-Brake System at a front wheel. *(Chrysler Corporation)*

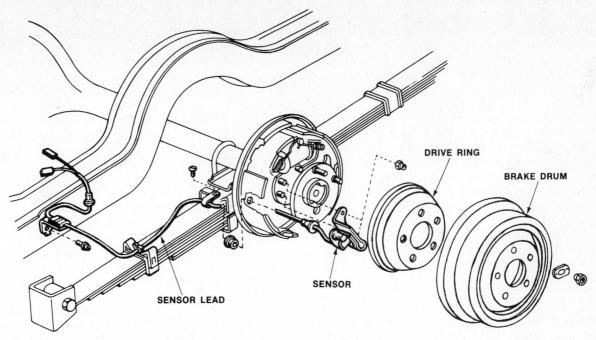

Fig. 25-26 Antilock mechanism for the Chrysler Sure-Brake System at a rear wheel. *(Chrysler Corporation)*

crash. During a crash, the air bags inflate in a fraction of a second so the driver and passengers are cushioned as they are thrown forward during the crash. Figure 25-28 shows the actions during the first few fractions of a second. Figure 25-29 shows the complete system for the passenger side of the front seat. The controls for this system are electronic. The action is triggered by a deceleratometer—a device that measures how rapidly the car is decelerating, or slowing down. It slows down very fast during a front-end crash. This causes the deceleratometer to signal the electronic control, which almost instantly releases the compressed gas in the container so the air bags are inflated.

⚙ **25-17 Anticollision radar** Radar works by sending out bursts of short radio waves. These waves bounce off any object at which the radar is pointed. The waves then come back to the radar. The time it takes for the waves to reach the object and return is measured electronically, and a computer then indicates the distance the object is from the radar. In highway patrol work, the officer sets up the radar, or it is mounted on the patrol car. The radar then measures not only the distance between the radar and the oncoming car but also how rapidly that distance is being cut down. In other words, it measures how fast the car is moving.

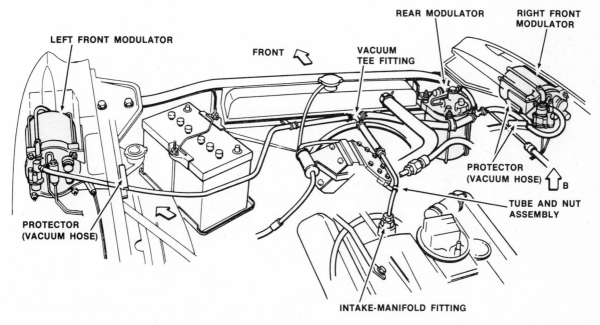

Fig. 25-27 Location of the modulators. *(Chrysler Corporation)*

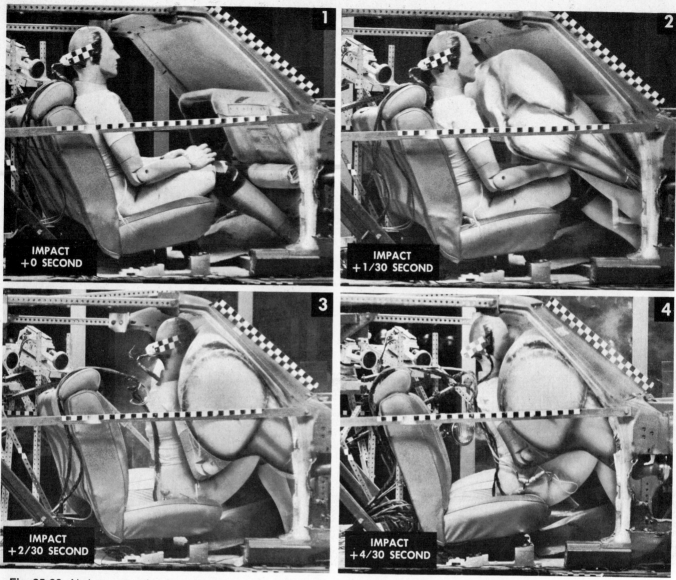

IMPACT +0 SECOND

IMPACT +1/30 SECOND

IMPACT +2/30 SECOND

IMPACT +4/30 SECOND

Fig. 25-28 Air-bag operation in a simulated front-end crash, using a test dummy in the passenger's seat. The entire sequence shown took place in 4/30 second. *(General Motors Corporation)*

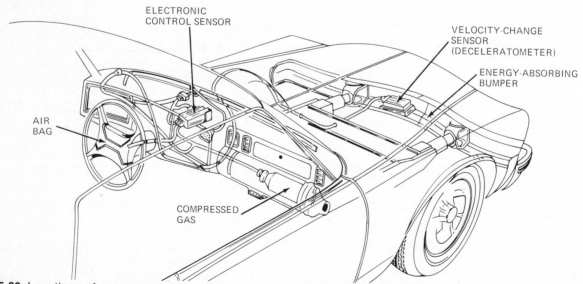

ELECTRONIC CONTROL SENSOR

VELOCITY-CHANGE SENSOR (DECELERATOMETER)

ENERGY-ABSORBING BUMPER

AIR BAG

COMPRESSED GAS

Fig. 25-29 Locations of components in an air-bag system. *(General Motors Corporation)*

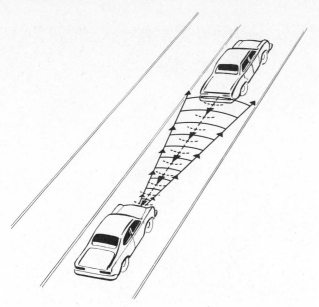

Fig. 25-30 The on-board radar in the car behind senses how fast the gap between cars is being narrowed. When the danger point is reached, the radar triggers electronic devices to sound an alarm and slow the car.

This same principle is put to work in the anticollision radar system (Fig. 25-30). The anticollision radar constantly measures the distance to the car up ahead and how fast the car is closing up the gap between. If the gap narrows to the danger point, the radar signals the throttle and brake so that the car is slowed down or stopped. In a similar way, if the car is headed into a stationary barrier or a wall, the anticollision radar will apply the brakes far quicker than the driver could. In other words, the electronic system works much faster than a human being can.

Figure 25-31 illustrates some technical aspects of the system. Car 2 has the radar system. The radar echo, plus the other factors shown, feed into the computer. The computer takes all these factors into consideration and solves the equation continuously. If the distance shortens too much, the computer sounds an alarm and can start braking. The system includes an adjustment that can be made as road conditions change. For example, if the road is wet or icy, it takes much longer to slow or stop the car, and this must be considered by the computer.

NOTE: Anticollision radar is not yet in production. When it will appear on cars depends on when the public is ready to accept it.

⚙ **25-18 Variable displacement engines** These are engines that are electronically controlled to run on all or only a few of the cylinders. Figure 25-32 shows an in-line six-cylinder engine which can run on all six cylinders (full displacement) or on only three cylinders (half displacement). Because of this action, the engine is known as a *dual-displacement engine*. The computer is fed information by sensors that measure intake-manifold vacuum, engine speed, throttle position, coolant temperature, and the transmission gear. When conditions are right, the computer activates three solenoids located above the valves in three of the cylinders. This

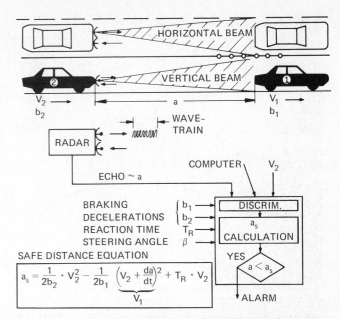

Fig. 25-31 Diagramatic layout of a radar system in a car. Shown are the variables that are fed into the computer and the equation the computer continuously solves. *(Robert Bosch GmbH)*

prevents these valves from opening. As a result, no air–fuel mixture can enter, and no exhaust gases can escape. The cylinders are inoperative, and the engine runs on three cylinders. There is a substantial saving in gasoline while at the same time the engine supplies enough power for steady-speed cruising. When conditions change so that more power is required, the computer deactivates the solenoids and the valves become free. Now, the engine runs on all cylinders.

There is also a V-8 engine in which the computer selectively cuts out one, two, three, or four cylinders. How many are cut out depends on the power demands on the engine. Thus, the engine becomes a four-, five-, six-, seven-, or eight-cylinder engine. Neither of these

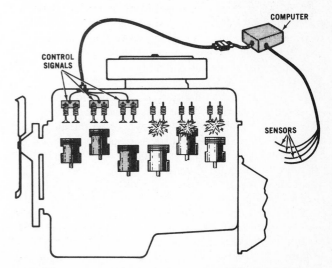

Fig. 25-32 Schematic drawing of a six-cylinder, dual-displacement engine. Under some operating conditions, when full power is not needed, the computer cuts out three of the cylinders. *(Ford Motor Company)*

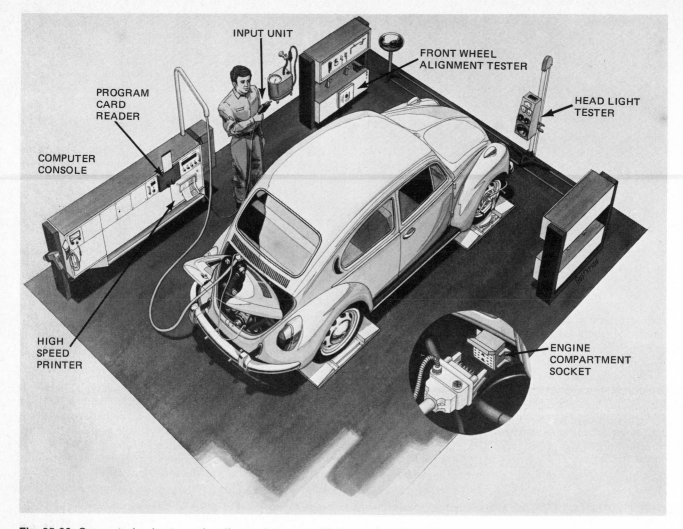

Fig. 25-33 Computerized automotive diagnosis system. *(Volkswagen of America, Inc.)*

engines is in production, but they are examples of the increasing use of electronics in automobiles.

⚙ 25-19 Electronic test equipment Just as the automobile control systems have gone electronic, so has testing equipment. The oscilloscope and timing light are electronic devices. Exhaust-gas analyzers have electronic devices that can sniff out and measure the pollutants in the exhaust gas. Some dynamic wheel balancers are electronic and use electronic circuits to spot out-of-balance wheels and to indicate where and how much weight to add and where to put it on the wheel. Now undergoing tests in research laboratories are engine testers that can be hooked up to operating engines to measure main-bearing clearances. Special electronic testers are used to check the electronic spark-advance and fuel-system control systems.

Many cars today have a diagnostic connector that can be connected to a computerized diagnostic system which will make a whole series of checks very quickly. Figure 25-33 shows one such system, introduced by Volkswagen. Wiring and sensors built into the car are connected by the computer through a socket in the engine compartment. The system checks more than 70 items. A special program card contains the specifica-

tions for the year and model of the car being checked. The computer compares the operation of car components with values it reads from the program card. The results of the test are recorded by a high-speed printer. This tells the technician and the driver what needs to be done to restore the car to top operating condition.

Figure 25-34 shows schematically the diagnostic connector for some Chevrolets. When a car with this arrangement comes into a shop which has the diagnostic tester, the technician can plug into the connector and make 35 electrical checks and tests in a few minutes.

Chapter 25 review questions

Select the *one* correct, best, or most probable answer to each question. Then check your answers against the correct answers given at the end of the book.

1. The windshield washer-wiper system requires:
   a. one electric motor,
   b. two electric motors,
   c. three electric motors,
   d. manifold vacuum to operate.

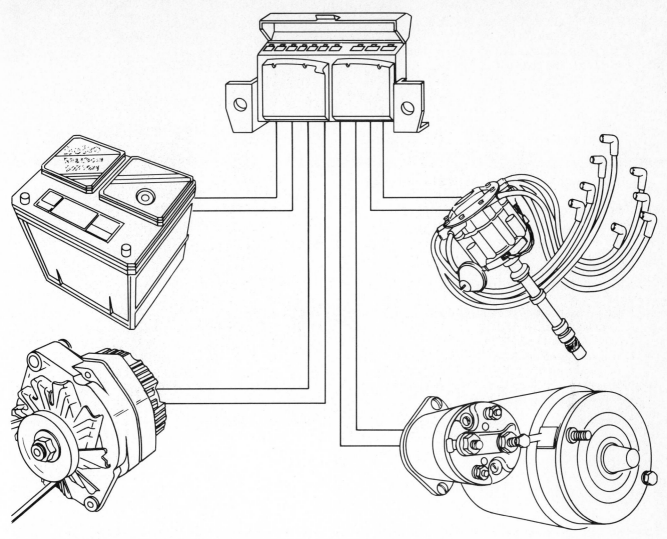

Fig. 25-34 Diagnostic connector. When connected to the shop testing device, it makes 35 electrical tests and checks. (*Chevrolet Motor Division of General Motors Corporation*)

2. Two-speed wiper motors have:
   a. one brush,
   b. two brushes,
   c. three brushes,
   d. four brushes.
3. The most common service required on the washer-wiper system, aside from keeping the washer reservoir filled, is replacement of the:
   a. motor brushes,
   b. motor bushings,
   c. governor control,
   d. wiper blades.
4. The electric fuel-pump control circuit includes a hydraulic switch which opens the circuit if the engine should stop. This switch is operated by hydraulic pressure from the:
   a. brake system,
   b. transmission,
   c. engine lubricating system,
   d. engine cooling system.

5. The purpose of the roll-over switch in the electric-pump control circuit is to shut off the pump in case the:
   a. car rolls over in an accident,
   b. air–fuel mixture is so rich the engine rolls,
   c. air–fuel mixture needs to be rolled back,
   d. fuel tank is overfilled.
6. The heated rear window has a grid of resistance wire:
   a. set between the inner and outer panes of glass,
   b. baked onto the inside surface of the back window,
   c. baked onto the outside surface of the back window,
   d. moulded into the glass.
7. The purpose of the diesel-engine glow plugs is to:
   a. glow to indicate that the engine is warm enough to start,
   b. turn on when the engine is overheated,
   c. improve combustion and reduce pollutants,

d. heat the combustion chambers of a cold engine to improve starting.

8. The purpose of the automatic level control is to:
   a. improve the handling of the car,
   b. improve the ride characteristics,
   c. maintain level of the car rear with changing loads,
   d. all these.

9. The purpose of the cruise control system is to:
   a. avoid arrest for breaking speed laws,
   b. improve gasoline mileage,
   c. maintain car speed preselected by the driver,
   d. prevent engine overspeeding.

10. The purpose of the diagnostic connector found on some cars is to:
    a. make it easier for the technician to spot trouble causes,
    b. simplify checking procedures,
    c. speed up the diagnostic procedure,
    d. all these.

11. The two basic types of front-seat adjusters are the:
    a. one way and two way,
    b. two way and four way,
    c. four way and six way,
    d. six way and eight way.

12. The hydraulic switch in the electric-fuel-pump control system is operated by:
    a. fuel-pump pressure,
    b. cooling system pump pressure,
    c. oil-pump pressure,
    d. brake-system pressure.

13. The purpose of the diesel-engine glow plugs is to:
    a. heat the engine combustion chambers for easier starting,
    b. keep the engine warm after it has started,
    c. prevent engine freeze up,
    d. warm the fuel oil so it flows easily during cold weather.

14. The automatic level control adjusts the height of the rear end of the car by:
    a. adjusting the air pressure in the rear shock absorbers,
    b. turning an air compressor on or off,
    c. bleeds air from the shock absorbers when loads are removed from the car,
    d. all of these.

15. The basic purpose of the antilock braking system is to:
    a. prevent braking malfunctions,
    b. keep tires from skidding to improve braking,
    c. prevent a thief from unlocking the system,
    d. prevent skidding by locking the wheels in a panic stop.

GLOSSARY

This glossary of automobile words and phrases provides a ready reference for the automotive technician. The definitions may differ somewhat from those given in a standard dictionary. They are not intended to be all-inclusive, but to cover only what specifically applies to the automotive service field.

ABDC After bottom dead center.

Ac See "Alternating current."

Accessories Devices not considered essential to the operation of the vehicle; for example, the radio, car heater, and electric window lifts.

Adjustments Necessary or desired changes in clearances, fit, or setting.

Advance The moving ahead of the ignition spark; this is produced by centrifugal, vacuum, or electronic devices in accordance with engine speed and intake-manifold vacuum.

Air–fuel mixture Name given to the air and fuel traveling to the combustion chamber after being mixed by the carburetor.

Air–fuel ratio Proportion of the air and fuel by weight delivered to the combustion chambers.

Air gap Small space between parts magnetically related, as in an alternator, or electrically related, as between the ground and center electrode of a spark plug.

Air–injection system An exhaust-emission control system. It injects air into the exhaust manifold to complete the burning of unburned hydrocarbons and carbon monoxide in the exhaust gases.

Alternating current An electric current that flows first in one direction and then in the other.

Alternator The device in the electric system that converts mechanical energy into electric energy for charging the battery, etc. Also known as an ac generator, the alternator produces alternating current (ac) which must be changed to direct current (dc) for use in the automobile.

Ammeter An electric meter for measuring the amount, or number of amperes, of current in an electric circuit.

Amperage The amount, in amperes, of current flowing.

Ampere (amp) A unit of electric current.

Antenna The device used to pick up radio signals.

Anticollision radar A system designed to electronically control the speed of a car so it maintains a safe distance from the car ahead.

Antilock system A system installed along with the brake system to prevent wheel lockup during braking and thus prevent skidding.

Arcing Name given to the spark that jumps the air gap between two electric conductors. An example is the arcing of the distributor contact points.

Armature A part moved by or through magnetism to produce motion, or to complete a circuit.

ATDC After top dead center.

Atom The smallest particle into which an element can be divided.

Autronic eye An automatic electronic device using a phototube to select the proper headlight beam during country driving.

Balancing–coil gauge An indicating device (fuel, oil pressure, engine temperature) that contains a pair of coils in the instrument-panel unit.

Ballast resistor A resistance in the ignition primary circuit to reduce battery voltage to the coil during engine operation. May be a separate ceramic resistor, a resistance wire, or a separate resistor built internally into an ignition coil.

Battery An electrochemical device for storing energy in chemical form so that it can be released as electricity. A group of electric cells connected together.

Battery acid Term applied to the electrolyte used in a battery, which is a mixture of sulfuric acid and water.

Battery cell Formed by covering a battery element with electrolyte; a cell has a specific gravity of approximately 1.300 when fully charged and a voltage of approximately 2 volts.

Battery efficiency The characteristic of a battery to vary the current it delivers within wide limits, depending on temperature and rate of discharge.

Battery element A group of unlike positive and negative plates assembled with separators. One element is used per cell.

BDC Bottom dead center.

Bearing The part which transmits the load to the support and, in so doing, takes the friction caused by moving parts in contact.

Bendix drive A type of starting-motor drive which screws into mesh with the flywheel teeth as the starting-motor armature begins to turn. It demeshes automatically as engine speed increases when the engine starts.

Bimetal A thermostatic bimetal element made up of two different metals with different heat-expansion rates. Temperature changes produce a bending or distorting movement of the element.

Bore The diameter of an engine cylinder; the diameter of any hole. Also used to describe the process of enlarging or accurately refinishing a hole, as to bore an engine cylinder.

Bottom dead center (BDC) The piston position at which the piston has moved to the bottom of the cylinder and the cylinder volume is at its maximum.

Brake horsepower (bhp) The power delivered by the engine which is available for driving the vehicle.

Brush A block of conducting substance, such as carbon, which rests against a rotating ring or commutator to form a continuous electric circuit.

BTDC Before top dead center.

Bushing A one-piece sleeve placed in a bore to serve as a bearing surface.

Cable Stranded conductor, usually covered with insulating material, used for connections between electric devices.

Cadmium–tip tester A battery tester using two cadmium tips which are inserted into the electrolyte of adjacent battery cells to determine cell voltage.

Calibrate To check or correct the initial setting of a test instrument.

Cam A rotating lobe or eccentric which changes rotary motion to reciprocating motion.

Camshaft The shaft in the engine which has a series of cams for operating the valve mechanisms. The camshaft is driven by gears or sprockets and chain from the crankshaft.

Capacitor See "Condenser."

Capacity The ability to perform or hold.

Carbon dioxide (CO_2) A colorless, odorless gas which results when gasoline is burned completely.

Carbon monoxide (CO) A colorless, odorless, tasteless, poisonous gas which results when gasoline is burned incompletely.

Carbon pile A pile, or stack, of carbon disks enclosed in an insulating tube. When the disks are pressed together, the resistance of the pile is decreased.

Carburetor The mixing device in the fuel system which meters gasoline into the airstream (vaporizing the gasoline as it does so) in varying proportion to suit engine operating conditions.

Cell Formed by suspending in electrolyte, in a compartment of a battery, an element of unlike positive and negative plates. The cell produces current at a voltage of about 2 volts.

Celsius In the metric system, a temperature scale on which water boils at 100 degrees and freezes at 0 degrees; equal to a reading on a Fahrenheit thermometer of $^5/_9(°F - 32)$. Also called *centigrade*.

Centigrade See "Celsius."

Centrifugal advance Mechanism in the distributor designed to advance and retard ignition timing by centrifugal force resulting from changes in engine speed.

Charging rate The number of amperes of current flowing from the alternator into the battery.

Circuit The complete path of an electric current, including the current source. When the path is continuous, the circuit is closed and current flows. When the path is broken, the circuit is open and no current flows. Term also used to explain hydraulic system operations.

Circuit breaker A protective device that opens an electric circuit to prevent damage when overheated by excess current flow. Some circuit breakers contain a thermostatic blade that warps to open the circuit when maximum current is reached.

Clearance The space between two moving parts, or between a moving and a stationary part, such as a journal and a bearing. Bearing clearance is considered to be filled with lubricating oil when the mechanism is running.

Coil In the automobile ignition system, a transformer used to step up battery voltage, by induction, to the high voltage required to fire the spark plugs.

Cold cranking rate A battery rating: the minimum amperes maintained by a battery for 30 seconds with a minimum voltage of 1.2 volts per cell, checked at a battery temperature of $0°$ F $[-17.8°C]$ and at $-20°$ F $[-28.9°C]$.

Cold rate A battery rating; the number of minutes a battery will deliver 300 amperes at $10°$ F $[-17.8°C]$ before cell voltage drops below 1.0 volt.

Combustion Burning; in the engine, the rapid burning of the air–fuel mixture in the cylinder.

Commutation In a dc generator, the effect produced by the commutator and brushes. The alternating current developed in the armature windings is changed by commutation to direct current.

Commutator The series of copper bars at one end of the generator or starting-motor armature. These bars are electrically insulated from the armature shaft and insulated from each other by mica. Brushes rub against the bars of the commutator to form a rotating connector between the armature windings and brushes.

Condenser In the ignition system, also called a *capacitor*. Connected across the contact points to reduce arcing by providing a "storage place" for electricity (electrons) as the contact points open. In an air-conditioning system, the radiatorlike device that allows the vaporized refrigerant to lose heat and return to a liquid state.

Conductor   Any material or substance that allows current to flow easily.

Constant–current charging   A battery-charging method in which an unchanging amount of current flows into the battery.

Constant–voltage charging   A charging method in which a constant voltage is applied to the battery. The charging current then tapers off as the battery approaches a charged condition.

Contact points   In the conventional ignition system, the stationary point and the movable point in the distributor which open and close the ignition primary circuit.

Cranking motor   See "Starting motor."

Crankshaft   The main rotating member, or shaft, of the engine, with cranks to which the connecting rods are attached.

Crankshaft gear   A gear, or sprocket, mounted on the front of the crankshaft, used to drive the camshaft gear, or chain.

Cross-firing   Jumping of the high-voltage surge in the ignition secondary circuit to the wrong high-tension lead so that the wrong spark plug fires. Usually caused by improper routing of the spark-plug wires, by faulty insulation, or by a defective distributor cap or rotor.

Cruise control   An electronic device which maintains a preset car speed.

Cubic centimeter (cm³ or cc)   A unit in the metric system used to measure volume; equal to approximately 0.061 cubic inch.

Current   A flow of electrons, or electric current measured in amperes.

Cutout relay   The device in the circuit between the generator and battery which closes when the generator charges the battery and opens when the generator stops.

Cylinder   A round hole or tubular-shaped structure in a block or casting in which a piston reciprocates. In an engine, the circular bore in the block in which the piston moves up and down.

DARS chart   Diagnostic and repair simplification chart which provides, graphically, methods of diagnosing and correcting troubles.

Dc   See "Direct current."

Delco Eye   A type of battery vent cap that, without having to be removed, signals low electrolyte level in the cell.

Detonation   In the engine, an uncontrolled second explosion after the spark occurs, with excessively rapid burning of the compressed air–fuel mixture, resulting in a spark knock, or pinging noise.

Dial indicator   A gauge that has a dial face and a needle to register movement; used to measure variations in size, movements too small to be measured conveniently by other means, etc.

Diaphragm   A thin rubber sheet used to separate an area into different compartments; used in the fuel pump, modulator valve, vacuum-advance unit, etc.

Diesel engine   An internal-combustion engine burning oil. The oil is sprayed into the combustion chambers and ignited by the heat of compression.

Dimmer switch   A two-way switch, usually mounted on the car floor; operated by the driver to select the headlight high beam or low beam.

Diode   A solid-state electronic device which allows the passage of an electric current in one direction only. Used in the alternator to convert alternating current to dirrect current for charging the battery.

Direct current   Current that flows in one direction and does not alternate.

Directional signal   A device on the car which uses flashing lights to indicate the direction in which the driver intends to turn.

Disassemble   To take apart.

Display pattern   See "Parade pattern."

Distributor   See "Ignition distributor."

Drop light   A portable light, with long electric cord, used in the shop to illuminate the work area.

Dry-charged battery   A new battery that has been charged and then stored with the electrolyte removed. To activate the battery at the time of sale, electrolyte must be added.

Dura–Spark system   A Ford ignition system designed to produce higher secondary voltages which produce stronger and longer-lasting sparks at the spark-plug gaps.

Dwell   The number of degrees of distributor cam rotation while the distributor points are closed.

Dwell meter   A precision electric instrument used to measure cam angle, or dwell, of the distributor cam as it rotates.

Dyer drive   A type of starting-motor drive, used on heavy-duty applications, which provides mechanical meshing of the drive pinion (as in overrunning clutch) and automatic de-meshing (Bendix drive).

Eccentric   A disk or offset section—of a shaft, for example—used to convert rotary motion to reciprocating motion.

Electric–assist choke   A choke which uses a small electric heating element to warm the choke spring, causing it to release more quickly. This reduces exhaust emissions during the startup of a cold engine.

Electric brakes   A type of brake system which uses an armature-electromagnet combination at each wheel. As the electromagnet is energized, the magnetic attraction between the armature and electromagnet causes the brake shoes to move against the brake drum.

Electric system   In the automobile, the system that

electrically cranks the engine for starting, furnishes high-voltage sparks to the engine cylinders to fire the compressed air–fuel charges, lights the lights, operates the heater motor, radio, and so on. Consists, in part, of starting motor, wiring, battery, alternator, regulator, ignition distributor, and ignition coil.

Electrochemical device A device that operates on both electrical and chemical principles. In the automobile, a lead-acid storage battery.

Electrode In a spark plug, the spark jumps between two electrodes. The wire passing through the insulator is the center electrode. The small piece of metal—welded to the spark-plug shell—to which the spark jumps is the side, or ground, electrode.

Electrolyte The mixture of sulfuric acid and water used in lead-acid storage batteries. The acid enters into chemical reaction with active material in the plates to produce voltage and current.

Electromagnet A coil of wire (usually with an iron core) which produces magnetism as electric current passes through it.

Electromagnetic induction The characteristic of a magnetic field that causes an electric current to be created in a conductor as it passes through the field or as the field builds or collapses around the conductor.

Electron One of the negatively charged particles that circle the nucleus of an atom. Movement of electrons is an electric current.

Electronic carbureted fuel system A fuel system with an electronic control which continuously adjusts the carburetor to prevent over-rich or over-lean air–fuel mixture.

Electronic engine control (EEC) system An electronic system that controls the spark advance and also the exhaust-gas-recirculation and the air-injection systems.

Electronic fuel control (EFC) system An electronic control system that continuously adjusts the carburetor to prevent an over-rich or over-lean air–fuel mixture.

Electronic fuel injection A fuel-injection system, used for injecting gasoline into spark-ignition engines, that uses an electronic control system to time and meter the fuel injected.

Electronic ignition system An ignition system, using transistors, which does not have mechanical contact points in the distributor but uses the distributor for distributing the secondary voltage to the spark plugs.

Electronic lean-burn (ELB) system An electronic ignition control system that provides voltages of sufficient strength and duration to burn lean air–fuel mixtures. It varies the timing, or spark advance, to suit engine operating conditions.

Electronic module Electronic control device.

Electronic spark–advance control An electronic system that takes the place of the mechanical ignition-system centrifugal and vacuum advances. The electronic system more accurately controls the advance to suit the engine operating condition.

Electronic spark control (ESC) An electronic system that guards against detonation in engines using turbochargers. It retards ignition timing if detonation begins to occur.

Electronic spark timing (EST) Also called, in one version, a *Microprocessed Sensing and Automatic Regulation* (MISAR) *system*. It controls the ignition spark advance electronically.

Element A substance that cannot be further divided into a simpler substance. In a battery, the group of unlike positive and negative plates, separated by insulators, that make up each cell.

Energizer Delco-Remy's name for their storage batteries.

Energy The capacity or ability to do work.

Engine A machine that converts heat energy into mechanical energy. The assembly that burns fuel to produce power, sometimes referred to as the *power plant*.

Exhaust–gas recirculation system An NO_x control system that recycles a small part of the exhaust gas back through the engine and thus lowers combustion temperatures.

Feedback–carburetor electronic engine control (FCEEC) system An electronic control system that continuously adjusts the carburetor to prevent an over-rich or an over-lean air–fuel mixture. The system also controls the operation of the air-injection system.

Feeler gauge Strips of metal of accurately known thicknesses used to measure clearances.

Fiber optics A system of transmitting light through flexible cables made up of very fine threads or fibers of glass.

Field coil A coil, or winding, in a generator or starting motor, which produces a magnetic field as current passes through it.

Field-frame assembly The round, soft iron frame in a generator or motor which has the field coils assembled into it.

Field relay A relay that is part of some alternator charging systems; it connects the alternator field to the battery when the engine runs and disconnects it when the engine stops.

Field winding See "Field coil."

Firing line The high-voltage vertical spike, or line, that appears on the oscilloscope pattern of the ignition-system secondary circuit. The firing line shows when the spark plug begins to fire and the voltage required to fire it.

Firing order The order in which the engine cylinders

fire, or deliver their power strokes, beginning with No. 1 cylinder.

Flasher A special type of automatically resetting circuit breaker used in the directional-signal and emergency-signal circuits.

Flywheel ring gear The gear fitted around the flywheel that is engaged by the teeth on the starting-motor drive to crank the engine.

Folo-Thru drive A type of inertia starting-motor drive similar to the Bendix drive except that it has a locking pin to hold the pinion in mesh until the engine starts.

421 tester A battery tester, designed originally for testing batteries with a one-piece cover, which applies timed discharge-charge cycles to a battery to determine its condition.

Friction The resistance to motion between two bodies in contact with each other.

Fuel system In the automobile, the system that delivers to the engine cylinders the combustible mixture of vaporized fuel and air. It consists of fuel tank, lines, gauge, carburetor, fuel pump, and intake manifold.

Fuse Device in an electric circuit to protect against excessive current flow which could overheat and damage the circuit.

Fuse block A special boxlike unit used for holding the fuses for the various electric circuits in an automobile.

Fusible link A type of fuse wire used to protect the main wiring harness against accidental damage from shorts or grounds.

Gap The air space between two electrodes, such as the spark-plug gap and the contact-point gap.

Gasket A flat strip, usually of cork or metal or both, placed between two machined surfaces to provide a tight seal between them.

Gassing Escape from a battery of hydrogen gas formed during battery charging.

Gear Mechanical device to transmit power, or turning effort, from one shaft to another. Gears contain teeth that interlace, or mesh, as the gears turn.

Gear ratio The relative speeds at which two gears (or shafts) turn; the proportional rate of rotation.

Generator A device that converts mechanical energy into electric energy; it can produce either ac or dc electricity. In automotive usage, the term applied to a dc generator (such generators are now seldom used).

Glow plug A small electric heater installed in the precombustion chambers of diesel engines to preheat the chambers for easier starting in cold weather.

Goggles Special glasses worn over the eyes to protect them from flying chips, dirt, or dust.

Ground Connection of an electric device to the engine or frame to return the current to its source.

Growler An electrical test instrument for checking starting-motor and generator armatures.

Guide–Matic An electronic device which automatically controls the headlights, shifting between upper and lower beams as conditions warrant.

Hazard system Also called *emergency-signal system*; a driver-controlled system of flashing front and rear lights, used to warn approaching motorists of a traffic hazard when a car has broken down.

HC Chemical formula for a hydrocarbon, such as gasoline.

Headlamps Lights at the front of the vehicle designed to illuminate the road in front of the vehicle.

Heat sink A device for absorbing heat from one medium and transferring it to another. The diodes in alternators are usually mounted in heat sinks which remove the heat from the diodes and thus prevent them from overheating.

High-discharge test A battery test in which the battery is discharged at a high rate while the cell voltages are checked.

High-Energy Ignition (HEI) system An electronic ignition system used by General Motors that does not use contact points and has all ignition-system components contained within the distributor. Capable of producing 35,000 volts, hence the name "High-Energy Ignition system."

High-tension cables The secondary or spark-plug cables, or wires, that carry high voltage from the coil to the spark plugs.

Horn A noise-making electric signaling device on the vehicle.

Horn relay A relay connected between the battery and horns; when energized by closing of the horn button, it connects the horn to the battery.

Horsepower (hp) A measure of mechanical power, or the rate at which work is done. One horsepower equals 33,000 foot-pounds of work per minute.

Hydrometer A test instrument, consisting of a float inside a tube, which measures the specific gravity of a liquid; used to measure the specific gravity of battery electrolyte to determine the state of battery charge.

Ignition In an engine, the act of the spark in starting the combustion process in the engine cylinder.

Ignition coil That part of the ignition system which acts as a transformer to step up the battery voltage to many thousands of volts; the high-voltage surge then produces a spark at the spark-plug gap.

Ignition distributor That part of the ignition system which closes and opens the circuit to the ignition coil with correct timing and distributes to the proper spark plugs the resulting high-voltage surges from the ignition coil.

Ignition switch The switch in the ignition system which is operated with a key to open and close the ignition primary circuit.

Ignition system In the automobile, the system that furnishes high-voltage sparks to the engine cylinders to fire the compressed air–fuel charges. Consists of battery, ignition coil, distributor, ignition switch, wiring, and spark plugs.

Ignition timing The timing of the spark at the spark plug, in relation to piston position.

Indicator A device used to make known some condition by use of a light or pointer; for example, the temperature indicator or oil-pressure indicator.

Induction Action of producing a voltage in a conductor or coil by moving the conductor or coil through a magnetic field (or moving the field past the conductor or coil).

Insulation Materials that stop the travel of electricity (electric insulation), or heat (heat insulation).

Insulator A device made of a material that strongly opposes electric current, or motion of electrons, through it.

Integral Built into, as part of the whole.

Jump-starting Starting a car that has a dead battery by connecting a good battery to the starting system.

Key A wedgelike metal piece, usually rectangular or semicircular, inserted in grooves to transmit torque while holding two parts in relative position; the small strip of metal with coded peaks and grooves used to operate a lock, as in the ignition switch.

Kilogram (kg) In the metric system, a unit of mass, or weight, equal to approximately 2.2 pounds.

Kilometer (km) In the metric system, a unit of linear measure equal to 0.621 mile.

Kilowatt (kW) In the metric system, a measure of power. One horsepower equals 0.746 kilowatt.

Kinetic energy The energy of motion; the energy stored in a moving body as developed through its momentum; for example, the kinetic energy stored in a rotating flywheel.

Knock A heavy metallic sound which varies with engine speed and is usually caused by a loose or worn bearing.

kW See "Kilowatt."

Laminated Made up of many thin sheets, or layers.

Lead A cable or conductor to carry current (pronounced *leed*).

Lead A heavy metal, used in lead-acid storage batteries.

Lead sulfate A hard, insoluble layer that slowly forms on the plates of a discharging battery. It may be reduced only by slow charging.

Level control A mechanism which returns the rear of the car to level after loads have been added or removed. Some are electronically operated.

Light An electric device that includes a wire in a gas-filled bulb which glows brightly when current passes through it; also called a *lamp*.

Lines of force Magnetic lines of force; the imaginary lines by which a magnetic field may be visualized.

Liter (L) In the metric system, a measure of volume equal to approximately 0.2642 U.S. gallon.

Load test The starting-motor test to measure current draw under normal cranking load.

Machining The process of using a machine to remove metal from a metal part.

Magna-Flux The process of using a special electromagnet and magnetic powder to detect cracks—which may be invisible to the naked eye—in iron.

Magnet Any substance that has the ability to attract iron. May be a natural magnet, a permanent magnet, or an electromagnet, which is dependent on a current flow for its magnetism.

Magnetic field The space around a magnet which is filled by invisible lines of force.

Magnetic lines of force See "Lines of force."

Magnetic pole The point where magnetic lines of force enter or leave a magnet.

Magnetic switch A switch with a winding which, when energized by being connected to a battery or alternator, causes the switch to open or close a circuit.

Magnetism The ability of certain substances, called *permanent magnets,* to attract iron. This ability can also be produced in other substances, called *electromagnets,* by a flow of electric current.

Magneto An engine-driven device that generates its own primary current, transforms that current into high-voltage surges, and delivers these surges to the proper spark plugs.

Mass production The manufacture of interchangeable parts in large quantities.

Matter Anything which has weight and occupies space.

Measuring The act of determining the size or capacity of an object.

Meter (m) In the metric system, a unit of linear measure equal to 39.37 inches. Also, the name given to a measuring instrument through which the substance being measured passes, such as an ammeter. Also, any device that measures and controls the discharge of the substance passing through it. For example, a carburetor jet is used to meter fuel flow.

Mica An insulating material used to separate the copper bars on starting-motor and generator commutators.

Micrometer A precision measuring device that measures small distances, such as crankshaft or cylinder bore diameter or the thickness of an object. Also called a *mike*.

Millimeter (mm) In the metric system, a unit of linear measure approximately equal to 0.039 inch.

Misfire See "Missing."

Missing A term that describes the engine in which the air–fuel mixture in a cylinder fails to ignite when it should.

Molecule The smallest particle into which a chemical compound can be divided.

Motor A device for converting electric energy into mechanical energy, for example, the starting motor.

Negative Name for one pole of a magnet or one terminal of any electric device. Also called *minus pole* or *terminal*.

Negative terminal The terminal from which electrons flow in a complete circuit. On a battery, the negative terminal can be identified as the battery post with the smaller diameter. The minus sign ($-$) is often used to identify the negative terminal.

Nitrogen oxide (NO_x) A by-product of combustion within the combustion chamber at high temperature and under heavy load. A basic air pollutant; automotive exhaust-emission levels of nitrogen oxide are controlled by law.

No-load test A starting-motor test in which the starting motor is operated without load; the current draw and armature speed at specified voltages are noted.

Nonconductor See "Insulator."

North pole The pole of a magnet from which the lines of force leave the magnet.

Nucleus The center of an atom; it has a positive charge (from the protons).

Octane rating A measure of antiknock property of gasoline. The higher the octane rating, the more resistant the gasoline is to detonation.

Ohm A unit of electric resistance.

Ohmmeter An instrument used to measure the number of ohms resistance in an electric conductor or circuit.

Oil-pressure indicator Oil gauge that reports to the driver the oil pressure in the engine lubricating system.

One-wire system On automobiles, the practice of using the car body, engine, and frame as a path for the grounded side of electric circuits, allowing the attached electric circuits to be of the one-wire type.

Open circuit A break, or opening, in an electric circuit which prevents the passage of an electric current.

Oscillating Moving back and forth, as the swinging of a pendulum.

Oscilloscope A high-speed voltmeter which visually displays pictures of voltage variations on a televisionlike picture tube, widely used to check engine ignition systems. Also can be used to check charging systems and electronic fuel-injection systems.

Overcharging Continued charging of a battery after it has reached a charged condition. This action damages the battery and shortens its life.

Overdrive A device in the power train, usually in the transmission, which introduces an extra set of gears into the power train. This causes the drive shaft to overdrive, or drive faster than, the engine crankshaft.

Overrunning-clutch drive A type of clutch drive which will transmit rotary motion in one direction only; when rotary motion attempts to pass through in the other direction, the then driving member overruns and does not pass the motion to the other member. Widely used as the drive mechanism for starting motors.

Parade pattern An oscilloscope pattern in which the ignition voltages are shown on one line, one after the other, reading from left to right across the scope screen in engine firing order.

Parallel circuit The electric circuit formed when two or more electric devices have their terminals connected together, positive to positive and negative to negative, so that each may operate independently of the other from the same power source.

Permanent magnet A piece of steel which continues to act as a magnet without requiring the use of an electric current to create a magnetic field.

Pickup coil In an electronic ignition system, the coil in which voltage is induced by the reluctor passing the permanent magnet.

Ping The sound resulting from sudden ignition of the air–fuel mixture in the engine combustion chamber; characteristic sound of detonation.

Planetary-gear system A gearset consisting of a central sun gear surrounded by two or more planet pinions which are, in turn, meshed with a ring (or internal) gear; used in overdrives and automatic transmissions.

Plate In a battery, a flat, rectangular part composed of spongy lead. Sulfuric acid in the electrolyte chemically reacts with the sponge lead to produce an electric current.

Plate group In a battery, the connecting together of all like plates in a cell; for example, all the positive plates in one cell form one plate group, and all the negative plates in that cell form another plate group.

Polarity The condition in an electric component or circuit that determines the direction of current flow.

Polarizing generator Correcting generator-field polarity so the generator will build up polarity in the proper direction to charge the battery.

Pole One end of a magnet.

Pole shoe The curved metal shoe around which a field coil is placed.

Positive Commonly accepted name for one pole of a magnet or one terminal of any electric device. Also called a *positive pole* or *terminal*.

Positive terminal The terminal to which electrons flow in a complete circuit. On a battery, the positive terminal can be identified as the battery post with the larger diameter. The plus sign (+) is often used to identify the positive terminal.

Post The point at which the cable is connected to the battery.

Power The rate at which work is done. A common power-measuring unit is the horsepower, which is equal to 33,000 foot-pounds of work per minute.

Power train The group of mechanisms that carry the rotary motion developed in the engine to the car wheels; it includes the clutch, transmission, drive shaft, differential, and axles.

Preignition Ignition of the air–fuel mixture in the engine cylinder (by any means) before the ignition spark occurs at the spark plug.

Primary The primary, or low voltage, circuit of the ignition system.

Primary winding The outer winding of relatively heavy wire in an ignition coil.

Printed circuit An electric circuit made by applying a conductive material to an insulating board in a pattern that provides electric circuits between components mounted on or connected to the board.

Proton A particle in the nucleus of an atom; protons have a positive electric charge.

Pulley A metal wheel with a V-shaped groove around the rim, which drives, or is driven by, a belt.

Quick charger A battery charger which will produce a high charging current and thus will substantially charge, or boost, a battery in a short time.

Raster pattern An oscilloscope pattern of the ignition voltages in which the cylinder traces are shown on the screen, one above the other, reading up from the bottom to the top of the screen in the engine firing order.

Reassembly Putting the parts of a device back together.

Recharging The action that takes place when electric current is forced into a battery in a direction opposite to that in which current flows from the battery when the battery is being discharged.

Rectifier A device which changes alternating current to direct current; in the alternator, the diodes.

Refractometer An instrument that measures specific gravity of a liquid, such as battery electrolyte or engine coolant, which gives a reading already adjusted for the temperature of the liquid being tested.

Regulator In the electric system, a device that controls generator output to prevent excessive voltage or excessive current output.

Reluctor In an electronic ignition system, the metal rotor, with a series of tips on it, which replaces the conventional distributor cam.

Reserve capacity A battery rating; the number of minutes a battery can deliver a 25-ampere current until the cell voltages drop to 1.75 volts per cell.

Residual magnetism The magnetism that remains in a material after the electric current producing the magnetism has stopped flowing.

Resistance That property of a material that opposes the flow of current.

Rotor A revolving part of a machine, such as the alternator rotors, disk-brake rotors, distributor rotors, and Wankel-engine rotors.

rpm Revolutions per minute.

Scope See "Oscilloscope."

Sealed-beam headlamp A headlamp which contains the filament, reflector, and lens in a single, sealed unit.

Secondary circuit The high-voltage circuit of the ignition system, consisting of the coil, rotor, distributor cap, spark-plug cables, and spark plugs.

Segments. The copper bars of a generator or starting-motor commutator.

Self-discharge Chemical activity in the battery which causes the battery to discharge even though it is furnishing no current.

Semiconductor A material that can act as a conductor under some conditions and as an insulator under other conditions.

Separator The thin sheet of wood, rubber, or glass mat that is placed between positive and negative plates in a battery cell to insulate them from each other.

Series circuit An electric circuit in which the same current flows through all devices; positive terminals are connected to negative terminals.

Series–parallel system A special starting system using, for example, a 24-volt starting motor, two 12-volt batteries, and a 12-volt alternator. For starting, the two batteries are connected in series for 24 volts; for charging, they are connected in parallel for 12 volts.

Shift lever The lever used to change gears in a transmission; also, the lever on the starting motor which moves the drive pinion into or out of mesh with the flywheel teeth.

Short circuit A defect in an electric circuit which permits current to take a short path, or circuit, instead of following the prescribed path.

Shunt A parallel connection, or circuit.

Silicone An insulating material, similar to rubber,

used to cover high-voltage ignition cables and to insulate other electric devices.

Slip rings In an alternator, rings that form rotating connections between armature windings and brushes.

Smog A term coined from "smoke" and "fog" which is applied to the foglike layer that hangs over many areas under certain atmospheric conditions. Smog is compounded from smoke, moisture, and numerous chemicals which are produced by combustion (from power plants, automotive engines, incinerators, etc.) and from numerous natural and industrial processes. Term used generally to describe any condition of dirty air and/or fumes or smoke.

Snap ring A metal fastener made in two types: an external snap ring which fits into a groove in a shaft and an internal snap ring which fits into a groove in a housing. Snap rings must be installed and removed with special snap-ring pliers.

Soldering The uniting of pieces of metal with solder, flux, and heat.

Solenoid The device which, when connected to an electrical source such as a battery, produces a mechanical movement. This movement can control a valve or produce other controlling movements.

Solenoid relay The relay that connects a solenoid to the battery when its contacts close; specifically, the starting-motor solenoid relay.

Solenoid switch A switch which is opened and closed electromagnetically, by movement of a core. Usually, this core also causes a mechanical action, such as the movement of a drive pinion into mesh with flywheel teeth for cranking.

Solid-state regulator An alternator regulator encapsulated in a plastic material and mounted in the alternator.

South pole The pole of a magnet into which the magnetic lines of force pass.

Spark line In an oscilloscope pattern of the ignition secondary circuit, the spark line shows the voltage required to sustain the spark at the spark plug and the number of distributor degrees through which the spark exists.

Spark plug The assembly, which includes a pair of electrodes and an insulator, that provides a spark gap in the engine cylinder.

Spark-plug heat range The distance heat must travel from the center electrode to reach the outer shell of the plug and enter the cylinder head.

Spark test A quick check of the ignition system, which is made by holding the metal spark-plug end of a spark-plug cable about $3/16$ inch [4.76 mm] from the cylinder head, or block, cranking the engine, and checking the spark.

Specifications The measurements, usually as recommended by the manufacturer, for the vehicle being serviced.

Specific gravity A measure of the weight per unit volume of a liquid as compared with the weight of an equal volume of water.

Specs See "Specifications."

Stacked pattern See "Raster pattern."

Stall test A starting-motor test of current draw with the starting motor stalled.

Starter See "Starting motor."

Starting motor The electric motor in the electric system that cranks the engine, or turns the crankshaft, for starting.

Starting-motor drive The drive mechanism and gear on the end of the starting-motor armature shaft used to couple the starting motor to and disengage it from the flywheel gear teeth.

Stator In the torque converter, a third member (in addition to turbine and pump) which changes direction of fluid under certain operating conditions (when stator is stationary). In the alternator, the assembly that includes the stationary conductors.

Steering-and-ignition lock A device that secures the ignition switch in the OFF position and also secures the steering wheel so it cannot be turned.

Stoplights Lights at the rear of the car, used to indicate that the brakes are applied.

Stoplight switch The switch used to turn the stoplights on and off.

Storage battery A lead-acid electrochemical device that changes chemical energy into electric energy; that part of the electric system which acts as a reservoir for electric energy, storing it in chemical form.

Stroke In an engine, the distance that the piston moves from BDC to TDC.

Sulfation The lead sulfate that forms on battery plates as a result of the battery action that produces electric current.

Sulfuric acid See "Electrolyte."

Superimposed pattern On an oscilloscope, name given to the pattern that shows the traces of all cylinders one on the other so that only one pattern, with the variations from it, can be seen.

Surface ignition Ignition of the air–fuel mixture in the combustion chamber produced by hot metal surfaces or heated particles of carbon.

Switch A device that opens and closes an electric circuit.

Synchronizer A device in the transmission that synchronizes gears about to be meshed so that there will not be any gear clash.

Tachometer A device for measuring engine speed, or rpm.

Tank unit A unit of the fuel-indicating system that is mounted in the fuel tank.

TDC Top dead center.

TEL Tetraethyl lead.

Temperature indicator A gauge that indicates to the driver the temperature of the coolant in the cooling system, thus giving warning of impending damage if the temperature goes too high.

Tetraethyl lead A chemical put into engine fuel which increases octane rating, or reduces knock tendency. Also called *ethyl* and *tel*.

Thermistor Heat-sensing electric device with a negative temperature coefficient of resistance. That is, as temperature increases, resistance decreases. Used as the sensing device for engine-temperature-indicating instruments.

Thermostatic gauge An indicating device (fuel, oil pressure, engine temperature, etc.) that contains a thermostatic blade (or blades).

Three-phase A term used to designate the three interconnected circuits in an alternator stator which produce alternating current.

Timing In an engine, refers to timing of valves and timing of ignition and their relation to the piston position in the cylinder.

Timing chain A chain, driven by a sprocket on the crankshaft, that drives the sprocket on the camshaft.

Timing gears A system of gears by which a gear on the crankshaft drives the camshaft by meshing with a gear on its end.

Timing light A light that is connected to the ignition system to flash each time the No. 1 spark plug fires; used for adjusting the timing of the ignition spark.

Top dead center (TDC) The piston position at which the piston has moved to the top of the cylinder and at which the center line of the connecting rod is parallel to the cylinder walls.

Torque test A starting-motor test in which the torque the starting motor can develop and the current that is drawn are measured with the specified voltage applied.

Torque wrench A special wrench that indicates the amount of torque being applied to a nut or bolt.

Transistor An electronic device that can be used as an electric switch; used in the control module in electronic ignition systems.

Transmission The device in the power train that provides different gear ratios between the engine and rear wheels, as well as reverse.

Transmission-controlled spark (TCS) system An exhaust-emission-control system which allows distributor vacuum advance in high gear only; widely used on General Motors vehicles.

Transmission-regulated spark (TRS) system Name used by Ford to identify an exhaust-emission control system similar to the GM transmission-controlled spark system; an exhaust-emission-control system which allows distributor vacuum advance in high gear only.

Trouble diagnosis The detective work necessary to run down the cause of a trouble. Also implies the correction of the trouble by elimination of the cause.

Tuneup The procedure of inspecting, testing, and adjusting an engine, and replacing any worn parts, to restore the engine to its best performance.

Turn signal See "Directional signal."

Twenty-five-ampere rate A battery rating; the length of time a battery can deliver 25 amperes before cell voltage drops to 1.75 volts, starting with electrolyte at 80°F [26.7°C].

Twenty-hour rate A battery rating; the amount of current a battery can deliver for 20 hours without cell voltage dropping below 1.75 volts, starting with an electrolyte temperature of 80°F [26.7°C].

Unit distributor An ignition distributor, used by General Motors, that uses a magnetic pickup coil and timer core instead of points and condenser. It also has the ignition coil assembled in the distributor as a unit.

Vacuum advance Ignition-spark advance resulting from partial vacuum in the intake manifold.

Vacuum-advance controls Any of several NO_x emission-control systems designed to allow vacuum advance only during certain modes of engine and vehicle operation.

Vacuum gauge In automotive-engine service, a device that measures intake-manifold vacuum and thereby indicates actions of engine components.

Vacuum switch A switch that closes or opens its contacts with changing vacuum conditions.

Valve tappet Valve lifter.

Valve timing The timing of valve opening and closing in relation to piston position in the cylinder.

Vibration A complete rapid motion back and forth; oscillation.

Voltage Electric pressure.

Voltage drop The drop, or reduction, in voltage across a resistance (a circuit, connection, electrical device, etc.)

Voltage regulator A regulating device that prevents excessive alternator or generator voltage by repeatedly inserting a resistance into the field circuit.

Voltmeter An electric meter for measuring the voltage of an electric device, such as a battery or alternator, or for measuring the voltage between two points in an electric circuit.

Warning blinker See "Hazard system."

Wire feeler gauge A round wire gauge used for checking clearances between electric contacts, such as distributor points and spark-plug electrodes.

Wiring harness A group of individually insulated wires wrapped together.

INDEX

ANSWERS TO REVIEW QUESTIONS

The answers to the chapter review questions are given here. If you want to figure your grade on any quiz, divide the number of questions in the quiz into 100. This gives you the value of each question. For instance, suppose there are 10 questions: 10 goes into a hundred 10 times. Each correct answer, therefore, gives you 10 points. If you answered 8 correct out of the 10, then your grade would be 80 (8×10).

If you are not satisfied with the grade you make on a test, restudy the chapter and retake the test. This review will help you remember the important facts.

Remember, when you take a course in school, you can pass and graduate even though you make a grade of less than 100. But in the automotive shop, you must score 100 percent all the time. If you make 1 error out of 100 service jobs, for example, your average would be 99. In school that is a fine average. But in the automotive shop that one job you erred on could cause such serious trouble (a ruined engine or a wrecked car) that it would outweigh all the good jobs you performed. Therefore, always proceed carefully in performing any service job and make sure you know exactly what you are supposed to do and how you are to do it.

CHAPTER 1

1. (c)   2. (b)   3. (a)   4. (a)   5. (c)
6. (a)   7. (d)   8. (c)   9. (b)   10. (a)
11. (c)   12. (b)   13. (c)   14. (c)   15. (b)
16. (a)   17. (b)   18. (a)   19. (c)   20. (c)

CHAPTER 2

1. (d)   2. (a)   3. (b)   4. (a)   5. (b)
6. (c)   7. (a)   8. (b)   9. (d)   10. (b)

CHAPTER 3

1. (d)   2. (c)   3. (a)   4. (b)   5. (b)
6. (c)   7. (c)   8. (c)   9. (d)   10. (a)
11. (a)   12. (c)   13. (b)   14. (b)   15. (a)

CHAPTER 4

1. (b)   2. (a)   3. (b)   4. (d)   5. (d)
6. (d)   7. (c)   8. (a)   9. (b)   10. (a)
11. (a)   12. (d)   13. (a)   14. (b)   15. (a)

CHAPTER 5

1. (a)   2. (b)   3. (b)   4. (a)   5. (d)
6. (a)   7. (b)   8. (d)   9. (b)   10. (b)
11. (d)   12. (b)   13. (a)   14. (d)   15. (c)

CHAPTER 6

1. (d)   2. (b)   3. (a)   4. (b)   5. (d)
6. (d)   7. (d)   8. (c)   9. (a)   10. (a)

CHAPTER 7

1. (a)   2. (d)   3. (a)   4. (b)   5. (d)
6. (c)   7. (b)   8. (d)   9. (a)   10. (d)
11. (c)   12. (a)   13. (b)   14. (a)   15. (d)
16. (a)   17. (c)   18. (c)   19. (c)   20. (a)

CHAPTER 8

1. (d)   2. (c)   3. (a)   4. (d)   5. (c)
6. (c)   7. (b)   8. (a)   9. (b)   10. (d)
11. (c)   12. (b)   13. (c)   14. (c)   15. (b)

CHAPTER 9

1. (d)   2. (a)   3. (c)   4. (b)   5. (b)
6. (d)   7. (a)   8. (c)   9. (c)   10. (c)

CHAPTER 10

1. (a)   2. (b)   3. (a)   4. (b)   5. (b)
6. (b)   7. (d)   8. (b)

CHAPTER 11

1. (b)   2. (a)   3. (d)   4. (a)   5. (a)
6. (c)   7. (b)   8. (d)

CHAPTER 12

1. (b)   2. (d)   3. (a)   4. (c)   5. (d)
6. (a)   7. (d)   8. (c)   9. (c)   10. (a)

CHAPTER 13

1. (b)   2. (d)   3. (c)   4. (b)   5. (a)
6. (a)   7. (b)   8. (b)   9. (a)   10. (d)

CHAPTER 14

1. (c)   2. (c)   3. (a)   4. (b)   5. (b)
6. (d)   7. (c)   8. (b)   9. (d)   10. (a)
11. (b)   12. (b)   13. (a)   14. (b)   15. (a)

CHAPTER 15

1. (d)   2. (c)   3. (b)   4. (d)   5. (b)
6. (d)   7. (a)   8. (b)   9. (d)   10. (b)
11. (d)   12. (c)   13. (a)   14. (d)   15. (c)

CHAPTER 16

1. (d) 2. (b) 3. (a) 4. (a) 5. (b)
6. (b) 7. (b) 8. (b) 9. (a) 10. (c)

CHAPTER 17

1. (d) 2. (c) 3. (b) 4. (c) 5. (a)
6. (b) 7. (b) 8. (c) 9. (b) 10. (c)

CHAPTER 18

1. (c) 2. (a) 3. (d) 4. (b) 5. (d)
6. (c) 7. (d) 8. (a) 9. (d) 10. (d)

CHAPTER 19

1. (a) 2. (b) 3. (c) 4. (d) 5. (c)
6. (b) 7. (a) 8. (b) 9. (b) 10. (d)

CHAPTER 20

1. (b) 2. (c) 3. (a) 4. (a) 5. (d)
6. (c) 7. (a) 8. (b) 9. (c) 10. (b)

CHAPTER 21

1. (d) 2. (b) 3. (c) 4. (a) 5. (b)
6. (c) 7. (b) 8. (d) 9. (d) 10. (c)

CHAPTER 22

1. (d) 2. (b) 3. (d) 4. (d) 5. (d)
6. (c) 7. (d) 8. (c) 9. (c) 10. (b)

CHAPTER 23

1. (c) 2. (d) 3. (a) 4. (b) 5. (b)

CHAPTER 24

1. (a) 2. (a) 3. (a) 4. (a) 5. (b)

CHAPTER 25

1. (b) 2. (c) 3. (d) 4. (c) 5. (a)
6. (b) 7. (d) 8. (d) 9. (c) 10. (d)
11. (c) 12. (c) 13. (a) 14. (d) 15. (b)